PEARSON mysocialworklab™

Save time and improve results!

MySocialWorkLab is a dynamic website that provides a wealth of resources geared to help students develop and master the skills articulated in CSWE's core competencies—and improve their grades in their social work courses.

MySocialWorkLab is available at no extra cost when bundled with any text in the **Connecting Core Competencies Series.** Visit **www.mysocialworklab.com** to learn more.

MySocialWorkLab offers:

- A complete **Pearson eText** of the book
- A wealth of engaging **videos**
  - **Brand-new videos**—organized around the competencies and accompanied by interactive assessment—that demonstrate key concepts and practices
  - **Career Exploration videos** that contain interviews with a wide range of social workers
- Tools for **self-assessment and review**—chapter specific quizzes tied to the core competencies, many written in the same format students will find on the licensing exam
- A **Gradebook** that reports progress of students and the class as a whole
- **MySocialWorkLibrary**—a compendium of articles and case studies in social work, searchable by course, topic, author, and title
- **MySearchLab**—a collection of tools that aid students in mastering research assignments and papers
- **And much more!**

In recent years, many Social Work departments have been focusing on the CSWE Educational Policy and Accreditation Standards (EPAS) to guide their accreditation process. The current standards, issued in 2008, focus on mastery of the CSWE's ten core competencies and practice behaviors. Each of the ten core competencies now contains specific knowledge, values, skills, and the resulting practice behaviors as guidance for the curriculum and assessment methods of Social Work programs.

In writing this text, we have used the CSWE core competency standards and assessment recommendations as guidelines for structuring content and integrating the pedagogy. For details on the CSWE core competencies, please see www.cswe.org.

For the core competencies highlighted in this text, see page iv.

Professional Identity

2.1.1 Identify as a professional social worker and conduct oneself accordingly.

Necessary Knowledge, Values, Skills

- Social workers serve as representatives of the profession, its mission, and its core values.
- Social workers know the profession's history.
- Social workers commit themselves to the profession's enhancement and to their own professional conduct and growth.

Operational Practice Behaviors

- Social workers advocate for client access to the services of social work;
- Social workers practice personal reflection and self-correction to assure continual professional development;
- Social workers attend to professional roles and boundaries;
- Social workers demonstrate professional demeanor in behavior, appearance, and communication;
- Social workers engage in career-long learning; and
- Social workers use supervision and consultation.

Ethical Practice

2.1.2 Apply social work ethical principles to guide professional practice.

Necessary Knowledge, Values, Skills

- Social workers have an obligation to conduct themselves ethically and engage in ethical decision-making.
- Social workers are knowledgeable about the value base of the profession, its ethical standards, and relevant law.

Operational Practice Behaviors

- Social workers recognize and manage personal values in a way that allows professional values to guide practice;
- Social workers make ethical decisions by applying standards of the National Association of Social Workers Code of Ethics and, as applicable, of the International Federation of Social Workers/International Association of Schools of Social Work Ethics in Social Work, Statement of Principles;
- Social workers tolerate ambiguity in resolving ethical conflicts; and
- Social workers apply strategies of ethical reasoning to arrive at principled decisions.

Critical Thinking

2.1.3 Apply critical thinking to inform and communicate professional judgments.

Necessary Knowledge, Values, Skills

- Social workers are knowledgeable about the principles of logic, scientific inquiry, and reasoned discernment.
- They use critical thinking augmented by creativity and curiosity.
- Critical thinking also requires the synthesis and communication of relevant information.

Operational Practice Behaviors

- Social workers distinguish, appraise, and integrate multiple sources of knowledge, including research-based knowledge, and practice wisdom;
- Social workers analyze models of assessment, prevention, intervention, and evaluation; and
- Social workers demonstrate effective oral and written communication in working with individuals, families, groups, organizations, communities, and colleagues.

Adapted with the permission of Council on Social Work Education

Diversity in Practice

2.1.4 Engage diversity and difference in practice.

Necessary Knowledge, Values, Skills

- Social workers understand how diversity characterizes and shapes the human experience and is critical to the formation of identity.
- The dimensions of diversity are understood as the intersectionality of multiple factors including age, class, color, culture, disability, ethnicity, gender, gender identity and expression, immigration status, political ideology, race, religion, sex, and sexual orientation.
- Social workers appreciate that, as a consequence of difference, a person's life experiences may include oppression, poverty, marginalization, and alienation as well as privilege, power, and acclaim.

Operational Practice Behaviors

- Social workers recognize the extent to which a culture's structures and values may oppress, marginalize, alienate, or create or enhance privilege and power;
- Social workers gain sufficient self-awareness to eliminate the influence of personal biases and values in working with diverse groups;
- Social workers recognize and communicate their understanding of the importance of difference in shaping life experiences; and
- Social workers view themselves as learners and engage those with whom they work as informants.

Human Rights & Justice

2.1.5 Advance human rights and social and economic justice.

Necessary Knowledge, Values, Skills

- Each person, regardless of position in society, has basic human rights, such as freedom, safety, privacy, an adequate standard of living, health care, and education.
- Social workers recognize the global interconnections of oppression and are knowledgeable about theories of justice and strategies to promote human and civil rights.
- Social work incorporates social justice practices in organizations, institutions, and society to ensure that these basic human rights are distributed equitably and without prejudice.

Operational Practice Behaviors

- Social workers understand the forms and mechanisms of oppression and discrimination;
- Social workers advocate for human rights and social and economic justice; and
- Social workers engage in practices that advance social and economic justice.

Research Based Practice

2.1.6 Engage in research-informed practice and practice-informed research.

Necessary Knowledge, Values, Skills

- Social workers use practice experience to inform research, employ evidence-based interventions, evaluate their own practice, and use research findings to improve practice, policy, and social service delivery.
- Social workers comprehend quantitative and qualitative research and understand scientific and ethical approaches to building knowledge.

Operational Practice Behaviors

- Social workers use practice experience to inform scientific inquiry; and
- Social workers use research evidence to inform practice.

Human Behavior

2.1.7 Apply knowledge of human behavior and the social environment.

Necessary Knowledge, Values, Skills

- Social workers are knowledgeable about human behavior across the life course; the range of social systems in which people live; and the ways social systems promote or deter people in maintaining or achieving health and well-being.
- Social workers apply theories and knowledge from the liberal arts to understand biological, social, cultural, psychological, and spiritual development.

Operational Practice Behaviors

- Social workers utilize conceptual frameworks to guide the processes of assessment, intervention, and evaluation; and
- Social workers critique and apply knowledge to understand person and environment.

Policy Practice 2.1.8 Engage in policy practice to advance social and economic well-being and to deliver effective social work services.

Necessary Knowledge, Values, Skills

- Social work practitioners understand that policy affects service delivery and they actively engage in policy practice.
- Social workers know the history and current structures of social policies and services; the role of policy in service delivery; and the role of practice in policy development.

Operational Practice Behaviors

- Social workers analyze, formulate, and advocate for policies that advance social well-being; and
- Social workers collaborate with colleagues and clients for effective policy action.

Practice Contexts

2.1.9 Respond to contexts that shape practice.

Necessary Knowledge, Values, Skills

- Social workers are informed, resourceful, and proactive in responding to evolving organizational, community, and societal contexts at all levels of practice.
- Social workers recognize that the context of practice is dynamic, and use knowledge and skill to respond proactively.

Operational Practice Behaviors

- Social workers continuously discover, appraise, and attend to changing locales, populations, scientific and technological developments, and emerging societal trends to provide relevant services; and
- Social workers provide leadership in promoting sustainable changes in service delivery and practice to improve the quality of social services.

Engage, Assess, Intervene, Evaluate 2.1.10 Engage, assess, intervene, and evaluate with individuals, families, groups, organizations, and communities.

Necessary Knowledge, Values, Skills

- Professional practice involves the dynamic and interactive processes of engagement, assessment, intervention, and evaluation at multiple levels.
- Social workers have the knowledge and skills to practice with individuals, families, groups, organizations, and communities.
- Practice knowledge includes
  - identifying, analyzing, and implementing evidence-based interventions designed to achieve client goals;
  - using research and technological advances;
  - evaluating program outcomes and practice effectiveness;
  - developing, analyzing, advocating, and providing leadership for policies and services; and
  - promoting social and economic justice.

Operational Practice Behaviors

(a) Engagement

- Social workers substantively and affectively prepare for action with individuals, families, groups, organizations, and communities;
- Social workers use empathy and other interpersonal skills; and
- Social workers develop a mutually agreed-on focus of work and desired outcomes.

(b) Assessment

- Social workers collect, organize, and interpret client data;
- Social workers assess client strengths and limitations;
- Social workers develop mutually agreed-on intervention goals and objectives; and
- Social workers select appropriate intervention strategies.

(c) Intervention

- Social workers initiate actions to achieve organizational goals;
- Social workers implement prevention interventions that enhance client capacities;
- Social workers help clients resolve problems;
- Social workers negotiate, mediate, and advocate for clients; and
- Social workers facilitate transitions and endings.

(d) Evaluation

- Social workers critically analyze, monitor, and evaluate interventions.

CONNECTING CORE COMPETENCIES **Chapter-by-Chapter Matrix**

Chapter	Professional Identity	Ethical Practice	Critical Thinking	Diversity in Practice	Human Rights & Justice	Research Based Practice	Human Behavior	Policy Practice	Practice Contexts	Engage Assess Intervene Evaluate
1		✔	✔				✔	✔		
2			✔	✔			✔			✔
3	✔	✔		✔					✔	
4		✔	✔		✔					✔
5	✔				✔			✔		✔
6	✔	✔		✔	✔					
7			✔	✔			✔			✔
8		✔					✔	✔	✔	
9				✔		✔			✔	✔
10			✔		✔	✔	✔			
11	✔					✔		✔		✔
12			✔		✔		✔	✔		
13	✔	✔		✔					✔	
14				✔	✔			✔		
15						✔				
16	✔						✔		✔	✔
Total Chapters	6	6	6	7	6	4	7	6	5	7

Generalist Social Work Practice

An Empowering Approach

Karla Krogsrud Miley
Black Hawk College

Michael O'Melia
St. Ambrose University

Brenda DuBois
St. Ambrose University

Allyn & Bacon

Boston Columbus Indianapolis New York San Francisco Upper Saddle River
Amsterdam Cape Town Dubai London Madrid Milan Munich Paris Montreal Toronto
Delhi Mexico City Sao Paulo Sydney Hong Kong Seoul Singapore Taipei Tokyo

Editor in Chief: Dickson Musslewhite
Executive Editor: Ashley Dodge
Editorial Assistant: Carly Czech
Director of Development: Sharon Geary
Development Editor: Deb Hanlon
Director of Marketing: Brandy Dawson
Senior Marketing Manager: Wendy Albert
Marketing Assistant: Kyle VanNatter
Advertising Director: Kate Conway
Advertising Manager: Sara Sherlock
Design Specialist: Robert Farrar-Wagner

Copywriter: Jonathan Andrew
Senior Media Editor: Melanie MacFarlane
Senior Production Project Manager: Pat Torelli
Editorial Production and Composition Service:
   Laserwords, Maine
Manager of Design Development: John Christiana
Interior Design: Joyce Weston Design
Cover Design: Joel Gendron
   Kristina Mose-Libon
Manufacturing Buyer: Debbie Rossi

Credits appear on page 486, which constitutes an extension of the copyright page.

Library of Congress Cataloging-in-Publication Data

Miley, Karla Krogsrud
  Generalist social work practice : an empowering approach / Karla Krogsrud
Miley, Michael O'Melia, Brenda DuBois.—Updated 6th ed.
     p. cm.
  ISBN-13: 978-0-205-78981-8
  ISBN-10: 0-205-78981-1
  1. Social service. 2. Social case work. I. O'Melia, Michael. II. DuBois,
Brenda, III. Title.
  HV40.M5223 2011
  361.3'2—dc22

                    2009047803

10 9 8 7 6 5 4 3 2   BRR 14 13 12 11 10

Allyn & Bacon
is an imprint of

www.pearsonhighered.com

ISBN-10: 0-205-78981-1
ISBN-13: 978-0-205-78981-8

Contents

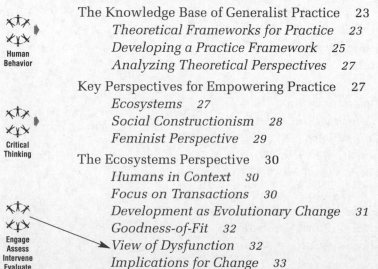

Ethical
Practice

Policy
Practice

Human
Behavior

Critical
Thinking

Human
Behavior

Critical
Thinking

Engage
Assess
Intervene
Evaluate

**Diversity
in Practice**

---

3. Values and Multicultural Competence   47

**Ethical
Practice**

**Professional
Identity**

**Diversity
in Practice**

**Practice
Contexts**

PART TWO: THE DIALOGUE PHASE: BUILDING RELATIONSHIPS AND DESCRIBING SITUATIONS

Diversity in Practice

Professional Identity

Human Rights & Justice

Ethical Practice

8. Defining Directions   182

PART THREE: THE DISCOVERY PHASE: ASSESSING RESOURCES AND PLANNING CHANGE

9. Identifying Strengths   207

**Research
Based
Practice**

10. Assessing Resource Capabilities   235

**Human
Behavior**

**Research
Based
Practice**

**Human
Rights
& Justice**

**Critical
Thinking**

PART FOUR: THE DEVELOPMENT PHASE: IMPLEMENTING, EVALUATING, AND STABILIZING CHANGE

Professional
Identity

Research
Based
Practice

Policy
Practice

Engage
Assess
Intervene
Evaluate

Human
Behavior

Critical
Thinking

Policy
Practice

Human
Rights
& Justice

Diversity
in Practice

Ethical
Practice

Practice
Contexts

Professional
Identity

16. Integrating Gains   411

Preface

This book organizes material into four parts. Part 1 creates a perspective for empowerment-oriented generalist social work practice. Parts 2, 3, and 4 describe and explain empowering processes that generalist social workers apply with clients at the micro- mezzo-, and macrolevels of practice.

Part 1, Social Work Practice Perspectives, describes how generalist social workers using an empowerment-based approach can meet the purposes of social work to enhance human functioning and promote social justice.

Part 2, The Dialogue Phase, describes the practice processes related to constructing and maintaining empowering client system–worker relationships, communicating effectively with diverse clients about their situations, and defining a purpose for the work.

Part 3, The Discovery Phase, presents solution-oriented processes for identifying client-system strengths and environmental resources and using them in planning.

Part 4, The Development Phase, features generalist social work skills for implementing, evaluating, and stabilizing change efforts.

Connecting Core Competencies Series

The updated edition of this text is now a part of Pearson Education's new *Connecting Core Competencies* series, which consists of five foundation-level texts that make it easier than ever to ensure students' success in learning the ten core competencies as stated in 2008 by the Council on Social Work Education. This text contains:

- **Core Competency Icons** throughout the chapters, directly linking the CSWE core competencies to the content of the text. **Critical thinking questions** are also included to further students' mastery of the CSWE's standards. Check out the table of contents and chapter opening outlines to see where the icons are located throughout the text. For easy reference, page iv also displays which icons are used in each chapter, in a chapter-by-chapter matrix.
- **An end-of-chapter Practice Test**, with multiple-choice questions that tests students' knowledge of the chapter content and mastery of the competencies. These questions are constructed in a format that will help prepare students for the **ASWB Licensing exam.**
- **Additional questions pertaining to the videos found on the new MySocialWorkLab** at the end of each chapter to encourage students to access the site and explore the wealth of available materials. If this text did not come with an access code for MySocialWorkLab, you can purchase access at: **www.mysocialworklab.com**

Acknowledgments

We are thankful for the encouragement and support offered by our colleagues, friends, and families. We especially thank David, Jane, and Jim! We are grateful for the technical assistance provided by the Prairie Area Library System and

Black Hawk College librarian, Charlet Key. We also express appreciation to Karen Hanson for her unwavering commitment to this project; to Pat Quinlin for her thoughtful direction and support; and to both for their diligent work during various stages of production. We also thank the reviewers who offered thoughtful comments on the first five editions of this book: Stephen C. Anderson, University of Oklahoma; Cynthia Bishop, Meredith College; Thomas J. Blakely, Western Michigan University; M. Jenise Comer, Central Missouri State University; Sherry Edwards, University of North Carolina, Pembroke; Sarah Hendrix, University of Kentucky and University of Louisville; Edward W. Ihle, Syracuse University; Robert H. Keefe, Syracuse University; Betty J. Kramer, University of Wisconsin–Madison; Doman Lum, California State University, Sacramento; Mark W. Lusk, University of Montana; Robert Madden, Saint Joseph College; Mary Harris Pegram, Bowling Green State University; Barbara Rio, University at Albany, State University of New York; Andrew Scharlach, University of California, Berkeley; and Eleanor Reardon Tolson, The University of Illinois at Chicago. The following reviewers provided useful comments as we engaged in preparing the sixth edition: Sylvester Bowie, California State University, Sacramento; Suzanne L. Cross, Michigan State University; Adele Crudden, Mississippi State University; and Andrea Scharlach, University of California, Berkeley.

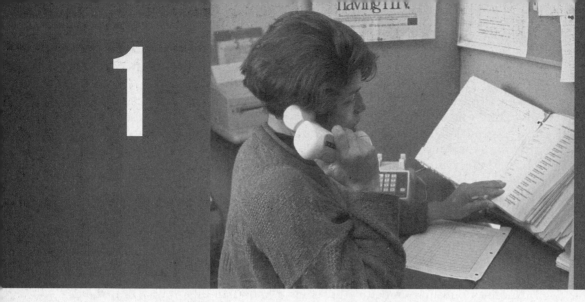

Generalist Social Work Practice

CONNECTING CORE COMPETENCIES *in this chapter*

| Professional Identity | **Ethical Practice** | **Critical Thinking** | Diversity in Practice | Human Rights & Justice | Research Based Practice | **Human Behavior** | **Policy Practice** | Practice Contexts | Engage Assess Intervene Evaluate |

"What's working well that you would like to see continue?" With this question, Andrea Barry, a family preservation worker, shifts focus in her work with the Clemens family. She carefully studies the reactions to her question on the faces of the family members who are gathered with her around their kitchen table. She reads caution, apprehension, maybe even a little anger, and yes, there it is, a growing sense of surprise, of intrigue with her approach. As a social worker with the family preservation program of Northside Family Services, Andrea has seen this before. Preparing to fend off the blame of abuse or neglect, families involved with the program are often taken off guard by the careful, non-judgmental phrasing of her questions. With the query about "what's working well," Andrea recognizes family strengths and looks toward the future, toward things families can still do something about. In other words, she sets the stage for empowering families by focusing on their strengths and promoting their competence.

Andrea's question embodies her view of how families might find themselves in this predicament. To continue to focus on "What are your problems?" doesn't make sense to Andrea, who sees family difficulties arising from the challenge of scarce resources rather than resulting from something that the family is doing wrong. As reflected in her question, Andrea believes that even those families referred by the Child Protective Unit for work with the family preservation program are actually doing a lot right. She regards families as doing the best they can with currently available resources. So, of course, in trying to overcome their present difficulties, the subsequent question becomes, "What can we do to build on your strengths?" rather than "What else is wrong?" Her approach presumes that all families have strengths and are capable of making changes; it prompts them into collaborating with her as partners in the change process.

Andrea has learned from experience that different families benefit from different constellations of resources for optimal functioning. Some family members need to understand themselves and each other better. Others need information about how to cope with the inevitable, and also the unexpected, changes that occur throughout their lives. Often, isolated families benefit from connections to the support of interpersonal relationships. Still other families need to access resources from within the community. Andrea teams with families to manage a network of social services, selecting among possibilities ranging from housing assistance to job training to crisis child care to child abuse prevention.

Andrea also recognizes the need to broaden her focus, to look beyond the needs of individual families to serve their best interests. Many times, families, confined by forces they consider to be beyond their personal control, seek a professional voice to speak out for them at the levels of government, policy, and resource allocation. They certainly need power and resources to take charge of their own directions in a world that has grown complex and confusing.

As Andrea provides opportunities for the Clemens family members to respond to her question, she reminds herself that this family is unique. She knows to attend to the ways that her clients are similar as well as to the ways they are different. As an African American woman, Andrea herself is sensitive to the confinement of prejudgments. The strengths the Clemens family members have to offer and the challenges they face are particular to their own situation. Demonstrating her cultural competence, Andrea thoughtfully examines the assumptions she makes about people based on their obvious similarities so she will not ignore their inevitable differences.

Clients have taught Andrea that individual differences themselves can be the keys to solutions. Social work practitioners accept the challenge to enable each client system to access its own unique capabilities and the resources of its particular context. Andrea's role in the professional relationship is that of partner to empower families with their own strengths, not to overpower families with her own considerable practice knowledge and skills. Andrea has learned to depend on each family system's special competencies to guide her in this empowering process.

Even though Andrea considers the Clemens family as a whole, she will not neglect her professional mandate to act in the best interest of the Clemens children. Ethical considerations and legal obligations compel Andrea to protect the children in this family. However, family service social workers simultaneously focus on the preservation of families and the protection of children. Andrea sees the needs of families and children as convergent. What benefits the family will help the children in their development. What benefits the children will contribute to the cohesiveness of the family. Theoretically, she sees the whole family system as her client and knows that any change in the family system will create changes for individual family members.

Andrea's work with the Clemens family reinforces her opinion that social policy that aims to keep families together is good policy. She always feels best when implementing a policy that reflects a professional philosophy that so neatly fits her own values. The policy of family preservation makes sense in Andrea's practice experience, as well. She has observed the trauma for families and children when children at risk are removed from their own homes. Reuniting them, even after positive changes occur, always seems to be a difficult transition. Research in the field of child welfare confirms Andrea's practice observations and lends support for the current policy of family preservation. Andrea believes that keeping families together makes good economic sense, too. She suspects that economic considerations are a major force motivating the development of policies that favor family preservation.

"What's working well that you'd like to see continue?" A simple question, yet it reflects Andrea Barry's empowerment orientation toward social work practice. Andrea has learned that even simple questions can have dramatic effects. Simple questions set the tone, bond relationships, and lead to successful solutions.

This chapter provides an overview of social work practice. It describes the underlying values, purposes, and perspectives that contribute to the empowering approach that Andrea Barry uses and explains what generalist social workers do. Specifically, this chapter

- Articulates the value base and purpose of the social work profession
- Defines generalist social work as an integration of practice, policy, and research
- Explains social work intervention activities at each system level of practice—micro-, mezzo-, and macrolevel, and the social work profession
- Differentiates the multiple functions and roles of generalist social workers at various system levels

The outcome is a foundation on which to build an understanding of social work practice from a generalist perspective.

SOCIAL WORK VALUES AND PURPOSE

Ethical Practice

Human dignity and worth and *social justice* are the centerpiece values of the social work profession. How are these professional values reflected in the definition of human rights?

Andrea Barry practices in family services—one of many fields of social work. Other practice arenas include school social work, medical social work, probation and other criminal justice services, mental health, youth services, child welfare, and housing and urban development, to name a few. The predominant fields of social work practice, representing more than 70% of the professional workforce, are mental health, medical health, child welfare, and aging services (NASW, 2005a).

All social work practitioners, regardless of their particular field of practice, share a common professional identity and work toward similar purposes. The National Association of Social Workers (1999a), in its *Code of Ethics,* defines this unifying purpose, or mission, of all social work as "to enhance human well-being and help meet the basic human needs of all people, with particular attention to the needs and empowerment of people who are vulnerable, oppressed, and living in poverty" (Preamble). To meet this purpose, social workers recognize that private troubles and public issues are intertwined.

Thus, social workers strive to both strengthen human functioning and promote the effectiveness of societal structures. This simultaneous focus on persons and their environments permeates all social work practice. As a social worker, Andrea Barry works with the Clemens family to facilitate the adaptive functioning of their family and preserve their unity. She also works to create a resource-rich and responsive environment that will contribute to the development and stability of the Clemens family. Both of these activities reflect Andrea's integration of the fundamental values of the social work profession. The overarching values of *human dignity and worth* and *social justice* shape her attitudes; the purpose of the profession directs her actions.

Human Dignity and Worth

Valuing the inherent human dignity and worth of all people reflects a nondiscriminatory view of humankind. The *Code of Ethics* (1999a) charges social workers to "treat each person in a caring and respectful fashion, mindful of individual differences and cultural and ethnic diversity," ". . . promote clients' socially responsible self-determination," ". . . enhance clients' capacity and opportunity to change and to address their own needs," and ". . . resolve conflicts between clients' interests and the broader society's interests in a socially responsible manner" (Preamble). Similarly, in their joint statement on ethics in social work, the International Federation of Social Workers (IFSW) and the International Association of Schools of Social Work (IASSW) affirm that human rights follow from respect for the inherent dignity and worth of all people. As such, social workers are expected to defend and uphold the physical, psychological, emotional, and spiritual integrity and well-being of all persons by

1. Respecting the right to self-determination—Social workers should respect and promote people's right to make their own choices and decisions, irrespective of their values and life choices, provided this does not threaten the rights and legitimate interests of others.

2. Promoting the right to participation—Social workers should promote the full involvement and participation of people using their services in ways that enable them to be empowered in all aspects of decisions and actions affecting their lives.

3. Treating each person as a whole—Social workers should be concerned with the whole person, within the family, community, societal and natural environments, and should seek to recognise all aspects of a person's life.

4. Identifying and developing strengths—Social workers should focus on the strengths of all individuals, groups and communities and thus promote their empowerment. (IFSW, 2004, Sec. 4.1)

Respectful interaction with others affirms their sense of dignity and worth. Social workers treat people with consideration, respect their uniqueness, appreciate the validity of their perspectives, and listen carefully to what they have to say. Ultimately, according people dignity and worth affords them the opportunities and resources of a just society.

Social Justice

Charity begins at home and justice begins next door.

—Charles Dickens

Social justice refers to the manner in which society distributes resources among its members. "Social justice prevails when all members of a society share equally in the social order, secure an equitable consideration of resources and opportunities, and enjoy their full benefit of civil liberties" (DuBois & Miley, 2008, p. 16). The IFSW and the IASSW (2004) detail the fabric of social justice:

1. Challenging negative discrimination—Social workers have a responsibility to challenge negative discrimination on the basis of characteristics such as ability, age, culture, gender or sex, marital status, socio-economic status, political opinions, skin colour, racial or other physical characteristics, sexual orientation, or spiritual beliefs.

2. Recognising diversity—Social workers should recognise and respect the ethnic and cultural diversity of the societies in which they practise, taking account of individual, family, group and community differences.

3. Distributing resources equitably—Social workers should ensure that resources at their disposal are distributed fairly, according to need.

4. Challenging unjust policies and practices—Social workers have a duty to bring to the attention of their employers, policy makers, politicians and the general public situations where distribution of resources, policies and practices are oppressive, unfair or harmful.

5. Working in solidarity—Social workers have an obligation to challenge social conditions that contribute to social exclusion, stigmatisation or subjugation, and to work towards an inclusive society. (Sec. 4.2)

Social injustice prevails when society infringes on human rights, holds prejudicial attitudes toward some of its members, and institutionalizes inequality by discriminating against segments of its citizenry. Encroachments on human and civil rights deny equal access to opportunities and resources, limiting full participation in society. Collectively, the injustices enacted by advantaged groups create conditions of discrimination and oppression for disadvantaged groups. Members of oppressed groups often personally experience dehumanization and victimization. Social workers understand the consequences of injustice and intervene to achieve individual and collective social and economic justice.

Defining Social Work

Social work is a profession that supports individuals, groups, and communities in a changing society and creates social conditions favorable to the well-being of people and society. The International Federation of Social Work (IFSW) defines social work:

> The social work profession promotes social change, problem solving in human relationships and the empowerment and liberation of people to enhance well-being. Utilizing theories of human behaviour and social systems, social work intervenes at the points where people interact with their environments. Principles of human rights and social justice are fundamental to social work. (IFSW, 2000)

Similarly, the Council on Social Work Education (CSWE), which accredits undergraduate and graduate social work programs, describes the purpose of social work:

> The purpose of the social work profession is to promote human and community well-being. Guided by a person and environment construct, a global perspective, respect for human diversity, and knowledge based on scientific inquiry, social work's purpose is actualized through its quest for social and economic justice, the prevention of conditions that limit human rights, the elimination of poverty, and the enhancement of the quality of life for all persons. (CSWE, 2008, p. 1)

Framing social work's commitment to respect for the dignity and worth all people and the profession's quest for social justice, the core values of social work also set the standards for what is desirable in practice. The National Association of Social Workers *Code of Ethics* (1999a) describes the professional values that guide social work practice:

- Service: helping people and solving social problems
- Social justice: challenging injustices
- Dignity and worth of the person: respecting inherent dignity
- Importance of human relationships: recognizing the importance of belongingness
- Integrity: being trustworthy
- Competence: practicing competently

Achieving the Purpose of Social Work

Social work focuses on releasing human power in individuals to reach their potential and contribute to the collective good of society; it emphasizes releasing social power to create changes in society, social institutions, and social policy, which in turn create opportunities for individuals (Smalley, 1967). This view conceptualizes the purpose of social work in relation to both individual and collective resources. The trademark of the social work profession is this simultaneous focus on persons and their impinging social and physical environments.

To this end, practitioners work with people in ways that strengthen their sense of competence, link them with needed resources, and promote organizational and institutional change so that the structures of society respond to the needs of all societal members (NASW, 1981). Additionally, social workers engage in research to contribute to social work theory and evaluate practice methods. To achieve these purposes, social workers engage in a variety of activities.

Box 1.1 The Ethic of Justice

Social justice describes circumstances in which all members of a society have equal access to societal resources, opportunities, rights, political influence, and benefits (Barker, 2003; Finn & Jacobson, 2003; Healy, 2001; Parker, 2003; Pease, 2002). Social justice prevails when all members benefit from the resources that a society offers and, reciprocally, have opportunities to contribute to that society's pool of resources. In contrast, social injustice is evident when a society denies certain population groups civil rights by excluding them from full participation in decision making, when it distributes institutional resources in deference to privilege and power, or when its members show prejudicial attitudes and discriminatory actions toward each other.

The philosophy of social justice is deeply rooted in the social work profession; however, political realities and ethical dilemmas confound workers' attempts to apply the principles of social justice in practice. As an example, Reisch (2002) describes problems associated with relating social justice principles to the social policy debates taking place in today's political and economic environment.

> Two fundamental problems are often overlooked, however, in discussions of applying justice principles to contemporary social policy debates. The first is the paradox of attempting to develop principles of justice within a political, economic, and social context based largely, if tacitly, on the preservation of injustice. . . . The second problem relates to the application of justice concepts based largely on the expansion of individual rights and individual shares of societal resources to the development of policies, programs, and modes of intervention that address group needs and concerns. (pp. 346–347)

Reisch highlights the tension between asserting individual rights and advancing the common good in allocating societal resources. Group and individual interests do not always converge. Social workers face dilemmas in choosing actions in practice that promote a social justice ideal.

Despite competing values, privileged interests, ethical contradictions, and political realities, social work ethics compels workers to promote social justice and challenge injustices through social change, particularly in their efforts with the most vulnerable groups in society. Empowerment-based practice principles also demand that workers address injustice and inequality as they affect all practice domains, processes, and activities. "Part of what is involved in becoming empowered is that people are not cowed into hopelessness and inaction by these existing inequalities. Thus is empowerment intrinsically linked to fighting against oppression and social justice" (Breton, 2002, p. 26). Guaranteeing access to services, the opportunity to experience social and economic privilege, an awareness of due process, a voice in policy formulation and implementation, and the power to influence resource allocation—all are trademarks of justice-centered and empowerment-based social work practice.

Social workers further the social justice ideal by expanding institutional resources such as adequate education, political participation, and economic self-sufficiency. Justice-centered workers also strive to promote fair health, education, employment, and social welfare policies and to organize social service delivery networks for client access, respect, and acceptance. Ensuring people equal access affirms human dignity and worth and creates an environment reflective of a just society.

First, social work practitioners engage with clients to assess challenges in social functioning, process information in ways that enhance their ability to discover solutions, develop skills to resolve problems in living, and create support for change.

Second, social workers link people with resources and services, a vital strategy in any change effort. More than simply connecting people with services, workers advocate optimal benefits, develop networks of communication among organizations in the social service delivery network, and establish access to resources. When necessary resources do not exist, practitioners generate new opportunities, programs, and services.

Third, the NASW charges practitioners to work toward a humane and adequate social service delivery system. To accomplish this, social workers champion the planning of pertinent programs by advocating client-centeredness, coordination, effectiveness, and efficiency in the delivery of services. Importantly, they strengthen lines of accountability and ensure the application of professional standards, ethics, and values in service delivery.

Fourth, social workers participate in social policy development. In the arena of social policy, workers analyze social problems for policy ramifications, develop new policies, and retire those that are no longer productive. They also translate statutes, policies, and regulations into responsive programs and services that meet individual and collective needs.

Finally, practitioners engage in research to further the knowledge and skill base of social work. Effective and ethical social work depends on practitioners using research-based theory and methods as well as contributing to the knowledge base of the profession through their own research and evaluation activities.

GENERALIST SOCIAL WORK

Policy Practice

Generalist social workers practice in the context of personal and collective issues. Why is policy practice important to their work in direct practice?

Generalist social work provides an integrated and multileveled approach for meeting the purposes of social work. Generalist practitioners acknowledge the interplay of personal and collective issues, prompting them to work with a variety of human systems—societies, communities, neighborhoods, complex organizations, formal groups, families, and individuals—to create changes that maximize human system functioning. This means that generalist social workers work directly with client systems at all levels, connect clients to available resources, intervene with organizations to enhance the responsiveness of resource systems, advocate just social policies to ensure the equitable distribution of resources, and research all aspects of social work practice.

The generalist approach to social work practice rests on four major premises. First, human behavior is inextricably connected to the social and physical environment. Second, based on this linkage among persons and environments, opportunities for enhancing the functioning of any human system include changing the system itself, modifying its interactions with the environment, and altering other systems within its environment. Generalist practitioners implement multilevel assessments and multimethod interventions in response to these possible avenues for change. Third, work with any level of a human system—from individual to society—uses similar social work processes. Social work intervention with all human systems requires an exchange of information through some form of dialogue, a process of discovery to locate resources for change, and a phase of development to accomplish the purposes of the work. Finally, generalist practitioners have responsibilities beyond direct practice to work toward just social policies as well as to conduct and apply research.

Levels of Intervention in Generalist Practice

Generalist social workers look at issues in context and find solutions within the interactions between people and their environments. The generalist approach moves beyond the confines of individually focused practice to the expansive sphere of intervention at multiple system levels. "In this process, all social work methods—traditional and innovative—are utilized, singly or in combination, to meet reality needs and to alleviate stresses in ways that enhance or strengthen the inherent capacities of client systems" (Brown, 1982,

p. 123). In generalist social work, the nature of presenting situations, the particular systems involved, and potential solutions shape interventions, rather than a social worker's adherence to a particular method.

The view of generalist social work is like the view through a wide-angle lens of a camera. It takes in the whole, even when focusing on an individual part. Workers assess people in the backdrop of their settings, and interventions unfold with an eye to outcomes at all system levels. Visualize potential clients and agents for change on a continuum ranging from micro- to mezzo- to macrolevel interventions, small systems to large systems, including the system of the social work profession itself (Figure 1.1). Generalist social workers view problems in context, combine practice techniques to fit the situation, and implement skills to intervene at multiple system levels.

Working with microlevel systems

Microlevel intervention focuses on work with people individually, in families, or in small groups to foster changes within personal functioning, in social relationships, and in the ways people interact with social and institutional resources. Social workers draw on the knowledge and skills of clinical practice, including strategies such as crisis intervention, family therapy, linkage and referral, and the use of group process. For instance, in this chapter's introductory example, Andrea Barry could work with Mr. and Mrs. Clemens to improve their parenting skills or refer them to a parent support group.

Although microlevel interventions create changes in individual, familial, and interpersonal functioning, social workers do not necessarily direct all their efforts at changing individuals themselves. Often, workers target changes in other systems, including changes in the social and physical environments, to facilitate improvement in an individual's or family's social functioning. These activities involve work with systems at other levels.

Working with mezzolevel systems

Mezzolevel intervention creates changes in task groups, teams, organizations, and the network of service delivery. In other words, the locus for change is within organizations and formal groups, including their structures, goals, or functions. For example, if, in working with the Clemens children, Andrea learns of their embarrassment at receiving lunch subsidies because the school physically segregates the "free lunch" students from the "full pay" students in the cafeteria, she can help them and other families who report similar concerns by working directly on the school's policy. Andrea's work with the school to address this demeaning and discriminatory practice represents a mezzolevel intervention. Effecting change in organizations requires an understanding of group dynamics, skills in facilitating decision

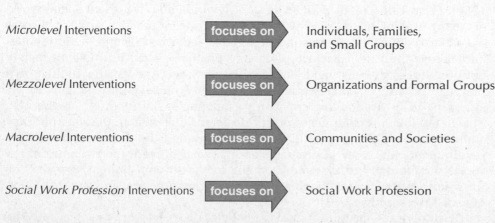

Microlevel Interventions   **focuses on** → Individuals, Families, and Small Groups

Mezzolevel Interventions   **focuses on** → Organizations and Formal Groups

Macrolevel Interventions   **focuses on** → Communities and Societies

Social Work Profession Interventions   **focuses on** → Social Work Profession

Figure 1.1
System Levels for Social Work Intervention

making, and a proficiency in organizational planning. Working with agency structures and the social service delivery network is essential for developing quality resources and services.

Working with macrolevel systems

Macrolevel intervention addresses social problems in community, institutional, and societal systems. At this level, generalist practitioners work to achieve social change through neighborhood organizing, community planning, locality development, public education, policy development, and social action. A worker's testimony at a legislative hearing reflects a macrolevel strategy to support a comprehensive national family welfare policy. Working with neighborhood groups to lobby for increased city spending on police protection, street repair, and park maintenance is another example of a macrolevel intervention. Social policy formulation and community development lead to macrosystem change.

Working with the social work profession

Finally, generalist practitioners address issues within the system of the social work profession itself. These activities project a professional identity, define professional relationships with social work and interdisciplinary colleagues, reorient priorities within the social work profession, or reorganize the system of service delivery. For instance, by supporting social work licensure and the legal regulation of practice, practitioners use their collective influence to ensure the competence of those persons who become social workers. Standard setting and accountability call for social workers to be actively involved in the system of the social work profession.

Policy and Generalist Practice

We must become the change we want to see.
—Mahatma Gandhi

Social policy determines how a society distributes its resources among its members to promote well-being. Social policies direct the delivery of health and human services. Policies particularly relevant to social work include government plans and programs in the areas of social welfare, economic security, education, criminal justice, and health care, among others (Barker, 2003). Social workers press for fair and responsive social policies that benefit all persons and advocate changes in policies affecting disenfranchised and oppressed groups whose dignity has been diminished by injustice.

Social welfare policies affect all facets of social work practice (Schorr, 1985). First, value-based policies implicitly guide how we orient social workers to the profession, the ways we educate workers for practice, and the choices we make to define the dimensions of practice activities. Second, policy shapes bureaucracy and the structure of agency practice—a culture that ultimately defines who gets services and what services they get. And, finally, in their own practice activities, social workers unavoidably make policy judgments by attending to or overlooking constantly changing social realities. To this list, Specht (1983) adds other major policy decisions that arise in the sociopolitical context of social work practice. These policy choices determine eligibility requirements, the array of programs and services offered, the structure of the social service delivery system, financing for health and human services, the form and substance of educating social work practitioners, and the regulation of social work activities.

To understand the impact of social policies on social work practice, consider how policy affects all aspects of Andrea Barry's practice in family preservation.

Box 1.2 Professional Image and a Social Justice Identity: A Policy–Practice Connection

The social work profession today faces a confusing and inaccurate public image, an image perpetuated by the portrayal of social work in the media (Freeman & Valentine, 2004; Zugazaga, et al., 2006). To address this concern about image, social work professionals may need to look inward. The bifurcation of the social work profession into two mutually exclusive divisions, one focusing on clinically based (micro) practice, and the other, on policy-oriented (macro) practice dilutes the social justice image of social work (Bisman, 2004; Dennison, et al., 2007; Dessell, et al., 2006; Johnson, 2004; Macdonald, et al., 2003; Olson, 2007; Reisch & Andrews, 2004; Specht & Courtney, 1994). Social workers debate questions that reinforce the notion of a dichotomy in social work practice. Should social work's emphasis be clinical work or policy practice? Does facilitating individual adaptation mean succumbing to social injustice? Do the long-range solutions of macropractice address the immediate needs of social work clients? Are social work solutions best found at the microlevel or macrolevel?

The past several decades show social work leaning more toward clinical than political practice, leading Karger and Hernandez (2004) to suggest that the profession has abandoned its engagement in public discourse, social commentary, political and social activism, and intellectual life. As a result, social workers "have little influence on the pressing issues of the day" (p. 51), particularly with respect to policy concerns about social justice. Searing (2003) charges social work "to reclaim its radical tradition. This asserts that the assessment of client's 'needs' should not only be driven by the availability of resources but should also be concerned with the reduction of inequality and social justice" (¶4) Furthermore, "if we want the profession of social work to pursue a social justice mission, which our official and espoused position suggests, then we need to take steps to ensure that the way we frame and conceptualize our practice is congruent with, and furthers, social justice principles" (Hawkins, et al., 2001, p. 11).

A generalist, empowerment method bridges the micro/macro split within the social work profession; it frames social work practice to meet the social justice mandate based on the following principles:

- The unifying purpose of social work is to enhance human well-being and to promote a mutually beneficial interaction between individuals and society
- The social work profession maintains an integrated view of persons in the context of their physical and social environments
- Social workers practice at the intersection of private troubles and public issues
- Social workers work with people to enhance their competence and functioning, to access social supports and resources, to create humane and responsive social services, to influence social policy, and to expand the structures of society that provide opportunities for all citizens
- Social workers have a partisan commitment to people who are vulnerable, oppressed, and living in poverty. The mandate of the social work profession is to ensure the fulfillment of the social justice contract between individuals and society, particularly for those groups that are disenfranchised
- A just society is one in which all members of society share the same rights to participation in society, protection by the law, opportunities for development, access to social benefits, and who, in turn, contribute to the resource pool of society
- Empowerment social work is simultaneously clinical (personal) and critical (political) (Miley & DuBois, 2005)

Social policies, framed at the legislative level in the amendments to the Social Security Act and implemented through state administrative procedures, define the goals and processes that Andrea implements in family preservation. Agency-level policy to design programs and services consistent with empowering principles and a strengths perspective further refines Andrea's approach to working with families. As a professional social worker, Andrea's direct practice with families falls within the policy guidelines established by the NASW standards for child protection. Policy choices at many levels—federal, state, agency, and worker—influence the day-to-day practice of social work.

Research in Generalist Practice

Research is a method of systematic investigation or experimentation, the results of which can enrich theory and refine practice applications. When clients are integrally involved in designing and implementing research, research processes themselves empower clients. Research informs social work practice in several ways. It contributes to the theoretical base for understanding human behavior and change. Further, research is a tool for designing intervention strategies, measuring intervention effectiveness, and evaluating practice. Research is essential for program development and policy analysis. Aware of the integral relationship between theory and practice, generalist social workers use research-based knowledge to support practice activities and directly conduct their own research and analysis. The press for evidence-based practice attests to the importance of the research–practice connection. The goal of evidence-based research is to identify effective intervention strategies and robust program models. Based on rigorous client outcome studies, best practices are emerging in all fields of social work practice.

Research enhances social work effectiveness, as illustrated in the example of Andrea Barry's work with clients in family preservation. Her coursework on empowerment-based practice, theories about families, and the dynamics of child abuse and neglect—all information rooted in decades of social work research—informs Andrea each time she interacts with her clients. Andrea regularly reads professional journals, especially *Social Work, Child Welfare, The Journal of Ethnic and Cultural Diversity in Social Work, The Journal of Evidence-Based Practice,* and *Families in Society,* to keep up with best practices within the field of child welfare. She also uses evaluation and research techniques to monitor her clients' progress toward goals and to assess her own practice effectiveness. Additionally, Andrea's work presents opportunities to add to the knowledge base of the profession as she and other family preservation workers carefully document the results of a new intervention program piloted by her agency. Research supports practice, and practitioners conduct research.

Advantages of a Multifaceted Approach

A pebble cast into a pond causes ripples that spread in all directions. Each one of our thoughts, words, and deeds is like that. We won't sit down and feel hopeless. There's too much work to do.

—Dorothy Day

Social workers realize many advantages from their generalist practice approach. Inevitably, changes in one system ripple through other interrelated systems as well. In other words, a significant improvement in a client or environmental system might precipitate other beneficial changes. A single policy change may have far-reaching benefits for an entire society. Research demonstrating effective change strategies in one situation may lead to broader implementations to assist others in similar situations. Because of their multidimensional perspectives, generalist practitioners are likely to uncover more than one possible solution for any given problem.

Generalist social workers see many possible angles from which to approach any solution. They analyze the many dimensions of any challenging situation to discover entry points for change. They also align the motivations and efforts of client systems with systems in their environments, synchronizing the movements of all involved to achieve the desired outcome. Generalist social work frames a way of thinking about both problems and solutions in context, and it describes a way of working with clients at a variety of system levels.

Generalist social workers use best practices with culturally diverse families.

SOCIAL WORK FUNCTIONS AND ROLES

Social worker roles direct the nature of interaction between practitioners and client systems. What is the common denominator of the roles associated with each of the functions of consultancy, resource management and education at the various client system levels?

Generalists work with systems at many levels, but what does that actually mean in their daily practice of social work? As a family preservation worker, Andrea Barry intervenes directly with individuals and families. She provides them with education, counseling, and linkage to needed community resources—activities associated with roles at the microlevel. Yet Andrea's work encompasses more than microlevel intervention. In her position, Andrea identifies gaps in the social service delivery network when resources families need are not available. As a result, she works with other professionals in child welfare to address social service delivery issues—a mezzolevel intervention. She and her interdisciplinary colleagues are developing a community education plan to promote effective parenting—a macrolevel strategy. Finally, Andrea systematically evaluates the effectiveness of her work and keeps abreast of child welfare policy initiatives. In doing so, Andrea demonstrates the integration of research, policy, and multilevel intervention that characterizes generalist social work practice.

Activities of generalist social work practice fall broadly into three related functions—consultancy, resource management, and education (DuBois & Miley, 2008; Tracy & DuBois, 1987). Within each function are associated roles that explicate the nature of the interaction between clients and social workers at various system levels. These roles define responsibilities for both client systems and practitioners. Interventions designed within this model cover the range of issues presented to generalist social workers by clients at all system levels.

Consultancy

Through consultancy, social workers seek to find solutions for challenges in social functioning with individuals, families, groups, organizations, and communities. Within the roles of the consultancy function of social work, workers and clients confer and deliberate together to develop plans for change. Practitioners and clients share their expertise with one another for the purpose of resolving personal, family, organizational, and societal problems. Consultancy acknowledges that both social workers and client systems bring information and resources, actual and potential, that are vital for resolving the issue at hand.

As a collaborative process, consultancy draws on the knowledge, values, and skills of social workers and clients to clarify issues, recognize strengths, discuss options, and identify potential courses of action. As consultants, social workers empower clients by respecting their competence, drawing on their strengths, and working with them collaboratively to discover solutions. These consultancy activities cast workers into the roles of enabler, facilitator, planner, and colleague (Table 1.1).

Enabler role

As enablers, social workers engage individuals, families, and small groups in counseling processes. An enabler encourages action by engaging in a helping relationship, framing solutions, and working for constructive and sustainable change. In other words, enablers are change agents who "use varying approaches in order to provide the conditions necessary for clients to achieve their purposes, meet life challenges, engage in their natural life development processes, and carry out their tasks" (Maluccio, 1981, p. 19). In the context of work with groups, social workers enable supportive interactions among group members to facilitate problem solving. As enablers, practitioners consult with individual and family client systems to improve social functioning by modifying behaviors, relationship patterns, and social and physical environments.

Facilitator role

Facilitators activate the participation of organizational members in change efforts. By facilitating group processes, social workers encourage competent group functioning, stimulate intragroup support, observe group interaction, offer constructive feedback, and share information about group dynamics. As facilitators, social workers enhance linkages within organizations and help them counteract apathy and disorganization (Pincus & Minahan, 1973). In

Table 1.1	**Consultancy Roles**	
Level	Role	Strategy
Micro-	Enabler	Empower clients in finding solutions
Mezzo-	Facilitator	Foster organizational development
Macro-	Planner	Coordinate program and policy development through research and planning
Social Work Profession	Colleague/Monitor	Mentor, guide, and support professional acculturation

Adapted with permission of the authors from *Information Model for Generalist Social Work Practice*, p. 2, by B. C. Tracy and B. DuBois, 1987. All rights reserved.

this role, practitioners may even target their own agency settings to increase the cooperation of staff and ensure the effectiveness of social service delivery.

Planner role

As social planners and community organizers, social workers understand community needs, recognize gaps and barriers in service delivery, and can facilitate a process for community-based or social change. Social planners use research and planning strategies to collect data systematically, explore alternative courses of action, and recommend changes to community leaders (Barker, 2003). Techniques for planning include needs assessments, service inventories, community profiles, community inventories, environmental scans, and field research to understand social problems and develop innovative solutions at the macrolevel.

Colleague and monitor roles

Through their colleague and monitor roles, social workers uphold expectations for the ethical conduct of members of their profession. Consultative relationships among social work practitioners lead to sound practice and professional development. As colleagues, social workers develop working partnerships with other practitioners through their participation in professional organizations such as the NASW and its local membership groups, and through their everyday contacts with other professionals. The *Code of Ethics* (NASW, 1999a) specifically casts social workers as monitors, charging them to review the professional activities of peers to ensure quality and maintain professional standards.

Resource Management

In the resource management function, social workers stimulate exchanges with resources that client systems already use to some extent, access available resources that client systems are not using, and develop resources that are not currently available. Resources are sources of power and provide the impetus for change at any system level. Resources are found within individuals, in relationships, and in social institutions.

Resources are not gifts bestowed by social workers. Instead, both social workers and clients play active roles in managing resources. Clients, as resource managers, take action to explore existing opportunities, activate dormant supports, and assert their rights to services. Social workers bring the resources of professional practice—the value imperative of equitable access to societal resources, the broad knowledge of the availability of resources, and a repertoire of skills to access and develop resources. Resource management is empowering when it increases the client system's own resourcefulness through coordinating, systematizing, and integrating rather than through controlling or directing. Social workers as resource managers function in the roles of broker, advocate, convener, mediator, activist, and catalyst (Table 1.2).

Broker and advocate roles

The professional mandate of the social work profession, "to help people obtain resources," lays the foundation for the roles of broker and advocate. As brokers, social workers link clients with available resources by providing information about resource options and making appropriate referrals. Competent brokers assess situations, provide clients with choices among alternative resources, facilitate clients' connections with referral agencies, and follow up to evaluate their efforts.

Table 1.2	**Resource-management Roles**	
Level	Role	Strategy
Micro-	Broker/Advocate	Link clients with resources through case management
Mezzo-	Convener/Mediator	Assemble groups and organizations to network for resource development
Macro-	Activist	Initiate and sustain social change through social action
Social Work Profession	Catalyst	Stimulate community service through interdisciplinary activities

Adapted with permission of the authors from *Information Model for Generalist Social Work Practice*, p. 2, by B. C. Tracy and B. DuBois, 1987. All rights reserved.

As advocates, social workers act as intermediaries between clients and other systems to protect clients' rights. Frequently, advocates function as spokespersons for clients in the bureaucratic maze of governmental structures. Advocates intervene with social service delivery systems or policy-makers on behalf of clients. Circumstances often press social workers to take on advocacy roles because the rights of social service clients have often been abridged.

Convener and mediator roles

Social workers often serve as conveners and mediators with formal groups and organizations to coordinate resource distribution and development. Conveners promote interagency discussion and planning, mobilize coordinated networks for effective service delivery, and advocate policies that promise equitable funding and just service provisions. As conveners, social workers use networking strategies to bring together diverse representatives to address collective goals such as in the examples of community task groups, interagency committees, and United Way panels. When controversy or conflicts of interest arise, social workers as mediators use their skills for negotiating differences and resolving conflicts. Conveners-mediators ally service providers in identifying service delivery gaps and encouraging proactive interagency planning, activities that are central to prevention efforts in social work.

Activist role

Generalist social workers are in positions to identify societal conditions detrimental to the well-being of clients—a view that informs the social worker as activist. According to Barker (2003), social activists alert the general public about social problems or injustices and garner support to alleviate these conditions. Social activists mobilize resources, build coalitions, take legal actions, and lobby for legislation. They create just social policies as well as initiate new funding or funding reallocations that address their identified priority issues. Engendering community support, activists empower community-based efforts to resolve community issues, redress social injustice, and generate social reform.

Catalyst role

As catalysts for change, social workers team with other professionals to develop humane service delivery, advocate just social and environmental policy, and support a worldview acknowledging global interdependence. Through professional organizations, social workers lobby at the state and federal levels and provide expert testimony. As catalysts, social workers initiate, foster, and sustain interdisciplinary cooperation to highlight client, local, national, and international issues.

Education

The social work function of education requires an empowering information exchange between a client system and a social work practitioner. Mutual sharing of knowledge and ideas are central to the educational function. Educational processes at all system levels reflect partnerships of co-learners and co-teachers. Collaborative learning presumes that client systems are self-directing, possess reservoirs of experiences and resources on which to base educational experiences, and desire immediate applications of new learning. The education function of social work respects the knowledge and experience that all parties contribute. Functioning as educators involves social workers in the activities of teaching, training, outreach, and research and scholarship (Table 1.3).

Teacher role

The teaching role in social work empowers client systems with information to stimulate competent functioning in all domains of living. Through teaching strategies, social workers strengthen clients with information to resolve current issues and to prevent other difficulties from emerging. To affirm clients' existing knowledge and skills, social workers select collaborative learning strategies to implement educational activities. Educational exchanges may occur in structured client–worker conferences, in formalized instructional settings, or in experiential exercises such as role plays.

Trainer role

As educational resource specialists for formal groups, trainers make presentations, serve as panelists at public forums, and conduct workshop sessions. Sometimes, trainers are organizational employees; at other times, organizations contract with social workers to provide specific training experiences. Effective trainers select methods and resource materials based on research about adult education, attitude change, and learning modalities. Successful training strategies require a careful assessment of staff-development needs, clear goals of what the organization seeks, the ability to convey information through appropriate training formats, and a concrete evaluation process.

Outreach role

In outreach roles, social workers inform a variety of audiences about social problems, describe social injustices, and suggest services and policies to

Table 1.3	**Education Roles**	
Level	Role	Strategy
Micro-	Teacher	Facilitate information processing and provide educational programming
Mezzo-	Trainer	Instruct through staff development
Macro-	Outreach	Convey public information about social issues and social services through community education
Social Work Profession	Researcher/Scholar	Engage in discovery for knowledge development

Adapted with permission of the authors from *Information Model for Generalist Social Work Practice,* p. 2, by B. C. Tracy and B. DuBois, 1987. All rights reserved.

As illustrated in Table 1.4, Andrea Barry engages in the functions of consultancy, resource management, and education at all client system levels. What specific verbal and written communication skills would Andrea need for her interventions with client systems?

address these issues. Workers disseminate information to inform the community about public and private social service organizations, thereby enhancing service accessibility. At the macrosystem level of community and society, the outreach role supports the prevention of problems. Increasing awareness of such issues as poverty, health care, disease control, stress, suicide, infant mortality, substance abuse, and family violence leads to early intervention and stimulates support for preventive actions. Using mass media, distributing posters and leaflets, conducting mailings, staffing information booths, and engaging in public speaking all bolster community members' awareness about programs and services. Sensitive to the unique needs of potential clients, outreach social workers provide multilingual, signed, Braille, and large-print announcements.

Researcher and scholar roles

The social work *Code of Ethics* (NASW, 1999a) specifically describes how professional knowledge and scientific research form the basis for practice. The *Code of Ethics* obligates social workers to contribute to the profession by conducting their own empirical research and sharing their findings with colleagues. Professionals also critically examine the social work literature to integrate research findings with their practice. Social workers contribute to and draw on research related to human behavior and the social environment, service delivery, social welfare policy, and intervention methods.

Integrating Generalist Functions

In practice, social workers interweave the functions of consultancy, resource management, and education. For example, in addition to counseling, consultancy may involve linking clients with resources and teaching them new skills. Similarly, even though education is identified as a separate function, educational processes are inherent in all other social work activities as well. Rather than compartmentalizing these roles, this trilogy of social work functions provides an organizing schema for generalist social workers to construct and integrate multifaceted interventions. Table 1.4 offers examples of how family service worker

Table 1.4	**Family Service Interventions. Case Example: Andrea Barry**			
	Microlevel	Mezzolevel	Macrolevel	Social Work Profession
Consultancy	Counseling with families	Facilitating organizational change to prevent burnout in child protective workers	Participating in child welfare community planning	Addressing ethical and legal issues in mandatory reporting of child abuse and neglect
Resource Management	Linking families with additional community resources	Coordinating service delivery planning among local agencies	Developing a stable funding base for child-welfare services	Stimulating interdisciplinary cooperation to develop resources
Education	Providing opportunities for learning anger control and positive parenting	Leading staff development training on mandatory reporting at local day care centers	Initiating public education regarding child-protective resources	Presenting family preservation research at a regional conference

Andrea Barry engages in consultancy, resource management, and educational interventions at all system levels.

LOOKING FORWARD

Generalist social work is a multifaceted approach to helping people overcome the challenges in their lives. Generalist social workers play many practice roles, contribute to social work research, and improve social policy in their efforts to promote human dignity and ensure social justice—the core values of social work. It is these core values that call people to social work. Adhering to these values becomes the litmus test for determining one's fit with the profession.

Proficiency as a social worker requires a coherent practice framework, resourceful ways to look at human and social system functioning, and dynamic processes for change. This book explains the perspectives and processes that are essential for the effective practice of an empowerment-oriented method of generalist social work. This chapter provides an overview of the purposes and values of the social work profession and descriptions of practitioner roles. The orientation to empowerment social work provides a foundation for examining an ecosystems perspective for generalist social work, infusing multicultural and strengths perspectives in practice, and implementing social work processes at many levels described in later chapters. Chapter 2 discusses social work theory in practice and articulates how various views, such as the ecosystems perspective and social constructionism, support an empowering generalist approach. Chapter 3 describes how values, expectations, and diverse cultural and ethnic influences filter our perceptions and affect our work. Chapter 4 explains the strengths perspective and empowerment and discusses their implications for generalist practice.

Chapter 5 introduces this empowering method of social work practice framed within three concurrent phases—dialogue, discovery, and development—each explicated by discrete practice processes. Through dialogue, workers and clients develop and maintain collaborative partnerships, exchange relevant information, and define the purposes of the work. In discovery, practitioners and clients locate resources on which to construct plans for change. Through development, workers and clients activate resources, forge alliances with others, and create new opportunities to distribute the resources of a just society. Chapters 6 through 16 delineate these phases, examine each process in full detail, and offer applications at the micro-, mezzo-, and macrosystem levels.

Succeed with **mysocialworklab**

Log onto **www.mysocialworklab.com** and click on the link to view the Interactive Skill Module videos. Answer the questions below. (*If you did not receive an access code to **MySocialWorkLab** with this text and wish to purchase access online, please visit* www.mysocialworklab.com.)

1. **Watch page 22 of the school social work module** where worker Terry suggests a micro-level intervention for a client's family. What other actions might Terry take that would indicate she is a generalist social worker?

2. **Watch social work client Faye in the domestic violence module, pages 5 and 11.** What do you see and hear that supports the hypothesis that Faye's situation is affected by social and economic oppression? What must change to create a more just society?

PRACTICE TEST

Professional Identity

1. Evaluate the perspectives of the following social workers and determine which perspective most closely aligns with the unifying purpose of social work:
   a. Bob says the social work's unifying purpose is to facilitate social action that results in social change
   b. Adreana believes that, as a social worker, her main focus of activity is providing advice to people with problems.
   c. Jake describes social work as including counseling and linking families with resources.
   d. Maria indicates that she helps individuals, groups, or communities to enhance their capacity for social functioning and to create societal conditions that support this goal.

Human Rights & Justice

2. Andrea Barry applies the ethic of justice to her practice of empowerment-based social work. Which of the following is LEAST characteristic of her thinking about the ethic of justice?
   a. Clients should be aware of their rights to due process.
   b. Clients should have a voice in formulating policies.
   c. Clients should be involved in decisions about allocating resources.
   d. The ethic of justice relates to issues of dignity and worth but not to oppression.

3. Duane Jackson facilitates a parenting group for young couples. This represents a(n) _____.
   a. a microlevel intervention
   b. a mezzolevel intervention
   c. a macrolevel intervention
   d. working with the social work profession

4. As a social worker at the Northside Family Agency, Jane coordinates a public education initiative on preventing child abuse This activity represents a _____.
   a. a microlevel intervention
   b. a mezzolevel intervention
   c. a macrolevel intervention
   d. working with the social work profession

5. Joel Diamond's work in organizational planning is most likely a _____.
   a. a microlevel intervention
   b. a mezzolevel intervention
   c. a macrolevel intervention
   d. working with the social work profession

Professional Identity

6. Maria Garcia regards social justice as an integral facet of her professional identity as a social worker. Which of the following is MOST likely true?
   a. Her professional activities are clinical but not political.
   b. Her professional activities are political but not clinical.
   c. Her professional activities are neither clinical nor political.
   d. Her professional activities are both clinical and political.

7. Carolee Goode links clients with the community-based services they request. Her work represents the social work role of _____.
   a. resource management   b. enabler
   c. broker   d. catalyst

8. Tim Stein lobbies for extending health care benefits to families who are uninsured. His lobbying activities reflect the _____ role.
   a. trouble maker
   b. activist
   c. enabler
   d. outreach worker

9. Dorothy Martin runs support groups for adolescent clients. Her work reflects the role of _____.
   a. facilitator
   b. enabler
   c. advocate
   d. outreach

Log onto **MySocialWorkLab** once you have completed the Practice Test above to take your Chapter Exam and demonstrate your knowledge of this material.

2

Human System Perspectives

CHAPTER OUTLINE

CONNECTING CORE COMPETENCIES *in this chapter*

| Professional Identity | Ethical Practice | Critical Thinking | Diversity in Practice | Human Rights & Justice | Research Based Practice | Human Behavior | Policy Practice | Practice Contexts | Engage Assess Intervene Evaluate |

In the deserts of the Southwestern United States, plants develop various ways to survive in the face of harsh, dry, and hot conditions. The creosote bush, for example, sends down a tap root 30 feet to drink from the water table. Other plants send out a network of fine roots just under the soil to capture every available drop of surface moisture. Still others have roots that emit toxins to choke out all available competition for scarce water. Each plant also has its own unique way to hang on to the precious moisture it captures. Some have tiny leaves that minimize evaporation, whereas others grow waxy and spiny surfaces that ward off those who seek to drink from their reserves. In the same environment, each different plant adapts uniquely.

In the mountains of New England, a beaver builds a dam to meet its own unique needs. But this change in the environment has ramifications beyond the beaver's life. The pond that results is a resource not only to the beaver but also to other creatures, such as frogs, fish, birds, and deer. When any organism modifies its environment, other organisms within the same ecosystem are affected and may benefit as well.

These examples from the field of ecology show the reciprocal connection between organisms and their environments. In addition, they illustrate the uniqueness and interconnectedness among living things. Human beings are more complex than desert plants or beavers, but they show similar patterns of relationship and adaptation. Consider the following example describing how Grady, a person who is unable to read, adapts to life in a literate world.

Grady is unclear about why he never learned to read. Sometimes he thinks it's because his family moved around so much, and he was always either out of school or way behind everyone else. Maybe it's because his father died when he was 12, and he stopped going to school altogether to work on his aunt's farm. Or maybe, Grady thinks, he just wasn't smart enough. One thing he has learned for sure—when you don't read, you keep it to yourself. People never give you a chance when they find that out. Besides, Grady is a proud man, and even the sound of the word "illiterate" leaves him feeling ashamed.

Not knowing how to read never stops Grady, though. He can get around on the bus—the routes are color-coded. He rides the red line to work and the green line to go to the grocery store. At the grocery store, he buys items that he can see directly or those that have pictures on them. Some aisles have cheaper food in them—generic products—but Grady seldom takes a chance with them because those boxes all look alike. Once he got some kind of box mix instead of the cereal he thought he was buying, and he couldn't read the directions to figure out how to make it. Grady can't make that kind of mistake very often. Money is too scarce for that.

One thing Grady does every day is buy a newspaper. He carries it, tucked under his arm, wherever he goes. No one would ever suspect he can't read then. He pulls it out on his break at work, chuckles to himself, and shares news items with his coworkers. The truth is, he listens to the news and sports every morning and evening so he can join in the conversations at work. Grady especially doesn't want the people at work to know he can't read; employers don't hire you if they figure out you can't read. Grady remembers how he pretended to forget his glasses when he picked up the job application, so he could take it with him and get help from his friend at the coffee shop to fill it out.

Grady has worked as a field hand at the local nursery for the last 5 years. It's a minimum-wage job, but it pays the bills at least part of the year. His boss and co-workers tease him about living "the good life," because Grady heads south each winter when the nursery shuts down. Grady smiles broadly when he talks about his sister's winter place right on the beach. In reality, he wanders homeless from place to place. He buys food with the money he earns doing odd jobs and panhandling. Sometimes, when he runs short of cash, he goes for days without eating.

Grady's co-workers cope with their winter layoff by signing up for unemployment benefits, food stamps, and short-term jobs through the local temporary employment office, but Grady doesn't see this as an option for him. There is no way to get any of those benefits without filling out the forms right there in the office. That means reading, and that is out of the question for Grady. Sometimes Grady doesn't like the limited choices he has, but he has found ways to adapt to his situation.

In all professional practice settings, social workers meet people like Grady, people who have developed styles of coping that fit their unique situations. Understanding behavior as resulting from this "ecological fit" of persons with their environments constitutes essential knowledge for social workers. Social work incorporates concepts from the science of ecology to help explain human behavior, social environments, and human diversity.

Ecology is one of the many disciplines that enrich the knowledge base of social work and guide practice activities. This chapter explains concepts from ecology and other theoretical perspectives to create an "ecosystems framework" for generalist social work practice. Specifically, this chapter

- Describes the contributions of multidisciplinary theories and perspectives that support the knowledge and skill base of generalist social work
- Summarizes the relationship between the person and environment as foundational to the ecosystems perspective for social work practice
- Explains the concepts from social systems theory for generalist social work practice
- Applies the steps of an ecosystems framework as a tool for generalist social work practice

The outcome is a dynamic view of human system behavior in the context of the social environment. Generalist social workers maintain this ecosystemic view throughout each phase of the practice process.

THE KNOWLEDGE BASE OF GENERALIST PRACTICE

Generalist social work, with its multileveled focus, requires extensive knowledge about the functioning of many types of human systems, necessitating a multidisciplinary preparation for practice. Areas of study most relevant to social work include biology, sociology, linguistics, psychology, ethology, communication, anthropology, economics, political science, history, and ecology (Table 2.1).

Theoretical Frameworks for Practice

Social workers draw from many diverse theoretical perspectives "to explain why people behave as they do, to better understand how the environment affects behavior, to guide interventive behavior, and to predict what is likely to be the result of a particular social work intervention" (Greene & Ephross, 1999, p. 5). To organize their perceptions of clients' situations, workers apply theories, perspectives, models, and orientations. Although some use these terms interchangeably, most consider theories more firmly grounded in research than the other concepts listed. A theory represents a plausible explanation about the relationship between a set of facts or circumstances and a framework for change

Table 2.1	Disciplines Contributing to Social Work Knowledge
Discipline	Research Domains
Anthropology	Culture and values Cross-cultural sensitivity Cultural and religious diversity Linguistics
Biological Sciences	Health and wellness Illness Chemical dependency Physical development, aging, and death Ecology Genetics Nutrition Physical environment
Economics	Distribution of goods and services Capitalism Socialism International finance Labor and trade Consumerism Welfare economics Employment theories Governmental fiscal policies
Psychology	Personality dynamics Gender roles Developmental issues Problem solving Perception Learning Memory Interpersonal relationships
Sociology	Structure and function of groups, organizations, and society Small group behavior Social stratification Discrimination and the "isms" Deviance Role theory Demographics Social change theory Family dynamics

Whether a theory is useful depends on the practitioner's ability to reflect on its relevance for the "in vivo" qualities of a particular relationship. This we might call practice wisdom.

—Howard Goldstein

(Sheafor & Horejsi, 2008). In contrast, perspectives, models, and orientations are more descriptive yet still useful for conceptualizing human system behavior and processes for change (Figure 2.1).

Theories and perspectives about human systems

Derived primarily from the social and behavioral sciences, theories about human systems provide a cogent understanding of how biological, psychological, social,

Figure 2.1

Selected Theories and Models for Social Work Practice

Addictions model	Family systems approach	Psychodynamic theory
Behavioral theory	Feminist perspectives	Psychosocial approach
Bureaucratic theory	General systems theory	Reality therapy
Case management model	Generalist approach	Remedial model
Cognitive-behavioral theory	Gestalt therapy	Self-help model
Communication theory	Human relations theory	Small group theories
Constructivism	Humanist theory	Social action model
Crisis intervention model	Integrative model	Social constructionism
Developmental theory	Interactional model	Social planning model
Ecological-life model	Learning theory	Solution-focused therapy
Ecosystems perspective	Locality development model	Strategic family therapy
Ethnic sensitive perspective	Management theory	Strengths perspective
Existential theory	Mediating structures model	Structural model
Family-centered practice model	Natural helping network theory	Symbolic interactionism
	Person-centered theory	Task-centered model
Family preservation model		Teamwork model
Family structural therapy	Problem solving model	Value clarification model

Human Behavior

To inform their practice, social workers draw upon a variety of theoretical perspectives, from the biological and social and behavioral sciences. Why is it important for social workers to critically evaluate the underlying assumptions of the theories they use?

cultural, economic, and political systems affect and are affected by human behavior and social structures. In practice, generalists sometimes use theories specific to the level of the client system. Examples include family life-cycle theory to assess issues in family development and conflict theory to describe group dynamics. At other times, social workers use more general theoretical perspectives that apply to all system levels. For example, the general systems perspective offers principles that apply to the functioning of all human systems—individuals, social groups, communities, and even complex bureaucracies. The general systems perspective combined with concepts from the field of ecology forms the ecosystems framework that supports this book's approach to generalist practice.

Theories and models of change

Knowledge about how change occurs in sociopolitical, organizational, community, group, family, and individual systems influences the ways that workers approach practice. Models of change define the interaction between the social worker and the client system, influence strategies the social worker selects, and describe "who should do what" to create the changes desired. Social justice–oriented practice models, including the empowering approach featured in this book, emerge from an understanding of oppression and its impact on individual functioning and potential.

Developing a Practice Framework

No one practice framework clearly represents "the social work view." A survey of social workers reveals tremendous diversity in perspectives guiding social work practice (Norlin & Chess, 1997). Practitioners in this study said they applied psychosocial and social systems theories most frequently, but many respondents also reported using principles from the psychoanalytic, behavioral, humanistic, and ecological perspectives. Significantly, a large proportion of these social workers do not implement a single theory in isolation but, instead, integrate concepts from several perspectives to construct an eclectic approach. Another study showed that experienced social workers each applied an average of eight distinct theories in their practice (Timberlake, et al., 1997).

All social workers develop frameworks for practice. A comprehensive framework for generalist practice interweaves personal and social work values, theoretical perspectives on human behavior, and orientations to change. Beginning practitioners launch their professional careers by adopting established models for practice. Over time, workers modify and update their approaches to incorporate evidence-based strategies and to match their own observations of what works.

Box 2.1 The Ethic of Critique

The ethic of critique involves a critical examination and understanding of sociopolitical and economic arrangements in the social world and the impact of these arrangements in defining human identity, beliefs, and interactions. How a person experiences the world results from the confluence of an internalized social identity as shaped by sociopolitical location and of structural arrangements within larger social and political environments. In critically examining social and political environments and their influences in constructing people's lives, practitioners and clients are analyzing organizational and institutional systems both as sources of stress and as potential solutions.

The critique of social arrangements focuses on issues of hierarchy and privilege, class distinctions and distortions, definitions of power, and the culture of silence and domination (Daniel, 2004; Starratt, 1994; Sue, 2004; Williams, 2006). "Critical reflection seeks to challenge the prevailing social, political, and structural conditions which promote the interests of some and oppress others" (Ruch, 2002, p. 205). The social work values associated with evaluating the sociopolitical and economic impact of a social arrangement include inclusion, anti-oppression, anti-discrimination, advocacy, human and social rights, democratic participation, and justice.

To critique is not necessarily to criticize, but rather, to view critically a given situation for its implications and consequences from a particular stance or theoretical perspective. The ability to critique is essential to apply social work theory to a client's situation in a way that respects client diversity and uniqueness. Without question, the social science theories and practice models that are pervasive in social work education and practice are replete with the dominant

thinking of white, middle-class men (Figueira-McDonough, et al., 2001). Without careful critique and reflection on theories, where they come from, and how they fit, workers are likely to apply knowledge and concepts that are irrelevant or even damaging to many clients, particularly those clients with minority status. Critical-evaluative processes relevant to the critique of social work practice include

▶ Reflecting on the explanations and thought processes by which a conclusion has been reached
▶ Sorting out differences between the personal values of the practitioner and the client and between personal views and professional perspectives
▶ Engaging in a rebuttal process that challenges assumptions made
▶ Identifying any reservations about the conclusions drawn
▶ Justifying one's line of reasoning (Osmo & Landau, 2001)

In many ways, to critique is to reflect on and to question the status quo—why something is arranged the way it is and why it can, or should, be different. Examining the "why" of a constructed social relationship and exploring the "why not" of some alternative relationship involves asking questions such as, Who defines the structural arrangements? Who holds the power? Who controls the resources? Which groups benefit or suffer? Who has the most to gain or lose from changing the social arrangement? Effective critique yields awareness and questions presumptions, assumed realities, and subtle norms. One cannot critically examine what one takes for granted.

Analyzing Theoretical Perspectives

To evaluate a theory's utility in practice, workers examine several aspects, including its knowledge base, description of change, role expectations for practitioners and clients, definition of problems, significant areas of focus, specific intervention methods, consistency with social work ethics and values, and effectiveness in application, as substantiated by research. Questions to address in assessing a theory's appropriateness include the following:

- What is the main focus of the theory? Is it relevant to the situation?
- To what system level does the theory apply?
- Does the theory apply widely to diverse situations or narrowly to particular cases?
- Does the theory further the worker's understanding of human system behavior or guide the worker's efforts in change activities?
- What research supports the theory? Are the samples in the research studies representative of diverse groups or of particular segments of the population?
- Is the theory congruent with the professional value base of social work?
- What assumptions does the theory make about clients, including their power, expertise, and roles?

The choices made about theory determine whether social workers function as agents of social control or, in contrast, empower clients to make changes in themselves, their situation, and social structures.

KEY PERSPECTIVES FOR EMPOWERING PRACTICE

The ecosystems perspective represents the current way many generalist social workers frame their practice. This view conceptualizes the exchanges between people and their physical and social environments (Germain, 1979, 1983; Germain & Gitterman, 1996; Gitterman & Germain, 2008; Siporin, 1980). Other perspectives fit well with the ecosystems framework to support an empowering approach to generalist practice. Social constructionism focuses on how people understand themselves and interpret what is happening in their lives. The feminist perspective advocates a political stance and drives a social worker's efforts to fashion a just society.

Ecosystems

The ecosystems view combines key concepts from ecology and general systems theory. Ecology "focuses specifically on how things fit together, how they adapt to one another" (Greif, 1986, p. 225). In ecological terms, adaptation is "a dynamic process between people and their environments as people grow, achieve competence, and make contributions to others" (p. 225). General systems theory "reduces highly complex social realities to manageable constructs [and] extends our knowledge about the diversity of human behavior" (Schafer, 1969, p. 26). It offers principles about how human systems operate and interact with one another. Together, ecology and systems theory describe the functioning and adaptation of human systems in their social and physical environments.

In the ecosystems view, persons and environments are not separate but exist in ongoing transactions with each other. We cannot simply add an understanding of persons to an understanding of environments. Instead, we must also examine the reciprocal interactions or transactions between the two. The ecosystems perspective describes the ways that environments affect people and the ways people affect their environments. The ecosystems view is compatible with various theories of human behavior, making it particularly useful as an organizational tool for synthesizing the many perspectives that social workers apply in practice.

Social Constructionism

Critical Thinking

Social constructionism is about meaning-making, that is, how we understand the events and experiences in our lives. How is the social work process affected by who constructs the meaning or defines the problem or issue?

Each of us selectively attends to, interprets, and acts on our beliefs about ourselves and the world around us, a concept embodied in the theory of social constructionism. Social constructionism centers on how people construct meaning in their lives, emphasizing social meaning as generated through language, cultural beliefs, and social interaction (Gergen, 1994). "Knowledge is created, not discovered, and context is all important" (Dean & Rhodes, 1998, p. 3). Each person understands events only as they are filtered through the "ecosystemic" layers of the social and cultural environment.

Cultural identity and social position influence the person you believe yourself to be and therefore the way you interpret the events in your life. The privilege of membership in an advantaged group offers a sense of fit with the world; it reinforces well-being and validates feelings of control. In contrast, members of cultural groups disadvantaged by oppression, prejudice, and stereotypes are likely to be encumbered by dominant cultural views. This control over norms held by the majority group is known as hegemony—an invisible force that offers privilege to dominant groups and maintains oppressive beliefs about nondominant groups (Mullaly, 2002). "Consequently, a person from an ethnic group in the minority may construct a sense of self that is influenced by this devaluation, lack of power, and discrimination in the societal context" (Greene, et al., 1996, p. 2).

Applying a social constructionist view, social workers can intervene at two different points in an oppressed client's life. First, workers can interfere with the internalization of disempowering beliefs by collaborating with clients to question socially generated "truths" and their relevance for the particular client. For example, the practitioner who questions how a female client's love of another woman can be "wrong" and validates the experience as "maybe something to celebrate" is working to disable the heterosexist bias that undermines the client's emotional experience.

Second, workers can advocate for social and political changes to liberate disadvantaged groups from the oppressive belief systems that delimit individual experience. Such would be the case if the worker in the previous example fought to legalize same-sex marriages, thus providing societal support for the client's loving feelings. The intervention at both the individual and the societal levels applies social constructionist thinking by operating to overturn the hegemony that contradicts the client's emotional reality and inhibits free choice.

Similar to social constructionism, the psychological theory of constructivism questions the assumption of a fixed and objective reality. Constructivism says that two people can interpret the same event very differently because each experiences a personalized, idiosyncratic view of what has occurred. Each person's unique perspective is rooted in individual history, current expectations, and sense of self. Like social constructionism, constructivism "questions the view of knowledge as something 'built up' within the mind through dispassionate observation" (Gergen, 1994), favoring instead the idea of each individual's creation of a unique reality. Both theories also view reality as maintained through language (Greene & Lee, 2002). In social work literature, the terms constructivism and social constructionism are frequently used interchangeably.

Feminist Perspective

A feminist perspective provides a significant foundation for social workers striving to achieve a just society in their practice (Baines, 1997; Carr, 2003; Gutiérrez & Lewis, 1998; Saulnier, 1996). Consistent with the ecosystemic perspective, a feminist view concretely links individual experiences with social forces. In essence, gender is an organizing system of power for interactions at all levels of society.

From a feminist perspective, the personal is political. Social forces perpetuate the subjugation of women, and this oppression is reflected in interpersonal relationships and interactions. To ignore this social reality is to participate in it. Feminism forces workers from a stance of neutrality into a position of advocacy for gender equality.

No singular feminist view exists, but rather a set of perspectives that have a core consistency. In addition to the gendered lens and the principle that personal is political, key elements of feminist practice, according to Hyde (2008) include

- Incorporating democratized processes and structures that promote collaboration, networking, and relationship building align with the value placed on egalitarianism by feminist practitioners
- Extending the focus beyond gender to eliminate all forms of oppression and "working toward the understanding of social problems and solutions through perspectives other than that of white, middle-class women" (p. 218)
- Understanding the transformational nature of change in social, economic, and political structures inherent in pursuing justice for all those who experience oppression and discrimination

The feminist perspective aligns with social constructionism, proposing that the oppressed position of women in our society results from a patriarchal construction of reality. Disempowering views held toward women are rooted in the constructions of dominant groups who ignore the experiences of those who are disadvantaged. The social worker's task becomes one of "deconstructing" a disempowering reality for women and "reconstructing" a new one that is sensitive to diversity and honors unique experiences.

Feminist views, likewise, are compatible with an ecological framework. Bricker-Jenkins (1991) says that "feminist practitioners lead with an assumption that individual and collective pain and problems of living always have a political and/or cultural dimension. That is, they reflect and express ideologies, relations, structures of power and privileges, or other salient features of the cultural milieu" (p. 279). A feminist perspective emphasizes the relationship between the personal and the political and augments the ecological systems approach of social work practice.

THE ECOSYSTEMS PERSPECTIVE

This book incorporates the ecosystems view as a way to frame the many theories and perspectives that support generalist social work practice. Three good reasons support our emphasis of the ecosystems view. First, because of its integrative nature, the ecosystems view draws on the strengths of many helpful theories to describe human behavior in all of its complexity. Second, it describes the behaviors of individuals, families, groups, organizations, local communities, and international societies as interconnected, making this an ideal perspective to support generalist social work practice. Third, the ecosystems view clearly focuses on how people and their environments fit, rather than forcing workers to place blame on either one for problems that arise (Gitterman & Germain, 2008). This accepting view of human behavior is consistent with the value base of social work; it allows workers and clients to join forces against the problematic fit of client and situation rather than judge clients themselves to be deficient.

The ecosystems perspective conceptualizes and explains human system functioning. Specifically, it

- Presents a dynamic view of human beings as systems interacting in context
- Emphasizes the significance of human system transactions
- Traces how human behavior and interaction develop over time in response to internal and external forces
- Describes current behavior as an adaptive fit of "persons in situations"
- Conceptualizes all interaction as adaptive or logical in context
- Reveals multiple options for change within persons, their social groups, and in their social and physical environments

Humans in Context

It is not the strongest of the species that survives, nor the most intelligent, but the one most responsive to change.

—Charles Darwin

The ecosystems perspective describes humans as very complex. We are biological, psychological, spiritual, social, and cultural beings with thoughts, feelings, and observable behaviors. We are initiators within our environments as well as responders to those same environments. We create our own traditions and legacies just as we inherit and respond to our cultural and ethnic heritage. The ecosystems view acknowledges that we react consciously and intentionally but also act unconsciously and spontaneously. We are complex wholes with internal parts and, at the same time, we are parts or members of larger groups. In the ecosystemic view, humans are neither completely powerful nor powerless. Instead, humans play an active role in creating events that shape their lives, a role tempered by environmental forces and conditions.

Focus on Transactions

Humans and their environments evolve in continuously accommodating responses to one another (Brower, 1988). Notice this two-way influence when you visualize the connection of a person interacting with the environment. This connection is called a transaction. Transactions are reciprocal interactions, "the processes by which people continually shape their environments and are shaped by them over time" (Germain, 1983, p. 115). The phrase "person:environment" symbolizes this mutual relationship (Gitterman & Germain, 2008). The colon emphasizes the dynamic interrelatedness of people in transaction with their social and physical environments.

Each of us takes part in innumerable transactions every day. When we talk with friends, have dinner with family members, or buy groceries, we are interacting with people around us. We are also part of larger systems that engage in transactions. Examples of transactions within larger systems include a social agency that trains a group of volunteers, sends staff members to a conference, or runs public service announcements on a local television station. Transactions are the means by which people and systems exchange resources with their environments. Therefore, productive transactions serve as sources of energy to sustain a system's functioning and fuel change. Deficient transactions inhibit growth and possibly even threaten basic sustenance.

Recognizing the significance of transactions reaffirms social work's focus on social functioning—"people coping with life situations [or the] balance between demands of the social environment and people's coping efforts" (Bartlett, 1970, p. 130). This definition describes flexible people adapting to their demanding environments. An empowerment-based view of transaction increases the emphasis on the reciprocal dimension of social functioning, the notion that both people and environments can change. Not only do people respond to environmental demands, but environments must also adapt to the demands of people.

Development as Evolutionary Change

The ecosystems perspective views human development as evolutionary. It describes how individuals and other human systems change and stabilize in response to internal and external forces. As humans grow physically, emotionally, and intellectually, their behaviors reveal and respond to these internal changes. The changes within systems are not the only determinants of human behavior. Instead, these internal experiences themselves affect and respond to contextual events.

Contextual influences

Individuals develop in a context in which other systems are evolving, too. Social groups, organizations, and societal and international institutions—entities that humans themselves help create—seem to take on lives of their own as they also grow and develop. These social systems act on and respond to individuals' behaviors. The effects are mutual. Neither the external nor the internal world has total responsibility for causing any particular human behavior. We create our world just as our world creates us.

When explaining human growth and development, certain contexts merit special note. Cultural identities powerfully influence how we view ourselves and how others view us. Race, ethnicity, culture, and socioeconomic and gender contexts can be stepping stones to success for the power elite; however, they may function as roadblocks for those who are oppressed. Burdening individual development with stereotypic expectations denies overwhelming evidence of in-group diversity and ignores other environmental influences. Humans develop in societies that congregate individuals into categories and value certain group memberships over others. Assumptions and expectations arising from membership in social groups influence self-perceptions, interactions with others, and access to social and economic resources.

Goodness-of-Fit

The ecosystems perspective explains behavior in terms of adapting to a situation. All individual and social systems evolve to fit the resources and demands of their worlds. "Our specific actions are best understood as our attempts to competently respond to the situations we encounter; we do the best we can given what we know about ourselves and what is needed in the situation" (Brower, 1988, p. 413). How we interact at any specific time arises from a synthesis of what is happening in the world within us, what is happening in the world around us, and how we interpret those events.

Various theorists characterize the nature of these transactions as an adaptive balance between persons and environments. Germain (1979) refers to this as "goodness-of-fit." Brower (1988) defines the concept of "niche," a comfortable and unique place where an individual exists interdependently with the environment. However described, we seek to behave in ways that fit ourselves and our situations best.

View of Dysfunction

Engage Assess Intervene Evaluate

From an ecosystems perspective, all behaviors make sense to some degree when they are considered in the context of the impinging social environment. How does this understanding of behavior as a transactional experience inform how social workers assess problems?

In the ecosystems view, the terms "maladaptive" and "dysfunctional" don't really apply. After all, if behaviors are adaptations to meet internal needs and the demands of environments, how can any behaviors be maladaptive? Even a 10-year-old child who carries a gun to the neighborhood playground is displaying a behavior understandable in the threatening environment of a violence-plagued community. Although behaviors like these are unacceptable and have negative consequences, all behaviors make sense when considered in context.

In contrast, describing a client's behavior as dysfunctional or maladaptive blames clients and neglects the reciprocal responsibility of environments for human behavior. Proposing a transactional view of dysfunction, Pardeck (1988) shifts the focus from individual pathology to the possibility of malfunctioning ecosystems. He suggests thinking in terms of maladaptive patterns of interaction, viewing problems in social functioning "as stemming from an interactive, reciprocal, and dynamic set of forces operating between the person and the ecosystem" (p. 95). Thus, the ecosystems view removes the blame from clients in favor of describing problems as transactional—a "fit" in a problem-producing context.

How problems arise

No human behavior occurs in isolation from other events. Rather, humans respond to multiple internal and environmental events simultaneously. In the world of gloves, we may be able to find that "one size fits all." However, in human behavior, we often find that a behavior that may be perfectly adaptive in one specific person:environment configuration is a mismatch in another. The third-grade boy who finds that swearing on the playground elevates his status among his peers will experience the ill fit of this behavior when the principal overhears him. Although the swearing may lead to this boy's identification as having a behavior problem in school, careful examination of his behavior and the situation shows clearly that it is not deviant per se but, rather, understandable in context. A focus on the interaction within the peer group leads to the alternative conclusion that he is socially astute.

Environmental resources and demands

Whether difficulties arise when people encounter physical, intellectual, psychological, emotional, or situational challenges depends on the responsiveness of the environment and the strengths of the particular human system. A nurturing and supportive environment often compensates for a system's limitations, enabling the system to achieve the goodness-of-fit that characterizes the ecosystemic view of health.

Consider the following examples. Given access to appropriate resources, such as a seeing-eye dog, modern technology, and a supportive social network, a person who is unable to see can construct a way to visualize and maneuver in a seeing world. Given direct payment to meet basic human needs for food and shelter, unemployed persons can concentrate on improving their employment situations, rather than resorting to crime or lapsing into depression. With social policies and legislation sensitive to human diversity, persons with disabilities have better access to the community at large. An example is the *Americans with Disabilities Act of 1990,* which mandates removal of architectural barriers in private businesses. A resource-rich, responsive environment transforms persons who may otherwise be labeled dysfunctional into contributors who can further enrich their environments.

Even persons who are gifted may encounter demanding environments that would immobilize the most well-prepared among us. Perfectly functional people become overwhelmed in times of great stress, such as war, grief, physical illness, or crises, and in the face of discrimination and oppression. Difficulties don't reside in persons or environments alone. Instead, gaps in the fit between persons and their environments define a situation as problematic.

By considering the responsibility of environments, the ecosystems view precludes labeling individuals or social systems as dysfunctional or pathological in favor of recognizing that simply no goodness-of-fit exists. That which the system lacks, the environment isn't providing. For that which the environment fails to provide, the system is unable to compensate with its own resources. Even a good adaptation in one particular context may not work effectively in others. The ecosystems view concludes that dysfunctional behavior is transitory, changeable, and related to the responsiveness of the environment.

Implications for Change

A human being is a deciding being.
—Viktor E. Frankl

How we work with people and their situations logically follows from how we perceive human behavior. If we believe the ecosystems model cogently explains how people develop strengths and vulnerabilities, then the choices we make in supporting growth and change will reflect this perspective. Ecosystemically oriented social work practice centers on changing and maintaining both client and environmental systems.

Multiple possibilities for change

A fundamental principle of ecosystems theory states that a change in one part of the system creates a change in another part of the system, which, in turn, changes the functioning of the entire system (von Bertalanffy, 1968). In other words, altering one part of any person:environment transaction affects the other transactional elements. For example, when social worker Jan Kim encourages Dorothy, a disgruntled resident of Northside Care Center, to organize a resident's council, a variety of related changes occur. Dorothy's mood improves as she directs her energy toward relating with the other residents. Once the council forms, they take charge of planning recreational and social events that match their own interests. They also lobby members of the management team to change policies regarding visiting hours and roommate assignments. Dorothy's son even comments about her remarkable adjustment to living at the care center. Count all of the positive changes! Prompting one productive change initiates a cycle that may have subsequent benefits throughout the entire transactional system.

Focus on strengths

The ecosystems perspective offers many intervention possibilities, yet social workers move cautiously to initiate change. Because human beings naturally evolve to work in harmony with their environments, it is likely that client systems are actually doing a lot right. One ecosystemic practice principle mandates social workers "to respect the balances and processes through which people and environments have adapted to each other's needs, while attempting to improve

---

Box 2.2 Opportunities, Risks, and Resilience: A Policy-Research-Practice Connection

No human system thrives in isolation. The successes or failures of individuals, families, groups, organizations, neighborhoods, and communities result from their unique interactions within their environments. The effective functioning of social systems is determined by the relative balance or imbalance of resources, opportunities, and demands within and between systems. Risks present within these interactions increase the likelihood of negative outcomes, whereas protective factors mitigate risks (Little, Axford, & Morepeth, 2004).

Interestingly, research shows that even people who have experienced extreme difficulties have the capacity, or resiliency, to overcome them (Greene, 2002, 2007; Harris, 2008; Williams, Davey, & Klock-Powell, 2003). Resilience is the ability to manage positively, even in the face of adversity. Resilient people are characteristically hopeful, have a sense of mastery, self-efficacy, and meaning in life, and are effective problem solvers. Based on a 20-year longitudinal study on competence and resilience, Masten (2005) identifies several environmental factors that enhance resilience in children. These factors include connections to adults who are competent and caring, connections with faith communities, availability of community resources, and educational opportunities.

Resources available to systems in their social and physical environments that foster well-being are described as environmental opportunities (Garbarino, 1983). Examples of such macrosystem opportunities include governmental assistance in times of emergencies, legislative support for social programs, and budgetary allocations for community infrastructures. In contrast, environmental risks, such as oppression and discrimination, disenfranchise many from society's opportunity structures. Environmental risks are ideologies or cultural alignments that work against the well-being of individuals and society. Shortages and barriers in resource provisions, social inequities, and lack of opportunities create social problems and pose environmental risks (Garbarino, 1983). Other examples of such risks include national economic policies that create inequities and increase poverty for some, and social policies that magnify racism, sexism, or other discriminatory practices. In short, a "macrosystem risk is a social event or a pattern that disrupts and impedes the caring community" (p. 15). Limiting environmental risks while expanding environmental opportunities promises social justice and supports empowerment.

Creating responsive environments rich in opportunity is a policy issue. Access to health care, adequate education, technical training, child care, civil rights, jobs, transportation, and comprehensive community-based services all benefit individual citizens and contribute to the general good. The lives of individual clients cannot improve without the opportunities of resource-rich environments to contribute to their clients' sense of power and well-being. This posture "embodies the profession's mission to improve societal conditions and to enhance social functioning. A resilience-enhancing approach underscores the need to seek resources and sources of natural support within clients' environments" (Greene & Cohen, 2005, p. 369).

Perspectives on risk, opportunity, and resilience have both research and policy implications for social work practice. Informed by research evidence about risk and resilience factors in individuals, families, neighborhoods, faith communities, and schools, social workers craft strategies that span system levels (Corcoran & Nichols-Casebolt, 2004). With respect to policies, social workers draw on research evidence and practice experiences to advocate social policies that provide the infrastructures for resource-rich environments.

transactional patterns that are maladaptive" (Siporin, 1980, p. 517). This challenges us to build on the strengths and competencies clients already have available. A strengths orientation (described fully in Chapter 4) is an essential tool for successfully applying an ecosystemic perspective.

HUMAN SYSTEMS

The systems with which practitioners work may be as small as a single element of the internal processes of one individual or as large as the entire human population. Generalist social workers develop skills to comprehend, support, and change behaviors of many kinds of human systems, because systems at all levels are potential clients and targets for change.

System Defined

Technically speaking, a system is "an organized whole made up of components that interact in a way distinct from their interaction with other entities and which endures over some period of time" (Anderson, et al., 1999, p. 294). More simply, a social system is a structure in which interdependent people interact (Greene & Ephross, 1999). Groups of people are identified as systems because they interact with each other in some definable way or are associated with each other because of shared attributes. In other words, a pattern of relationships or shared characteristics separates one group from other groups in the environment. This definition of system encompasses groups as different as a street gang, a Girl Scout troop, residents of a nursing home, employees of a corporation, and social work professionals. These and all other social systems, small and large, share common features.

Systems as holons

All social systems are *holons.* This means that each system is a part of a larger system, while, at the same time, it is composed of smaller systems (Anderson, et al., 1999). A family is a social system that is only one part of the neighborhood suprasystem in which the family resides. Children and parents within this family are also systems themselves within the context of the larger family system. All of these systems—the children, the parents, the family, and the neighborhood—are holons that share systemic properties.

Subsystems and environments

To clarify the idea of systems within systems, we define two important concepts: *subsystem* and *environment.* The smaller systems within every system are subsystems. Children and parents make up subsystems of the larger family system. Similarly, each individual within a family is actually a subsystem. Conversely, the larger system that encompasses a social system is that system's environment. The environment influences and provides the context for the systems functioning within it. The neighborhood is one example of the social environment for a family system. Broadening the focus to an even larger picture, the community is the social environment for both neighborhoods and families (Figure 2.2).

All systems have subsystems and environments. All systems are also subsystems, while, at the same time, they are environments. For example, the family is a system itself, but, in switching the focus, this same family is also the environment of the children within it. Another perspective shift leads us to describe this

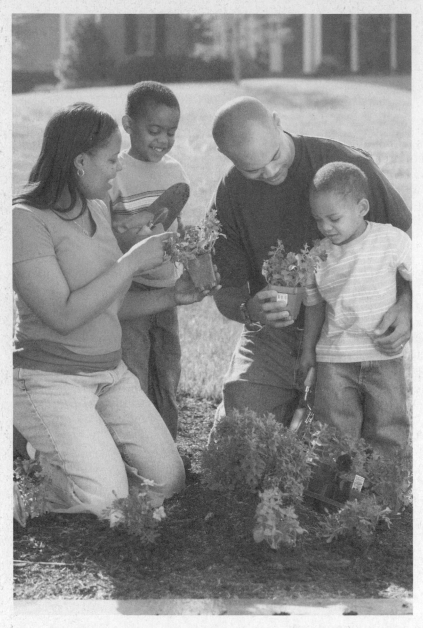

The family unit is a primary human system.

family as a subsystem of the neighborhood in which it lives. Whether we label a system a "subsystem," "system," or an "environment" is relative and changes as we shift our point of focus.

Dimensions of Systems

The complex behavior of human systems gives rise to several helpful ways for viewing them, including the system's structure, interaction, biopsychosocial dimensions, and cultural elements. *Structure* refers to the organization of the system at a point in time. *Interaction* puts this organization into motion and shows how the system operates as its components respond to and affect each other. *Biopsychosocial* dimensions feature the biological, cognitive, and affective characteristics of persons. The *cultural* view appraises the influences of ethnicity and culture on human functioning. Each dimension helps social workers describe human behavior in productive ways and conceptualize creative possibilities for change (Figure 2.3).

A Structural View of Systems

How individuals and subsystems within a system arrange themselves is the structure of the system. Structure is not actually visible; we discern it by observing two variables that characterize the structural arrangements of any system—closeness and power. Closeness refers to the closed or open nature of system boundaries, whereas the distribution of power aligns the system hierarchy. When we ask, "How close or distant are members?" we discover the boundaries of a system. When we ask, "Who's in charge?" we uncover the hierarchy for distributing power within a system. Considering both boundaries and hierarchies offers a complete picture of a system's structure.

Boundaries

Boundaries define systems. In other words, boundaries distinguish the interior of the system from its environment. Human systems' boundaries are not visible like boundaries that mark real estate properties. We deduce their location and

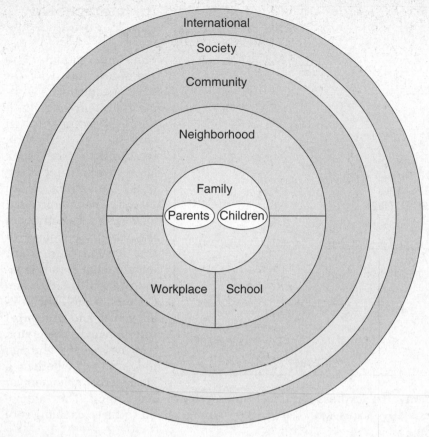

Figure 2.2
Subsystems and Environments
Whether social workers define a particular system as an environment or a
subsystem depends on which system they identify as the focal system.

characteristics by observing how the system operates (Anderson, et al., 1999).

Boundaries vary in permeability or, in other words, in how many transactions they allow between systems. Consider the analogy of a fence. If the fence is short and full of gates, the system and its boundary are "open." Open systems interact frequently and exchange resources with their environment, offering the potential for meeting systems' needs and the risk of being overwhelmed by demanding environments. If the fence is a high stone wall with no entry or exit, the system and boundary are "closed." Having no access to the environment, closed systems may seem protected, but they must meet all of their needs by drawing on resources from within their own systems. With such limited access to additional resources, closed systems may deplete their resource supplies.

Boundaries also differentiate people within a given system. Internal boundaries, which exist around various individuals and subgroups within a larger system, define subsystems. For example, for most social agencies, boundaries define administrative, supervisory, and direct service subsystems. Particular agencies may also distinguish other subsystems such as "experts" and "novices"; professionals, paraprofessionals, and clerical staff; or direct and indirect service providers. These internal boundaries have different degrees of permeability. Like boundaries that define systems, subsystems boundaries vary on a continuum from open to closed. The level of closeness within a system is a significant element in understanding the system's structure.

Hierarchy

Hierarchy indicates which individuals and subsystems in a particular system have status, privileges, and power. Typically, hierarchy describes who is in charge in business or formal organizational systems. By looking at organizational charts, formalized procedures, and position titles such as president, director, or supervisor, you can clearly define hierarchy in formal organizational systems. Describing hierarchy in other systems may be more difficult. Although titles such as "mother," "father," or "ringleader" may give clues about power and control within the system, these titles may not match the system's actual distribution of power. Observing who makes decisions and who initiates actions provides a more accurate picture of hierarchy. Examining the power distribution and the boundary construction in any given system offers structural information about that system.

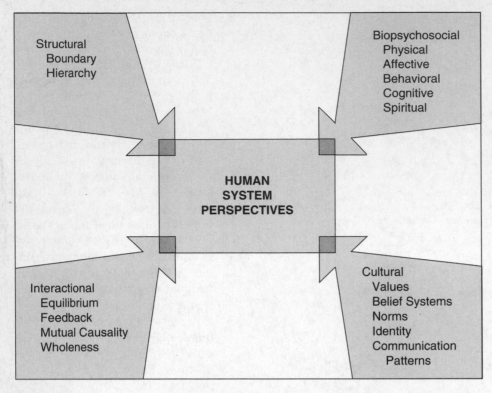

Structural
Boundary
Hierarchy

Biopsychosocial
Physical
Affective
Behavioral
Cognitive
Spiritual

**HUMAN
SYSTEM
PERSPECTIVES**

Interactional
Equilibrium
Feedback
Mutual Causality
Wholeness

Cultural
Values
Belief Systems
Norms
Identity
Communication
Patterns

Figure 2.3
Elements of Human
Systems

An Interactional View of Systems

The interactional view examines the way in which people relate within a system and with their environments. In contrast to structure, which offers a static look at systems, interaction puts the structure in motion. The interactional view traces the activity of the various members of the system and their environment as they communicate with each other. Communication includes all verbal and nonverbal interpersonal behavior. Any message sent through the system, whether a clear verbal statement or a subtle nonverbal expression, affects the system's functioning. The interactional perspective focuses on the ways systems respond to these exchanges of information.

Equilibrium

The tendency of a system to interact in ways that maintain its balance or equilibrium is a key concept in the interactional view. Events that temporarily knock a system out of balance leave it scrambling to regain its previous equilibrium or lead it quickly toward establishing a new one. For example, funding cuts require a social service provider's immediate response. It is likely that the agency's first action is an attempt to maintain the status quo by locating new funds. If this isn't possible, the agency may look internally, cutting staff positions and redistributing the workload to ensure survival and maintain system balance. Rebalancing can also occur if this agency system changes its relation to the environment. The agency may decrease the services it offers to the community, thereby reaching a new balance without overloading the remaining staff. Whatever the agency does to regain equilibrium, one thing is clear—changes in funding, staffing, or programming create other changes in the internal functioning of the system as well as in its ability to work with clients.

Repetitive interactions provide evidence of a system's current equilibrium. Identifying, reinforcing, and modifying various patterns is one way to change a system. Social workers attempt to stabilize productive interactional patterns while interrupting those in which difficulties reside. As an example, consider a social worker who suggests that a father allow his teenager more privileges, attempting to interrupt the pattern of restriction and rebellion that has characterized the parent–child relationship. As the teen responds responsibly and the father reinforces the change through increased privileges, the worker encourages this new, more rewarding pattern.

Feedback

Feedback provides a continuous flow of information. On the one hand, some information fits neatly with the system's existing way of doing things. The system assimilates this feedback, reinforcing the current pattern. On the other hand, incompatible information forces the system to change to accommodate the discrepancy. In other words, two forms of feedback exist—information that maintains the existing equilibrium and information that induces change toward a new equilibrium.

Social workers provide both kinds of feedback. They offer reinforcing feedback to maintain the existing strengths. An example is when a social worker facilitating a group comments on the group members' acceptance of diverse views, as a way to encourage continuing respect for members' differences. In contrast, workers also introduce system-altering feedback to disrupt problematic patterns, clearing the way for new possibilities. When a social worker confronts a citizen's advisory committee with its inequitable distribution of community development funds, this worker provides feedback to disrupt the status quo and seek a new, more equitable pattern of distributing funds. Social workers offer feedback carefully to work toward desired goals.

Mutual causality

Human systems influence their environments and are influenced by them. In other words, one person does not cause the behavior of any other; people participating in a particular interaction mutually work out how they will relate to each other, a concept described as mutual or circular causality. For example, social workers who constantly instruct and advise clients on how to change their lives bear some responsibility for their clients' lack of initiative. Likewise, clients' withdrawn and dependent behavior contributes to overfunctioning by social workers.

Although theoretically, all members of a system have some degree of power and share some responsibility for the behavior of the system, an important note of caution is found here! Social workers remain particularly vigilant when considering the principle of mutuality in relationships characterized by large discrepancies in power. Clearly, social work ethics does not allow the conclusion that persons who are victimized are to blame for the acts of others. The principle of mutual causality does not free those who abuse others from responsibility for their own behaviors or blame victims for having no access to power.

Wholeness

Closely related to mutual causality is the axiom of wholeness, which postulates that a change in one part of a system will precipitate changes in other parts of the system. This rule extends beyond the system's boundary to describe how a system changes in response to its environment, as well as how an environment responds to changes in those systems within it. Consider the previous example of the agency and its funding cuts. A change in the environment, which, in this case, takes the form of reduced funding, has ramifications throughout the agency system and subsequently reemerges to affect the environment in terms of the agency's ability to serve its clients.

This interactional perspective on systems fits neatly into an ecosystems view. Concepts from ecology describe the ongoing balancing act of systems with their environments. The evolution to reach the "goodness-of-fit" necessitates that systems continue to change and stabilize in response to feedback. To keep a comfortable balance, a system must at times resist change and, at other times, go with the flow. Likewise, the environment responds to the feedback sent out of the system.

Biopsychosocial Dimensions

All social systems have distinctive human qualities based on the biopsychosocial characteristics of their individual members. Similar to social systems, individual human beings are multidimensional. Longres (2000) identifies two domains of individual functioning, the biophysical and the psychological. He further divides the psychological into cognitive, affective, and behavioral components. Others add spiritual dimensions to this list (Canda, 1988; Krill, 1988). The mutual impact of these internal subsystems on one another reflects the same principles that apply to larger social systems.

This biopsychosocial view of systems holds special significance for change processes. As thinking and feeling beings, we have options and to some extent the power to choose our responses to what is happening in our lives. These options may be limited by individual and environmental conditions, but, within a reasonable range, we are able to make choices about how we view ourselves and interpret the events around us.

A biopsychosocial view applies to more than individual functioning. Multiperson systems, composed of thinking and feeling individual members, also have cognitive and affective dimensions that can lead to change. The neighborhood whose residents "believe" that a neighborhood watch program can ensure personal safety and property rights will activate and participate in such a program. Families who "feel" pride in their reputation and accomplishments will risk activities that have the potential to add to their accomplishments, further contributing to a greater sense of pride. This psychosocial view of social systems expands the options for social workers and clients. Workers can help clients construct new ways of perceiving and responding to events.

Cultural Influences

Diversity
in Practice

All human beings are influenced by the multiple cultures in which they hold membership. What effect does this cultural imprint have on how we regard and interact with others?

Every individual and social system exists within a web of other interlocking and overlapping human systems. These contextual systems vary with respect to size, type, and degree of influence. Each of us carries the imprints of those systems of which we are a part. As members of the human race, we have universal similarities. As members of different racial, ethnic, gender, religious, cohort, community, and other groups, we also develop differences. The relative influence of each of these systems contributes to the diversity that characterizes individual human identities and behaviors.

The concept of culture speaks to the influence that these various external system memberships exert on human behavior.

> Culture is not an easy concept to define, but it generally incorporates all the symbolic meanings—the beliefs, values, norms, and traditions— that are shared in a community and govern social interactions among community members or between members and outsiders. The values and norms of the various social classes, of religious denominations, of gays and lesbians, of ethnic and racial groups constitute their cultures. (Longres, 1995, p. 74)

Every human system has cultural dimensions. Social groups at every system level have unique ways of interacting and patterns of understanding (Anderson, et al., 1999). Each of us incorporates influences from the multiple cultures in which we participate.

Every human being identifies cultural memberships in multiple contextual systems. Race, ethnicity, gender, socioeconomic class, religion, sexual orientation, age group, geographic location, political affiliation, occupation, and lifestyle are several of the cultural dimensions that influence human behavior. Cultural influences are profound. Not only do we build our own identities around the various groups of which we are members, but frequently others view us more in terms of our general cultural attributes than of our own unique identities.

Cultural influences on systems

Our cultural memberships affect the way others treat us. Human societies do not afford the same status and privileges across cultural categories. Privileged groups sometimes disenfranchise members of other cultural groups. For example, in the United States, someone identified culturally as male, white, and heterosexual simply has more opportunities and fewer constraints than someone whose cultural group memberships include female, African American, and lesbian.

Generalizations based on memberships in cultural systems also obscure individual differences. Although membership in a particular cultural group usually indicates certain similarities among group members, individual members hold other cultural group memberships as well. Add these multicultural influences to each person's unique physical, cognitive, and affective attributes, and the result is diversity among members within even the most influential of cultural groups. Simply put, no two people are alike! The multiple influences of simultaneous cultural contexts individuate even members of the same family. Think about your own family if you're not convinced. Can you identify cultural differences among family members? Every human system internalizes elements of the multiple contexts in which it exists. Each and every one of us is a virtual "melting pot" of cultural influences.

ECOSYSTEMS: A CONCEPTUAL FRAMEWORK FOR PRACTICE

The ecosystems perspective provides a way to comprehend human diversity and explicates the relationship between humans and their environments. The views of human systems as structural, interactional, biopsychosocial, and cultural entities offer a comprehensive and sometimes complex understanding of system behavior. A simple way to organize the ecosystems perspective into a user-friendly framework for generalist social work practice involves a five-point schema (O'Melia, 1991):

- Identify the focal system.
- What's happening inside the system?
- What's happening outside the system?
- How do the inside and outside connect?
- How does the system move through time?

A closer look reveals the universality and usefulness of this simple framework (Table 2.2).

Identify the Focal System

All aspects of generalist practice involve human systems. Social workers practice within systems such as agencies, departments, institutions, and various other organizations. Social workers interact with client systems, including individuals, couples, families, groups, organizations, and communities. Social workers also target changes in environmental systems to benefit their clients. Practitioners themselves are members of personal and professional

Table 2.2   Ecosystems: Conceptual Practice Framework

Questions	Description
What's the focal system?	Identifies the system on which the ecosystems analysis will focus—can be an individual, family, group, organization, or community.
What's inside the system?	Explores the structure, interaction, biopsychosocial dimensions, and cultural features within the focal system.
What's outside the system?	Delineates the network of other systems and resources in the focal system's environmental context.
How do the inside and outside connect?	Examines the transactions between the focal system and systems in its context.
How does the system move through time?	Observes adaptation and changes occurring in the process of the focal system's development.

From *Generalist Perspectives in Case Coordination* by M. O'Melia (May, 1991). Used with permission of the author.

systems that may support or inhibit their work. In effective generalist practice, workers understand the functioning of and resources within each of these systems, including their settings, their clients, their communities, and themselves.

The ecosystems view recognizes the complex configuration of these nested and interlocking systems. To ignore the multiple influences present in any situation is to offer only a partial account of why things are the way they are, what resources exist, and how things might change. Acknowledging these influences requires a step-by-step analysis that begins with a well-defined reference point, which we call the focal system.

What we determine to be the focal system depends on our purpose or activity. If we are trying to increase our self-understanding, we may focus on ourselves, including our own thoughts, feelings, and interactions with others. If we are beginning work with a new client, the developing professional relationship requires attention and becomes the focal system. If we are assessing a client system's functioning in its own ecological context, the client is the focal system. If we are implementing intervention strategies, we may identify a system in the client's environment as the focal system. In generalist social work practice, the system in focus may vary during the process.

What's Happening Inside the System?

After determining the focal system, we next analyze the system's internal functioning. A structural perspective offers information about the system's membership, boundaries, and hierarchies. Highlighting the interactional view provides information about how system members communicate, the patterns they develop, and the ways they maintain balance. Exploring biopsychosocial dimensions provides information about system members' physical health, thoughts, and feelings. Considering the cultural influences of values, beliefs, attitudes, communication patterns, and norms adds to our understanding of functioning inside the focal system.

What's Happening Outside the System?

Exploring context is essential to understanding any situation. All systems exist in the context of an *ecosystem*—a set of interconnected, interdependent, and interactive systems that affect one another. Identifying important environmental influences begins to explain the focal system's behavior and reveals possible targets for intervention. Because ecosystems are also systems, workers can describe and analyze ecosystems by applying the same perspectives used for describing any system—structural, interactional, biopsychosocial, and sociocultural.

Although many systems share aspects of the same environments, the particular ecosystem of any one system is a unique configuration, idiosyncratic to the focal system. Consider the following examples of the ecosystems of potential client systems. For one 8-year-old child, relevant environmental systems may be the child's immediate family, extended family, peer group, neighborhood, school, and church. For a different 8-year-old child placed in foster care, relevant environments include the child's biological family, foster family, social worker, case management team, foster children's support group, and the family court system. On another level, significant contextual systems for a public housing project include the community, city government, local social agencies, and federal housing departments, to name a few. The ecosystem of any system varies over time as it evolves and adapts.

How Do the Inside and Outside Connect?

The viability of any human system depends on its success in interacting with its environment. Social workers need personal and professional backing. Clients need information, resources, and support. This interface of the system with the environment—the system:environment transaction—is a major target for assessment and intervention.

To illustrate how this relates to professional practice, consider the example of Tony Marelli. As a social worker for the Northside Addictions Recovery Center, Tony is experiencing feelings of burnout. Significant events in Tony's connections to his environment contribute to this situation. The Addiction Recovery Center's loss of a state grant has forced layoffs and a redistribution of work to remaining staff. Tony's workload has increased from 25 to 35 clients as a result. Normally, the agency has a supportive collegial and supervisory system with which Tony exchanges ideas about his experiences with clients, but the overload has sent everyone scrambling. Consequently, the workers hardly have time to talk to one another.

Look closely at the changes in Tony's connections to the world around him. The previous balance of Tony (the inside) with his clients and co-workers (the outside) is now skewed. His boundaries have opened wide to clients and have closed with respect to his professional support network. For Tony, more resources are going out, and fewer are coming in, obviously contributing to his burnout. This ecosystemic analysis also points the way toward what might be done to ease Tony's situation. Changes in Tony's workload or his relationships with colleagues may be solutions. Analyzing Tony's transactions with his environment offers insights into what is currently happening and stimulates thinking about the possibilities for change.

How Does the System Move through Time?

The ecosystems perspective emphasizes the evolutionary nature of human systems. Systems at every level, from individual to society, move along their developmental paths in response to expected and unexpected events. Both kinds of events, predictable and surprising, affect systems. How systems negotiate these changes as they move through the context of time merits careful review. Social workers incorporate historical and developmental contexts by gathering enough information about the focal system to understand the system's evolution.

Many evolutionary changes occur naturally, including physical maturation and other developmental transitions. Erikson (1963) describes expected stages of psychosocial development for individuals. Carter and McGoldrick (2005) expand this notion of developmental change to families and examine the mutual influences of individual and family life cycles. Another theorist describes the natural path of group development as sequential, passing through stages of forming, storming, norming, performing, and adjourning (Tuckman, 1965, cited in Anderson, et al., 1999). Systems at all levels evolve in predictable and adaptable ways.

Nodal events

Other changes are unexpected and can create temporary havoc in systems as they struggle to regain equilibrium. Consider how the sudden death of a child in a family system immediately disrupts the family's sense of how things should be and requires extensive adjustment in the way the family operates. These unexpected changes, called nodal events, have a dramatic effect on a system's development (Carter & McGoldrick, 2005). The addition or loss of a member or a significant change in a member's role profoundly affects the system as a whole. Such is the case in birth, marriage, death, and serious illness. Examples of nodal events in larger systems are organizational expansion and downsizing. In a community, nodal events can include a change in leadership, plant closings, or the receipt of federal grants. Nodal events can improve a system's functioning or challenge its capabilities.

Applying the Ecosystems Framework

This ecosystems framework provides ways for social workers to organize information about "what is" in a way that hints at "what might be." Specifically, this framework guides practitioners as they build effective relationships with clients, assess client functioning, and implement change activities.

Dialogue: Building relationships with client systems

By identifying the professional relationship as the focal system, workers can develop and monitor how they relate to clients. The structural perspective allows workers to question issues of power and closeness: Does the client system have sufficient power in the relationship with the worker to ensure feelings of control, an experience of competence, and a guarantee of self-determination? Is the relationship sufficiently close to encourage an open and honest sharing of information yet distant enough to ensure professional integrity and encourage independence? By applying this framework, workers can construct empowering and respectful relationships with client systems.

This framework also helps workers monitor the effects of outside forces on their work with clients. Obviously, the relationships of social workers and clients respond to influences in their respective ecosystems. Cultural contexts are particularly important. Analyzing cultural dimensions can help workers recognize and confront their own biases and sensitize them to relate to clients in culturally appropriate ways.

Discovery: Assessing functioning

The ecosystems framework is a tool for assessing a client's situation, regardless of the particular level of client system. Observing a system from structural, interactional, biopsychosocial, and cultural points of view offers considerable information for understanding individuals, families, groups, and communities. Assessing the client system's progress as it evolves through time contributes additional clues about important historic events, the system's ability to adapt, and its future direction.

Development: Planning and implementing change

Knowing the specific ways that systems function reveals entry points for social workers and clients to initiate change. Altering internal aspects of a system's functioning, changing environments, or modifying the connections between the two all hold potential for creating change. Social workers and clients carefully analyze these possibilities to construct plans and carry out activities, enhance client competence, activate environmental supports, create alliances, and expand opportunities.

LOOKING FORWARD

Conventional wisdom says that theory is essential in organizing and justifying actions that social workers take. Current debate questions whether theory supported by empirical research is really so necessary for effective practice. A social constructionist might say that a professional's theoretical explanation of events is only one construction of reality and contains no more "truth" than the explanation offered by the client system. Favoring the professional view over the client's perspective may be oppressive and contrary to the social work values of acceptance and client self-determination.

The ecosystems perspective is an adaptable framework for social work practice. It broadens our view of human behavior and suggests ways for practitioners to conceptualize, plan, and evaluate their work. Social workers apply the ecosystems perspective flexibly to fit the characteristics of client systems. Identifying the focal system is the first step. From there, social workers and clients proceed to examine other aspects of the system:environment configuration. Possibilities for understanding and change are present in every element of the ecological milieu.

The ecosystems perspective presented in this chapter is foundational to the empowering approach to social work practice featured in subsequent chapters. The ecosystems perspective offers a way of thinking about human systems and their functioning. Feminism and social constructionism provide additional lenses to filter our perceptions. Chapter 3 describes how attitudes, expectations, professional and personal values, and cultural identities influence professional practice. Social workers must inventory their own values and cultural backgrounds to prepare for value-based, culturally competent practice.

Succeed with PEARSON mysocialworklab

Log onto **www.mysocialworklab.com** and click on the link to view the Interactive Skill Module videos. Answer the questions below. (*If you did not receive an access code to* **MySocialWorkLab** *with this text and wish to purchase access online, please visit* www.mysocialworklab.com.)

1. **On pages 16 and 17 of the school social work module,** client Michelle discusses being raised in the U.S.

by Portuguese parents. Use an ecosystemic perspective to describe Michelle's family experience applying the concepts of system, boundary, and hierarchy.

2. **On page 13 of the group work video,** group member Anna describes how body type and weight are judged differently in the U.S. and Belize. Use a social constructionist perspective to explain these differences in meaning.

PRACTICE TEST

Human Behavior

1. The ecosystems perspective _____.
   a. applies only to plant life and physical environments
   b. provides a framework for viewing the ways that environments affect people and the ways people affect their environments
   c. examines the linear relationships between people and their environments
   d. offers singular strategies for change

2. Which perspective identifies gender as the organizing concept for interactions at all levels of society?
   a. ecosystems
   b. constructionism
   c. feminism
   d. social constructivism

3. Ask "Who's in charge in this family?" to learn about family _____.
   a. structure
   b. affect
   c. biopsychosocial dimensions
   d. culture

4. When Georgina observes patterns of communication among group members, she is focusing on the _____ of the group system.
   a. homeostasis
   b. interaction
   c. biopsychosocial dimensions
   d. culture

Critical Thinking

5. Kennedy Brown applies the ethic of critique to his practice as a generalist social worker by _____.
   a. evaluating sources of stress within organizational systems
   b. criticizing organizational and institutional systems as sources of problems
   c. analyzing institutional systems as sources of potential solutions
   d. examining the influences of socio-political-economic arrangements on clients' situations

6. A group of friends within a larger group of employees are _____ of the employee group.
   a. holons
   b. environments
   c. subsystems
   d. boundaries

7. Crystal Riez observes that in some families the children make the rules and the parents comply. This observation provides structural clues about family _____.
   a. interpersonal interactions
   b. hierarchy
   c. boundaries
   d. biopsychosocial dimensions

Engage Assess Intervene Evaluate

8. Assessing factors such as the influence of gender, class, and life style focuses on the _____ dimensions that influence human behavior.
   a. economic
   b. political
   c. cultural
   d. institutional

9. Toni's relationships with her clients are professional rather than personal. Based on a structural view of systems, you conclude that Toni maintains appropriate _____.
   a. interactions
   b. authority
   c. hierarchies
   d. boundaries

10. Since Sandy Davis, a social worker at Families United, applies the person:environment perspective, her work will _____.
   a. take into account factors related to families rather than their environments
   b. focus on environments rather than on the families
   c. consider factors related to both families and their environments
   d. make decisions independent of families and their environments

Log onto **MySocialWorkLab** once you have completed the Practice Test above to take your Chapter Exam and demonstrate your knowledge of this material

Answers

1) b 2) c 3) a 4) b 5) d 6) c 7) b 8) c 9) d 10) c

3

Values and Multicultural Competence

CONNECTING CORE COMPETENCIES *in this chapter*

| Professional Identity | Ethical Practice | Critical Thinking | Diversity in Practice | Human Rights & Justice | Research Based Practice | Human Behavior | Policy Practice | Practice Contexts | Engage Assess Intervene Evaluate |

By the first time social workers and clients actually talk together, both have already been formulating their expectations about each other and the work ahead. Both bring values, attitudes, and assumptions that will undeniably influence their interaction with each other. Effective social workers acknowledge these existing frames of reference.

To create empowering experiences, practitioners examine their value base, develop their cultural competence, and even take it one step further by purposefully constructing a set of presuppositions about clients that will influence their work productively. This chapter explores the ways that social workers prepare themselves both professionally and personally for relationships with clients, particularly in the areas of values and diversity. Specifically, this chapter

> ▶ Describes how expectations and personal perspectives influence our perceptions, interactions, and relationships
> ▶ Delineates the values and principles of social work practice that guide workers to build ethical relationships with clients
> ▶ Considers the influences of a social worker's personal resources and self-awareness on professional practice
> ▶ Explores multicultural competence for social work practice
> ▶ Assesses cultural competence at the personal, agency, and community levels

Value-prepared, culturally competent social workers prepare to form relationships that activate clients' resources, respect their contributions, and maintain professional integrity.

FRAMES OF REFERENCE

Research documents that what people expect to happen influences how they respond, a phenomenon called the "placebo" effect. Experiments repeatedly demonstrate how positive changes in behavior result from participants' expectations that improvements will occur. Our expectations are influential in shaping how we understand experiences and in swaying our responses.

What others expect of us influences our responses, too. In a classic educational study, Rosenthal and Jacobson (1968) found that a diverse group of children randomly labeled "bloomers" lived up to their teacher's expectations. You can imagine the results if those same children had been labeled difficult or slow. Whether preconceived notions are positive or negative, their effects are often dramatic. What we expect powerfully shapes our sense of self, influences our behavior, and constructs the reality in which we interpret events.

Our values, culture, and patterns of thinking as well as our expectations of situations and others' expectations of us all contribute to our frames of reference. These factors serve as filters through which we view, interpret, and respond to our situations. For example, several people can witness the same incident, yet each perceives or explains the situation differently. Our actions and reactions to others reveal our frames of reference.

Your Frame of Reference Shows

Fundamentally, all social work activities, at any system level and in any field of practice, have a common core. Social work depends on interaction and communication with others. As social workers, we purposefully and spontaneously interact with clients. Within this interaction, our communication unavoidably and automatically reveals our frame of reference. Two facets of communication—its constancy and its influence on relationships—deserve careful attention in preparing for empowerment-based social work practice.

Communication is constant

Because assumptions influence outcomes, social workers should interact in ways that demonstrate positive expectations. They should communicate only messages that help clients accomplish their goals. This sounds simple enough, but the very nature of communication makes communicating productively a challenging task. As a matter of fact, "one cannot not communicate. Activity or inactivity, words, or silence all have message value" (Watzlawick, et al., 1967, p. 42). Think about the implications of this simple concept. We are always communicating. In the way we look, the way we sit, the words we select, the information we choose to notice, and in countless other ways, we automatically send messages to one another.

Communication defines relationships

Messages are more than simple bits of information. Communication theorists believe that every message communicated has two sides: content and relationship (Watzlawick, et al., 1967). This means that a message both provides information and defines something about the relationship of the communicators. The relationship aspect of communication says, "This is how I see myself . . . this is how I see you . . . this is how I see you seeing me" (p. 52).

Communicating in empowering ways

What social workers truly feel and sincerely believe about themselves and about clients emerges in social work interactions. Professionally constructed relationships are not merely role plays. On the contrary, they are genuine relationships in which the values, beliefs, and opinions of social workers and clients show through. Furthermore, "the language social workers use to describe their work and the problems to which their work responds is a powerful tool in making visible the relational aspects of oppression and in shaping the ways [clients] are seen" (Dietz, 2000, p. 376). In light of this, social workers acknowledge the complex, continuous, and unavoidable nature of communication. They understand that "words serve as lenses that have the power to shape, to filter, or indeed even to 'create' what it is we see in front of us" (Laird, 1990, p. 213).

If a worker's implicit or explicit messages reflect little confidence in a client or judgments about a client's culture, these messages undermine empowerment and countermand goals for promoting competence. Conversely, to the extent that social workers implicitly and explicitly relay messages of confidence, acceptance, and respect for diversity, their communication empowers.

PROFESSIONAL VALUES AND PRACTICE PRINCIPLES

Personal and professional values are a significant component of a social worker's frame of reference and have been since the beginning of the profession in the early twentieth century (Reamer, 2008). Some even assert that values matter more than techniques (Freud, 1999). Values shape thinking and direct our actions as social workers through practice principles. These principles guide the day-to-day practice of social work (Table 3.1). They include acceptance, individualization, nonjudgmentalism, objectivity, self-determination, access to resources, confidentiality, and accountability.

Table 3.1	**Social Work Practice Principles**
Acceptance	Conveys positive regard for clients' strengths and potential for growth
Individualization	Affirms each client's unique and distinctive characteristics
Nonjudgmentalism	Maintains nonblaming attitudes toward clients
Objectivity	Promotes professional caring, concern, and commitment in working with clients
Self-determination	Upholds clients' rights to exercise their own decision making
Access to services	Promotes and fosters access to resources and opportunities
Confidentiality	Respects clients' rights to privacy
Accountability	Ensures competent professional conduct and comportment

Acceptance

Social work practice principles guide the day-to-day work of social workers. What ethical conflicts or issues could arise as workers strive to uphold each principle in their practice with clients?

The principle of acceptance charges social workers to go beyond merely tolerating clients to regarding clients positively. Social workers demonstrate acceptance when they affirm clients' perspectives and value what clients contribute to the work. They treat clients with respect and dignity, realizing that clients have unique strengths and resources to offer. Acceptance facilitates change. According to Berlin (2005), "our attempts to assist the client to undertake positive change are most likely to be effective when the client feels both cared for and recognized as a free agent" (p. 485).

According to Tillich (1962), an existentialist theologian who wrote about the philosophy of social work, the type of love shown in acceptance is different from charity, as charity makes no critical demands. Instead, he associates acceptance with *agape* or *caritas,* the Greek and Latin words for love. The regard for others shown in *agape* or *caritas* "is critical as well as accepting, and it is able to transform what it loves" (p. 15). Social workers whose practice reflects acceptance authenticate the worth and dignity of client systems, expect clients to use their capacities for growth, and build on their strengths.

Individualization

Valuing individualization means recognizing that all humans have a right "to be individuals and to be treated not just as a human being but as this human being with personal differences" (Biestek, 1957, p. 25). Although practitioners do rely on general information about human behavior gleaned from research, they carefully differentiate the distinctive qualities and circumstances of each client system. Social workers' sensitivity toward diversity prevents them from deducing too much about clients from background information, knowing that any cultural characteristic is only one of several individual and group identities clients hold. Individual members of any cultural group have distinctive stories to tell.

Oppression, discrimination, and cultural or ethnic stereotyping seriously impede individualization. The principle of individualization prompts social workers to customize their generalized view to accommodate individual differences. A social worker who individualizes clients, their situations, and their diversity resists applying labels or using stereotypes. Individualizing means focusing on each client's unique characteristics and treating clients as persons with rights and dignity rather than "objects," "cases," or "the next appointment."

Nonjudgmentalism

Think for a moment about conversations in which you feel blamed, evaluated, or condemned. Do you try to justify your behavior? Are you so aggravated that you stop listening? Do you feel as if the person with whom you are talking isn't really listening to you or understanding your situation? Judgmental attitudes and behaviors tend to shut down communication processes, create barriers to relationships, and cast doubts about abilities. "In situations where service users—and practitioners—feel defended, guarded, and self-protective, it can be difficult to establish a sound foundation on which to build future work" (Trevithick, 2003, p. 169). Nonjudgmental social workers neither blame clients nor evaluate them as good or bad. Instead, the worker lets clients make their own value decisions.

Being nonjudgmental does not mean that social workers never make judgments about what clients are doing. Social workers inevitably filter what they learn about clients through their own professional and personal value screens, as all relationships are value based (Dolgoff, et al., 2004). However, social workers are careful to help clients examine the value issues of their decisions through their own value screens, not the worker's. Social workers applying an ecosystemic perspective readily recognize that diversity of choices is a natural result of the many influences that create human behavior. Culturally competent practice requires workers to avoid applying their own values and suspend making judgments in favor of learning the client's worldview—a perspective in which the client's behavior makes sense. Adopting a nonjudgmental perspective, practitioners recognize circumstances that provoke judgment and blame, acknowledge that their personal values and beliefs are not likely to apply to the circumstances of others, and work to set aside their personal opinions.

Objectivity

Objectivity, individualization, and nonjudgmentalism are all closely related. To ensure objectivity, practitioners separate their own personal feelings from a client's situation. They listen openly to avoid distorting a client's story with their own biases and refrain from prejudicially labeling the client. They also avoid the pitfalls of extreme reactions, responding neutrally with neither cold detachment nor emotional overidentification. Taken to an extreme, objectivity devolves into being aloof, dispassionate, or indifferent.

Empathy expresses the objective caring and commitment that competent social work practice requires. A social worker's honest feedback that describes rather than evaluates a client's behavior reflects objectivity, too. Self-awareness helps sort out the worker's personal perspective and provides insight from which to draw for empathy with the client's situation. In keeping with the principle of objectivity, social workers invest themselves in their work with clients, yet maintain a professional perspective.

Self-Determination

The NASW *Code of Ethics* (1999a) upholds clients' rights to make their own decisions. This freedom to choose and decide reflects the principle of self-determination. Simply, self-determination is the freedom to make choices. Actualizing this freedom to choose depends on the presence of options and resources. Scarce resources limit opportunities for choice and, therefore, limit a client's potential for self-determination. Empowerment-based social work practice creates opportunities for clients to exercise choice and helps clients recognize their privilege to decide. Involving social service consumers at all levels of decision making quells potential encroachments on self-determination: "If practitioners align themselves with the interests of consumers, including consumer input and control, the result will be greater self-determination among clients and less ethical discord regarding paternalism within the helping professions" (Tower, 1994, p. 196).

Self-determination also presupposes freedom from coercion. When social workers impose solutions, give direct advice, assume the role of expert, treat clients as subordinates, or in other ways control decisions, they thwart client self-determination. Upholding self-determination doesn't mean abandoning clients, abdicating responsibility, or failing to provide direction. Social workers committed to client self-determination actively guide rather than coercively direct the helping process. Social workers who advocate self-determination foster collaboration, affirm client strengths, activate resources, and expand opportunities.

Access to Resources

Without choices and resources, people lack power. Honoring dignity and self-determination hinges on clients having access to resources (Hopps, et al., 2000). Guaranteeing clients access to alternatives and opportunities is a fundamental practice principle and requisite of empowerment. The profession's *Code of Ethics* (NASW, 1999a) mandates social workers to advocate the development of opportunities for oppressed and disadvantaged populations and to promote policy changes that improve social conditions. These efforts reveal workers' commitment to social justice and uphold client self-determination by providing rightful access to the resources that society offers.

To promote access to resources, social workers ensure that their practice settings demonstrate sensitivity to diversity. Workers urge their agencies to incorporate multicultural illustrations into their brochures, to provide multilingual staff and literature, to create information forms that are sensitive to lifestyle diversity, and to design office spaces that are comfortable and accessible to people with disabilities. Access to services is a reality only when clients can see that the agency is adapting to their styles and needs.

Confidentiality

All clients have a right to privacy, a right to have what they share held in confidence by the practitioner and protected by the agency. Confidentiality extends to all identifying information, case records, and professional opinions about clients' situations (Barker, 2003). As an ethical principle, confidentiality guides professional behavior and forms the basis for trustworthy professional relationships. Workers make exceptions only if clients give their express consent to disclose information or if laws compel workers to reveal information. Respecting privacy by maintaining confidentiality builds trust and demonstrates respect for client systems, two essential ingredients for developing collaborative partnerships.

Accountability

The *Code of Ethics* (NASW, 1999a) clarifies professional roles and relationships at various levels of responsibility in relation to clients, colleagues, employers, employing organizations, the social work profession, and society.

Our identities as social workers leave us accountable for our personal and professional conduct. Accountability requires that practitioners be proficient in the performance of professional practice. It means that workers regard the service obligation of social work as primary and, thus, prevent discriminatory and inhumane practices. To be accountable, social workers act with professional integrity and impartiality, and they use sound protocols in practice and research.

To meet the standards of accountability, social workers must know relevant laws and their implications for social work practice. A continuum of legal technicalities—from the program and procedural requirements of policy initiatives to federal and state laws to the specifics of case law—applies to particular fields of social work practice. Social workers increase their professional accountability when they familiarize themselves with laws related to the general practice of social work as well as those related to their specific fields of practice.

Value Conflicts in Practice: An Example

Values and principles guide professional behavior, yet making the most ethical choice is not always easy in practice. Hingsburger (1990) relates the story of Sylvia, a client with mental retardation, placed as a volunteer in a nursing home. Difficulties developed when Sylvia did her job so effectively that visitors to the facility would sometimes mistake her for a nurse, a situation that upset the professional staff and led to a meeting with Sylvia's employment counselor and the nursing home manager.

> The manager had come to the meeting with a compromise. Sylvia could come back to work if she wore a tag that said, "Retarded Volunteer." This was unquestionably unacceptable. Negotiation occurred, and the employment counsellor offered the alternative of having Sylvia wear a tag that said, "Volunteer." It made sense that in a medical establishment one be able to quickly identify medical staff for emergencies.
>
> A week or two of calm went by and the second call came. Sylvia was to be fired. Again the counsellor pleaded for a meeting and got an audience with the manager. Sylvia had become a problem. Some of the nurses didn't like her and didn't want anything to do with her. The only compromise that could be reached was stunning. The employment counsellor was told that Sylvia could come to work if, and only if, she followed the following rules. First, she would speak to no staff except for the head nurse on duty. Second, she would take her breaks early in the cafeteria by herself. Third, she would clean up after herself after breaks. Fourth, she would come to work fifteen minutes late so as not to arrive with any of the other staff. These conditions were brought to a meeting.
>
> We all sat there and discussed this. Sylvia and her mother were very quiet and we basically said that the placement was over. We needed to find another place. I asked Sylvia if she understood. She looked at me and said, "I'm going back to work. I'm going to do what they say." This was unacceptable and Sylvia was being unreasonable. "No Sylvia, they want me to teach you to never be with or speak to any staff there. I can't do that." Sylvia didn't care what I could or could not do. She said something that no other client before or since has ever said. "You work for me. Teach me.". . . I taught her.

We put staff back in and reinforced her for solitary behaviour. She was taught how to clean up in the cafeteria and when to contact the head nurse. I hated doing this. A month later I arrived at the group home to find Sylvia waiting at the door for me, "What!!!" Sylvia's excitement knew no bounds. "What?" I asked. "One of the nurses said good morning to me." I listened to her voice and looked in her eyes. I saw the eyes of every liberationist who has ever known victory. I saw courage. I saw strength. I saw faith. (pp. 119–121)

In this example, the worker's acceptance and respect for Sylvia made it difficult to recognize Sylvia's right to make her own choices. Value conflicts such as this are frequent in social work, especially in practice with clients like Sylvia whom workers may feel the need to protect. When social workers experience ethical conflicts, they apply theories and principles for ethical decision making; consult clients, colleagues, supervisors, and ethics committees; and sometimes obtain legal advice to make informed choices about their actions.

PERSONAL VALUES AND RESOURCES

The personal values and resources of social workers support the professional helping process. A singular emphasis on having professional knowledge, techniques, and skills denies the importance of the "person" of the social worker. Personal attributes of warmth, honesty, genuineness, openness, creativity, sensitivity, commitment, and optimism are all assets for workers in engaging clients and building relationships.

Use of Self in Social Work

A repertoire of intervention techniques without positive personal qualities makes us merely technicians, not social workers, featuring the "science" of worker in our title rather than emphasizing the "art" of the social.

The social worker's self is very much involved in the process of helping others. One of the commonly accepted goals in learning social work is the "conscious use of self," which requires self-discipline. Self-discipline necessitates knowledge of the self. There can be no escaping this aspect of the involvement of the self in the social work process, particularly in direct practice. To deny it is simply not to recognize its presence. Social workers are often aware of what is called personal style in their work. The expression of personal style really says, in effect, that this is how I can best use who I am in the social work relationship with this other person. (Imre, 1982, p. 93)

Personal styles of practitioners are resources for working with clients. Reflective social workers inventory their personal values and resources as a way of preparing to work with clients.

Increasing Self-Awareness

Because so much of our personhood finds its way into practice, self-awareness is an essential quality for every social work practitioner. To prepare for practice, we identify and accept our own strengths and areas for growth. To heighten our self-awareness, we examine a broad range of personal characteristics, such as our

Self-awareness is essential for practitioners to maintain professional boundaries and works to benefit others. How can over-identifying with the client's issues affect the professional relationship?

lifestyle, moral codes, values, family roots, manner of meeting personal needs, attitude toward change, response to various life circumstances, as well as the personal biases and stereotypes we hold (Johnson & Yanca, 2007). In addition, understanding our own cultural history and identity is a prerequisite for culturally sensitive social work. As practicing professionals, social workers refine their self-awareness through feedback from supervision, reviews by peers, team consultations, interactions with clients, and educational opportunities.

The benefits of self-awareness

Our knowledge of "self" allows us to discern our inner core, our needs, thoughts, commitments, and values and, at the same time, to observe ourselves. The very fact of "who we are affects what we see in our clients and the ways that we hear and tell their stories" (Dean, 1989, p. 121). Therefore, social workers learn to know themselves—their personal stories that reveal their attitudes, values, and beliefs—and step back and observe themselves to use themselves most effectively in the helping process. Social workers "always return to the need to be self-aware and self-knowing, for authentic dialogue with and true understanding of our clients, as well as for effective helping" (Siporin, 1985, p. 214).

When social workers are aware of their own perspectives, thoughts, and aspirations, they carry a supportive base of personal resources into each new relationship with a client. They acknowledge their own needs and actively pursue their own goals in their personal lives. In this way, social workers are able to enter and endure professional relationships in which their own needs are contained to work to benefit others.

Values and Principles in Action: A Practice Example

Personal qualities develop over a lifetime of relating, communicating, and reflecting. Expanding self-awareness of personal qualities blends with professional values, knowledge, and skills as social workers prepare to interact with clients. In the example that follows, note how Paul Quillin reflects on his own readiness as he anticipates his work with a new client system. Follow Paul's thinking as he applies the professional practice principles of acceptance, individuation, nonjudgmentalism, objectivity, and self-determination while still maintaining his own personal values. Take note as to how he uses his self-awareness as a tool for empathy and as a way to build positive expectations about his clients.

Paul Quillin is one of several social workers at Northside Family Services (NFS) who gather weekly to share ideas and strategize new ways to deliver agency programs and services. The discussion at the last team meeting revealed that several gay and lesbian clients had expressed common concerns about parenting issues. In some ways, their issues include the usual parenting challenges; however, for these parents, the usual translates into complex realities made more difficult by the societal context of prejudice and discrimination. The workers concur that they and their clients have no easy answers for gays and lesbians in a homophobic society.

Brainstorming possible strategies, the workers report many examples of their clients' assertive, creative, and effective responses to the difficult situations. It seems only logical that these clients might benefit from the mutual support that group meetings could offer. When the social workers subsequently poll potential group members to determine their interest in a support group, they discover an enthusiastic, affirmative response. This sets the stage for Paul's work with the new support group for gay and lesbian parents.

Using self-awareness

As Paul reads through the referrals, he anticipates who the group's members might be and what he himself has to offer. Paul reflects on what he knows about people who are gay or lesbian. Narrow definitions of homosexuality lead to limited descriptions of sexuality. Understood more broadly in the context of social oppression, being gay or lesbian has dramatic implications. Paul realizes that each prospective group member is likely to experience the stress, anxiety, and fear that often accompany people's awareness that their sexual orientation evokes unpredictable responses from others. These responses range from acceptance to ignorance and misunderstanding, to imposing labels of pathology, to antagonistic acts of rejection, ridicule, and violence.

Paul's own identity as gay allows him to empathize with the struggles that are likely to characterize the life experiences of the support group members. Paul recognizes the strengths that he develops as he accepts and asserts his identity in the face of discrimination. Paul recounts that his own process of coming out increased his self-awareness, respect for human diversity, and ability to assert himself even when others disagree with his point of view. Although Paul knows that his own personal experiences will be helpful in his work with the support group, he tempers his thinking with the realization that his life doesn't actually match the lives of others. Similar sexual orientations do not mean that Paul and the support group members are all similar. Paul fully expects that group members have developed many distinctive personal strengths as a result of confronting the array of challenges in their own lives.

Respecting what clients bring

Consider the diverse array of resources that clients can offer to each other as the support group convenes. Members of the group will include Rita and Stephanie, who have been partners for 10 years. They met in graduate school when they were members of a lesbian activist group. They remain politically active. Both women have supportive extended families and friends. Rita's two children (Thomas, who is 11, and Ursala, who is 13) have always regarded Stephanie as a parent. They have grown up accepting their parents' lifestyle but now find themselves in uncomfortable struggles with their friends about their family. Previously, both parents had assertively intervened when the children reported incidents of discrimination against them. But lately, Ursala resists their assistance and keeps to herself. Both parents would like to reinitiate the support that was previously accepted by their daughter.

Vince has been a single parent to 8-year-old William since his wife abandoned the family shortly after William was born. Vince is quite accomplished as a single parent, balancing his job as an attorney with an active social life and responsible parenting. He has received much support and assistance from his family and friends in the care of his son. Currently, Vince is considering moving in with Andrew, with whom he has been in a committed relationship for 2 years. Although he is comfortable with this move for himself, he wonders about its effect on William. The three of them have fun together, but William isn't sure where Andrew fits into his dad's life. Vince wants to maintain an atmosphere of openness and honesty with his son, but doesn't know what and how much to say. Vince is apprehensive about how to explain his decision to William, wonders about how to include Andrew in their daily family life, and is uncertain about the reactions of other family members and friends.

Barb teaches Language Arts and coordinates the reading program at the local middle school. Her divorce was a difficult one, finalized just a little more than a year ago after an extensive battle for custody of 6-year-old Carissa. Barb has come to understand and accept her sexual orientation gradually. At this time, she is open with only a few close friends. She has expressed many concerns about the consequences of others finding out that she is a lesbian. She worries about questions like: What about the custody of her daughter? Could her ex-husband use this against her? What about her job? The school district's policies are unclear about protection for employees, and her experiences with some of the parents make her cringe at the thought that they would find out about her sexuality. Barb is looking forward to discussing these issues with other group members, but she is cautious with concerns about privacy and confidentiality.

Each person offers considerable resources that may be useful to the group and its members. Rita and Stephanie have successfully negotiated a working relationship as partners and parents. Vince may benefit from learning about their experiences. As an attorney, Vince has relevant knowledge for Barb. He may be able to inform her decisions about the risks involved in her coming out and the implications for her custody of Carissa and her employment as a teacher. Rita and Stephanie's openness about their sexuality may offer an experiential model for the transitions happening in Barb's life. Even Barb herself, although tentative in her decision to come out, clearly has important resources for the other group members. She brings a first-hand view of adolescence from her training and years of experience as a middle-school teacher. Barb's insight into teenagers and their relationships may enlighten Rita and Stephanie as they struggle to cope with the changes in their parenting of 13-year-old Ursala. This list of potential resources is only a beginning. As the support group works together, its members will reveal again and again that they possess distinctive knowledge that is a reservoir of resources on which they can draw.

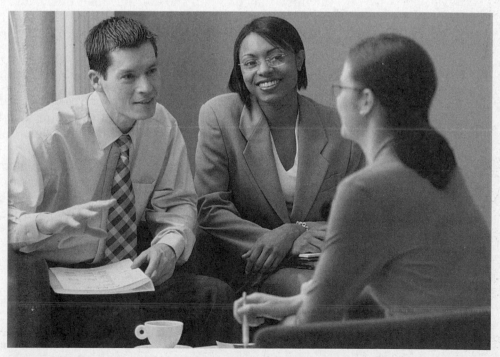

Social workers support each other in increasing their self-awareness and multicultural competence.

How Values Influence Practice

Paul's consideration of the support group members offers only general help in anticipating the exact value system that each new group member will bring. Being parents and gay or lesbian does not prescribe common beliefs or values. Differences within a group are often as striking as differences between groups. For example, members will likely have differing views on whether asserting one's identity as gay or lesbian is a personal or political matter. Each probably maintains different views on parenting, what is important for children to know, and how involved parents should be in their children's lives. Regardless of their particular beliefs, each has valid perceptions to support the way that he or she feels.

When the group convenes, Paul Quillin will consciously avoid imposing his own values on the group. Instead, he will identify and validate the value perspectives held by group members and encourage members to assert their unique views. Paul will help group members sort through and accept value differences as they form relationships, describe their perspectives, and develop solutions to their challenges.

Forming relationships

Values influence the formation of professional relationships. Values often bond social workers with client systems when their respective value systems are similar. However, differing values may distinguish social workers from client systems. Differences test a worker's ability to demonstrate acceptance and affirm client self-determination. If Paul imposes his own values on the group, members will likely withdraw and fail to invest their resources in the group's efforts.

Also consider the interaction within the support group. Similar values among members will probably lead to cohesion, mutual respect, and congruent goals. Discrepant values among members may lead to disagreements and stalemates unless members can develop an atmosphere of acceptance and curiosity in which they question and enhance their own belief systems by incorporating the perspectives of other group members. The existing values of the support group members will intermingle to create group norms, which ultimately affect the behavior of each group member.

Viewing situations

The way clients view their situations reveals their long-standing, deeply held beliefs and values. Often, the issues at hand are value laden, charged with conflicts and ethical dilemmas (Goldstein, 1987; Siporin, 1983, 1985). Frequently signaled by the word "should"—"What *should* I do?"—or denoted as a quandary about determining the right answer, these moral dilemmas are fraught with inner turmoil, intrapersonal conflict, and, sometimes, labels of immorality (Goldstein). Consider the support group members. Rita and Stephanie question how they *should* parent Thomas and Ursala. Vince is trying to decide how he *should* incorporate his partner Andrew into his family life. Barb is grappling with whether she *should* be open about her sexual identity. These issues all raise questions that have value issues at their core. Clients respond to challenges and solutions within the context of their values and beliefs.

Screening possible solutions

Clients screen options for change through the values they hold. What may be a viable solution for one may conflict with the values of another. Clients most readily apply change strategies that are congruent with their existing belief systems. An ethical social worker suggests options that are a good fit with clients' values or, as an alternative, guides clients to reconsider their value systems and broaden the range of acceptable solutions.

Values can change when people are exposed to different views. The dissonance that new information and perspectives creates can alter beliefs and lead to behavioral changes. For example, a father's newly acquired understanding of sexual orientation may change his perspective on whether he should welcome his gay son's life partner as a member of the family. Whatever beliefs currently guide a client system's behavior, perceptive social workers recognize that these beliefs inform a client's perspective, prescribe the dimensions of possible solutions, and influence the social worker–client relationship.

Values and Diversity

Values are not random; they develop over a lifetime. Each of us demonstrates values molded by family, friends, ethnic group, cohort group, neighborhood, region, and a host of other cultural influences. Recognizing and accepting a client's values requires social workers to be informed about human diversity.

Box 3.1 The Ethic of Anti-oppressive Practice

Oppression may be the single most disabling social force affecting social work clients. Recognizing oppression exposes "a systematic and deliberate strategy to suppress the power and potentiality of people by legitimizing and institutionalizing inhumanistic and person-delimiting values such as materialism, fragmentation, individualism, and inordinate competition" (Scheile, 1996, p. 286). Oppression results in social exclusion and damage to individuals' aspirations and abilities (Pierson, 2002; Washington & Paylor, 2000). "Cultural oppression suppresses the experiences, values, ideas and interpretations of marginalized groups about the causes and resolutions of social problems" (Graham, 2002, p. 43).

Anti-oppressive practice redresses oppression and social exclusion through its focus on the liberation, emancipation, and enfranchisement of members of vulnerable and oppressed groups (Baines, 2000; Cooper, 2001; Hick, 2002; Hyam, 2003; Langlery, 2001; Tang, 2003). Although the term, anti-oppressive practice, is not part of the language used in the NASW *Code of Ethics* (1999a), it clearly reflects the social-justice mandate. "The promise of anti-oppressive practice is that it prioritizes considerations of equity and social justice across a wide range of social difference" (Williams, 2002, p. 20). Anti-oppressive practice brings clarity in an actionable way to the social justice ideal.

The ethic of anti-oppressive practice holds social workers accountable to confront social inequality, to advocate anti-discriminatory practices in policy and procedural implementation, and to practice from a value base of social inclusion and individual respect. Gil (2002) believes that the

transformation of unjust and oppressive societies into just and free ones would require major changes in patterns of people's actions, interactions, and social relations. In turn, such changes seem to depend on prior changes of people's consciousness, which would be conducive to alternative patterns of actions and relations. (p. 46)

Rose adds that

challenging oppression requires social workers to support individuals in naming their experiences of oppression, examining the effects of oppression, and challenging oppression both personally and politically. (1990, cited in Dietz, 2000, p. 371)

Anti-oppressive practice differs from anti-discriminatory practice, distinguished by its actions to challenge disabling and exploitive relationships. Anti-oppressive practice is directly related to altering power dynamics. "Its use of power is three-dimensional since it acknowledges structural inequality and exploitative legal, social and economic relationships, and seeks a fundamental realignment of power relationships in the wider social context" (Braye & Preston-Shoot, 1995, p. 107). Empowerment is also about who has power and how that power is used. Central to implementing an empowerment method is understanding how those in power use oppression to maintain the status quo and in working to overturn power imbalances in personal interaction, professional relationships, and social structures.

MULTICULTURAL COMPETENCE

Diversity
in Practice

The responsibility to resolve difficulties in cross-cultural relationships rests with social workers, not clients. How do social workers develop into competent multicultural practitioners?

Social work values and principles are essential to working successfully with diverse clients, but good values alone are not sufficient for competent multicultural social work practice. Without ongoing efforts to develop capabilities in cross-cultural practice, even accepting, well-intentioned, and professionally principled practitioners make significant errors in relating to culturally diverse clients. Putting social work values into practice requires knowledge of the dynamics of diversity and skills for working with diverse populations.

"Culture is the lens through which all things are viewed, and to a great extent culture determines not only how but what is viewed and how it is interpreted" (Briggs, et al., 2005, p. 95). In essence, culture plays a pivotal role. It determines how clients "express and report their concerns, how they seek help, what they develop in terms of coping styles and social supports, and the degree to which they attach stigma" to their issues (Huang, 2002, p. 4). "Culturally different behaviors are not equivalent to social-skill deficits or behavior disorders" (Cartledge, et al., 2002, p. 117). Coming from different worlds can lead to misunderstandings and leave workers and clients feeling alienated from one another—the antithesis of collaborative partnerships that characterize empowerment-oriented social work. Although both workers and clients experience difficulties in cross-cultural relationships, adjusting to those cultural differences is the responsibility of social work practitioners.

Cultural Diversity Defined

Preservation of one's own culture does not require contempt or disrespect for other cultures.

—César Chávez

Cultural diversity, in its broadest sense, describes the phenomena of human differences as generated by membership in various identifiable human groups. Pinderhughes (1995) describes culturally diverse populations as including all who differ from the white middle-class norm "by ethnicity and/or race as well as those who are socially different, such as people in poverty, gay men and lesbians, and people who are physically or developmentally challenged" (p. 132). Social workers understand that the dimensions of diversity have many facets, including practice without discrimination with respect, knowledge, and skills related to clients' "age, class, color, culture, disability, ethnicity, gender, gender identity and expression, immigration status, political ideology, race, religion, sex, and sexual orientation" (CSWE, 2008, p. 5).

Sometimes, social workers apply the term diversity more specifically to emphasize differences in race or ethnicity. Race refers to physical characteristics, with special attention to skin color and facial features, whereas ethnic group members share common cultural attributes such as language, ancestry, or religion. In a society that categorizes, segregates, and discriminates based on race and ethnicity, these differences may be especially difficult for social workers and clients to bridge.

None of us, regardless of our primary cultural identity, is monocultural. Our own cultural uniqueness derives from membership in multiple cultures such as cultures associated with gender, occupations, clubs and organizations, geographic regions, ethnicity, and religion, to name a few. Members of a group generally share some values or rules of behavior for participation and/or membership in that group. However, individual members of the same group also possess many qualities and behaviors that differentiate them from each other. If we consider the multitude of sociocultural variables affecting both workers and clients, we can unequivocally conclude that most social work relationships are, in fact, multicultural.

Proficient Multicultural Practice

Citing the works of others, Lee and Greene (1999) distinguish between culturally competent and culturally sensitive approaches to multicultural practice. Cultural competence targets social worker knowledge for development, focusing "on a particular cultural group, with the purpose of developing culture-specific concepts, knowledge, and techniques within the specific context" (p. 23). In contrast, achieving cultural sensitivity is more value centered. Implementing a culturally sensitive approach requires a worker's genuine appreciation of the client's uniqueness and universalistic respect for the client's humanness. A third possibility for success in multicultural practice is a skill-based approach we describe as cultural responsiveness. To be culturally responsive, social workers use dialogue skills that place the client's construction of reality at the center of the conversation. Clients take the role of cultural expert, leaving the worker as an inquisitive and respectful learner. A competent, sensitive, and responsive approach to multicultural practice is rooted in the knowledge, values, and skills of generalist social work; it is cultivated through years of experience interacting with those who are culturally different.

Cultural Competence

The NASW (2001a) *Standards for Cultural Competence* indicate that cultural competence is "the process by which individuals and systems respond respectfully and effectively to people of all cultures, languages, classes, races, ethnic backgrounds, religious, and other diversity factors in a manner that recognizes, affirms, and values the worth of individuals, families, and communities and protects and preserves the dignity of each" (p. 11). This standard requires social workers to be aware of their own and their clients' cultural and environmental contexts, to value diversity, continually to refine skills that enhance the cultural strengths of others and draw on informal networks of support, and to advocate systems of service delivery that are in and of themselves culturally competent. In sum, "cultural competence is gaining knowledge about cultures AND engaging in a comprehensive process that includes: listening to client and families, understanding practices and priorities of the involved organizations, overturning institutionalized disadvantages to certain groups of people, and working for justice" (Clowes, 2003, p. 22).

Cultural Sensitivity

Culturally sensitive practice shifts the emphasis from acquiring extensive knowledge about various cultural groups toward developing the worker's attitude of acceptance, respect, and appreciation for each client's cultural uniqueness. Practitioners who are culturally sensitive demonstrate social work values in action and display a willingness to learn about the cultural worlds of their clients. In maintaining an open and inquisitive style, workers become lifelong learners about human diversity, defining multicultural competence as a process of becoming rather than an achievement or end product (Castex, 1994a; Green, 1999; Sue & Sue, 2003). Cultural sensitivity implies that social workers recognize that the multiple facets of clients' life experiences affect their values and priorities.

Box 3.2 Cultural Competence: A Research–Practice Connection

Culturally competent delivery of social services is essential to achieve the goals of the social work profession. Changing demographics, human differences rooted in gender, race, culture, ethnicity, age, sexual orientation, religion, physical and cognitive ability, and other dimensions demand that social workers transcend human differences in relating to diverse clients.

Contemporary research on multicultural competence reveals the difficulty of achieving cultural competence and shows that social workers and clients alike believe that workers fall short of realizing this goal. For example, in a survey of providers who serve Asian Americans with developmental disabilities and their families, 44 of the 112 workers who were surveyed reported significant barriers to delivering culturally appropriate services (Choi & Wynne, 2000). Obstacles included language differences resulting in communication difficulties, cultural variance in defining what it means to have a disability, and diverse expectations about the responsibilities of family members and social service providers. Another exploratory study of caregivers' perspectives on their workers' cultural competence provides mixed reviews (Walker, 2001; Walker & Cook, 2002). Although most respondents indicated that service providers had done fairly well in respecting clients' cultural values, nearly half of those respondents who were minorities described interactions with service providers as disrespectful. Their words echoed a need for service providers to be more aware of the realities of racism, oppression, and discrimination: "Don't say, 'Just put it behind you.' That does not validate the reality of what people of color experience with racial prejudice" (p. 36). Additionally, about 20% of respondents with low incomes reported instances in which they perceived a worker's disrespect, inferring from such labels as "lazy," "loser," and "trash."

Other studies provide guidance about the essential elements included in culturally effective practice. Based on a large-scale study of services in multiple Systems of Care sites, Gomez (2002) reports that respondents assessed workers' cultural competence based on perceptions of service providers' demeanor of caring and commitment: "Families judged the cultural competence of their providers in terms of the respect, honesty, trust, support, equality, acceptance, and mutual growth that their relationships engendered" (p. 13). Notably, those service providers judged less culturally competent had adopted a deficit view in their approach. Another study by Kulis and colleagues (2005) shows that program modifications to incorporate specific cultural elements have benefits. Their randomized control study evaluated the effectiveness of keepin' it REAL, a substance abuse prevention program that uses culturally grounded prevention strategies. Results indicate that "the Latino and multicultural versions of the intervention provided the clearest benefits to Mexican and Mexican American students" (p. 140).

Research also identifies areas for continued professional development. Based on her survey of Native American social workers and social work students, Weaver (1999) compiled results from many tribes to delineate key characteristics of cultural competence for working with First Nations people. Increased knowledge is necessary to recognize within-group diversity among Native Americans and to know both the history and contemporary realities of specific Native American clients. Weaver identifies developing patience for listening and tolerating silence as important skills, coupled with the expression of traditional social work values of respectfulness, nonjudgmentalism, and open-mindedness. Napoli (1999) expands this list, emphasizing trust, the role of spirituality, differing perceptions of time, variable meanings in communication, and the value of community over individuality as core components of culturally competent services for Native Americans.

The daunting need for cultural competence is transparent. Our success in meeting the need has been limited. Keeping informed of current research is one way in which social workers can develop their abilities to be culturally responsive and respectful in their practice with diverse populations.

Cultural Responsiveness

A culturally responsive approach accentuates key practice skills as a method to achieve multicultural competence. Extensive knowledge about a client's culture is not the key. Rather, the answer lies in the worker's abilities to frame the conversation without overriding the client's perspective. "The worker's expertise lies in applying the skills necessary to access the client's cultural expertise. The ability to elicit and accept client stories without imposing the worker's assumptions, biases, or interpretations is the starting point" (O'Melia, 1998). This approach suggests that "one way to learn about a culture is from the client," by using attitudes of "cultural naiveté and respectful curiosity" (Dyche & Zayas, 1995, p. 389). By applying client-centered responding skills, workers initiate "a discovery procedure, a way of accessing and learning about the world of people different from ourselves" (Green, 1999, p. 82).

A GENERALIST VIEW OF CULTURAL COMPETENCE

Social workers do not function in isolation, but, rather, in a professional context that includes colleagues, agencies, and the community in which they work. What happens in these contextual systems influences the capability of workers to practice in culturally sensitive ways. Cultural competence requires a systemic effort—the synchronization of values, knowledge, skills, and attitudes at the worker, agency, and service network levels—as well as the incorporation of these attributes into practices, policies, services, institutions, and community functioning (Raheim, 2002). Culturally competent practice begins at the personal level of the worker and must be supported by both the agency and the community to sustain an ongoing and successful effort.

Practitioner-Level Cultural Competence

Workers themselves bear primary responsibility for developing competence in multicultural social work. Key elements of this personal level of competence include (1) self-awareness, both in terms of values and cultural background, (2) knowledge of other cultures coupled with the skill to adapt general knowledge to specific clients, and (3) the ability to identify and articulate the power and privilege differentials that characterize intercultural relationships.

Self-awareness

Truly to know others, you must first know yourself. The abilities of workers to sort out differences among values and cultural dimensions begins with an intensive review and articulation of their own personal values and cultural heritage. Culturally competent social workers continuously refine their self-awareness. They acknowledge the ways in which their own biases influence their professional practice. Practitioners determine how similarities as well as differences between themselves and clients affect their perceptions and professional judgments. They also reflect on the nature of their own spiritual beliefs (Canda & Furman, 1999; Gilbert, 2000; Hodge, 2000; Ortiz, et al., 2000). An extensive consideration of our own cultural identities is a requisite for developing a culturally competent repertoire of practices. Complete the cultural self-inventory in Figure 3.1 as a way to begin to envision the cultural lens through which you perceive the world and the clients with whom you will work.

Earlier, this chapter described the pervasive influence of values and principles in social work practice. Nowhere are value differences and conflicts more evident than in cross-cultural social work. In this context, certain values are pivotal, such as one's position on assimilation and cultural pluralism (Devore & Schlesinger, 1999). Assimilation is the process by which cultural minorities absorb characteristics of the dominant culture, whereas pluralism refers to

Figure 3.1   Cultural Self-Inventory

Personal Identity
- What are your ethnic identities?
- Of which other cultural groups are you a member?
- Which cultural memberships are most influential in the way you define yourself?
- What characteristics or behaviors do you display that indicate the influences of these cultural identities?
- What values are associated with these cultural memberships?
- Do you feel positively or negatively about these identities?
- Have you ever experienced discrimination based on your cultural memberships?
- What privileges do your cultural memberships afford you?

Spiritual Beliefs
- What are your spiritual beliefs?
- What led you to these beliefs?
- How important are spiritual beliefs in your daily life?
- How do these beliefs influence the way you perceive others who hold different beliefs?
- How do your spiritual beliefs influence your choices and behaviors?

Knowledge of Others
- What other cultural groups are present in your community?
- What do you know about the beliefs, values, and customs of members of these other cultural groups?
- What is the source of this knowledge?
- Have your interactions with people from these cultures reinforced or altered this knowledge base?
- What stereotypes or prejudices do you hold about other cultural groups?
- What is the source of your biases?
- What are you doing to increase your knowledge about people who are culturally different from you?

Cross-Cultural Skills
- Are you currently involved in relationships or activities in which you have ongoing interactions with people from other cultures?
- What is your comfort level while interacting with people who are culturally different from you?
- Are you able to talk with people who are culturally different from you about these differences?
- What languages do you speak other than your own primary language?
- What words, phrases, or nonverbal behaviors do you know that have different meanings in different cultures?

respecting and maintaining cultural distinctions among different groups (Green, 1999). Questions to ask yourself to sort out your view on this issue include

- As a worker, do you help maintain the cultural integrity of the people with whom you work, or do you expect them to adapt to the dominant norm?
- Which do you see as more beneficial—cultural assimilation or cultural pluralism?
- Which more closely matches your views of what society should be?
- Which is easier for you to implement in practice?
- How is your perspective similar to or different from those of your clients?

Awareness of others

None of us enters any relationship without expectations about the cultures of those with whom we are about to relate. These presuppositions have many sources. Our knowledge of other cultures develops throughout our lives, influenced by our families, our neighborhoods, the media, and our own history of experiences with others. Some of us have had extensive contact with people who are culturally different from ourselves, whereas others of us have been isolated in more secluded monocultural worlds. Whether diverse or narrow, our experiences leave us with preconceived notions, stereotypes, and prejudices that taint our views even when, as students of social work, we accumulate knowledge about others through academic preparation, volunteer work, and field experiences.

Identifying our views about others combined with acquiring more formal knowledge begins to build a more realistic understanding of cultural differences. The more we articulate and question our preconceived notions as we examine various cultures, the more we experience alternative ways of knowing, feeling, and behaving. However, no single practitioner can know all that is relevant to know about every cultural group. Instead, workers can initiate interactions with others in the community while systematically monitoring what they observe and how they react to their experiences.

Studying cultural groups Multicultural competence requires processes by which practitioners can continue to educate themselves about the particular groups and individuals with whom they work. One way in which workers might increase their awareness of diverse cultural groups is to use the anthropological approach of naturalistic observation. Green (1999) says:

> The route to greater appreciation of the role of culture in human behavior requires direct observation and participation in naturalistic settings, away from the confines of offices and their imposing routines. For instance, the practitioner who has failed to attend a black church service or talked with a black minister might not understand black clients as well as he or she could. The worker serving American-Indian clients who has not spent enough time in an Indian home seeing how extended families take care of their children and their elderly, or how ritual practices are used for preserving traditional ways, really doesn't know enough about Indian clients (p. 97).

By observing people interacting within their cultural contexts, workers can identify those values, resources, skills, and supports indigenous to their communities of practice. Green (1999) suggests three concrete steps:

1. *Preparing to enter an unfamiliar community.* Social workers first review the literature about the particular ethnic group, including research studies, statistical information, and ethnic literature and poetry. They can also study the particular community through social mapping.

2. *Using key respondents as cultural guides.* In this step, workers identify resourceful indigenous people who are willing to articulate what they know to an outsider, develop trusting relationships with them, and learn about their lives in the ethnic community.

3. *Observing while participating.* Finally, workers use their relationships with key community members to become involved in the ethnic community's activities. Informed by a research orientation and directed by clear-cut goals, this observation focuses on important attributes of the ethnic community's functioning, placing special emphasis on available leadership, resources, and preferred methods for solving problems.

Experientially generated knowledge of the cultural groups with whom practitioners will work, placed in the context of the dominant cultural perspectives to which these various cultural groups must respond, is an essential supplement to the "textbook overviews" by which most practitioners begin their journey to cultural sensitivity.

Social workers need to expand their base of knowledge about the cultures to include becoming familiar with the diverse religious and spiritual traditions of those with whom they work. Competent "working knowledge of cultures requires an understanding of indigenous belief systems as related to spirituality and religion" (Ortiz, et al., 2000, p. 21). Specifically, social workers can

- Increase their awareness of spirituality in themselves and their clients
- Respect differences resulting from religious diversity
- Clarify points of religious bias and the implication of this bias for practice
- Appreciate the significance and meaning of religious metaphors
- Identify the resources of other professionals who have sensitivity and skill for working with particular aspects of religious diversity (Miley, 1992)

Status and privilege

A fully functional multiracial society cannot be achieved without a sense of history and open, honest dialogue.

—Cornel West

Cultural group membership means more than differences of values, attitudes, and behaviors. Membership in some culture groups also confers differences in status and privilege. A socially and economically stratified society such as that of the United States does not afford all groups equal status or privileges. Many of us have the luxury of ignoring this fact. "Power differences are less apparent to the privileged, who can more readily accept a view of American society as classless and color-blind—the myth of the playing field" (Akamatsu, 1998, p. 129).

To develop collaborative cross-cultural relationships, both workers and clients must neutralize the impact of the wider society as to whom society has granted greater status. To do so, practitioners must understand "the dynamics of power and powerlessness and how these forces operate in human functioning. Moreover, practitioners must be able and willing to apply such knowledge to themselves as well as clients" (Pinderhughes, 1995, p. 133). For example, do you recognize the privileges or restrictions that society assigns you based on your own cultural identity? How might these privileges affect your practice with people from other cultures?

Certain cultural characteristics—such as race, gender, religion, and economic class—are weighted more heavily in determining social privilege and ranking societal status. Most Whites are oblivious to White privilege and the underlying racist ideologies inculturated in the institutional structures of society (McIntosh, 1998). White privilege is particularly insidious: "Because of the embeddedness of racism in our society, White skin privilege is a camouflage for those who are not targeted. Not perceiving themselves as unknowing, they may never think, or may feel vaguely reluctant, to ask for information" (Akamatsu, 1998, p. 131).

Religion is often overlooked as a source of privilege; however, in the United States, those belonging to Christian religious groups are often rewarded with signs of status and power. Schlosser (2003) contends that even "discussing Christian privilege is 'breaking a sacred taboo,' because both subtle and obvious pressures exist to ensure that these privileges continue to be the sole domain of Christians" (p. 47). Christian privilege is likely invisible to those who are Christian, virtually a nonconscious ideology. However, Christian privilege is transparent to those who profess a faith other than Christian or no faith at all. People who are members of religious minority groups may feel that "their religious identity is not valued, and, subsequently, they feel discrimination and oppression because of their religious group membership" (p. 47).

History reveals a plethora of instances of gender stereotyping, gender bias, and discrimination based on sex. "Hidden assumptions about sex and gender remain embedded in cultural discourses, social institutions, and individual psyches that invisibly and systematically reproduce male power in generation after generation" (Bem, 1993, p. 2). Bem calls the sexist assumptions of andro-centrism (men are human, and women are "other"), gender polarization (men are masculine, and women are feminine), and biological essentialism (biologi-cal destiny) the lenses of gender. "Not only do these lenses shape how people perceive, conceive, and discuss social reality, but because they are embedded in social institutions, they also shape the more material things—like unequal pay and inadequate day care—that constitute social reality itself" (p. 2).

Sexism interacts with other types of oppression and exploitation, such as racism, heterosexism, and classism. Women of color face the double jeopardy of racism and sexism. Lesbians must deal with the patriarchy inherent in sex-ism as well as in heterosexism and its corollary, homophobia. Classism multi-plies the oppression and discrimination experienced by the expanding ranks of women who are poor.

Becoming a competent cross-cultural social worker

In summary, learning to be a competent cross-cultural practitioner is an evolu-tionary process that begins with awareness and increases with each interaction with clients. Workers first attempt to understand their own cultural filters. Next, they build a knowledge base of other perspectives through literature reviews and field research. Third, workers analyze the impact of cultural iden-tities on the power dynamics of the worker–client partnership. Finally, practi-tioners continue to fine-tune their cultural sensitivity through their ongoing practice experiences with unique client systems.

Agency-Level Cultural Competence

Practice Contexts

Agencies need culturally responsive policies, prac-tices, and services. How can agencies involve consumers in evaluating attempts to create cul-turally sensitive policies and deliver culturally competent services?

The agency setting is crucial in supporting workers' attempts to deliver cultur-ally sensitive services. A culturally competent agency prepares its workers with the necessary training and skills for diversity-sensitive practice, and it promotes multicultural awareness and functioning in all aspects of its organi-zational structure and program delivery. Specifically, culturally competent agencies infuse multicultural influences into their policies, orientations to practice, structures, resource networks, and physical environments.

Agency policies

Organizational policies guide an agency's operations, including hiring and training staff, evaluating program effectiveness, and defining criteria for eli-gibility for services. Reflected in these policies are cultural attitudes and assumptions. Agency policies may simply ignore diversity issues, adopting a dominant cultural perspective by omission, or these policies may reflect sensi-tivity to the cultural elements inherent in all human interaction.

Multiculturally sensitive administrators actively seek to employ a staff that reflects the cultural and social diversity of the community (Gutiérrez & Nagda, 1996). This means hiring diverse staff at all levels of the agency, including administrative, supervisory, direct service, clerical, and maintenance personnel. Ideally, hiring policies and procedures will ensure processes for actively recruiting culturally diverse staff members. Interviewers will incorporate interview questions that evaluate the cultural sensitivity of prospective employees, and ongoing training will provide opportunities for all agency personnel to develop the specific cultural knowledge and skills that are relevant to the community.

Eligibility guidelines can either enhance or restrict access to services. Culturally competent policies ensure the accessibility of services to all potential clients. Culturally sensitive agencies recognize the difficulty that many people, particularly those who have been historically disenfranchised, have in connecting to traditionally delivered social services. In response, an agency develops inclusive policies to promote access to diverse clients through the creative design of service delivery—such as locating services in various neighborhoods and offering concrete, pragmatic aid as part of its program (Lum, 2004).

Culturally aware agencies also structure their program evaluation methods for maximal participation by the consumers of their services. Evaluation procedures are most effective when they request input from clients through consumer satisfaction surveys, seek direct feedback from clients in other forums, and ask clients to provide specific information regarding their perceptions of the cultural sensitivity of the agency's practices.

Orientation toward practice

An agency's theoretical orientation affects the ways that workers view clients and their situations. In social constructionist terms, workers construct the world in which they interact with clients by selecting which theories and perspective to apply. Not all these choices are equal in terms of cultural sensitivity. For example, an agency that implements an intrapsychic approach may overlook the social etiology and ramifications of the client's situation. Multicultural competence at the agency level means developing programs and services based on theories that place clients in cultural and social contexts. Competent agencies develop programs and procedures that focus on client strengths, use culturally sensitive assessment instruments, consider culture a resource, and make use of ethnically oriented indigenous helping networks (Miller & Gaston, 2003).

Gutiérrez and Nagda (1996) recommend that organizations adopt an ethnoconscious approach. This approach "combines an ethnic-sensitive orientation and an empowerment perspective on practice. . . . At its center is a concern with power and confronting social inequality through work with individuals, families, groups, organizations, and communities" (p. 205). Even when agencies serve clients primarily on the individual and family level, addressing macrolevel issues—including policy, social inequity, and the distribution of resources—is an essential ingredient of multiculturally sensitive practice.

Structures

The way in which an agency organizes itself, particularly in determining the roles that clients play, affords opportunities to facilitate cultural competence. At its best, an agency can structure "client collaboration and partnerships in organizational governance, program development, staffing, and evaluation" (Gutiérrez & Nagda, 1996, p. 207). Involving diverse clients in agency operations ensures synergistic multicultural interchanges in all aspects of agency functioning, operations, and governance.

The distribution of power within the agency is an important structural component. Traditional organizations maintain rigid vertical lines of authority, hierarchial structures that likely mirror the inequities of the larger society (Bailey,

1994). In contrast, a flatter organizational structure encourages the sharing of power through consensus-based decision making. It also enhances opportunities for mutual influence among management, direct service, and support staff. When the agency's organizational structure allows workers to have greater control over their practice, workers, in turn, are more likely to respond similarly with their clients, encouraging them to participate more fully in planning, evaluating, and developing services (Adams & Krauth, 1994). When clients have a greater influence on services, agencies meet clients' needs more consistently, regardless of the variations in culture they represent.

Physical environment

The culturally competent agency is accessible in every way. This means that it is physically accessible to persons with disabilities. It is verbally accessible to those who speak languages other than English. It also is conveniently located in neighborhoods where clients live, has offices on major public transit routes, offers clients transportation, or provides outreach services.

Even the ways that an agency decorates and furnishes its offices and promotes its programs affect whether clients will perceive the agency as culturally open or as an agent of majority control. See Figure 3.2 for a list of questions to evaluate the degree of an agency's cultural competence. These expressions of an agency's perspective can be critical to helping clients feel comfortable, or they can edge clients toward a more guarded mode of interaction.

Resource networks

All social work organizations connect to a network of services, both to refer clients to services and to receive referrals from other agencies. For an agency to be considered culturally competent, this continuum must include "more than the network of community agencies and referral services. It includes institutions, individuals, and customs for resolving problems that are indigenous to the client's own community" (Green, 1999, p. 92). Examples of indigenous resources include churches, schools, clubs, local healers, neighborhood leaders, and culturally oriented media.

Culturally competent agencies are also active participants in their larger environments. Agencies need to connect with legislative bodies to advocate clients' rights and social justice reforms (Gutiérrez & Nagda, 1996). Agencies should also work to build coalitions with other community groups and organizations working toward social change.

Figure 3.2   Cultural Inventory for Agencies

- Can persons with disabilities access the agency readily? Consider those with difficulties in walking, hearing, and seeing as well as those with intellectual and emotional challenges.
- Does the agency display art work that is culturally diverse?
- Is the reading material available in waiting areas of interest to a variety of cultural groups?
- Do story books, games, dolls, and other toys appeal to both boys and girls as well as children from various cultural backgrounds?
- Are brochures and orienting information multilingual and do they contain pictures which reflect the diversity of the agency's clients? Are forms and brochures available in large print format?
- Are agency materials nonracist, nonsexist, and nonheterosexist?
- Do agency materials define concepts inclusively? For example, does its literature on family life define family to include blended families, extended families, and families with same-sex parents?
- Does the agency staff represent diverse cultural groups?

Community-Level Cultural Competence

Both workers and clients respond to the same community context. In some ways, each cross-cultural practice relationship is a microcosm of the status of similar relationships in the community. A community that discriminates in housing, segregates its schools, and maintains separateness in cultural events fixes distinct boundaries between cultural groups—a chasm that workers and clients must bridge to form working partnerships. A community that values pluralism, celebrates its diversity, promotes cross-cultural interactions, and works toward social justice facilitates the work of social workers and clients. Even practitioners working at the individual and family level can, in generalist fashion, play an activist role in the community-at-large to encourage cross-cultural interactions, awareness, and respect.

LOOKING FORWARD

Professional practice principles, personal values, cultural attributes, individual belief systems, and expectations permeate the relationships of social workers and clients. The social worker–client relationship is potentially a complex web of personal–professional–relational transactions. Social workers must resolve conflicts between their personal values and professional obligations, between their cultural backgrounds and those of clients, between their own perspectives and clients' perspectives, and between the values of social work and those of society.

Workers' expectations that develop from personal and professional preparation and their anticipation of what clients will bring to the process will influence the relationship. A positive view of clients, appreciation of cultural diversity, understanding of ethical principles, and heightened self-awareness prepare social workers to construct effective relationships with clients. These filters become increasingly important as practitioners engage clients in the social work processes explicated in later chapters. These are not the only filters through which workers view clients and their situations. Chapter 4 discusses the strengths perspective and empowerment, which also orient a worker's views and approach to practice.

Succeed with **PEARSON mysocialworklab**

Log onto **www.mysocialworklab.com** and click on the link to view the Interactive Skill Module videos. Answer the questions below. (*If you did not receive an access code to* **MySocialWorkLab** *with this text and wish to purchase access online, please visit* **www.mysocialworklab.com**.)

1. **Watch the entire group work module** (page 26) to examine a worker's underlying values and professional principles. Which of her responses demonstrate the professional principles of acceptance, individualization, nonjudgmentalism, and self-determination?

2. **Watch the group work module on page 13** to explore the impact of cultural differences on a client (Anna) whose family has immigrated from Belize. What steps can the worker take toward cultural competence in her work with Anna?

PRACTICE TEST

1. Based on communication theory, Jamie knows that all messages convey elements of both ____.
   a. content and relationship
   b. messages and non-messages
   c. significance and insignificance
   d. power and authority

2. Practitioners review their frames of reference to ____.
   a. create a false sense of professionalism
   b. impress clients with their broad-base of knowledge
   c. send messages consistent with respect for clients' competence
   d. avoid communicating spontaneously

Ethical Practice

3. As a social work student, your most important task with respect to your values is to ____.
   a. eliminate your personal values from your professional perspective
   b. regard your value perspective as ideal
   c. heighten your self-awareness of your own value perspective
   d. dismiss your own perspective on values as irrelevant

4. When Alexis treats her clients and their situations with respect, her practice behavior reflects the social work principle of ____.
   a. objectivity
   b. individualization
   c. accountability
   d. acceptance

5. Asking a client "Why did you do that?" MOST likely contradicts the social work principle of ____.
   a. self-determination
   b. individualization
   c. accountability
   d. nonjudgmentalism

6. As a member of the agency diversity task force, Kenesha recommends revising intake forms so the forms are more sensitive to life style differences.

Kenesha's recommendation demonstrates the ethical charge to promote ____.
   a. self-determination
   b. access to resources
   c. accountability
   d. self-determination

Research Based Practice

7. Drawing on evidence-based protocols to direct practice interventions and program development exemplifies the practice principle of ____.
   a. objectivity
   b. nonjudgmentalism
   c. accountability
   d. confidentiality

Diversity in Practice

8. Research indicates that families judged their service providers as culturally competent by all of the following characteristics EXCEPT:
   a. honesty
   b. deficit view
   c. supportiveness
   d. respect

9. With respect to privilege, which of the following statements is MOST accurate?
   a. Race, but not cultural group membership, confers privilege.
   b. Power differences are more apparent to people who have privilege than to those who do not.
   c. Religion is never a source of privilege.
   d. The dynamics of privilege, power, and powerlessness influence social work practice.

10. Which of the following is LEAST likely a facet of agency-level cultural competence?
    a. Accessible physical environment
    b. Policies that demonstrate respect for diversity
    c. Culturally sensitive orientations to service delivery
    d. Self-awareness

Log onto **MySocialWorkLab** once you have completed the Practice Test above to take your Chapter Exam and demonstrate your knowledge of this material.

Answers

1) a 2) c 3) c 4) d 5) d 6) b 7) c 8) b 9) b 10) d

4

Strengths and Empowerment

CONNECTING CORE COMPETENCIES *in this chapter*

| Professional Identity | Ethical Practice | Critical Thinking | Diversity in Practice | Human Rights & Justice | Research Based Practice | Human Behavior | Policy Practice | Practice Contexts | Engage Assess Intervene Evaluate |

A good conference can be energizing, and this one, "Empowerment and the Strengths Perspective," is giving Mark Nogales a real boost. Mark's 8 years as an outreach worker in the Community Support Program of the County Mental Health Center sometimes leaves him in need of professional revitalization. Facilitating the community integrated-living arrangements for persons with chronic mental illnesses has its challenges. But today's conference is crystallizing something for Mark that he has been sensing for some time now. People's lives get better when you focus on what they can do rather than on what they can't. Mark has learned that his clients, often identified more by their pathological labels and diagnoses than as the unique individuals that Mark knows them to be, bring considerable talents and skills to the challenges in their lives. Mark openly acknowledges and celebrates the diverse resources each client reveals. And now, this conference on the strengths perspective clearly says that the very process of activating client strengths is the quickest and most empowering path toward increasing client competence.

Mark's undergraduate study of social work taught him to implement a process focused on solving problems. "Good social work practice," the words of his first social work professor still echo, "has a beginning, a middle, and an end." More specifically, Mark knew this professor was talking about a well-organized social work process that begins with a concrete definition of problems. Mark built his early practice by using this framework offered by experts in the field.

As a practicing social worker, Mark is learning from other experts in the field—his clients. These experts are teaching him to look beyond their presenting problems, to shift the attention of the work from solving problems per se to developing strengths and finding solutions. This gradual transition has been a natural evolution for Mark and his clients, a subtle, yet significant shift in Mark's orientation toward practice.

Simply put, Mark sees the impossibility of trying to solve the problems of chronic mental illness, which are, by definition, unchangeable and lifelong. Besides, working closely with the people defined as his clients, Mark has discovered that the various labels of mental illness assigned to them hold little meaning to the relationships he forms with them. Each of his clients is unique. Mark's work with them reflects his awareness that diversity in approach is a natural response to a clientele so distinct in lifestyle, personality, and aspirations as to defy the deficiencies implied in the categories by which they are grouped.

The common message to Mark from his clients is consistent and clear. They respond in positive ways when Mark accepts their challenges and accentuates their talents. Mark is learning it. His clients are proving it. His practice experience is validating it. And now, at this conference, the "experts" in the social work field are promoting it. Practice processes that focus on client strengths rather than on deficits actualize empowerment.

Mark's orientation to strengths reveals his respect for his clients. He affirms their capacity and creativity to discover ways to manage their own challenges. When trying to accomplish something, it only makes sense to make use of all the resources available. Building on resources reflects the growing trend in social work to practice from a strengths perspective. When social workers incorporate the strengths perspective, their orientation simply represents *"good, basic social work practice"* (Saleebey, 2000a, p. 81).

Adopting a strengths perspective influences the ways that social workers view client systems and involve them in the change process. This chapter discusses the strengths perspective and empowerment as the foundation for an empowering approach to generalist social work practice. In detail, this chapter

- Describes the strengths perspective and discusses the implications of this view for practice
- Defines empowerment as a process and desirable goal of social work intervention to address issues of social injustice
- Explains how an orientation toward strengths and empowerment shapes social work practice

Understanding the strengths perspective and empowerment prepares social workers to implement an empowering approach with clients that emphasizes their abilities and ensures their active participation in change processes.

STRENGTHS PERSPECTIVE

Client strengths are resources in working for change and the focus of a contemporary approach to social work practice. The strengths perspective subscribes

> to the notion that people have untapped, undetermined reservoirs of mental, physical, emotional, social, and spiritual abilities that can be expressed. The presence of this capacity for continued growth and heightened well-being means that people must be accorded the respect that this power deserves. This capacity acknowledges both the being and the becoming aspects of life. (Weick, et al., 1989, p. 352)

All people have a natural power within themselves that can be released (Weick & Chamberlain, 2002). When social workers support this inherent power, they enhance the probability for positive growth. People strive toward the development of their potential, mastery, and self-actualization (Maluccio, 1981). This humanistic view leads social workers to recognize "each person's multipotentialities—that is, actual as well as latent resources, strengths, and creativity" (p. 11).

The strengths perspective is consonant with social work's fundamental values regarding human worth and social justice. A focus on strengths is essential to operationalizing social work's professional value base:

> Focusing and building on client strengths is not only a counterweight to the prevalence of the deficit model. It is an imperative of the several values that govern our work and the operation of a democratic, just, and pluralistic society including distributive justice, equality, respect for the dignity of the individual, inclusiveness and diversity, and the search for maximum autonomy within maximum community. (Saleebey, 2002b, p. 264)

By adopting a strengths perspective, workers infuse values into their practice. Actualizing fundamental social work values, such as human dignity and worth, respect, and self-determination, naturally promotes clients' strengths and potential capabilities (Cowger, 1992). Simply stated, applying a strengths perspective creates an atmosphere that accords client systems dignity and support.

Ethical Practice

The strengths perspective assumes that every client has the capacity for growth and change. How can social workers reconcile the assumptions of the strengths perspective with their biases about clients who have a history of abusive behavior or other social deviances?

Practice Assumptions

Currently, the strengths perspective brings together principles and techniques that highlight the resources and promote the resourcefulness of clients (Saleebey, 2002b). Strengths-oriented social workers believe that the strengths of all client systems—individual, familial, group, organizational, and societal—are resources to initiate, energize, and sustain change processes (see Figure 4.1). Workers draw on the resources available, both within client systems and in their environmental contexts, to promote more effective functioning.

Key Transitions

Words construct the meaning of our experiences. The particular words we use to describe social work, the metaphors we select to elaborate the process, and the labels we assign to categorize information are extremely significant. Words influence how we think, interpret situations, envision possibilities, and conduct day-to-day activities. The evolution of social work practice from "expert treatment" to a practice process that promotes strengths compels us to enrich our professional language to reflect these changes. Rappaport (1985) supports a shift in language, advocating "a language for helping that is steeped in symbols that communicate the powerful force for change contained within ourselves, our significant others, and our communities" (p. 16).

One example of the paradigm shift is the movement toward asset-based assessments and planning. The asset-based approach shifts the focus away from identifying risk factors to promoting protective factors. This shift signals a move in thinking from problem-focused to strengths-based, from at-risk to resiliency, from individual to family and community context, from dependency to self-efficacy, and from alienation to connectedness (NASW, 2002b). Social work that focuses on strengths and emphasizes collaboration transforms the way that professionals conceptualize their practice of social work. To apply the strengths perspective, practitioners need to reexamine their orientation to practice, their views of client systems, and their interpretation of the issues clients present. Practicing from a strengths perspective prompts social workers to examine two key transitions—the transitions from pathology to strengths and from a preoccupation with the past to an orientation toward the future.

Pathology or strength?

You can build little of lasting value on pathology, but you may build an enduing edifice out of strengths.

—Dennis Saleebey

Social workers who focus on strengths do not ignore the difficulties that clients bring. The point is not whether problems are part of the helping process; they are. When social workers orient their view of clients toward strengths, they question the centrality of focusing on pathology. Narrowly focusing on problems and pathology blocks the ability to uncover strengths. Negative frames of reference obscure the unique capabilities of client systems (Pray, 1991). For example, the problem of "a half glass of water" is that the glass is half empty. If we fail to recognize that the glass is half full, we may go thirsty because of our oversight.

Figure 4.1 Assumptions of a Strengths Perspective

Social workers who subscribe to the strengths perspective:
- Acknowledge that clients have existing reservoirs of resources and competencies to draw upon
- Recognize that each client has a distinct capacity for growth and change
- Define problems as occurring within the transactions between systems rather than residing in deficient system functioning
- Hold that collaboration augments existing strengths to build new resources
- Affirm that clients know their situations best and, given options, can determine the best solutions for their challenges
- Maintain that positive change builds on a vision of future possibilities
- Support a process to magnify mastery and competence rather than correct deficits

Good reasons exist for social work's long-standing focus on pathology. After World War I, the social work profession ushered in an era of practice based primarily on the psychoanalytic perspective and the medical model. This approach, replete with its own language set, served the profession well. Widely accepted, the model helped social work achieve professional status, gain society's sanction by providing psychiatric services to veterans and their families, and establish a definitive theoretical and technical base for practice. As its title implies, the medical model adopts the medical practice of predicating any prescriptive treatment on a diagnosis. Transposed to the arena of social work, the medical model views presenting problems as "pathologies" that require "diagnosis" by a social work "expert" to recommend and carry out the proper course of "treatment." Although helpful as an organizing framework for practice, the medical model falls short of acknowledging the reciprocal nature of human interaction in environmental context. Instead, the medical model presumes individual fault, failure, personal inadequacy, and deficiency.

Diagnosing "pathology" does more than obscure people's strengths. It creates labels that conveniently describe the presenting "pathological" behaviors. This may prompt social workers to move from the construct of a "person with a pathology" to the stigmatizing conceptualization of a "pathological person." Clients, whose behavior society judges immoral—those involved in child abuse, domestic violence, incest, or other criminal acts—are themselves labeled immoral (Goldstein, 1987). Clients who have been victimized, and, thus, called "victims," begin to take on the diminished, impotent persona of the victim role. When careless social workers belittle their clients by evoking labels such as "welfare cases," "those people," "the handicapped," or "run-down communities," even their images of clients become depersonalized and dehumanized.

Maligning clients with unfavorable and impersonal labels generates images of stagnation with no potential for regeneration, renewal, or change. The labels social workers use influence their sense of a client's worth and even shape their ideas about what course of action to take. "Professionals have to let go of their grip on labels and their reliance on taxonomies, both of which are often misused to the point of pigeonholing people and communities as well as professional reactions, thwarting the potential for social action" (Breton, 2002, p. 31). Pathological labels establish negative expectations that diminish the chances for positive change. Collectively, pejorative labels and stereotypes assign categorical meanings, block visions of potential, and constrict plans for service delivery and social policy. When social work practitioners shift their orientations to strengths, they escape the many pitfalls of focusing on pathology.

Past or future?

The shift in perspective from problems to challenges also refocuses our view from a look at the past to an eye on the future. An intervention process based on the medical model searches the past to detect when, why, and how client systems went wrong. In contrast, strengths-oriented social workers explore the present to discover the resources that clients currently have that they can use to take charge of the future. Take careful note of this shift—*from the past to the future.* This change from *what was* to *what can* and *will be* reorients our thinking about the entire process of social work practice.

Life doesn't stand still. No matter how stuck we may feel, we have little choice but to go on, as life continues to present its challenges and possibilities. Clients have all gone on and are continuing on despite previous events that may have stretched their capabilities. The ecosystems perspective describes the ongoing evolution of human systems as they adapt to difficult circumstances in productive ways or even as they cope in ways that further complicate their situations. Regardless of its positive or negative direction, change is always occurring. When clients and social workers begin their work together, they can only influence the current situation and the direction of future evolution; they cannot alter past events. What's done is done. What's yet to come is still in question.

None of us can stop the clock or reverse time to rewrite an episode in our past. Our lives just keep happening. If we become mired in looking backward, we are likely to be blindsided to presently occurring events. As an alternative, if we face toward the future, we have opportunities to review what we currently know, apply skills we have developed, and determine what additional resources are available to meet upcoming challenges. No rules say that all past problems must be uncovered and resolved or all deficits erased to move forward. Focus on an approach that permits forging ahead to a more promising future in which past difficulties fade in the light of success.

Applying a Strengths Perspective

To apply a strengths perspective, practitioners need a clear understanding of how to focus on the present and to incorporate a vision of the future. Consider the example of how Olivia Adams builds on her present strengths to construct a workable future.

Olivia, a 24-year-old client of Mark Nogales, resides in a supportive living arrangement and attends a work activity program sponsored by the County Mental Health Center where Mark is employed. Olivia presents herself as withdrawn and socially awkward and seldom interacts with others at the center. Although she is very capable of performing her assigned tasks, she isolates herself. Mark could dwell on the etiology of Olivia's timorous behavior, but instead Mark uses a forward-looking perspective that considers what is, not what was.

Mark believes that the unique way that Olivia copes is a potential resource for directing the future. In withdrawing from social situations, Olivia shifts her attention away from others toward solitary activities. Olivia is gifted with incredible memory skills, especially remembering dates. Fascinated with holidays and celebrations, she can easily recite dates for every U.S., Mexican, and Canadian holiday and religious observance. Her interest also extends to significant dates in the lives of persons with whom she is acquainted. Olivia recalls birthdays and wedding anniversaries of everyone in her extended family. She reminds Mark on a weekly basis of the upcoming birthdays of clients and staff associated with the work activity program. Mark recognizes this significant strength in Olivia.

One of Olivia's goals is to develop her social support network. As a first step, Mark and Olivia plan a way to increase Olivia's contacts with friends at the center by building on Olivia's unique capacity for remembering dates. The work activity program has a policy of granting paid leave for both clients and staff on their birthdays. Olivia's new job will be to acknowledge each individual's birthday by personally delivering the agency's birthday greeting and the letter granting paid leave. One can easily imagine the positive exchange that accompanies this interaction. As Olivia uses her talents productively, she becomes more confident in interpersonal relationships and develops friendships through her contacts with co-workers.

In viewing client systems as resourceful, social work practitioners demonstrate their respect for what clients have to offer. Mark Nogales discovers and activates the strengths present in his clients' current situations and in their previous adaptations to life events. Mark and his clients draw on these strengths as well as the resources available in the community network to achieve their goals.

This orientation toward client strengths and environmental resources is an essential backdrop for implementing practice processes that empower change.

EMPOWERMENT

Social work pioneers in the settlement-house movement planted the seeds of empowerment. However, the problem-focused, medical genre of social case-work practice overshadowed empowerment as a practice process in the decades

---

Box 4.1 The Ethic of Power

Power is a dynamic inherent in all social interaction. Sharing power in relationships is generative; it unleashes the strengths and resources of participants and builds on and creates new energy and information through synergistic interaction. In contrast, power imbalances deplete individual and relationship resources. In situations of oppression and domination, more powerful groups in society control access to power and opportunities, suppress beliefs of less powerful people about their capacity, and deny those oppressed their rights to exercise power, thereby wasting essential human potential to contribute to community. Social control is a central issue in social work practice today. In fact, Sophie Freud (1999) contends that many clinicians are lured into thinking that social control is "good practice" for the "good of the client." Empowerment practice recovers this potential, emphasizing the critical use of power to achieve social rights and social justice, promote human well-being, and create a humane society.

Empowerment social work practice provides perspectives, frameworks, and methods to assist people who are disenfranchised to access and exercise power as well as a context for people who are oppressed to re-experience their worth and potential as a prelude to taking social and political actions. Social workers recognize two dimensions of power—potential and actual. Power as potential is the capacity of one's ability to effect or produce change. Power as actually exercised involves attempting, doing, or saying something to produce change (Webb, 2000). Social workers also acknowledge the multilevel nature of power and empowerment, "a confluence of the individual, the interpersonal, and the sociopolitical, in which the experience of power in each sphere continually replenishes the others" (O'Melia, 2002).

The exercise of power requires attention to the environment, because power can be sustained or diminished depending on interactions within the interpersonal, social, and cultural contexts. For example, feelings of personal adequacy and influence are short term if not reinforced by experiences within larger contexts. To guide practitioners in working with clients to activate their personal, interpersonal, and political power, DuBois and Miley (2008) propose the following tenets for empowerment social work practice:

1. Empower people, individually and collectively, to utilize their own problem-solving and coping capabilities more effectively.
2. Support a proactive position in regard to social and economic policy development to prevent problems for individuals and society from occurring.
3. Uphold the integrity of the profession in all aspects of social work practice.
4. Establish linkages between people and societal resources to further social functioning and enhance the quality of life.
5. Develop cooperative networks within the institutional resource system.
6. Facilitate the responsiveness of institutional resource systems to meet health and human service needs.
7. Promote social justice and equality of all people in regard to full participation in society.
8. Contribute to the development of knowledge for the social work profession through research and evaluation.
9. Encourage an information exchange in those institutional systems in which both problems and resource opportunities are produced.
10. Enhance communication through an appreciation of diversity and through ethnically sensitive, non-sexist social work practice.
11. Employ educational strategies for the prevention and resolution of problems.
12. Embrace a worldview of human issues and solutions to problems. (pp. 54–56)

after World War I. Today, the integration of empowerment into practice mandates social workers to move beyond diagnosing deficits toward emphasizing strengths and to create solutions that incorporate elements of social action.

Empowerment is a complex concept that has personal and political implications. On a personal level, empowerment refers to a subjective state of mind, feeling competent and experiencing a sense of control; on a *political level*, it refers to the objective reality of opportunities in societal structures and the reallocation of power through a modification of social structures (Swift & Levin, 1987). Empowerment is a process whereby individuals, families, organizations, communities, and societies increase their personal, interpersonal, and/or political power to realize improvements in their situations (Gutiérrez, 1994; Parsons, 2008). Empowerment has personal, interpersonal, and structural dimensions that apply to social systems at all levels (Rappaport, 1987). (See Table 4.1.)

Personal Dimensions of Empowerment

Personal empowerment embodies our own sense of competence, mastery, strength, and ability to effect change.

> [Empowerment] suggests a sense of control over one's life in personality, cognition, and motivation. It expresses itself at the level of feelings, at the level of ideas about self-worth, at the level of being able to make a difference in the world around us, and even at the level of something more akin to the spiritual. It is a process ability that we all have, but

Table 4.1	**Dimensions of Empowerment**
As a Concept	As a Process
Personal	Actualizing
Competence	Becoming
Mastery	Collaborating
Feelings of Control	Respecting
Esteem	Consciousness-Raising
Goodness of Fit	Discovering
Interpersonal	Acknowledging
Interdependence	Enhancing
Sense of Influence	Strengthening
Partnership	Developing
Social Support	Activating
Respected Status	Connecting
Sociopolitical	Creating
Privilege	Constructing
Citizens' Rights	Expanding
Control of Resources	Integrating
Access to Opportunities	
Social Justice	

which needs to be released, similar to the way our bodies can be self-healing when endorphins are released. We all have it as a potential. It does not need to be purchased, nor is it a scarce commodity. (Rappaport, 1985, p. 17)

Essentially, people who experience personal power perceive themselves as competent (Gutiérrez, 1991). Competence is the ability of any human system to fulfill its function of taking care of itself, to draw resources from effective interaction with other systems, and to contribute to the resource pool of the social and physical environment.

A transactional view of competence

On the surface, words used to describe human competence, such as efficacy, mastery, and accomplishment, seem like self-appraisals. Without looking beyond individuals, we are left wondering, "Effective in what way?" "Mastery over what?" or "Accomplished in what endeavor?" Rather than being individually derived, feelings of competence arise from the goodness-of-fit between systems and their environments. In contrast, a sense of helplessness, ineffectiveness, or inadequacy results from the lack of fit between systems and their social and physical environments. It is not the system alone, but, rather, the system in the context of the environment that defines the competence.

From a transactional view, personal empowerment and competence result from the interplay between a system's assets and needs and the environment's resources and demands. A sense of power results from a good fit between a system and its environment, a fit that offers support, security, protection, and resources (Hopps, et al., 1995). A transactional view of human competence highlights the interdependence of individual, interpersonal, and environmental factors in competent system functioning.

Personal competence in a political context

A transactional understanding of competence prompts social workers to design and implement empowerment-oriented strategies that deal with both internal and contextual barriers (Breton, 1993). However, competence is a necessary but not sufficient condition for empowerment: "When personal competence is isolated from the interpersonal, social and structural contexts in which it manifests, and when individual rights are not coupled with responsibilities towards others' rights, the outcome can be nefarious as often as it can be benign" (p. 31). Personal competence coupled with personal responsibility is not enough. Empowerment requires access to societal resources.

Human Rights & Justice

Feelings of competence derive from a goodness-of-fit between individuals and their social environment. What role does protecting human rights and promoting social and economic justice play in achieving this goodness-of-fit?

Interpersonal Dimensions of Empowerment

Although we may experience empowerment as a feeling within, it emerges from our interactions with others. *Interpersonal empowerment* refers to our ability to influence others (Gutiérrez & Ortega, 1991). Our successful interaction with others and the regard others hold for us contribute to our sense of interpersonal empowerment.

The social power of positions, roles, communication skills, knowledge, and appearance contribute to a person's feelings of interpersonal empowerment (Gutiérrez, 1991). Therefore, interpersonal power comes from two sources. The first source is power based on social status—for example, power based on race, gender, and class. The second is power achieved through learning new skills and securing new positions, key features of empowerment. Both reshaping the

Participating in recreational activities is a source of personal and interpersonal empowerment for children with disabilities.

societal ascription of power and enhancing personal skills expand our experience of interpersonal power.

Sociopolitical Dimensions of Empowerment

Empowerment is easy to define in its absence; powerlessness, real or imagined; learned helplessness; alienation; loss of a sense of control over one's life. It is more difficult to define postitively only because it takes on a different form in different people and context.

—Julian Rappaport

Empowerment also has *structural dimensions*, meaning that it involves our relationships with social and political structures. When, as a result of their interactions with their environment, people increase their access to and control of resources, they experience empowerment (Leonardsen, 2007; Rappaport, et al., 1992). Having access to resources and opportunities develops individual strengths and accentuates interpersonal competence.

All human systems require an ongoing, expansive set of resource options to keep pace with constantly changing conditions. The more options available, the more likely systems can master their challenges. The fewer the options, the greater the vulnerability of systems. In regard to communities, "the better the resources that have been developed, the more successful the community will be in developing effective responses to problems it encounters; e.g., crime, unemployment, housing problems" (Solomon, 1976, pp. 19–20). Competent social systems contribute to the effective functioning of their members and likewise function as opportunity structures for other systems in their environments.

Blocks to sociopolitical power

Power blocks at three levels deny access to opportunities and thereby undermine competent functioning (Solomon, 1976, 1987). First, power blocks deny "access to resources needed to develop some critical personal resource" (1987, p. 81); inadequate health care is a barrier to good health. A second power block barricades sources for learning technical and interpersonal skills; people fail to qualify for jobs or promotions as a consequence of inadequate educational opportunities. The third power block denies a valued social role; "discriminatory employment practices may prevent a father from obtaining a job adequate to support the family" (p. 81). In groups and communities, these blocks can produce powerlessness, resulting in "the inability to use resources to achieve collective goals" (1976, p. 19). Powerlessness usurps a system's energy and blocks access to a sufficient mix of personal, interpersonal, and contextual strengths, resources, and support to achieve empowerment.

To expect individuals to seek a higher "empowered state" without considering whether they have a minimal level of resources needed even to exercise choice mocks empowerment (Clark, 1989). However, even having access to resources is insufficient for empowerment, as people also need opportunities to contribute to their communities as respected citizens to experience empowerment fully (Breton, 1993). The goal of empowerment should include "the creation of structural conditions under which people can choose to 'give to' their community as well as 'take from' their community" (p. 29).

People are more likely to overcome barriers to power by making structural changes in political and social institutions than by changing themselves (Solomon, 1976). Achieving structural changes creates new opportunities to redistribute resources equitably and to give and take within a competent society.

Power

Having power means having access to information, choosing actions from many possibilities, and acting on one's choices. Power is the ability to obtain the resources one needs to influence others and to effect changes in how resources are distributed in such systems as families, organizations, or communities (Gutiérrez, 1991). The personal, interpersonal, and sociopolitical dimensions of power intertwine. The experience of power within one realm contributes resources for accessing power in another.

Powerlessness

Like power, powerlessness is multidimensional. Personal, social, and political factors all "play into the cyclical nature of powerlessness which keeps certain individuals and groups oppressed, impairing individual functioning and the functioning of family and community systems" (Dodd & Gutiérrez, 1990, p. 65). Blocks to power at one level can impede access to power at another.

Powerlessness combines "an attitude of self-blame, a sense of generalized distrust, a feeling of alienation from resources for social influence, an experience of disenfranchisement and economic vulnerability, and a sense of hopelessness in sociopolitical struggle" (Kieffer, 1984, p. 16). However, hope exists. Someone who feels powerless is not empty of resources, as "competencies are already present or at least possible, given niches and opportunities . . . [and] that what you see as poor functioning is a result of social structure and lack of resources which make it impossible for the existing competencies to operate" (Rappaport, 1981, p. 16).

Oppression

Powerlessness and oppression go hand-in-hand. Oppression involves economic, social, and psychological power over and exploitation of others—individuals, groups, social classes, religious groups, and nation-states (Gil, 2002; Hodge, 2007). Oppression is the injustice that results from the domination and control of resources and opportunities that entitles favored groups and disenfranchises others (DuBois & Miley, 2008).

Oppression results in injustice or "the consequences of domination and exploitation: multidimensional inequalities and development-inhibiting, discriminatory, and dehumanizing conditions of living" (Gil, 2002, p. 36). Such conditions include poverty, unemployment, inequitable access to housing, health care, education, and other exploitations and discriminatory actions. By imposing categorical judgments, dominant groups in society classify other groups as less worthy, affording them little prestige, few possibilities, and limited resources. Racism, classism, ableism, heterosexism, regionalism, sexism, ethnocentrism, and ageism are all interrelated expressions of oppression, exploitation, and injustice (Table 4.2).

Victim blaming

Victim blaming compounds the insidious experience of oppression. According to Ryan (1976) in his book, *Blaming the Victim,* victim blaming occurs in two different ways. One way labels victims as inferior, genetically defective, or unfit. The other casts blame for inferiority on environmental circumstances. Victim blaming is "a brilliant ideology for justifying a perverse form of social action designed to change, not society, as one might expect, but rather society's victim" (p. 78). Specifically, Ryan says:

> All of this happens so smoothly that it seems downright rational. First, identify a social problem. Second, study those affected by the problem, and discover in what ways they are different from the rest of us as a consequence of deprivation and injustice. Third, define the differences as the cause of the social problem itself. Finally, of course, assign a government bureaucrat to invent a humanitarian action program to correct the differences. (pp. 8–9)

Although "do-good" helpers recognize the impact of social problems, they probe those who "have the problem," designate them different from others, and label them "incapable," "unskilled," "ignorant," and "subhuman." People who subscribe to this view believe that changing "those people" is requisite to solving social problems (Ryan, 1976). They unjustly blame those who experience the effects of social problems, rather than recognizing that these difficulties

Table 4.2	**Prejudicial Attitudes Contributing to Oppression**
Racism	Ideology often based on negative stereotyping that perpetuates individual and institutional discrimination against members of racial groups
Sexism	Based on sex role stereotyping and cultural beliefs that one sex is superior to the other
Classism	Elitist attitudes about persons based on their socioeconomic status or class
Heterosexism	Prejudice and discrimination directed against persons who are homosexual
Ableism	Prejudicial attitudes and behaviors that result in unequal regard for persons because of their physical or mental disability
Ageism	Negative stereotyping of persons based on their age
Regionalism	Generalizations about the character of individuals or population groups based on the geographic region of their origin or residence
Ethnocentrism	Condescending belief that one's own ethnic group, culture, or nation is superior to others

result from oppression, discrimination, and injustice. These are sociopolitical issues that require sociopolitical solutions.

Persons who experience blame, shame, and stigma often assimilate this negativity into their self-images (Patten, et al., 1989). Self-blame may lead people to feel incompetent, dependent, and rejected (Janis & Rodin, 1980). Ironically, people who feel victimized may identify with the oppressors, conclude that these charges are accurate, and apply the derogatory labels to themselves. In general, feelings of powerlessness increase, often resulting in low self-esteem, alienation, and despair.

Social work clients and oppression

Social work clients often find themselves trapped by powerlessness and oppression. In today's world, social workers likely deal with clients who are "profoundly vulnerable and disempowered . . . overwhelmed by oppressive lives, circumstances and events they are powerless to control" (Gitterman & Shulman, 2005, p. xi). Simon (1994) links powerlessness and oppression to empowerment-based social work practice:

> Client empowerment presupposes an existing condition of client disempowerment and marginality. Fitting subjects, therefore, of empowerment social work are socially despised persons, families, and groups. They may be poor in a county that values economic success, black in a culture that privileges white skin, chronically ill in a nation that equates health with productivity and productivity with merit, or old in a land that cherishes the vigor of youth and shuns symbolic and material reminders of human mortality. (pp. 24–25)

Oppression, discrimination, injustice, and experiences of powerlessness are the very circumstances that call for the application of empowerment-based social work practice (DuBois & Miley, 2008; Gutiérrez, 1994; Lee, 2001; Solomon, 1976). Therefore, social workers confront the multiple dimensions of oppression present in society that discriminate by race, ethnicity, socioeconomic status, level of ability, gender, sexual orientation, age, health status, or any other status that is held in low regard by those who have privilege and power.

Empowerment as a Concept and a Process

To address these issues of oppression, injustice, and powerlessness, strengths-oriented social work practice incorporates empowerment as both a concept and a process. As a *concept,* empowerment constructs a framework for understanding the personal, interpersonal, and sociopolitical dimensions of any given situation. Empowerment offers a perspective to assess the interconnections between personal circumstance and political realities.

As a *process,* empowerment describes how practitioners actually approach their work. The process of empowerment represents the ways by which systems—individuals, families, groups, organizations, and communities—gain control over their situations. In other words, empowerment is a process by which people procure personal, interpersonal, and sociopolitical resources to achieve their goals.

The process of acquiring power does not necessitate a struggle or relinquishment of power by one group in favor of another. Empowerment is a geometrically expansive rather than a zero-sum commodity. Empowering—the process of empowerment—means recognizing, facilitating, and promoting a system's capacity for competent functioning. Empowering also implies taking actions that respond to the linkages among the personal, interpersonal, and sociopolitical dimensions of empowerment.

EMPOWERMENT-BASED PRACTICE

Working toward the goal of empowerment significantly affects the way social workers practice. First, workers apply an ecosystems perspective and a strengths orientation in practice. This means that workers consider client situations in context, search for client strengths and environmental resources, and describe needs in terms of transitory challenges rather than fixed problems. Second, as generalists, social workers draw on skills for resolving issues at many social system levels and respond to the interconnections between personal troubles and public issues. Instead of dwelling on vulnerabilities, empowerment-based practice accentuates resiliencies. An empowering approach liberates client systems from the encumbrances of eliminating problems to the promises of generating solutions. Empowerment-based practitioners join with clients as partners and rely on clients' expertise and participation in change processes. They discern the interconnections between client empowerment and social change. These changes are not trivial! They redirect every phase of the practice process.

The Paradox of an Empowering Process

Social workers empower clients toward feelings of competence and control of resources. Take note, however, as the idea of empowering others is a fundamental paradox (Gruber & Trickett, 1987). Social workers cannot bestow empowerment on other systems from star-tipped wands. Empowerment is not something one person can give to another (Simon, 1990). Only those seeking power can initiate and sustain the process. "Others can only aid and abet in this empowerment process. They do so by providing a climate, a relationship, resources, and procedural means through which people can enhance their own lives" (p. 32).

Even if one could bestow power, bestowing power, in itself, would be disempowering! Empowerment-based social workers actively involve client-partners in collaborative processes to release the resources of change. Empowerment, by definition, requires the full participation of clients. Rather than given away, empowerment draws on both internal and external resources; it generates from within systems and their environments.

Collaboration and Partnership

An orientation toward strengths and empowerment compels social workers to redefine their relationships to embrace the notion of collaboration and partnership (Greene, et al., 2005). Without this redefinition, overzealous social workers assume responsibility for solutions and often ascribe responsibility for failures to clients.

The role of the expert supported by a socialization process of revering authority figures and teaching that the expert is in charge has the unintended side effect of ascribing to the professional an unrealistic amount

Box 4.2 Empowerment: A Practice–Research Connection

Empowerment as a concept unites social workers in a shared vision of human competence in a just and resourceful world. Empowerment as a method is less universally understood or consistently practiced. Research shows the variability of an empowerment method as implemented in practice and answers critical questions about empowerment.

What are the similarities and differences in the ways workers implement an empowerment approach? In Ackerson and Harrison's (2000) qualitative study of eight seasoned social workers, respondents all described empowerment as microlevel intervention, including self-determination, choice, and the ability to act on choices; only half referred to macrolevel dimensions of empowerment in social, institutional, and political systems. These results support earlier evidence by Gutiérrez and colleagues (1995a) that practitioners were more likely to apply empowerment-based concepts in microfocused ways. This limited focus on individual or psychological empowerment stands in contrast to the theoretical literature that defines empowerment as multidimensional with a full complement of social, political, and economic components (Breton, 1994; Rappaport, 1987). Theoretically, empowerment reaches beyond individual clients to include sociopolitical dimensions (Cohen, 1998; Rapp, 1998) and the organizational context of practice (Gutiérrez, et al, 1995b). Empowerment in practice may fall short of this multidimensional ideal.

In what settings does an empowerment approach work best? Research findings in child welfare and mental health demonstrate the positive impact of empowerment methods. Meta-analytic research included a review of 56 studies of child welfare services to determine elements of program effectiveness with respect to family wellness and the prevention of child abuse (Macleod & Nelson, 2000). Those home visitation and intensive family preservation programs that achieved high levels of involvement by participants, incorporated empowerment strategies, and emphasized social support measures showed the best outcomes. A small-scale qualitative study analyzed the meaning of social support to participants in consumer-run mental health agencies (Hardiman, 2004). Analysis of the narrative themes uncovered personal agency, organizational empowerment, a shared sense of ownership, and a deeply felt sense of community in peer networks of caring as significant benefits to participants.

What do clients tell us about empowerment? A qualitative study of psychiatric consumers found that empowering processes at multiple levels facilitated recovery (Nelson, et al., 2001). Conditions identified as empowering included personal motivation; supportive relationships with mental health workers, in natural support networks, and self-help groups; responsive mental health agencies and receptive communities; advocacy for social change; and social policies that provide adequate mental health resources.

What benefits are there in a group approach to empowerment practice? Parsons (2001) gathered data through focus groups and intensive interviews with women involved in two social work groups, one focusing on domestic violence and the other on poverty. Despite differences in goals, members in both groups experienced similar benefits from group membership working to "foster interdependence, interaction, and behaviors that facilitate changes, such as learning about the problem, acquiring new skills, having the courage to take risks, taking small steps, resolving conflict, and engaging in collective action" (p. 175). These studies confirm that personal well-being and social action intertwine. As these examples show, social workers advance the knowledge base of social work when they connect practice and research.

of responsibility for the solution of the client's problems. . . . Then, when they do not succeed, they tend to rationalize in terms of the mysteries of scientific expertise and/or to blame the clients and call for more thorough compliance with their decisions. (Lenrow & Burch, 1981, p. 243)

Empowerment liberates social workers from an elevated status, emphasizes collaborative partnerships, and delineates mutual responsibilities.

For clients, collaboration is a resource for power. Rollo May (1972) in his book, *Power and Innocence*, identifies nutrient power or "power for the other" and integrative power or "power with the other" as positive manifestations of power. "Both of these positive expressions of power suggest collaboration in a

Engage Assess Intervene Evaluate

Establishing a collaborative relationship between the social worker and client is the hallmark of the empowerment process. In what ways does engaging clients as partners in the intervention process enhance their sense of power in the professional relationship?

common enterprise in which cooperation becomes a form of power" (Weick, 1980, p. 183). In other words, social workers who share power with clients, free clients to access their own power; the cooperation within the professional relationship itself becomes a new source of power. Collaboration is the hallmark of empowerment (Figure 4.2).

Clients or consumers?

The terms social workers use to describe their clients shape the expectations for their roles and define the nature of professional relationships. Over the years, practitioners have assigned many different labels to persons or groups who use social services, including "supplicants," "patients," and "those receiving help." Each of these labels characterizes clients as "people who need fixing." Furthermore, these labels imply that professionals are experts who have the knowledge, power, and authority necessary to supply, heal, or treat, leaving receivers of services as "have-nots" who passively acquire supplies, healing, or treatment.

Some use the term "consumer" to emphasize a client's active role (Gummer, 1983). Viewed as consumers, social work clients seek information, make choices, and contract for what they need from public or private organizations or corporations through fees, vouchers, or citizens' rights (Tracy & DuBois, 1987). "Consumerism offers a way that, in combination with other strategies for equalizing power and control between givers and receivers of services, can revitalize and relegitimate our social welfare institution" (Gummer, 1983, p. 934). Tower (1994) elaborates, stating

the basic doctrine of consumerism within human services systems is that individuals who have direct experience with a particular life condition

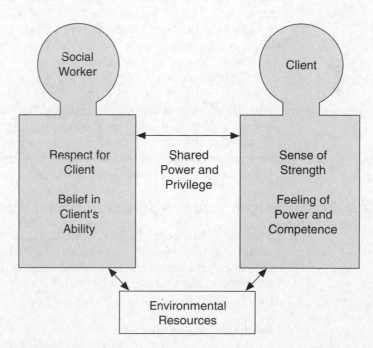

Figure 4.2
Elements of Empowerment in the Social Worker-Client Relationship
An empowering social worker-client relationship has personal, interpersonal, and sociopolitical elements.

(for example, aging, disability, mental illness) are more knowledgeable about their own needs and interests than are their professional counterparts. When individuals redefine their role from that of patient, client, or recipient of goods and services to that of consumer, their sense of control over their own lives is elevated. (p. 192)

Others criticize the term, "consumer," as conveying passive, compliant consumption. On the receiving end, those labeled consumers may believe they need to be on guard as "buyers must beware." Consumer may also imply a consumer market strategy of rationing services rather than an empowerment model of service-user involvement (Adams, 1997). In its most empowering construction, the concept of consumer conveys the idea that a person or other social system seeking services has both rights and responsibilities, yet negative connotations about consumerism restrain widespread use of this term in social work.

The most widely accepted term for those using social services is "client" (Aho El Nasr, 1989). In fact, use of the term "client" predominates social work literature, codes of ethics, and international documents. Numerous other professional groups apply the term client when referring to those who engage their services. Critics contend that client suggests a subservient position to the professional expert, thus lending too much power to the "expert" professional. However, in general use, the term client affords dignity. Consider the example of an international business client or the client of a corporate attorney. Only in relation to social work does "client" seem to take on negative connotations. Perhaps, it's not the word "client" that conjures negative images, but society's view of social work itself that taints any term we choose.

Today, several different terms are in vogue, depending on the context. Some alternatives used in agency practice include neighbors, participants, residents, parents, members, students, and citizens. Writers vary among the use of the term "client," which reflects a professional relationship, "client system," which broadens the concept beyond individuals to include multiperson systems, and "consumers of social services," which emphasizes active participation and rights.

Carefully chosen words embody a sense of reciprocity. Any term chosen should clearly recognize that clients are people first, and our relationships with them should encompass the dignity and respect of collaborative partnerships. In this text, we use the terms "client" along with "client systems" to emphasize the various system levels in generalist social work and "partners" to acknowledge their collaborative participation. We also, without apology, refer to practitioners as social workers!

Characteristics of Empowerment-Centered Social Workers

Several characteristics distinguish empowerment-centered social workers, including their focus on context, affirmation of collaboration, emphasis on strengths and opportunities, integration of practice activities at multiple system levels, incorporation of a politicized approach, and commitment to reflection in practice.

Focusing on context

Empowerment practice is based on a transactional view of human behavior, one that describes people in continuous interaction with the sociocultural, political, and physical environments. Focusing on context influences all facets of work. For example, in assessment, workers and clients identify the contextual elements that contribute to the problems that clients face. To intervene, workers can join with clients to block negative environmental influences, help clients to respond differently to environmental pressures, or directly address environmental challenges, creating benefits for specific clients and the community.

Affirming collaboration

Collaboration is at the heart of empowering relationships, reflecting attitudes of mutual respect and modalities of shared power. In sharp contrast to the expert paradigm in which workers are expected to eliminate or control clients' problems, in the collaborative paradigm, workers and clients function interdependently to address challenges within a client's situation. Moreover, the collaborative quality extends beyond the worker–client relationship to define the structure of how the worker relates to colleagues, agencies, community, and society.

Emphasizing strengths and opportunities

A social work process that focuses on strengths activates resources rather than corrects deficits. The strengths perspective emphasizes the importance of envisioning a future goal and examining the present and the past to gather resources and create opportunities to reach that desired outcome. In dialogue with clients, workers respond in ways to re-center the view to highlight strengths, skills, solutions, and opportunities.

Integrating practice activities at multiple system levels

The systemic concept of wholeness states that a change in any part of the system can influence the situation and will likely reverberate throughout the system to create other changes. This implies that a problem experienced at the individual level may respond to changes in the environment. For maximal impact, workers and clients synthesize simultaneous interventions—in other words, coordinate several forces at multiple levels to achieve a positive change. In sum, the empowerment method demands contextually framed generalist interventions in considering the multiple opportunities for change.

Incorporating a politicized approach

"The personal without the political is not empowerment" is the mantra of empowering social work. A political context constantly shapes the human condition. All human interaction is politicized by the implicit negotiation for power and privilege in meaning-making within relationships. Empowerment-based workers integrate a political perspective into direct practice, mobilizing clients through work in groups to initiate social action that addresses organizational, community, and social policy issues.

Committing to reflective practice

To be reflective means to be perceptive and to exercise good judgment. Applied to social work practice, reflection involves a continuous process of thinking, doing, and reflecting—a process that incorporates feedback to garner insight and refine actions. Reflective practice is not only effective practice, but it is also ethical practice.

Empowerment-Oriented Strategies

Empowerment-oriented social workers assume that a client's issues reflect a lack of congruence between the system's capacities and environmental demands. They acknowledge the imbalance between the pool of personal, interpersonal, and societal resources and the system's need for these resources to meet the challenge. They select multilevel strategies that heighten the availability of personal, interpersonal, and sociopolitical resources. In the tradition of empowerment-based practice, this means selecting strategies that increase self-efficacy, develop skills, discern connections between personal difficulties and public issues, enhance collectivity, and take actions to create sociopolitical changes.

Integrating clinical and political practice

The purpose of empowerment social work is to promote a just society in which all members share the same rights to participation in society, protection by the law, opportunities for development, and access to social benefits, and who, in turn, contribute to the resource pool of society. From an empowerment perspective, the mandate of the social work profession is to ensure the fulfillment of the social justice contract between individuals and society, particularly for those groups that are disenfranchised. The assessment of clients' "needs" not only should be driven by the availability of resources, but also should be concerned with the reduction of inequality and promotion of social justice. Empowering social workers are both clinical and political in their efforts to create social conditions favorable to the well-being of people and society (DuBois & Miley, 2004; Miley & DuBois, 2004, 2005, 2007a, 2007b) (see Table 4.3).

Using group modalities

Many practitioners conclude that working with clients in groups maximizes empowerment and promotes social justice (Breton, 1994, 1999, 2004; Gutiérrez, 1995; Home, 1999; Lee, 2001; Malekoff, 2008; McNicoll, 2008). Work in small groups "is the perfect environment for raising consciousness, engaging in

---

Table 4.3 Empowerment Social Work: Clinical and Political

Empowerment-oriented social workers are both clinical and political in their efforts to strengthen human functioning and relationships and to create conditions favorable to the well being of people and society.

	Clinical Social Work	Political Social Work
Purpose	To ensure social participation	To protect social rights
Focus	The needs of the client	The rights of the client
Goal	Personal and interpersonal effectiveness	Socioeconomic-political justice
Strategies	Microlevel, direct practice, individual and family change	Macrolevel, indirect practice, social policy change, social and economic justice
Interventions	Counseling, casework, group work, case management	Advocacy, legislative initiatives, economic development, policy practice
Theme	Contributive Justice: What a person owes to society • Contribute to the resource pool of society • Fully participate in society	Distributive Justice: What a society owes its citizens • Provide resources and opportunities • Right to basic resources for living

mutual aid, developing skills, problem solving, and experiencing one's own effectiveness in influencing others" (Dodd & Gutiérrez, 1990, p. 71).

Hearing others tell stories similar to one's own has a dramatic effect, particularly for those who have experienced oppression. In addition to the support and mutual aid offered through group work, "the collective view of experiences tends to reduce self-blame, increase the tendency to look for causes other than personal failure, and bring about a sense of shared fate and consciousness raising" (Cox & Parsons, 1993, p. 37).

Developing a critical consciousness

Critical Thinking

Developing a critical consciousness about the interconnections of the personal and political is another essential component of empowerment-oriented practice (Keenan, 2004; Hernandez, et al., 2005; Lee, 2001; Sewpaul, 2008). Breton (2002) explains the interconnection: "For it is correct to postulate that empowerment necessarily involves both conscientization (change at the personal level) and social action (change at the collective level), then the term psychological empowerment would seem to quality as a consummate oxymoron (so would the term political empowerment, for that matter)" (p. 26). Furthermore, Breton argues that conscientization "requires that the inseparability of private troubles and public issues be addressed—and that is done more effectively in groups" (p. 27). Through their work with groups, social workers implement consciousness-raising strategies, contextualize experiences, reduce self-blame, and provide opportunities for group members to evaluate and assume responsibility for the consequences of their choices (Simon, 1990). Furthermore, when this dialogue occurs in the context of a group, group members form a solidarity that can mobilize energy and lead to collective actions (see Figure 4.3.).

Empowerment social work is both clinical and political. In what ways do these dual activities contribute to fulfilling the social justice contract between individuals and societies?

Engaging in praxis

Praxis involves cyclical processes of reflection, action, and reflection. Social workers and clients take actions and then pause to observe and reflect to guide the next step. As the work unfolds, reflection and action intertwine in praxis. According to Carr (2003), "empowerment is an inherently interpersonal process in which individuals collectively define and activate strategies to gain access to knowledge and power" (p. 18). Praxis, with its alternating phases of collective dialogue and action, is a fundamental element of empowerment.

Taking action

Social action is the key to sociopolitical empowerment and a legacy of the social work profession (Aubrey, 2004; Breton, 2006, Cox, 1991; Franco, et al., 2007; Jacobson & Rugeley, 2008). Collective action strives to reallocate sociopolitical power so that disenfranchised citizens can access the opportunities and resources of society and, in turn, find meaningful ways to contribute to society as valued citizens.

Social action is not exclusively the domain of the macropractitioner. Generalist practitioners working primarily with microlevel clients also make efforts to improve conditions in communities, bureaucracies, and society. For example, they may act as advocates to speak out with clients at the institutional and political level to influence changes in social policies. In these ways, practitioners work in collaboration with clients to create social and political change.

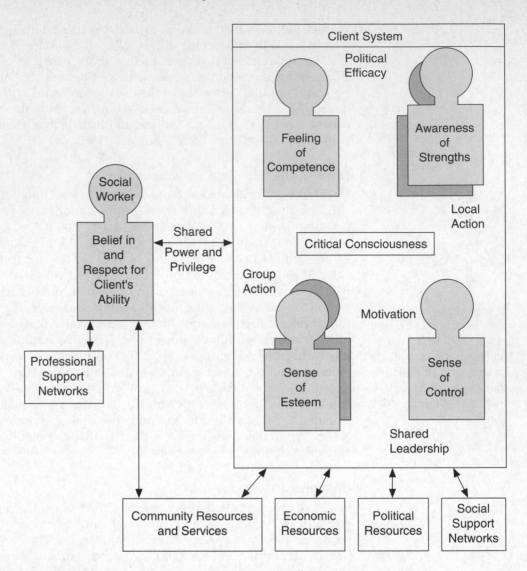

Figure 4.3
Developing a Critical Consciousness
Alliances among individuals create opportunities for developing social bonds, enhancing personal competence and political efficacy, and achieving a critical consciousness as requisites to collective social action.

LOOKING FORWARD

Understanding diversity involves a process of critical questioning about issues of powerlessness, oppression, and discrimination. This approach goes beyond merely examining the demographic differences of diverse population groups to exploring the commonality of the experience of victimization and exploitation. Only in this way can social work practitioners step outside of their own perspectives into clients' worldviews.

When social workers view clients through the perspective of strengths and competence, they discover and appreciate the uniqueness and diversity inherent in all human systems. They affirm that client systems already have potential—knowledge, experiences, and resources—from which to draw. When social workers magnify client strengths, they heighten motivation and involvement as collaborative partners. When clients get in touch with their own strengths, they discover solutions in the personal, interpersonal, and sociopolitical dimensions of their situations.

As described in this chapter, an orientation to strengths and empowerment is essential to implement an empowering approach to generalist practice. Chapter 5 describes how social workers transform these perspectives on practice into a coherent approach that empowers clients at all system levels.

Succeed with PEARSON **mysocialworklab**

Log onto **www.mysocialworklab.com** and select the **Interactive Skill Module** videos from the left-hand menu. Answer the questions below. (*If you did not receive an access code to* **MySocialWorkLab** *with this text and wish to purchase access online, please visit* www.mysocialworklab.com.)

1. Empowering social workers engage clients as partners, discover their strengths, and seek their feedback. **Compare pages 6, 7, and 9 of the group work module** to pages 4, 6, 7, and 9 of the child welfare module. Which is more empowering? Offer examples to support your conclusion.

2. Empowerment-based group workers raise consciousness among members to link individual problems to social issues. **Read about group purpose in the group work module (page 3).** How would you connect a teenage girl's self esteem to larger social issues?

PRACTICE TEST

Human Behavior

1. _____ is the ability of any human system to fulfill its function of taking care of its members, to interact effectively with other systems, and to contribute to the resources in the environment.
   a. A social system
   b. Personal empowerment
   c. Competence
   d. Structural empowerment

2. Practitioners applying a strengths orientation do all of the following EXCEPT _____.
   a. work in partnerships
   b. highlight strengths
   c. focus on dysfunction
   d. believe clients' perspectives

3. Which of the following is most accurate?
   a. Negative frames of reference mask the unique capabilities of client systems.
   b. Social workers who focus on strengths ignore clients' difficulties.
   c. Social workers and clients can alter past events.
   d. Power is not necessarily a dimension of all social interactions.

4. The medical model is LEAST likely to _____.
   a. focus on strengths
   b. establish a theoretical base for practice
   c. suggest basing treatment on a diagnosis
   d. develop a technical base for practice

5. Maria believes that all people have strengths. By this, she means that _____.
   a. people have the capacity for growth
   b. people are strong-willed
   c. people can change if they only try
   d. weak people can rely on strong social workers for help

6. A sense of mastery, strength, and the ability to effect change are MOST likely related to _____ empowerment.
   a. personal
   b. interpersonal
   c. structural
   d. environmental

7. Chanda's ability to influence others represents _____ empowerment.
   a. personal
   b. interpersonal
   c. structural
   d. institutional

Engage Assess Intervene Evaluate

8. Of the following, which is LEAST likely an empowerment-oriented strategy?
   a. using group modalities
   b. taking action
   c. developing a critical consciousness
   d. emphasizing clinical as separate from political

Critical Thinking

9. The cyclical process of reflection, action, and reflection is _____.
   a. praxis
   b. critical consciousness
   c. social action
   d. political practice

10. Empowerment as a process involves _____.
   a. understanding oppression.
   b. recognizing personal, interpersonal, and sociopolitical dimensions of situations
   c. implementing the methods of social work
   d. considering the interconnections between personal circumstance and political realities

Log onto **MySocialWorkLab** once you have completed the Practice Test above to take your Chapter Exam and demonstrate your knowledge of this material.

Answers

1) c 2) c 3) a 4) c 5) a 6) a 7) b 8) d 9) a 10) c

5

An Empowering Approach to Generalist Practice

CHAPTER OUTLINE

CONNECTING CORE COMPETENCIES *in this chapter*

| Professional Identity | Ethical Practice | Critical Thinking | Diversity in Practice | **Human Rights & Justice** | Research Based Practice | Human Behavior | **Policy Practice** | Practice Contexts | **Engage Assess Intervene Evaluate** |

An empowerment orientation shapes the processes that structure social work practice. Empowering processes move clients to center stage—positioning them as the authors of their stories as well as the directors and producers of the action. This leaves workers in the roles of accentuating clients' "unique coping and adaptive patterns, mobilizing their actual or potential strengths, emphasizing the role of natural helping networks, and using environmental resources" (Maluccio & Libassi, 1984, p. 52). Changes accomplished by clients through such processes are likely to endure, because they are "funded by the coin of their capabilities, knowledge, and skills" (Saleebey, 1992, p. 6).

The method of generalist practice described here empowers clients. Consistently, it demonstrates confidence in the abilities of client systems, builds solutions on their capabilities, and acknowledges the essential role of social and political change in empowerment. This approach also recognizes the incredible diversity of strengths that various client systems possess. This shift prompts social workers to view clients as resources, "as human beings with assets and potentialities that can be mobilized on their own behalf, and also to help clients to see themselves as resources" (Maluccio, 1981, p. 15).

This chapter presents an overview of the empowerment method of generalist social work practice. Specifically, it

- Summarizes the perspectives that support a generalist, empowering approach
- Describes phases of dialogue, discovery, and development that guide the activities of social work practice
- Details processes and skills for each phase of the empowerment method
- Offers examples that apply the generalist model to practice with clients at the micro-, mezzo-, and macrolevels
- Features a full-length integrative case example for multilevel generalist social work practice

When generalist practitioners use an empowerment approach, clients rediscover their own strengths and gain access to resources within their environment.

ELEMENTS OF AN EMPOWERING GENERALIST APPROACH

The empowerment method of generalist social work draws on the practice perspectives presented thus far. This approach applies the ecosystemic perspective and reflects social work values. It actualizes the strengths orientation through its assumptions of client expertise and consistent emphasis on collaborative roles for both clients and practitioners. Ultimately, it works to achieve empowerment for clients at the personal, interpersonal, and political levels of human experiences.

Infusing an Ecosystems Perspective

The ecosystems perspective examines the interplay of human systems with their environments both to understand what is happening and to develop strategies for initiating change. Consistent with the ecosystems perspective, the empowerment method guides social workers and clients to view challenges and strengths in context, to identify the many possible paths to solutions, and to recognize that change in any given system reverberates through other system levels. Each phase of this approach accommodates the transactional nature of social work by considering the interaction of client systems in context. Informed by an ecosystemic perspective, workers are able to locate resources for change present in the entire ecosystem in which their relationships with clients exist.

Reflecting a Social Justice Commitment

All social work practice is political. Social workers participate in defining whether a society is just. If social workers impose dominant cultural views about human behavior, function to control deviance as defined by majority values, and offer expert solutions to client problems, they reinforce and perpetuate oppression. In contrast, if social workers align with client worldviews, define problems transactionally, and seek solutions in social and political change, they nudge society in the direction of social justice. Processes within this empowerment-oriented approach consistently reveal the requisite client-centeredness and focus on environmental conditions necessary to meet social work's commitment to social and economic justice.

Applying a Strengths Orientation

As a lens for viewing clients, the strengths perspective shifts the view of clients from one of pathology toward one of potential. The fundamental question switches from "what is wrong" to "what is available" within clients and their environments to achieve desired changes. Strength-oriented social work processes describe methods for clients to discover what might be useful in the present for constructing a more positive future. Cultivating client strengths and resources throughout all phases of the practice process is essential for implementing an empowerment-based approach to social work practice. However, simply adopting a strengths perspective is insufficient in many situations. Activating client strengths becomes most effective in a socially and economically just environment in which opportunities are accessible to all.

Collaborating with Clients

An orientation toward strengths redefines the social worker–client relationship. Recognizing client expertise, social workers partner with clients. Workers and clients collaborate to create a vision of what they hope to accomplish, and then concentrate their efforts to search for resources to reach that goal. Collaboration entrusts clients with rights and responsibilities, encouraging clients to discover their own solutions and to remain in charge of their own changes. "Clients, by contrast, who empower themselves in collaborative 'alliance' with social workers, to use Bertha Reynolds' conception, have retained crucial control of the purpose, pace, and direction of the work" (Simon, 1990, pp. 32–33). In an empowerment-focused approach, clients feel their own sense of power in the social work process and carry these feelings of competence and control beyond the boundaries of their relationships with social workers.

Box 5.1 The Ethic of Praxis

Praxis involves a continuous process of action–reflection–action, "the meeting place of theory and practice, the juncture at which words and actions meet and discourse and experience merge" (Stacey, 2001, p. 209). Drawing on the work of Paulo Freire (1973a, 1973b, 1990), social workers configure praxis as integral to developing a critical consciousness about oppression and its impact (reflection) and to implementing solutions for achieving social justice (action).

Applied in practice, a praxis process ensures that clients can describe their experiences with oppressive conditions through dialogue with others. Through this reflective discourse about their experiences, clients discover possible actions to take at the personal, interpersonal, and political levels. In this way, praxis "is used to consolidate and deepen the work of developing critical understanding and a vision for social change" (Lee, 2001, p. 89). Then, in the development phase, clients and social workers initiate actions to achieve the vision and reflect on the processes and outcomes of the change effort. These phases involving dialogue, discovery, and development frame the processes of an empowerment-based approach.

Praxis is not a linear process with a defined end point, but rather, it is a continuous looping of action–reflection–action. Social workers and clients take actions, then pause to observe and reflect to guide the next step. As the work unfolds, reflection and action intertwine in praxis: "As clients are actively involved in change, they are also reflecting upon and analyzing their experiences. The results of this analysis is then integrated into the development of future efforts" (Dodd & Gutiérrez, 1990, p. 70).

Decisions made in the collaboration of workers and clients are not simple choices between what is right and what is wrong. Political realities, ethical contradictions, and systemic interaction complicate the simplest choices, leaving workers and clients to ponder the meaning and impact of what they are doing. Actions taken may define clients as powerful or vulnerable, may activate social and political forces opposing equity and change, or may lead to inequity or injustice for others. Ethical and effective social work actions require the reflective stance by workers and clients suggested by a praxis process.

Constructing an Empowering Reality

Human Rights & Justice

Empowerment social work reflects a commitment to social and economic justice. What injustices and oppressive social conditions do social workers address in their quest for a just society?

Consistent with a social constructionist perspective, research demonstrates that a professional's prehelping attitudes and beliefs and the help-giving practices of social service programs influence a client's experience of empowerment (Dunst, 1993). This research also affirms that positive attributions and program orientations make a difference in a social worker's effectiveness. The empowerment method of practice introduced in this chapter consistently describes social work processes in language that frames a future-oriented, solution-saturated, and client-validating reality.

Effective social workers purposefully construct an empowering "practice reality" by orienting themselves toward client strengths, empowerment, and collaboration. They develop productive assumptions about clients and the practice process, including:

Assumptions about Human Systems

- All people deserve acceptance and respect.
- Clients know their situations best.
- All human system behavior makes sense in context.
- All human system behavior is motivated.
- Challenges emerge from transactions between human systems and their physical and social environments rather than reside in clients themselves.
- Strengths are diverse, including personal feelings of worth, cultural pride, successful relationships, and resourceful interdependence within a community.

Assumptions about Change

▶ Change is not only possible, but it is also inevitable.
▶ A small change in one part of the ecosystem may initiate a chain of beneficial changes.
▶ Challenges are likely to have many solutions.
▶ You don't have to solve a problem to find a solution.
▶ Enduring change builds on strengths.
▶ Strengths and the potential for growth characterize all human systems.
▶ Given niches and opportunities, human systems cultivate competencies.
▶ Collaborative relationships stimulate feelings of power and lead to actions.
▶ Cultural differences are resources offering broader perspectives, additional options, and possibilities of synergistic solutions.

When social workers believe that clients have the rights to their own beliefs, that they have made choices and can make new choices, and that they have the potential to achieve their goals, these expectations prepare workers to implement an empowering practice process.

PHASES AND PROCESSES OF EMPOWERING PRACTICE

Each of the various methods of social work practice describes a coherent framework to guide the progress of workers and clients as they strive to achieve desired goals. Likewise, this empowering approach offers an organized and deliberate, yet dynamic and flexible, structure for practice. The empowerment method frames practice as moving through phases of dialogue, discovery, and development and suggests specific activities to accomplish within each of these phases. Table 5.1 describes the processes that comprise the dialogue, discovery, and development phases.

The Dialogue Phase

Engage Assess Intervene Evaluate

The empowerment method of social work comprises activities for practitioners in the phases of dialogue, discovery, and development. What activities do clients contribute in each process of the empowering method listed in Table 5.1?

Successful social work requires conversation, an ongoing dialogue with clients about their situations, goals, and strengths. Through this exchange, practitioners define their relationships with clients as a collaborative partnership to which both will contribute. In this phase, social workers and clients fully discuss the challenging situation and clarify the purpose of their relationship. In the dialogue phase, practitioners and clients collaborate to

▶ Build partnerships based on acceptance, respect, and trust
▶ Define their respective roles
▶ Discuss clients' experiences with challenging situations
▶ Define the purpose of their work together
▶ Activate client motivation for change
▶ Address crisis needs

In the dialogue phase, workers and clients talk with one another to assess what is happening and develop a preliminary vision of the way clients would like things to be. These processes require open and respectful exchanges of information. Specific processes associated with this phase include forming partnerships, articulating situations, and defining directions.

Table 5.1	An Empowering Approach to Generalist Practice	
Phase	Process	Activities
Dialogue	Forming Partnerships	Building empowering social worker–client relationships that acknowledge clients' privileges and respect their uniqueness
	Articulating Situations	Assessing challenging situations by responding to validate clients' experiences, add transactional dimensions, and look toward goals
	Defining Directions	Determining a preliminary purpose for the relationship to activate client motivation and guide the exploration for relevant resources
Discovery	Identifying Strengths	Searching for client strengths in general functioning, coping with challenging situations, cultural identities, and overcoming adversity
	Assessing Resource Capabilities	Exploring resources in clients' transactions with the environment including connections to family, social groups, organizations, and community institutions
	Framing Solutions	Constructing an achievable plan of action that utilizes client and environmental resources and leads toward desired goals
Development	Activating Resources	Implementing the action plan by mobilizing available resources through consultancy, resource management, and education
	Creating Alliances	Forging empowering alliances among clients, within clients' natural support networks, and within the service delivery system
	Expanding Opportunities	Developing new opportunities and resources through program development, community organizing, and social action
	Recognizing Success	Evaluating the success of the change efforts to recognize achievements and inform continuing actions
	Integrating Gains	Wrapping up the change process in ways that resolve the relationship, celebrate success, and stabilize positive changes

Forming partnerships

Forming partnerships describes the process in which workers and client systems define their working relationship to reflect the purposes of social work and standards of ethical codes (Chapter 6). For the process to be empowering, social workers and client systems resolve power and authority dilemmas to structure their relationship in an egalitarian way, maximizing their respective contributions. Social workers and clients become collaborators, working together to understand situations and accomplish change.

Articulating situations

In the process of *articulating situations,* workers and clients develop a mutual understanding of what prompts clients to seek social work assistance (Chapter 7). To do so, social workers actively listen to what clients say and respond to both the information and feelings within these messages. They recognize cultural variations inherent in communication processes and place client perspectives at the center of the process. In work with larger systems, practitioners use group process techniques, surveys, and other tools to maximize the participation of and to ensure input from all members.

Defining directions

In *defining directions,* practitioners and clients orient their work to achieve a specific purpose (Chapter 8). This concrete sense of direction determines which of the client's resources and strengths are useful in constructing solutions. Defining a desired direction motivates clients to participate. While clients are describing their situations and the outcomes they seek, alert social workers screen for issues requiring immediate attention such as trauma, homelessness, family violence, child abuse and neglect, substance abuse, and the threat of suicide to determine the need for immediate action.

The Discovery Phase

During the discovery phase, clients and social workers continue to assess, systematically exploring resources on which to build solutions. These resources may be present within client systems or in the context of their social and physical environments. Working as partners, social workers and clients also organize the information gathered to develop plans for change. Specifically, they

- Explore clients' strengths as resources for change
- Examine resource possibilities in clients' environments
- Collect relevant information from collateral sources
- Assess capabilities of available resource systems
- Specify outcome goals and concrete objectives
- Construct a plan of action
- Negotiate a contract for change

In the discovery phase, client systems and practitioners explore personal and institutional resource systems to set goals and contract for change. Universally applicable to clients at all social system levels, discovery processes include identifying strengths, assessing resource capabilities, and framing solutions.

Identifying strengths

The process, *identifying strengths,* presumes that client strengths function as cornerstones for change and therefore should be noted early and often (Chapter 9). Exclusively focusing on problems traps workers and clients into thinking that nothing works. Scanning for strengths sets a positive tone and conveys expectations of success. Listening to clients describe their challenges with an ear for strengths leads workers to discover clients' abilities, resourcefulness, and creativity, as well as strengths found in interpersonal relationships, culture, organizational networks, and community connections. When workers accentuate strengths, clients experience hope and feel empowered to contribute as full partners to the change effort.

Assessing resource capabilities

The process of *assessing resource* capabilities adds transactional dimensions to the understanding of clients' situations (Chapter 10). Workers and clients jointly assess personal, interpersonal, familial, group, organizational, community, societal, and political systems to detail a positive, broad-based view of the client system in transaction with its environment. Through this strength-oriented assessment, workers and clients discover what resource systems they might activate to reach the outcomes they seek.

Framing solutions

The discovery phase culminates in *framing solutions,* a process in which social workers and clients develop plans for action (Chapter 11). Action plans contain explicit statements about what clients hope to achieve, as well as concrete strategies for achieving their goals and objectives. Developing this comprehensive plan signals the transition from understanding what is happening to acting on this information to make desired changes. A detailed action plan guides the implementation of activities throughout the development phase.

The Development Phase

Action indeed is the sole medium of expression for ethics.
        —Jane Addams

In the development phase, practitioners and clients intervene to activate interpersonal and institutional resources, create alliances with other systems, and expand opportunities through resource development. This approach empowers clients with their own abilities and the resource of their environments with a goal of recognizing and stabilizing the positive changes achieved. Together, workers and clients

- Operationalize the plan of action
- Increase the experience of power within client systems
- Access resources necessary to achieve goals
- Create alliances among persons and organizations to accomplish the plan
- Enhance opportunities and choices by creating additional resources
- Evaluate ongoing progress and outcomes
- Identify and generalize achievements and gains
- Wrap up the professional relationship

Major activities in the development phase work to organize and expand resources, reach outcome goals, measure achievements, and conclude the formal intervention process. This implementation phase includes the processes of activating resources, creating alliances, expanding opportunities, recognizing success, and integrating gains.

Activating resources

In *activating resources,* workers and clients collaborate to put the agreed-on plan into action (Chapter 12). Clients make connections with necessary interpersonal and institutional resources, experiment with new behaviors and interactions, and carry out the tasks developed in their meetings with workers. Social workers organize and monitor intervention activities, motivate clients to participate in the plan, facilitate cooperative efforts in multiperson client systems, detail options

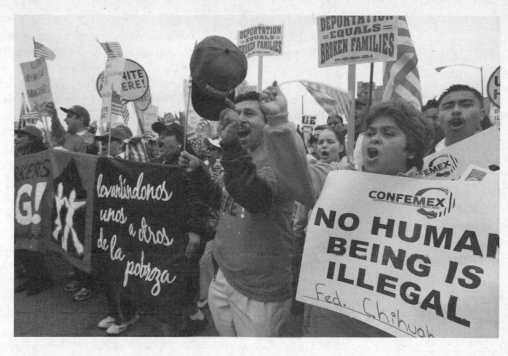

Joining with others in support of a cause promotes social change.

and choices, and provide helpful feedback to clients. Workers play a variety of roles as they consult on strategies, work with clients to manage resources, and oversee educational activities.

Creating alliances

Alliances generate new resources to fuel change. By *creating alliances,* social workers and clients align the efforts of clients in empowerment groups, strengthen the functioning of clients within their natural support networks, and organize the service delivery network (Chapter 13). These alliances bring emotional support to clients and build bases of power for social change efforts. Social workers also benefit from alliances through their collaboration with colleagues, supervisors, and professional organizations. Social workers who feel supported and experience their own power are most likely to engender these same feelings in their clients.

Expanding opportunities

Generalist social workers understand the need to develop resources at all system levels. Through the process, *expanding opportunities,* workers and clients team to create resources that redress social injustice (Chapter 14). Possibilities for change in the service delivery network include refining access to existing social services and creating new programs. Practitioners and clients work to develop just social policy at the agency, local, state, and national levels; they use community organizing and social action strategies to inspire political reforms and legislative changes.

Recognizing success

All effective plans of action include procedures for evaluation. The process, *recognizing success,* highlights the numerous ways to measure the achievement of goals and evaluate service effectiveness (Chapter 15). Evaluating outcomes guarantees a worker's accountability to client systems and practice settings, credits clients with their contributions to the success, and functions as part of the process to bring closure to professional relationships. Measuring success gives clients and social workers a sense of their accomplishments and helps both clients and social workers generalize the success of a particular endeavor to cope with other situations that each will confront. Formal research increases the knowledge base and contributes to the development of the social work profession.

Integrating gains

The final process of *integrating gains* emphasizes that clients grow, develop, and change even after their efforts with social workers end (Chapter 16). The ultimate measure of the success of any social work endeavor is whether clients can independently continue the progress initiated within the professional relationship. To encourage continued success, workers facilitate a closure process that helps clients review the work, express their thoughts and feelings about ending, and recognize the transferability of the strategies implemented to managing other events.

From Solving Problems to Promoting Competence

This model for empowerment-based practice draws its organizational framework from the problem-solving model. Like problem-solving, empowerment-based practice guides workers through activities of building relationships, defining

---

Box 5.2 Social Work Imperatives for the Next Decade: A Policy–Research–Practice Connection

In March 2005, the National Association of Social Workers convened the Social Work Congress 2005, "Vision to Action," in Washington, D.C. Cosponsored by several social work organizations, the Congress brought together 400 social work leaders to discuss social issues and frame the profession's response for the next decade. Working from a vision statement framed by the sponsors, "Social work expertise is highly valued for helping the global community protect and advance the well-being of all people, at every stage of life," the participants identified 12 imperatives for professional action that will inform social work strategies through 2015 (NASW, 2005d). The imperatives set priorities in areas of practice, including aging services, child welfare, health care, behavioral health, advocacy, social action, and policy practice. Furthermore, the directives call on social workers to take actions to ensure professional competence, to address social injustices and human rights issues, to participate in political action, to promote cultural competence, and to engage in research partnerships. In sum, the imperatives charge social workers to

- Ensure excellence and a qualified workforce for practice with older adults and children

- Increase professional involvement in political and policy decision making with respect to behavioral health issues
- Address social injustice and human rights violations
- Advocate for universal health care
- Raise professional standards and increase academic rigor to strengthen the value proposition of social work
- Mobilize to become more involved in politics, policy, and social action
- Enhance the profession's influence in corporate and political arenas
- Develop research partnerships with practitioners and communities to strengthen connections between research and practice
- Acknowledge and confront the racism present in social work practice
- Endorse culturally competent practice interventions and research methods

Clearly, the imperatives delineated by the Vision to Action Congress demonstrate the integration of social work practice, social welfare policy, and intervention research. Over the next decade, many opportunities will arise to promote social justice and human rights as social workers implement corresponding strategies.

Table 5.2	**Empowering Processes and Traditional Problem Solving**
Problem Solving	Empowering Processes
Engagement	Forming Partnerships
Problem Identification and Assessment	Articulating Situations
	Defining Directions
	Identifying Strengths
	Assessing Resource Capabilities
Goal Setting and Planning	Framing Solutions
Implementation	Activating Resources
	Creating Alliances
	Expanding Opportunities
Evaluation	Recognizing Success
Termination	Integrating Gains

We must adjust to changing times and still hold to unchanging principles.
—Jimmy Carter

purposes, assessing situations, planning, and implementing change. In contrast, however, the empowering approach reconstructs traditional problem solving into a process of seeking solutions, using language and concepts that emphasize strengths, empowerment, and working in partnerships with clients at all system levels to promote competence (Table 5.2).

This approach emphasizes strengths rather than deficits, solution seeking rather than problem detecting, competence promotion rather than prescriptive directives, and collaborative partnerships rather than professional expertise. It sets a different tone from deficit-based practice and reflects the contemporary paradigm shift in social work practice to strengths and empowerment. Empowerment influences *assessment*—how we describe the client system, *intervention*—what we do to create change, and the *underlying process*—the way we gather information, organize our work, and implement strategies for change. An empowering approach consistently operates on the presumption that clients have strengths, that environments hold potential resources, that social structures can change as well as client systems, and that clients should participate as full partners in all aspects of change processes.

PROCESSES IN ACTION: PRACTICE EXAMPLES

To understand the application of this empowering practice approach, read the following three examples carefully. Each example demonstrates the phases of dialogue, discovery, and development as applied to a different type of client system. Examine the actions of the social workers to discover the underlying theories, perspectives, competencies, and values that support their work. Specifically, look for generalist thinking, an ecosystemic perspective, respect for cultural diversity, and an orientation to strengths. Notice how the same processes apply at various client system levels, demonstrating the generalist application of this approach.

An Example at the Microlevel

Professional Identity

Generalist social workers practice at multilevel systems. What do Kay Landon, Margo Suarez-Rand, and Leon Casey, the three social workers in the generalist practice examples, have in common?

On her way to the intake appointment, Kay Landon recalls her conversation with Helen Ingersoll. Helen sounded desperate when she made the appointment. Kay could hear the feelings of helplessness as Helen described events leading to her call. Helen's husband Jack is recovering from a work-related head injury that occurred 6 months ago. Things are not going well. Helen is overwhelmed. Jack's progress is slow, and the doctors are talking about "permanent disability." Helen is out of energy and nearly out of hope.

Kay empathizes, but she feels anything but hopeless. From Kay's experiences with other clients in Northside Prevention Services' Family Support Program, she knows that situations like these feel stressful. But, paradoxically, these challenges also bring out capabilities in clients they may not realize they have. Helen Ingersoll has been coping with this traumatic situation for 6 months with little assistance. She obviously has a great deal of strength. Kay is not willing to count Jack out either. The concept of "permanent disability" is one that Kay cannot quite grasp. Maybe Jack is not capable of things that he used to be able to do, but Kay will look for what he still can do. Kay has observed it so often that she assumes it: All clients bring strengths to the social work process.

Dialogue

When Kay arrives, she doesn't have to knock. Helen greets her at the door. Helen is clearly motivated. Once they are seated in the living room, Kay introduces herself and asks to meet Jack. Helen is unsure whether Jack should join them because he can be "unpredictable." Kay's response, "I guess we're all somewhat unpredictable at times," puts Helen at ease; and she leads Jack into the room. Kay begins the meeting by clarifying who she is, what the Family Support Program has to offer, and answers the couple's questions about the services.

Next, it's the Ingersolls' turn to talk. Kay allows them to lead the way, responding attentively to encourage them to keep talking. She clarifies information that confuses her and reassures them that she understands what they say. Kay learns much as Helen and Jack describe their situation in their own way.

Only a few months ago, Helen and Jack Ingersoll were experiencing the kind of life they had planned. Having launched the second of their two children, they were settling into the "good life," relaxing with friends, pursuing individual interests, enjoying time together, and looking ahead to early retirement and travel. Jack was working at the power company and had only 3 years remaining to retire with full benefits. Helen worked part-time as a substitute teacher.

Then, the unexpected happened. Helen was stunned to receive the call about Jack's accident. He had slipped from a utility pole and fallen to the ground. The head and back injuries Jack sustained left him with numerous problems. Even now, his mobility remains limited, he requires assistance in many activities of daily living, and he has trouble remembering things. His condition requires Helen's constant care. This event reverberates throughout every aspect of the couple's lives.

As Kay gathers information, she readily identifies Helen's stress. The months of adjustment have taken their toll. Helen reels off a list of complicated issues. Tending Jack's needs leaves her exhausted. Even though she provides loving care, she endures Jack's frequent criticism and resistance, so uncharacteristic of his "old self." Helen doesn't understand Jack's angry outbursts and seeming lack of motivation to do things for himself. She feels confined to the house and socially isolated. She is frustrated by her inability to return to work, watching their bills pile up as their income decreases. Jack describes his feelings of depression and anger at his helplessness. He admits that he is sometimes difficult and that conflicts interrupt their previously tranquil relationship. For Jack and Helen, these problems seem insurmountable.

As Helen and Jack complete their story, Kay responds, "What resilience! How have you been able to make it this far?" At first, Helen and Jack hesitate. Then each begins to describe what has gotten them through the last few months. Helen talks about the emotional support that her children offer, even though they live out of state. She mentions a friend from church who stops by weekly with a covered dish. Jack credits Helen for her support and endurance. And he admits that occasionally there are good days; in fact, today is one of them. Sometimes, he believes that he just might get "back to normal." Both see their caring relationship as a source of strength throughout the entire ordeal. As the Ingersolls describe what is working, Kay notices a lightening of the mood and the looks of affection the couple exchange with each other.

When Kay asks, "So, what are you looking for from me?" Helen takes the lead. She explains that even though she knows things will never be the same, she still wants them back to the way they were. When Kay asks Helen to be more specific, Helen explains that she would like to be able to do some things on her own again. She wants greater financial stability, maybe even to return to work. Jack states that he would like to take care of himself better so that Helen can get out more. Kay believes these are workable goals and agrees to work with the Ingersolls to achieve them.

Discovery

With a direction in mind, Kay continues her exploration to assess what resources the Ingersolls have to facilitate this effort. Having identified the Ingersoll couple as the focal system, she seeks additional information to discover *what is happening inside the system.* Previously, the Ingersolls enjoyed times together as well as maintaining their separate interests. Now, Jack's health care needs throw them together intensively around the clock. This circumstance blurs the boundaries that define them as distinct individuals. Consequently, each suffers a loss of independence and identity. The sense of equality and partnership previously characteristic of their marriage is disrupted. Jack feels dependent on Helen; and Helen feels trapped by the care Jack needs. Kay observes that both are held hostage by the challenge of Jack's physical condition. To Kay, the couple's depression and conflicts make sense in terms of their feelings of powerlessness. Kay also recognizes that in spite of their difficulties, they show genuine concern and caring for each other.

What is happening outside of the system also influences this couple's experience. At first, the Ingersolls' family and friends showed support. However, as time passes, their attention dwindles. The couple's children are concerned, but they live out of state and can offer only long-distance support. Early on, numerous friends stopped by and called. Now, only one friend visits regularly. Kay notes that the potential for natural support exists but is not fully activated. Kay knows of several community programs assisting people in this situation, yet Helen and Jack have sought no other outside help. Finally, Kay discovers what contributes to the couple's financial instability. Disagreement over liability among the Ingersolls' insurance company, the manufacturer of the utility tower, and Jack's employer have stalled any kind of settlement for the injury.

How does the inside connect to the outside? Kay identifies that Jack's accident has initiated a sequence of events, isolating this couple from the resources of their environment. Before, the Ingersolls were free to work, interact with friends, and pursue individual interests. Now, Jack's injuries confine them to a shrinking world, just as their needs for outside support increase. The pressure builds for Jack and Helen as they run out of reserves.

The information Kay gathers shows that, in the past, the Ingersolls had been artful in negotiating life's expected transitions. Not every family system *progresses through time* with the success evident in this couple's affection, achievements, and accomplishments. Kay sees this adaptability as a strength the couple has yet to rediscover.

Together, Kay and the Ingersolls analyze this information. They identify the power that Jack's health holds over the couple. They recognize the financial bind imposed by Helen's lack of opportunity to work and the unresolved insurance claim. They acknowledge the significance of the disruptions in their relationships with family and friends, and they note the absence of helpful social services. All agree that these are issues for focus as they plan a strategy for change.

Building on this analysis, Kay helps Helen and Jack set concrete goals to guide their work together. They decide to stabilize their financial situation by resolving the insurance claim and freeing Helen to return to work. They also will access community services to relieve Helen's responsibilities, giving her more time to spend with friends and for herself. Finally, they will coordinate a network of health-related services to improve Jack's physiological functioning. As they articulate each phase of this plan, Kay works with Helen and Jack to generate specific objectives and activities to pursue each of these goals.

Development

Kay and the Ingersolls collaborate to get things moving. Kay provides information about available resources, and the Ingersolls take charge of contacting and organizing the services they select. They access in-home physical therapy. A respite worker comes 1 full day each week, allowing Helen time for her own pursuits. Helen uses part of this time to attend a Northside Hospital "mini-course" on caring for persons with head injuries. She talks with others having similar experiences and learns about people recovering from head trauma. Helen also spends time with friends; she comes home with renewed energy and more patience for Jack. As Helen feels better, Jack's mood improves. He no longer feels stuck. He participates in rehabilitation activities and a support group for persons with head injuries. He develops new skills in self-sufficiency, which restore some feelings of control and reduce Helen's caregiving duties.

The goal of financial stability requires Kay to seek additional help. She locates a trained legal advocate, Quyen Nguyen of the Center for Citizens' Rights, who works to resolve the intersystem conflict over liability for John's accident. Quyen facilitates the flow of information among Jack's doctors, the insurance company, Jack's employer, the manufacturer of the utility tower, and the Ingersolls. Through advocacy and mediation, Quyen influences the participants to negotiate an acceptable settlement and avoid a lengthy court process.

Kay encounters obstacles in her efforts to assist Helen back to work. She finds no respite services providing care on short notice to match Helen's unpredictable work schedule as a substitute teacher. The only respite care in Northside has few openings and limits regularly scheduled care to a maximum of 1 day per week. Kay reports this gap in service to the Northside Network, a consortium of social service providers in the Northside community, to encourage resource-development efforts to increase respite services.

While implementing the plan, Kay and the Ingersolls monitor the progress they are making. Kay emphasizes the success the Ingersolls are achieving. The Ingersolls have regained their momentum. In meetings with Kay, they now report their progress rather than request assistance. Kay realizes that the Ingersolls are planning a future again rather than looking back at what they have lost. Although their lives have changed course, they have overcome many hurdles and have the power to continue on their own. Kay wraps up her work with Helen and Jack by reviewing their success and celebrating their achievements.

An Example at the Mezzolevel

Mezzolevel practice focuses on change within organizations and formal groups. Such change may be initiated internally by workers who are part of the organization or by persons outside of the organization functioning as consultants or educators. Social worker Margo Suarez-Rand functions at the mezzolevel in her role as Training Director for the Area Association for People with Disabilities (APD). As part of her job, Margo is responsible to plan and implement initial orientation and training for direct service personnel in the agency's residential and day programs, as required by state regulations and as part of the agency's mission to provide quality care for the individuals the agency serves. Although Margo's training program has developed over a number of years and is approved by state regulators, Margo questions the effectiveness of the training in teaching the skills and attitudes necessary for working with APD's clients.

Recently in monthly meetings with frontline supervisors, Margo has heard complaints about the lack of readiness of newly hired direct service staff, most of whom have no previous work or life experience with people with disabilities. Margo cringes to hear reports that some direct service personnel are treating clients in demeaning ways, using discriminatory language, or ridiculing their behaviors, and others abandon programs designed to teach clients life skills in favor of doing things for clients because "it's just easier." To Margo, this anecdotal information suggests that, even though the training program teaches a philosophy of client empowerment and includes clear instruction on how to implement this perspective in client treatment, the training may not be producing the outcomes that she seeks. She sees it as her responsibility to check into this situation further.

Although Margo operates within the overriding mission of APD and shares the vision of improving the quality of life for the individuals APD serves, her "client system" is really the agency system itself. As a social worker, Margo functions at the mezzolevel, working to strengthen the organization and its response to its clientele. Margo's organizational client system benefits from processes similar to those used with clients at other system levels. In the example that follows, note how Margo (like microlevel social worker Kay Landon in the previous example) guides her mezzolevel client thought phases of dialogue, discovery, and development as she works to achieve the desired outcomes.

Dialogue

At this point, Margo has only a vague idea that the training program may not be working well. Her current concerns are based on conversations with a few frontline supervisors. She recognizes that, although this information is useful, it does not represent the full view. She will need to establish some sort of *dialogue* that accesses a more complete picture of what is currently happening before she can move to assess what part of the training works and what should change.

Dialogue at the individual and family level usually involves a direct in-person exchange with the people involved. Dialogue at the organizational level is more complex, involving more people with differing perspectives. Margo must plan carefully to get a comprehensive and useful view. With whom should she talk? What methods would be best to ensure a productive and open exchange of information that fully articulates the current situation and defines a direction for improvement?

A systemic view guides Margo's decisions about whom to talk with and how to get information. Because her agency client is composed of several subsystems, Margo considers newly hired and recently trained staff, their immediate supervisors, and more experienced staff as useful subsystem perspectives. Margo's empowerment orientation also leads her to explore the client viewpoint. After all, who can better assess how staff members improve the quality of life for clients than the clients themselves?

Margo currently uses written surveys to evaluate trainees' perceptions of the training, and many trainers use written tests to measure learning. In mezzolevel social work, social workers frequently use assessment instruments such as surveys and tests to generate and exchange information. At ADP, these surveys report positive outcomes, but Margo believes that she does not receive the depth of information about the training she needs to refine. She determines that a series of focus groups may be a way to understand the situation better.

A focus group is a facilitated small group discussion centered on key questions of interest, recorded and analyzed to identify salient issues and conclusions. Acknowledging that the quality of information accessed through focus groups partly depends on participants' comfort in openly sharing their views, Margo looks for group facilitators who are neutral to the process. How free would various stakeholders in the program be to share opinions about the training when talking to the Training Director? So, Margo partners with faculty and students from a social work program at a nearby university.

The student facilitators begin by holding informal discussions with selected members of the constituent groups, including representatives of recently trained staff, supervisors, experienced staff, and clients. Through this initial dialogue with key informants and discussions with Margo, a series of key questions takes shape that will guide the focus group discussions. What current training content is most useful? What learning processes work most effectively? What do trainees actually learn that they are able to apply directly in their new positions?

During the focus group sessions, student facilitators use responding skills to fully articulate the thoughts and feelings of participants. They formulate well-phrased questions to access more complete and concrete information, and they encourage widespread participation among group members. Later, the students transcribe audio recordings of the meetings to allow a qualitative analysis of key themes and issues. These focus groups provide a forum for Margo's dialogue with her mezzolevel client system, a way for Margo to discover the strengths of the existing training program and lend direction to plans for improvement.

Discovery

A social service agency is a human system that has structures, functions, and policies that affect the transactions within it. An agency has its own culture that shapes rules, norms, and interactions within the agency system. Significantly, an agency also functions within an environmental context that influences its internal operations. Questions addressed within the focus groups help Margo gather internal and contextual information on agency functioning as well as to assess how these dynamics affect the training program's effectiveness. Margo will combine conclusions drawn from the focus groups with other assessment measures to provide a comprehensive view.

The focus groups help Margo answer the assessment question, *what's happening inside the system*? She notes the strengths of the training program, as indicated by the qualitative analysis of the group discussions. Most new and experienced frontline staff report the training program's success in orienting them to the state-mandated documentation and reporting requirements as well as agency personnel policies. Frontline supervisors agree with the conclusion that staff are proficient in paperwork and procedures. Staff participants also concur that the training helps to develop skills in providing personal care for clients, teaches them basic signs to communicate with clients who use American Sign Language, and prepares them with self-defense responses in case of aggressive client behaviors.

The focus group discussions also reveal significant challenges. Newly trained staff report that a lot must be accomplished with not enough time to do everything. They turn to the more experienced staff for guidance, and they quickly learn to "document, document, document." To keep your job on the front lines, experienced workers say you need to stick to procedures. It's not so much what you do, but your ability to keep supervisors and the state people off your back that is necessary to succeed in direct service. This bureaucratic culture predominates; when choices must be made, client care takes a back seat. New workers also report that it is a big adjustment to learn to relate to clients with developmental disabilities. Workers reveal their fears about what clients "might do," and they describe how their friends and families wonder how they can work with "those people."

To understand this focus group information further, Margo broadens her analysis to examine *what's happening outside the system* and how this affects transactions within the agency staff system. The clients' focus group reports are the first place she looks. Clients describe that staff are frequently hard to find because they are always "hanging out in the office" rather than in the program areas. Clients also report that staff members are unresponsive to their requests and sometimes irritable, saying they "are too busy right now" to deal with clients. Clients also report that staff sometimes hurt their feelings, treating them like "little kids."

Continuing her assessment, Margo examines the *context* to consider other influences. The emphasis placed on administrative work at the expense of client programs leads her to examine the increase in state requirements and the close scrutiny by state inspectors of client files and agency procedures. She takes a historical view to examine *changes in the system over time* and recognizes that, as the state worked to de-institutionalize services in favor of community-based care, much of the state's complex bureaucracy has followed clients to community agencies. State functions have evolved from direct service to agency monitoring. Inspectors focus more on documentation than on client services and quality-of-life measures.

Margo looks to the training modules she teaches directly and notes that, to meet state mandates, she has increased the content on paperwork and procedures, leaving her less opportunity to teach about program philosophy and treatment. Further discussion with other trainers leads Margo to conclude that this shift is common across many aspects of the training. Margo recognizes the issue of "goal displacement," a common organizational problem that develops over time. As more attention is given to the functioning and the survival of the agency, the client-centered mission begins to fade from view.

Turning her attention to the staff members' fears and client complaints about staff insensitivity reminds Margo that oppression is a daily experience for the clients of ADP. Stereotypic views, discrimination, and prejudice about people with developmental disabilities is rampart in the culture at large. Newly hired staff bring these cultural biases in with them, and the initial training may not be doing enough to confront these oppressive views and guide people to a more sensitive response. Interestingly, the focus groups of experienced staff and supervisors showed little fear or bias. Margo concludes that daily interaction with clients over time cultivates new attitudes, as reflected in one supervisor's statement that "working here has opened me up to how beautiful all people are—I can't imagine working anywhere else."

To begin her planning process, Margo reviews all of the information she has gathered and summarizes the key strengths and needs of the training program. She focuses on three areas in setting goals. First, she determines to shore up the current strengths of the program by setting a goal to maintain the high level of staff compliance with paperwork and procedures. Margo doesn't want to change something that's working as she makes attempts at improvement.

Second, Margo sets a goal to increase the successful implementation of client-centered programming by direct service staff. Two objectives flesh out this goal. The first objective—to maintain the existing training approach in teaching personal care for clients and sign language—is based on the assessment of these as existing strengths in staff functioning. The second objective within this goal—to increase the implementation of client developmental programs—will require modification in the training approach and additional emphasis. Some redistribution of workload requirements may also be necessary to optimize the chances for success.

Finally, Margo sets a goal to increase the humane treatment of agency clients by newly hired workers. She immediately sees the significant challenge associated with success in this arena, because social injustice toward people with developmental disabilities is deeply ingrained in the wider society. But if all people committed to social justice avoided the difficult goals, society would never have achieved the gains of the civil rights and women's movements. Besides, Margo recognizes that she is not alone in this endeavor. The more experienced staff and the clients themselves are resources to assist her in addressing the wider social issue of oppression of people with disabilities.

Development

Within the development phase, social workers and clients collaborate to implement the action plan. Margo and her agency client launch a multifaceted strategy to achieve the goals and objectives specified in the discovery phase and to evaluate the impact of their efforts.

The first goal—to maintain staff expertise with paperwork and procedures—is the easiest to achieve. To discover what works and continue it is always easier than to acknowledge a failure and guess how to improve things. To meet this "stay-the-course" goal, Margo needs only to activate existing resources. She teams with other agency trainers to identify those parts of the training program focused on paperwork and procedure and identifies strengths of the training program to ensure that upcoming changes will not interfere with their current success in these areas.

The second goal—to increase the successful implementation of client-centered programming—requires more work. Margo convenes the same group of trainers to enlist their expertise in this effort. She challenges them to improve training on the programmatic aspects of agency functioning. She structures the intervention for success by asking each trainer to convene a team of experts—an alliance of training instructor, experienced staff, supervisor, new direct service employee, and client—to redesign the content of each targeted training module. Margo knows that creating such an alliance will give voice to the differing perspectives, leading to changes that will benefit all stakeholders. Margo, herself, takes responsibility to discuss with her own supervisor a possible redistribution of workload requirements to free direct service personnel for more client interaction and programming.

Margo also addresses the goal to create a more affirming environment for agency clients. She implements a two-pronged approach aimed both at new employees and at the wider community pool of potential employees. She accesses experienced direct service employees as training "associates" to talk about their transformation in attitude toward clients. Margo encourages each to tell his or her personal story of professional and personal development within ADP and share his or her feelings about agency clients. Margo also seeks clients as experts to train new hires about who clients are and what they expect from staff.

The clients are a key resource in another arena to address the social justice goal. As part of an ADP community integration program, a group of clients has formed a "Speak Up" group—a social action coalition of clients who present information about people with developmental disabilities to community groups, issue press releases to local media, and offer training to individuals with disabilities in public speaking and legislative testimony. She asks this client group to join with ADP's employee recruitment and hiring efforts to initiate a re-socialization process about persons with developmental disabilities from the first point of entry into the ADP system. Because her assessment showed clearly that interaction with clients was effective in reducing bias, Margo figures the sooner the better for employees to begin to relate positively to the clients they will serve.

As Margo coordinates this agency-wide effort to improve the training program, she continually evaluates the process and the progress. She meets regularly with those involved to monitor the impact of the changes she has initiated. Each group with whom she meets identifies what is working and should continue and also notes what is not working and should be modified. Changes in training judged to be effective are written into the training program modules, thereby institutionalizing them into the agency's culture and functioning.

As time goes on and the stakeholders begin to agree that "they are getting it right," Margo moves to wrap up this particular intervention into the training program. She recognizes that the procedural changes in hiring, the changes in the training content and process, and the cultural changes in agency atmosphere will work to stabilize the improvements initiated during this concentrated effort. Deciding to add periodic focus groups to the ongoing evaluation of the training program will give Margo another tool she needs to monitor the effectiveness of the training program as it evolves.

An Example at the Macrolevel

Leon Casey's job as a community prevention specialist at the Neighborhood Development Association (NDA) prompts him to keep abreast of community issues. At first, the neighborhood conflict between a Caucasian resident and his new African American neighbor seemed to Leon like an isolated incident. But when subsequent events occur—the fights between groups of Latino and Caucasian students at the high school, the charge of police brutality by an Asian American claiming racial discrimination, and now a cross burning on the front lawn of Northside's only synagogue—a trend emerges. After the civil rights commission contacts Leon with the same concerns, Leon directs his efforts toward the simmering ethnic and intercultural tensions in his client system—the Northside community.

Dialogue

Leon quickly convenes a meeting of relevant community members to function as key informants about this challenging issue. Participants include the community liaison from the Police Department, the chairperson of the Civil Rights Commission, the current president of the Ecumenical Council, the director of the Gay and Lesbian Alliance, a representative from United Way, the chairperson of a neighborhood action council, and the rabbi from the site of the cross burning. Each participant can offer additional examples of cultural intolerance, and the group members agree that the Northside community must promote a greater acceptance of diversity.

Participants agree to work together to reduce intercultural tension. They form themselves into a steering committee to assess the situation further and develop a strategy for change. Leon facilitates this committee, exploring ways to articulate this challenging situation in more detail. Members agree to host community forums at their respective sites to encourage citizen participation in the assessment process. Leon's role is to coordinate the scheduling of these events. He will use the outreach capabilities of NDA to announce these forums to the public. Leon also trains forum observers to record information offered by citizens at the various meetings and to compile the results for the steering committee's consideration.

Discovery

Leon facilitates the steering group's assessment processes, helping them complete a strengths-based ecosystemic assessment. This means Leon guides the group to look for strengths and resources within the community rather than focusing solely on its challenges. Leon also orients group members to consider the community's interactions with its environment as potential resources for change.

The community forums help Leon understand *what is happening inside the system*. Citizens report additional acts of racial and cultural hatred. Observers note several angry interchanges at the forums among citizens from different cultural groups. On the positive side, citizens describe several exceptions to these problems—successful cross-cultural community events and acts of kindness and friendships among diverse people, counteracting the trend toward intolerance. Those attending the forums want the community to respond quickly before the incidents "get out of hand" or "somebody really gets hurt."

Leon leads the steering group to consider *what's happening outside the system* and *how the inside is connecting to the outside.* Group members are all familiar with national events that create a context of racial and cultural divisiveness. An anti-immigration sentiment pervades national opinion; homophobia leads to regressive social policies and laws; white supremacy groups grow in popularity; and movements promoting English as the only language evidence the trend away from cultural pluralism.

Conversely, not all that is happening in the environment of the Northside community is bleak. Other cities, responding to the same pressures, have begun efforts to increase cultural acceptance in their communities. In a phone survey of similar-sized municipalities, Leon learns of several strategies used in other areas that are yielding positive results. He carefully records the information and asks these municipalities to send pamphlets, brochures, newspaper articles, program evaluation results, and other written information about their efforts.

Compiling the information obtained from the community forums and the telephone survey, steering committee members work together to construct a plan of action. They confirm their original purpose by setting a goal to increase acceptance of cultural diversity in the Northside community. To meet this goal they articulate two objectives including (1) to form a Quick Response Team to deal with hate crimes, and (2) to establish a Mediation Center. These objectives are concrete steps toward the goal of cultural tolerance.

Development

Steering group members divide up their efforts to achieve both objectives simultaneously. Some members complete activities to form the Quick Response Team. After studying the composition of such teams in other locations, steering group members determine criteria for team membership. Qualifications include skills in crisis response, conflict resolution, bilingualism, and cultural competence. Subsequently, steering committee members poll social service agencies and other community organizations to see whether they have qualified personnel and whether they are willing to donate their resources.

In response to these inquiries, the Quick Response Team begins to take shape. A large pool of team members assembles. Each individual response team includes at least one representative from the police department, a person skilled in mediation and conflict resolution, and a person or persons fluent in the languages and familiar with the cultures of the citizens involved. Other members from the larger pool of volunteers stand available to supplement teams as necessary in specific situations.

Leon's own agency takes a coordinating role with the team. The Northside Development Association uses its resources to supply office space and an emergency phone line. NDA will also serve as the center for the ongoing recruitment and training of the response team members.

Other steering committee members work on the second objective. They secure a site for the Northside Mediation Center when the rabbi volunteers space at the synagogue. They also visit other mediation centers in nearby communities to gather ideas for how to organize the Mediation Center. Once they develop a tentative plan for the center, the steering committee holds a public meeting at the proposed site to elicit additional input.

The steering committee integrates the information gathered from other mediation centers, adds the perspectives from the citizen's forum, incorporates its own ideas, and then proposes a model for organizing and operating the Mediation Center. Members vote to approve the proposal and then focus their efforts on launching the new program. Steering group members use their community networks to locate both private and public sources of support, including technical expertise, funding, and volunteer mediators.

Finally, steering committee members combine their efforts to determine the interface between their respective projects. Clearly, the Quick Response Team and the Mediation Center have complementary roles. Committee members negotiate a service agreement by which the Quick Response Team focuses on crisis situations and refers citizens to the Mediation Center for more lasting solutions to their conflicts.

Once the team and the center are operational, the committee seeks ways to end its work and ensure that both services remain established as ongoing programs in the community services network. The Quick Response Team will continue to function as part of the Northside Development Association. The Mediation Center will remain at the synagogue and be governed by a board of directors that includes some members from the original steering committee and other volunteers recruited from the community.

The steering committee also agrees to follow up on its work. In 6-month intervals, they will review evaluations of the two new programs and examine police reports to assess whether cultural tolerance is increasing.

MULTILEVEL INTERVENTION IN GENERALIST PRACTICE: AN INTEGRATIVE CASE EXAMPLE

Even when specializing at a particular level of practice, a generalist social worker will recognize viable interventions in other domains. Consider the following example of Alisha Shelton, a school social worker at Northside Elementary, who, while working with first-grade student Benita Alvarez, extends beyond the microlevel of practice to intervene at the mezzo- and macrolevels as well. Generalist social workers see multiple opportunities for change and sometimes intervene at all levels of practice to maximize potential benefits for clients and achieve social justice.

Intervention at the Microlevel

Policy Practice

Policy implications are evident in the micro-, mezzo-, and macrolevels of social work practice. What policy threads are woven in the practice example of school social worker Alisha Shelton?

In response to teacher Dorothy Campbell's concern, school social worker Alisha Shelton meets with Benita Alvarez, a first-grade student who has recently enrolled in Northside Elementary. The referral stems from Benita's reticence. According to Mrs. Campbell, Benita "hasn't said a word" in the 2 weeks she has attended. Mrs. Campbell sees Benita as compliant with instructions but thinks that Benita may have hearing loss, autism, retardation, or some kind of speech difficulty, or maybe Benita is simply shy or not fluent in English. Benita nods or shakes her head in response to questions or instructions given by Mrs. Campbell. She stays isolated from the other students and converses with no one.

Before meeting with Benita, Alisha checks with school administrators. She learns that Benita transferred to Northside 3 weeks after the term began. Benita's mother Isabella Alvarez, together with a friend, had registered Benita, but Isabella had produced no school records or offered any information about previous school attendance. Isabella spoke only Spanish, and her friend, Ann, translated during the registration process. When asked about previous school experience, Isabella's response was evasive, saying the family had recently moved around a lot.

After registration, the school nurse coordinates with the County Health Department for a physical exam and the immunizations required for school enrollment. Benita is placed in Mrs. Campbell's first-grade class based on her chronological age and her mother's report that first grade is the appropriate level. Mrs. Campbell receives instructions to assess Benita carefully to determine whether placement in the first grade is appropriate. Observing Benita's 2 weeks of silence leads Mrs. Campbell to question the placement, precipitating the referral to Alisha.

Benita behaves predictably in her first meeting with the social worker. Alisha does most of the talking, with Benita nodding occasionally or whispering a brief response. It seems to Alisha that Benita hears her well and also understands English, yet she demonstrates considerable shyness or a great need for privacy. Benita will offer little information about her life or her family, but she does respond to direct questions indicating that "things are OK" with school, Mrs. Campbell, and the other students. Alisha knows she needs to access other perspectives on Benita to determine what might help Benita at school. She decides to make a home visit.

Because no phone is listed on Benita's record, Alisha drops by the Alvarez home to schedule an appointment. Alisha intends to bring an interpreter to the family appointment but believes she knows sufficient Spanish to set a meeting time. Isabella answers the door cautiously and does not invite Alisha in. Standing on the front step, Alisha introduces herself to Isabella, describes her role and relationship to Benita, and clarifies the purpose of the proposed meeting. They agree to a time for Alisha to return with an interpreter.

Returning for the appointment with interpreter Carmen Mendes, Alisha is greeted at the door by Isabella's friend Ann. Ann explains that she knows Isabella from church, and Isabella has asked her to be present. Isabella and Benita are waiting in the kitchen. Through the interpreter, Alisha again explains who she is and the purpose of the visit. Alisha notes that although Carmen translates everything to Isabella, Isabella frequently looks to her friend Ann for reassurance about what she is hearing. From this observation, Alisha concludes that language is not the only obstacle to communication. A great need exists on Isabella's part to include someone she trusts in the discussion. With Ann to offer reassurance, Isabella grows more comfortable. Isabella begins to talk about Benita more freely, and Alisha is able to do a brief assessment of Benita's developmental functioning.

At home, Alisha observes a very different Benita. As Isabella grows more trustful, Benita becomes more animated. Benita converses readily with her mother in Spanish and talks intermittently with Ann in English. Clearly, Benita is bilingual and not really shy at all in the comfort of her own home. As Alisha queries Isabella about Benita, the two tease one another playfully. Alisha sees the affection. She also notes that Benita will answer some questions herself without waiting for Carmen to translate and then will share the content with her mother. Benita is beginning to look like a typical first grader to Alisha. Perhaps the adjustment to school will come more easily as Benita's comfort increases. Alisha refocuses her efforts in this familiar setting to build an easy rapport with Benita, hoping to bridge that same level of comfort to school.

Next, Alisha shifts her assessment to the family. Immediately, Alisha notices uneasiness once again invade the conversation. Alisha learns that Benita is Isabella's only child and that Isabella's husband Roberto is at work. Isabella reports that the family originated in Guatemala and migrated to the Northside community, drawn by the promise of employment at a local food-processing plant. Although Alisha seeks more detailed information, none is forthcoming. Isabella remains silent about how long the family has lived in the United States and their path from Guatemala to Northside.

Noting the modest living situation, Alisha expects that Benita may qualify for the subsidized school lunch program. She explains how Isabella can apply by simply offering some proof of the family's income. Isabella resists, saying that whatever help she needs she can get from the church. Then Isabella stands up, indicating that she is ready to end the meeting. Alisha honors the preference and arranges to meet with Isabella again in a couple of weeks to help facilitate Benita's transition to the new school.

Back at school, Alisha reflects on her conversation in the Alvarez home and develops both a hypothesis about what is going on and a plan of action. She first notes the strengths. Benita is developmentally appropriate, perhaps gifted. She is bilingual and likely understands what others are saying to her in class. She lives in an affectionate household, and her mother Isabella shows both motivation and ability to parent in an uplifting way. An obvious goal is to generalize Benita's feelings of comfort and competence at home to the school environment.

Alisha also notes areas of concern. A significant difference appears between Benita at home and Benita at school. What is inhibiting Benita's integration into the classroom? Alisha believes that Isabella's pattern of sharing information in their meeting provides some clues. Isabella is very cautious, especially when talking about anything not directly related to Benita's performance at school. Perhaps a family rule exists about sharing too much. Could it be that Benita is permitted to be herself in the family setting but instructed to keep to herself in the outside world?

It strikes Alisha that she has seen this caution before in other immigrants. Many tread carefully when interacting with those they perceive to be authorities. Some bring memories of oppressive actions by officials in their countries of origin. Others fear that their status in the United States leaves them vulnerable to prosecution. Alisha recalls a previous student who was born in the United States but whose parents had entered the country without proper documentation. She respected the resistance the parents showed, recognizing the risks if their immigration status were discovered: deportation and possibly losing their child to state custody. The situation of the Alvarez family feels similar to her. Are concerns about immigration status the central theme that affects both Isabella's reluctance to share information and Benita's behavior at school?

Alisha concludes that Benita is probably appropriately placed and simply needs to gain comfort in the school environment to activate her potential. So Alisha develops a three-part plan. First, she places Benita in Alisha's first-grade girls' group, a group designed to help members develop social skills and build self-esteem. Second, she meets with Mrs. Campbell and Benita together to help Benita feel safe in the classroom and also to help Benita and Mrs. Campbell develop a more comfortable relationship. Alisha feels that she already relates effectively with Benita and hopes to help Mrs. Campbell do the same. Third, Alisha continues to visit with Benita and Isabella at home as a way to sustain a comfortable rapport with the family and to update Isabella on Benita's progress.

In many ways, this intervention plan is successful. Benita blossoms in the girls' group. Her comfort increases, and she makes friends. Isabella remains dedicated to her daughter's success, keeping regular appointments with Alisha and supporting Benita. But the goal of assisting Mrs. Campbell to relate well with Benita falters. Benita remains detached in class. Alisha earlier recognized that progress in the classroom could be slow. When first responding to the plan, Mrs. Campbell had said, "I don't know why I should have to take time to meet with her individually. Students like her take up way too much of my time. All this effort, and in 6 weeks they'll be moving away. That's just how those people are."

Noting Mrs. Campbell's resistance, Alisha determines two things. She will need to move cautiously with Mrs. Campbell not to alienate her further. Alisha remembers a former professor's advice that astute social workers respect a client's resistance and work to understand it before rushing ahead with a plan. Second, Alisha must craft an appropriate response to what Mrs. Campbell is saying. The teacher's words are likely rooted in bias, but exactly who does Mrs. Campbell mean by "those people" and what can Alisha do about it?

Intervention at the Mezzolevel

Within the next week, Alisha gets her answer by walking into the teachers' lounge. Mrs. Campbell is there, as are other teachers. The conversation is about immigration, specifically illegal immigration. Many teachers are siding with Mrs. Campbell, saying "those people" should be stopped at the border because they are taking American jobs and using up social and educational resources without contributing anything. Other teachers are expressing different views, saying things like, "but we all come from immigrants" and "diversity in the United States is a good thing" and "they are doing jobs no American will take."

Alisha moves further into the room and joins the conversation. She refrains from offering her own opinions, responding instead to what others are saying, helping the teachers to articulate their views. Participating in this dialogue, Alisha begins to understand that Benita's experience in the classroom may not be an isolated one. Several teachers express their desire to withhold efforts from "undeserving" students who they presume to be undocumented immigrants. Alisha realizes that this negative preconception is likely affecting Benita's comfort in the classroom, and she recognizes that other students at Northside Elementary may have similar disempowering experiences as well.

Frequently, when an individual client's behavior is viewed in context, a different perspective emerges. Rather than focusing exclusively on the individual needs of Benita, Alisha now sees the need for intervention at a different level—the mezzolevel of practice. Mezzolevel practice addresses challenges within the functioning of formal groups and organizations. Northside Elementary is such a system. Alisha can see the benefits that would accrue for Benita and others if teachers' views were more empathic.

Alisha takes her concerns to the school administration, saying that teachers need a better understanding of the changing demographics of the student population, particularly the needs and experiences of those who have immigrated. The timing for this discussion is good. The building principal mentions that school personnel are planning the next in-service day, and they are exploring various topics around the theme of student diversity. A focus on the experiences and rights of immigrant students is timely. He asks Alisha to join the in-service planning committee and share her ideas.

The in-service planning committee is a district-wide task group responsible for organizing relevant training for staff and teachers in the school system. They are receptive to Alisha's thoughts about immigration issues yet are unsure how to proceed. Alisha volunteers to develop a survey to assess the learning needs of those who will attend. The results will help the committee plan an event and suggest which expert presenters might speak directly to the concerns and attitudes of those who will attend. Alisha develops a brief survey and pretests it with a few staff in her building. She also develops a cover letter explaining the purpose of the survey and its confidential nature. Finally, she distributes sufficient copies of the survey and cover letter to each building in the district for teachers and staff to complete.

Frequently, assessment at the mezzolevel requires social workers to use such tools as surveys to access accurate assessment information. After compiling the results and analyzing the survey data, Alisha returns to the in-service committee with the concrete information necessary to plan a relevant and useful training event. The survey shows that school personnel are generally aware that all immigrants, documented and undocumented, have rights to school attendance. Beyond that fact, their knowledge is limited. Very few understand what rights immigrants have to access other community and social services. Even fewer show knowledge of the larger social issues that have increased the flow of immigration in recent times. Many teachers express resentment about increasing class size and the specialized instruction sometimes required to accommodate foreign-born students.

These data lead the committee to plan a two-pronged event. First, an immigration attorney will explain the legalities of immigration. The attorney will also discuss the rights of immigrant families and how immigration status determines eligibility for community services and social benefits. Second, an immigration rights activist will discuss the global social and economic dynamics contributing to the current immigration wave. The focus here is to enlighten attendees on the possible motivations and experiences of recent immigrants, by using current research and facts to examine the validity of myths and biases pervasive in the popular media. Perhaps this will lead to greater empathy and understanding by school personnel for the students with whom they work.

The in-service is a success, according to the attendees' evaluation forms and comments. Alisha herself learns much. From the attorney, she learns that immigration is a complex issue. Those immigrants who are undocumented are entitled to very little except public education and necessary medical care. Even those who have legally migrated to the United States and are on a direct path to citizenship are prohibited in many states from accessing certain social welfare benefits such as Temporary Aid to Needy Families (TANF). Alisha hears that the rights of legal immigrants vary tremendously depending on their particular immigration status. For example, Alisha is surprised to learn that undocumented immigrants arrested for violation of immigration law are not guaranteed legal representation.

The immigration rights activist offers a powerful message to those attending. One by one the activist presents common myths about immigrants and dispels them with current research and facts. Two misconceptions stand out in Alisha's mind—that undocumented immigrants don't pay taxes and that immigrants in general draw more from the U. S. economy than they contribute. Neither is true. All immigrants do pay taxes in the form of income, property, and sales taxes at the state and local levels—the very taxes that pay Alisha's salary in the Northside school system. Moreover, through their employment and entrepreneurship, immigrants likely contribute more to the American economy that they ever recoup in public benefits. Many immigrants arrive during prime working age and enter the U.S. workforce without ever having drawn on the resources of the public educational system. Even undocumented workers receiving pay checks contribute to Social Security and Medicare funds from which they will never be able to draw benefits.

Why is there such a wave of immigration at this time? The social activist points to recent international trade agreements such as NAFTA as a primary cause. Just as the movement of jobs to Mexico has depleted many employment opportunities in the United States, the subsequent movement of jobs from Mexico to the cheaper labor pool in China has brought increased unemployment to Mexico and other Latin American countries. Loss of family farms to corporate agricultural conglomerates has similarly affected both the United

States and Mexico. Individuals seeking to support their families are not to blame for the immigration controversy. Globalization, corporate interests, and trade agreements may be creating some of the circumstances that disenfranchise working people in both North and South America.

Alisha feels increased empathy for all of those affected by the immigration issue. Importantly, the in-service changes the conversation in the school environment. Several teachers thank Alisha for broadening their understanding. Even Mrs. Campbell's demeanor seems gentler when Alisha stops by to monitor Benita's progress in the classroom. The intervention at the school-system level seems to have trickle-down benefits for individual students.

Intervention at the Macrolevel

The positive impact of the in-service gives Alisha a feeling of accomplishment. She feels proud that she has met the ideals of the social work profession by recognizing the opportunities for change, both in the person and in the environment. Yet, what Alisha learns that day also leaves her with an unsettled feeling. Her work is not finished. The situations in which immigrants such as Benita find themselves seems fundamentally unfair. To Alisha, the treatment of immigrants is more than a legal issue; it is a human rights issue. Laws governing immigration should change. The societal response to immigrants—whether documented or undocumented—should be brought into line with global economic and social realities. Alisha feels strongly about these convictions.

Alisha realizes that intervention on a broader scale than possible in her position as a school social worker is necessary to ensure the well-being and to respect the human dignity of clients like the Alvarez family. Although Alisha recognizes the need for change at the macrolevel, she must honor the boundaries of her professional position. A political stance about immigration falls outside her contracted role with the school system, yet Alisha's professional identity as a social worker extends beyond her job. She feels the pull of social justice and seeks to expand her efforts beyond her work environment.

Alisha is a member of two professional organizations—the National Association of Social Workers (NASW) and the School Social Worker Association (SSWA). Both groups serve multiple functions for their members and their clients. They implement social-action efforts and employ lobbyists to press for legislation that benefits social work practice. Alisha specifically remembers the attention given to the rights of immigrant students at the last SSWA annual program meeting. SSWA is the place to start. So Alisha contacts the political action committee of the SSWA.

The response from the political action committee is immediate, informing Alisha they are recruiting members for a newly formed subcommittee on immigration. Clearly, Alisha is not the only school social worker interested in the immigration issue. They invite Alisha onto the subcommittee, and she readily accepts. Attending her first meeting, Alisha realizes that considerable progress has already been made. They have completed many elements of the dialogue and discovery phases by researching current laws about immigration, surveying their own members about issues and preferences regarding their work with immigrant students, talking with congressional representatives about immigration reform, and looking broadly at the social policies of other countries to assess how they answer questions posed by immigration.

Alisha sees that immigration is a complex issue affected by both state and federal laws. The subcommittee recognizes this complexity and forms task groups to work toward goals at both governmental levels. At the state level, the group decides to focus on extending social service eligibility to all residents regardless of citizenship. At the federal level, they agree to support a humane path toward citizenship for undocumented current residents who intend to remain in the United States. Current laws criminalize the lack of documentation. The subsequent prosecution and deportation for those convicted frequently leads to community turmoil and family disruption. The subcommittee decides to support a program of amnesty for current residents and emphasize community preservation and family well-being in any immigration reform.

To achieve these goals, subcommittee members develop a multifaceted plan. Taking action at the federal level, the SSWA lobbyist will work to influence members of Congress to fashion an accessible and fair legalization process for undocumented residents. Some subcommittee members will organize an e-mail and letter writing campaign in support of this new federal legislation. At the state level, other members of the subcommittee will contact their own state representatives, pressing them to introduce legislation to offer social welfare benefits to all residents without regard for immigration status. Still other members will recruit key informants and prepare them to participate in state legislative hearings when the legislation comes to the floor.

Alisha helps those preparing for the legislative hearings. She works to locate professional experts who will present evidence to prove the benefits of the proposed changes. She also seeks to identify clients who are willing to offer their perspectives about the detrimental impact of current laws. Finally, Alisha prepares to speak herself about her experiences as a school social worker in seeking to support the humane treatment of children adversely affected by the current policies.

Subcommittee members know that this will be a lengthy process. Such a complex problem as immigration reform will require a complex solution that accounts for many conflicting views and attitudes. Meanwhile, interested school social workers will continue their efforts at the microlevel by supporting individual students and at the mezzolevel by creating affirming school environments until such a time as a public solution at the macrolevel can be achieved.

LOOKING FORWARD

The approach to generalist practice presented in this chapter provides a framework for working with clients at all system levels. These processes incorporate a contextual view of situations, a partnership view of the social worker–client relationship, and a solution-focused view of outcomes.

Theoretical orientations to human behavior and change combined with social work values and skills prepare social workers for practice. The ecosystems perspective in unison with a strengths orientation provides the foundation for the empowering approach to generalist social work practice. This paradigm frames practice within dialogue, discovery, and development phases and distinguishes empowering processes to implement in each. Practitioners use this approach to structure their work with clients, while maintaining flexibility in its implementation to fit the unique circumstances of each client system, accounting for the level of the system, cultural diversity, and the particulars of clients' situations.

The remaining chapters fully describe this approach to generalist social work practice. These chapters explore the conceptual base, delineate collaborative roles for workers and clients, consider cultural diversity, apply skills to all levels of human systems, and highlight ethics for each empowering process. Chapter 6, Forming Partnerships, describes the social worker–client relationship and offers specific guidelines for translating positive expectations and assumptions about clients into empowering partnerships with them.

Succeed with **PEARSON mysocialworklab**

Log onto **www.mysocialworklab.com** and select the **Interactive Skill Module** videos from the left-hand menu. Answer the questions below. (*If you did not receive an access code to **MySocialWorkLab** with this text and wish to purchase access online, please visit* **www.mysocialworklab.com**.)

1. **View page 13 of the group work module.** Here a worker uses a group approach to address Anna's concern about body type. How might the worker also intervene on this problem at other levels of practice including individual, family, community, and society?

2. **Contrast pages 4, 6, 7, and 9 of the child welfare module with pages 18, 19, and 20.** Earlier pages depict a problem-centered investigation of potential child abuse. Later pages show more empowering actions. Which worker behaviors are empowering? Which are not?

PRACTICE TEST

Critical Thinking

1. Which of the following statements is NOT an assumption about change from an empowerment perspective?
   a. Enduring change builds on strengths.
   b. Change is inevitable.
   c. You must solve a problem to find a solution.
   d. There are likely multiple solutions to any one challenge.

2. Julio Montez is learning about praxis as an element of social work practice. Which of the following statements is LEAST likely an element of praxis?
   a. Praxis has a defined end point.
   b. Praxis involves reflection.
   c. Praxis includes an element of action.
   d. Praxis is a continuous looping process.

3. The initial or engagement phase of empowering practice is called the _____ phase.
   a. discovery
   b. development
   c. dialogue
   d. relationship building

4. Assessing the resources of clients in the context of the social and physical environments occurs during the _____ phase of empowering practice.
   a. discovery
   b. development
   c. dialogue
   d. competence clarification

5. Practice activities associated with intervention and evaluation are involved in the _____ phase of empowering practice.
   a. discovery
   b. development
   c. dialogue
   d. activating

6. Kay Landon and the Ingersolls are creating a plan of action. This work is a part of the _____.
   a. development phase
   b. discovery phase
   c. planning phase
   d. dialogue phase

7. When Tony Marelli and his client end their working relationship, their final work together involves the empowering process called _____.
   a. recognizing success
   b. integrating gains
   c. terminating the relationship
   d. framing solutions

8. Since Janet Crause is interested in mezzolevel practice, she will be applying a generalist approach to practice to facilitate changes in a(n) _____.
   a. family group
   b. support group
   c. organization
   d. community

Policy Practice

9. When school social worker Alisha Shelton becomes involved in addressing the legal and human rights issues related to undocumented immigrants, she is participating in _____ activities.
   a. microlevel
   b. mezzolevel
   c. macrolevel
   d. discovery level

10. When Kay Langdon and the Ingersolls agree on a preliminary purpose for their work together, they are _____.
    a. framing solutions
    b. defining directions
    c. assessing resource systems
    d. articulating situations

Log onto **MySocialWorkLab** once you have completed the Practice Test above to take your Chapter Exam and demonstrate your knowledge of this material.

Answers

1) c 2) a 3) c 4) a 5) b 6) c 7) b 8) c 9) c 10) b

6

Forming Partnerships

CONNECTING CORE COMPETENCIES *in this chapter*

| Professional Identity | Ethical Practice | Critical Thinking | Diversity in Practice | Human Rights & Justice | Research Based Practice | Human Behavior | Policy Practice | Practice Contexts | Enga Asse Inter Eva |

Relationships between social workers and clients are fundamentally relationships between human beings. Whether working with an individual or a whole community system, social workers are connecting with other humans to achieve mutual purposes. The relationships formed by social workers and clients differ from social relationships. Although they are friendly, social workers and clients are not friends. Although these relationships are genuine, they have designated purposes and defined endings. In addition to being spontaneous and personable, social work relationships are deliberate and professional. Successful professional partnerships are complex and directed toward goals. Social workers and clients carefully construct and monitor their relationships to ensure that they meet the purposes for which they exist.

Within the helping relationship, participants establish trust, sort out their respective roles and responsibilities, and develop patterns of interaction necessary to engage in a process for change. To the extent that this relationship nurtures and encourages mutual participation, it is empowering. Practitioners and clients work together as collaborative partners, with each serving as a resource for the other.

When the social work relationship is a partnership, the relationship, itself, is an empowering resource for change. "Partnering" with clients means initiating the working relationship on a basis of "collaboration, trust, and shared power; accepting the client's definition of the problem; identifying and building upon the client's strengths; actively involving the client in the change process; experiencing a sense of personal power within the helping relationship" (Gutiérrez, 1989, p. 7). To meet the purposes of this collaborative partnership, practitioners need a conceptual understanding of the relationship, effective communication and interpersonal skills, abilities to relate cross-culturally, and social work ethics and values to guide their transactions. This chapter discusses how workers develop relationships with clients that are collaborative and empowering. In detail, this chapter

- Describes the qualities and structure of an empowering worker-client partnership
- Articulates the initial steps of developing a working partnership with a client
- Lists the characteristics that distinguish a worker-client relationship from a social relationship
- Guides workers to consider how power, privilege, and culture influence the achievement of a worker-client partnership
- Explains confidentiality and its impact on worker-client relationships

Practitioners who apply these concepts will build partnerships with clients that encourage openness and collaboration in all phases of the professional relationship.

COLLABORATION AND PARTNERSHIP

To actualize the strengths perspective and encourage empowerment, social workers and clients must collaborate as partners. Working with clients as collaborative partners is grounded in the tradition of the social work principle of self-determination (Sullivan, 1992). Empowerment-based social workers respect what client systems already know and can do (Evans, 1992). In short, they recognize client strengths and competence. Graybeal (2007) says that "the art of collaboration depends on finding ways to acknowledge, understand, and incorporate the client's world view into every aspect of practice" (p. 519) and concludes that "the art of practice is embedded in the capacity of the individual practitioner to form working alliances with clients, and to abstract from the generalities of accumulated knowledge to the particulars and the exigencies of a moment in time" (p. 521).

The phrase, "begin where the client is," expresses a fundamental social work practice imperative. Strengths-focused social workers interpret "begin where the client is" as a charge to discover potential strengths and resources, support developing competencies, and base constructive solutions on what already works for the client. This view has profound implications for relationships between social workers and clients.

The Dilemma of Social Workers as Experts

If we are to reject a culture of dependency on experts, we need to use a different vocabulary.

—Julian Rappaport

Reverence toward social workers as experts fabricates a hierarchy of haves and have-nots. In this view, proficient social work experts have the knowledge, insight, and ideas to bestow on inept clients who lack these qualities. Proactive professionals take charge of passive clients. Masterful social workers commence action and ineffectual client systems are acted on. Interpreted bluntly, the expert professionals are the champs, and the clients are the chumps!

Social workers beware! Traps exist in this definition of social workers as experts and clients as passive recipients, so no successful way out is available. If clients don't improve, then, of course, social workers are to blame. If clients get better, then social workers get the credit along with the responsibility of being the champion of keeping clients' lives on track. Ultimately, when expert social workers win, passive clients lose their sense of competence and independence. Weick (1983) further describes the insidious nature of this dependency or process of "giving over":

> The process of human judgment has been radically overturned, and, as a consequence, knowledge that is naturally accessible to people because it is personal knowledge is no longer admitted or accepted by them. The result is that their knowledge about themselves becomes partially or wholly hidden. In addition, whatever information they give to the professional is without meaning until the professional confers meaning on it. What is seen, therefore, at the base of the giving over process, is a willingness to give someone else power to define one's personal reality. (p. 468)

This configuration depicts a hierarchy of power and authority. The worker is the expert authority with decision-making power, and the client comes to depend solely on the power resources of the social worker or struggles with the worker to gain a share of the power. This one-sided perspective on expertise is the antithesis of empowerment!

The Rewards of Clients as Experts

Social workers bring professional expertise about change processes to the relationship, but they are not the sole experts. Social workers who practice from an empowerment perspective realize that social workers and clients have complementary roles and recognize the value of clients' experiences and competencies. According to Labassi and Maluccio (1986), clients bring their own assets and potentialities, whereas social workers contribute knowledge about strategies to facilitate change and information that will assist clients in making choices and achieving their goals. An empowerment view summons social workers to suspend any tendency to disbelieve clients and to acknowledge clients' expertise. Clients are the most qualified experts about their own situations. Quite simply, they know their situations and capabilities best.

The Social Worker's Role

Viewing clients as experts on their own situations directs workers to redefine their roles in more egalitarian and consultative ways (Cox & Parsons, 1992). Informed by an egalitarian view, social workers take on the roles of working in partnerships with clients, whereas, from a consultative view, social workers act as mentors in their interactions with clients. Social work clients in Cohen's (1998) study varied in their preferences for partnerships and mentorships. Some liked a more *client-directed* approach, as reflected by the partnership agreement. Others preferred a *client-centered* approach "with workers using their expert knowledge and skills to provide clients with advice and guidance" (p. 438). Significantly, all clients in Cohen's study expressed dissatisfaction with authoritarian workers. Clients clearly wanted to be in charge of what happened in the relationship, even when that meant they could decide when they wanted workers to be in charge.

Clients' power in defining the relationship is central to an empowerment approach. Well-meaning professionals who control the helping process and make decisions for their clients undermine clients' efficacy. Paternalistic actions impede empowerment! To this end, workers continually monitor their behavior for paternalistic tendencies by asking

1. With what degree of concentration do I listen to and consider the explicit and implicit communications of the clients or constituents to whom I am responsible?

2. Do I silently discount the opinions of any client, client group, or constituent? If so, why so? And what can I do to exchange my silence for dialogue with that person or group?

3. When I recommend a particular course of action to a client, do I take ample care and time to elicit from him or her alternative proposals before seeking agreement on the nature and sequence of steps to be taken?

4. Has any client given me feedback that I have been remote, intimidating, or inaccessible? If so, what more can I learn from that person about the basis for her or his impression of my unavailability?

5. Do I use acronyms, abbreviations, proper names, or specialized language that are foreign to clients in their presence without defining these terms?

6. When circumstances force me to rush a client or constituent or to keep him or her waiting, in what ways do I make amends?

7. When my professional duty requires me to violate a client's preferences, do I explain my actions and reasoning to that client in as open, direct, and respectful a manner as possible?

8. When I feel protective of a client, do I inspect the situation with special care to make sure that I am not underestimating the client or exaggerating my own importance or capability?

9. When I find myself thinking primarily about the problems that a client faces, do I make a conscious effort in my contemplation to pay closer attention to his or her strengths and imagination? (Simon, 1994, pp. 188–189)

Empowerment demands the centrality of the perspectives of client systems in all aspects of social work practice. Collaborative social workers not only begin where the client is, but they also continue to stay with the client system's perspective throughout all phases of the change process.

Agency Influences on Worker–Client Relationships

The organizational context influences the degree to which social workers and clients can achieve a true partnership. "The question remains as to whether social work practice can fully realize the goals of shared power, mutuality, and collaboration associated with feminist and empowerment-oriented practice models when client/worker relationships are embedded in a hierarchical power structure that simultaneously transcends and impacts on power relationships within the dyad" (Cohen, 1998, p. 441). Workers may need to intervene within their own agencies to ensure that they have the necessary power to share with clients. Agencies can provide support through policies favoring collaborative methods and training initiatives designed to equip workers with partnership skills (Marsh & Fisher, 1992). Only when social workers, themselves, experience empowerment in their professional lives can they implement an empowering approach to practice.

MAKING INITIAL CONTACTS

Effective social workers begin immediately to promote a client's hopes and active participation. Workers do not wait until implementing action plans to facilitate empowerment. Instead, they consistently act in empowering ways from the outset. Practitioners encourage clients to become full partners by responding to clients with reflective listening skills, offering clients assistance that corresponds to their perceived needs and encouraging their active participation in all facets of decision making (Dunst, 1993). Even in the apparently routine tasks of beginning the relationship, workers and clients are already setting patterns that will influence the success of their work.

Recognizing What Clients Bring

Clients experience a variety of thoughts and feelings as they enter working relationships with social workers. Perhaps clients have had previous relationships with helping professionals. Maybe they have specific knowledge about the agency, social workers, or the type of service, predisposing them to trust or resist services. Many clients are directed to social workers by others. The way that clients feel about these referral sources also influences their preconceptions. Each of us approaches new relationships based on our previous experiences. With clients, whatever stories precede their entry into a professional social work relationship inevitably define that partnership.

Maluccio's (1979) research examined clients' perceptions at the time they initiated contact with a family service agency. As might be expected, these new clients reported feelings of distress, discomfort, and confusion. Additionally, they described feelings of hope for finding a solution in comments such as "straighten things out," "get quick answers," and "find a snappy solution" (p. 5). Interestingly, clients also reported they received encouragement from other professionals or family friends who prompted their contact with the worker. Clients' initial expectations reflect discouragement about their own abilities to overcome their problems combined with optimism and encouragement about working with social workers.

Other commentary on clients' perspectives emphasizes the significance of effective communication and interpersonal ambiance (O'Donnell & Giovannoni, 2006; Scheyett & Diehl, 2004). After reflecting on the stigma and dehumanizing effects of chronic and persistent mental illness, consumers indicated that social workers were more helpful "when they could convey optimism and belief in the consumer's abilities, when they asked consumers for their ideas and opinions about what might help a particular problem, and they gave consumers choices and options" (Scheyett & Diehl, p. 443). They recommended that social workers ask such questions as "What kinds of things are important to you?" and "What do you think should happen?" (p. 443). In a study of Family Resource Center service delivery strategies, O'Donnell and Giovannoni found that the highest client satisfaction ratings reflected clients' perceptions of the warmth and interpersonal relationship skills of staff. Engaging clients in respectful conversations sets the stage for collaborative partnerships.

Social workers should take heart, as many clients do enter professional relationships with seeds of trust and hope. Even clients whose lives have predisposed them to distrust and suspicion often remain alert to clues that this professional relationship may hold promise. The fact is that ambivalence characterizes the approach of most people to any new relationship. It makes sense that we should begin with a "maybe yes" and "maybe no," or a "wait and see" attitude. Social workers cannot predetermine the expectations of clients or head off their feelings of ambivalence; however, social workers can influence first impressions either reinforcing hope or inadvertently accentuating negative feelings. Workers must examine their own predisposition toward clients and construct productive assumptions about client potential if they wish to reveal optimism and confidence from the moment of the first contact.

Initiating Collaboration

Early interactions reveal more than a worker's expectations for success. How the worker organizes the meeting around the client's experience and what the worker discusses about the client's responsibility in the process also begins to shape the degree to which the client collaborates. A worker who commandeers the early phases of the relationship may initiate a cycle of dependency throughout the work. In contrast, a worker who openly discusses the need for the client's active participation, invites a client's expertise, and elicits a client's perspective sets a pattern for partnership. Practitioners launch empowering relationships within the first meeting when they communicate positive expectations about success and accentuate the need for client participation.

Beginning Steps: A Practice Example

During their first meeting with a client, workers have much to accomplish. Tasks include making a personal connection, clarifying the purpose of the meeting, describing the worker's role, exploring the client's issues, and wrapping up the meeting with a clear direction that defines the next step. Shulman

(2006) also stresses the need for workers and clients to discuss issues related to power and authority. Workers use their natural abilities to implement these processes flexibly to match the unique characteristics of each client system. As an example of this beginning process, Karen McBride, a Case Manager at the Northside Hospital Outreach Program, goes through the steps of initiating a relationship with the Fuentes family, her newest client.

The referral

The medical social worker in the emergency room at Northside Hospital referred the Fuentes family to Karen only a few days before. Doctors there had treated Juanita Fuentes for a broken leg—injured while Juanita was helping her mother, Rosa Hernandez, down from their second-floor apartment to a taxi waiting below. Mrs. Hernandez, herself, was not injured. But Juanita, even while being treated for her own injuries, talked about her concern for how she would manage to take care of her mother while her leg mended. Her own daughter Nora was not that helpful. And her husband? Well, Humberto had to work; sometimes he was away from home for days at a time. Karen's job as case manager would be to discover with the Fuentes family how best to meet the needs of Mrs. Hernandez and ensure the well-being of the family while Juanita's leg was healing.

Thinking ahead

As Karen walks up the street to the Fuentes family's apartment, she can feel her anxiety increase. The relative quiet she left in her office has given way to throngs of people, aromas of spicy food, and the sounds of Latin music—it's all a bit strange to Karen. Her pace quickens. Her eyes focus straight ahead. Karen realizes that she is clutching her briefcase tightly. She has to admit it. She feels uncomfortable, out of her culture, so to speak. It makes sense that she would feel this way in a place so different from her own suburban home and even different from the quiet city street where her office is located.

Karen recognizes that her feelings of strangeness might approximate the feelings of the Fuentes family members when she, a 28-year-old white, suburban social worker arrives at their door. Logically, they might be uncomfortable or have doubts about whether someone who is so young and from a different culture can really understand and respect their situation. Karen will have to work quickly to help the family feel comfortable with her as a person and a professional. Karen's own feelings will help her empathize with the family's response to her.

Karen also contemplates the purpose of her visit and the family's potential reactions. Even though the intent of the outreach program is to help families cope effectively with their medical difficulties, not all clients begin as eager participants. Karen wonders if Juanita will see this visit as an intrusion into her private affairs or as a threat to her way of caring for her mother. Karen doesn't yet know what previous experiences this family may have had with outside assistance, but this will certainly affect their initial comfort with her, too.

As a case manager, Karen has initiated relationships with many clients before. All are strangers to her at first, but they soon become people that she likes, respects, and often admires. But bridging that initial distance between having no relationship and forming a working partnership characterized by mutual respect, trust, and effective communication is no small leap, especially across a cultural gap. Working together with the Fuentes family will again test Karen's abilities to clarify the boundaries of the professional relationship, accept views and lifestyles other than her own, and give clients the freedom to move in directions that work best for them.

Diversity in Practice

Social workers and clients are likely to differ in many ways. How might differences in culture, life experience, and privilege affect a worker's ability to partner with a client?

Telephone work

The receptionist in the Northside Hospital's Outreach Program scheduled this appointment. The hospital social worker referred Juanita while she was still at the emergency room because the Fuentes family had no phone, and subsequent contact would be difficult. When Karen schedules appointments herself, she directly and succinctly identifies who she is, where she works, and why she is calling. She states her purpose and clearly outlines the client's privileges of how to respond.

With the Fuentes family, Karen would have described her purpose to assist the family to discover ways to care for Mrs. Hernandez while Juanita recovered. She would have assured the family that they were in control. For example, she would have told them that setting an appointment with her was completely their choice and, even if they met with her once, they were under no obligation to continue to see her or to do what she might suggest. Karen attends to power issues with each client from the first phone call to the last contact. She treats clients as partners from the beginning to the end of their work together.

Meeting and greeting clients

Without the advantage of an initial phone contact, Karen will have to work quickly to orient the Fuentes family to the purpose of her visit. This family needs to know who she is and what she is doing there. When Juanita Fuentes opens the door, Karen is direct: "Mrs. Fuentes? I'm Karen McBride from the Northside Hospital Outreach Program. We have an appointment, arranged the day you were at the hospital." Juanita obviously is expecting her. Karen follows as Juanita maneuvers on crutches through the kitchen to the living room where Mrs. Hernandez is waiting. As Juanita introduces Karen to her mother, Karen again explains her presence to the older woman. If Karen expects Mrs. Hernandez to be a contributing partner to their discussion, she has to include her in the conversation from the outset.

Within this brief introductory interchange, Karen learns two important aspects of relating to this family. She notes that Mrs. Hernandez speaks halting English. Karen will need to speak clearly and concretely to facilitate Mrs. Hernandez's participation. Karen also learns to call Juanita by her first name after Juanita requests that she do so. A respectful relationship always begins by addressing people in the ways they prefer.

Physical arrangements

Juanita's choice to meet in the living room is a good one. Everyone seems comfortable, and Karen can easily interact directly with either Juanita or Mrs. Hernandez. If this had not been the case, Karen would have requested a rearrangement. Building relationships with a family or group requires direct interactions with each member. When conducting a meeting in a client's home, Karen balances her respect for the family's style, property, and privacy with her own preferences for an arrangement that facilitates family involvement. Karen wants all relevant family members in the room and actively participating. She finds it more empowering to talk with people than about them.

When Karen asks Juanita's permission to turn off the television, she completes her physical preparation for the session. Karen's comment—"I want to make sure I can hear everything you have to say, and the TV may be distracting. Would you mind if we turned it off?"—shows her respect for the family. Karen consistently defines the meeting as work that requires a client's full attention. In her own office, she doesn't take phone calls or interact with other staff when meeting with clients. Families have her full attention, and likewise, she wants theirs. In home visits, Karen also wants the meeting to be focused and productive. When phone calls or visitors interrupt home meetings, Karen lets clients handle the interruption, but then discusses the need to control interruptions and focus on the meeting, or reschedule if necessary.

Karen accepts the cup of coffee that Juanita offers. Her agency's previous policy restricted workers from accepting gifts of any kind from clients. Now there is flexibility to accept gifts of hospitality in culturally appropriate and friendly ways. Clients have their own traditions of initiating relationships with workers, and Karen is sensitive to defining relationships mutually rather than rigidly structuring the visit to meet her own needs. With the Fuentes family, Karen briefly socializes, describing her trip over from the office and inquiring about Juanita's leg before getting down to business. Her experience has taught her that it is culturally appropriate with most Latino clients to establish social contact first.

Getting down to business

After the brief social exchange, Karen proceeds with the task at hand. Karen never assumes that clients know all about the social service network. Even from an insider's view, Karen still finds it confusing. For Juanita and Mrs. Hernandez, the connections between Karen's visit, Juanita's trip to the hospital, and her need for assistance in caring for Mrs. Hernandez may be hazy. Again, Karen repeats her name as she hands each of the women one of her business cards. She describes her role and the purpose of the agency for which she works. She clearly traces how she comes to be with them on this day. She recounts Juanita's conversation with the hospital social worker, the worker's call to the Northside Hospital Outreach Program, the appointment made by the receptionist, the information being passed on to Karen, and her arrival at their door. Karen wants to demystify the social work world for this family, a world she hopes they will learn to activate for themselves.

When both women indicate they understand who Karen is, she hands them each a brochure describing her program's services. Karen is pleased that the pamphlet is multilingual. She notices that Mrs. Hernandez follows along in the Spanish language section as Karen highlights important features of the program. Karen stresses that participating in these services is voluntary and has no direct costs to clients. She also talks about confidentiality, assuring the family that she keeps their information private as long as no one in the home is in danger. Karen points out the guarantee of confidentiality and the exceptions as stated in the program brochure. When she completes her explanations, she asks the women if they have questions. Both agree that they understand. Karen notices that their nonverbal messages also indicate they are clear on what she is saying.

Respecting the client's perspective

Having completed this general business, it's time to get down to specifics, and that means Karen turns over the dialogue to Juanita and Mrs. Hernandez. Her simple statement of "Now, it's your turn" immediately activates both women, who relate their own parts of the story of Juanita's injury and the difficulties they are having. Karen is careful to respond to each woman, validating their different views and encouraging their continued sharing. Karen has dual goals to understand the specifics of this family's situation and, simultaneously, to initiate a supportive relationship. To do so, she responds with warmth, acceptance, respect, and empathy.

Karen even attends to building relationships with family members who are not present in the room. When Juanita defends Humberto as hard working and caring, yet unable to help with her mother, Karen accepts her view. When Juanita describes her 17-year-old daughter Nora, who still lives at home, as unwilling to help, Karen's neutral response, "So Nora doesn't think that her help is the answer here," reveals a nonjudgmental acceptance of the choices that Nora is making while indicating to Juanita that she is listening. Karen knows that families work in the ways they do for good reasons. When building relationships with new clients, Karen accepts their current functioning as workable under the present circumstances. She also makes sure that she allies herself with every family member—even those not in the room—because a working relationship with each member of the client system will most likely elicit everyone's best cooperation and contributions.

Continuing the relationship work

The initial interchange between Karen and the Fuentes family focuses on launching and defining the social worker–client relationship. However, the dialogue of the first few minutes does not complete the work of building the relationship. Within this first meeting, Karen will continue to shape the partnership as she talks with them to understand their challenges, identify their existing resources and strengths, and clarify the purpose of their work together. In subsequent meetings, Karen will maintain her focus on the quality of the relationship so that the family continues to feel comfortable enough to share their thoughts, express their feelings, and assert their priorities. No matter what phase of the work, Karen will integrate her professional skills with her personal qualities to ensure that her relationship with the Fuentes family remains a resource for its members.

QUALITIES OF PROFESSIONAL PARTNERSHIPS

The workers' human qualities are emphasized by clients more than his or her technical skills.
—Anthony Maluccio

With whom do you find yourself talking freely, sharing your innermost thoughts, and revealing the depth of your feelings? Whom do you trust? What characteristics draw you to others? What makes some people approachable and others not? Personal qualities and communication styles can enhance or detract from interpersonal relationships. Likewise, social workers' personal qualities either support or inhibit their success in developing and maintaining empowering relationships with clients.

Research validates the importance of personal qualities in building professional relationships. In his book *Learning from Clients,* Maluccio (1979) reports that "the worker's human qualities are emphasized by clients more than his or her technical skills" (p. 125). Those personal qualities most valued by clients include empathy, genuineness, acceptance, objectivity, and concreteness. Others agree that social workers need to invest themselves in their relationships with clients in genuinely caring ways. As one consumer put it, "'Maybe we need a different definition of friendship here—that the relationship should be friendly and caring, but doesn't have to involve lots of camaraderie or going fishing together. I know you have limits, but let's have a real relationship'" (Scheyett & Diehl, 2004, p. 443). Results of a study by Hopps, Pinderhughes, and Shankar (1995) indicate that workers' attributes of caring and flexibility supported positive outcomes with clients. Competent social workers successfully blend their personal characteristics with professional skills when they respond with genuineness, acceptance, respect, trustworthiness, empathy, sensitivity to diversity, and purposefulness.

Box 6.1 The Ethic of Care

At its essence, "social work is social caretaking" (Weick, 2000, p. 401). To care is to feel interest or concern, to provide encouragement or guidance, or to render some assistance. Caring feelings and actions characterize all supportive interpersonal relationships, and they are appropriate qualities in social worker–client relationships as well. The ethic of care embodies social work's concern with maximizing human potential, respecting human dignity, and treating each client as a unique individual. Caring is a "basic moral principle" in social work, "a basic good which social work practice is designed to implement" (Imre, 1982, p. 103). The ethic of care fits with the core social work values of acceptance and respect for human dignity.

A client's felt experience of care goes beyond a worker's simple interpersonal response. Genuine caring is demonstrated in an environment that supports individual achievement and affords the opportunities and resources for personal well-being. Focusing on individual care without regard to ensuring a caring society abandons the core social work purpose of social justice and results in professionals who are "unfaithful angels" (Specht & Courtney, 1994). Without an eye to creating a caring context, a worker's individual care response may function to control or pacify clients. Clients are defined as victims, and a worker's caring response leaves clients as the dependent recipients of professionals' paternalistic and maternalistic deeds.

Ethically based and reflective caring does more than support clients as they take risks to improve their situations. Caring stirs workers and clients to take action. Research focusing on motivations for social activism among a group of women uncovered a relationship between social activism and the ethic of care (Faver, 2001). The three central motivations for social activism—"to ensure rights, to fulfill responsibilities, and to restore relationships and build community"—were founded on a concern for others, not only those immediately known to those activists interviewed, but also on a concern for socially, culturally, and geographically distant others fueled by a recognition of interconnectedness and interdependence. The ethic of care is not separate or distinct from justice; rather, it is an integral component of just social work practice (Orme, 2002).

Genuineness

Professional Identity

Social workers represent the social work profession. What are the defining professional qualities of social work that practitioners demonstrate in their relationships with clients?

Social workers seek to create a comfortable atmosphere in which clients can "be themselves." Certainly, clients are most likely to do so if workers are doing the same. When workers are genuine, they initiate authentic relationships with their clients. Drawing on the definitive works of Truax, Mitchell, Carkhuff, and Rogers, Fischer (1978) describes genuineness as a characteristic that facilitates communication and builds open relationships. Genuineness refers to social workers "being 'real.' This means, simply, that at any given moment, workers really are whatever their responses denote. . . . In fact, genuineness may be best understood as the absence of phoniness, as nondefensiveness, as congruence, and as spontaneity" (p. 199). Who social workers are as people shows through and enhances their professional roles.

Workers who lack genuineness fail to connect with clients in productive ways. Clients in Maluccio's (1979) study described such workers as "too nice, phony, put on. Too low key. Too calm and collected. Doing [a] job as a job. Above it all, almighty. Mechanical. Businesslike" (p. 124). These comments depict ingenuine social workers as distant, indifferent, and contrived. In contrast, genuineness liberates social work practitioners to "be themselves" (Egan, 2002).

When Karen McBride interacts with Juanita Fuentes and Mrs. Hernandez, she does so honestly as a concerned person rather than a mechanical professional. When Mrs. Hernandez remarks, "Well, you know, that's the Mexican way," Karen responds with "I'm not really sure—could you explain it to me?" Karen is aware of herself, her similarities and differences from her clients, and her clients' reactions to her. She openly acknowledges these differences rather than distancing herself from the interaction to appear "professional."

Genuineness is different from total honesty. Being genuine does not mean that workers disclose everything they are thinking and feeling about clients. Instead, it means that what workers share is "a real aspect of themselves, not a response growing out of defensiveness or a merely 'professional' response that has been learned and repeated" (Fischer, 1978, p. 199). Being genuine also is not the same as being personal. Professional relationships differ from social relationships. Although social workers are friendly and genuinely interested in their clients, they find other ways to expand their networks of friends. In responding genuinely to clients, social workers maintain the qualities of purpose and standards of ethics that define relationships as professional.

Acceptance and Respect

Social workers draw on their personal qualities of acceptance and respect in building relationships with clients. Workers who demonstrate acceptance affirm the worth of others while at the same time holding them accountable for the consequences of their behaviors (Barker, 2003; Berlin, 2005). Respectful social workers regard clients as partners, listen to their opinions, communicate cordially, honor cultural differences, and credit clients as having strengths and potential.

Social workers also manifest acceptance through behaviors that communicate unconditional positive regard and nonpossessive warmth. Nonpossessive warmth involves

> communication of respect, acceptance, liking, caring and concern for the client in a nondominating way . . . Thus, the client is accepted as a person with human potentialities: nonpossessive warmth involves valuing the client as a person, separate from any evaluation of his or her behavior and thoughts. . . . Rather [than approving or sanctioning behavior], it means that despite such thoughts and behaviors, workers are able to communicate, in both the form and content of what they say and how they act, that they appreciate the meaning of such thoughts and behavior to their clients and deeply prize their clients as individuals. (Fischer, 1973, pp. 196–197)

Unconditional positive regard and nonpossessive warmth are one-way expressions. Social workers demonstrate them without expecting anything in return. However, experience confirms that when social workers consistently treat clients in accepting and respectful ways, clients respond in kind.

A positive view of humankind makes it easier to accept and respect others. The ecosystems perspective offers such a view. As you will recall from Chapter 2, this framework explains all human behavior as evolutionary, adaptive, and functional in context. Social workers appreciate and even admire the unique and creative ways clients match their particular resources with the demands of their environments.

The ways that social workers communicate with clients reveal their acceptance and respect. Accepting workers restrain from asking judgmental "why questions" that critique clients' previous choices. Instead, workers use words such as "what, who, when, where, and how" to arrive at a mutual understanding of events without leaving the impression that clients are doing something wrong. Acceptance means that social workers listen carefully to comprehend rather than critique what they see and hear. Respect means that social workers recognize that clients are doing the best they can under their present circumstances.

Names and respect

One concrete way of showing respect is in the way that social workers treat clients' names. Some workers address all members of client systems by their first names in an attempt to create a friendly atmosphere. But Smith (1996) cautions against this approach, especially in cross-cultural relationships, based on her observations: "Well-meaning white social work interns sought to convey warmth and concern by addressing their older African American clients on a first-name basis. The clients were often angered and insulted by what was perceived as a lack of respect" (p. 291).

In their study of cross-racial social worker–client relationships, Proctor and Davis (1994) also concluded that workers should "address the client by his or her last name" (p. 317). Workers are free to address clients other than in the more formal style of using last names in instances in which clients specifically request workers to call them by their first names or nicknames.

Examining naming practices in describing groups of people is also imperative. Do clients prefer to be described as African American or Black? Hispanic, Latino, or the more specific Mexican American? Weaver (2000) provides another example when she describes the significant distinction in meaning for indigenous people between their identification as part of a tribe or a nation, noting "the term 'tribe' has been used to minimize the social structures and civilizations" of American Indians while "the term carries with it a stronger sense of sovereignty" (p. 8). Culturally competent ways of relating to clients require sensitivity to the meanings associated with naming practices and honors clients with the privilege of naming themselves.

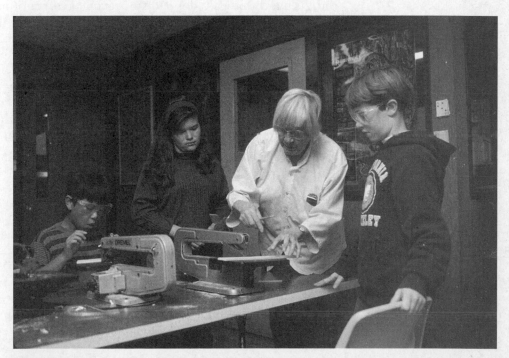

Genuineness, trustworthiness, and acceptance and respect are essential qualities in helping relationships.

Trustworthiness

The presence or absence of trust or the ability to take risks in the context of interpersonal relationships affects the social worker–client relationship. To reach goals, clients must feel comfortable enough to exchange something that they know for some new way of doing things that has unknown potential. Taking these risks requires trust. Trustworthiness is a multidimensional personal quality based on the client's perception of the worker's reliability, honesty, credibility, sincerity, and integrity. It springs from a nonthreatening and open personal approach nestled in the context of professional expertise.

Many factors contribute to developing trust. Trust is reciprocal. In other words, "to get it you must give it." For clients to trust social workers, social workers must trust clients. Social workers trust clients to be experts about their own situations, as open and honest as is currently possible, and motivated to make necessary changes. Each of us knows our own experience best. When others recognize and validate our experience, we begin to trust their value and to see the potential rewards of a relationship with them. Clients who experience a social worker's trust are more likely to trust the resources the worker has to offer.

Interactions influence the movement of trust along a continuum from no trust to complete trust. As social workers follow through on their own commitments, meet a client's expectations, and demonstrate their acceptance of a client's perspectives, trust increases. When social workers violate a client's developing sense of trust through what the client perceives to be distortion, insensitivity, or betrayal, trust plummets and struggles to recover. Trust builds slowly over time through repeated trustworthy acts, but plunges in the blink of an eye. Parents can tell you that it takes a lifetime of relating to build enough trust to give their teenager the keys to the car and only one night of drinking and driving to have to start building trust all over again.

Each social worker–client relationship begins with a different level of trust. Individual differences depend on preconceived notions, personality variables, and cultural norms. A client's previous experience with trusting others influences how trust in the worker evolves. Perceived similarities and differences between clients and social workers as well as current levels of comfort or stress also affect a client's capability to trust. Wherever on the continuum trust begins, it evolves continuously in the relationship. Trust increases or decreases with respect to the experiences of clients and social workers within and outside of professional relationships. Practitioners develop trusting relationships with clients purposefully, by deliberately behaving in trustworthy ways.

Empathy

Clients experience support and trust when social workers respond with empathy. Empathy is "the helper's ability to perceive and communicate, accurately and with sensitivity, the feelings of the client and the meaning of those feelings" (Fischer, 1973, p. 329). For a client to experience the worker's empathy, a worker must accurately distinguish the client's situation and simultaneously "feel with the client, understand how his or her own feelings are different from the client's and hold in abeyance any cognitive distortion such as stereotyping or value judging" (Pinderhughes, 1979, p. 316). Empathic communication reflects respect and nonjudgmental acceptance.

Empathy differs significantly from both pity and sympathy. To understand this difference, visualize a response showing pity. Do you see someone patting another on the head while lamenting, "Poor you?" Responses flavored with pity suggest others are helpless and incapable. Feeling sorry for someone clearly indicates pity. Likewise, sympathy grows from viewing others as weak and vulnerable. Showing pity and sympathy defines a hierarchy of those who are competent and capable and those who are unfortunate and needy. When social workers express pity or sympathy, they disempower clients.

In contrast, when social workers respond with empathy, they validate the perspectives of clients. Clients experience the affirmation of having someone join with and understand their thoughts and feelings. Empathy communicates that social workers are with clients. Empathic support brings the power of affiliation to clients who are struggling to meet life's challenges. "Empathy is being able to finish a [client's] sentence. Being empathic, though, is not finishing that sentence" (Book, 1988, p. 423). Empathy is an "act of loving imagination" (Keith-Lucas, 1972) that empowers clients to work toward goals experiencing their competence, efficacy, and responsibility.

Cultural Sensitivity

With so many systems involved on both sides of this transactional relationship, social workers and clients find much in common as well as much that is different. Successfully responding to both similarities and differences is central to building cross-cultural relationships. Social workers should maintain an openness to cultural similarities and differences without judging attitudes, values, or behaviors as either inherently right or wrong (Nakanishi & Ritter, 1992). Perceived similarities lead to a sense of understanding, empathy, and trust. Similarities bond relationships and establish rapport. Sharing such characteristics as race, ethnicity, religion, or other defining characteristics may create commonalities that contribute to, but in no way ensure, a cognitive match (Walker, 2001).

Discussing cultural differences

Discovering differences is inevitable. The ways workers and clients differ are infinite; possibilities include gender, age, race, ethnicity, lifestyle, socioeconomic status, religion, and values, among others. With larger client systems, differences multiply geometrically. These differences affect the dynamics of the helping relationship. Perceived differences may lead to questions about the ability to achieve a mutual understanding. Social workers acknowledge differences directly and respect the client's worldview. Rather than viewing cultural differences as threatening, empowering social workers explore these differences as resources in generating culturally relevant solutions.

Accepting cultural differences is not as easy as we might like it to be. Cultural memberships define the very ways that we view the world. Western thinking tends to value human control over nature, an orientation to the future, individual autonomy, competition, and the work ethic. In contrast, ethnic minorities often have a nonwestern perspective that values the natural environment, links to the past, community well-being, and extended family (Lum, 2004).

These differences in values, perspectives, and experience are enormous. They make cross-cultural relationships vulnerable to miscommunication and conflicting goals. Bridging cultural gaps requires appreciation of diversity, client-focused responding, and open communication. Practitioners may hesitate to ask direct questions about cultural background, racial identity, sexual orientation, prejudice, or discrimination, out of concern they might offend clients or appear incompetent (Rogers, 1995; Smith, 1996; Woody & Green, 2001). However, research on cross-cultural communication has found that clients are more likely to respect workers who are able to talk openly about cultural differences. Respondents in one study "interpreted such questions as a sign of interest and respect" (Smith, p. 296). Proctor and Davis (1994) found that levels of rapport with clients increased when workers acknowledged and spoke directly with clients about their difficulties in comprehending cultural differences or life circumstances presented by the client.

Box 6.2 Relationships and Effectiveness: A Research-Practice Connection

What works in helping clients reach their goals? What techniques have proven effective? The press for accountability by workers and services to achieve desired outcomes propels social work researchers to investigate what works. Contemporary research reinforces the conclusions of past studies that a strong and positive helping alliance, that is, a close and respectful relationship between worker and client, is the key to effectiveness, possibly exceeding the importance of the particular change strategies implemented. This conclusion generalizes across fields of practice.

In the field of child welfare, studies reveal the pivotal role relationships play in achieving successful outcomes. Dore and Alexander (1996) completed an extensive review of research on family preservation services to evaluate the impact of relationship factors in three areas of practice—individual work with clients, couple and family practice, and group work. They concluded, "there is substantial evidence that the helping alliance that forms between client and worker is directly related to positive therapeutic outcome" (p. 350). Dawson and Berry (2002), too, identified factors from child welfare research shown successfully to engage parents in helping processes, lead to successful outcomes, and prevent out-of-home placements of children. Interestingly, worker behaviors associated with honoring client preferences and increasing client skills have the most positive effects. These behaviors include "setting of mutually satisfactory goals, providing services that clients find relevant and helpful, focusing on client skills rather than insights, and spending sufficient time with clients to demonstrate skills and provide necessary resources" (p. 312).

Studies conducted with parents of children with disabilities also point to worker–client collaboration as central to effective helping. Itzhaky and Schwartz (2000) found that a partnership relationship, as defined by the parents' participation in decision making at the case and organizational levels, was a key element in producing a positive outcome. Dunst and colleagues (2002) also concluded that the benefits of participatory help giving, including strategies that facilitate clients' active involvement in identifying goals and planning courses of action, are more significant than specific strategies in promoting client empowerment. When comparing client outcomes in family-centered programs in the United States and Australia, Dempsey and Dunst (2004) reached a similar conclusion. Family members in both countries underscored the significance of both the relational and participatory dimensions of help giving for family empowerment.

Research also shows the power of relationships in group work practice, both worker-to-member relationships and member-to-member relationships. In her research, Parsons (2001) identified key elements associated with relationships in women's groups—support through acceptance, validation, and interdependence. "To be accepted and nurtured and to have a chance to be in an interdependent relationship with others in the group appeared to facilitate the women's acceptance of themselves and encouraged them to be less blaming of and to believe in themselves" (p. 169). Parsons notes that even though the one worker clearly defined her role as a consultant on strategies for social change, members of the social action group still valued their relationship with the worker highly, identifying her as "someone who was there for us." One member reflected, "When you need someone to talk to, she is there and she listens. She asks you, well, what do you think you are going to do?" (p. 167).

For nearly a century, the social work profession has placed relationship at the heart of social work practice. Now, current research validates this tradition, proving the importance and the power of the relationship between practitioners and clients in achieving successful outcomes.

Purposefulness

In her classic book, *Social Casework: A Problem Solving Process,* Perlman (1957) defines the benchmark of a professional relationship as "its conscious purposefulness." Social work relationships are grounded in the values and purpose of the profession. In general, social work relationships strive to fulfill the profession's mission to improve quality of life by achieving a goodness of fit between persons and their physical and social environments. In particular, each unique client guides the direction and defines the parameters of the relationship with the social worker.

CONSTRUCTING EMPOWERING RELATIONSHIPS

To the extent that social workers and clients are able to achieve a true partnership, the relationship empowers. This type of partnership develops when both partners have control over their own lives. Each can choose to behave in ways that are congruent with their own particular beliefs and intent at any given time. Freedom springs from mutual respect, acceptance, and a constant sense of permission to "be who you are." Achieving this openness ensures equality and leads to an unguarded dialogue in which new perspectives, options, and choices surface continually. With such relationships come rights, responsibilities, and considerations of power.

Recognizing Rights

Being partners guarantees certain rights and privileges. Partners have permission to view situations in their own ways along with the privilege to cooperate with or resist others' viewpoints or requests. For example, considering a client's point of view does not require social workers to sacrifice their own integrity, value base, or professional roles. In other words, social workers' acceptance, respect, and nonjudgmentalism do not signify their approval of a client's behavior. Neither is the client under any mandate to accept the view of the social worker as anything but information on how someone else sees things.

All clients have rights (Figure 6.1). Even clients coerced into social work services maintain their privileges to think the way they think, feel the way they feel, and, to the extent that their behavior doesn't hurt themselves or others, behave the way they choose. Inside empowering social worker and client relationships is a shared belief in equality and common goals, yet freedom to hold differences in perspective.

Taking Responsibilities

Responsibilities accompany privileges. Credible social workers bring professional ethics, knowledge, and skills to their partnerships with clients. They take care of their own needs and wants outside the context of professional relationships. Within professional relationships, they work in an efficient and goal-directed manner, using practice-tested, research-based, and ethically sound strategies.

Clients, too, take responsibility. They are responsible for deciding what goals to select and for approving what strategies to use. When clients have control, then the choices they make belong to them, along with credit for their success.

Figure 6.1   Clients' Rights

Clients have rights:

- To be treated with dignity and respect
- To privacy through confidentiality
- To participate as collaborative partners in the change process
- To receive culturally sensitive treatment
- To have an equitable share of societal resources
- To view their challenges from their own perspective
- To participate in gathering and analyzing information
- To set their own goals
- To resist what social workers want
- To choose from among the various alternative interventions
- To negotiate the distribution of roles and responsibilities for themselves and the social worker
- To collaborate on evaluation processes
- To help determine time frames and know costs involved

Clients' active involvement in decision making not only leaves them accountable but promotes their sense of competence as well (Dunst, 1993).

Dual relationships

Serious problems and ethical issues arise when social workers assume secondary roles or dual relationships with clients, such as a personal friendship, business partnership, or sexual relationship (Hardina, 2004a; Johner, 2006; Mayer, 2005; Reamer, 2003a, 2003b, 2008; Ringstad, 2008; Strom-Gottfried, 1999, 2003). Dual relationships extend beyond relationships with individual clients. Social workers who work with macrosystem clients as consultants, grant writers, board members, and volunteers also need to attend to issues of conflict of interest.

The NASW *Code of Ethics* (1999a) explicitly condemns dual relationships and places the responsibility for setting clear boundaries on social workers: "Social workers—not their clients, their clients' relatives or other individuals with whom the client maintains a personal relationship—assume the full burden for setting clear, appropriate and culturally sensitive boundaries" (Section 1.09b).

Practitioners who engage in dual relationships risk disciplinary hearings and sanctions by the NASW and state licensing boards. Practitioners who commit sexual misconduct may find themselves subject to criminal action or a civil suit for malpractice. Moreover, because insurance companies consider sexual misconduct a flagrant breach of professional conduct, these practitioners may find themselves without the benefits of liability insurance coverage (Kurzman, 1995). In any form, dual relationships have the potential to exploit clients, cloud the judgments of professionals, and result in charges of professional misconduct.

Discussing Rights and Responsibilities

When social workers openly take their own responsibilities and privileges seriously and leave space for clients to do the same, they begin to balance and distribute power in the relationship. Empowering social workers directly state their philosophy of practice, clarify their perceptions about the corollary roles of social workers and clients, and talk specifically about their confidence in clients' abilities to reach their own goals. Discussing approaches and roles enlightens clients as to the expectations of the relationship and frees them to contribute to the process.

All social workers make conscious and deliberate choices about how to practice; however, these practice theories, principles, and intervention strategies are not their private domain. Clients have the right to know the approach of the particular professional with whom they're working. Practitioners should prepare an understandable explanation of their practice philosophy to share directly with clients. If workers' approaches and clients' preferences are a "mismatch," clients can seek to work with other professionals who practice in ways clients prefer.

When social workers formulate a clear picture of what they do, their blueprint clarifies the roles of "worker" and "client." In the example that follows, note how one social worker explains the collaborative process of an empowering practice approach:

Client: I'm here to find out what you think I should do.

Worker: Okay, but I need your help. The way I see things, you have a lot to offer to what we are going to be doing. In fact, you know your situation best. I count on you to let me know what's happening in your life outside of this relationship, where you want to end up, and make choices about what you think might work best.

Client: Sounds like I'm doing all the work. What will you be doing?

Worker: We both have responsibilities. You can count on me to help you make sense out of what we discover and locate resources that you might need. You bring the expert knowledge about your life. I'll be a guide who, hopefully, can work with you to put it together in a way that will get you where you want to go. Does that make sense to you?

Empowerment-based, strengths-focused social workers convey the expectation that client systems are active participants. When clients indicate that they want to sit back and let social workers do all the work, empowering social workers take time to explain the logical impossibility of this approach. Workers openly discuss the implications of dependency, reveal their belief in client strengths, and candidly admit that they are unable to implement the social work process without the client's contribution.

Augmenting Power

Collaborative partnerships evolve. Many clients enter social work relationships humbled by their perceived inability to handle challenges on their own. Some clients initially expect to give over their power to social workers. Social workers report that clients often request "answers" to their dilemmas even before the social workers have any realistic possibility of understanding their difficulties. Developing solutions takes work, not magic.

"Social worker as magician" is a fictitious role that has no roots in empowering social work practice. Social workers resist the temptation to take over clients' situations by offering quick fixes, standard cures, or free-flowing advice. Only when clients explore and discover their own power and options does the social work relationship engender maximal benefits. Even when clients enter the relationship relinquishing their power, social workers move quickly to shift the locus of power from worker-centered to client-controlled. Ultimately, successful clients conclude their work with practitioners with both the responsibility and the credit for the choices they made. The best preparation for enhancing competence is a growing pattern of control by clients that increases over the duration of the professional relationship.

Power differentials in the social worker–client relationship can, in and of themselves, oppress clients (Sakamoto & Pitner, 2005). Social workers actively guard against the temptation to take over the process. Social workers who seek to empower rather than to dazzle client systems restrain themselves from trying to solve clients' problems, be experts, and perform extraordinary feats. Amundson, Stewart, and Valentine (1993) describe the "temptations of power and certainty" to which helping professionals fall prey, based on their role and status and the needs of clients for the quick relief of a "pat answer." Being obsessed with expert knowledge blocks social workers from comprehending clients' actual real-life experiences. "As an antidote to undue emphasis upon power and certainty," they suggest "embracing curiosity and the desire to empower" (p. 117). The resulting approach frees social workers from imposing their own standards of what they consider "best" in favor of respecting and appreciating diverse solutions selected by the client.

Balancing power through self-disclosure

One way to help clients experience equality within the social work relationship is with the worker's selective use of self-disclosure. Workers who expect clients to be trusting and open may need to risk demonstrating these qualities first. "Appropriate self-disclosure can produce a mutual, rather than imbalanced, expectation of information sharing and contribute to a sense of good will toward the client" (Proctor & Davis, 1994, p. 317). Workers seeking to share power should "engage in the reciprocal self-disclosure expected by clients from particular cultural groups—for example, American Indians, some Puerto Ricans, and African Americans" (Pinderhughes, 1995, p. 138).

When Clients Feel Powerless

Rarely do clients engage social work services with the sense that they are in charge of their environments. Their feelings and thoughts are evident when clients say things like, "The world is getting me down," or "Nothing I do seems to make a difference." The research by Hopps, Pinderhughes, and Shankar (1995) found that many clients feel overwhelmed by persistent, intractable powerlessness in the face of "poverty and other circumstances—drugs, violence, physical abuse, joblessness" (p. 8). Admittedly, in the early phases, the power dynamics of clients and their situations are often skewed against clients. Clients exhibit feelings of powerlessness in various ways, including anger, guardedness, self-hatred, aggression, passivity, humor, or manipulation (Pinderhughes, 1995).

Clients may perceive themselves as being carried along by external events rather than actively shaping their futures. Social workers accept the challenge of reversing this trend. They strive to build relationships in which clients recognize and use strengths to take charge of themselves and change their situations.

Clients view their roles in the social worker–client relationship in different ways. Some may be ready to operate as full partners in the process; others feel beaten down and dependent and look for social workers to lead the way. Research helps us understand why some clients feel helpless and disempowered when they enter relationships with social workers (Abramson, et al., 1978; Seligman, 1975). Simply, experience has taught them to be helpless because their previous attempts have failed. People who learn that their efforts make little or no difference lose motivation. They give up and turn over the responsibility for decision making to someone else or to chance. When social workers yield to the temptation to rescue those who appear dependent and helpless, they often create harmful effects in their attempts to be helpful (Dunst & Trivette, 1988). They add to clients' experiences of helplessness.

Many times clients approach social workers dependently because their previous experiences with other helping professionals have convinced them that their role is one of passive acceptance of assistance. Help can backfire in four ways and set up clients to be helpless (Coates, et al., 1983):

- Help undermines clients' competence when it lessens their control over their lives
- "Help may foster helpless recipients by directly hindering the acquisition and maintenance of important and useful skills" (p. 254)
- Help seekers often lower their opinions of themselves and their capabilities in response to receiving help, because needing to "have help" implies incompetence
- "Recipients may have their problem solved by the help, but still become helpless, convinced they could not succeed on their own" (p. 255)

To be "helpful," workers guide clients to their own power to help themselves.

Collaborating with Oppressed Clients

Human Rights & Justice

Many social work clients are members of oppressed groups. What actions can social workers take individually and collectively to advance the rights of these clients?

Many social work clients enter the relationship burdened by the experience of oppression. When oppression denies people their own dignity and access to the resources of society, they feel disempowered. These feelings interfere with the development of a working partnership, especially when clients view workers as similar to their oppressors. According to Pinderhughes (1979):

The cross-racial and cross-ethnic helping encounter compounds the consequences of the power differential. For the client, intervention by a member of a group he or she regards as the oppressor may reinforce the powerlessness experienced in a moment of need. Intervention by a worker whom the client sees as inferior may also reinforce the client's sense of helplessness. Power issues related to differences in ethnicity, class, sex, age, and other social markers may exaggerate the power inherent in the helping role in a way that causes the worker to misperceive the client. (p. 315)

Ultimately social workers and clients may choose to work on oppression as a goal of the relationship, but what can workers do to get over this initial hurdle? Dean (1993) advises that no way is known for social workers to ignore the power that they hold in these situations, even if it is subtle and implied in dominant cultural values and prejudices. Rather than denying them, workers do best by acknowledging these difficult issues and incorporating dialogue about them into the conversation.

The goal of any social work relationship is simple—it's for clients and social workers to resolve difficult situations. Clients are supposed to take charge of their own worlds in enlightened and fruitful ways. Social workers should be proficient in networking resources, advocating clients' rights, and creating macrolevel changes. Establishing an equal partnership is challenging for workers relating to clients who feel helpless, coerced, or oppressed. However, effective collaboration helps clients realize their goals.

Voluntary and Involuntary Clients

The client system's status as voluntary or involuntary profoundly affects the relationship dynamics of power and closeness. Voluntary clients choose to participate freely, based on their perceived notion that social work assistance will help. Involuntary clients are forced by others who hold enough power over them to insist on involvement in social work services (Ivanoff, et al., 1994; Rooney, 1992; Trotter, 2004). Examples of involuntary clients include persons convicted of crimes, parents ordered to receive services to regain custody of their children, and those whose use of substances necessitates mandated treatment. In some ways, all clients are involuntary. Would people decide to seek social work assistance if they weren't stuck on something that they would have preferred to solve on their own?

Although clients who are voluntary may choose social work services in desperation, nevertheless, they participate with the power of choice to address their challenges in their own ways. They can choose to work with this particular social worker, shop for another, or try a totally different approach. They have choices to remain or to leave the relationship, and they are free to behave in openly powerful ways. Collaborative partnerships are easier to form with clients who are voluntary, as their voluntary status places them on more equal footing as partners from the outset.

In contrast, consider those clients coerced into social work services because they have infringed on the rights of others. In these instances, social workers function as agents of social control as well as advocates for clients' rights. Clients begin the relationship in a "one-down" position, feeling more like prisoners than partners. To develop partnerships with involuntary clients, social workers quickly move to offer them honest and direct information about the structure of the helping relationship and their privileges within it.

Owning up to the reality of the coercive nature of the relationship reflects the social worker's genuineness and trustworthiness. Acknowledging that mandated clients still maintain rights shows the worker's acceptance, objectivity, and respect. This open discussion about limits and privileges is a beginning step toward ensuring equal footing for clients. Chapter 8 provides more extensive information about how workers develop and maintain collaborative relationships with mandated clients.

Partnerships with Larger Systems

Forming empowering relationships with larger client systems—such as groups, organizations, and communities—draws on all the skills already described and more. Building trusting relationships with program participants and members of organizations, neighborhoods, and communities is as important as building trust in work with individuals, families, and groups (Gutiérrez, et al., 2005). Workers also assist client systems to maximize power by encouraging cohesive development and distribution of leadership. This means that workers facilitate feelings of power in as many members of the system as possible, including those members who may initially feel that their contributions are insignificant.

Workers guide group interactions so that a particularly powerful member does not overshadow the worker's efforts to form working partnerships with other members of the client system. Similar to when a social worker's directive approach inhibits the contributions of clients, dictatorial members of larger group systems are likely to stifle the contributions of other group members. Therefore, with multiperson client systems, workers make direct connections to each group member, seek and accept the contributions of both active and less active members, and encourage each member to take part.

RESPECTING CONFIDENTIALITY

**Ethical
Practice**

Ethical social workers respect a client's right to confidentiality. However, the promise of confidentiality is not absolute. What situations affect a client's confidentiality rights?

Workers promote a client's power when they maintain confidentiality. Many describe confidentiality as the cornerstone of the social worker–client relationship (Reamer, 1998). Generally, confidential information is information deemed private. To maintain confidentiality, workers restrain from disclosing information about clients to others. Fulfilling the ethical obligations of confidentiality demonstrates respect for clients and builds trust. Ethical codes and legal requirements prescribe the nature of confidentiality in professional social work practice. The NASW *Code of Ethics* (1999a) obliges social workers to "respect clients' right to privacy. Social workers should not solicit private information from clients unless it is essential to providing service or conducting social work evaluation or research. Once private information is shared, standards of confidentiality apply" (Section 1.07a). Furthermore, laws at the federal, state, and local levels regulate professional responsibility for confidentiality. The following section explores differences between absolute and relative confidentiality, consents for releasing confidential information, and instances and implications of violating confidentiality.

Absolute and Relative Confidentiality

Given the significance of privacy for the sanctity of professional relationships, many conclude that confidentiality is unconditional, yet usually limits exist to confidentiality in social work practice.

We can distinguish two types of confidentiality, absolute and relative. With absolute confidentiality, professionals never share information in any form with anyone. Workers neither record information about clients in any type of report nor orally share information about clients with supervisors, agency-based colleagues, or any other professional. Few circumstances afford absolute confidentiality. More likely, the principle of relative confidentiality guides practice. Relative confidentiality allows sharing of information within agencies, such as in supervision, case conferences, and team meetings. However, relative confidentiality still presumes that, with some exceptions, workers do not share information outside the agency context without the explicit permission of the client (Figure 6.2).

Violating Confidentiality

Some workers unwittingly violate confidences (Houston-Vega, et al., 1997; Wilson, 1978). One common violation is discussing client or work setting situations with their own family and friends under the guise that not using names or identifying detail protects confidentiality. Family and friends are under no constraint to keep shared information confidential. Informal sharing with colleagues in public settings such as social gatherings, coffee-break rooms, or the shopping mall also presents serious problems. Additionally, inappropriate remarks, such as judgmental commentary about another client or an agency, may irrevocably damage working relationships. Phone calls taken during sessions with clients, although not necessarily revealing confidential information, distract and send messages about the potential for divulging private information. Finally, accidental or careless revelation of records or identities occurs in numerous ways, including leaving confidential records unattended on a desk

Figure 6.2   Exceptions to Confidentiality

- Evidence of child abuse or neglect
- Legal mandates for reporting elder abuse or neglect
- Threats by clients to harm themselves or others
- Clients' needs for emergency services
- Guardianship hearings or committal procedures requiring information
- Quality assurance procedures, internal audits, or peer reviews of nonidentifiable case records
- Consultation with colleagues, consultants, and attorneys
- Lawsuits filed against social workers by clients
- Other exceptions, as prescribed by laws and regulations

or in an unlocked file; working on records in public places; greeting a client by name in a public place; discarding unshredded records and notes; or even taking work home. Additionally, using unprotected means of communication, such as cellular phones, answering machines, fax machines, or E-mail can result in breaches of confidentiality.

If social workers break confidentiality, they seriously violate standards of professional ethics. In many states, if social workers violate confidentiality, they break the law. Possible consequences include professional sanctions and disciplinary actions, loss of professional licenses and certifications, misdemeanor charges, and civil lawsuits.

Informed Consent for Releasing Information

Clients can grant a worker permission to release confidential information through a process called informed consent. For a client's consent to be "informed," the worker must fully reveal the conditions, risks, and alternatives of sharing information. However, obtaining consents for the release of information is not without controversy. Questions arise, such as, What constitutes a valid consent? Is it ever appropriate to use a blanket consent? Is it appropriate to respond to a client's request for immediate disclosure if time constraints preclude having a written consent in hand? Do circumstances ever not require social workers to obtain informed consent?

What is proper procedure when a third party and not the client requests information? Is a social worker obligated to inform clients of the results of a request for information or of the potential consequences of not agreeing to sign the form? Can clients withdraw their consent? (Reamer, 1998; 2003). State and federal statutes, regulations, and policies, as well as court decisions and case law, stipulate the parameters for disclosing information. Additionally, cultural values influence clients' conceptualization of confidentiality and the propriety or even obligation to release information to others (Meer & VandeCreek, 2002; Palmer & Kaufman, 2003).

Consent forms clearly detail the nature of the information exchange. Workers should make copies of the completed and signed consent form for the client's case file, the client, and the professional requesting the information. Specific steps social workers take in obtaining informed consent include

1. Determining client competence
2. Providing service information
3. Ensuring client understanding
4. Documenting informed consent (Houston-Vega, et al., 1997, p. 53)

Privileged Communication

Privileged communication provides the legal ground for confidentiality (Dickson, 1998). Simply put, clients claim legal privilege, and ethical social workers maintain confidentiality. Legal privilege protects a client's private communication with a social worker by prohibiting the professional from divulging information in court. Establishing privilege often involves the following elements:

- The client invokes privilege to prevent the social worker's testimony or records being used as evidence in a court of law
- The social worker asserts privilege at the client's request. When a client waives this right, the social worker is not legally bound to maintain silence in court
- The judge considers Wigmore's Principles, relevant statutory and case laws, and client waiver and entitlement to determine whether privilege applies

By invoking privilege, clients restrict professionals from revealing confidential information in courts of law. In the absence of privilege, court officials compel social workers to testify and document their evidence with written records. Because it holds communication sacrosanct, the legal right of privilege enhances the effect of confidentiality in the social worker–client relationship (Kagle, 1990; Schroeder, 1995).

Safeguarding confidentiality conscientiously protects a client's legal right to privilege. However, privileged communication does not afford the absolute protection of privacy, as numerous exceptions exist, even in states that grant the status of privilege to clients of social workers.

Statutory provisions

Federal, state and local laws, which may or may not agree, stipulate conditions of privilege. In regard to federal cases, a U.S. Supreme Court ruling on Jaffee v. Redmond indicates that clients can now claim protection from disclosure of confidential exchanges with licensed social workers in federal courts (NASW, 2005g). "Jaffee prevents an attorney for the plaintiff from using the discovery process to invade a social worker's privacy and prevents harassment" (Alexander, 1997, p. 388). It also offers full protection to social workers who practice on Native American reservations whose clients face lawsuits or charges in federal courts.

All states and the District of Columbia grant some form of testimonial privilege to psychotherapist–client communications; many states include clinical or licensed social workers in the definition of "psychotherapist" (Alexander, 1997). However, most states do not grant social workers the right to absolute confidentiality. Typically, for clients to establish privilege, the social worker involved must either be licensed or registered or be supervised by someone who is. In some states, privilege extends to social work students; in other states, it does not. Because laws stipulate conditions required for privilege to apply, social workers should learn the implications of the laws governing their specific area of practice. The serious legal implications of these issues press social workers to familiarize themselves with situations in which privilege applies, as well as with the exceptions.

Various laws regarding licensure, professional regulation, and human-service activities designate conditions for confidentiality and privileged communication. "There are a number of federal and state laws that impose different confidentiality requirements depending on the practice setting" (Saltzman & Furman, 1999,

p. 451). In general, stipulations for federal funding restrict social workers from disseminating records and other information in such practice areas as education, medical and health care, criminal justice, and other public services. More specifically, in the public service arena, restrictions apply to child abuse, foster care, adoption, family preservation, Temporary Assistance to Needy Families (TANF), child support, and child custody. Other areas protected by privilege often include work in parole and probation, services to persons with developmental disabilities, practice in home health agencies, and services for persons with AIDS and HIV-related disorders. Federal laws regulating substance abuse treatment stipulate strict confidentiality, forbidding staff from even revealing whether someone is a client and mandating a secure record-keeping system.

Exceptions to privilege

Like other laws, privilege laws contain exceptions. Based on the NASW model licensure law, social workers are obligated to testify about confidential communications with clients when

1. The client, or someone acting on the client's behalf, waives privilege, giving written consent for disclosure.

2. The client brings charges against the social worker.

3. The client reveals in confidence the contemplation of a crime or harmful act.

4. The client is a minor who may have been the victim of a crime. (Kagle, 1990, p. 56)

Certain types of court proceedings, such as commitment hearings, child abuse cases, and trials for serious crimes, abrogate or, in other words, invalidate privilege (Saltzman & Furman, 1999). Subpoenas for records or court appearances require responses. Saltzman and Furman (1999) advise that "one may respond by claiming confidentiality or privilege. If the claim is contested, there will be a court hearing, and a judge will decide if the claim is valid or if the records must be turned over" (p. 461). Search warrants require immediate compliance, although ways may exist to persuade law enforcement officers to wait for a court ruling.

In addition, privilege does not apply when clients know from the outset that social workers may be called on to testify. Frequently, this is the case with involuntary clients. For example, various situations—such as family violence, child custody disputes, criminal activity, or mental health issues—in which social workers gather information on behalf of the court exclude privilege. The presence of another person when private information is shared, called the "third-party rule," may also limit the legal right to privilege (Dickson, 1998).

Balancing Accountability and Privacy

Numerous factors influence the extent to which social workers maintain confidentiality. Codes of ethics and standards for professional practice emphasize that confidentiality is necessary to create the atmosphere of trust in which clients are free to reveal their situations. Statutory regulations, case law, judicial interpretations, and agency policies and procedures provide guidelines that support confidentiality. However, these same guidelines demand that professionals balance matters of privacy with the requisites of accountability and the rights of others.

Particularly difficult ethical dilemmas and legal quandaries emerge with the trend toward managed care, the reliance on computer technology, and challenging social issues (Congress, 1999; Madden, 2003; Millstein, 2000). For example, managed care officials demand "confidential" information about cases as a requisite to funding (Rock & Congress, 1999). Increased utilization of technology, computerized databases, and computer networks creates the potential for breaching confidentiality (Gelman, et al., 1999; Gewirth, 2001; Reamer, 2001, 2005, 2008). The press of "duty to warn" and "informed consent" in an age of pandemic disease and violence increases social workers' risks of violating confidentiality (Dickson, 1998). Finally, circumstances under which social workers breach confidentiality may further discriminate against clients from various oppressed population groups.

LOOKING FORWARD

Social work values mandate that people be treated with acceptance and respect. The shift toward a more egalitarian partnership between social worker and client system actualizes this value in the professional relationship, but in relinquishing the role of expert, workers are placed in the quandary of who to be.

The social worker–client relationship sits at the intersection of many influences and opportunities. Empowering social workers recognize these possibilities and work directly to take full advantage of their potential. To do so, workers carefully construct partnerships with clients that encourage open sharing, collaboration, and active participation. Workers use their personal qualities and professional expertise in the process of developing this relationship. They also maintain the integrity of the relationship by orienting it to the goals that clients seek and by maintaining clients' rights to confidentiality.

Although social workers define the professional partnership in direct ways, clients experience the relationship most profoundly when discussing their situations. Chapter 7 details the processes that social workers use to talk with clients about the challenges they face. Workers consider both clients' thoughts and feelings in this process. The ways that social workers gather information can contribute to clients' feelings of competence and hope as well as activate clients to continue to invest in the relationship.

Succeed with **mysocialworklab**

Log onto **www.mysocialworklab.com** and select the **Interactive Skill Module** videos from the left-hand menu. Answer the questions below. (*If you did not receive an access code to* **MySocialWorkLab** *with this text and wish to purchase access online, please visit* **www.mysocialworklab.com**.)

1. **On page 12 of the school social work module**, worker Terry explains confidentiality to client Michelle. How would you explain confidentiality in response to Michelle's question, "What will you tell my parents about what I'm telling you?"

2. **Watch pages 4, 6, and 7 of the child welfare module** to understand the worker's dilemma in building a partnership while investigating potential child abuse. Clearly, the worker takes charge. What else could the worker do to forge a more equal partnership with this client?

PRACTICE TEST

Engage Assess Intervene Evaluate

1. When social worker Sonja Hearn met with Mrs. Jacobs, she began by saying: "Mrs. Jacobs? I'm Sonja Hearn from the Northside Hospital Outreach Program. You and I worked out a plan for follow-up care before you were discharged from the hospital and we agreed that I would stop by your home to talk with you today." Sonja's strategy most likely reflects _____.
   a. greeting Mrs. Jacobs
   b. orienting Mrs. Jacobs to the purpose of her visit
   c. being overly concerned with the authority of her position
   d. a dual relationship

2. Mrs. Jacobs appreciates that social worker Sonja Hearn is a reliable professional, not one who makes empty promises. Mrs. Jacobs notes Sonja's capacity for _____.
   a. genuineness
   b. empathy
   c. respect
   d. trustworthiness

3. Of her experience with her social worker, Gina Block says, "Jennifer listens carefully to what I'm saying. She seems to understand me rather than feel sorry for me." Based on Gina's comments, social worker Jennifer Miller is successful in communicating with _____.
   a. genuineness
   b. empathy
   c. pity
   d. respect

4. Of the following situations, which is LEAST likely considered a dual relationship?
   a. Social worker Dick Jenson was attracted to his client Danielle, but waited until their last appointment to ask her to go to dinner to "celebrate."
   b. Social worker Joy Fielding agrees to counsel her neighbors who are having marital difficulties.
   c. Mental health social worker Sue Greene agrees to receive a referral from a friend employed by Northside Family Services.
   d. Social worker Karen Lundeen accepts a client's proposal to exchange lawn work for the counseling fee.

Diversity in Practice

5. Medical social worker Kim Cates reviews the record of a client whom she will meet for the first time. The client, an eighty-five year old African American woman, recently fell down steps and sustained injuries for which she will need continued care after her discharge from the hospital. Kim notices that there are several names in the record and wonders what name she should use. To be culturally appropriate, Kim should address her client by calling her _____.
   a. Isadorra
   b. Izzie
   c. Miss Izzie
   d. Mrs. Jackson

6. Of the following situations, which is NOT a violation of confidentiality?
   a. consulting with colleagues in the break room about a difficult case
   b. greeting a client by name at the shopping mall
   c. reporting suspected child abuse to the child protection agency
   d. after procuring a release of information, sending a client's records to a colleague via e-mail attachment

Ethical Practice

7. Because she is embarrassed by her situation, an involuntary client asks if licensed social worker Judith Weinberg will promise never to reveal any information about their sessions to anyone under any circumstances. Based on the principals of confidentiality and privileged communication, how will Judith MOST likely respond?
   a. "Of course I understand your embarrassment and I promise you absolutely never to reveal any information about you to anyone."
   b. "Since I am a licensed social worker, state law grants me privilege so I'll absolutely be able to keep that promise."
   c. "I certainly understand why you may ask me to keep our sessions absolutely confidential; however, you do need to keep in mind that I may be called upon to testify in court."
   d. "I can promise that unless there are extenuating circumstances, I won't share information outside the agency without your explicit consent."

Log onto **MySocialWorkLab** once you have completed the Practice Test above to take your Chapter Exam and demonstrate your knowledge of this material.

Answers

7

Articulating Situations

CONNECTING CORE COMPETENCIES *in this chapter*

| Professional Identity | Ethical Practice | **Critical Thinking** | **Diversity in Practice** | Human Rights & Justice | Research Based Practice | **Human Behavior** | Policy Practice | Practice Contexts | **Engage Assess Intervene Evaluate** |

153

While articulating situations, clients and social workers develop a mutual understanding of what they are getting together to do. An open and respectful dialogue identifies the issues clients confront and elucidates the contexts in which these difficulties occur. During this mutual exchange, clients and social workers define and strengthen their working partnership.

Social workers and clients share responsibility in articulating situations. Clients take the lead in telling their stories. Social workers respond to clarify and organize the information clients offer. By choosing responses to determine goals and to locate resources for change, social workers infuse purpose into the dialogue while demonstrating respect for the clients' expertise and privilege of self-definition. This exchange requires a delicate power balance between social worker and client, made more complex in the context of social work with larger systems, such as organizations and communities.

An effective social worker focuses the information exchange to describe what is currently happening, to determine goals, and to locate resources for change. This chapter describes how social workers respond to access clients' perspectives. Specifically, this chapter

- Frames an empowering style of communication to meet the purposes of social worker–client conversations
- Analyzes communication processes and the influences of culture, emotion, and other experiences on effective communication
- Demonstrates various ways for social workers to elicit and organize information offered by clients
- Identifies how workers effectively respond to client feelings expressed verbally and nonverbally
- Delineates specific approaches for workers to communicate with clients who are angry, silent, curious, and evaluative
- Contrasts the skills necessary for responding to individuals with those necessary for responding to larger groups

Workers implementing these client-focused dialogue skills are able to initiate and maintain empowering relationships with diverse clients.

EMPOWERING DIALOGUE

A man, recently paroled and saddled with a felony record, can't find a job. A girl refuses to return to school after her fight with a teacher. A downtown redevelopment group wants to attract customers to its revitalized town center, an area that has become a gathering place for people who are homeless. A public housing project's reputation for crime and drug traffic complicates a cycle of low occupancy rates, reduced income, and spotty maintenance, further decreasing the attractiveness to potential residents. Each of these client systems faces very different situations that challenge their capabilities to respond.

In articulating the significant dimensions of any of these situations, social workers face choices of how to respond. What information is most relevant? Which avenues of exploration will be productive in leading toward desired goals? What kind of conversation will work best to guide the change process and to establish a working partnership that merges social worker and client expertise?

Box 7.1 The Ethic of Discourse

Discourse is the exchange of ideas, beliefs, and practices that both shape and challenge what we think is true or real about our personal and social situations. In this way, we say the perception of our situation is socially constructed. The context of discourse is the network of social relations within which the communication and interchange of ideas occurs, a context shaped by social inequality and privilege. Through discourse, people express views and opinions, confer and deliberate, modify their perceptions of reality, and reason together. In other words, people tell and retell their stories, narrated with personally defined, culturally shared, and socially ascribed meanings. These stories shape people's views of themselves and their possibilities.

More than the simple telling of one's story, discourse is a synergistic process of continuous reinterpretation of the socially constructed meaning of that story as told in the context of conversation with others. Through such social exchange, people grow stronger as they willingly incorporate divergent points of view and new ideas that validate their behaviors and perceptions, and they yield to pressure from others to adopt alternative interpretations that may limit their reach. Through social interaction, discourse becomes the means by which dominant groups promote self-serving ideologies, limit social participation, impose meaning, and construct "realities" for less-powerful others.

Discourse emphasizes the use of language and the influence of context in giving meaning to one's experiences and in defining one's place and value in those experiences. Language and context define self and social identity, assign social location, and channel individual access to resources. As such, there is power in both language and context. Power is evident in such examples as word usage, intonation, labels, nonverbal signals, body posturing, and the use of space. The contextual power behind discourse includes social structures, hierarchical relationships, economic privilege, ascribed social roles, dominant ideologies, and social institutions and the ways these dimensions have been socially constructed (Fairclough as cited in Webb, 2000). Sexism, racism, heterosexism, ageism, and ableism frame discourse in ways that disadvantage vulnerable groups.

Listening and Responding

Communication leads to community, that is, to understanding, intimacy and mutual valuing.
—Rollo May

Social workers are active participants in conversations with clients, focusing their attention to understand and articulate the meanings clients intend. Workers listen carefully and then respond directly to access a clear image of the client's world and to communicate interest, appreciation, and concern. The best comments by social workers build on and validate what clients have shared. Clients experience a worker's empathy and respect if the worker can describe the situation as the client sees it. Practitioners learn how to respond to clients by listening to them first.

Social workers demonstrate their acceptance of clients and foster collaboration when they emphasize responding. By using responding skills, workers hold their own views in check in favor of eliciting the client's perspective. Responding in a client-focused dialogue is a "culturally responsive" way to interact, leaving to the client the role of cultural expert. When clients take the lead, they set a cultural tone for the work by revealing their language, style, hopes, and beliefs. Encouraged by a social worker's responses, clients disclose their own theories about events as well as their motivations and priorities.

A social work professional has a responsibility to maintain the defined purpose of any relationship with a client. Social work practice is best when it is client-focused and goal-directed. In conversations with clients, social workers deliberately choose responses that are useful in meeting the purposes of the relationship.

PROACTIVE RESPONDING

To assist workers in conversations with clients, O'Melia (1998) suggests the concept of proactive responding. Proactive responding weaves three related dialogue skills:

1. Responses to articulate the current situation and its impact from the client's perspective

2. Responses to define a positive outcome to direct the work, and

3. Responses to identify strengths and resources available for goal achievement. (p. 2)

These proactive responses maintain the client's central position as expert on the situation while allowing the worker to infuse a strengths orientation into the process. These responding skills assist clients to describe their current situations and to locate existing strengths and resources.

Describing the Current Situation

Clients and their situations make the most sense when we view them from the client's point of view and in context. A social worker's responses to access the client's unique perspective and relevant contextual information reflect the integration of two theoretical views—social constructivism and the ecosystems perspective. A social worker's best responses validate clients' experiences and expand clients' views about their situations.

Eliciting the client's reality

We have already discussed the difficulty of anticipating another's experience. Inevitable differences in perspectives arise, generated by cultural group memberships and individual uniqueness. The differing realities between social workers and clients press workers to withhold their views in favor of eliciting the client's perspective. The worker takes on the role of student to be educated rather than informed cultural expert (Leigh, 1998). As a student of the client's construction of reality, the worker responds reflectively with interest and curiosity until achieving a mutual understanding.

Discussing transactions

The social justice imperative directs workers to explore the social, institutional, and political contexts of client situations. Workers examine the goodness-of-fit of persons and their environments rather than investigate failures in the functioning of client systems themselves. When clients say they have failed, a worker immediately responds to link this "failure" to its context, in which other explanations of the client's experience become evident.

Placing a situation in its systemic context has two major advantages. First, this view assumes no fault or inadequacy on the part of clients. A gap simply exists between what client systems currently need and what their environments presently offer. Removing the need to pinpoint blame frees clients to cooperate rather than fend off the perception of judgment and blame. Second, when we describe situations transactionally, we scan the entire ecosystem in developing resources for change.

Examining the contextual features of situations reveals targets for solutions. Consider a girl who refuses to return to school after a fight with her teacher. A linear view looks first to the child and second to the teacher to see what and who is wrong. In contrast, the transactional view explores other elements of the ecosystem that may be supporting the transaction. Perhaps the girl has concerns about her elderly grandmother's health. Maybe she is reluctant to admit that she is having difficulty reading. Possibly her teacher is succumbing to pressures of increased class size and decreased student support services. Maybe racial and ethnic bias is predisposing other children in the class to pick on her. Events happening within the ecosystem provide clues for assessment and focus for solutions.

Situations involving larger client systems also have transactional dimensions to explore. For example, the task group seeking to revitalize the downtown area looks beyond the immediate concern of a few businesses and a few customers to understand the issue more fully. A social worker would guide group members to examine the impact of the city's investment in a new shopping mall on the other side of town, the loss of jobs created when the area's major employer consolidated and moved its operations to another state, the influx of people who are homeless into the downtown area drawn by the empty buildings, and the shifts in population from the town center to suburban areas. When social workers respond to describe situations in concrete transactional terms, the area in which they search for solvable problems expands.

Orienting Toward Goals

The second important response by a social worker shifts the conversation to refine the direction of the work. When clients present their problems, social workers respond by asking how this problem gets in the way. This takes a first step toward defining where clients would like to go (see Chapter 8, Defining Directions).

To shift the focus toward the future, social workers frame clients' situations in terms of challenges, rather than problems. Challenges differ significantly from problems; challenges orient us toward the future. Consider Zeb, a client recently paroled and looking for employment. The problem Zeb presents is his felony record. This fact about his past will not change. Focusing on this problem engenders feelings of guilt and powerlessness. However, Zeb's challenge is getting a job. Notice the perspective shift from what's wrong to what should happen. Despite Zeb's past, finding a job is still a future option. Similar to how you would assist any recent college graduate seeking a job, the social worker assesses Zeb's motivation and interest, defines his current capabilities, and determines his needs for additional job skills to increase Zeb's marketability in the eyes of potential employers. There may be no way to expunge the problem of a criminal record, but multiple approaches exist to the challenge of securing employment.

The concept of challenge steers workers away from the notion of eliminating a problem fixed in the past toward overcoming or avoiding hurdles in the pathway leading to a future goal. Previous problems are significant only if they interfere with achieving a desired future. Examine this shift in perspective: the concept of challenge reorients workers to move quickly beyond talking about what is wrong. Instead of dwelling on past problems, social workers encourage clients to articulate where they are going (goals) and what might help them get there (strengths and resources).

Searching for Strengths and Resources

A third effective response by social workers pivots toward a discussion of client strengths and environmental resources available to achieve goals. Social workers consistently choose responses that direct attention to what clients are doing right, what they have accomplished, and what resources may contribute to the effort (see Chapter 9, Identifying Strengths, and Chapter 10, Assessing Resource Capabilities).

Consider the example of an aging public housing project. The social worker's conversation with residents identifies their sense of helplessness about their situation—a reality of substandard living conditions, neglect by the housing authority, and periodic incidents of violence. But as the worker responds to reorient the conversation to how residents cope with their situation, a new picture emerges. Through this shift in direction, the social worker learns that the difficult conditions have contributed to a strong sense of community; some residents have researched their rights as tenants and are poised to assert themselves at the next meeting of the housing authority, and other residents have organized a neighborhood watch program. These newly articulated strengths of the neighborhood can contribute to achieving the solutions that residents seek.

Human system behavior adapts in context. Likely something works in each client's situation. Always finding it more empowering to validate and improve than to denigrate and redirect, social workers respond to clients with positive possibilities in mind. What's good about what clients are doing? The answer is "probably a lot."

Sizing Up Situations

Only clients truly know their situations. As clients share, workers respond to articulate more fully the client's perspective and structure the dialogue. Social workers respond proactively to access clients' thoughts and feelings, consider issues with respect to goals, and locate strengths and resources for solution development (Figure 7.1).

Figure 7.1   Proactive Responding

Proactive responses maintain the client's central position as an expert on the situation while allowing the worker to infuse a strengths orientation into the conversation. Social workers using proactive responding combine attentive listening with reflections, clarifications, summaries, and occasional questions to access information about what is going on, to define what the client hopes will happen, and to locate resources available to assist in the effort. Specifically, Proactive responding weaves three related dialogue skills, including:

Responses to articulate the current situation

- What is happening from the client's point of view
- Other associated events that may be related
- Other people involved in or affected by the current situation
- The impact the events are having on the client's life
- How the client makes sense out of what is happening

Responses to define a positive direction

- How the client would like it to be instead
- What it would look like if things were working in that way
- Indicators that would signal that things are beginning to improve

Responses to identify strengths and locate available resources

- Times in the past when things were working in the desired way
- Times currently when things are working best or even a little better than usual
- What the client sees as personal strengths, specifically those related to goals
- What is available in the environment that could be resource
- Other people who might contribute to the effort and what they could do
- Coping methods the client uses to manage the situation
- Client's ideas about what others might do in a similar situation

EXCHANGING INFORMATION

By definition, all communication processes involve exchanges of information between senders and receivers (Figure 7.2). Senders *encode* messages. In this process, senders consider their thoughts and feelings and symbolically represent them in words and actions. The actual verbal and nonverbal delivery of these words and actions transmits a message to the receiver. Receivers, in turn, *decode* or interpret the messages they receive based on their perception of the message. When receivers respond to a sender's message with messages of their own, a dialogue begins. As conversations unfold, receivers become senders and senders become receivers, trading roles as they respectively encode, transmit, and decode messages. Communication is effective to the extent that senders clearly transmit and receivers accurately understand messages. Successful communication depends on the active participation and cooperation of both senders and receivers.

Verbal Communication

There is more than a verbal tie between the words common, community, and communication.
—John Dewey

Several theorists contribute to our understanding of the human experience of remembering and reporting events (Bandler & Grinder, 1975; Johnson, 2006). When something happens, we perceive it and tuck it away in our minds for future reference, but already the event that actually occurred and the representation we store in our memory differ, as our attention is selective. The complexity of events defies our capabilities to absorb all the details. We see what we see, hear what we hear, feel what we feel, and we remember it selectively. Others

Dialogue Information Loop

Sender — Message → Receiver

Sender
Encodes Message: Translates Thoughts and Feelings into Words and Action

Decodes Message

Receiver
Decodes Message: Interprets Message Based on Perception of Meaning

Encodes Response: Sends Feedback Message

Feedback

Figure 7.2
Communication Processes

witnessing identical events do the same, resulting in a different perception of the event. Each of us constructs idiosyncratic memories, unique compilations of events as we perceive them.

Memory stores general information rather than precise, meticulous details. Then when we retrieve information, we fill in the gaps to reconstruct events logically, as we expect they would have happened (Loftus, 1979). In other words, when we report these events from memory, we are likely to leave out significant features or even embellish the details. Moreover, we can't possibly share everything we are thinking; there wouldn't be enough time. Most likely, we tailor our remarks to the requisites of specific conversations. Our motives for presenting information, the effect we seek, and our feelings further influence the choices we make in what and how to share. Rather than report our entire memory of events, we selectively delete, generalize, and distort information as we pass it along (Bandler & Grinder, 1975).

When clients express their thoughts about events, naturally, they share only bits and pieces of their stories. Social workers respond to help clients rediscover events in fuller, more productive detail.

Words are ambiguous

In talking with clients about their situations, workers choose their words carefully, as words either facilitate partnerships or block communication processes. For example, when social workers use jargon, technical terms, and vocabulary unfamiliar to clients, these esoteric words elevate social workers into expert roles and leave clients feeling as if they have nothing to offer. When social workers use complex, enigmatic terminology, they puzzle clients. One client who participated in a focus group for a child welfare research project talked about the importance of communicating on a level with clients this way: "I mean being personal and friendly and just being down on our level or whatever. It's just really the most important thing they can do" (Drake, 1994, p. 598).

Even when clients and social workers use the very same words, they may not mean the same thing (Kadushin & Kadushin, 1997). For example, the words, "eligibility," "referral," and "privacy" can invoke disparate meanings and reactions. Even common words such as "soon," "later," "possibility," and "likely" leave room for alternative interpretations. Workers choose words with an ear for what fits naturally with the world of the client system and continually check in with clients to ensure mutual understanding.

Critical Thinking

Effective communication is essential for successful social work practice. What is effective communication and how does a social worker achieve it?

Nonverbal Communication

Words are only part of the messages we communicate. When we talk, we also send nonverbal messages. Humans rely heavily on nonverbal communication to convey and interpret meaning (Burgoon, et al., 1996). Nonverbal messages accompany every verbal expression and sometimes stand on their own. Body posture, facial expressions, eye contact, head and body movements, and other attending behaviors, as well as voice tone, inflection, and intensity, all contain nonverbal messages.

Nonverbal communication can be purposeful, but generally it is spontaneous. Nonverbal messages often communicate information that would otherwise go unsaid. Long-standing research indicates that nonverbal behavior influences communication processes more prominently than do verbal messages, generating about two-thirds of any communication's meaning (Birdwhistell, 1955). What you think and how you feel shows through in how you behave.

Social workers encourage or inhibit clients by their nonverbal responses to them. Nonverbal messages qualify otherwise neutral information. How we say words conveys information about our attitudes, making nonverbal messages particularly important in cross-cultural work. "Minority clients are likely to be particularly sensitive to the degree of congruence between a worker's verbal and nonverbal messages" (Proctor & Davis, 1994, p. 317). When there's a mismatch between verbal and nonverbal messages, we tend to believe the nonverbal ones.

Influences on Communication Processes

A number of factors influence communication processes by creating lenses through which we view and interpret messages. These include culture, assumptions, expectations, emotions, and distractors.

Culture

Culture powerfully influences communication processes. Consider the example of a social worker asking a client the simple question, "What does your family think about this?" Who pops into your mind as you consider your family's reaction? If you are Latino, you might think of your extended family, including your godparents (Falicov, 1996). If you are Asian American, you probably consider your extended family with an emphasis on your husband's or father's side (Nakanishi & Rittner, 1996). If you are Native American, you may think about a multihousehold, extended kinship network with tribal connections, including those in areas far away (Weaver & White, 1997). If you are African American, you might include blood relatives and long-time friends in the community network as part of your family (Hines & Boyd-Franklin, 1996). If you are European American, you probably flashed on an image of your nuclear family (McGoldrick, 1989). Cultural backgrounds trigger differences in meaning that confound social workers in their attempts to communicate effectively with clients, and they create communication gaps among members of multiperson client systems.

Culture influences some facets of nonverbal communication, whereas other facets are universally expressed and understood. For example, cross-cultural research discovered that people from different cultures usually interpret certain facial indicators of emotion—surprise, disgust, anger, fear, sadness, and happiness—similarly (Ekman & Friesen, 1975). This research reported remarkable agreement across cultures about communicating and interpreting these facial expressions of emotion. However, cultural differences prescribe variations in the meaning of other types of nonverbal behaviors.

People from varying cultures attribute different meanings to gestures, eye contact, and even voice intonation. For example, many North American cultural groups interpret direct eye contact as a sign of support, interest, and respect, yet some Native Americans and Asian Americans interpret direct eye contact as rude and intrusive (Lewis & Ho, 1975). However, be cautious in overgeneralizing, because in a changing and assimilating society, cultural "rules" have exceptions. For example, some Native Americans avoid eye contact. Although this "may have been true for a few tribal cultures (but not all), most American Indian children in urban areas are far removed from such traditions" (Franklin, et al., 1995, p. 187).

Additionally, some cultural groups are more sensitive to contextual features of communication, including nonverbal elements:

High context cultures, such as traditional Chinese and Japanese, pay great attention to the surrounding circumstances or context of an event; thus, in interpersonal communication, the elements of phrasing, tone, gestures, posture, social status, history, and social setting are all crucial to the meaning of the message. (Chung, 1992, p. 29).

Given this variability in cultural meaning, social workers must decipher what verbal communications and nonverbal behaviors will work with each client system.

Assumptions

Social workers' assumptions may interfere with their understanding clients' messages. For example, a practitioner working in foster care observed sparse interaction between a mother and her children during a supervised visit and assumed that the mother's behavior was aloof and disinterested. Talking with the mother after the visit, the social worker learned that the mother wanted to be "a good mom," so she let the kids play video games, but was disappointed in her lack of opportunity to interact with them. "There's always the danger when we don't check things out, that we may think we understand a client's meaning and act as if we do, when we are actually not at all in accord" (Dean, 1993, p. 137). Careful clarification circumvents the pitfalls of assuming meanings.

Expectations

Past experiences create expectations that filter perceptions of here-and-now situations. Both workers and clients hold expectations for the helping encounter. A client may negatively interpret a social worker's message simply based on bad experiences with other helpers. Or, a social worker who observes particular patterns of communication in a single-parent family may presume that these patterns apply to all single-parent families, overlooking individual differences. Bits and pieces of past experiences influence how people send, receive, and interpret messages. Unchecked, categorical generalizations distort information and severely restrict the ability to communicate effectively. To counteract the effect of negative expectations, social workers listen carefully and consciously send messages of acceptance and respect.

Emotions

Communication also involves emotional elements. Frequently, emotions affect how we send, receive, and remember information. For example, stress narrows our focus, distracts our attention, limits our ability to recognize alternatives, and increases our inaccuracies and misinterpretations (Baradell & Klein, 1993). Other research indicates that our moods may even influence our ability to recall information. For example, in a well-known experiment on emotions and memory, Bower (1981) found participants remembered more words when their mood during "input" matched their mood during "retrieval."

On the receiving end, strong emotions may blur our ability to listen accurately. Over-identifying with emotions confuses our own stories with those of the message sender. We project our own circumstances into our understanding of the messages we receive. In other words, caught up with personal emotions, we may interpret information through the masks of our own emotions. Most communications convey emotion, but strong emotions held by either senders or receivers can undermine the effective sharing of information. Social workers take extra caution to communicate effectively in emotionally charged interchanges.

Distractors

Distractors confound communication processes. For example, background noise interrupts concentration, covers up softly spoken messages, and hinders communication with persons who have a hearing loss. Repetitive sounds, such

Box 7.2 Social Work with Immigrants and Refugees: A Research–Practice Connection

In 2006, there were about 10.6 million refugees and asylum seekers in the world (USCRI, 2007). Nearly one-half of the refugees are from Afghanistan, Iraq, Sudan, and Somalia. Additionally, about 12.8 million people were displaced within their own countries because of civil wars, famine, and natural disasters.

Social workers in all fields of practice are likely to work with immigrants and refugees. Additionally, specialized immigrant services, such as neighborhood centers, case management services, and refugee resettlement programs continue to emerge to meet the increased demand. In contrast to the century-old settlement house emphasis on assisting immigrants to assimilate into "American ways of life," the contemporary goal balances assimilation with respect for an immigrant's culture of origin. To this end, social workers encourage immigrants to draw on the resources and strengths of their own culture, while at the same time, they assist them in transitioning to life in American society (Balgopal, 2000).

Research highlights a variety of challenges in working with immigrants and refugees. Trust building is often difficult because many immigrants are survivors of war and torture (Behnia, 2004). Successful cross-cultural communication is also important. In a study by Russell and White (2001), "all immigrant clients interviewed indicated that the ability to communicate innermost feelings was essential in remedying their sense of social isolation" (p. 81), yet to achieve such an intimate level of communication, workers and clients must overcome language and cultural barriers.

A survey of 226 Asian Indian immigrants age 50 and older explored factors mitigating stress related to adjustment to life in the United States. Diwan, Jonnalagadda, and Balaswamy (2004) found protective factors within the immigrants' cultural context, including the bonds of friendships, a secure cultural identity, religious faith, and personal sense of mastery. They concluded that promoting social integration and addressing spiritual concerns are useful strategies for increasing well-being among immigrants, suggesting that practitioners should solicit information about how well connected clients are to others and to explore their sense of spiritual well-being.

Ely's (2004) review of the literature on domestic violence among immigrant women in the United States reveals the complexities faced by social workers. She found, for example, that "humiliation and dishonor are perceived by many immigrant women to be more harmful than enduring domestic violence" (p. 227), leaving these women reluctant to disclose the violence to social workers. In addition, not knowing exceptions in immigration law, these women fear that sharing information may jeopardize their immigration status. The social isolation that often accompanies abuse in any culture makes it less likely these women will know about available resources or protections against deportation under the Immigration Act of 1991 and the Violence Against Women Act of 1994. Ely recommends that social workers develop culturally competent education and advocacy programs that foster open communication and a safe environment for self-disclosure.

Because of ethnic strife in their own country, most Ethiopians of Jewish descent have immigrated to Israel. Stress, low self-esteem, and intergenerational conflicts often mark their acculturation experiences. Ringel, Ronell, and Getahune (2005) report that Ethiopian adolescents' integration into Israeli culture is complicated by cultural and generational differences in communication styles. They report that Ethiopian culture emphasizes nonverbal communication in contrast to an Israeli culture that prizes verbal exchange.

These research studies demonstrate the necessity and challenge of effective communication when working with immigrants and refugees requiring a worker's understanding of the nuances of language, silence, context, and meaning.

as the ticking of a clock, accentuate silence. Odors, too, may distract us. Certain odors evoke deeply imbedded memories and shift our attention away from the present to the past of our own personal associations. Interruptions such as telephone calls, intercom messages, and requests to step outside suggest to clients that they are of secondary importance. In home visits, distractors, such as radios and televisions, neighbors dropping by, or other household activities, may interrupt the flow of communication. When social workers feel the press of their own agenda or environmental distractions interfere, they take steps to remove the distractions to facilitate productive conversations.

ACCESSING THE CLIENT'S PERSPECTIVE

Diversity in Practice

Social workers use responding skills to access a client's perspective. What factors make these skills especially important for situations in which clients are culturally different from social workers?

Central to success in any social work endeavor is an exchange of information that describes the client's situation in a useful way. With individual, family, and small-group clients, this exchange takes the form of conversation. Social workers and clients talk directly with each other. With formal systems, organizations, and communities, workers implement other methods to articulate the situation. Dialogue with larger systems may involve formal meetings, public forums, focus groups, or written surveys.

No matter what form this exchange of information takes, two key purposes orient the conversation. First, workers seek to articulate the situation as the client sees it. The idea is to access the client's perspective untainted by the worker's biases. Second, workers nudge the conversation toward a broader view, broad enough to place situations in environmental context and to reveal strengths and resources for change.

In successful conversations, workers learn what clients know and, in the process, help clients organize and understand this information in useful ways. To accomplish this, workers listen carefully to what clients say and encourage them to say more.

Clients constantly communicate verbally and behaviorally, telling and showing workers how they think and feel. This abundance of information forces social workers to respond selectively. Empowering social workers choose responses that demonstrate acceptance and respect while encouraging clients more fully to articulate their situations. Through their responses, social workers send their own messages, explore what clients are thinking, and reflect what clients are feeling.

RESPONDING TO THOUGHTS

In everyday conversations, we may share our thoughts freely, trying to get others to understand our points of view. In professional conversations, social workers initially withhold their thoughts in favor of learning about the client's experience. Social workers deliberately offer responses to guide clients to describe their situations in concrete and transactional terms. A social worker's purposeful selection of responses

- Helps workers clearly comprehend clients' challenges
- Promotes clients' understanding of their own situations
- Pursues information relevant to clients' goals
- Develops and maintains a respectful partnership that gives clients control over their own directions
- Encourages all members of multiperson client systems to share their views

Workers can choose from a continuum of responses that range from nondirective to focused questions. As a general rule, social workers use the least intrusive responses when clients concretely describe events in context and consider them in the light of their goals. Social workers use more direct strategies for responding when clients remain ambiguous or repeat information.

Responses that elicit the client's perspective without imposing the worker's view include: allowing space, nonverbal behaviors, verbal utterances, restatements, clarifications, summary clarifications, requests to continue, and questions (Figure 7.3). These responding skills are useful for person-to-person interactions at all levels of social work practice.

Figure 7.3
Response Continuum for Generalist Social Work

Allowing Space

If you want to hear what clients have to say, give them the space to talk. The dialogue between social workers and clients includes moments of silence. Quiet spaces give clients chances to formulate words to express their thoughts and feelings.

Allowing space may prove difficult. Most of us are socialized to fill the gaps in conversations. Add these personal tendencies to our pride in professional expertise, and we may feel the pressure to have answers. To allow space, social workers resist the temptation to describe what they see or what they can guess in favor of giving clients opportunities to express their own thoughts and feelings.

Multiperson client systems

Allowing space has special significance in working with multiperson client systems. Here, social workers do more than control their own contributions in ways that leave individual clients with opportunities to talk. Workers actually temper the contributions of actively verbal members to create space for more cautious members to contribute. Frequently, less talkative members of a system have the greatest impact. People who aren't talking have opportunities to observe and think. People who participate less frequently have the most new information to offer. Recognizing the potential resources of all members of a multiperson client system, practitioners work to create space to ensure that all members have chances to contribute.

Nonverbal Responses

Just as social workers observe clients carefully to see what they are saying nonverbally, clients pay attention to social workers' faces, hands, and bodies. The ways workers sit, the looks they give, and how they express themselves send messages to clients. Workers can show empathy, support, and comprehension through nonverbal responses while clients talk.

Nonverbal responses send powerful, yet ambiguous messages. Each of us may interpret them differently. For example, an attentive posture may encourage clients to continue to articulate their views. A hand gesture in the direction of a member of a client system who is not contributing may invite their participation. However, members of some cultural groups may view close attention or gestures as threatening or demanding. To discover whether a client receives the intended message, social workers screen their nonverbal behavior for cross-cultural meanings and observe how clients react.

Single Word Responses

Sometimes, it doesn't take much for social workers to keep people talking about their situations informatively. Simple, one-word responses or even verbal utterances convey an attentive and accepting tone and keep clients talking. Examples include:

- ◗ Mmhmm . . .
- ◗ OK
- ◗ Yes!
- ◗ All right
- ◗ Aaah . . .

When social workers use simple phrases with positive connotations, they nonjudgmentally validate what clients are saying and encourage clients to continue sharing.

Restatement

Social workers can respond by repeating a client's last few words or a significant phrase. This restatement functions as a perception check, verifying that workers have listened and understood. Even when social workers misunderstand what clients are talking about, restatements encourage clients to modify their messages, clarify, and continue to add more information.

Sometimes restatements cast information in a new light. In offering restatements, social workers select certain parts of the client's message. In this way, workers use restatements purposefully to develop a transactional view, provide glimpses of strengths, and forge a sense of direction toward goals.

Client: I don't know what to do. Seems like every time I take him to the store, he throws a fit.

Worker: Every time you take him to the store . . .

***

Good listening skills prompt clients to engage in dialogue about their situations.

Client: Sometimes I can handle it, sometimes I can't.

Worker: Sometimes you can handle it.

With restatements, workers can also guide the focus of the conversation by emphasizing parts of the response with voice inflections or by adding an inquisitive tone.

Client: My mom always complains, nags, and picks on me.

Worker: Your mom always picks on you?

* * *

Client: I've been thinking about what I need to do to make a career change.

Worker: You're thinking about a career change?

Social workers use restatements sparingly. This type of response may fail to move conversations forward. Stringing together several restatements parrots the client and may be irritating or even sound sarcastic. Social workers select restatements to emphasize clients' conclusions and ensure they are hearing what clients are saying.

Restating what clients say is particularly important with multiperson client systems. This response inserts conversation breaks and discourages any one member from monopolizing exchanges, especially when the worker looks around at other members while restating the contribution. Restating what one member says emphasizes information clearly for other members of the client system to consider. When social workers use restatements, they demonstrate respect, model effective listening skills, and give other members of the client system the opportunity to respond.

Clarification

Engage Assess Intervene Evaluate

More than an initial joining, a social worker's genuine engagement with a client is an ongoing dynamic process that may strengthen or weaken as the relationship progresses. What skills work best to strengthen engagement during the information gathering phase?

Clarifying is a more active way for social workers to check their understanding. Kadushin and Kadushin (1997) describe this as "paraphrasing" (p. 128). Here social workers may say, "So, what I hear you saying is . . ." followed by their best attempt to paraphrase and simplify what the client has just shared.

Client: You can't imagine the burden I feel caring for my father who has Alzheimer's. I never get out anymore. He needs around-the-clock care, can't find his way around the house, repeats the same question again and again, and doesn't sleep much. I'm afraid he's going to get out when I'm not looking, but I just can't keep my eyes on him 24 hours a day.

Worker: So, what I hear you saying is that you are having a tough time caring for your father 24 hours a day.

Clarifying what clients say has positive effects. It lets clients know that social workers are listening and understanding. Clarification can also add to clients' understanding of their situations.

Conversely, a client may think the clarification off-base. This challenges clients to try again to explain their thoughts.

Client: Men just always want to be in charge.

Worker: So, men are controlling your life.

Client: Not really. I do what I want. But my husband never listens to my opinions about how he should handle the kids' even though what I do works better.

Worker: Oh, I see. You're talking about your husband and how he relates to the kids. You would like him to handle them the way you do.

Client: That's right.

Clearly there are benefits when clients discover new ways to comprehend and explain their situations. When social workers respond by clarifying, clients and workers begin to see the situation more clearly.

Summary Clarification

When social workers identify important themes or clusters of information, they pull this content together to summarize as well as clarify. To use the summary clarification technique, social workers say things like:

> ▶ Let me see if I'm getting this all right. There seem to be three common issues that the residents are most concerned about.

Or, in keeping with a strengths-oriented perspective:

> ▶ So, it seems like each time your boss confronts you, you find ways to respond assertively yet respectfully.

In each response, the worker does two things—groups information in a logical way and uses words other than the client's to frame the situation. This response "clears the agenda of items that they have adequately discussed so that [they] can devote attention to items that [they] have not" (Kadushin & Kadushin, 1997, p. 150). Summary clarifications organize the work, prioritize the activity, and develop a focus on goals.

Request to Continue

Sometimes the best response is simply to ask clients to keep talking. Politely, many clients pause for the worker to talk, to make a contribution. When social workers sense that it's their turn to talk, they do so without interrupting clients' thinking. When needed, workers can unobtrusively request clients to continue by using short prompts like:

> ▶ Go on . . .
> ▶ Tell me more . . .
> ▶ Please, continue . . .
> ▶ So . . .
> ▶ And, then . . .
> ▶ Anyone else want to comment . . .

When clients are doing a good job of expressing and organizing what they want to say, social workers do less so as not to interfere with the flow of information.

Workers sometimes respond with requests for more specific information, such as:

> ▶ Tell me more about the time when things were getting better.
> ▶ I'd like to talk about parts of your life other than school.

▶ It does seem like the move to the new neighborhood was significant. Please talk more about that.

▶ Let's explore the economic and political ramifications of the policy proposal.

Note that when asking for specific information, social workers guide clients to focus on either important issues or areas which seem confusing:

▶ I'd like to understand better about what you were doing differently.

▶ Please help me understand specifically what is happening at work.

▶ I want to hear more about the recreation resources for community youths.

▶ Help me clear up my confusion about the task force's definition of homelessness.

Requests to continue also give workers direct opportunities to highlight strengths and help clients consider areas of resources that may lead to solutions:

▶ Could you go over that part again about the new approach you tried?

▶ So, you're a successful student. Tell me more.

▶ Let's focus on the steps the neighborhood watch has taken that seem to be working.

Additionally, social workers broaden descriptions by requesting that clients discuss contextual elements:

▶ I'd like you to tell me what else is happening in your life at this time.

▶ So, could you list for me who else attended the public forum?

▶ Tell me more about the new policies your agency developed.

Emphasizing certain topics as important makes these requests for specific information powerful responses. When social workers choose this type of response early in their work with a client, they strive to focus on issues the client presents, rather than leap away from the client's agenda.

Questioning

Questions function to open new areas of exploration or to pursue more specific, detailed information. As responses, questions merely follow up on what clients have already said. Well-framed questions invite clients to survey what they know rather than confess how they have failed. Specific questions can focus clients directly on their strengths. When social workers construct their questions carefully, they can elicit important information and still let clients lead the way.

Well-trained social workers know that respecting clients' power while asking questions is a practice skill requiring extensive preparation. Envision what it's like to be questioned. Do hot lights and smoke-filled rooms spring to mind as you are being interrogated and forced to justify yourself to the uniformed figures circling around you? Certainly, this is not the atmosphere that social workers want to create as they gather information from clients. Experienced practitioners use questions selectively and phrase them carefully!

Phrasing questions is important

Depending on how social workers ask questions, clients experience them as intrusive and confrontational or as interested and supportive. Questions that seek descriptive information begin with words such as "who," "what," "when," "how often," and "in what way." These questions lead to important concrete and contextual information. In contrast to the judgmental message of "why" questions, "who," "what," "when," "how often," and "in what way" questions seek readily available information that increases understanding.

Social workers avoid questions beginning with "why." "Why" questions force respondents to account for their behavior, although often people do not know "why" they've acted as they have (Kadushin & Kadushin, 1997). When social workers use "why" questions, they cast doubts on the choices clients have made and produce defensive postures. Consider how the following questions elicit a greater understanding of what clients are saying. When a client says, "He always lets me down," social workers can respond by asking:

- Who is the "he" that you're talking about?
- In what way does he let you down?
- How does this interfere with what you are trying to accomplish?
- What do you think is getting in his way?
- Always? Is there ever a time when he doesn't?

Notice the common elements of these questions. Each question follows up directly on the client's assertion. Each seeks to elicit concrete information about the client's thinking and the events that are occurring. The worker doesn't search for whom to blame, look for why the behavior occurs, or question whether the representation of the event is "really" true. Each question demonstrates acceptance of the client's experience and the associated feelings. Questions work best when they relate directly to what clients say and when answers will add new information.

Combining Responses

In practice, social workers weave combinations of these responses together to articulate a client's thoughts fully. Some clients offer considerable information with little prompting. Others need more direct approaches to explain their situations in concrete and helpful ways. Empowering social workers choose the least directive responses possible that still keep the conversation on track. The more clients offer their own, the less directive social workers become.

Practice Example

Learning responding skills prepares practitioners to talk with clients. Review the following dialogue to see the skills and to discover the orientation to the future, transactional focus, positive tone, and variety of responses with which Alex Anderson, a practitioner from Northside Prevention Services, responds to Don who calls their telephone hotline.

Alex: Hello. This is the Listening Line. I'm Alex.

Don: Hi. I'm Don.

Alex: Hi, Don. (allows space for client to continue)

Don: You probably want to know why I'm calling.

Alex: Whatever you'd like to tell me.

Don: Well, I've got this problem.

Alex: OK.

Don: You see, I'm the child of an alcoholic.

Alex: Uh-huh.

Don: And my life is a mess.

Alex: In what way, a mess?

Don: I can't seem to get anywhere.

Alex: Some place specific in mind?

Don: Yes, a place that's not so lonely.

Alex: A place that's not so lonely. Who might be there?

Don: Friends, family . . . mostly family.

Alex: Mostly family.

Don: My parents and my sister.

Alex: Seems like you're missing your parents and your sister.

Don: Sometimes.

Alex: I'd like to hear more about your parents and sister.

Don: What do you want to know?

Alex: I guess I'd like to hear the things you think are most important.

Don: Well, I haven't seen them for a while.

Alex: A while?

Don: About six months.

Alex: So, it's been about six months, since . . .

Don: The big fight.

Alex: The big fight?

Don: Yes, my fight with Dad.

Alex: (waits for client to continue)

Don: The fight where he kicked me out . . . or I left . . . I'm not real sure.

Alex: Kind of a mutual thing, huh?

Don: Yes. I guess I just needed some space, but I really wasn't ready for quite this much. Besides, I get concerned about Anna.

Alex: Anna?

Don: My sister.

Alex: So you're concerned about your sister Anna?

Don: Yes, having to deal with my parents and their drinking. It's a lot for a 13-year-old.

Alex: So, tell me more.

Don: Well, you probably know the story. Mom and dad go out and drink and then come home and pick on us kids. I used to take most of the heat, but since I moved out I'm sure they're doing it to Anna.

Alex: So let me get this straight. You are calling with a couple of concerns. First, you are kind of missing contact with your family since you haven't seen them for six months. And secondly, you are wondering how your sister is coping with your parents' drinking since you left.

Don: You got it.

Alex: Anything else?

Don: I guess not.

Alex: Seems like you are thinking about changing this situation.

Don: I'm not liking the way things are.

Alex: So is this call the beginning of changing things or are you also doing other things to change this situation?

Don: Well, I wrote my folks a letter, but I didn't mail it.

Alex: You wrote your folks a letter?

Don: Yes, I worked on it a long time.

Alex: What do you think you'll do with it?

Don: I might mail it. I might deliver it in person. I might throw it away.

Alex: You do have a lot of options.

Don: I do, don't I?

Alex: Seems like it.

Don: You know, now that I have written it out, I could probably even talk to them directly about it.

Alex: Is that what you want to do?

Don: I'll have to think about it.

Alex: Well, you seem like a thoughtful person. I have a sense that you'll figure out what to do next.

Don: Well, it's time to do something. I'll just have to decide what.

Alex: Is that something that you want my help with?

Don: Not right now I don't think.

Alex: OK? Sounds like you're on the way to solving this one.

Don: I think maybe you're right.

Alex: Anything else to talk about with me?

Don: Not right now.

Alex: Feel free to call back if you want to keep thinking out loud, if you're looking for a referral someplace, or whatever.

Don: Thanks. I will.

Alex: Good luck, Don.

Alex gently steers Don toward a positive, transactional, and forward-looking orientation. To do this, Alex uses deliberate responses that maintain the centrality of Don's message. An effective social worker learns communication and listening skills to respond to clients in ways that balance respect for their views while moving them forward toward resolutions.

RESPONDING TO FEELINGS

The human experience of feeling differs from the experience of thinking. We acknowledge this difference by contrasting what is in our hearts with that which is in our heads. Both information from our heads and from our hearts fuel positive growth and change. All events have associated feelings. As social workers, we encourage clients to identify and articulate feelings by responding to feelings that we observe.

Identifying and expressing feelings benefits everyone. Feelings provide clues about where we stand on things and information about what works. Expressing feelings allows us to be close to and validated by others. The consequences of not expressing feelings include loss of information, sense of isolation, projection of emotions into situations where they don't fit, and even physical and emotional illnesses (Johnson, 2006). When social workers assist clients in accessing their feelings, they empower clients with new information, acceptance, and a sense of control.

The Experience of Feelings

Sharing our thoughts and describing our feelings are very different experiences. For example, running into an old friend at a conference is an observable event that may engender an entire constellation of feelings from surprise to joy to awkwardness. We can readily share our thoughts about the event by remembering and reporting. But when describing the associated feelings, we may be plagued by their ambiguity. For some of us, expressing feelings is more difficult than describing thoughts. As we try to articulate how we feel about the event of running into an old friend, we may struggle with the task.

Feelings arise from events occurring within us or outside of us. Feelings may be ambiguous and sometimes surprising or contradictory. Clients may struggle with expressing their feelings, and social workers, likewise, may have difficulty reading the emotions clients express. Social workers and clients work together as partners to identify, verbalize, and validate feelings.

Identifying Feelings

Clients have abundant feelings—about themselves, their situations, and their social workers. All of these feelings are important in guiding the social work process. Social workers prepare to respond to a client's affect by learning to identify the multiple ways people express feelings and by understanding the cultural implications of such expressions.

With some people, talking about feelings is easy. They relate comfortably on the affective level, expressing feelings directly, articulately, and automatically. But more consistently, clients express feelings nonverbally through facial expressions, voice tone, body posture, and choices of words. Social workers observe for feelings and select responses to clarify verbal and nonverbal expressions of emotion.

Verbalizing Feelings

As clients describe the events in their lives, the associated feelings show up, either tumbling out verbally as part of the reporting of events or surfacing in nonverbal behaviors. Feelings vary in intensity—from mild to strong, and from barely noticeable to preoccupying. When social workers see clients express feelings, they respond with verbal reflections to identify the feeling and its intensity. Social workers make educated guesses about a client's feelings and invite clients as experts to either validate or correct these perceptions.

By following a simple strategy, social workers use reflective skills to identify feelings (Figure 7.4). First, workers scan the client's information and behavior for the feeling. Second, they tentatively attach a descriptive label to the feeling. Third, workers enhance the client's understanding of the feeling by connecting it with the precipitating event or behavior. Clients benefit from information that links feelings to thoughts. For example, a social worker may say:

- It seems like you're feeling proud of things you've accomplished to this point, especially your success in parenting.
- I may be detecting a note of sarcasm when you talk about the possibility of your promotion.
- I'm sensing a glimmer of hope when you describe your new approach.
- Look's like you're really angry that the state cut back your funding.
- Seems hopeless since each time you complain to the police, nothing seems to change.

As workers offer hunches about what feelings clients may be experiencing, they make their suggestions tentatively. Workers are actually guessing when they reflect a client's feelings. Only clients know for sure whether the worker's hunch accurately reflects their emotional experiences. Social workers must check out their perceptions. In the subjective world of feelings, only clients can know for sure!

Notice that nowhere in the process of accessing and expressing feelings do workers directly ask "How do you feel?" Experienced social workers will tell you that the most likely response to "How do you feel?" is an honest "I don't know." Right now, ask yourself the question, "How do I feel?" There is nothing like direct questioning about feelings to send every emotion you are experiencing running for cover. Many of us just go blank or struggle to find the right words. Pursuing feelings directly from clients often obscures them, rather than bringing them out. Social workers nurture feelings with hunches and observations rather than chase them with probing questions.

Validating Feelings

Clients are always right about their feelings. Each human being is the sole expert about how he or she feels. Feelings don't have to make sense; they are

Figure 7.4 Constructing a Reflection of Feelings

Step #1	Observe for feelings in verbal and nonverbal expression.
Step #2	Tentatively identify the feeling in words.
Step #3	Connect the feeling expressed to the associated events or thoughts.
Step #4	Reflect the feeling to the client verbally using some variation of the formula: It seems that you are feeling _____(the feeling)_____, when you talk about _____(the event or thought)_____.
Step #5	Wait for the client's response to agree or disagree with the reflection.
Step #6	If the client agrees, accept and validate the feeling. If the client disagrees, go through the steps to try again.
Step #7	Remember that feelings are always correct. You need not approve or disapprove of them. Simply, accept them.

entirely personal and subjective experiences. And importantly, feelings do not mandate behavior. Consider this dramatic example. Even when a father reveals to his social worker that he has sexual feelings toward his daughter, he has done nothing wrong unless he acts on those feelings. In fact, by expressing this feeling he is actually doing something right. In doing so, he creates the opportunity to take charge of his feelings rather than have his feelings lead him toward problematic behavior. Social workers acknowledge even this feeling, reinforce the client's trust in sharing, and work quickly to enable the client with the capability to make other choices.

SPECIAL ISSUES IN RESPONDING

Certain actions by clients deserve special consideration; they call for thoughtful responses by social workers. Experienced social workers learn successful ways to respond to clients' anger, silence, questions, and feedback.

Responding to Anger

Predictably, anger is expressed in many social work encounters. Challenging situations can lead to frustration, disappointment, pain, and sadness—all feelings closely associated with and sometimes expressed by anger. When we hurt, we lash out. When clients hurt, social workers are frequently the targets. Self-confident social workers encourage and validate clients' expression of anger even when it volleys directly toward them. Additionally, workers respond to expressions of anger as opportunities to look for other associated feelings and information.

We each have our own degree of comfort with expressing and responding to anger. When clients express anger, social workers respond as they respond to any other feeling they observe: they reflect the feeling to heighten clients' awareness and invite them to clarify their responses.

- You seem angry . . .
- I can see you are upset . . .
- Makes you mad, huh?

Practitioners connect the feeling to the associated events, in ways such as:

- You seem angry, when you talk about the way the media put down your neighborhood.
- When I mention Child Protective Services, I can see your anger.
- Seems to me that you're upset about my suggestion to get information from your probation officer.

Finally, social workers recognize, accept, and validate feelings of anger. They accept the feeling as okay, even good to express, with phrases such as:

- I can understand how this makes you angry. I appreciate that you trusted me enough to share that.
- Feels good to get angry sometimes.
- Go ahead, talk about it. It's okay to be mad.

Generally, when people express anger, this outward expression reflects internal pain. Often, people respond to their own experience of pain by defending their vulnerability with anger. Social workers reach beyond the expression of anger to identify and reflect a client's internal turmoil and pain rather than simply leaving this emotion at the surface level:

- You look angry, but it seems to me you feel sad.
- Makes you mad to feel so helpless, doesn't it?
- I'd probably be fighting back too, if I felt so vulnerable.

Workers respond to anger with the same empathetic, reflective, and informative style used to respond to all feelings.

Sometimes, when clients express anger toward social workers, their anger contains a specific message. In other words, the anger is not misplaced or symbolic of internal pain, but the client is actually upset at something the worker is or is not doing. Maybe the social worker is trying to get too close too fast. Maybe the worker is missing the point or not responding in ways that show understanding and empathy. Maybe the worker is falling prey to prejudices and stereotypes and not seeing clients for who they really are. Here, too, nondefensive responses clarify feedback:

- So, you're upset with my questions?
- You're angry because I interrupted you?
- In your view, I'm just another white person who can't understand a black man?

Anger communicates important information. Workers examine clients' anger for the feedback it provides.

Responding to Silence

In responding to silence, remember the rule in communication: "one cannot not communicate" (Watzlawick, et al., 1967, p. 49). Even silent clients tell us things about themselves. "One of the most significant sounds that requires listening to is the sound of silence and the associated messages of omission. What interviewees avoid saying is as important as what they do say. Not talking is a special way of talking" (Kadushin & Kadushin, 1997, p. 214). Consider these possible meanings of silence: "I don't want to be here." "It's hope-less." "Leave me alone." "I don't trust you." "I don't trust words." "You might think you are in control, but you can't make me talk." "I don't understand a thing you're saying." According to Laird (1993):

> Meanings and forms vary cross-culturally, in the ways that silence is used linguistically to foster talk, display anger, suppress or hide difference, maintain control, achieve certain ends, manage emotions, or as part of culturally institutionalized rituals. Silence can spring from fear, from loneliness, from resistance, from the will to survive, from the effort to escape stigmatization, from choice, from strength, from the desire to manipulate others. Silence is as powerful if not more powerful in intersubjective discourses as talk. (p. 248)

Silence is ambiguous, so, in responding, the worker's empathy and imagination come into play. Social workers formulate hunches about what clients mean by considering contextual elements, nonverbal cues, and the client's characteristics. If a client is involuntary, a lack of trust and the need for some control is likely. If a client is adolescent, withdrawal from and resistance to adults is age appropriate. If the client smiles blankly, a polite lack of understanding may be evident. If the client is Japanese American, silence may show respect for the social worker (Sue & Sue, 2003). If clients have been victimized by severe oppression or abuse, their poverty of words may reveal the void in their sense of self (Belenky, et al., 1986). If the client is a recent immigrant, language and cultural differences may show up in silence. Workers make their best determination about what clients are saying with their silence, verbalize it, and wait for clients to modify the guess to a more accurate view.

Social workers respond verbally to a client's silence, phrasing their responses in ways that invite clients to talk. Social workers may say:

- Must be tough for you to be here just because someone told you you had to come.
- Kind of seems hopeless to try again on something that you've been trying to deal with for so long.
- I can understand how it might be hard to trust a stranger, especially an older person like me. Take your time. Only tell me things when you are ready.
- Is this making sense to you? Could I ask you to explain what you hear me saying?
- ¿Comprende usted? ¿Habla usted inglés?

Whether clients respond verbally or nonverbally, workers continue to converse, providing clients with ample opportunities to talk.

Responding to Questions

Clients ask questions, too. Frequently, clients have questions about the social worker's credentials, the agency's procedures, or what the worker is saying. Questions are good signs. They often indicate a developing partnership in which clients feel free to assert their needs and express their curiosity. When clients actively take charge of eliciting information, they exercise their power. Workers encourage clients' power by acknowledging their rights to information and by providing appropriately direct and honest answers.

Certain questions require cautious responses. Frequently, clients seek advice with questions: "What would you do if you were in my situation?" "So which one of us is right?" "What should I do?" Social workers who fall prey to this invitation to be experts find themselves trapped by the dependencies they create in clients. An empowering response is one that recognizes the client's need for assistance evident in the advice-seeking question, yet returns the responsibility for solutions to the partnership. Social workers can say:

- I know you'd like me to give you the answer. Trouble is I don't have it.
- I appreciate your confidence in me, but this must be a tough issue or you would have solved it without me.
- Maybe when I know you and your situation better I can let you know what I think, but right now you know a lot more than I do about what is going on.
- I don't know who's right. Probably you both have valid points.

Social workers always respond to questions, but may choose responses that respect the client's expertise.

Responding to Feedback from Clients

As social workers, we benefit from candid appraisals by clients. Clients know best what helps and what does not. Asking clients to make comments concerning both us and the practice process functions as an empowerment strategy. This means accepting clients' positive commentaries as well as their negative perceptions of who we are as people and professionals.

Social workers learn skills to accept feedback. They prepare themselves for nondefensive listening. They respond with appreciation and enthusiasm to feedback from clients.

> ▶ I appreciate your honesty in telling me when I'm off base.
> ▶ Thanks for trusting me enough to share that with me.
> ▶ I appreciate you saying how much you enjoy coming here. I think we make a good team, too.
> ▶ So, you think I'm not understanding your point of view. I'm glad you let me know. What's the piece you think I'm missing?
> ▶ I can understand how it might be difficult to talk to a man about this. How can we make it easier?

Client feedback orients the professional relationship and defines the direction of the work.

RESPONDING TO LARGER CLIENT SYSTEMS

Generalist social workers respond to client systems of all sizes. At all levels of practice, workers respond to clients to elicit their views and to validate their feelings. Practice with any client requires a worker's "one-with-one" conversational ability. Dialogue with larger client systems places workers in a matrix of conversations.

When practitioners work with larger client systems, they must balance the rights of individuals with the rights of others. This ethical challenge raises numerous questions. For example, is it acceptable for one person within the client group to be the spokesperson? Does everyone need to contribute equally? What if people disagree? How does the social worker respond to each individual member of a system, yet respect the functioning of the group? Two skills—facilitating discussion and respecting existing functioning—provide answers to these questions.

Facilitating Discussion

Human Behavior

Generalist practitioners work with a variety of client systems including client groups. How do the dynamics of group interaction affect the skills and methods workers require to access information in the group setting?

Social workers coordinate traffic when responding to multiperson client systems. They actively involve themselves with the client group to influence "who talks when about what." Social workers guide the interaction so that only one person talks at a time, members listen and respond to one another, all members have opportunities to express their views, and the contributions of all members receive respect. To accomplish this, social workers use a variety of methods.

Workers model effective communication by responding in ways that make the thoughts and feelings of all participants more concrete. Workers frequently summarize the group's discussion, highlighting areas of agreement and clarifying options. When others interrupt, contradict, or let one person monopolize, social workers take more active roles. When more than one member talks at once, social workers may say:

> ▶ I love people who talk, but I need it one at a time so I can take it all in.
> ▶ I see you both have information. Who wants to start?
> ▶ Whoa. There is a lot of enthusiasm here. Good! I want to hear what each of you has to say.

Or social workers may respond nonverbally and

- ◗ Attend to the person who was first talking through eye contact and body posture; then, immediately turn to elicit the view of the person who was interrupting at the first available pause
- ◗ Acknowledge the member's desire to contribute with a hand gesture that holds back the person's contribution temporarily; then, wave them on to share when possible

When people's different views lead to conflict, workers may say:

- ◗ You both have interesting views. I guess there's more than one way to look at this situation.
- ◗ You know, no two people see the same thing the same way. You both may be right.
- ◗ Well, that's two ways to look at it. Anyone have another way?
- ◗ It's great when people disagree. It always gives you more options.

When one member monopolizes, workers recognize the mutual responsibility of the talking and the silent members by responding:

- ◗ Thanks for all the information. You're really working hard here. Maybe somebody else should take it for a while.
- ◗ Well, I think I understand your views. I'm going to need everyone's opinion for this to work. Who's up next?
- ◗ You really have a good grasp of the situation. What can the rest of you tell me?
- ◗ That was a bold move to go first, and now you get to relax and listen while the others talk.

Social workers respond in ways that appreciate contributions yet redirect interactions. Workers validate contributions, encourage participation, and organize the flow of information.

Respecting Existing Functioning

When one member of a client system says more or less than another, this does not mean that social workers must intervene. Workers trust that systems have their own style of relating. How each system member contributes may actually draw on the strengths of the system. Some client systems work best with a combination of talkers and listeners, up-front doers and behind-the-scenes planners. For example, within a given family, a parent who spends more time with the child concerned logically has more to contribute to describing events.

Formal client systems, such as organizations, likely have prescribed interactional processes. With such clients, workers show respect for the organization's structure and practices. For example, if an organization decides through a consensus process that a certain committee will speak for the group, rights of individuals are still assured. As long as the system operates in a way that respects the contributions of all its members, workers have no reason to interfere.

LOOKING FORWARD

Articulating situations means detailing challenging issues from the client's perspective and placing these events in environmental context. A challenge model adds future, transactional, and positive dimensions to the problems clients face. The process of articulating situations is one piece of what practitioners do to "begin where the client is." But "where clients are" is not exclusively a place of problems. Even when things look bleak, not everything is going wrong. Clients have resources even in the most difficult times.

For workers to discover available strengths within clients and their environments, they must first help clients define a positive direction by setting desired goals. Chapter 8 presents processes to assist clients in describing positive directions for effort. In the context of these preliminary goals, workers can focus the search for relevant resources.

Log onto **www.mysocialworklab.com** and select the **Interactive Skill Module** videos from the left-hand menu. Answer the questions below. (*If you did not receive an access code to **MySocialWorkLab** with this text and wish to purchase access online, please visit* www.mysocialworklab.com.)

1. **Watch the school social work module, pages 16 and 17.** Social worker Terry gathers information about client Michelle's family. Critique Terry's responding skills in this interview. Which responses work best to elicit information and engage Michelle?

2. **Turn off your computer's sound to watch pages 4, 6, 7, and 9 of the group work module.** Observe the group's leader and its members. What do you "hear" from facial expression and body language? Replay the pages, now with sound. Critique your ability to understand non-verbal communication.

PRACTICE TEST

1. When social worker Alex Anderson responds to his client by saying, "Help me understand more about what you do differently," he's using the strategy from the response continuum called _____.
   a. allowing space
   b. restatement
   c. clarification
   d. request to continue

2. Which of the following statements describes a benefit of responding with a restatement?
   a. Restatements are effective as perception checks.
   b. Restatements provide "quiet spaces" for clients to formulate their words.
   c. Restatements convey one-word responses to keep the conversation going.
   d. Restatements open new areas of conversation.

Engage Assess Intervene Evaluate

3. Of the following questions, which is the LEAST appropriate for gathering information from a client who expresses being let down by a partner?
   a. In what ways does your partner let you down?
   b. Why do you respond that way to your partner?
   c. Is there a time when your partner hasn't let you down?
   d. What seems to be getting in your partner's way when you feel let down?

4. Which of the following is NOT phrased as a challenge?
   a. Louise needs the respite from caregiving provided by the adult day center
   b. Ann's family is dysfunctional
   c. Ryan and Lee are rebalancing their relationship after adopting their first child.
   d. Members of the Northside Community planning commission are exploring ways to make their community supportive of aging in place.

5. Meeting the Lopez family for the first time, social worker Cassandra Ruez observes a number of silences. Cassandra interprets these silences as _____.

   a. a need to end the session quickly because the family is telling her through their silence that they have nothing more to say
   b. an indication that the family wants her to take over the conversation
   c. an opportunity to evaluate the nonverbal behavior and formulate a response that invites family members to talk
   d. an invitation to asking probing questions, such as "Why is it so difficult for you to talk right now?"

6. Social worker Albert Smith wonders whether he fully understood what his client has told him. To determine whether he is understanding his client accurately, Albert should _____.
   a. task his supervisor to clarify the meaning
   b. use a perception check to facilitate understanding
   c. empathize with the client to promote effective communication
   d. evaluate his accuracy by reconstructing the session

Diversity in Practice

7. Yamada Tāro pays a great deal of attention to the details of communication such as posture, social status, phrasing and gestures. His cultural heritage reflects a _____.
   a. contextual culture
   b. low context culture
   c. detail oriented culture
   d. high context culture

Critical Thinking

8. While leading a team meeting, social worker Tammy Feldon encounters a lively discussion among team members reflecting conflicting points of view. Tammy should _____.
   a. use nonverbal eye signals to express her displeasure
   b. redirect the team members attention to another agenda item
   c. regard the different points of view as options and solicit additional ideas
   d. control the conversation to avoid conflict

Log onto **MySocialWorkLab** once you have completed the Practice Test above to take your Chapter Exam and demonstrate your knowledge of this material.

Answers

1) c 2) a 3) b 4) b 5) c 6) b 7) d 8) c

8

Defining Directions

CONNECTING CORE COMPETENCIES *in this chapter*

| Professional Identity | **Ethical Practice** | Critical Thinking | Diversity in Practice | Human Rights & Justice | Research Based Practice | **Human Behavior** | Policy Practice | Practice Contexts | Engage Assess Intervene Evaluate |

It's the second Tuesday of the month, and members of the Northside Network are gathering for their monthly brown-bag luncheon. Established less than 3 months ago, the Northside Network is a consortium of human service agencies with representatives from all over the Northside community. Network members are quickly discovering that, in spite of the differences in the services that each provides, they really have much in common. As part of the same community, they confront similar community problems and draw from the same selection of resources and opportunities to serve clients.

During the first two meetings, members of the group get to know one another, and they organize a structure to guide the functioning of the group. Now it is time to look ahead. Members have yet to decide a specific purpose for the Network. Miriam Andovich calls the meeting to order, part of her role as facilitator, and she guides the group to develop a coherent direction for action.

Miriam works in the AIDS prevention project at the Northside Alliance for Family Health, and today, she is the facilitator for the Northside Network—a role that rotates among the group's members. Miriam shifts her focus to the group as a whole and uses many of the same generalist practice skills to facilitate its functioning as she uses with clients in the AIDS prevention project. Miriam suggests that the group begin today's work with a brief structured experience she calls "the Network News." She asks that each member take 2 minutes to update the others about newsworthy events at their agencies. Miriam believes that for the group to decide where they are going, they should first establish where they are.

One by one, workers describe current issues affecting the agencies they represent. Tony Marelli announces that the Addictions Recovery Center has new funds for in-school prevention programming, but so far no schools have applied. Mark Nogales describes his organization's concerns about a reduction in participation by county residents in the programs of the County Mental Health Center. Kay Landon notes that the Family Support Program is seeking funds to hire interpreters and bilingual staff. Andrea Barry describes the frustration workers in the Family Preservation Program are experiencing in helping clients locate low-cost housing. The waiting lists for public assistance housing are growing, and low-cost private rentals are virtually nonexistent. All Network members contribute their own perspectives on what's happening in the Northside community.

As members report, Miriam writes their comments on large sheets of paper mounted on the wall behind her. Next, she poses the question: What are our common concerns? As members offer their ideas, Miriam responds in ways to encourage interaction, to summarize and clarify what members say, and to guide members to synthesize ideas. Soon, similar opinions about "getting rid of so many restrictions to services" and "simplifying intake processes" lead the members to identify the umbrella issue of accessibility of services as an apparent unifying theme. Miriam sums up the group's direction by saying, "So, our purpose will be to increase the accessibility of our services for both urban and rural county residents." A quick poll of the members confirms this common purpose. Members act to make their consensus an official agreement or "contract" by proposing it as a formal motion, approving it with a unanimous vote, and recording the transaction in the minutes.

Identifying accessibility as the central issue focuses the group's discussion. Ideas surface concerning community education about available services, services at no cost to clients or based on the clients' abilities to pay, better transportation for clients to reach agencies, staff and community training on cultural sensitivity, more in-home services, and the need to examine restrictive eligibility requirements for various programs. Members acknowledge each idea's merit but agree that choosing specific "solutions" right now is premature. No one can say with certainty what poses significant barriers or what actions will have the greatest influence on service accessibility. Members will need a more detailed assessment to determine what activities will do the most good.

Before adjourning, several members volunteer to participate on a committee to develop a community resource assessment plan. Implementing this assessment, members will discover which factors currently enhance accessibility and which create obstacles. The more complete assessment information will then contribute to the members' efforts to develop a workable and concrete plan of action.

Miriam's interaction with the Northside Network illustrates how a practitioner assists a community-based organization to define a direction for its work. The same processes apply to practice at other system levels. Both clients and social workers participate in developing a mutual direction. Clients bring their own motivations, sense of destination, and rights to self-determination. Social workers balance their respect for client privileges with their own vision of what could be. Clients benefit from this early effort to define a mutual purpose. "Only when people start creating scenarios of possibility do they move in directions more satisfying to them and the problems become lost or much less influential" (Saleebey, 1994, p. 357).

This chapter describes how social workers and clients define a direction for their work. It also examines priority issues that may arise requiring an immediate response. In detail, this chapter

- Demonstrates skills that guide a worker and client to reformulate a problem statement into a goal
- Uses methods to understand and activate a client's motivation
- Explains how a collaborative social worker interprets and responds to a client's resistance
- Summarizes effective social worker responses to crisis events that require immediate action

Agreeing to a common purpose for the relationship activates clients to participate in the change process and directs the search for available resources.

TRANSFORMING CHALLENGES INTO DIRECTIONS

Empowerment presumes that the worker does not hold the answers to the client's problems.

—Lorraine Gutiérrez

Defining a direction describes the process of negotiating a mutually agreeable purpose or preliminary goal. It logically precedes other actions taken by workers and clients to assess resources or develop an intervention plan (Figure 8.1). In other words, workers and clients postpone setting very specific goals at this early juncture in lieu of establishing a more global expectation about the outcomes of the work. This beginning agreement about the purpose of the relationship guides the dialogue toward gathering enough information to frame a concrete intervention plan with more specific goals and objectives—a plan informed by a goal-focused assessment.

Strength-oriented social workers recognize the benefit of a vision of the future, so they move quickly to "define directions" with their clients. Oftentimes, clients begin the dialogue at intake by describing what they hope to achieve. In the case of an individual or family client, a practitioner might come to an agreement with the client within a few short minutes of beginning

Figure 8.1
The Process of Defining Directions

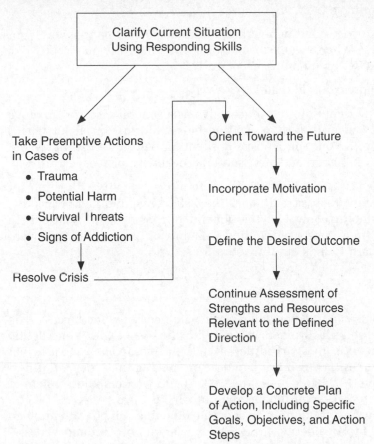

the initial interchange. In contrast, the diversity of perspectives in larger client systems will likely require more dialogue before participants can negotiate an agreed-on direction. With client systems at any level, workers may need to nudge clients beyond describing only their present difficulties toward considering future possibilities about how things should be.

Reshaping a report of a challenging situation into a clear direction informs social workers and their clients in several ways. First, clients are most likely to achieve outcomes that they can clearly envision (Walter & Peller, 1992). Second, workers learn what clients want, an important context in which to view the information clients offer. For example, understanding a client's overall purpose helps to determine the significance of problematic events and also to identify resources for building a solution. And finally, pausing to consider a preliminary sense of direction gives a generalist social worker time to explore the transactional dimensions of the situation, thereby broadening the field of potential solutions to all system levels.

Orienting Forward, Not Back

Clients seeking services most often want some change in their present situations. Solution-oriented social workers urge clients to go beyond simply identifying what they want to change to project in detail how they would like to be. Setting overall goals directs helping relationships away from describing problems toward constructing solutions, from what is to what will be.

Social workers assist clients in visualizing what they want by shifting the conversation from what is not working to the more empowering view of a desirable outcome that clients can achieve. Observe the dialogue in which Vanessa, a social worker in the State's Child Protective Unit, responds to focus Kim toward the future.

Vanessa: I understand that you are here to talk about ways to stop hitting your son when he talks back.

Kim: That's right. He'll report me for child abuse if I do it again.

Vanessa: OK. If you're not going to hit your son when he talks back, what do you see yourself doing instead?

Kim: I guess I'll do nothing.

Vanessa: By doing nothing, do you mean that you will allow him to talk back while you just stand there and ignore him or will you just walk away? What exactly are you hoping to do?

Kim: I'm not really sure. I know I can't hit him. I'll get in trouble. He's getting too big and it doesn't help anyway. I really wish he just wouldn't talk back. Then I wouldn't have to do anything.

Vanessa: Seems like you're telling me that the first step will be to ignore your son or walk away when he talks back, but in the long run you'd really like to have him talk with you more respectfully.

Kim: That's right. How can I do that?

Vanessa: I'm not sure right now, but it does give us a general direction to move in. We probably need to start by getting more information about what's going on with you, your son, and your situation before we can figure out specific ways to help you and your son talk together more respectfully.

In this example, Vanessa and Kim quickly determine a positive direction for their work. Notice how Vanessa facilitates this task by responding in ways that enable Kim to maintain control of the general purpose of the relationship while, at the same time, gently reorienting Kim away from describing current dilemmas and forward to look at future solutions.

Framing the Search for Resources

Outcomes that clients can imagine and describe are necessary for success. The role of solution-focused practitioners is "to invite clients to explore and define two matters: (1) what it is they want different in their lives (goals), and (2) what strengths and resources they can bring to bear on making these desired differences a reality" (Berg & De Jong, 1996, p. 377). Social workers know where to steer assessment processes after the desired outcome is clear.

You can see how helpful defining a concrete outcome can be in framing an assessment process by considering the previous example of Kim and Vanessa. Knowing what Kim wants leads Vanessa to focus directly on those resources Kim has to help her talk with her son more respectfully. Vanessa can now ask Kim about exceptions, times when she either walked away before hitting her son or was able to discuss issues with him in a calm manner. Recognizing an exception or a resource is only possible in the context of how Kim wants things to be. Defining the purpose of the relationship is a necessary prerequisite to discovering useful resources. Chapters 9 and 10 outline specific strategies and suggest tools for assessing client strengths and environmental resources in the context of a clearly defined direction. Chapter 11 details the process of analysis and planning.

Integrating Transactional Dimensions

Setting very specific goals before developing an ecosystemic understanding is premature from the point of view of generalist practice. Planning too quickly can overemphasize the responsibility of clients to make changes while underestimating the potential of social and physical environments to hold solutions. In other words, we may be asking clients to change themselves (because that is now what we know most about) while ignoring the possible benefits of modifying the context.

Reconsider the previous example. What if Kim's unemployment adds stress or fears for her son's safety in the neighborhood and a sense of desperation to her parenting? What if the community's discrimination against Vietnamese immigrants or the housing authority's policy of refusing housing to families without credit histories contributes to an underlying tension in the household that triggers aggression in any difficult interaction? If, early on, a social worker and client set goals that narrowly focus on changing the client's behavior, significant transactional elements may go undetected as possible paths to solutions. Completing a broader ecosystemic assessment before establishing more concrete goals and plans of action gives flexibility and adds a generalist focus to the process.

CONSIDERING CLIENT MOTIVATION

Some social workers summarily dismiss unsuccessful outcomes with a simple, "This client isn't sufficiently motivated." This attitude fails to consider the notion that all behavior is motivated, including seemingly "unmotivated" behaviors such as disinterest in service plans, resistance to change, or withdrawal from service. Simply, client behavior, like all human behavior, is motivated toward some end, even if it is not in the direction social workers anticipate.

Clients go where they are motivated to go within the boundaries of the resources and constraints present. Naturally, goals likely to enhance motivation are those that clients believe will result in more satisfying situations. Workers help clients envision desirable outcomes that will motivate their participation and provide a continuing incentive for following through.

A Transactional View of Motivation

Social work has traditionally defined motivation as an individual attribute, something that clients either have or do not have, bring or fail to bring. Contemporary social work understands motivation as a transactional concept rather than a personal trait. Social workers move beyond the tendency to assess behavior as unmotivated or resistive. Instead, they examine the interactions among the client system, the social worker, and the environment for clues to understand the underlying motivation of behavior. Social workers share responsibilities for stimulating clients' motivation to participate in and continue the work.

Motivating Clients Who Have Given Up

To succeed, people need a sense of self-efficacy to meet the inevitable obstacles and inequities of life.

—Albert Bandura

Many clients need a motivational boost to succeed. These clients have learned that despite their best efforts, their attempts fail. Life has convinced them they are helpless. Researchers have observed this phenomenon of learned helplessness, documenting that a prolonged lack of success results in a lack of motivation to continue to try (Abramson, et al., 1978; Seligman, 1975).

Clients in oppressive situations are most vulnerable to experiencing this state of learned helplessness. Social structures disenfranchise these clients and block them from their rightful share of societal resources. Workers can address this situation in four steps by

- Listening to and validating the client's frustrating experiences
- Framing an achievable direction
- Expressing belief in the worker's and client's abilities to reach the desired outcome
- Searching for resources to effect sociopolitical change

Recognizing feelings of hopelessness

Oppression is a real event in the everyday lives of many people. To begin a motivational process with clients who experience oppression, social workers must first recognize and validate the reality of oppression as clients tell their stories. Workers can also share how other clients were able to overcome their hopelessness and achieve their goals. For example, Saleebey (1994) describes the efforts of social work students placed in public housing to spread "tales of survival under difficult conditions; stories about compassion, about 'grace under pressure'; tales of accomplishment; and word pictures of people acting effectively with dignity" (p. 356).

Visualizing positive outcomes

Workers help clients who feel hopeless to define a positive direction. Clients benefit from looking ahead, as looking ahead provides an optimistic context in which to view their present difficulties. Research documents that setting goals increases motivation. Bandura and Cervone (1983) describe a relationship between feelings of self-efficacy, motivation to achieve a self-prescribed goal, and gains in performance. In other words, people made the most progress when they had clear visions of where they were going, participated in defining the direction, and believed that they could achieve their goal. For clients to maintain motivation, they need a sense that the end product is in sight.

Expressing hope and optimism

Practice Contexts

Negotiating desirable and meaningful goals with clients is a core social work skill. How does the agency context influence what goals social workers might set with clients?

To motivate a client who feels hopeless, workers bring hope to the situation. Underlying the worker's efforts to instill hope is the worker's belief that the client can achieve. Assumptions that all clients have strengths and recognition of the transactional and transitory nature of challenges contribute to expectations that positive changes can occur even for clients who initially view their situations as hopeless. A worker's optimism that a client can succeed is contagious. It begins to construct a reality of alternatives and options that previously seemed unavailable to clients.

Aligning Worker and Client Motivations

Because all human behavior is motivated, we can conclude that clients and workers alike bring motivations to the professional relationship. When workers and clients unite to move in the same direction, this alliance itself becomes a powerful resource in the process. Each validates the sense of purpose in the other. Each contemplates and initiates actions toward the desired outcome. Each has an investment in reaching a common destination. But when workers and clients are heading in different directions, even the most vigorous efforts of one can be neutralized by the energetic efforts of the other. Before clients and workers forge a path ahead, they need to talk enough about where they are going to agree on a mutual direction.

Motivating Larger Systems

Work with larger systems builds on the motivation of individual members. In large client systems, the key is to activate maximal involvement by as many members as possible. In the example of the Northside Network that opens this chapter, all members will report the group's activities to their own colleagues to generate enthusiasm and receive additional input. They will also update their supervisors, administrators, and boards of directors about the Network's activities to retain their agencies' official sanctions. Each agency will want assurances that the goals of the Network mesh with its own particular mission. A good fit in terms of goals and agreement with the methods chosen will motivate agencies to support the Network's efforts.

Nominal group technique

Sometimes, workers define directions with large client systems by using structured processes. Nominal group technique is a formal strategy that motivates participants and combines their efforts in setting directions. This quick and efficient process works best with six to nine people (Toseland & Rivas, 2002). However, it can easily be adapted to work with larger organizational and community groups by running the process several times and combining the results.

Nominal group technique offers a way of generating information about a specified issue, eliciting responses from participants by using a round-robin strategy, discussing the ideas participants contribute, and, finally, establishing priorities through a mathematical rank-ordering process. The steps for using this technique include:

1. Before the process begins, prepare a clear statement of the issue or problem to which the group will respond.

2. Provide a copy of the statement for participants and ask them to list their responses without conferring with each other.

3. Have participants share their responses one at a time. Record each response so that all participants can view the list of responses. This is a brainstorming strategy in which participants simply report their responses without discussing them or evaluating them. Participants may add new ideas that occur to them during this step.

4. Beginning with the first item on the list and proceeding in order, discuss each item to eliminate the overlap among ideas and to clarify the meanings of the responses.

5. Ask participants to select a predetermined number of items from the list that they consider most important. This step reduces the number of items from which participants select their "top priorities."

6. Finally, ask participants to rank-order the items they consider in the "top five," using 5 for the highest ranked item and 1 for the lowest. Record the ratings for each item and calculate the total points assigned to each. Ideas receiving the highest point totals are the ones the group identifies as most important.

Nominal group technique has important advantages as a decision-making process in that it always reaches a conclusion, considers several alternatives, and encourages participation and discussion. As a planning tool, nominal group process assesses needs while increasing collaboration between the worker and the group members (Gerdes & Benson, 1995). It accommodates the motivation of each individual member and, thereby, activates a widespread commitment to the group's direction.

COLLABORATING WITH CLIENTS WHO RESIST

Considering the motivations of clients leads us to look at resistance. When social workers see resistant behaviors in clients, they explore them for the messages they contain. Clients may be sending messages that they want to change direction or that environmental obstacles are blocking their participation. Behaviors that look uncooperative on the surface merit careful attention. They indicate important information about clients, social workers, and the environments in which they operate.

Resistance is Motivated

Human Behavior

A generalist social worker might say that a client's resistance is understandable in context. What does it mean that a client's resistance is contextually-based?

Resistance from clients is expected. "Resistance to change in general and resistance to being influenced in particular always occurs when individuals, groups, and systems are required by circumstances to alter their established behaviors" (Anderson & Stewart, 1983, p. 1). Certainly, this description makes sense in terms of ecosystems theory. Human systems evolve in ways that represent their best attempts to master their current situations. Why would clients readily change behaviors that have logically developed and provided them with stability and equilibrium? "However great the distress people feel, they resist asking for help, and having asked for help, they resist being influenced by the professionals they have employed to help them" (p. 1).

Look more closely at the assumptions inherent in the assertion that clients always resist. Do we mean that clients are resisting changes, or do we mean that clients are resisting what social workers want them to do? If social workers want to go in one direction and clients want to go in another, who is resisting whom? In his work as a family therapist, de Shazer (1989) talks about resistance when he says: "Attributing blame to either party of an interaction is theoretically unsound. Such a split between members of a system inevitably creates imaginary opposition. But clinically, both therapists and clients are in it together" (p. 231). Resistance indicates that clients and social workers are not synchronized. It may reveal a client's motivation to move in a different direction.

Resistance is communication. It often communicates a message that social workers are overstepping their partnership agreements. In other words, at times, clients may rebel against the directions that workers propose simply because they don't want to be told what to do. Any parent experiences those periods in children's lives—the "terrible twos" and adolescence—in which no matter how right parents are, they're wrong. Social workers are not parents to clients. Rather, they are partners with them. When clients respond with resistance, social workers cooperate by clarifying just where clients are leading them.

Cooperating with Resistance

Reconsider the framing of social work relationships as collaborative partnerships, incorporate the assumption of client expertise, and then the notion of client resistance melts away. When clients want to go in directions other than those that workers choose, empowering practitioners yield and let clients lead the way. Clients have the privilege to resist. Social workers respect and cooperate with clients who resist. Resistance clearly demonstrates that clients have power! Why would empowering social workers want to invalidate such an expression?

Social workers respond to a client's expression of resistance in ways that clarify, organize, and encourage. Workers may say:

- I have the sense that you are not agreeing with me. Please help me understand where I'm off base.
- I keep trying to pull the discussion back to our prepared agenda; however, it seems like this group wants to move in a different direction. I'd like to understand more clearly where you're headed.

▶ I'm confused. Earlier, I understood that you wanted to protest how the worker at the public aid office is treating you, and now I'm hearing you say that you want to leave well enough alone. In which direction are we going?

Each response acknowledges that social workers have a part in creating resistance. Each response also demonstrates how workers "go with the flow" by turning the responsibility for defining the direction back to the client.

Overcoming Environmental Resistance

Even when clients have a high level of investment and see their outcomes as very desirable, their investments may falter under the burden of environmental constraints. Social workers may misread clients' behaviors as resistance in these situations. Instead, others may be trying to thwart clients' efforts; their access to resources needed for their successful achievement of goals may be limited or nonexistent; or the practicalities of service delivery such as transportation, costs, and location may be prohibitive. Social workers and clients maintain creativity and flexibility in aligning interpersonal and service delivery resources to overcome these very real barriers. They may need to target social or environmental impediments to motivation to clear the way for the clients to invest fully in the process.

Consider the example of Twyla, who sporadically attends a mothers' support group. The worker's initial impulse is to confront Twyla for her lack of commitment to the group. However, assessing more closely reveals the nature of Twyla's "resistance." In discussing the issue, Twyla describes her husband's anger over her attendance, her difficulty in locating child care, and the undependable car that she drives. Each one of these environmental factors influences her attendance at group meetings. In view of these obstacles, even Twyla's sporadic attendance demonstrates a great deal of motivation to participate. To increase Twyla's attendance, the worker needs to target the issues of child care, transportation, and her husband's attitude.

COOPERATING WITH MANDATED CLIENTS

Policy Practice

Social policy affects all social work clients. What effects might social policies have on a social worker's practice with a mandated client?

Clients mandated to receive services are involuntary participants in social worker–client relationships. They are pressured by legal authorities to work with a practitioner they haven't chosen to deal with problems they may not believe are important, real, or anybody's business but their own. The majority of clients served in child welfare agencies, probation offices, delinquency intervention programs, and many types of mental health services approach these services involuntarily.

Equalizing power within the helping relationship is a major challenge for social workers in forming partnerships with involuntary clients. The client's sense of powerlessness generated by the specific mandate is often complicated by a life-long experience of oppression because "members of oppressed groups are disproportionately represented among involuntary clients" (Rooney, 1992, p. 21). Seeking to increase an involuntary client's experience of power in a context in which someone else is in charge requires the worker to take direct actions that restore the client's feelings of control. So practitioners move quickly to frame a positive experience, to reconfigure the relationship for collaboration, and to define a mutual direction in which the client's goals are primary.

Constructing Workers' Expectations

Previously, we discussed the powerful role that expectations play in human interaction. Without reflective consideration, three damaging presuppositions are likely to invade a worker's thinking about mandated clients: (1) "they are 'bad' people," (2) "they won't cooperate no matter what I do," and (3) "they will be unsuccessful." In working with mandated clients, workers must carefully prepare their assumptions to construct an atmosphere conducive to collaboration.

Regarding mandated clients as "bad" people obviously violates the social work principles of nonjudgmentalism and acceptance. This posture also fails to apply an ecosystemic understanding that orients workers to examine not just the person but the person in the situation as the focus of inquiry. This vision of where the problem is located—in the person or in the situation—is a key element in encouraging involuntary clients to cooperate with services. Rooney (1992) describes this as the contrast between the deviant/pathological perspective (the problem is within the individual) versus the structural perspective (the problem is within how the individual relates to the environment). Workers who demonstrate their belief in a structural perspective will most likely achieve collaboration with clients who are involuntary.

Research has also shown that mandated clients can achieve success equal to or greater than the outcomes of voluntary clients (Rooney, 1992; Burke & Gregoire, 2007). Mandates to change may actually act as powerful motivators for clients to confront issues that they have ignored or been unable to face without assistance. Workers must recognize the feasibility of a successful outcome, communicate this expectation to clients, and anticipate clients' cooperation to set the helping relationship on a positive course.

Structuring a Working Partnership

Mandated clients enter social work relationships convinced that the practitioner and referral source are functioning as one. Consequently, a client's feelings of powerlessness and resentment experienced with legal authorities transfer immediately to the worker. The client is likely to perceive the initial structure of the helping relationship as one-sided—with the client on one side of the relationship and the worker and mandating authority partnered on the other. For workers to initiate a collaborative relationship, they must take action to restructure this initial configuration by talking directly about the worker–client relationship.

In many respects, working with mandated clients makes social workers involuntary participants as well. Workers acknowledge this reality and discuss it openly with their clients. The purpose of this discourse is to shift how the client perceives the role of the worker in relation to the referral agency—the "common" outside force. Social workers must draw boundaries between themselves and the coercive referral source to find the common ground on which to build partnerships with clients. To this end, workers carefully articulate their own roles in relation to the client (as differentiated from the referral source), clearly define the client's privileges in the newly established relationship, and ascertain the client's motivation and goals to recenter the relationship on the client's needs and aspirations.

Distinguishing worker roles

To structure the relationship for collaboration, the worker finds ways to ally with the client's perspective. Consider the example of a men's support group, one component of a Batterer's Education Program. These men, ordered to the

Box 8.1 Ethic of Autonomy

Self-determination derives from the ethic of autonomy. Autonomy recognizes personal initiative, free choice, voluntary action, and power and authority in governing one's life. Necessarily, the ethic of autonomy includes two dimensions—one, a sense of capability for independent action, and two, independence from undue influence or control by others (Barker, 2003). For social workers, this translates into a practice mindset that perceives clients as capable and into actions that promote voluntary participation by clients in assessment, planning, and change activities.

By applying the principle of self-determination, social work practitioners uphold the "right and need of clients to freedom in making their own choices and decisions" (Biestek, 1957, p. 103). Self-determination acknowledges that sound growth emanates from within, or as Hollis (1967) says:

> for this growth from within to occur, there must be freedom—freedom to think, freedom to choose, freedom from condemnation, freedom from coercion, freedom to make mistakes as well as to act wisely. Strength to understand and to act upon one's understanding comes only as one actually experiences and exercises the freedom to direct one's own thoughts and behaviors—and that is what we mean by self-determination. (p. 26)

Although self-determination arises within, it can be stifled in a hierarchical relationship. Paternalism and maternalism both undermine autonomy in social work practice. When social workers act paternalistically, they impose their preferences and decisions on clients based on a belief that they "know best" or know what is in the best interest of the client. Maternalism is based on good intention gone awry—unintentional control exercised through overpowering caring behaviors. Collaborative social workers avoid skewed power relationships, freeing clients to define the direction of the change effort.

A worker's commitment to the ethic of client self-determination and autonomy is tested in situations in which a client's capacity is limited by disability or crisis. A social worker's respect for client autonomy depends on clients' abilities to make choices that "do no harm" to themselves or other people. Risks associated with any action need to be fully disclosed and explored. Clients need to make informed and carefully considered choices in exercising their rights to self-determination. Practitioners need to minimize the risk of benign neglect or underserving the client by over-respecting clients' autonomy (Austin, 1996). Social workers do have responsibilities to assess a client's capacity for making decisions, including recognizing the influence of crisis events that render clients temporarily incapable of good judgment, situations that warrant workers taking charge to prevent clients from harm.

For a worker to honor a client's autonomy requires more than a careful assessment and implementation of a client's preferences among limited choices. Client self-determination may be curtailed by agency rules, standards, or eligibility requirements, and in the context of social policy by legal restrictions or mandates. A client will experience the benefits of autonomy only when choosing among alternatives in a context in which genuine opportunities are available. This reality orients social workers to mezzo- and macropractice interventions to create an environment in which good choices and productive alternatives exist. The NASW (1999a) *Code of Ethics* requires that social workers "respect and promote the right of clients to self-determination" but also recognizes that workers must "engage in social and political action that seeks to ensure that all people have equal access to the resources, employment, services, and opportunities they require to meet their basic human needs and to develop fully." Client autonomy exists only in an atmosphere of social justice that affords clients rights and their share of societal benefits.

group by the courts, differ from each other in many ways, yet they share a common desire not to be there. They are frequently resentful of the judge's order and sometimes angry at those who they perceive have contributed to their predicament. Workers who attempt to partner with this group by placing themselves in a similar social control role discover closed boundaries when trying to build relationships with group members.

Workers can expect a certain amount of resistance from involuntary clients, initially in terms of acknowledging that a problem exists and then in response to worker-initiated change attempts (Slonim-Nevo, 1996). Workers with nonvoluntary clients must weigh the use of the legal authority to force cooperation against the risk of increasing the client's sense of powerlessness.

Articulating client roles

Recently stripped of power, involuntary clients may withhold information to gain some sense of control. Direct talk about power issues can reopen communication. When initiating relationships with involuntary clients, social workers move quickly to identify just what power clients do hold by providing answers to questions such as:

- What realistically do clients control?
- Within the boundaries of the relationship, what privileges do clients have?
- What are the potential sanctions clients may experience for self-disclosure?
- What are the consequences for clients who refuse to participate?

Discussing the client's legal situation clarifies the expectations affecting both clients and practitioners. Within these boundaries, social workers and clients may still have choices about methods for removing the mandate. In defining what the worker and client will do, mandated clients benefit from descriptions of how the work will proceed, from the generation of a realistic array of options and choices that may work under the circumstances, and from active participation in defining objectives and tasks (Rooney, 1992).

Defining a Motivating Direction

Involuntary clients enter professional relationships compelled by someone else's decision—the motivation to participate is external—yet, these clients are not without their own motivation. At a minimum, mandated clients want to get someone off their backs, regain control over their lives, or prove that they don't need anybody's help. Social workers openly accept these underlying goals of mandated clients as reasonable and focus on what clients can do that will result in their freedom and independence.

Motivational congruence between clients and workers is a key factor in achieving successful outcomes (Rooney, 1992). When clients' goals vary from those set by authorities, workers respond to shape a mutual agenda. Social workers may say:

- I believe it when you say that you don't need to be here. What do you think you need to do to convince the Child Protective Unit that you can handle things?
- You're absolutely right. No one can tell you what to do. I certainly don't intend to. What is it that you think we need to be doing?
- It looks like we're stuck together for at least five sessions. Is there something you would like to work on because you're here anyway, or do you just want to wait it out?

Initially, practitioners may accept a client's goal to escape the legal entanglement precipitating the mandate. Consider a simple example. When the court forces parents to use social work services to control their daughter's truancy, the worker accepts the family's goals of getting court and school officials off their backs. When the social worker explores how to make that happen, the family's roles and responsibilities become apparent. Defining an initial direction in terms of how others will change may motivate an involuntary client. As the work continues, the social worker refines this direction, by helping clients discover actions within their control to take as a means to change how others respond.

TAKING PRIORITY ACTIONS

Certain situations demand immediate action by social workers. When clients' safety is uncertain, others are at risk, basic survival needs are unmet, or clients are emotionally overwhelmed by recent events, social workers may choose to take charge. This doesn't mean that social workers strip clients of their control; however, it does mean that social workers ensure the welfare of everyone concerned. Recent trauma, self-destructive behaviors, abuse, threats toward others, needs for food or shelter—these are all situations that direct social workers to seek guidance from their colleagues and supervisors and take definitive actions.

Responding to Trauma

Ethical Practice

Ethical social workers sometimes take charge of clients in situations requiring priority actions. How is "taking charge" ethical in consideration of the social work principle of client self-determination?

Trauma is a sudden occurrence that requires specialized and immediate attention. When environments are overwhelming, people need help quickly. Traumatic events temporarily overload their abilities to cope. Experiencing violence, unexpected death, dramatic loss, or the aftermath of war can leave people floundering and in need of immediate support. To respond to trauma, social workers play transitional roles, lending their support, guidance, strengths, and skills until clients can reconnect with their own abilities to take charge.

In dealing with the aftermath of trauma, social workers acknowledge they are unable to alter the actual occurrence itself. Instead, workers focus on clients' responses to the traumatic event. Unloading visual images, hearing stories again and again, encouraging the outpouring of thoughts and memories, accepting and validating feelings—social workers use responding skills to help clients work through trauma. Workers reassure clients that their intense feelings of vulnerability, fears of loss of control, and emotional overload are natural responses in their situation.

Social workers play active roles in responding to crises and trauma. They take the lead in decision making, offer facts and information to counteract misconceptions arising from the intensity of the experience, activate natural support networks on the client's behalf, and break down the issues facing the client into discrete units to dispel the overwhelming nature of the problem (Sheafor & Horejsi, 2006). Workers also access concrete resources such as food, shelter, or clothing to supplement any that the client may have lost. Social workers take direct actions to stabilize clients who are experiencing crises; however, workers also strive to return control to these clients as the urgency of their crises subsides.

Larger system considerations

When a natural tragedy such as a tornado, hurricane, earthquake, flood, or fire strikes, communities may call on social workers to respond. When an organization suffers the dramatic loss of a member or members, many system members may need assistance at once. In general, the same responses used with individuals are also appropriate in responding to trauma in mezzo- or macrosystems. Community or organization members need to unload the trauma, describe their personal experience with the events, release their feelings, and receive tangible support. When workers are unable to respond to each affected system member directly on an individual basis, they use the existing structures and functions of the client system to offer crisis services.

Most organizations and communities have already developed emergency plans in preparation for immediate implementation when crisis or disaster strikes. However, when such a plan doesn't exist, or it poorly fits the situation, social workers move quickly to activate the existing resources of the community. First, workers locate key community members in the various subsystems of the community—churches, schools, social agencies, clubs, businesses, and neighborhood organizations—that are already functioning to support community members. Having identified key leaders, workers educate these members about the dynamics of the trauma and the locations of necessary resources. These community members, in turn, provide support in the various contexts in which they are already operating.

Imagine how the Northside Network might respond to a severe storm causing extensive damage and injury in the Northside community. The group would recognize that many people would require immediate assistance to alleviate the impact of such a crisis—people unfamiliar with what services are available. The Network could respond by creating an emergency services information and referral committee from among its members. This new committee would have experienced and knowledgeable social workers who could function as a central clearinghouse for information about specialized disaster services as well as coordinate the work of the many agencies involved. Working with local media on an aggressive public information campaign about available services could also be part of the Network's response. To cope with a community-level crisis situation, social workers first work on facilitating connections among service providers and then extend these connections to those in need.

Consider another example of responding to a crisis in an organization. When all members of a family perish in a tragic house fire, the principal of the local elementary school where the three children attended calls the trauma team from the County Mental Health Center for assistance. The social worker, Georgia Betts, immediately convenes a meeting of school personnel including

Social workers are among the first responders in disaster relief efforts.

administrators, teachers, counselors, cafeteria workers, maintenance workers, and bus drivers. Each of these people already plays an important role in the everyday functioning of the school and directly interacts with students. At this meeting, Georgia begins by processing the trauma with those assembled, recognizing that everyone gathered has experienced this loss. Next, she provides information about various direct and indirect ways that students may demonstrate their grief. Georgia further describes how to encourage students to express themselves and how school personnel can respond to students in ways that accept and validate the students' feelings. Finally, she arranges a referral process for students who need individualized attention. By using the existing resources of the organizational system, the worker effectively responds to this trauma within the context of a larger system.

Responding to the Threat of Suicide

At some time in their careers, most practitioners will work with a client who considers committing or actually commits suicide (Freedenthal, 2008). Statistics show that nearly 30,000 persons commit suicide each year (NIMH, 2004). Research further suggests that for every death by suicide, as many as 8 to 25 suicide attempts occur.

Although suicide is not confined to any one particular group, a statistical analysis does show certain trends with respect to race, gender, and age. Typically, rates of suicide among Whites are higher than those of most minority groups (NCHS, 2007). Further, a review of data confirms a gender difference, showing suicide rates to be higher among White men when compared with White women. Although more women attempt suicide, men are four and a half times more likely to commit suicide. Data also reveal that for Whites, the highest rate of suicide is among those 65 years of age and older; whereas for African Americans, suicide rates peak between 20 and 44 years of age.

Data reveal a trend toward an increased incidence of suicide in persons age 15 to 24; suicide is the third leading cause of death in this age group (NCHS, 2007). Suicide is also the fifth leading cause of death among children ages 10 to 14. Recent studies on suicide among gay, lesbian, and bisexual youths indicate that the rate of suicide for these youths is slightly higher than that for heterosexual youths the same age (DeAngelis, 2002). Proctor and Groze's (1994) research discovered that this risk could be mitigated by positive functioning in the areas of self-perception, family interactions, and social relationships. Their research demonstrates that it is not a homosexual identity itself, but the social response of homophobia that places gay and lesbian youths at risk.

Recognizing signals

Competent practitioners learn to recognize the signals that suicidal clients send. Sometimes these signals are direct; at other times, messages are subtle and require careful attention to detect. Types of suicidal messages include:

Verbal direct:	"I will shoot myself if you leave me."
Verbal indirect:	"A life without love is a life without meaning."
Behavioral direct:	Hoarding pills by a chronically ill, severely disabled person.
Behavioral indirect:	Giving away prized possessions, loss of appetite, insomnia. *(Evans & Farberow, 1988, p. 63)*

Box 8.2 Social Work Response to Disaster: A Policy-Practice Connection

Social workers and other mental health providers function as first responders in times of community crises including natural disasters, such as flood, earthquake, hurricane, tornado, or fire; acts of terrorism; epidemics such as SARS; industrial disasters; or school violence. These catastrophic events precipitate large-scale relief efforts requiring the mobilization and deployment of a full spectrum of emergency responders. Social workers are well equipped to meet such challenges. "Of all the allied human health and human service professions, social work is uniquely suited to interpret the disaster context, to advocate for effective services, and to provide leadership in essential collaborations among institutions and organizations" (NASW, 1996, p. 83).

The generalist perspective frames an effective social work response to a community disaster. At the microlevel, workers supply immediate assistance to survivors. As members of a disaster response team, social workers provide crisis intervention to persons directly affected. Reassurance, accurate information, concrete assistance, and casework services are the social work activities that best fit the needs of people distressed by sudden tragedy. Practitioners recognize that, in the initial aftermath of the event, people more often need postdisaster support and assessment for referral rather than intensive trauma debriefing and psychotherapy. Current research shows that immediate psychological debriefing may have long-term adverse effects on the recovery of survivors and witnesses (Robbins, 2002; Scurfield, 2002).

Social workers also "help the helpers" by talking with rapid responders such as paramedics, firefighters, police officers, National Guard personnel, forensic technicians, morticians, and disaster relief workers. This mezzolevel activity addresses the needs of organizations and their members. Frontline emergency responders often require counseling to mitigate the effects of secondary trauma. Experience has shown that in the months after their deployment to a disaster assignment, emergency personnel often experience emotional health issues, including problems with coping and symptoms of posttraumatic stress.

At the macrolevel, social work professionals play key roles in planning, policy formulation, coordination, and evaluation. Many social workers affiliate with national or international agencies in the forefront of disaster management and operations, such as the American Red Cross, International Red Cross and Red Crescent Societies, the World Health Organization, and the U.S. Federal Emergency Management Agency (FEMA). In addition, social workers participate in disaster drills sponsored by local public health agencies or community safety and preparedness teams (North & Hong, 2000). They provide leadership in coordinating networks of service providers in the three major phases of the disaster—prewarning preparation, the disaster event, and the recuperative efforts in rebuilding the community (Galambos, 2005). Social workers implement disaster research protocols to assess damage, identify populations at risk, and delineate safety, health, and mental health needs. As policy analysts, social workers assist in evaluating disaster service policies and procedures with respect to their responsiveness to the health and mental health needs of survivors, witnesses, and responders. Based on those evaluations, social workers engage with disaster management teams to craft more effective policies and procedures.

Reports of clustering events such as a history of previous attempts or even a recent attempt by a friend or family member may also signal an increased risk for suicide (Evans & Farberow, 1988). Aggressive thoughts toward themselves or others, family dysfunction, lack of social support, parental ambivalence, neighborhood violence, and history of sexual and psychological abuse are possible correlates with suicidal tendencies in preadolescents (Jackson, et al., 1995).

Certain changes in functioning may indicate that clients are contemplating suicide (Lamb, 1990; Bloch, 1999). Sudden changes in personal-care habits, appetite, or sleeping patterns; increased use of alcohol or drugs; lethargy or agitation; risk-taking behavior; or school failure are all possible indicators. Preoccupation with ideas about death, getting personal affairs in order, describing how the world would be a better place without them, or giving away personal belongings are also clues to suicidal intent. Finally, Lamb cautions that the sudden elevation in mood of a previously depressed person may reveal a feeling of resolution at having made the decision to commit suicide.

Social workers must sort out facts from misconceptions in assessing a client's risk of suicide (Evans & Farberow, 1988). People who frequently talk about suicide may carry through and, having attempted suicide unsuccessfully, may try again. Talking directly to people about their suicidal thoughts is important. Direct talk does not precipitate suicidal behavior, and it may help prevent it. Mistakenly, people assume that only the wealthy and those in families in which others have made this choice attempt suicide. Trapped in a web of circumstances, anyone of any socioeconomic status could be at risk.

Although any of these signs may alert social workers to possible suicidal thinking, no one sign is definitive. Many of these behaviors correlate with other issues as well, and some may indicate no problem at all. Studies about suicide inform practitioners about trends and signs, but only clients are experts on what they are really thinking. When workers suspect suicidal thinking in clients, they consult with their supervisors and get further information from clients to assess the actual risk.

Taking action

When social workers sense that a client is contemplating suicide, they directly discuss their concerns with the client. Workers may say:

- Are you thinking about harming yourself?
- Are you telling me that you're considering suicide?
- I heard you mention killing yourself. Are you really thinking about that?
- I'm noticing several changes in the way you are handling things, sort of like you are giving up. What are you trying to tell me?

Many workers hesitate to pose these questions, fearing that such direct discussion will foster suicidal behavior; however, this is not the case. By directly talking with clients about what they are hearing and seeing, a social worker gives clients permission to talk openly about any self-destructive thoughts.

In discussing suicidal thinking with a client, social workers strive to assess the seriousness of the client's threats. The most important factor for determining the potential of a suicide threat is the individual's plan (Aguilera & Messick, 1982). Workers should consider three important elements:

- Is it a relatively lethal method?
- Does the individual have the means available?
- Is the plan specific? (pp. 116–117)

Risk of suicide is greater when plans are detailed and specific, and when the methods chosen are lethal and readily available. In response to a client who is seriously contemplating suicide, social workers quickly involve support systems for themselves and for the client. Within their own professional support systems, workers seek the advice and counsel of their supervisors, colleagues, or consultants to gain outside perspectives and receive emotional support. Social workers consider whether the client requires hospitalization or, as an alternative, whether to activate the client's natural support system to prevent the suicidal act. Sometimes, the worker and the client enlist friends or family members to accompany the client at all times until the client's self-destructive feelings pass. This strategy is sometimes referred to as putting the person "on watch." Whatever choices social workers make, they ensure that clients are not left alone with their suicidal thoughts and feelings of hopelessness.

Responding to Threats toward Others

Sometimes, social workers learn that clients are planning violent actions toward others. Clearly, when clients threaten violence, they reveal their frustration, stress, and sense of limited options. Ultimately, practitioners will work to help clients alleviate their anger and expand their vision of possible solutions. But, first, workers must intervene to prevent the potential harm.

Violence is not in the best interests of clients or society. Actions derived from the principle of protection of human life supersede all other obligations (Loewenberg, et al., 2000). If social workers truly believe that clients will commit violent acts, they are ethically and legally bound to prevent clients from carrying out their plans. Workers strictly adhere to the agency's procedures for reporting the potential harm.

Discussing violent thoughts and feelings with a client tests a social worker's ability to remain nonjudgmental. This is not to say that social workers maintain a permissive attitude toward violent acts. Instead workers discuss the client's thinking openly and neutrally. In this way, workers can encourage continued sharing, relieve pressure, and introduce other less dangerous options for coping. Even if a client persists in planning violence, this open discussion of violent impulses allows workers to assess the reality of what the client may do and supplies information on which to build preventive responses. Similar to dealing with potential suicide by clients, workers seek supervisory support and consider using in-patient services.

Duty to warn

Under most circumstances, social workers keep what they hear from clients confidential, but in the case of potential violence, social workers function as agents of social control. In these situations, confidentiality is abridged. When clients threaten others, workers take charge and document their actions carefully (Madden, 2003; NASW, 2005e). A landmark court decision made in California, *Tarasoff v. The Regents of the University of California* (1976), set the stage for legislative initiatives and court decisions in other states. This decision stipulates that

> When a therapist determines, or pursuant to the standards of his profession should determine, that his patient presents a serious danger of violence to another, he incurs an obligation to use reasonable care to protect the intended victim against such danger. The discharge of this duty may require the therapist to take one or more of various steps, depending upon the nature of the case. Thus it may call for him to warn the intended victim or others likely to apprise the victim of the danger, to notify the police, or to take whatever other steps are reasonably necessary under the circumstances. (in Ca. 3d 425, 431 (1976) cited in Dickson, 1998, pp. 148–149)

Three criteria invoke duty to warn under *Tarasoff:* (1) a client seriously threatening to do bodily harm, (2) the client's ability to carry out the threat, and (3) an identified victim (Gothard, 1995). However, legal obligations vary from state to state. Many states have enacted specific duty-to-warn laws:

> These statutes create a duty for certain professionals to warn or protect third parties and establish liability for the professionals' failure to do so in specific, limited circumstances. At the same time these statutes limit liability; if the professional follows the steps provided by the statutes, no

> monetary liability or other action can be taken against the professional. These statutes vary as to which professionals are subject to the duty, which threats will activate the duty, which victims are owed the duty, and how the duty can be discharged. (Kopels & Kagle, 1993, p. 109)

Duty-to-warn laws differ in their definitions of foreseeable threats, stipulations of obligatory actions, requirements to notify law enforcement officials, and mandates for involuntary hospitalization (Houston-Vega, et al., 1997). Proceeding under duty to warn "does not mean that social workers need to immediately warn all potential victims of any threat to danger" (Kopels & Kagle, 1994, p. 220). However, it does compel social workers to act legally and ethically and proceed according to the principles of standard practice: "assessing the client situation, with particular attention to factors that indicate imminent danger; fully documenting decisions and actions; and, where indicated, developing and implementing a plan of action that protects identifiable third parties" (p. 220). Thorough documentation of the assessment and actions that details facts, observations, and verbatim accounts of interactions offers some protection against malpractice (Houston-Vega, et al., 1997). Prudent responses include such actions as obtaining the client's consent to warn potential victims, consulting an attorney who is familiar with state laws, disclosing only enough information to substantiate the warning, and/or asking the client to consider a voluntary hospitalization (Reamer, 1994). At first glance, duty to warn may seem contrary to principles of empowerment. However, consider the consequences of allowing clients to commit acts of violence. Ultimately, if clients harm others, both clients and those they harm lose power to determine the courses of their lives.

Responding to Child Abuse

When social workers suspect that children in families are being abused, they take appropriate actions to ensure children's safety and prevent further harm. Child maltreatment takes on many forms, including physical abuse, neglect, emotional abuse, and sexual abuse. *Child Maltreatment 2006* (USHHS-ACYF, 2008) reports that child protection agencies confirmed reports that 905,000, or 12.1 of every 1,000 children in the United States, experienced some form of child abuse or neglect. About 1,500 children died as a consequence of maltreatment. Social workers most likely to deal with these issues are those in child protective services working under mandates to investigate reports of potential abuse or those working in hospital settings. Even social workers in other practice settings encounter clients in situations in which abuse is occurring. Therefore, all practitioners need to know about how to identify abusive situations and how to respond.

Recognizing signs of abuse

Social workers may become aware of child abuse in several different ways. Sometimes, workers hear reports of events directly from children or parents that describe harsh discipline, events, or "accidents," which prompt workers to obtain further details to assess the child's safety. At other times, social workers observe physical evidence of abuse in the form of bruises, scratches, burns, or other injuries. Many times they hear about abusive events from people outside of the client's family, such as friends, extended family members, or neighbors.

Some evidence of abuse is more subtle. Research provides assistance in identifying risk factors, including spousal abuse, unemployment, single parenthood, illness or developmental disabilities, preterm birth, history of intergenerational abuse or family violence, and addiction (Bethea, 1999; Freisthier, et al., 2006; Toth & Cicchetti, 2005). Child welfare records implicate the misuse of alcohol or other drugs in between 40 and 80 percent of the founded cases of child maltreatment (CWLA, 2001).

Children may show behavioral signs that indicate they are being abused, including such diverse personal actions as aggression, self-destructive behaviors, retreat, or withdrawal. How children relate to adults also provides clues to abuse. Children may demonstrate fear of physical contact or affection, extreme dependence and attachment, and excessive attention to parental needs. Children who are abused sometimes reveal problems in social functioning, such as difficulties in learning, even though they have no apparent learning deficits, lack of concentration and low energy at school, depression, impulsive behavior, or noncompliance (Lowenthal, 1999). Sexual acting out and evidence of parental neglect are other possible indicators of abuse.

Taking action

Social workers do not immediately assume that families with these characteristics are experiencing family violence. Yet, workers are cautious not to overlook signals of abuse. When practitioners fail to notice abuse, they unknowingly contribute to it. When social workers detect issues of abuse, the safety of the person being abused takes priority.

Social workers seek more information when they suspect abuse. In some instances, they may need to see members separately to encourage family members to speak openly and freely, and to protect vulnerable family members from reprisals by abusive members. Workers proceed cautiously when persons who are abused and perpetrators are present at the same interview, because revealing information could precipitate retaliation. Children need reassurance about what will happen to them and their family members. Workers carefully refrain from making judgmental comments about perpetrators after the abuse is reported, because the child may have ambivalent emotions of anger and affection about the person involved. As workers respond to information about abuse, they recognize their important role in comforting and protecting those threatened.

Reporting suspected child abuse

Statues, case law, and administrative regulations and procedures vary from state to state. Although all states have mandatory reporting laws that require social workers and other designated professionals to report instances of child maltreatment, these laws offer general guidelines rather than specifying those conditions that warrant reports (Goldman & Salus, 2003). States also differ on the actual reporting process—whether reports are by phone or written document and with whom reports are filed. Typically, a state department is charged to provide child welfare services, including prompt investigation and follow-up services with families as their situations require.

Responding to Elder Abuse

Estimates of the prevalence of elder abuse and exploitation in the United States reported in *Elder Mistreatment: Abuse, Neglect, and Exploitation in an Aging America, 2003,* indicate that between 1 and 2 million adults age 65 and older have been mistreated (NCEA, 2005). The National Center on Elder Abuse's (1998) first national incidence study uncovered an "iceberg effect." Reported cases of elder abuse represent the "tip of the iceberg," whereas the majority of incidents are "hidden" or not disclosed to authorities. For every reported case of mistreatment, exploitation, or self-neglect, about five go unreported. A disproportionately large number of these situations involve people older than 80 years. Those who are physically or cognitively frail are particularly vulnerable. Relatives, including spouses and adult children, are the most likely perpetrators of domestic elder abuse.

Most states have enacted reporting laws that designate certain professionals as mandatory reporters of the abuse of adults who are dependent, as defined by age, mental, or physical disabilities (U.S. Department of Justice, 2001). Only some reporting laws designate penalties for noncompliance. States vary as to which agencies take responsibility for receiving and investigating reports of elder abuse and the abuse of other dependent adults. Designated agencies include units of state human service departments, local social service agencies, and law enforcement officials (Tatara & Kazmeskus, 1997).

Several factors complicate both identifying and reporting elder abuse. Many older adults, particularly those who are frail, are homebound and away from public scrutiny. Additionally, older adults may be reluctant to bring charges when a family member or loved one on whom they rely has committed the abuse. They may believe they themselves are to blame, or they may be concerned that reporting will ultimately lead to a nursing home placement. Social workers may also experience dilemmas in weighing an older adult's competency for self-determined decision making, and their own duty to protect a client's safety and well-being.

Responding to Intimate Partner Violence

Violence within marital or couple relationships also requires priority action. Abuse may be physical, psychological, sexual, or economic. Practitioners use caution in working with families in which such violence is happening for fear that changes in any part of the family system may escalate the occurrence of violence. With families experiencing violence, social workers deal with safety issues first, before addressing other concerns. Findings from the National Violence Against Women Survey suggest that violence is a serious public health issue for women (Tjaden & Thoennes, 2000). Of the women surveyed, 22.1 percent report intimate partner violence during their lifetime, as compared with 7.4 percent of the men surveyed. In the United States, about 1.3 million women are assaulted by an intimate partner each year. Studies indicate that involvement in partner violence leads to increased risk for children becoming the objects of aggressive parenting (Salzinger et al., 2002).

Research identifies a number of factors associated with increased risk for couple violence (NCIPC, 2006). Rates of violence are greater among cohabiting couples than among married couples. Younger couples are more at risk than older couples. Experiencing abuse as a child predicts domestic violence, either as a victim or a perpetrator. Partner abuse occurs in all socioeconomic groups; however, prevalence is greater in situations of poverty, unemployment, or underemployment. Finally, substance abuse increases the risk for intimate partner violence (Catalano, 2007; CDC, 2006).

When workers believe that violence is occurring, they may need to meet separately with those at risk to elicit honest information in a secure setting and take immediate action to minimize further harm. An extensive knowledge of community service networks helps workers to ensure the safety of persons threatened by domestic violence. Many communities have domestic violence programs that coordinate multilevel services, because these clients are likely to require legal assistance, court protection, transitional housing, financial resources, and counseling support. Whether these services are relevant to a client depends on the degree of the cultural competence of the community (Pyles & Kim, 2006).

Responding to Survival Needs

All human beings have universal needs for food, shelter, warmth, and sleep. Struggling to meet these basic needs blocks people's abilities to accomplish anything else. Maslow (1970) describes this as a hierarchy of needs. This hierarchy has implications for social workers as they prioritize actions. For example, helping a client return to school to achieve the goal of obtaining a GED before dealing with a client's homelessness and needs for food and shelter makes no sense. When social workers recognize that a client is lacking the necessities for survival, they focus on stabilizing essential supports before working on other issues. "Advocacy/empowerment and primary relationship building alone cannot compensate for homelessness, malnutrition, lack of medical care, and social isolation" (Klein & Cnaan, 1995, p. 210). All social workers need to know about the support services in their communities that provide immediate shelter, food, and financial assistance to network clients for life-sustaining assistance.

Responding to Signs of Addiction

Substance abuse and addiction accompany many situations that challenge clients' abilities to cope and frequently preempt their capabilities to address other concerns. Sometimes, mood-altering substance use springs from dissatisfactions with life. At other times, addiction may have physiological roots and create a wave of associated issues blocking abilities to function effectively.

Not all people who use substances are addicted. A probability study of adults in the United States indicates that 14 percent of all adults report alcohol dependence at some time during their lives. The *2006 National Survey on Drug Use and Health* (SAMHSA, 2007), a large-scale random sample survey, found that 22.6 million Americans, or 9.2 percent of the population ages 12 and older, were classified as experiencing substance dependence or substance abuse. "Of these, 3.2 million were classified with dependence on or abuse of both alcohol and illicit drugs, 3.8 million were dependent on or abused illicit drugs but not alcohol, and 15.6 million were dependent on or abused alcohol but not illicit drugs" (p. 69). Previous studies have shown "more than 6 million children lived with at least one parent who abused or was dependent on alcohol or an illicit drug" (Office of Applied Studies, 2003, p. 1). Nearly 10 percent of children 5 years of age and younger lived with a parent who was substance dependent.

Characteristically, involvement with alcohol and drugs takes on three different forms: use, abuse, and dependency. Persons who are users likely use alcohol and drugs for pleasure and an enhanced sense of well-being (Griffin, 1991). Users become abusers when "the drug and its effects interfere with the individual's ability to carry out expected responsibilities" (p. 88). Drug dependency occurs when the "individual persists in using drugs, disregarding any negative consequences and exhibiting tolerance to the drug and withdrawal symptoms when he or she cannot have the drug" (p. 88). A worker who discovers that clients are using drugs and alcohol discusses this openly to determine the extent of the involvement and the impact of use. If clients show signs of abuse or dependency, they will probably need assistance from drug treatment programs before continuing to work toward other goals.

Even when confronting substance abuse, social workers seek balance to respect a client's right to self-determination, securing the client's cooperation in making referrals for drug and alcohol assessment and treatment. All treatment for substance abuse requires motivation and participation by clients to be successful. Although social workers may support a client through the process of seeking treatment for substance abuse, as much as possible, workers activate the client's capabilities for accessing treatment services. Sometimes, social workers recognize that the dependence is disabling and the client is unable to acknowledge the need or activate personal resources for change. At these times, social workers contact members of a client's natural support network to arrange treatment.

LOOKING FORWARD

Defining directions represents a turning point in the partnership of clients and workers. They now agree on which way they are going. Setting preliminary goals focuses the partners on what to do next. It answers the question of whether workers and clients need to take priority actions to prevent immediate harm or cope with crisis situations. If the current situation allows, the partners can now proceed to look for strengths, resources that may be available to work toward desired outcomes. Articulating situations and defining directions clarify "where the client is" and predict where the partnership is going.

The dialogue phase sets the stage for implementing the discovery processes of identifying strengths, assessing resource capabilities, and planning possible solutions. In the discovery phase, social workers and clients will combine their expertise to generate new information, consider resources available within clients and their environments, and frame possible solutions. Practitioners and clients conduct an organized search for opportunities to overcome restraints and work to recognize strengths and resources to meet defined needs. Identifying strengths, the topic of Chapter 9, initiates these discovery processes.

Log onto **www.mysocialworklab.com** and select the **Interactive Skill Module** videos from the left-hand menu. Answer the questions below. (*If you did not receive an access code to **MySocialWorkLab** with this text and wish to purchase access online, please visit* www.mysocialworklab.com.)

1. **Watch the school social work module (pages 4–7)** in which social worker Terry sees client Michelle's

resistance. Recalling that resistance is transactional, why might this client resist? Does Terry's behavior increase or decrease Michelle's resistance?

2. **Watch pages 4, 6, and 7 of the child welfare module** to observe a child abuse investigation. What does the worker look for when assessing child abuse and neglect? What signs might a child exhibit that he or she is experiencing abuse?

PRACTICE TEST

1. Social worker Gil Gomez and the Martinez family are at the point of their work together when they are defining a direction. In this process Gil and the Martinez family are ___.
   a. setting specific concrete goals and objectives for their work together
   b. agreeing on the preliminary purpose or goal for their work together
   c. solidifying the original purpose of the relationship
   d. exploring the reasons for the family's difficulty

2. Marcy Quinn is highly motivated to complete her college degree. Systems-oriented social workers regard her behavior as ___.
   a. genetic
   b. a characteristic that increases as anxiety increases
   c. a personal trait that remains relatively constant across the life span
   d. influenced by interactions

Research Based Practice

3. Social worker Alisa Adamson meets with the Brown family to resolve conflicts over providing in-home care for Mrs. Brown's mother. At the first session, the Browns say, "just tell us what to do to get through this crisis!" Based on the research by Bandura and Cervone, Alisa should ___.
   a. immediately detail a step-by-step plan to resolve their crisis
   b. explore the history and origin of the conflict with Mrs. Brown's mother
   c. maximize self-efficacy by working with the Browns to set their own goals
   d. refer the Borwns for marital counseling

4. The Northside Planning Commission asked social worker Jalyn Thomas to chair a citizen task force on "elder friendly" communities. The group is charged with identifying ways the community already supports its aging population and with visioning possible community development initiatives. To ensure everyone

on the task force has a voice, JayIn considers implementing a(n) ___.
   a. process of assimilation
   b. administrative control technique
   c. nominal group technique
   d. process using paradoxical injunctions

5. Daryl's attendance at the "Committed Fathers" group is so sporadic, that social worker Adam French wonders if Daryl's behavior actually reveals a lack of commitment and resistance to change. With respect to resistance, Adam should realize that ___.
   a. Adam needs to go over the purpose of the group again with Daryl to help him align with the group
   b. Daryl's behavior reveals something about his motivation, but it may not be what Adam is assuming
   c. Daryl's behavior is typical of an involuntary client
   d. Adam needs to confront Daryl directly about his lack of commitment and resistance to change

Human Behavior

6. His supervisor suggests that Jake apply a structural perspective to understand clients mandated to participate in the anger management group. From the structural perspective, Jake will conclude that the clients' issue with anger is a product of ___.
   a. genetic inheritance
   b. pathological personalities
   c. transactions with their environment
   d. diminished personal control

Ethical Practice

7. With respect to issues such as a client's threat to harm another person or a worker's suspicion of child or elder abuse, all social workers should ___.
   a. not reveal this information to anyone to maintain trust and ensure absolute confidentiality
   b. work with the client involved to resolve the underlying issues
   c. automatically call the police
   d. proceed according to their legal obligations as mandated by state law

Log onto **MySocialWorkLab** once you have completed the Practice Test above to take your Chapter Exam and demonstrate your knowledge of this material.

Answers

1) b 2) d 3) c 4) c 5) b 6) c 7) d

Identifying Strengths

CHAPTER OUTLINE

CONNECTING CORE COMPETENCIES *in this chapter*

Professional Identity | Ethical Practice | Critical Thinking | Diversity in Practice | Human Rights & Justice | Research Based Practice | Human Behavior | Policy Practice | Practice Contexts | Engage Assess Intervene Evaluate

Even clients in the toughest situations reveal resiliency and resources to strength-focused social workers. When social workers acknowledge these strengths, they cement working relationships with clients and energize the process with possibilities. However, the process of identifying strengths in clients is not simple. So accustomed are we to detecting problems, we may overlook indicators of client strengths as they pass right before us.

Read the following excerpt about Chad as he describes what prompted him to seek assistance at the Northside Addictions Recovery Center. Assess your ability to identify Chad's strengths.

> Two weeks ago, I felt like I couldn't go on—that's when I decided to call you. I'd just been laid off and the kids were driving me crazy. I could feel it creeping in—that craving for a drink. I've been sober for 18 months now, but I still think about it every day. Both of my parents had the same problem and at Alcoholics Anonymous they say it's hereditary. Maybe there's no escaping it and I'll die young just like they did. I've needed a drink so bad that I can't stay home, especially with the kids getting on my nerves. I called my friend in to take care of the kids and I hit the pavement, putting in applications all over town—14 to be exact. I don't think any of them will pay what my accounting job paid, but I still can go back and be a mechanic or even be a waiter again, at least temporarily. I don't know what I'll be doing, but I have to do something. I just can't sit around. I'll go crazy. My brother tells me I'm running away from my problems. What do you think?

If you are a problem-focused practitioner, you might agree with Chad's brother. You might think that Chad fits the description of a multiproblem client. After all, he is the adult child of two alcoholics, a recovering alcoholic himself who is craving a drink, recently unemployed, and frustrated with his children.

Switch your focus to recognize Chad's strengths. Do you notice the fact that he lost his job two full weeks ago and still hasn't had a drink? Do you realize that he is already on the move to getting another job, has actually put in applications, and has a wide range of skills to draw on including abilities as an accountant, a mechanic, and a waiter? Do you recognize his social support—a friend to take care of his children and a brother to talk with about his issues? Do you acknowledge that he has overcome the adversity of growing up in an alcoholic family? This is only the beginning of the list of strengths that Chad reveals in these few statements.

If you can recognize Chad's strengths, congratulate yourself on your own strengths. You are well on the way to becoming an empowering practitioner. Recognizing and validating client strengths is fundamental to empowering social work practice—in constructing relationships and in building solutions. This chapter equips practitioners with the knowledge and skills to identify and utilize client strengths in the practice process. In detail, this chapter

- Argues the value of focusing on client strengths in social work practice
- Gives examples of strengths potentially present in individuals, families, groups, organizations, and communities
- Exhibits dialogue skills for social workers to shape conversations to discover client strengths
- Analyzes strengths shown by ethnic group members as discovered through social work research

♦ Delineates strengths unique to various population groups including women, gays and lesbians, older adults, those with religious affiliations, and persons with disabilities
♦ Identifies strengths developed by clients in coping with adversity and oppression

INFUSING A STRENGTHS PERSPECTIVE

The strengths orientation shifts the way social workers view and respond to clients. Strength-focused workers assume client competence and expect to discover client system strengths. To infuse a focus on strengths, practitioners must understand the diverse and contextual nature of strengths and know where to look for strengths in client systems.

What Are Strengths?

Practice Contexts

All social agencies use practice models, agency protocols, and paperwork to structure a social worker's practice. In what ways might these influences affect the ability of a social worker to implement a strengths perspective in practice?

To many of us, our strengths are obvious. We recognize them easily and use them to manage our lives and realize our goals. Readily identified strengths include natural talents, acquired capabilities, and skills demonstrated in daily life. However, not all strengths are so apparent. Strengths may surface more subtly as cultural attributes, as coping responses in difficult times, or as luck in achieving goals.

Strengths-oriented social workers develop skills to identify strengths relevant for each level of client system—individual, family, group, organization, neighborhood, or community. Locating resources requires looking diligently and creatively for anything that may be useful in activating confidence and achieving goals. Workers find client strengths "in the context of clients' personal history, their immediate social environment, the larger societal matrix, the mix of individual characteristics, and the meanings clients ascribe to their experiences" (McAuaide & Ehrenreich, 1997, p. 201).

The contextual nature of strengths

What may be an asset for you may be a deficit for others; conversely, what may be an asset for others may be a deficit for you. For example, the ability to bring patience, persistence, and a sense of accomplishment to a repetitive task may benefit a person who assembles nuts and bolts in a developmental training program, but these same talents may constrain a worker with a temporary employment agency which demands quick adaptation and flexibility to learn new tasks on a daily basis. Strengths are relative; "they cannot be isolated from the situation in which they are expressed" (McAuaide & Ehrenreich, 1997, p. 203). A social worker's transactional view helps discover strengths in how client systems' abilities mesh with their situations.

Consider the example of African American families. Several writers describe the extended family network present in many African American families as a source of strength and support (Billingsley, 1992; Boyd-Franklin, 1989, 1993; Hill, 1997; Wright & Anderson, 1998). This knowledge leads social workers to consider possible extended family resources in their work with African American clients. However, whether the extended family is functioning supportively is specific to each African American client. To understand the resources of a particular client's situation, workers consider questions such as:

♦ What is actually happening in this client's situation?
♦ Are extended family members present?

> ◗ Are they involved with the client's family?
> ◗ Does the client believe that involvement of extended family members helps or interferes?

Workers bring knowledge about potential strengths to each encounter, but only clients can define what is working for them.

Why Identify Strengths?

Identifying client strengths has many advantages. Most important, accentuating strengths highlights possible resources for achieving goals. It also contributes to the process in other important ways. Specifically, identifying strengths solidifies the client–social worker partnership, functions as a generally enhancing intervention, and increases clients' motivation to invest in the process.

Acknowledging strengths to build partnerships

Examine the relationships in your own life. In which of these relationships do you experience equality? Of course, you've probably identified those relationships in which you feel that you have something to offer, in which others recognize the potential of your contributions. To engage clients as contributing partners, workers communicate their understanding that clients have resources to offer to the process. Identifying and acknowledging their strengths invites clients into professional relationships as collaborators.

Building productive relationships requires a degree of openness as well as a sense of equality. Clients often withdraw when social workers narrowly focus on problems. Revealing more and more of what is going wrong increases clients' feelings of vulnerability and heightens their defensiveness. When the defensive walls go up, exchanges of information dry up. A worker who balances gentle and accepting explorations of challenges with a recognition of strengths encourages clients to bring along feelings of success and power as they explore areas of vulnerability.

Acknowledging a client's strengths early in the developing partnership becomes especially important in cross-cultural relationships. Obvious cultural differences cast doubts on the abilities of clients and workers to relate successfully. Typically, clients wonder how these differences will affect their relationships with social workers. For example, questions include: Will the worker operate from a value base that devalues the client's worldview, choices, or lifestyle? Will the worker see cultural differences as threatening or something to change to move the client into the mainstream? Is the worker informed enough about the client's culture to place information in a cultural context?

Recognizing strengths as a general intervention

The perfect solution for a particular issue requires a carefully tailored, specifically designed strategy that fits the unique circumstance of each client system. Although there may be several potential solutions to any one dilemma, there is no universal strategy to fit every situation. However, certain actions that social workers can take are likely to give any client system a general boost. Accentuating client system strengths is one of those actions.

Assuming that client systems have resources postures attention toward strengths. It means that social workers enter each working relationship wearing magnifying glasses to notice strengths, helping to create an empowering atmosphere in which good things exist and other good things are possible. A sense of hope and optimism facilitates workers' and clients' beliefs that change and success are possible—a thought that can become a reality in the context of their work together.

Self-esteem is a concept that receives much attention in education and parenting. Teachers and parents are supposed to behave in ways that enhance children's positive self-esteem, feelings of self-worth, and belief in their abilities. The theory says that children who feel better about themselves demonstrate higher achievement, feel more secure in experimenting, and experience greater success. Self-esteem accrues based on one's accomplishments, self-affirmation that one is doing something right, and outside recognition of one's abilities. Identifying what clients are doing right enhances their feelings of esteem and amplifies their sense of power.

Identifying strengths as a motivational tool

People change when they are motivated to change and when they believe they have the capabilities and resources to do so. This axiom leads us to see client motivation and confidence as essential to success. A strength-oriented approach to social work heightens clients' sense of competence, hope for the future, and motivation for change (Saleebey, 2002c). Offering compliments to acknowledge strengths and resources heightens clients' motivation and stimulates connections to their capabilities.

Experienced practitioners indicate that people stretch to prove the truth of compliments but recoil to defend against criticisms. Workers who comment on client strengths keep clients stretching toward success.

Balancing Strengths and Challenges

Talking about strengths does not mean that workers ignore information clients provide about problems. Clients need to unload their difficulties before opening their eyes to more positive views. Interestingly, even problem talk frequently reveals strengths and potential solutions. "To find solutions you must talk about the problem in a solvable way" (Durrant & Kowalski, 1992, p. 111).

Typically, clients let social workers know if they move too quickly to identify strengths and possible solutions. Clients question the shift in direction and work harder to convince the worker that their problems are difficult. They have not yet said all they have come to say; they think the worker hasn't heard enough about the situation to lead toward the way out. When clients have exhausted their stories, workers can redirect the focus of conversation by summarizing and clarifying the client's perspective, asking if there is anything else, and seeking permission to move in a more positive direction. Social workers may say

> ▸ I'm hearing that this marriage has changed in the last few months, that you don't seem to find much time to be together, and when you are together, you don't seem to have much to talk about. Is there anything else? If not, I'd like to find out more about those times before when your marriage was working the way you wanted.
> ▸ I guess "support group" isn't a very accurate name for what seems to be happening in the group right now. You all seem to agree that you are beginning to pull back, share less about what you are really thinking and feeling, and you don't know clearly what you want out of it yet. Am I hearing you right? Well, that's one good thing—we seem to have consensus about that. What else do we have that we might build on?
> ▸ We all agree that the Council is getting bogged down on defining homelessness. However, several agency representatives to the Community

Housing Council have clearly outlined the problems associated with lack of affordable housing, limited shelter space, and the complex referral process. Is this the common ground we're looking for to move our efforts forward?

When workers move too quickly to accentuate strengths, clients think workers are missing the point or minimizing their issues. Durrant and Kowalski (1992) say:

> We do not believe that talking about the problem ("working it through") leads to change; however, we are clear that not talking about it sometimes leads to clients feeling unheard. Therefore . . . we are alert to our clients' lead and to signs that they need to know that their situation has been understood and their experience validated. (p. 110)

Social workers set a pace that matches client readiness by acknowledging the significance of problems before tilting the conversation toward strengths.

Looking for Strengths

Social workers find client strengths when they are prepared to look for them. Familiarity with research about human resiliency provides workers background information about what might be helpful. Knowledge about the unique capabilities of specific cultural groups also puts workers on alert for identifying strengths. The rest of this chapter details knowledge and skills essential for detecting and accentuating client strengths. Specifically, sections address looking for strengths in general functioning, in the context of challenges, in cultural contexts, and in coping with adversity.

HIGHLIGHTING STRENGTHS IN GENERAL FUNCTIONING

Recognizing clients' capabilities builds confidence, motivation, and feelings of power. To identify general strengths, workers keep many questions in mind, such as:

- What are the outstanding qualities of this client?
- In what ways does the client demonstrate power?
- How and with whom does the client successfully build alliances?
- What special or unique characteristics distinguish this client from others?
- What skills does this client system have to connect to its environment?
- What resources support the client?
- In what ways does the client contribute to the social and physical environments?
- How has the client been able to adapt to changes?

These questions consider the qualities that characterize competence of any human system in its environmental context. Clients—including individuals, families, groups, organizations, and communities—draw on internal and environmental resources to adapt and progress.

Strengths in Individuals

Workers locate an individual's personal strengths by exploring cognitive, affective, physical, and cultural attributes. Intelligence, problem-solving skills, and creativity are important cognitive resources. Affective strengths may include positive feelings of self-worth, abilities to identify and express emotions, optimism,

Box 9.1 Service Users' Involvement: A Policy–Practice Connection

A strong belief that clients should remain in charge of social service decisions related to their situations, and therefore, their lives, provides a major impetus for the empowerment-oriented service user's movement in England, Ireland, and other western European nations. Persons involved in this movement, which promotes service-user autonomy in decision making, includes the self-described mental health system survivors, older adults, persons with learning difficulties and persons with disabilities (Beresford, 1999; Beresford, & Croft, 2003; Braye & Preston-Shoot, 2005; Evans, 2004; Valokivi, 2004). Initially focused on promoting personal control, many service user movements have now begun to expand their activities to affect larger system change. Shaping Our Lives, an example of one British organization in this movement, draws on the expertise of persons with disabilities to influence policy and program research, planning, and evaluation (Turner, 1997). Reflecting an understanding of empowerment as both a personal and a political process, service users set specific goals including advocating personal decision making and control, creating responsive programs and services, redressing discrimination and social injustice, and promoting social change.

Closer to home, Weiman, Dosland-Hasenmiller, and O'Melia (2002) describe the consumer-led transformation of one social service agency located in a midwestern urban community in the United States. This not-for-profit community-based agency provides day programs, community employment, and residential support for individuals whose primary service issue is mental retardation. Training personnel with a curriculum based on empowerment philosophy and principles, particularly listening and responding as mentors to "clients as experts," fostered changes in the organizational culture of the agency. Staff-in-training were afforded hands-on opportunities to put mentoring principles into practice through their work with consumer groups. One such consumer group, We Can . . . Speak Out!, convened a conference open to any community member to learn the process of speaking for oneself, hosted forums for congressional candidates, and participated in voters' rallies. Participants' experiences have been so powerful that they initiated and achieved a change in their agency designation from "consumers" to "individuals" and now sit on a committee to screen all applicants for employment at the agency.

As a policy directive, the service-user movement presses for clients to be involved in research efforts, not simply as participants, but as full partners in control of the research process. In the United Kingdom, many private and public funders of social research now stipulate service user involvement as a requirement of funding. According to Fisher (2002), the benefits of user-controlled research lie in "the possibility of technical enhancements to the processes of defining the research 'problem,' in ensuring that appropriate data are sought and are accessible, in defining outcome measures, and in recognizing relevance during analysis" (p. 310).

Consumers of social services now play increasingly prominent roles in developing policies, defining practice priorities, and serving as research-partners. Genuine service user power has important benefits for enhancing service delivery at every level. Beresford, Brough, and Turner (2001) pose a series of questions to evaluate the authenticity and inclusiveness of initiatives that involve service users:

- How *available* are publications, discussion documents, reports, and learning materials?
- How *respected* are contributions from service users?
- How *equal and valued* are the discourses of service users and their organizations?
- How *included* are services users? (p. 120).

Infusing empowerment theory into the day-to-day practice of social work honors the voices of clients by ensuring meaningful roles for service users in policy, practice, and research.

and sensitivity. Special physical talents, athletic skills, an attractive appearance, endurance, and good health are all physical qualities that benefit individual functioning. And one's cultural identities may be a source of pride contributing to a positive sense of self and belonging. Additionally, spirituality serves as a reservoir of strength, as "it can provide emotional consolation, inspiration, guidance, structure and security. It can foster personal responsibility, identity, respect for ethical codes, meaningful ritual, and community building" (Gotterer, 2001, p. 188). Each of these personal strengths contributes to individual well-being and also enhances interpersonal interactions.

Interpersonal strengths are evident in an individual's natural support network. They include rewarding relationships with immediate family members and extended family support. Friends, neighbors, employers, teachers, ministers, rabbis, and other spiritual leaders—all may provide important resources for individual well-being. An individual's abilities in building social alliances such as good communication skills, warmth, trustworthiness, and commitment underlie successful interpersonal relationships.

Rewarding connections to community, institutional, and recreational resources can also function as strengths. When people are aware of available resources and feel privileged to access them, they are positioned well to build productive connections to the environment—an important source of sustenance for individual functioning.

Strengths in Families

No one single formula guarantees a family's success. Families have different styles depending on their structure, membership, cultural influences, ethnic heritage, and a host of other environmental variables. However, 25 years of research by Beavers and Hampson (1990, 1993) shows trends in family interaction that generally function as strengths:

> These families show consistently high degrees of capable negotiation, clarity of individual expression, respect for individual choices and ambivalence, and affiliative attitudes towards one another. Each member appears competent, acknowledged, and assured; the resultant product is a group of individuals who are spontaneous, enjoy each other, and are allowed clear and direct expression of feelings, attitudes, and beliefs. (1990, pp. 30–31)

Notice that nowhere in this description of family competence is it necessary for there to be two, heterosexual, married, or biological parents or even children, for that matter. Families representing many structures and lifestyles can function competently. The nature of its interaction and the support that each member gives to and receives from their family defines its health.

Collecting information from more than 10,000 family members from every state in the United States and more than 22 countries, Olson and DeFrain (2006) discovered remarkable cross-cultural similarities with respect to family strengths. Factors contributing to family satisfaction and resilience include appreciation and affection, commitment, positive communication, time together, spiritual well-being, and the ability to cope with stress and crisis.

Strengths in Groups

In successful groups each member contributes to the group's overall functioning and, in return, receives the benefits of group membership. To accomplish this balance, groups require the strengths of clearly understood goals, effective communication among members, distributed power, appropriate decision-making procedures, conflict resolution skills, and cohesiveness (Johnson & Johnson, 2006). Competently functioning groups also have similar relationships with their environments, accessing and contributing resources in reciprocal exchanges.

Other qualities of group interaction that constitute strengths depend on the group's specific purpose. For example, a task group draws on particular skills of its members that are most relevant to the task at hand. A support group benefits from members' abilities to articulate feelings and demonstrate empathy. A social action group depends on members' feelings of power and their connections to powerful resources in the community at large. A successful committee finds strengths in efficient operating procedures and diversity among members to stimulate creativity. Social workers discover group strengths by examining the individual qualities of members, the dynamic interaction among members, and the group's relationship to its environment.

Strengths in Organizations

There are many possibilities for identifying strengths in larger systems including human services agencies and other organizations. For example, in a social service agency, we may discover talented employees, a good training program, a dedicated volunteer pool, supportive and active clientele, a motivated and dedicated board of directors, a sound program evaluation system, or lucrative relationships with community foundations.

Organizations draw on the strengths of their mission, reputation in the community, family-friendly personnel policies and practices, sound financial management, well-maintained facilities, and receptive administrators. When faced with critical issues such as corporate expansion or downsizing, organizations can rely on their strengths to see them through difficult periods of change.

Strengths in Communities

A community's strengths include an appreciation of its diverse population, shared community values and standards, timely and deliberate response to community problems, and availability of resources. Strengths are also found in well-maintained infrastructures, adequate transportation systems, affordable housing, equitable tax levies, committed office holders, and a sound economy. A community that provides resources services and social connectedness to meet residents' needs and activates its citizens to participate in city government, community projects, and long-range planning has the resources in place to resolve upcoming issues. The adaptive capacities of resilient communities draw on networks of resources to equitably support all community members (Norris, et al., 2008).

Assessing strengths of a community is similar to exploring resources of other systems. Social workers inventory the community's assets and audit its capacity for development. To respect diversity, workers remain open to culturally specific clues to community strengths. For example, murals in Latino communities are social indicators of community strengths, both in terms of the content they present and the process by which they develop (Delgado & Barton, 1998). Workers assess both what the community gives to its members and how members contribute to the community in return.

SOLUTION-FOCUSED DIALOGUE

Asking about what is working, in addition to fleshing out what is not, seeks readily available information about possible strengths and solutions. Social workers may say:

- ▶ So what have you been doing to try to solve this?
- ▶ What works, even for a little while?
- ▶ What are you learning about your situation?

In assessment, empowerment-oriented social workers emphasize client strengths. What knowledge and skills are most effective in identifying the strengths that clients bring to the change effort?

▶ Is there anyone who seems able to cope with what's going on? What are they doing?

▶ Are there ever times when things just seem to be going better for no apparent reason?

▶ What have you discovered about yourself as you work on this issue?

▶ Do you remember a time when this problem didn't exist? Tell me what was going on then.

Each of these questions moves clients beyond ruminating about problems by expanding the focus of the dialogue toward solutions.

Many social workers have shifted from problem-centered to solution-centered dialogue with clients. Focusing on solutions, particularly in interventions with individual, couple, and family system clients, is the subject of numerous contemporary books and articles (Berg, 1994; DeJong & Berg, 2002; de Shazer, 1985, 1988; Walter & Peller, 2002). In addition, Berg and Miller (1992) have been working in the area of substance abuse, Schott and Conyers (2003) in psychiatric rehabilitation, Newsome (2005) and Franklin and Gerlach (2007) in schools, and Lee and colleagues (2007) with domestic violence offenders, demonstrating that these solution-focused approaches can be effective with even the most difficult issues. Solution-centered dialogue shows potential in work with other systems as well. Bloor and Pearson (2004) present such an application to work in organizations, and Cohen (2007), to work with groups.

Similarities exist among the approaches of various writers about useful conversational strategies to discover client strengths and potential solutions. Each approach compels workers to (1) create an atmosphere conducive to possibilities; (2) look for exceptions to the occurrence of the problem; (3) survey clients' information for incremental steps in the direction of goals; and (4) search for transferable skills and solutions.

Creating a Solution-Saturated Atmosphere

Myriad influences affect the atmosphere and tone of the transactions between clients and social workers. Solution-focused social workers deliberately tend to the climate of their working relationships to instill confidence, optimism, and the idea that success is inevitable. Positive assumptions enhance this atmosphere significantly. When practitioners assume that clients have competence, that challenges are transitory, and that clients have coping skills that they have demonstrated in the past and will do so again in the present and the future, workers promote hope and orient clients toward strengths and solutions.

A social worker's skills can ensure a success-saturated climate. Recognizing that language defines meaning, social workers choose words carefully to reveal their assumptions that clients can and will succeed. Giving direct compliments works well, lending a respectful tone in which people experience their potential. Nonverbal messages also contribute to a positive atmosphere. Workers can show their enthusiasm and hope through emotional expression, gestures, and voice tone as a way to convey optimism and positive expectations.

Searching for Exceptions

Sometimes problems entrench clients; it seems like everything is going wrong and nothing is going right. However, "nothing always happens; nothing is always the same" (de Shazer, 1985, pp. 161–162). This concise statement alerts social workers to look for exceptions, for indicators of when things are going well or when difficulties abate, even if only briefly. To search for exceptions, workers may say:

▸ What is happening on those days when things seem less impossible?

▸ So, most of the time you feel down. What about the other times?

▸ The residents raise a number of concerns about the recent deterioration of the neighborhood. What continues to be positive about the neighborhood?

▸ So, these signs of worker burnout have been going on for almost six months. What was different at the agency before things started going wrong?

The way the "exceptions question" works is simple. Workers "focus on the who, what, when, and where of exception times instead of the who, what, when, and where of problems." (De Jong & Miller, 1995, p. 731).

Detecting Incremental Steps

Probably the strengths most often missed by workers and clients alike are resources that are just developing. Often, clients are experimenting with new behaviors to overcome their current problems. Workers explore these attempts to discover times when clients feel hopeful and identify those that hold even a glimmer of clues about what might work.

Success builds one step at a time. Clients may be capable of accomplishments that are not in and of themselves enough to resolve the current difficulties, but which, nevertheless, may be steps in the right direction. For example, in trying to overcome an early rift that has divided it into subgroups, members of a support group may demonstrate excellent listening skills. Although the worker recognizes that the support group is not fully accomplished in resolving conflicts, the worker helps members notice that their abilities to listen are essential strengths for negotiating resolutions.

If workers and clients can decide where they are going, they can survey the current situations for signs that clients are moving in the right direction. To discover incremental steps, workers first help clients define a direction toward goals (a process presented in Chapter 8). Second, workers guide clients to search their situations for times when they are inching in that direction. Workers may say:

▸ What is the first thing you will notice when things are getting better? Does that ever happen now?

▸ If this problem disappeared overnight, what would clue you in when you woke up in the morning? Do you remember a time when that thing was happening?

▸ So you want everybody on both sides of this blended family to talk openly about how they think things should be organized. I've noticed that everyone has done that here today. Could we talk about how that happened so that we might help it continue?

▸ When the community and school linkage project began, only a few parents were actively involved. Since that time, the project staff has worked to increase the roster of parents. How can we maximize on this effort?

Sometimes clients cannot describe where they want to go or even what the first step might be. They need opportunities to observe themselves in action to discover if they are making any progress or having any success. In such situations, workers direct clients to examine the events between meetings to notice what is happening that clients would like to see continue.

Searching for Transferable Skills

Clients often demonstrate abilities in other areas that they can generalize to the situations at hand. Consider the mother who is short-tempered with her child but who shows great patience and restraint in caring for her aging father. Clearly, the skills and tolerance in both caregiving situations have similarities. Recognizing the success in one situation may help generate solutions in the other.

Or, at another system level, consider the example of a community that quickly activates considerable resources in times of natural disaster such as a flood, tornado, or hurricane, but isn't drawing on those same assets to resolve the ongoing crisis in a neighborhood plagued by high crime rates, crumbling streets, and deteriorating housing stock. Strengths in one aspect of functioning hold promise for resolving other areas of need.

RECOGNIZING CULTURAL STRENGTHS

Each of us draws strength from a variety of internal and external resources. We feel strong when we have a clear sense of who we are and where we fit into our world. Likewise, we feel our strength when we are secure that others support the ways we think and believe and we can count on the backing of others around us. All these elements are present in the various cultural identities we hold.

Recall that culture is an aspect of all groups, but is most specifically applied to describe membership in a particular racial or ethnic group. Culture not only encompasses values, beliefs, customs, and traditions, but it also includes survival strategies (Lum, 2004). Recognizing cultural strengths in clients has potential to activate powerful internal and external resources. It also reveals the worker's acceptance of diversity and bonds cross-cultural relationships. Acknowledging cultural strengths has many benefits. Unfortunately, "cultural resources are probably those least used by professional social workers in their encounters with clients" (Green, 1999, p. 95).

Strengths in Diversity

The concept of dignity implies that human beings have a right to be respected.

—Frederic Reamer

What is it that makes us overlook valuable cultural resources? Is it our discomfort with differences that encourages us to emphasize how we are similar to our clients and ignore those differences that we sense may threaten the bond of professional relationships? Is it that we are so accustomed to looking at cultural identities as the roots of prejudice, stereotypes, and oppression that we choose instead to minimize and gloss over rather than accentuate and celebrate our cultural and ethnic diversity? Whatever the reasons, it's time to recognize that ethnicity can function as "a source of cohesion, identity, and strength as well as a source of strain, discordance, and strife—the family, rituals and celebrations, language, and ethnic institutions all provide a source of comfort for many members of ethnic groups" (Devore, 1987, p. 95).

A logical explanation for the lack of attention to cultural strengths is the difficulty of building a knowledge base to detect them. Studies, such as one offered in the *Harvard Encyclopedia of American Ethnic Groups,* list as many as 106 separate ethnic groups in the United States alone (Devore, 1987). How could any of us possibly know the unique strengths and capacities that characterize each of these distinct groups? Add to that the individual differences

Box 9.2 Ethic of Respect

Respect, when genuinely present in a relationship, validates identity and worth, facilitates comfort and sharing, and encourages assertiveness and risk-taking. These are all qualities that collaborative social workers would like to introduce into their relationships with clients. Showing respect goes beyond demonstrating mere acceptance of person and situation toward a place of admiration for someone's skill, ability, and value. Respecting another person is a spontaneous response, one that either occurs or doesn't, based on one's experience in relationships. Social workers are challenged by the ethic of respect to discover in all clients respectable qualities that can be genuinely and openly appreciated.

Acceptance leads social workers "to recognize clients as knowledgeable in their own right and to accord them full standing in a dialogical process through which both clients and workers can learn from each other" (Berlin, 2005, p. 499). Berlin cautions that acceptance is neither passive nor placating. It "is also expressed when [social workers] exert power on behalf of a client's human rights and take actions to ensure that he or she can gain access to the concrete conditions of dignity and respect" (pp. 485–486).

The NASW *Code of Ethics* (1999a) charges social workers to demonstrate respect to clients and colleagues, but offers little guidance on how to achieve such a stance. However, the strengths orientation does provide direction to practitioners to achieve a genuinely respectful interaction. The recognition that all people have strengths and innate power that can be tapped (Weick, 2002) and that they have latent potential and creativity (Maluccio, 1981) leads workers to the assumption that clients have qualities that merit respect. Whom do you respect? What specifically leads you to this position? When you discover people's capabilities and talents, respect follows.

Identifying a client's strengths requires cultural competence. NASW *Standards for Cultural Competence* (2001a) acknowledge that "cultural competence is never fully realized, achieved, or completed, but rather cultural competence is a lifelong process for social workers who will always encounter diverse clients and new situations in their practice" (p. 11). Voluminous cultural knowledge is not necessary to respond in a sensitive way to diverse clients. On the contrary, a position of "not-knowing" or cultural naïveté is likely the best stance (Dyche & Zayas, 1995). Accepting one's own lack of understanding of socially, racially, and ethnically diverse groups and subsequently seeking knowledge directly from clients positions workers effectively to achieve cultural competence (Dean, 2001; Walker & Staton, 2000; Weick & Chamberlain, 2002). Culturally competent workers recognize strengths in the traditions, values, and beliefs from which cultural group members rely for shared identity, community belonging, and even survival. In short, cultural resources are strengths and clients are the ultimate cultural experts on their own strengths—something to respect about clients.

Social workers must also respond to the power differentials that characterize intercultural group relationships (Green, 1999). Strengths of those who are oppressed may not surface in relationships skewed by power and privilege. "In the context of culture and diversity, privilege is a phenomenon evolving from historical oppression. Its most singular quality derives from unearned advantages that are enjoyed by members of a group simply by virtue of membership in it" (Dewees, 2001, p. 35). The professional group membership of social workers creates a distinct difference in power and privilege, a divide across which practitioners must reach to discover clients' strengths and to show respect.

among clients, even in the same ethnic groups, and the task of recognizing cultural resources stymies even the most competent and motivated among us.

Of particular importance for antioppressive social workers are strengths present in the characteristics of nondominant groups. By virtue of their power, the dominant cultural group enjoys the privilege of prescribing mainstream cultural values and beliefs, thereby setting societal standards and norms. As a result, members of diverse cultures viewed through this dominant lens are likely to be judged most harshly, their strengths obscured or underestimated.

What workers perceive as right or wrong, health or dysfunction, strength or weakness carries the imprints of their own cultural and ethnic backgrounds. With this restricted view, practitioners may actually interpret something that functions as a strength for a particular client as a deficit instead. Consider the Euro-American social worker who determines that the 24-year-old Puerto Rican woman who stays home to assist with her family is having a problem growing up and leaving home. The worker's value of individual autonomy contrasts sharply with the Puerto Rican view of family interdependence (Ramos-McKay, Comas-Diaz, & Rivera, 1988). In this situation, the worker sees this cultural characteristic as a problem to be solved rather than as a resource for this client and her family. The worker totally misses the point. Learning about various cultures and ethnic groups alerts workers to possibilities, but workers should maintain caution in zealously applying general information to any client's specific situation to avoid stereotyping.

ETHNIC GROUP STRENGTHS

Diversity in Practice

What may function as a strength for a client in one culture may be viewed as a deficit in another cultural context. How does this statement make sense? What are concrete examples of this?

Similar resources characterize many ethnic groups in the United States, including African Americans, Latinos, Asian Americans, and Native Americans (Lum, 2004). These attributes include the centrality of family, support of the extended family and kinship network, clear vertical hierarchy in families, and the importance of religion and spirituality. Many of these qualities differ from the predominant Euro-American characteristics of independence, autonomy, egalitarianism, and rationality. This contrast demonstrates the need for learning about various racial, ethnic, and cultural groups, but workers should refrain from adopting the simplicity of this overgeneralization. Detecting cultural strengths is not a simple exercise in categorical thinking, but rather arises from careful study of nuances, of the similarities and differences within and among various groups. The sections that follow highlight some of the strengths the cross-cultural literature reveals about ethnic groups.

Intergenerational kinship bonds are among the strengths of African American families.

African Americans

African Americans currently account for about 12.8 percent of the total population in the United States (U.S. Census, 2007). Previous attention to African Americans focused on "pathology" and judgmentally defined how they differed in their functioning from the cultural majority. Another look reveals these same differences as potential sources of strength (Wright & Anderson, 1998). For example, Boyd-Franklin (1992) lists eight major strengths that social workers are likely to discover when working with African Americans, including: (1) extended family support; (2) the centrality of religion or spirituality; (3) the high value placed on children; (4) adaptability of family roles in response to changing circumstances; (5) informal adoption; (6) cultural loyalty; (7) high priority on education coupled with a strong work orientation; and (8) strong females. Additional strengths include achievement orientation, strong work ethic, flexible family roles, kinship bonds, self-help and mutual aid, political empowerment tradition, and adaptability in coping (Billingsley, 1992; Hill, 1997).

Strengths in African American clients become more visible through an Africentric worldview that reflects values different from Eurocentric culture.

> These beliefs are manifested in behaviors such as sharing a communal orientation; living In harmony with nature; demonstrating cooperativeness and avoiding competitiveness, control, and confrontation; being flexible about time and not bound to exact time units; and using spiritual faith in daily activities. (Jackson & Sears, 1992, p. 186)

The Africentric perspective places high value on interdependence of individuals with their environment. Practitioners working with African Americans remain alert for resources available within the context of family, social, and community networks. Consistent with the Africentric view, the emergent models of African American families "suggest that a greater value be placed on socioemotional factors such as support, caring, loyalty, religion, and spirituality, and less focus on socioeconomic indices to assess family stability" (Barnes, 2001, p. 450).

A recent survey on religious affiliations in the United States indicates that compared with other major racial and ethic groups, Black Americans "are the most likely to report a formal religious affiliation" (Pew Forum on Religion and Public Life, 2008, p. 8). This strong religious orientation suggests that ministers and the church community are essential community resources for African Americans (Bliss, et al., 2008; McNeal & Perkins, 2007; Moore & Miller, 2007). In sum, working effectively with African American clients means appreciating their cultural values and traditions and broadly assessing individual functioning in extended family and community contexts.

Latino Americans

Latino and Hispanic American are general terms applied to many cultures of Spanish descent. Latinos trace their ancestors to places such as Mexico, Cuba, Puerto Rico, other Central and South American countries, and even parts of the Southwestern United States that were formerly Mexican territory. The common Spanish language heritage and categorical grouping by the U.S. government links these cultures, but comparisons reveal numerous cultural differences (Castex, 1994b). Currently, people of Hispanic origin comprise the largest ethnic minority group in the United States, accounting for about 15 percent of the total population (U.S. Census, 2007) The size of this population group will more than double by 2050, when projections indicate people of Hispanic-Latino origin will constitute 29 percent of the U.S. population and 60 percent of the population growth (Passel & Cohn, 2008).

Mexican Americans

Mexican Americans represent the largest Latino group and the second largest ethnic group in the United States. Mexican American families frequently function within extended family networks that can include godparents and members of other families (Falicov, 1996; Morales & Salcido, 1998). These extended family members share such family tasks as "nurturing and disciplining of children, financial responsibility, companionship for lonely and isolated members, and problem solving" (Falicov, 1996, p. 175). In contrast to more assimilated ethnic groups, Mexican Americans continue to maintain much evidence of biculturalism and bilingualism. Mexican Americans resist assimilation into the U.S. cultural mainstream because of their proximity to Mexico, which provides "a constant infusion of persons and culture" (Martinez, 1988, p. 183).

One of the major strengths of Mexican American families is a quantitative rather than a qualitative difference from other ethnic groups (Martinez, 1988). There are simply more family members available to provide support and resources. The tendency toward having many children, including extended family members as active participants in family activities, events, and decisions, and adding nonrelated individuals to the family in the form of godparents establishes a natural support network that is readily accessible.

Observable differences occur between the "public view" and "private reality" of Mexican American families (Falicov, 1996). For example, many Mexican Americans have a more egalitarian distribution of power in marital relationships than the male-dominated cultural stereotype indicates. The strong value placed on children coupled with the mother's role in child rearing frequently sets up an in-home reality of an in-charge woman, whereas the family maintains a public image that the man is in charge. This observation again alerts workers to the need to check out any general cultural conclusions with concrete information from each unique client system.

Mexican Americans frequently show the same high degree of spirituality that is present in other Latino cultures, such as Cuban and Puerto Rican. "Catholicism provides an order to social behavior that has a stabilizing and adaptive effect on individuals and families, and . . . it also offers a source of explanation and control in an inchoate world" (Martinez, 1988, p. 190). Moreover, intricate interconnections and interdependencies exist among the personal physical, mental, and spiritual domains. Knowledge of this connectedness offers spirituality as a strength and a beginning point of change for Latino clients.

Other Latino cultures

Similar to Mexican Americans, Puerto Rican and Cuban Americans show strengths in extended family support, respect for older family members, and a tendency toward cooperation over competition (Bernal & Shapiro, 1996; Garcia-Preto, 1998; Weaver & Wodarski, 1996). Regardless of these similarities, resist the temptation to group all Latino cultures together or risk overlooking more subtle cultural differences that distinguish these groups. For example, Cuban Americans show greater tendencies toward autonomy and individuality than other Latino cultures (Bernal & Gutiérrez, 1988). Because music plays a more prominent role in the lives of Puerto Ricans, some suggest that interventions using music fit well when working with Puerto Rican clients (Ramos-McKay, et al.,1988).

Asian Americans

The ethnically and culturally diverse groups described together as Asian Americans combine to form one of the fastest growing ethnic groups in the United States (Scommegna, 2004). Demographic projects indicate that the size of the Asian American population in the United States will triple by 2050, increasing from 14 million to 41 million or from five percent to nine percent of the population (Passell & Cohn, 2008). Like those ethnic groups clustered as Latino, the description "Asian American" represents various people who trace their origins to countries such as the Philippines, China, Vietnam, Korea, Japan, India, Laos, Cambodia, other Asian countries and the Pacific Islands. Unlike other ethnic groups in the United States, many Asian Americans do not suffer from negative stereotypes of dysfunction. Rather, they are stereotyped as a "model minority," an overgeneralized myth of unilateral brilliance and success. "According to this 'model minority' image, Asian Americans' cultural traits—diligence, frugality, and willingness to sacrifice—propel their upward mobility and win them public accolades" (Crystal, 1989, p. 405).

The "model minority" image has its drawbacks, as does any group stereotyping. It obscures individual differences and diminishes assistance to Asian Americans whose lives do not mirror the myth. Lorenzo, Frost, and Reinherz (2000) identify the depression, withdrawal, and social problems of Asian American adolescents that sometimes lie beneath the model minority image. And the minority status peripheralizes members of this group from the societal mainstream (Oyserman & Sakamoto, 1997). However, the model minority image does reflect a general awareness that there are strengths present in Asian cultures. Family unity, support for family members, particularly in times of crisis, and strong informal support networks such as churches, clubs, and family associations are strengths common among Asian Americans. A review of the social work literature by Fong and Mokuau (1994) shows general agreement that Asian American and Pacific Islanders hold respect and concern for others in higher regard than individual self-concerns. Considering this cultural emphasis on natural support networks, social workers may seek solutions through the resources of "priests, doctors, indigenous healers, and elders in their work with Asian clients" (p. 412).

The centrality of the family emphasized in many ethnic cultures is perhaps strongest among Asian Americans. Core family values among Asian Americans include family loyalty, unquestioning respect for parents, and "the unspoken obligatory reciprocity that arises out of human relationship, such as kindness and helpfulness" (Ho, 1987, p. 25). Other Asian values include preserving family honor and avoiding shame (McLaughlin & Braun, 1998; Nakanishi & Rittner, 1996). The quest for harmony in all human relationships is an essential value that can function as a powerful resource which compels Asian American clients toward cooperative resolutions (Browne & Broderick, 1994). Social workers must withhold their tendency to push clients toward self-assertion in a cultural context where group interest supersedes individual action and solutions lie in collaborative endeavors.

Native Americans

Although difficult to classify, American Indians and the Alaska Native population number about 4.3 million, about 1.5 percent of the population of the United States (Ogunwole, 2006). More than 500 Native nations exist; four have populations of more than 100,000: the Cherokee, Navajo, Chippewa/Ojibway, and Sioux.

Many differences distinguish the Native groups; however, one can identify common values and strengths. Within traditional Native American families, "closeness, collective problem solving, equal responsibility for young children, sharing of resources and of labor are all a way of life evolving out of the clan system in which the family was the core and the clan the extension" (Blount, et al., 1996, p. 269). The extended family is integral to Native groups' sense of family and community. Family members value generosity, sharing, and giving, and respect the wisdom and leadership of elders (Weaver & White, 1997). Social workers who overlook extended family resources among Native Americans miss opportunities to provide culturally appropriate services. Red Horse (1982) describes a classic case example in which a child protection unit proceeded to place an "at-risk" child in a foster home 40 miles away from the child's natural mother without ever discovering the extended family resources available less than 5 miles away. These resources included many family members who "offered their homes for foster placement services, guaranteed transportation for visits between mother and child during a period of family therapy, and provided ongoing assistance with parenting" (p. 19).

Many American Indians also find strength in tribal traditions. Garrett (1993–1994) says that tradition embedded in myths and "stories shared by the Indian elders teach culturally related values for learning and encourage that we all get along with each other" (p. 21). These stories emphasize cooperation and respect over personal achievement and "the interdependence of the family, clan, and tribes, rather than on personal gain or wealth" (p. 20). Encouraging the relating of these stories meets an identified need in Native American children to acquire information about cultural heritage (Franklin, et al., 1995). Social workers can ask Native American clients to tell stories about their heritage to discover strengths in tribal and familial histories.

As in other diverse cultures in the United States, spirituality functions as a guiding force. "Spirituality sets the tone for seeking harmony and congruence among mind, body, and spirit" (Red Horse, 1982, p. 18). Peaceful coexistence with natural forces is a key component of Native American spirituality (Yellow Bird, et al., 1995). Spiritual leaders have a significant influence on tribal members and are resources for Native American clients and for professional practitioners. Culturally sensitive social workers recognize that although these leaders may not be professionally trained helpers, they nevertheless "are trained in very rigorous cultural ways and are quite adept in working with Indian clientele" (Red Horse, p. 18).

Again, workers cautiously apply any general conclusions about Native Americans to specific clients because "researchers emphasize that there are large intragroup differences among American Indians and intergroup differences among tribes" (Franklin, et al., 1995, p. 183). Two major factors influence cultural differences among people described as Native American (Dykeman, et al., 1995; Grimm, 1992). First, distinctive differences in values and traditions are associated with various tribes. This "diversity among indigenous people may be best expressed in the relationship that each nation has with its natural environment" (Yellow Bird, et al., 1995, p. 131). Second, Native Americans show much variation in degree of assimilation into Euro-American culture. Such differences alert social workers to listen carefully for clues as to the possible values and resources in their work with Native Americans.

STRENGTHS IN CULTURAL GROUP MEMBERSHIPS

Variations in ethnicity are not the only qualities that distinguish cultural groups. Gender, sexual orientation, age, religion, abilities, and other characteristics also lead to groupings that classify and possibly even stereotype cultural group members. Culturally competent social workers learn to identify the unique strengths potentially present in people of many different cultures, including women, gays and lesbians, older adults, people with religious affiliations, and people with disabilities.

Women

Slightly more than half of the U.S. population is female. The proportion of women in the labor force has expanded dramatically over the last several decades, yet women are shortchanged in the market place. Even though their wages have increased, women still earned about 23 percent less than men in 2006 (Webster & Bishaw, 2007). According to the National Poverty Center, more than one-fourth of all female-headed households have incomes below the poverty level (http://www.npc.umich.edu/poverty/). Older women are particularly vulnerable to poverty. Issues affecting women, such as poverty, homelessness, domestic violence, inadequate child care provisions, and depression, have at their core social and economic inequities. Women show strengths in their abilities to face this social injustice.

Feminism adds a perspective on the strengths of women as survivors of patriarchy, inequalities, and oppression (Simon, 1994). Hanmer and Statham, two feminist social work scholars from Great Britain, urge a view of women "as active, resilient, and enduring actors in their own behalf rather than as sorry objects of other people's words or actions" (as cited in Simon, p. 171). Women discover self-worth in their abilities to survive. "Survival involves more than perseverance of living a life of quiet desperation; it means assertion, however unobtrusively this may be expressed. Survival means taking on what has to be confronted, preferably in your time, on your grounds, around your issue" (p. 172).

Categorical definitions of what it means to be feminine or masculine separate women and men. To be feminine is to be interdependent, peaceful, egalitarian, emotional, nurturant, and concerned about others, in contrast to masculine tendencies to be independent, rational, decisive, achievement-oriented, aggressive, and concerned about rights and responsibilities. These "appropriate" characteristics demonstrating femininity and masculinity are socially defined, yet they are often assumed to be biologically determined. Gender stereotypes are value based and can have negative effects.

Western culture has traditionally assigned characteristics associated with masculinity a superior status. Although masculine characteristics may support the patriarchal values of rugged individualism, competition, and the work ethic, masculine characteristics fall short in promoting cooperation, communication, and interpersonal relationships. This brand of sexism devalues feminine traits and masks the feminine strengths of both women and men. Nurturance, emotional investments in others, cooperation, and communication abilities that respect and honor others are the very elements that support self-growth, strengthen families, enhance interpersonal relationships, and promote "caring" structures within neighborhoods, organizations, communities, and society. These qualities are strengths for social workers to acknowledge in women and in men.

Women of color

Women of color experience disproportionate rates of poverty and homelessness. From their perspective, these injustices are more likely related to racism, classism, and ethnocentrism than to sexism, factors ignored by traditional feminist perspectives (Gutiérrez & Lewis, 1998). For women of color, institutional racism, not sexism, is the most critical factor in their experiences of oppression (Lum, 2004). Strengths abound in their abilities to survive oppression and "leverage political power" (p. 111). An exploratory study by Aguilar and Williams (1993, as cited in Lum) revealed "strengths of women of color that derive from their personal, family, and community traits" (p. 30), including hard work, pride in accomplishments, significant support systems, spirituality, optimism, self-motivation, and persistence. Factors identified in the research that contributed to the success of these women were "the achievement of goals, job satisfaction, self-esteem, education and skills, family support and stability, personal strengths, ethnic/racial pride, and community and professional commitment" (p. 31).

Gays and Lesbians

All social work practitioners will interact with clients and colleagues who are gay or lesbian. Estimates indicate that about 10 percent of the U.S. population are gay men or lesbian women. Census 2000 enumerated 594,000 same-sex unmarried partner households, defined as "sharing living quarters and [having] a close personal relationship with each other (Simmons & O'Connell, 2003). These data also show that same-sex unmarried partner households are more likely situated in metropolitan than in rural areas geographically dispersed throughout the United States. Social work requires a broad-based acceptance of sexual diversity with an openness to recognize the strengths of gay and lesbian clients.

Of course, the strengths of gays and lesbians mirror those of other people. They derive strengths from personal qualities, interpersonal relationships and connections within their communities. But acknowledging and asserting a homosexual orientation in a homophobic society requires unique struggles, creative adaptations, and the ability to take risks. To function successfully in both gay and straight communities, gays and lesbians inevitably learn to be bicultural (Lukes & Land, 1990).

Many gays and lesbians demonstrate considerable strengths in achieving developmental milestones. Developmental processes are complex for gays and lesbians because they must grow into an identity that is not socially sanctioned, a process not faced by heterosexuals (Sullivan, 1994). Gays and lesbians show strengths in recognizing and accepting a sexual identity that varies from the dominant norm, in coming out to others, in maintaining committed partnerships without legal sanction, and in asserting their identities in their social environments. At each developmental phase, gays and lesbians must resolve their own personal ambivalence and risk social rejection—unjust dilemmas imposed by a homophobic society but, nevertheless, situations that elicit assertion, creative adaptation, and personal strength.

The abilities of gays and lesbians to create families outside of the traditional family models is another significant strength. Ainslie and Feltey (1998) note that lesbian couples tend to be independent, self-reliant, assertive, and more flexible in defining gender role expectations suggesting "the possibility of a very positive childrearing environment in lesbian families" (p. 329). Their study concludes that children in lesbian families show acceptance of differences and express a high degree of social consciousness about issues such as racism, sexism, and nonviolence.

Besieged by misunderstanding, discrimination, and oppression, gays and lesbians have initiated numerous activities to redress these injustices. "The gay and lesbian community shows extraordinary strength and courage in its ability to initiate social action, educational, and advocacy activities in response to AIDS as well as to issues related to violence, and discrimination" (Newman, 1994). Abilities in community organizing and political activism typify the potential power that social workers discover in many gay and lesbian clients.

To recognize successfully the strengths of gay and lesbian clients, workers reject negative value judgments rooted in dominant cultural norms, explore their own biases and homophobic tendencies, and openly have dialogues with others about sexuality. This is an important aspect of social work practice because "the issues surrounding the gay population exemplify the core social work principles of self-determination and the basic need of full social and civil rights for all oppressed people" (Newman, 1989, p. 209).

Older Adults

Recent census studies in the United States predict that the number of adults 65 years and older will increase from the present 37 million in 2005 or about 12 percent of the population to 81 million or about 19 percent of the population by 2050 (Passell & Cohen, 2008). The subgroup of the oldest old, those 85 years of age and older, is 40 percent larger than it was in 1900. Projections indicate that this age group will increase from 5.3 million in 2006 to 21 million in 2050 (Federal Interagency Forum, 2008).

People often associate growing older with sensory loss and changes in mobility; however, for most older adults, these changes are neither as cumbersome nor as apparent as many imagine. Successfully coping with a lifetime of events, older adults show signs of resilience physically and emotionally. This realization is enculturated in beliefs by Asian and Pacific Islanders, who see older adults "as family decision makers and the keepers of family and cultural wisdom" (Browne & Broderick, 1994, p. 254). As people grow older, they accumulate life experiences, gain perspective, and amass the knowledge of a lifetime.

To discover strengths within older adults, social workers encourage them to talk about their lives, including their current interests and occupations, as well as those from the past (Kivnick & Stoffel, 2007). To detect the unique strengths of older adults often overlooked in standardized needs-based assessment processes, Kivnick and Murray (2001) have developed a life strengths interview guide. Nine key questions guide workers. Example questions include:

- What makes a good day for you?
- What about yourself has always given you confidence or made you proud?
- What kinds of help do you give to others?
- What lessons have you learned about how to cope with life from day to day?
- Who are the people that are especially important to you these days? (p. 32)

Reminiscing provides older adults with opportunities to retell their life stories. Kivnick (1988) says: "Sifting through these newly revealed old treasures allows interrelated parts of the whole that has been the one and only life cycle" (p. 64).

Religious Affiliations and Spirituality

Although there is a loud public outcry about the decline of values in contemporary culture, religious culture is flourishing in the United States. Recent studies conducted by the Pew Research Center (2001) found that 9 of 10 Americans pray and that 64 percent believe religion is very important. Studies also conclude that 87 percent of Americans never doubt the existence of God (Pew Research Center, 2003). Results of the American Religions Identification Survey, 2001 (Kosmin, et al., 2002), a randomized phone survey of more than 50,000 Americans, indicate that overall, 75 percent of the adults surveyed define themselves as either religious or somewhat religious. A comparison of selected groups reveals that African Americans are most likely to define themselves as religious or somewhat religious (81 percent). For many people in the United States, religion and spirituality are significant influences and potential sources of strength, resilience, and meaning in life (Bhul et al., 2008; Cummings & Mac-Neil, 2008; Gall, 2006; Hodge, 2003; Lazar & Bjorch, 2008; Miles, et al., 2007; Revheim & Greenberg, 2007).

Although specific beliefs and practices vary considerably, religious affiliation and spirituality have resources to offer. Affiliating with a community of faith provides a network of personal relationships and concrete support in times of need. Specifically, "spiritual beliefs and practices strengthen the ability to withstand and transcend adversity" (Walsh, 1999a, p. 38), and are virtual wellsprings for healing and resilience (1999b). Common beliefs, stories of the faith, holy days, and ritual celebrations forge a sense of communal identity and purpose. In African American churches, research reveals a "haven which children can learn about their heritage from other African Americans who valued and nurtured them" (Haight, 1998). As in other non-Western traditions, the interconnectedness within community is implicit in Hinduism, as the interdependent social body is a manifestation of the sacred order or Hindu dharma (Hodge, 2004). Community is also a common theme among the various traditions of Islam (Hodge, 2005a). Within the Muslim community, individualistic Western values, such as self-reliance and autonomy are subordinate to "group success, community development, interdependence, and consensus" (p. 161). Compassion, love, and forgiveness—themes in most religions—contribute to personal and interpersonal healing. Commitment to a faith can initiate a sense of meaning, renewal, and hope for the future. Religious commitment may encourage concern for the welfare of others and, for some, foster a zeal for redressing social injustices.

Persons with Disabilities

The U.S. Census estimates that 41 million people in the United States, ages five or older, not living in institutions, or about 15 percent, have a disability (Rehabilitation Research, 2007). Nearly half that number have a disability classified as severe. Many persons with disabilities face challenges in accomplishing life tasks. For example, 25.3 percent of all those between 18 and 64 years of age who have a work limitation had incomes below the poverty line in 2006. Not only do physical or mental conditions limit their opportunities, according to the social model of disability, but the social context imposes restrictions (Barnes & Mercer, 2004; Lester & Tritter, 2005; Oliver, 1996, 1997; Sapey, et al., 2005; Woolfson, 2004). Stigma, interpersonal degradation, and social marginality lead others to underestimate the capabilities of persons with disabilities as they strive to fulfill meaningful social roles.

The challenge for social workers is to recognize that people with physical, cognitive, and psychological disabilities are also people with abilities. "A collaborative approach to practice with people with disabilities must be founded on the fact that they are people first and disabled second" (Gilson, Bricout, & Baskind, 1998, p. 194). Individuals draw strengths from their own personal resolve, positive self-images, aspirations, priorities, creativity, supportive relationships with family members and friends, successful rehabilitation, and use of adaptive devices. Progressive legislative mandates—such as the Americans with Disabilities Act to remove architectural, transportation, and communication barriers—further ensure the full participation of persons with disabilities in community life.

Clients as Resources for Understanding Cultures

A general knowledge of culture and ethnicity sensitizes practitioners to the diversity of potential resources within special populations, but, even among people with similar cultural identities, workers remain cautious about overgeneralizing. "The capacity for individualizing the client within a specific cultural matrix is the genius and the challenge of effective cross-cultural social work" (Green, 1999, p. 92).

Luckily, as practitioners work to incorporate clients' cultural strengths, they have key respondents with them in the same room. Clients themselves are the best sources of information about their cultural strengths and resources. When social workers bring general cultural awareness, openness to differences, and good listening skills, along with permission for clients to be themselves in a cultural sense, workers learn how to relate to clients in their ethnic and cultural contexts.

UNCOVERING STRENGTHS IN ADVERSITY

Since the advent of psychoanalysis, helping professionals have searched the past to account for why things have gone wrong in the present. In this view, the scars of adversity and dysfunction accumulate to overwhelming proportions. Strengths-oriented social workers acknowledge that, in spite of the adversity, somehow people continue on their way. Clients who experience victimization are also, by definition, survivors.

"The view that past traumatic experiences are a source of problems in later life is certainly plausible—at least here in the West. The opposite view that past ordeals are valuable learning experiences is equally sensible" (Furman & Ahola, 1992, p. 23). Surviving trauma such as is the case in oppression, victimization, or family disruptions takes strength, courage, and resources. Practitioners working with survivors of any sort have opportunities to explore their clients' success in making it this far.

Surviving Oppression

Groups described as cultural minorities all share similar histories and experiences with respect to oppression. Oppression is "the systematic, institutionalized mistreatment of one group of people by another for whatever reason" (Yamato, 1993, p. 207). Racism, sexism, ageism, ableism, heterosexism, regionalism, and classism are all various forms of oppression. Each form of prejudice and discrimination denies a particular group access to their fair share of society's resources, violating human rights and principles of social justice.

Certainly, social workers strive to overcome such social injustice, operating at the macrolevel to create changes in social policy to increase universal access to resources and opportunities. They also work on their own professional styles to identify and eradicate tendencies to perpetuate oppressive practices in their

Research Based Practice

A strengths-based social worker might believe that a person's victimization frequently leads to the development of resilience and strengths. What steps could a social worker take to test this hypothesis by using social work research?

relationships with clients. Prevention of oppression is the preferred approach, but the simple fact is that social work practitioners deal with many clients who have already been affected by oppressive forces. On a client-by-client basis, social workers must look beyond the damage that oppression may have caused to applaud the strengths that these same clients have brought to bear in handling injustice.

Successful coping skills

Did you notice the predominance of strengths present in family, informal, and natural support networks as you read about various ethnic and cultural groups? Persons denied access to the benefits of society at large learn to cope in other ways. They group together. They help each other out. To meet their own needs, they set up their own informal institutions to circumvent the discriminatory formal institutional processes. The informal adoption practices of African Americans exemplify one such informal "child welfare system."

The "victim system" significantly affects racial and ethnic minorities (Pinderhughes, 1982). Victimization can impose a trap; however, surviving victimization requires adaptability, flexibility, and strength. Social workers acknowledge the magnitude of the impact of oppression and, at the same time, do not neglect the possibilities of positive adaptation.

One such positive adaptation is the strong extended family network present in African American families, which has roots in their African heritage and developed in response to slavery, threat, and oppression (Boyd-Franklin, 1992). Another adaptive coping skill is the example of "vibes." African Americans, because of the often extremely subtle ways in which racism manifests itself socially, tune in to very fine distinctions among such variables in interactions. Because of this, many African Americans have been socialized to pay attention to all the nuances of behavior and not to just the verbal message.

Survival and coping strengths develop in response to oppression. "We African Americans have a history of drawing upon inner and extended family resources to survive from one generation to the next, no matter what the obstacles and indignities" (Franklin, 1993, p. 37). Franklin suggests ways to draw out these strengths. For example, ask African American clients to describe the survivors known to them in their own family histories and guide them to search for these same qualities in themselves. A strong connection to history and legacy by African American clients draws on the support of their cultural identity and their success even in the face of the past abuse of slavery.

Responding to clients who are oppressed

All oppressed groups have overcome difficult odds. Clients benefit from exploring the ways they accomplished this. To do so, workers acknowledge and empathize with clients' feelings of oppression, yet urge them on toward the ways they have been able to handle this unfair treatment. Workers may say:

- ▶ I know you're right that it's not easy to be an African American in a racist community, but somehow you seem able to cope. How is it that you manage so well?
- ▶ It does seem like the school picks on you because you're different. Are there other Mexican American students that you know that seem to get by? What are they doing to cope?
- ▶ I agree that this neighborhood doesn't seem to get the same services that the rest of the city gets. I'm so impressed with the way all of you work together, pool your resources, and find ways to cope in spite of their

neglect. Maybe we can use some of the resources this group has already developed here to advocate with city officials for better treatment.

In each example, the worker does not underestimate the devastating impact of social injustice, but neither does the worker ignore that clients are making it in spite of the adversity.

Surviving Violence

Silence in the face of injustice is complicity with the oppressor.
—Ginetta Sagan

Many social work clients have experienced various forms of violence including intimate partner violence, war, natural disaster, or political upheaval. Such trauma can be devastating. But each survivor of such an event has found ways to get through each day in spite of the difficult circumstances. Social workers can assist these clients by first helping them unload their pain, and then by directing clients' attention back to their capabilities and areas of power.

Domestic violence

Providing immediate assistance to victims of domestic violence is a preemptive social work action leading social workers to ensure safety and to provide emotional support, medical services, and legal advocacy before moving toward long-term recovery. Even with an effective response to the crisis event, a client who experiences such intimate violence may continue to have adverse consequences as the person moves on with life. Being violated by traumatic events tests personal strength. Clients who have survived incidents of such violence in the near or distant past have already passed the test.

Danis (2004) notes some of the many strengths demonstrated by women who have experienced abusive relationships, including risk-assessment skills, persistence in working to resolve their relationships, loyalty to and protectiveness of their children, supportive informal helping networks, and spirituality, among others. Key to surviving this kind of intimate violence is the restoration of power and choice (Peled et al, 2000). Many women in these situations already demonstrate the power to cope, as evidenced by the positive self-regard and their refusal to accept blame for the abuse (Hensley, 2002).

War

Veterans returning from overseas wars suffer significant effects from the horror and stress of war-related activities. Posttraumatic stress disorder (PTSD) and traumatic brain injury (TBI), along with physical injuries, are frequent consequences of the war zone experience (DOD, 2007). Many veterans also experience disruption in family and community relationships on their return home. Yet, each returning soldier has a survival story that illustrates how he or she has drawn on significant skills and resources in the process. One of the social worker's tasks is to bring these strengths to the forefront.

Certainly, responsible social workers screen for difficulties that veterans may be facing, but strength-based practitioners also recognize the significant accomplishments of coping with such dire circumstances. The 2007 *Report of the Department of Defense Task Force on Mental Health* questions the current system of health care for veterans, citing its use of the disease-based medical model as possibly a poor fit for the psychosocial symptoms experienced by many veterans. Reacting to this report, Wheeler and Bragin (2007) suggest that

it is time for social work to bring its methods of inquiry to bear on the development of and advocacy for culturally informed, strengths-based, biopsychosocial approaches to work with veterans and others affected by violence. Such approaches, coordinated with public health care systems, would maximize opportunities for veterans . . . to emerge as contributing members and leaders in their communities. (p. 299)

Forced migration

All immigrants face the stress of adapting to a new culture. Refugees who are forced from their homes by violent political upheaval or devastating natural disasters, such as hurricanes, typhoons, or drought, confront challenges beyond the expected cultural adaptation required of those who voluntarily migrate. Most refugees have little time to prepare for the events that dislodge them from their homes. Escape from the situation usually involves fear, anxiety, and witnessing traumatic events. Many refugees spend months or even years in temporary camps or shelters that offer subsistence living standards and are frequently rocked by food shortages, water scarcity, and disease.

The evidence is compelling. In one study more than 70 percent of refugees fleeing political violence in Sri Lanka reported being hurt in their homelands through physical abuse, emotional trauma, and torture (Weaver & Burns, 2001). Another study revealed that Vietnamese parents who had endured refugee camps raised children more prone to violence than expected compared with normative data (Spencer & Le, 2007). Social workers are challenged to counteract the negative consequences associated with forced migration by recognizing the less-salient characteristics that reveal client strengths.

Where do social workers look for strengths in refugees? Using teachers' observations of refugee children, one study directs workers to recognize that students who were refugees may act with unusual respect and also to notice that their parents will likely become involved immediately in any issues affecting their children (Szente, et al., 2006). Other experts direct the search for resilience toward exploring each phase of the refugee's migration, including the reasons for leaving the home country, experiences in transit, and the resettlement experience in the new community (Pine & Crachman, 2005). Through this careful retracing of the refugee's path, a strength-focused social worker can highlight the adaptive mechanisms used by the refugee during each phase and consider how these demonstrated abilities may benefit the refugee in facing current challenges.

Diversity in survivors' experiences

Social workers need to be alert to the different ways that people from various cultures cope. "Too often, the active coping strategies of clients who have little social power are misinterpreted as passivity and giving up" (Holzman, 1994, p. 95). Workers acknowledge that there is no right way to respond to violence, but recognize that survivors draw on their own developed strengths as they cope.

Although workers may readily see strengths in viewing clients who are survivors, not all clients are ready to openly acknowledge that they have gone on. On a cautionary note, workers should not move too quickly to point out the successful ways clients are coping. Clients may first need to experience a worker's empathy and understanding before being able to benefit from a worker's admiration.

Surviving Family Disruption

The impact on children of families that experience disruption is a contemporary issue that receives much attention, giving rise to such support groups as Adult Children of Alcoholics (ACOA) or Adult Children of Dysfunctional Families. Many helping professionals trace the difficulties adults experience to origins in problematic family dynamics. In some ways, we are all affected by the dynamics of our families of origin. Each of us develops in unique familial and other social contexts. Each of us carries the impact of these interpersonal systems with us. Each of us also makes choices about how we respond and incorporate these influences. Think about your own life, the ways your family has affected and is affecting you, and the choices that you make to respond.

Strength-oriented social workers acknowledge the inevitable power that families have over children, yet also realize that all persons develop their own way to cope. "Care should be taken not to assume that each person who was abused as a child will necessarily be under extreme distress as an adult" (Busby, et al., 1993, p. 338). "Strength can emerge from adversity" and result in resiliencies that promote well-being (Wolin & Wolin, 1993, p. 15). Workers certainly empathize with difficult family experiences, but also press further to explore a client's response to this history. Workers may say:

- Growing up in an alcoholic family does leave its mark, and I see that you have a good job, a nice home, and people who care about you. How have you managed all of this?
- It must have been terrifying to know that your father was determined to commit suicide. What did you do to overcome that fear and anxiety?
- Growing up in your family meant that you had to grow up fast, almost like you never really got to be a kid. Have you found ways to relax and have fun now that you are in charge of your own life?

Workers do not underestimate the difficulty of childhood abandonment, neglect, or trauma, nor do they undervalue the strengths survivors have developed in response.

LOOKING FORWARD

People become social work clients for many reasons, at times because of actions deemed unacceptable by societal standards. These clients often bear labels such as child abuser, batterer, or perpetrator, descriptions that stir negative feelings in the most accepting social worker. Implementing a strengths perspective means that workers shift their focus even with these clients to acknowledge their capabilities and successes.

Identifying strengths is a companion process to articulating situations and defining directions. Social workers simultaneously elicit information about what brings clients to them while also searching to discover the resources available to achieve solutions. A social worker's ability to identify strengths springs from preparation to recognize client strengths in general functioning, in specific responses to the challenging situations, in cultural memberships, and in historical adversity.

Clients do not stand alone in mustering their capabilities to meet their challenges. They also have the resources of their social and physical environments. Chapter 10 describes additional assessment processes for social workers to discover what else clients and environments have to offer.

Succeed with **PEARSON mysocialworklab**

Log onto **www.mysocialworklab.com** and select the **Interactive Skill Module** videos from the left-hand menu. Answer the questions below. (*If you did not receive an access code to* **MySocialWorkLab** *with this text and wish to purchase access online, please visit* www.mysocialworklab.com.)

1. **Carefully watch page 13 of the group work module** in which group member Anna describes her problem of cultural dissonance. In this process Anna also

reveals many strengths. What do you notice? What questions might you ask to uncover additional strengths?

2. **In the child welfare module (page 15)**, a client describes a childhood of neglect, a model after which she styles her own neglectful mothering. What can the worker do to help this client recognize that these same experiences may have also produced resilience and strengthened her resolve to do better?

PRACTICE TEST

1. Which of the following statements is LEAST true about strengths?
   a. Strengths can be imbedded in culture.
   b. Strengths are personal rather than contextual.
   c. A strength for one person could be a deficit for another.
   d. Strengths are relative to situations.

2. Interested in applying the strengths perspective to her work with clients, social worker Chandelle Tomas has learned that _____.
   a. accentuating strengths has merits, but does little for building working relationships
   b. working through problems leads to change
   c. not everyone has strengths
   d. not talking about problems can leave clients feeling unheard

Human Rights & Justice

3. Mariel Ziaere and her family recount their harrowing escape from a country besieged by civil war. To apply an empowerment perspective, their social worker should _____.
   a. empathize with the family's feelings, yet urge them to look at how they have managed
   b. acknowledge that adversity likely creates long-term dysfunction
   c. understand that the family will necessarily be hostile toward people with authority
   d. help the family gain insight into how they contributed to their own victimization

Research Based Practice

4. In their research on families, Beavers and Hampson found that competent families _____.
   a. express positive emotions instead of negative ones
   b. are most likely two-parent families
   c. are able to negotiate differences
   d. are families that have a history of few problems

Practice Contexts

5. Of the following characteristics, which is LEAST likely a strength of a social service organization?
   a. hiring talented administrators
   b. maintaining a sound reputation in the community

   c. investing capital in programs rather than program evaluation research
   d. adopting family friendly personnel policies

6. Social worker Cecil Aronson uses solution-focused dialogue in his work with clients. Of the following conversation starters, which would he NOT use?
   a. Tell me what you've been doing to solve this problem.
   b. I'm wondering, what works, even for a little while?
   c. I'd like to know in detail what the problem is so that we can discover a solution.
   d. You've probably been learning about yourself while you've been working on this issue. I wonder what you've been learning.

7. de Shazer's idea that *nothing always happens and nothing is always the same* presses social workers to _____.
   a. create a solution-saturated atmosphere
   b. search for exceptions
   c. design a plan based on incremental steps
   d. motivate clients to change

8. At present, _____ are the largest minority group in the United States
   a. African Americans
   b. Asian Americans
   c. Latino Americans
   d. Native Americans

9. Social worker Janeal Howard is employed as a case manager at Northside Aging Services. She will meet with Miss Ada Long, a 90-year-old African American who is currently home-bound. To plan for her first visit, Janeal draws knowledge about older adults and strengths of the African American culture. Given this general background information, Janeal should explore the resources likely available to reduce Miss Long's isolation her connections with _____.
   a. neighbors
   b. church "family"
   c. friends from civic organizations
   d. older siblings

Log onto **MySocialWorkLab** once you have completed the Practice Test above to take your Chapter Exam and demonstrate your knowledge of this material.

Answers

1) b 2) d 3) a 4) c 5) c 6) c 7) b 8) c 9) b

10

Assessing Resource Capabilities

CHAPTER OUTLINE

CONNECTING CORE COMPETENCIES *in this chapter*

Professional Identity   Ethical Practice   **Critical Thinking**   Diversity in Practice   **Human Rights & Justice**   **Research Based Practice**   **Human Behavior**   Policy Practice   Practice Contexts   Engage Assess Intervene Evaluate

When you consider moving into a house, you want to see more than one room. No matter how impressed you are with that one room, you still want to explore the entire house—the other rooms, the attic, the basement, the yard. You may even want to stroll around the neighborhood. Because you know that the ambience of one room alone does not define the experience of living in the whole house, you ask to see it all. Life in one room responds to and affects the rest of the house, the yard, and the neighborhood, just as life in the entire house, yard, and neighborhood responds to and affects life in one room.

Clients may not lead social workers around to the "other rooms, yards, or neighborhoods" of their lives unless workers ask for a tour. A generalist assessment does more than articulate clients' situations and identify their strengths. Regardless of the level of the client system, an assessment of resources at all system levels broadens the area of potential solutions. When social workers guide clients to look beyond their immediate situations to explore contextual systems more thoroughly, they discover new information, resources, and opportunities. Discoveries enable social workers and clients to decipher the relationships among events and identify untapped, yet accessible, resources.

An empowering generalist assessment does more than simply list client and environmental resources. The inquiry of assessment, itself, creates change. As a result, social workers move cautiously to explore and respond productively. The choices clients and social workers make about what to explore begin to shape the possibilities for the solutions they will frame. The processes used in exploring set expectations for clients' involvement in change. Collaboration in this process activates clients to take charge of their own inquiry and builds momentum in their support networks to sustain the change effort.

This chapter discusses ways that clients and workers assess resources available to clients in their environments. Specifically, this chapter

- Explains social work assessment from a strengths-based generalist perspective
- Frames assessment from an ecosystemic perspective
- Scrutinizes assessment information using questions from an ecosystemic perspective
- Articulates the use of social work tools relevant to each level of social work practice
- Describes techniques for social workers to enhance assessment information through observation
- Defines procedures for workers to record information in an effective and ethical manner

An assessment of available resources leads practitioners and clients to distribute their change efforts wisely, selecting strategies that draw on client strengths and activate environmental resources

EXPLORING RESOURCE SYSTEMS THROUGH ASSESSMENT

Social workers and clients assess resource systems to discover gold, not causes or reasons. They work to clarify areas of competence in client:environment transactions. Assessment clarifies three facets of these transactions: (1) clients' unique capacities, capabilities, and potential; (2) environmental characteristics and resources; and (3) changes that need to be made to enhance transactions (Labassi & Maluccio, 1986). In the spirit of empowerment, assessment is a process for discovering resources. Like strengths, resources are relative, identifiable only in context. The actual ways clients interact with their social and physical environments determine what functions as resources for them. To complete an assessment, the partners explore broadly for resources that may be present in the environment, in the interactions of clients with others, and even in other challenges that clients are facing.

Recognizing Environmental Resources

Problem-based assessments encourage individualist rather than ecological accounts of clients.

—Dennis Saleebey

Social workers often locate resources in a client system's physical and social environments. For individuals, environmental resource systems may include family, friends, neighbors, co-workers, supervisors, classmates, teachers, social groups, school, church, social agencies, organizations, and the community. For a nonprofit organization, contextual resource systems may include consumers, funding bodies, foundations, professional organizations, local colleges, and other agencies in the service delivery network. For any human system, regardless of size, environmental resources are essential for survival and well-being.

Every part of our lives contributes to or hinders our ability to maneuver successfully through life. Consider your situation as an example. What in your environment facilitates your work? Likely you are reading this book as part of a social work class. Does the instructor frame this information in such a way that enhances your understanding? Do you have classmates with whom you will discuss this material to augment your comprehension? Do you have children for whom your spouse, partner, or friends provide child care so that you can study? Do you have a quiet place to read—the school library, your own room, or a picnic table in the park? The presence or absence of these supportive resources has a lot to do with your success in completing your studies.

Look further and you will also discover other systems that provide resources. How is it that you find yourself in this classroom? Is your family providing financial support? Are you receiving government loans or grants to pay expenses? Are you getting scholarships from community organizations, your church, or the college to defray your costs? Are you working to pay your own way, so that your place of employment is a resource to guarantee your education? Does your ethnic or cultural identity place a high value on educational achievement? The presence or absence of these environmental resources influences whether you have the opportunity for academic success and a career as a social worker. Resource systems—from personal support networks to institutional systems—contribute to even the simplest transaction. Recognizing resources requires awareness of environmental contexts, sensitivity to cultural differences, and openness to a broad range of possibilities.

Turning Challenging Situations into Resources

Certainly, not all aspects of ecosystems are resources per se. A comprehensive assessment frequently leads to a different kind of discovery—the discovery of other problems or challenges, but challenges can actually be resources rather than additional constraints. The key is how workers respond. Disempowering responses stack the newly found problems on the others already described. Visualize how this leads to stigmatizing clients with labels such as "multiproblem" or to ascribing blame for "who is causing what." Contrast this response with a more empowering perspective that suggests that recognizing common links among challenging events provides new insights about situations and expands options for change.

Notice in the example that follows how an ecological assessment uncovers additional challenges yet enlarges the arena of potential solutions. An African American woman, Latasha, consults with a social worker about her feelings of depression. Latasha shares her frustration and disappointment in not securing a job in law enforcement despite her obvious qualifications and credentials. Broadening the search for resources to local law enforcement agencies reveals a new challenge—a pattern of discriminatory hiring and promotion practices with respect to women and people of color. Discovering this additional challenge of institutional sexism and racism links Latasha's depression, her unemployment, and the discriminatory hiring practices. Latasha's options for change now expand beyond the personal realm to include political and legal strategies for confronting the discrimination. Latasha's exercise of political power is now an option—an avenue to restore her sense of personal control and relieve her depression.

Collaborating to Search for Resources

Social workers guide clients through an exploration of resource systems, but who or what guides social workers? Environmental contexts are enormous. A thorough examination of inside realms, outside environments, and the relationships between systems and their contexts literally goes on forever. After all, while you are examining any system, it remains dynamic, everchanging, and constantly evolving, even in response to the discovery process itself.

Take care, however, not to fall prey to the trap of certainty that classic diagnosis or categorical labels invite. Merely labeling behavior oversimplifies complex dynamics of human interactions and tends to limit options. Amundson, Stewart, and Valentine (1993) advocate a questioning and tentative attitude rather than a precise and expert posture to maintain an empowering frame during assessment. They say: "Our certainties about the world may also restrict and constrain us. . . . In trying to be helpful there is the temptation to enact our privilege, to impose upon others normalizing standards or to be blinded to diversity by the 'professional' certainties of our practice" (p. 111).

This advice leads social workers to offer their reflections in tentative and thought-provoking ways and encourage clients to do the same. Workers purposefully share their thoughts to stimulate new interpretations, develop usable theories, and suggest possible directions in ways that encourage mutual discourse. However, rather than stating the certainties, social workers offer hunches and possibilities with phrases such as:

▸ I wonder if . . .
▸ Is it fair to say that at this time . . .
▸ I have a hunch that I'd like your opinion about. Have you ever considered . . .
▸ I'm noticing that Hector's legal problems started at the same time your father died. From your point of view, does it look like . . .
▸ As I've listened to the Task Force's discussion, I believe that at this time you've identified three major areas to consider for action . . .
▸ There may be more, but I seem to hear two different ways of interpreting this situation.

Social workers' insights may, indeed, "unstick" client systems. However, for clients to remain in charge of meaning, social workers phrase their comments in ways that level authority and invite a client to support or disagree with their hypotheses. In recognizing a client's expertise, social workers do not abandon their theoretical knowledge and practice wisdom. Instead, reflective practitioners recognize that the authority of their knowledge has potential to disempower clients. As Hartman (1992) advises: "We need not discard our knowledge, but we must be open to local knowledge, to the narratives and the truths of our clients . . . to honor and validate our clients' expertise" (p. 484).

To define the scope of a comprehensive assessment, practitioners rely on clues from clients. Through dialogue, workers and clients maintain an informed perspective on what to assess and the ability to screen for what else they need to know. To assist clients in this exploratory process, workers implement assessment processes that include applying theoretical frameworks, using tools, adding new viewpoints, and conducting observations.

APPLYING THEORETICAL FRAMEWORKS

Social workers use frameworks drawn from theories about human system behavior and theories of change to organize the search for resources. Some assessment frameworks apply to human systems at all levels, whereas others are specific to particular situations. The ecosystems framework introduced in Chapter 2 is an example appropriate for generalist practice because it flexibly applies to any system level.

Organizing Assessment by Using a 5-Point Ecosystemic Schema

The ecosystems framework can organize the search for resources into a simple 5-point schema. Applying this strategy, practitioners begin by clearly identifying the focal system. From there, the framework guides workers and clients to explore what happens inside this system, what happens outside this system, how the inside and the outside of the system connect, and what happens as the system progresses through time. Applying this framework to any client system produces a dynamic explanation of its functioning in context and uncovers available resources (Figure 10.1).

Practice Example: Franklin Courts

Human Behavior

In the Franklin Courts case example, social worker Damon Edwards applies an ecosystemic view of human behavior to structure his assessment. What characteristics of this ecosystemic schema make it a good fit for an assessment from a social work perspective?

The following example demonstrates how applying the ecosystems framework organizes the activities of Damon Edwards and the residents of Franklin Courts to assess the situation in the housing complex.

The referral

The residents of Franklin Courts are angry. During a routine preschool screening, six children living at the low-income housing complex tested positive for lead contamination. The media reports that parents demand action! The Housing Authority says only that "they will look into it." Damon Edwards, a social worker in the outreach and advocacy services division of the Neighbors United Neighborhood Development Program, is also "looking into it." Fiona Grant, the grandmother of one of the six children, called Damon about the situation. Damon already knows Mrs. Grant from his work with the youth recreation program. She is a powerful and energetic resident of Franklin Courts. Damon is pleased that Mrs. Grant sees him as a resource. Damon doesn't know what he will find in his meeting with the residents that Mrs. Grant promises to gather. However, he has a way to look at the situation that will give him a sense of

Figure 10.1   Ecosystems Assessment Framework

An ecosystem assessment is a multi-faceted description of client system functioning in context. Social workers combine respectful listening with clarifications, summaries, selective questions, and validating feedback to access information framed by the questions below.

Identify the focal system

- Who are the system's members?
- What characteristics define their membership in the system?

Inside the System

Structural Dimensions: Closeness

- What are the subsystems?
- Who supports whom?
- Are members close to one another or isolated?

Structural Dimensions: Power

- What is the system's hierarchy?
- Who is in charge?
- Who makes decisions?
- Who enforces decisions?
- Do members function autonomously or interdependently?

Interactional Dimensions

- How do members communicate?
- Do members talk directly to one another or do they route messages through third parties?
- Do members offer constructive feedback to one another?
- What are the rules and norms for behavior?
- Does everyone share responsibility?

Biopsychosocial Dimensions

- Are members physically healthy?
- What are the special physical abilities and needs of members?
- How do issues of development and maturation affect the functioning of the system?
- How do members feel?
- Do members share their feelings openly?
- How do members think?
- Do members share their own thoughts and respect the contributions of others?
- What are the individual strengths of various members?

Cultural Dimensions

- What are the various cultural influences?
- What are the cultural strengths of members?
- Do common cultural identities bind members together?
- How do cultural differences influence the relationships within the system?
- What are the predominant beliefs and values of members?
- Are there cultural influences on communication?

Spiritual Dimensions

- What spiritual and/or religious traditions influence the system?
- How do system members define spiritual concepts?
- What meanings evolve from spirituality?
- What spiritual strengths are present?
- What resources are available through connections with religious or spiritual communities?

Outside the System

- What systems are influential in the environment of the focal system? Consider from among the following depending on the level of the system:
  - Family and extended family members
  - Friends, neighbors, natural support networks
  - Neighborhood, community
  - Organizations, groups

Outside the System

- Social agencies
- Social institutions
- Economic systems

Figure 10.1 *Continued*

- Government bodies
- Policies, laws, regulations
- How are these influential systems connected to one another?
- What are the influences of the physical environment?
- What potential resources exist that the system currently does not access?

Inside and Outside Connections

- Does the focal system's boundary tend to be open or closed?
- What information flows across this boundary?
- Does the system acquire necessary resources from the environment?
- What does the system contribute to the environment?
- Are some members more connected to the outside than others?
- Does the system have power in relationship to outside systems or is it overpowered by environmental demands?
- What outside systems provide stability?
- What outside influences tend to disrupt the system's functioning?
- What is the system's view of the larger environment? Does it see it as threatening or friendly?
- How is the system's cultural identity viewed in the larger environment?
- Is the system at risk of discrimination or oppression?

Movement through Time

- What is the expected development of the system?
- What physical, psychological, emotional, cognitive, moral, and systemic transitions are occurring at this time?
- How is the system handling these transitions?
- What nodal events characterize the system's development?
- How did the system respond to these nodal events?
- Does the system flexibly adapt to meet the needs of members?
- Does the system flexibly adapt to changing environmental demands?
- Were there times in the past when the system worked the way members would like?
- What development changes are expected in the near future?

---

what's going on and direction for ways he might contribute. Damon applies an ecosystems framework to ensure a generalist approach to assessment.

What's the focal system?

As always, Damon first identifies the focal system. In this situation, he knows that he will work with a group system. Mrs. Grant was acting on behalf of all the concerned residents. This, coupled with the urgency of the issue at hand, the common goal of the residents, and the fact that residents are already beginning to function in a collective manner, indicates that group action will be a likely strategy for success.

Identifying the group of residents as his client allows Damon to continue to frame his approach. He will need to look inside the group, at its membership, to discover its resources. He will also need to look outside the group to understand environmental opportunities and constraints. Damon doesn't yet know the kinds of linkages this particular group of residents has to resources in the community, but, certainly, exploring these connections will be important. Finally, Damon will examine the group's process and organizational structure. Theory informs him about effective group development. Damon's task will be as much to encourage the growth of the group itself as it will be to work toward the group's goals.

What's inside the system?

At the first meeting of the Franklin Courts group, Damon discovers that the crisis of the high lead levels in the children and the potential for further lead contamination has indeed activated the residents of Franklin Courts. Twenty-four

Box 10.1 Ethic of Contextual Practice

The empowerment paradigm underscores the importance of context by locating social work practice at the intersection of persons and their social, cultural, and physical environments. Social beliefs and values, social institutions, social structures, relationship networks, and features of the physical environment combine to create a person's experience. These elements prescribe a personal and social life that can be either oppressive or empowering (Kondrat, 2002; Moos, 2003; Mulroy, 2003; Polack, 2004; Saleebey, 2004).

"Social life is essentially spatial and contextual. Both oppressive and empowering relationships take place within, are constrained or supported by, and indeed may fundamentally reflect the particularities of the environments in which they are situated. The environments of daily life are themselves bearers of social messages and social scripts; they mark the bodies of those who occupy them in particular and differential ways. Social beliefs about people, their rights and responsibilities, and their place in the world, are translated into and expressed through spatial arrangements and structures. Relationships of power are thus made concrete and tangible in the material world" (Kemp, et al., 2002, p. 17).

Considering environmental contexts is pivotal in understanding the sources of client stress as well as in identifying resources for framing solutions. Contextual social work practice involves "practice both with and within context" (Fook, 2002, p. 143). This idea means that social work practice must emphasize

▶ The need to understand the *nature of contexts* in developing relevant practice strategies

▶ The idea of *positionality* being able to assume a reflexive stance, simultaneously outside and within contexts

▶ The need to develop an ability to work with *whole contexts,* rather than simply a number of disparate players within a contex

▶ The need to develop practice and practice theory/knowledge which is *transferable* across different contexts

▶ The need to *reframe our skills in contextual terms* (p. 143)

The ethic of contextualized social work practice encompasses the understanding that "physical and social environments are deeply implicated in patterns of social opportunity and constraint, and it is essential that social workers be able to read them in this way" (Kemp, et al., 2002, p. 20).

An empowerment practice approach depends on a "critical analysis of the relationships between people and their environmental contexts, transformation of perspectives and beliefs about one's social and physical circumstances, and the ability to act differently within one's wider environments, including in relation to oppressive social and environmental conditions" (Kemp, et al., p. 18). Ignoring context is unethical, because it fails to recognize the environmental influences that limit and undermine client choice. Social workers using an empowerment method acknowledge that their practice encompasses the whole context rather than just the individuals within it (Fook, 2002). The ethic of contextual social work practice prompts workers to widen their lens to identify and modify contexts that bind personal experience. Intervening focuses beyond individual adaptation to change social situations and political contexts.

adults attend the meeting; three other residents are babysitting so other parents can attend. Much is happening inside the group. Certain members have taken leadership roles. Mrs. Grant is obviously the spokesperson. She convenes the meeting and seems to be in charge of the agenda. When the group adjourns, Mrs. Grant along with three other influential group members volunteer to meet with Damon to plan and bring back recommendations to the group's next meeting. Also, smaller groups are beginning to form around specific issues of concern. The parents of the six children need to arrange immediate specialized assessment of their children's health. Several other residents want to press for an investigation into the source of the contamination and prevent further exposure. Damon quickly sees the possibility for task-oriented subcommittees to work concurrently in multiple directions rather than having the whole group continue its debate over what specific outcome to seek first.

What's outside the system?

Outside of the group, not too much is happening yet to address the concerns of the Franklin Courts residents. Despite the Housing Authority's promise to look into the lead contamination, the residents have heard nothing from them. The media have expressed interest but have not yet provided extensive reports. On a positive note, the doctor who discovered the problem is sympathetic and willing to support the group's action. And, of course, because the group called Damon, the resources of Neighbors United are accessible to them.

How does the inside connect to the outside?

Damon sees the group's relationship to the community as a resource to develop. Certainly, the group's connections with other systems need strengthening. For example, somewhere in the city's administration, the Housing Authority is accountable to a higher office; the Franklin Courts' group would benefit from a strong relationship with whomever this might be. Making this important link will increase the group's power in working with the Housing Authority. Damon also considers the doctor and the media as resources the group should continue to activate.

How does the system move through time?

Observing the group's developmental progress shows that it is maturing naturally in a productive way. The way the group itself organized child care during group meetings concretely demonstrates its positive development. Damon can build on the group's robust beginning. He will strive to clarify and cultivate the evolving structure and interaction of the group to maximize collaboration among members. Damon is beginning to understand the group's potential and direction.

Focusing on the residents' group as the client system, looking at its resources inside and out, assessing the group's transactions with its environment, and tracing the group's progress as it develops through time—all facets of an ecosystems assessment—contribute to Damon's broad view of what is happening with this particular group. The ecosystems framework offers a way to conceptualize the group throughout the entire process from assessing the situation to implementing strategies for change.

ORGANIZING ASSESSMENT: APPLYING ECOSYSTEMIC QUESTIONS

Questions arising from an ecosystemic perspective elucidate client system functioning in context, including information about the structural elements, interactions, psychosocial dimensions, cultural influences, and physical environments of the client system. The following sections list these questions and relate them to an ecosystems perspective.

Assessing Structures

Recall that the structural perspective on human systems examines the configuration of the ecosystem—the arrangement of interactions between the client system and its physical and social environments. The two most important structural elements are power and closeness or, in systemic terminology, hierarchies and boundaries. Assessing the hierarchies and boundaries of the client's ecosystem leads social workers and clients to understand which components may constrain the client and which hold resources for change.

Who has the power?

By definition, the success of an empowering social work process depends on clients gaining a sense of power and control. Identifying where the power currently lies is essential to this effort. Even when clients temporarily feel powerless, those persons or systems that contribute to powerlessness are potential sources of power. In other words, if you know where the power is, you know where client systems can get it. An assessment of the ecosystem identifies sources of power.

Consider the following example. A homeless family temporarily stays with a distant relative while waiting for an opening in a rent-subsidized housing complex. But policies at the city's housing authority require that families living in public shelters receive priority in renting available units. Although this policy has merit, it holds this homeless family hostage, leaving them only the alternative of moving from their temporary living arrangement into an overcrowded and understaffed shelter to become eligible for placement. Clearly, the housing authority and its policies have the power. Assessing this power distribution helps the worker and the family generate new strategies, which range from advocacy with the department to political strategies to initiate policy changes at the state level.

Another place to look for power is in the client system itself. Sometimes, clients do exercise power and competence in certain areas of functioning, but feel inadequate in others. For example, the neighborhood group that can organize a neighborhood watch program likely has many of the resource capabilities necessary to lobby a school board to institute cultural sensitivity training for teachers to meet the challenge of discriminatory educational practices and harsh discipline of ethnic minority students. When the answer to "where is the power?" is "with the client," the emphasis shifts from using the identified power in one area to meet the challenge in another. Workers and clients contemplate the following questions to discover power resources:

- Who or what has power?
- How does the client access it?
- Who or what can help the client gain power?
- What might get in the way?
- What power resources does the client already possess?
- What will the client do with the power?

What connections are working?

Alliances within and between systems are important sources of support and assistance. Assessing who is close to whom, what resources clients use successfully, and what supports are already available to clients defines areas of the client's functioning to maintain, strengthen, and develop. For example, the existence of a supportive extended family is a resource for an individual client seeking a job. Extended family members may be willing to increase their support and provide child care, financial assistance for specialized training, transportation to fill out job applications, or encouragement during the stressful time of applying, interviewing, and waiting for a job offer. Existing connections are likely to be resources that social workers and clients can expand.

Assessing existing connections may also reveal that the client's boundaries are currently too open to other forces but, if redefined, have potential to become resources. For example, consider Craig, a divorced father who has custody of his three children. Acknowledging the importance to his children of a strong relationship with their mother, Karen, Craig agrees to an open visitation policy whereby Karen can visit the children in his home whenever she chooses. When Craig and his social worker review the assessment information, they find that Craig has trouble establishing rules and enforcing discipline with the children, and Karen's unpredictable visits complicate this difficulty. Assessing this information identifies the need to renegotiate this boundary—to close it up somewhat—to maintain the relationship with the children's mother as a resource, yet fit her visits into an effective routine for the household.

A boundary assessment identifies how connections are working for the client. The answers to questions about boundaries supply information about the client's alliances with people and resources. Questions to consider include:

- What significant connections does the client have?
- Are these relationships functioning effectively?
- Could these connections serve as resources to address the client's current situation?
- What connections might need to be changed for them to function as resources?
- What might prevent the client from renegotiating these connections?

What connections are missing?

When assessing how clients connect with others, the connections they lack also become evident. Just as open boundaries allow access to resources, closed boundaries block clients from obtaining resources. A lack of connections to interpersonal and community resources forces clients to meet all their needs on their own, a situation that is likely to deplete their energies rather than sustain their sense of power. Factors preventing a client from connecting to resources include insufficient information, inaccessible resources, financial constraints, ineligibility, transportation needs, suspicion, and fear.

Consider the example of Marian, a woman who feels powerless to have friends, spend time alone away from home, or buy anything for herself without permission. Marian feels trapped by the rigid control and physical power exerted by her husband, Doug. However, a comprehensive exploration of her ecosystem also reveals that Marian is unaware of the Domestic Violence Center, believes that she is not eligible for the woman's support group at her church, and no longer maintains contact with her own family of origin because they don't like Doug. All these components of Marian's ecosystem—her husband Doug, the domestic violence program, the church group, and her own family of origin—have potential to be resources of power.

Think about the options created by identifying the missing connections. The worker recognizes that Doug is pivotal in this issue. He is disconnected from the social work endeavor and possibly from understanding Marian's situation. Obviously, if Doug changes his behavior toward Marian in ways that respect her freedom, she will gain a sense of power. The worker can connect Doug to Marian by inviting him to participate in the social work process. Even if the dynamics of this marriage are such that Doug chooses not to change or refuses to join the effort, the outside sources of support including the domestic violence program, the church, and her family may function to give Marian resources for survival should she decide to confront or leave Doug. Assessing Marian's world locates disconnections from these sources of power and identifies options for initiating empowering connections.

Questions that uncover missing connections include:

▶ Who is significant to the client system but uninvolved who might be invited to join the effort?
▶ What potential resources are present that the client might consider in new ways?
▶ What resources does the worker know about that the client doesn't?
▶ What is blocking the client from connecting to resources which might help?

Assessing Interactions

An assessment of interactions examines how people and their environments relate and evolve. Remember that human systems behave in ways that seek harmony and balance. What happens in a client system somehow is adaptive in its context. The interactional perspective leads us to contemplate just how things make sense.

Is this the way things should be?

Many times changes that seem unnatural are actually naturally occurring events and transitions in human system development. Examples of life-stage changes are Erikson's (1963) stages of psychosocial development, Carter and McGoldrick's (1989) family life cycle, Papernow's (1993) stages of stepfamily development, and the natural evolution of groups reported by many authors (Johnson & Johnson, 2006; Schriver, 2004). Knowledge that these changes are expected and desirable is a resource that social workers have available to share with clients.

Consider the example of the social worker hired to consult with a delinquency prevention agency. The agency recently received funds to develop a case management system to coordinate services for first-time offenders and attempt to divert them from prosecution by the juvenile justice system. Assessment reveals that for 2 months, the four-member team worked cooperatively, but, just when they seemed to be getting comfortable with each other, their meetings began to erupt with conflict. The social worker assesses the conflict and recognizes the disequilibrium that naturally evolves in a group as it forms. By helping the team learn conflict-resolution skills to continue its natural development, the worker assists team members to translate their differences into creative resources for developing the new program. To recognize natural transitions, workers and clients consider questions such as:

▶ What physical, cognitive, and psychological transitions are occurring in members of the client system?
▶ Do family life cycle transitions apply? Group development transitions? Organizational development transitions?

Assessment provides opportunities for clients to tell their stories.

▶ Is the event or behavior expected based on the client system's stage of development?

▶ What changes need to occur to facilitate a smooth transition?

What have we got to lose?

The question, "What have we got to lose?," considers the consequences of change. Recall the ecosystems view of dysfunction: even apparently problematic behavior may be working adaptively somewhere else in the client's ecosystem. As an example, consider the boy whose academic failure at school activates his parents to sit with him in the evening to help with homework, to visit his teacher to confer about his learning difficulties, and to advocate with the school board to hire a reading specialist for the district. Clearly, the boy's behavior is a resource in connecting him to his parents and connecting his parents to the school system.

What would happen if the boy's behavior suddenly improved? These resources might be lost, leaving him isolated and unnoticed. Consider what life will be like if the problem is resolved (Cowger, 1992). Also explore the negative consequences of change (Papp, 1983). She says the worker "should obtain a slow-motion picture leading up to, during, and after the occurrence of the problem" (p. 20). In this way, workers can assess the potential effects problems have in the system. This information provides insight into how the system is balanced and what changes might occur as solutions develop. To consider how difficulties affect a client's situation, workers contemplate:

▶ How is the system responding to the situation?

▶ Is there anything good that happens as a result?

▶ What solutions has the client attempted?

▶ What else will change when the client overcomes the difficulty?

Assessing Thinking and Feeling

Human beings think and feel. We respond not only to the structure and functioning of the social systems in which we participate, but also to the ways we interpret what happens in these various contexts. An assessment of thinking and feeling results in a clearer understanding of the cognitive and affective factors that influence human behavior.

What do you think?

Assessing how the client system functions in its ecosystemic context offers new ways to think about events. Typically, clients bring a particular theory about what is going on to the social work relationship. An assessment of thinking processes sheds new light on these previously fixed notions and theories. When social workers and clients reframe and reconceptualize, they generate many new ways to explain situations. Generating alternative ideas and hypotheses leads to multiple options for change. Questions that disclose aspects of thinking include:

▶ What explanations does the client system offer? Do all members of the client system hold the same view?

▶ Does the client hold notions that, if reframed, would incorporate new possibilities?

▶ How might changes in thinking lead to changes in behavior?

How does it feel?

Assessing feelings supplies intuitive hunches about whether social workers and clients are on the right track. Feelings are prominent, as "people have feelings about themselves and their plight, about making decisions, and taking definitive action. People have feelings about having feelings, and all of these are inextricably bound to definition and resolution of the problems they are facing" (Middleman & Wood, 1990, p. 59). Feelings can be a source of energy for change; unattended, they can be obstacles. Accessing affective responses taps into clients' motivations, comfort, and spontaneity. Questions that uncover dimensions of feelings include:

- What clues do verbal and nonverbal messages offer about the feelings the client is experiencing?
- In the case of multiperson client systems, are the emotions members express similar or different from one another?
- In what ways are feelings affecting thinking?
- How does the synergy of emotions amplify or diminish the energy available to invest in solutions?

Assessing Cultural Influences

The cultural identities of any particular system influence the way it interacts with other systems. The cultural influences internalized by various system members contribute to diversity within a given social system. A complete assessment of an ecosystem requires an exploration of cultural elements.

What about the big picture?

One aspect to consider in assessing cultural influences is to examine critically how clients fit into the larger picture. Because not all racial, ethnic, gender, or other cultural groups currently receive equal access to the resources of society, the relationship of the culture of the client system to the macrosystem deserves special consideration. Social workers overlook powerful influences when they fail to recognize oppression and discrimination. Helping clients adapt to an environment marked by prejudice and injustice disempowers. Instead, ethical practitioners craft macrosystem interventions to redress injustice. Assessing cultural influences raises the critical consciousness of social workers and clients to the impact of discrimination and oppression and serves as a catalyst for social action and social change. To understand the sociopolitical influences on client systems, workers and clients consider questions such as:

- In what ways do prejudicial attitudes such as racism, sexism, ageism, classism, ableism, heterosexism, and regionalism affect the client's circumstances?
- What roles do discriminatory practices, procedures, and policies play in the client system's situation?
- How has oppression directly and indirectly blocked the client's access to the power?
- What strengths can the worker and client discover in the ways the client adapts to experiences of discrimination and oppression?

How does the system fit together?

Culture also affects the internal functioning of each client system. One qualitative study voiced the views of immigrant clients and their social workers in emphasizing the importance of the workers' abilities to see cultural identity as multifaceted. Workers respond to clients' overlapping roles in ways that acknowledge the uniqueness of individuals rather than their salient cultural membership (Russell & White, 2001, p. 87). Simply applied, even members of the same immigrant family are culturally distinct, possibly leading to the assessment of family conflict as a cross-cultural issue. The stress ethnic group members experience as the result of living in two cultures is sociocultural dissonance (Chau, 1989). A similar dynamic occurs in the blending of stepfamilies with conflicting lifestyles (Visher & Visher, 1996). And, certainly, cultural differences are likely to exist among members of larger group, organizational, and community systems. Cultural information is a resource to clients and workers in externalizing the issues rather than personalizing the conflicts. To understand the role of culture, workers consider answers to questions such as:

- What different cultural perspectives are operating?
- Do these cultural perspectives agree or conflict with one another?
- Are factors such as the reasons for and experiences of immigration involved?
- In what ways are intergenerational perspectives a factor?
- To what extent does the experience of living in two cultures result in sociocultural dissonance?

Assessing Spiritual Dimensions

Although historically included as an important dimension of assessment, practitioners have often considered spirituality superfluous to the secular domain of practice. However, when we consider spiritual dimensions, we discover that "many clients' innermost thoughts and feelings are rooted in spiritual beliefs which, rather than being a separate issue, serve as the foundation for the seemingly mundane activities of everyday life" (Gotterer, 2001, p. 187). With respect to social work in health care, the accrediting body for health care, the Joint Commission on Accreditation of Healthcare Organizations, requires spiritual assessment as a standard of care (Hodge, 2006).

According to Canda and Furman (1999), "spirituality relates to a universal and fundamental aspect of what it is to be human—to search for a sense of meaning, purpose, and moral frameworks for relating with self, others, and the ultimate reality" (p. 37). Spirituality may be experienced as either a part of or separate from organized religion. Although some people may identify particular spiritual concerns, spirituality

> involves streams of experience that flow through all aspects of our lives . . . Spiritual beliefs influence ways of coping with adversity, the experience of pain and suffering, what is labeled as a problem and the meaning of symptoms. They also influence how people communicate about their pain; their beliefs about its cause and future course; their attitudes toward helpers—clergy, physicians, therapists, faith healers; the treatment they seek and their preferred approaches to acceptance or change. (Walsh, 1999b, p. 3)

Research indicates that spirituality is a vital force for dealing with issues related to chronic illness, disability, and death (Canda, 2001, 2002; Reese, 2001), aging processes (David, 2001), substance abuse (Friedman, 2000), adversity and trauma (Farley, 2007; Williams, 2004), and empowerment (Leight, 2001).

To identify dimensions of spirituality, Hodge (2001a) recommends an anthropological approach to assessment—basic questions to initiate conversations about spirituality and interpretive questions to understand in more depth the ways in which spirituality influences emotion, behavior, beliefs, a sense of communion with the Ultimate (for some, God); sense of right, wrong, guilt, and forgiveness; and insight or intuition. Questions in the initial framework include:

▶ Describe the religious/spiritual tradition you grew up in. How did your family express its spiritual beliefs? How important was spirituality to your family? Extended family?

▶ What sort of personal experiences (practices) stand out to you during your years at home? What made these experiences special? How have they informed your later life?

▶ How have you changed or matured from those experiences? How would you describe your current spiritual or religious orientation? Is your spirituality a personal strength? If so, how? (p. 208)

Assessing Physical Environments

Research Based Practice

Workers apply social work research through all phases of practice. In what ways might the use of evidence generated through research influence assessment processes?

The final piece to consider in assessing human systems is the influence of physical environments on client functioning. Workers may not have opportunities to view personally their clients' homes, places of work, or neighborhoods and, furthermore, may neglect to inquire about what these settings are like. "Yet not knowing how or if clients are able to meet such needs as privacy and personal space leaves workers poorly equipped to evaluate the full meaning of clients' behavior" (Gutheil, 1992, p. 391). Deficiencies, obstructions, lack of privacy, and other environmental factors can all contribute to the stress clients experience. The physical environment plays an important role in group dynamics, too. Arrangement of physical space, lighting, and ventilation all make a difference in how group members interact. Physical environments can augment or restrict client functioning and, therefore, are important factors to assess.

Have you looked around this place?

Consider the situation of Deanna, a client with retardation, who seeks assistance to balance her budget. Deanna's caseworker carefully evaluates Deanna's competencies in budgeting and is pleased to see that Deanna has appropriate math skills, demonstrates a good awareness of frugality, and organizes her bills effectively. But when the worker visits Deanna at home, the major issues are much clearer. The old apartment building in which Deanna lives clearly needs maintenance. The windows are not sealed properly, the thermostat is broken, and nearly every faucet leaks. The assessment of Deanna's physical environment leads the social worker to the resources of the city building inspector, the apartment owner, and the utility company in helping Deanna with her budgeting problems.

In assessing physical environments, workers and clients can discover resources and constraints. To weigh the effects of the client system's physical environment, workers ask questions such as:

▶ In what ways does the client system's physical environment enhance or curtail its ability to function?

▶ How does the client system respond to the stress that results from factors in the physical environment?

▶ What modifications to the physical environment would be helpful to the client system? Which are most realistic to pursue?

▶ Who has the decision-making authority to ensure that these modifications will be made?

Putting the Pieces Together

Answers to these assessment questions construct a contextually based vision of a client system's situation. Considering these various dimensions offers a comprehensive view of human system functioning—structure, interaction, psychosocial elements, and cultural influences in the context of the social and physical environments.

Box 10.2 Assessment: A Research–Practice Connection

Creating a plan for action, based on a comprehensive assessment, is a collaborative project connecting clients' desires and ideas with social workers' professional knowledge and expertise. As part of their responsibility in assessment and planning processes, competent practitioners consider what the social work research says about what might be going on and what might help. Imagine you are working with an African American adolescent who is identifying himself as gay. He is dealing with a homophobic school environment and contemplating coming out to his family. What does social work research tell you to consider, to avoid, to suggest, and to do?

Based on their review of the literature, Morrison and L'Heureux (2001) advise practitioners to assess the adolescent for risk of suicide and self-injurious behaviors. They note higher suicide risks in youths who come out at an early age, have a history of sexual or physical abuse, exhibit nonconformity to traditional gender stereotypes, and report emotional and psychological conflict about their sexual orientation. In addition, Morrison and L'Heureux recommend examining the client's microsystem to assess both risk and protective factors. They note the increased risks associated with "homophobic and heterosexist attitudes in teachers, peers, religious leaders, and family members" (p. 43). They also identify a decrease in self-destructive behaviors when gay, lesbian, transgender, and transsexual (GLBT) adolescents are connected to affirming environments including community services providing support to the GLBT community.

Research conducted by Merighi and Grimes (2000) found that the coming-out process for an African American youth may have key similarities to development of a gay identity in other ethnic groups. In their work to compare the coming out process for African, European, Mexican, and Vietnamese American gay males, ages 18–24, the researchers discovered that all participants "described the importance of preserving and upholding strong family relationship as a salient factor in their decision to come out" (p. 39). In this case social work research leads social workers to generalize the coming-out experience across cultural differences, emphasizing family response as a core assessment area for working with gay adolescents from any cultural and ethnic background.

Understanding expected milestones for gay identity development is another useful planning framework, one that offers support in normalizing some of the client's feelings. Flowers and Buston (2001) offer such a model based on their examination of 20 retrospective accounts of gay identity formation during adolescence. This qualitative study suggests that adolescent gay development can be understood by examining salient themes as these adolescents progress through phases Flowers and Buston label "defined by difference, self-reflection and inner conflict, alienation and isolation, living a lie, telling others, and wholeness and integrity" (p. 51). As a social worker informed by research, you can identify your client as thinking about moving to the phase of "telling others" and help prepare him for possible fallout, as this same study notes that "a new series of difficulties may emerge" including the possibility that "parents may reject or abuse their children" after such disclosure (p. 61).

Social workers wishing to empower clients are careful in their use of social work research to understand their clients. Applying research to assessment and planning neither replaces careful listening to clients as they describe their thoughts and feelings, nor supplants the need for comprehensive assessments of clients' unique situations. Clients' unique understandings of their own situations deserve the same consideration as information from research. Research simply provides clues for workers and clients that can guide assessment and planning activities and provide insight into possible intervention outcomes.

USING ASSESSMENT TOOLS

Assessment tools are also useful in structuring the search for resources. Specifically tailored to the purposes and characteristics of client systems, they include such diverse instruments as written questionnaires, standardized psychological tests, visual diagrams, behavioral checklists, role plays, games, toys, dolls, and community resource assessment instruments.

Assessment tools help to describe situations and identify strengths, stimulate discussion, and facilitate sharing of diverse viewpoints in multiperson systems. By using assessment instruments, workers can screen for issues requiring immediate attention, establish baseline information against which to measure subsequent change, and meet agency record-keeping requirements.

Because assessment tools mediate conversations between clients and social workers, they are particularly useful for clients who experience difficulty expressing their thoughts and feelings directly. For example, children who have been sexually abused frequently find it easier to express their experiences by drawing pictures, playing with dolls, or telling stories rather than candidly speaking about their personal experiences with sexual abuse. Shy adolescents may readily complete written forms describing their family relationships rather than struggle to articulate their thoughts and feelings directly. Studies suggest that computerized assessments prompt clients to disclose more candid information (Ferriter, 1993). Assessment tools provide an intermediate step—a way to be close in a mode that allows a safe distance.

Assessment tools may be essential with larger systems to ensure that all those involved have a voice. Formalized procedures such as surveys, polls, and forums can access a broad base of information for assessment. The following section describes assessment tools that may fit a client's situation, including social histories, genograms, eco-maps, culturally sensitive assessment, social network maps, and group, organizational, and neighborhood, and community assessment frameworks.

Social Histories

The client's fiction or story, like our own, reveals with purpose or intention a particular world view.

—Howard Goldstein

A social history organizes information about the history and current social functioning of individuals and families. Additionally, this standardized report describes the congruence between a client's needs and the formal and informal resources currently available (Sheafor & Horejsi, 2008). The exact format varies with the requirements of the practice setting. Some agencies use outlines to structure detailed narrative reports (Figure 10.2). Others use fill-in-the-blank forms that require brief comments in each of several categories. In general, social histories organize demographic data as well as information about personal history and life events. Social histories include information about: (1) the client system; (2) the client's concerns, needs, and associated problems; and (3) strengths and limitations of the client in context (Johnson & Yanca, 2007). As an alternative to traditional social history models, Kivnick and Murray (2001) detail a life strengths interview model for assessing older adults. Questions expand to focus on assets such as strengths and abilities, values and interests, cultural beliefs and practices, contributions, and protections and supports. Extending assessment to include assets shifts attention to a pool of valuable resources that can be drawn on to minimize deficits and expand the base of strengths.

To complete a social history, workers may choose to structure interviews to match the social history format. Other times, they facilitate conversations with clients that permit the information to flow naturally. Here, the social history

Figure 10.2 Social History Outline, Individual Client

Client:

Worker:

Date of Report:

1. Identifying information: (preferred name, address, phone, date of birth)
2. Referral information: (source of referral; reason for contact, including challenges faced and previous attempts to resolve; other professional or indigenous helpers currently involved)
3. Individual functioning: (developmental status; current physical, cognitive, emotional, psychological, and interpersonal capabilities; areas of need)
4. Cultural functioning: (race/ethnicity; primary language and languages spoken; significance of cultural identity, cultural strengths, experience of discrimination or oppression)
5. Family information (names, ages, involvement with client, including spouse/partner, parents, siblings, children, and extended family members)
6. Family interaction: (extent of support, family perspective on client, client perspective on family, and relevant family issues)
7. Natural support network: (significant relationships—names and nature of involvement)
8. Physical environment: (housing situation, financial stability, transportation resources, neighborhood)
9. Nodal events: (situation and client's response to deaths of significant others, serious losses or traumas, significant life achievements, other events)
10. Education: (dates, places, and years of education completed; accomplishments, degrees, and credentials)
11. Employment: (current job, type of work, lengths of employment, previous experience, skills, and special training)
12. Medical history: (birth information, illnesses/accidents/surgery, medications used, family medical and genetic issues, physical limitations, diet, alcohol and drug use)
13. Religion: (denomination, church membership, extent of involvement, spiritual perspective, special observances)
14. Social activities: (interests, clubs/organizations, preferred recreation, travels)
15. Future plans: (client's perspective on current situation, goals, personal and environmental resources to meet goals, constraints to goal attainment)

outline serves as a checklist to ensure that all necessary information has been included. Either way, workers inform clients that they are completing a social history and detail how the information will be used.

Social histories, as completed written products, are invaluable resources. For example, in a nursing home, various members of the staff including the social worker, activity director, dietician, physician, or family liaison may use the social history as a reference in planning or coordinating services with the resident. Clearly, this indicates the need for accuracy and clarity in the finished product. Sheafor and Horejsi (2008) say that good social history reports are brief, simple, useful, organized, confidential, and objective. In addition, they should be relevant and should focus on client strengths.

Genograms

Genograms visually represent family chronology (Hartman, 1978, reprinted in 1995; McGoldrick & Gerson, 1985, 1989). As schematic diagrams, genograms provide summaries of information about family history, marriages, deaths, geographic locations of family members, structure, and demographics (Figure 10.3). Completed genograms look somewhat like family trees, especially when they

Figure 10.3
Genogram of Fiona Grant's Family
A genogram illustrates family structure and relationships. Genograms list family members in at least two generations, including their names, ages, and dates of marriages and divorces. Workers and clients can also annotate genograms with other information to meet their specific purposes.

include information about several generations. Workers and clients annotate genograms to communicate information about "the sources of nurturance, stimulation, and support that must be available in the intimate and extended environment to make possible growth and survival" (Hartman, p. 113).

By highlighting familial information, genograms aid our understanding of relationship patterns, transitional issues, and life cycle changes. To gather information for genograms, workers ask clients to share family stories and traditions. Adding chronological information about nodal family events furnishes additional information about family transitions and identifies points where families have coped with change over the course of time. To incorporate a multicultural perspective, one can add dimensions of diversity to genograms by including "stories of generation, gender, ethnicity, race, class, and migration" (McGill, 1992, p. 344). Genograms are also useful to identify multiple cultural influences, trace intercultural blending through the generations, and emphasize the unique cultural history of any family (Congress, 1994; McCullough, et al., 2004). Additional modifications incorporate a solution focus (Zide & Gray, 2000), dimensions of spirituality (Frame, 2001; Hodge, 2001b;), and a socially constructed view of family (Mercier & Harold, 2003; Milewski-Hertlein, 2001).

Numerous areas of practice consider genograms essential for assessment. Constructing genograms with older adults affords them opportunities for life review. Practitioners working in medical settings use genograms to trace patterns of health and wellness. And, genograms adapt to many aspects of child welfare as they can be used to trace adoption histories or record foster care placements or short term, in-home family-preservation services (Walton & Smith, 2001). Genograms offer clues about intergenerational relationships and propose sources for family support, especially in relation to end-of-life care (Waldrop, 2006). Consistent with the strengths perspective, genograms can also reveal the patterns of family strengths over time and highlight exceptions to family legacies considered problematic (Kuehl, 1995).

Eco-Maps

Eco-maps graphically picture the ecological context of the client system (Hartman, 1978, reprinted in 1995; Hartman & Laird, 1983). Eco-maps focus specifically on the major systems with which clients are involved to depict their relationships with these systems visually. In other words, eco-maps portray transactions between the client and other systems: the exchange of resources, the nature of system relationships, the permeability of boundaries, and connections to the social service delivery system and other contextual supports (Hartman & Laird, 1983). To construct an eco-map, Hartman recommends placing the client's household in the middle of the eco-map and adding systems with which the client interacts to the parameters of the map. Lines connecting the systems portray the nature of the relationship and the direction in which energy flows (Figure 10.4). In this way, eco-maps provide information about available resources, existing constraints, and potential new connections.

The eco-map is a tool that encourages collaboration in the worker–client relationship (Hartman & Laird, 1983). Using eco-maps also instigates interaction among family members. "The process of mapping invites lively, active discussion. After all, it is the family's map, and no one knows their world quite the way they do" (p. 185). Furthermore, visual representations accentuate information, offering clients new perspectives. For example, "an eco-map full of stressful relationships showing all of the arrows pointing away from the family may lead a client to say, 'No wonder I feel drained—everything is going out and nothing is coming in!'" (p. 185). Comparing the eco-maps of family members can offer insight into the differing experiences and perceptions of the various family members (Harold, et al., 1997).

Because eco-maps frequently identify changes to make and resources to develop, workers and clients can use them to set goals and construct plans of action. Eco-maps can graphically illustrate change by contrasting a client's initial and concluding eco-maps. Workers also note how eco-maps externalize problems and diminish a client's sense of blame. Eco-maps demonstrate that social workers want to understand clients' unique circumstances and resources rather than search for their inner faults (Hartman & Laird, 1983). A generalist application of the eco-map places a group, organizational, or community client system at the center and maps its transactions with related systems (Mattaini, 1993).

Culturally Sensitive Assessment

For individual and family assessment that is sensitive to cultural differences, social workers augment traditional models of assessment that are more individualistically focused with collectively focused models that begin by exploring the influences and resources in the macroenvironment. One such model is the "Person-In-Family-In-Community Model" (Fong, 1997). Applying this model, social workers assess clients in the context of their families and social systems.

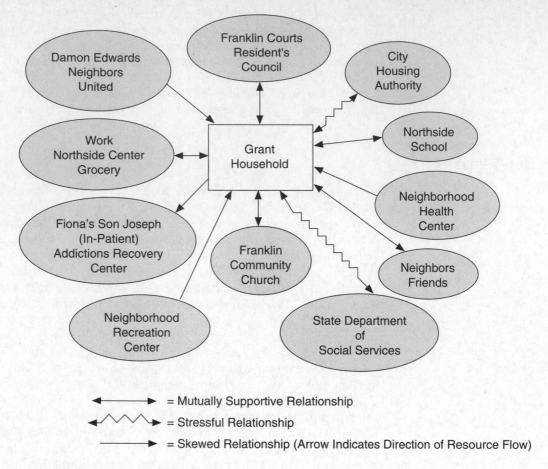

= Mutually Supportive Relationship

= Stressful Relationship

= Skewed Relationship (Arrow Indicates Direction of Resource Flow)

Figure 10.4
Eco-map of Fiona Grant's Household
An eco-map illustrates a human system in context. It identifies significant environmental systems and describes the nature of the relationships. Constructing an eco-map helps clients to clarify environmental resources and constraints.

To apply this model, social workers assess cultural influences in six areas. They

1. Identify the family's place of origin and the continued influence of their societal background

2. Explore the family's affiliations with their ethnic community and their attitudes toward social services

3. Determine in which community and family organizations, including ethnic social organizations, the family holds memberships

4. Detail the family's formal and informal roles, expectations for family members' behaviors, decision-making and power structures, and change agents

5. Analyze the subgroup structures in the extended family and their influence on family dynamics and family members

6. Examine how individual family members are influenced by family roles, obligations, and responsibilities (Fong, 1997)

Social Network Maps

Social network mapping is a tool for assessing social support that pictures a client's social support networks and quantifies the nature of support from the client's point of view (Tracy & Whittaker, 1990). To implement this technique, clients first identify members in their support network, including immediate family or household members, extended family, friends, and neighbors, as well as more formal organizations such as work, school, clubs, church, and other services. Then, by using a sorting technique and responding to specific questions, clients describe how they perceive the support they receive from others. Social network mapping assesses:

- Who provides social support
- Kind of support available
- Gaps in relationship resources
- Opportunities for reciprocal exchanges
- Presence of negativism and stress that produces criticism
- Barriers to using available resources
- Priority of social support in relation to other challenges

Group Assessment

The defining element of any group is its purpose. Group assessment, therefore, focuses on the "fit" between a group's functioning and its purpose. The purposes of client groups vary from those focused on support or therapeutic treatment to those organized for skill development, task completion, or social change. Areas of group functioning to explore include group culture, cohesion, norms, communication, leadership, decision making, controversy, and conflict.

Framework for group assessment

Effective groups share common qualities, such as productive communication, good listening skills, appreciation of member diversity, distributed leadership, participatory decision-making procedures, and skills for managing controversy. Similar to other human systems, a group's interaction must be assessed in its context to create a comprehensive view, including the group's goals and resources, interaction patterns, and relationships with various environmental systems.

Group Goals and Resources

- Identify the purposes of the group
- Determine members' motivation to meet the group's purposes
- Inventory group members' resources to achieve purposes
- Explicate the values, beliefs, and cultural affiliations of group members
- Characterize group consciousness about relevant issues

Group Interaction

- Measure group cohesion and communication effectiveness
- Assess members' respect for differences in perspectives and opinions
- Identify prevailing group norms
- Describe the group's decision-making processes
- Assess the distribution of power and leadership within the group
- Consider the group's ability to manage conflict and controversy

Group–Environment Relations

▶ Describe the matrix of environmental systems that influences the group and individual members
▶ Determine the accessibility of environmental resources
▶ Analyze the impact of race, class, gender, and other cultural identities on group interaction

Organizational Assessment

An organization is a formal group that joins together to make use of collective resources and skills to achieve a common purpose or goal. Social workers implementing organization assessments may consider an organization as a client, as a context for social service delivery, or as a target for change.

Framework for organizational assessment

Like any social system, organizations may be assessed by considering their internal characteristics and the demands and resources of their environments.

Organizational Goals and Structures

▶ Identify the mission, purpose, goals, and the history of the organization
▶ Describe the organizational governance and decision-making structures
▶ Define the perspectives or principles that guide leadership and managerial staff
▶ Characterize the organizational culture and membership and/or constituencies

Organization–Environment Relations

▶ Detail the economic, political, demographic, fiscal, cultural, legal/governmental, and technological environments of the organization
▶ Characterize the fit between organizational purpose with tasks and the needs and resources of the environment
▶ Describe the opportunities and threats posed in the environment
▶ Identify relevant policy issues that have an impact on organizational functioning

Organizational Competence

▶ Describe how the organization evaluates its achievement of its purpose and goals, and how the organization uses that feedback to enhance effectiveness
▶ Assess the organizational capacity for innovation or change
▶ Identify mechanisms for strategic planning and continuous quality improvement
▶ Characterize the organizational strengths and weaknesses

Force field analysis

Force field analysis, a creative problem-solving technique developed by Lewin (1951), applies to organizational assessment, community development, and strategic planning. This strategy is based on the theory that forces within a system either drive toward or restrain change. Either removing restraints or enhancing those forces currently driving toward solutions fuels change (Bargal, 2000; Pippard & Bjorkland, 2004; Wagner, et al., 2001). Force field analysis is useful for understanding forces that promote or block change and then creating

Figure 10.5
Force Field Analysis
Social workers apply force field analysis to evaluate the counter-
vailing factors that support or oppose change, including such forces
as stakeholders, funding, policies, and other contingencies.

strategies to strengthen forces that promote change and reduce those forces that create barriers Analysis of the forces identified provides insight into weighing the pros and cons of potential actions (Figure 10.5). Steps for implementing a force field analysis include

1. Frame target for change
2. Delineate the forces that support the change
3. Delineate the forces that oppose the change
4. Assign weights to each force identified based on their relative influence
5. Develop a plan of action, including goals, objectives, and strategies to enhance or diminish forces
6. Implement the plan
7. Assess progress toward achieving objectives and viability of strategies
8. Evaluate outcomes

Neighborhood and Community Assessment

Needs assessment differs from asset mapping. Social workers and planners conduct needs assessments to document problems, identify unmet needs, and establish priorities for service and resource development. Asset mapping in a community or neighborhood, on the other hand, involves assessing capacities, resources, and assets. This includes taking an inventory of the individual, associational, and institutional capacities (Kretzmann & McKnight, 1993). In contrast to the traditional community "needs" assessment, a community asset inventory focuses more on what a community has than on what is missing. This shift in emphasis from community problem solving to community capacity building positions localities for implementing asset-based community development strategies.

A comprehensive neighborhood or community assessment includes information gathered through a variety of methods (Kettner, et al., 1985). Community surveys include questionnaires administered face-to-face or mailed to a representative sample of the community population to solicit opinions and collect data about community life. Key informant studies involve structured interviews, surveys, or focus groups with individuals identified as having expertise on the subject under study. Community forums are open scheduled meetings held to solicit the views of a broad representation of community members. Telephone poll surveys are conducted over the phone with members of representative households. Statistical indicators profile the community using a collation of census data, demographic and population statistics, and social and economic indicators.

Framework for community and neighborhood assessment

Social workers find community studies useful for inventorying sources of strengths and assessing community competence. A community assessment is also useful for assessing distinct neighborhoods within a larger community. The assessment includes such elements as a community or neighborhood profile, an inventory of assets, and an audit of the capacity for development.

Community Profile

- Summarize the history of the community
- Describe the geographical and jurisdictional boundaries of the community
- Explicate the dominant values, traditions, beliefs, and standards of the community
- Characterize the relationships among community members

Community Inventory of Assets

- Prepare a demographic profile of the community population
- Describe the political/power, economic, religious, education, social welfare, and criminal justice institutions
- Inventory the talent and resource pool of community members
- Inventory the resources in the health and human services delivery system including its agencies, programs, and volunteer initiatives
- Describe the housing, transportation, and recreational resources of the community

Community Audit of Capacity for Development

- Delineate the strengths of the community
- Identify the major community problems
- Evaluate sources of oppression and discrimination
- Evaluate the degree to which the community resources meet the needs of its members
- Assess community competence: How well does the community respond to resident needs? In what ways do community members contribute to the well-being of the community? How does the community relate to other communities and the region?

Focus groups

Focus groups have been widely used in qualitative research activities that emphasize incorporating respondents' voices around such issues as domestic violence (Dziegielewski, et al., 2005); racism and discrimination (Johnstone & Kanitsaki, 2008); lesbian, gay, and bisexual youth in foster care (Clements & Rosenwald, 2007); and consumer responses to mental health services (Oatts-Chandler & Nelstrop, 2008), They also have utility as strategy for macrolevel assessment and as a basis for strategic planning (Kramer, et al., 2002).

Figure 10.6   Considerations in Using Assessment Tools

- What is the purpose of the tool?
- Is the tool a good fit for the unique circumstances of the client system?
- What is the cost in terms of time, effort, and money?
- Are clients fully informed about the tool's purpose and procedure? Do they give their consent to participate?
- Does the tool require special training or certification to administer?
- What is the client's role?
- Will clients see and discuss the results?
- Will the proposed tool provide useful information or does it merely attach a label to the client's behavior?
- How will the results be used?
- Does the tool provide reliable and valid information?

Human Rights & Justice

In assessment, social workers consider various issues when choosing the right tools to understand client situations. How might the choices social workers make about assessment tools be reflective of workers' efforts to work toward social justice?

Several features distinguish the focus group strategy, including the characteristics of participants and the processes involved in expediting the strategy (Quible, 1998). Focus groups ideally involve 6 to 12 participants in a 1- to 2-hour discussion session that is recorded. Participants share an interest or affiliation; however, they may or may not know each other. Focus group phases include (1) *planning,* to define the objective, identifying and recruiting participants, and developing general interview guidelines; (2) *conducting,* to design the setting to enhance participation and to facilitate the process in a way that builds trust and elicits different points of view; and (3) *analyzing and reporting,* to transcribe the sessions, conduct a content analysis, and write the final report.

Tools as Resources for Empowerment

Empowerment-based assessment uses tools to discover resources. These tools do not produce products that diagnose or categorize clients and herd them into particular intervention initiatives. Instead, workers use assessment tools to enrich, motivate, and inform clients. Before implementing any tool, practitioners fully explain it, including its administration and purpose. They also share results and discuss implications with clients (Figure 10.6).

ADDING VIEWPOINTS

All clients enter social work services with their own particular views of their situations. No matter how openly social workers and clients talk, what clients know and report, what social workers hear and deduce is but a small part of the available information. Soliciting the viewpoints of others provides fresh perspectives and adds indispensable heterogeneity to the information base. Clients and social workers access alternative views by bringing in significant others and collecting information from other professionals.

Bringing in Significant Others

Rather than just talking about what happens in particular environments, social workers and clients have options for inviting others from that environment to present their views. For example, if an adolescent girl has trouble leaving home for a job-training position, her parents' views may enlighten. If a parolee has one last chance to avoid a return to jail, a joint meeting with the parole officer may clarify expectations and impending repercussions of the legal system. If a state legislature is considering welfare reform, the views of constituents presented in legislative testimony are influential.

Certain situations lead logically to involving others within the client's ecosystem. When practitioners work with young children, elderly clients who are frail, or persons with severe developmental disabilities or chronic illnesses, it makes sense to include persons most intensively involved in caregiving roles. A client's cultural background also may provide practitioners with clues about other significant people to involve. As an example, with Native American clients, extended family members are a source of strength whose perspectives may be helpful (Dykeman, et al., 1995).

Accessing information directly from collateral resource systems has several advantages. More than simply contributing alternative views, it provides clients with direct access to new information within the supportive atmosphere of the social work relationship and affords social workers a clear view of clients in transaction with significant others. Bringing in others begins the process of activating the natural support network on behalf of clients and involves those who are likely to experience effects as client systems change. Involving others affords clients opportunities to witness the motivations, resources, and strengths of social supports. This information will be important as clients and social workers attempt to shift the functioning of the ecosystem into patterns that help clients reach desired goals.

Contacting Other Professionals

Many clients are involved with more than one type of formal system, so additional perspectives may be available from psychiatrists, psychologists, physicians, nurses, teachers, ministers, and other helping professionals. Choosing which of these perspectives to access depends on several factors. Those resources clients consider most significant and acceptable clearly direct these choices, because clients themselves control the flow of information between professionals. If the social worker and client anticipate that a particular helping system may be a future target for change, this may be a particularly good time to initiate contact, assess, and involve that system.

Often, social workers and clients discover needs for more information or additional evaluations. No one professional has expertise in every aspect of human behavior. Instead, each profession makes its own particular contribution. Depending on the client's situation, it may be appropriate to consult with physicians, psychologists, occupational therapists, addiction specialists, urban planners, or a myriad of other professionals and organizations. Rather than limit their views of situations, social workers expertly open doors to new perspectives.

The way practitioners access information from other professionals makes a difference. Without exception, social workers must obtain a client's permission, as documented by a signed release of information, to legitimate communication with others about the client. This means clients themselves decide whether to give social workers permission to gather information from significant others, records, or other professionals. Clients need to know who is being contacted, what information is sought, why the information is required, and what consequences result if they refuse to permit the contact. Although social workers have a clear responsibility to gather information from other professionals, they share this task with clients as much as possible. Practitioners mutually discuss possible sources of information or consultation with clients and, when feasible, encourage clients to handle the arrangements. When clients discuss, arrange, and follow through on gathering additional information from other professionals, they assume their rightful roles and responsibilities in this process.

ASSESSING THROUGH OBSERVATION

The client system, itself, is an important resource for generating new information. Think about it. Any client system's functioning is a dynamic demonstration of its ability to draw on internal and environmental resources. Clients and workers can use this to their advantage by designing ways to observe clients in action.

Observations by Clients

Significant issues warrant observation. Frequently, social workers and clients are operating on vague generalities that require "all or nothing" solutions rather than concrete data that can lead to a more client-specific approach. Social workers and clients construct observations to objectify and update assessment information.

Consider the following example. Tanya confides to Kennedy Brown, the social worker at OPTIONS—an agency providing services for older adults—that her elderly father, Reginald, has lost his ability to take care of himself. This "all or nothing" kind of thinking leads Tanya directly to the single option of placing her father in a nursing home. A new understanding emerges when Tanya observes and charts what Reginald still does for himself as well as what she does for him. With the all-or-nothing thinking, nursing home placement was a fait accompli. Considering more objective observations leads Tanya and Kennedy to redefine the situation and select viable options from community-based services to promote Reginald's independence by maintaining him in his home.

Deciding what to observe

Notice, in the example above, how Tanya observes not only what Reginald is unable to do but also what he can still do for himself. Strengths-oriented workers check their tendencies to suggest that clients go out and observe only their problems. What kind of effect can you predict if clients observe "the problem" and learn everything that they can about it? Instead, imagine asking clients to review their situations for times when things are going well. Which is the more productive observation, the focus on problems or the focus on exceptions? What do clients discover as they watch the successful parts of their experiences? Consider these examples:

- When a neighborhood group believes the city council is not listening to them, selected group members can attend council meetings to see who the council does heed and what approaches these other people use.
- When domestic partners who are both employed disagree on who is doing more housekeeping, a structured observation not only provides objective data but also clarifies the extent of household tasks necessary if the couple chooses to renegotiate their distribution.

Involving others in observing clients

Some clients—including infants, people with advanced Alzheimer's disease, or those with profound developmental disabilities—are unable to conduct observations themselves. In these cases, social workers may coordinate such observations with other professionals or members of the client's natural support network. When workers involve others in observing, they obtain the client's consent and carefully include the client in the planning process.

Observations by Workers

Observing our own reactions to clients and observing how clients interact with others provides additional assessment information. Workers monitor their own responses, clients' interactions with others, and the interactions within multiperson client systems.

Observing our own reactions to clients

As social workers, we learn what responses to expect in ourselves as we relate to clients. To learn about clients, we ask ourselves about our thoughts, feelings, and reactions. For example, do we look forward to meetings with clients? Do we feel hopeful or invigorated? Do we distance ourselves or become angry? Do we feel an urge to "take care" of clients? Do we call clients to remind them of appointments, give them rides back and forth, or tell them what to do rather than discuss possibilities? Social workers who are self-aware identify the dynamics of their own responses to differentiate those provoked by personal issues from those triggered by clients. To remain objective, social workers strive to keep personal responses separate and share their observations about clients constructively.

Observing how clients interact with others

The potentially rich information embedded within direct interactions prompts social workers to invite significant others to meetings with clients. Consider Robert, a client in the community integrated employment program of the Area Association for People with Disabilities. Robert complains to his case manager that his sister, Barbara, always rifles through his personal belongings. Robert agrees to the worker's suggestion that they invite Barbara to talk with them together. When Barbara explains that she is only separating the laundry, a clearer picture emerges. By observing the interaction between Robert and his sister, the worker discovers a pattern of caretaking in which Barbara seems to assume Robert isn't capable—Barbara leads Robert into the office, tells him where to sit, and answers all questions directed to her brother. The worker also notes that Robert's passive response validates his sister's view and encourages her controlling behavior. These observations provide resources for developing a plan for working out the conflict between the siblings.

Observing multiperson client systems

Working with multiperson client systems offers a firsthand view of how the system functions. Systems reveal their structures and interactional patterns both subtly and directly. Observing who initiates conversations, who contributes the most, who has the last word, and toward whom members look when it's time to respond discloses clues about who's in charge. Observing who supports whom and who sits by whom indicates the subsystem arrangement and closeness among members. These patterns provide direct information about group structure, process, and development.

Reconsider the earlier example of Damon Edwards and the residents of Franklin Courts. Much of what Damon was able to assess came from the transactions that he observed rather than from the questions that he asked. He discovered the group's power structure by noting the nods of agreement when Mrs. Grant spoke. When he asked for volunteers to form a steering committee, indigenous leaders came forward, prodded by those around them who recognized these members as natural choices. Damon also identified existing subgroups by observing how members were seated, who came to the meeting together, and who shared common issues and concerns. Finally, Damon was able to assess the group's development by their abilities to function as a team in planning child-care arrangements, the respectful ways members listened to one another, and the clear sense of direction that the group had already developed. Clients are always telling workers about themselves. Alert practitioners observe these messages for the assessment information they convey.

RECORDKEEPING

Critical Thinking

Seen merely as paperwork, recordkeeping can easily be devalued as unimportant in practice. However, used effectively, recordkeeping can function as a critical reflection on practice. What steps can social workers take to keep records in ways that offer a critical perspective on their work?

In many ways, records are resources for clients, social workers, agencies, and even the social work profession. Records provide a coherent and organized data base for assessment. Records, like maps, are resource guides. It's hard for people to know how far they've come, unless there's a record of where they started. Likewise, it's hard for people to know which turn to take if they don't have some sense of their destination. A well-constructed record provides concrete evidence of change, information for assessment, and indications for future action.

Records serve as the basis for individual reflection, supervisory discussion, and peer consultation. Agency administrators aggregate data from records to evaluate current programs and plan for the future. Usually, agencies are accountable to funding bodies for grant-funded service provisions. Accurate records support statistical documentation and provide measures of quality assurance. Finally, effective social work records facilitate practice and program evaluation research. This section examines several facets of recordkeeping including the role of recording, types of recording techniques, and ethical and legal issues associated with recordkeeping.

Recording

Recording assists social workers and clients in numerous ways. By keeping track of contacts, activities, and plans, records aid memory. By organizing relevant information and arranging priorities, records ensure continuity. By carefully documenting case activities, records detail productivity and provide an essential component of professional liability risk management. When their clients give permission or when legal constraints mandate, records enhance a worker's ability to share accurate information with other professionals. Finally, records offer legal protection to workers because they concretely document professional activities.

Rather than being a mundane, tedious activity, effective recordkeeping is a useful analytic tool. "Recording provides evidence of the quality of thought and action that have gone into the delivery of service" (Kagle, 1987, p. 463). Writing reports requires us to cluster ideas, develop themes, and organize our thoughts. Writing clarifies our thinking. Whereas statistical records document case activities, descriptive case records individualize accounts of process, impressions, and plans. Records form a baseline against which to measure change.

Valuable records contain objective facts and relevant case-related information and documents, such as letters and releases of information. To avoid malpractice suits, never record anything derogatory about a client (Barker & Branson, 1992).

When we communicate with others via written documents, our documents make a significant impression. Poorly prepared documents detract from their content and may not be taken seriously. People evaluate our ideas by scrutinizing the document's format, presentation of ideas, grammar, and style. Some social service administrators consider written communication skills a top priority in their list of qualifications for prospective employees. Factors such as a pleasing format, clear and effective presentation of ideas, correct grammar, and a style that is ethnically sensitive and nonsexist establish credibility (Figure 10.7). Effective social workers prepare records carefully.

Types of Recording Formats

Social work records are prepared for a diverse audience, including colleagues, supervisors, third-party payers, clients, and court officials. Some records summarize information about goals, objectives, activities, and outcomes; others narrate a detailed account of progress toward goals. Some records are abbreviated, using outlines, checklists, or abridged forms; others incorporate extensive documentation details. Some records are written to comply with court mandates and/or contractual stipulations; others are kept to meet agency standards. The purposes of the record dictate its format, content, and style.

Note taking

Good records begin with gathering accurate information. Some circumstances require note taking. For example, factual data such as names of family members, committee members, birth dates, meeting times, or specific follow-up tasks may be difficult to remember without a written record. Typically, asking clients for permission to take even limited notes reduces their defensiveness. Effective requests include:

▶ I'd like to keep these details straight. Is it all right with you if I take a few notes?
▶ Does anyone object to my taking notes during our discussion so that we have a record of our decisions?

Figure 10.7   Tips for an Appropriate Writing Style

- Avoid all derogatory labels (for example, ethnic or racial slurs)
- Demonstrate gender sensitivity
  - Use generic terms to describe people including words such as mail carrier, service person, chairperson, etc.
  - Use the phrases "he or she," "his or her," or "them"
- Maintain nonjudgmentalism
- Refrain from using jargon or slang
- Use concrete descriptions rather than diagnostic labels, generalizations, or subjective wording
- Use active voice
- Proofread your final draft by reading aloud

▶ This is a pretty long form to fill out. Do you want me to read the questions to you? Do you want to read along with me? I could give you a blank form and you could just tell me the answers and I'll write them down. What do you think would work best?

There is pressure to remember detail, yet a need to take notes in ways that have minimal effect on the process (Kadushin & Kadushin, 1997). By involving clients, social workers convert note taking from a display of expert authority into an empowering strategy. Taking only selective notes during actual meetings with clients requires conscientious social workers to record notes soon after. Noting even a few details will enhance the accuracy of recollection in completing formal reports.

Activity logs

Probably the most widely used style of record is a simple and organized log of contacts between workers and clients. This type of record is most useful in keeping the worker and client focused on relevant tasks and forms a data base for worker and agency accountability. Although the content of these records varies across practice settings, most include information about client goals, activities completed, future plans, people involved, and time invested. Examine the activity log of Rita Garcia, a social worker with the state's Child Protective Unit, who uses this record to document her work with Opal Zander (Figure 10.8). Although not offering detailed accounts of her activities, Rita's logs keep her on task and remind her of the sequence of important events when she presents court testimony. She also uses her logs to organize follow-up details.

Process recording

Process recordings review contacts with clients by including descriptive, specific details. More often found in educational than paid employment settings, process recording applies to any system level, builds self-awareness, refines assessment

Figure 10.8   Sample Activity Log

Worker: Rita Garcia			Client: Zander Family	
Date	**Time**	**Contact**	**Task/Activity**	**Action Required**
6/19	.25	Call from Smith/DCS	Requested emergency placement for Zander children—4 siblings	Find home for sibling group
6/19	.25	L. Jones	Confirmed Jones will provide foster placement for all four kids	
6/19	.50	Smith/DCS	Discussed disposition of case	Smith will pursue court action
6/19	1.50	Zander children	Provided transport to Jones' home	Call Jones 6/20
6/20	1.75	Opal Zander	Intake: Discussed procedures and requirements. Set goals for family reunification	Schedule joint meeting with team 6/21 (Families United office, 10:30)
6/21	2.25	Team meeting	Set visitation and determined plan of action including (1) moving out of boyfriend's house into transitional housing, (2) secure employment to achieve financial independence	Zander will contact Northside Shelter and the Women's Resource Center

skills, and supports learning to work effectively with clients (Kagle, 1991). Process recordings support social workers in becoming reflective practitioners and enhance their conscious use of self (Graybeal & Ruff, 1995; Neuman & Friedman, 1997). Consonant with the strengths perspective, social workers can modify process recordings to incorporate commentary on client strengths (Walsh, 2002). A number of innovative options for process recording go beyond formal written reports. These include audio- and videotaping, verbal descriptions, role plays, drawings, and in-session and one-way mirror observations by others (Graybeal & Ruff, 1995).

Content for properly prepared written process recordings includes the verbatim dialogue, comments on the social worker's reactions and feelings, analyses and interpretations of the transactions, and the supervisor's comments (Neuman & Friedman, 1997). Process recordings need to be written immediately. To organize process recording, one can divide legal-size paper into three or four columns or on a computer, format recording columns using a "landscape" setting to align the paper horizontally. Practitioners evaluate their experiences in the interviewer's column; supervisors provide constructive feedback in the instructor's comments column. Examine the process recording completed by Rita Garcia as she works with Opal Zander toward the goal of increasing Opal's employability (Figure 10.9).

Summary recording

Summary recordings such as progress notes, intake summaries, and referral reports are more typical of the recordkeeping requirements of day-to-day social work practice. Frequency and format depends on agency policy, stipulations of

Figure 10.9   Excerpts from a Processs Recording

Client: Opal Zander	Date: 7/12 (Individual Session # 8)	Interviewer: R. Garcia
Verbatim Account	**Interviewer's Response**	**Analysis**
I called the GED center.	Oh?	Opal's taking the initiative. Want to keep my responses minimal while supporting her efforts.
I can start anytime. They call it "study at your own pace."	Good!	
Not going to cost me any money. They've even got a bus token deal.	Mmhmm . . .	
And, something called a resource center for women like me.	For women like you . . .	Emphasizing Opal's connection with other women in program to increase its appeal.
I think so. I said, "I'm nervous and I've been having some hard times." And, then the lady I was talking to said, well I could try it out. So, I've been thinking . . . (pauses a bit)	Yes?	
Well, I've been thinking about whether I should wait until I get the kids back or start now. I even made this list to decide (list shows lots of pluses).	Looks like you're thinking about starting pretty soon.	Emphasizing Opal's efforts in thinking this through. But did I jump in too soon with this?
The way I see it, I've got some time on my hands right now. And, this GED program gives me a chance to do something positive. I sure need that. And, maybe I can make some friends, like we talked about last time, at that women's center.	I'm really impressed with how you're taking charge.	Opal sees she's making a difference, can build on this for parenting, too. How could we connect this with reunification goals?

accrediting bodies, government regulations, and grant requirements. Typically, effective summary recordings include

- Identifying data such as the client's name and identifying number, date of the interview, date the summary is being written, and social worker's name
- Reason for the meeting
- Summary account
- Description of the salient issues
- Worker's impressions
- Follow-up plans and/or goals (Wilson, 1980)

Content focuses exclusively on the client rather than on the worker's responses and reactions. Summary content describes outcomes thematically rather than in step-by-step details.

Ethical and Legal Issues in Recordkeeping

Records document courses of action. However, sharing this information with clients and other professionals raises numerous ethical and legal issues, as does the use of computers for recordkeeping.

Electronic records

Although computers streamline the processing and sharing of information and facilitate the collection of data, ethical issues abound (Gelman, et al., 1999; Reamer, 1998). Because the computerized data bases maintained in social work practice are likely to contain an abundance of confidential information, safeguards to maintain security and to preserve confidentiality are vital. For social workers in health and mental health, ensuring confidentiality for health records is the law. The Health Insurance Portability and Accountability Act of 1996 (HIPAA) stipulates the legal regulations and mandated compliance procedures to ensure privacy of electronic protected health information (NASW, 2005f; 2004a; 2001b). Security measures regulate access to data bases through the use of passwords and other "locked file systems," monitor the access to information afforded by computer networks, and rigorously protect the privacy of information on the computer screen. Professionals ensure that storage of computerized information is as safe as the records stored in their locked filing cabinets and that records on their computer screens are as private as the records in their files.

Clients' access to records

The NASW *Code of Ethics* (1999a) indicates that clients should have reasonable access to their records. Specifically, the code indicates that social workers should provide reasonable access to official records that concern them and, when sharing this information with clients, should protect the confidentiality of other persons noted in the records. Clearly, this code upholds clients' rights to access their records.

Several pieces of federal legislation also champion clients' rights to access their records. For example, the Federal Privacy Act of 1974 (Public Law 93-579), the Freedom of Information Act, and the Family Educational Rights legislation of 1974 (known as the Buckley Amendment) specify guidelines with respect to accessing records from educational institutions or from other federally funded or administered programs. These laws set a precedence that carries over into the private sector (Kagle, 1990, 1991). Both Family Service America and the

Child Welfare League of America encourage member agencies to grant clients access to their own records (Gelman, 1992). These codes, laws, and guidelines prescribe the principle; agency policies and procedures furnish detailed directions as to how clients proceed to access their records.

Social workers need to keep in mind the effect of reading the written reports as they prepare clients' records. Workers always write records with the understanding that the records could be read by clients or various third parties (Saltzman & Furman, 1999). Although some professionals struggle with the implications of fully sharing their written impression with clients, research findings indicate "that there is a qualitative improvement in both recording practices and relationships as a result of client participation" (Gelman, 1992, p. 76).

LOOKING FORWARD

Assessment processes infuse professional theory and expertise into the work of social workers and clients. Such processes are empowering to the extent that they contextualize the issues that clients face and locate resources to achieve goals. In contrast, assessment processes that elevate the social worker's expertise or reduce client situations to stigmatizing labels undermine a client's progress.

Assessment requires social workers and clients to think about what they are doing in theoretical and practical ways to organize their information into a usable format for planning. Clients contribute to this process by offering their theories, interpretations, and feelings to the assessment. Social workers contribute by integrating theoretical understanding, professional supports, and research information. Social workers can enhance the assessment by keeping written records.

The organized description of client needs and resources that comes from assessment begins to frame the options that the partners have for development and change. Framing solutions, the subject of Chapter 11, takes planning further. To frame solutions, the partners articulate goals, focus on change, consider multiple levels of intervention, and concentrate their energies toward the outcomes they seek.

Succeed with **PEARSON mysocialworklab**

Log onto **www.mysocialworklab.com** and select the **Interactive Skill Module** videos from the left-hand menu. Answer the questions below. (*If you did not receive an access code to* **MySocialWorkLab** *with this text and wish to purchase access online, please visit* www.mysocialworklab.com.)

1. **On pages 9, 10, and 16 of the school social work module**, worker Terry helps a client clarify her current problem and describe its context. What other questions should Terry ask to complete a comprehensive ecosystemic assessment?

2. **Watch the entire school social work module accessed via page 26.** Create a progress note to record the information shared in the session. Which information is most significant, and what should be included in the professional record?

PRACTICE TEST

1. Employed by Neighbors United, social worker Damon Edwards works with a small group of Franklin Court residents, including neighborhood leader Fiona Grant to assess the needs of the housing complex. In this example, the focal system is _____.
   a. only Mrs. Grant, the neighborhood leader
   b. all of the residents of Franklin Courts
   c. parents who live in Franklin Courts
   d. residents of Franklin Courts who make up the selected group

2. If Damon Edwards applies an ecosystems framework to assess Franklin Courts, which of the following questions is he LEAST likely to include in his assessment plan?
   a. Who influences decisions at Franklin Courts?
   b. What cultural strengths do the members contribute to Franklin Courts?
   c. What are the problems at Franklin Courts?
   d. How does the physical environment influence Franklin Courts?

3. To graphically depict the broad ecological context of Franklin Courts, Damon Edwards most likely completes a(n) _____.
   a. social network map
   b. genogram
   c. eco-map
   d. community inventory

4. A new social service administrator at Families United, Abby Youngman utilizes an ecosystems framework to better understand the agency. If Abby wants to include a question that will help her understand how the agency system has moved through time, which question should she ask?
   a. What systems outside the agency influence how it functions?
   b. How does the agency adapt to changing demands in the environment of the social service delivery system?

   c. How do cultural differences influence the relationships within the agency?
   d. How do employees and managers communicate?

Human Rights & Justice

5. Abby Youngman believes that privilege, prejudicial attitudes and discrimination affect the participants in Families United programs and services. To understand these sociopolitical influences, Abby needs to ask questions related to _____ analysis.
   a. structural
   b. interactional
   c. cultural
   d. psychosocial

Practice Contexts

6. Abby Youngman decides to assess factors within the agency organization that support or resist change. The strategy that most closely aligns with this type of assessment is a(n) _____.
   a. eco-map
   b. force field analysis
   c. social network map
   d. genogram

7. As a social worker at Northside Aging Services, Jay Hendricks wants a way to visually depict the complicated intergenerational family relationships of the Martinez family. To do so, he considers using a _____.
   a. force field analysis
   b. genogram
   c. social network map
   d. social history

8. Mental health social worker Addison Wakely knows she needs to ask her clients' permission in order to release any information about them to a different agency. When she seeks this informed consent from clients, she is upholding the ethical principle called _____.
   a. professionalism
   b. respect
   c. confidentiality
   d. access to services

Log onto **MySocialWorkLab** once you have completed the Practice Test above to take your Chapter Exam and demonstrate your knowledge of this material.

Answers

1) d 2) c 3) c 4) b 5) c 6) b 7) c 8) c

11

Framing Solutions

CONNECTING CORE COMPETENCIES *in this chapter*

| Professional Identity | Ethical Practice | Critical Thinking | Diversity in Practice | Human Rights & Justice | Research Based Practice | Human Behavior | Policy Practice | Practice Contexts | Engage Assess Intervene Evaluate |

During assessment, generalist social workers discover abundant information about what is available, what enhances, and what constrains client systems. Assessment processes often generate such a wealth of information that workers and clients must pause to sift through and organize these discoveries into a coherent plan before taking action. To plan solutions, social workers and clients work collaboratively to address such questions as: What exactly are we trying to accomplish? Who needs to be involved? What are we going to do? There is no single correct answer to any of these questions. Even when we know exactly where we want to go, we can probably plan many routes to get there.

Framing solutions means planning, that is transforming assessment material into manageable strategies for change. From a generalist social work perspective, planning can be complex because a generalist sees multiple options for solutions at each system level. However, when approached in a thoughtful and organized fashion, generalist planning is never a "dead end." Other possible approaches or other aspects of the situation always are amenable to change.

This chapter describes how social workers and clients develop comprehensive plans of action. Specifically, this chapter

- Identifies appropriate roles for workers and clients in a collaborative planning process
- Distinguishes goals from objectives
- Articulates processes for constructing action plans including rules for writing measurable objectives and considerations for choosing intervention strategies
- Analyzes contracting as a dynamic and empowering process

Successful completion of a comprehensive plan of action prepares social workers and clients with an explicit guide for their intervention efforts.

COLLABORATIVE PLANNING PROCESSES

A comprehensive helping program is one that is multitarget, multilevel, and multiphasic in its design.

—Max Siporin

A plan of action describes what social workers and clients hope to accomplish and how they intend to do it. A complete plan contains several components. It has goals and objectives, possible targets for change, various strategies designed to reach those goals and objectives, a timeline, and evaluation guidelines. Action plans delineate activities that specify what social workers and clients will do, with whom, in what locations, and when. The more concrete the plan, the greater the likelihood of accomplishing its purpose. The more flexible the plan, the more the partners can tailor it to changes that occur during its implementation.

The ecosystems perspective naturally leads workers and clients to construct multidimensional plans. Siporin (1975) sums this up succinctly, saying that a comprehensive action plan is "multitarget, multilevel, and multiphasic in its design" (p. 259). Siporin elaborates, describing a plan's many component parts, including

- Broad goals and concrete, measurable objectives
- A prioritization of objectives into immediate, intermediate, and long term
- Strategies to use and actions to take to meet objectives
- Time frames for implementation
- Identified targets for change

> ◗ An inventory of necessary resources such as financial, programs, or staff
> ◗ Clear division of responsibility for actions among the client system, social worker, and others
> ◗ Evaluation criteria and procedures
> ◗ Processes for altering the plan
> ◗ A defined point of resolution

Pulling together such a detailed plan of action requires the full participation of both clients and social workers. They openly discuss the information they have discovered, reexamine their goals, and mutually generate ideas about how to accomplish them. Both clients and social workers actively invest in planning processes, but each brings different expertise and plays a different role. Clients are experts on what they want and on what they are willing to do. Social workers contribute technical skills for constructing plans and knowledge of the resources available for implementing them.

Client Expertise in Planning

Clients bring significant expertise to the planning process. They are content experts—they know what they want. They are *motivation experts*—they can describe what they are willing to do. They are skill experts—they can demonstrate their own capabilities.

Clients have ultimate power over a plan's acceptability. Social workers may suggest, but clients have the right and the responsibility to say what they can and will do. They can give the "thumbs up" or "thumbs down" on the proposed plan. Clients maintain the privilege of selecting the outcomes and strategies they desire. Collaboration guarantees that plans are relevant to what clients want, and the involvement of clients ensures that the very process of constructing a plan activates clients toward its achievement.

Plans as motivators for action

Good plans motivate clients. They incorporate client-centered goals—statements of outcomes desired by clients. To respect self-determination and activate clients' participation, goals and strategies must naturally emerge from the collaborative efforts of workers and clients. Workers help clients clarify and operationalize their chosen goals in ways that retain the motivational quality of these goals (Gold, 1990). Goals and plans motivate clients when clients assume their ownership. To "own" their plans, clients need to see them as relevant and participate in their construction.

Worker Expertise in Planning

Workers are both technical and resource experts in the planning process. As technical experts, practitioners apply planning models to organize goals and ideas for change into coherent action plans. To do so, workers listen carefully to what clients want and help break down these goals into workable units. In other words, workers translate vague, abstract goals into measurable and attainable objectives. Practitioners also guide clients to articulate fully specific strategies in ways that clarify the roles of clients and workers, determine who else should be involved, set time frames, determine evaluation criteria, and specify a schedule to review progress. In planning, workers are technical experts who design a framework with clients to flesh out with the content of clients' situations and aspirations.

Workers are also resource experts in the planning process. Practitioners keep informed about what resources might be available beyond the social work relationship. In essence, effective social workers are resource directories, vital links to other resources in the community. Informed social workers help clients consider possible options available in other programs, other persons to access who have relevant skills, and even indigenous community resources that are outside of the formal network of social services.

Issues Affecting Collaborative Planning

Professional Identity

Social workers and clients collaborate to construct action plans. What are the similarities and differences in roles that workers and clients play in this process?

As much as possible, workers strive to develop action plans that reflect what clients themselves want to do and are hoping to accomplish. However, three issues affect a worker's ability to collaborate in this way with all clients. These factors include the participatory ability of the client, powerful forces outside of the social work relationship system, and other people who will be affected by the plan.

Participatory abilities of clients

Sometimes, the particular challenges of clients limit their abilities to participate fully in planning (Linhorst, et al., 2002). Those with overwhelming physical, cognitive, or emotional challenges may be currently unable to define where they are going, what they are willing to do, or what skills and abilities they can contribute. When this is the case, workers use their best judgment to make choices based on their awareness of the client's situation and what they believe to be the client's best interest. Workers also call on others in the client's life to assist with this process. If the client has a significant natural support system of family and friends, it is likely that they have already been involved in other parts of the process and can continue to participate in planning.

Even when involving other persons in planning, workers strive to ascertain what the client wants. For example, if the planning concerns medical treatment for a hospice patient who is physically unable to participate, any advance directives previously expressed to workers, family members, and friends should be in the forefront of the planning process. For clients who are developmentally disabled or too young to comprehend the process fully, workers still include them and encourage them to express their views.

Outside influences on involuntary clients

Not all clients are free to plan changes that they want. Involuntary clients frequently come encumbered with predetermined goals and limits on their options. For example, a client may be participating in an alternative counseling program to avoid prosecution. Or, a parent may want to regain custody of children placed in foster care and be court-ordered to resolve personal issues and acquire parenting skills. In these cases, the social worker and client must consider the mandates of others. The participation of those representing such outside forces can be direct, such as ordering specific activities or treatments; or it may be indirect, allowing workers and clients to develop their own plans subject to review and approval. In either case, workers accept the responsibility of incorporating into the plan the view of whatever authority is requiring the social work intervention.

When social workers accept involuntary clients, they agree to work within the boundaries set by the mandating agent. That does not necessarily mean that clients and social workers have no influence. Social workers should not ignore their implicit power. Those in authority have shown their trust in the worker enough to believe that social work expertise is what is necessary to facilitate change. Why else would they have ordered the client to work with the social work practitioner? If workers believe that clients would benefit from a different strategy or a plan, they may choose to advocate new orders. In this way, social workers balance the desires of the client with the orders of authorities in developing plans that are compatible and agreeable to both.

Considering significant others

Social workers consider the perspectives of others even when clients are voluntary. If the client is a 15-year-old youth who wants to move out of the house, the views of the legal guardian are pivotal. If the client is one partner in a committed relationship, social workers use their expertise to anticipate the impact of the proposed plans on the other partner and discuss this view with the client. With the client's permission, workers may even go so far as to invite the partner's direct commentary on the developing plan. Changes in the client will inevitably affect people in relationships with the client. The success of the plan ultimately depends on the cooperation that clients receive from those around them.

Planning with larger systems also considers the potential effect of the plan on others. For example, if the client system is a task group in the community, the foresighted worker encourages group members to seek the opinions of their constituents before implementing the plan. If the client is a social agency, the practitioner encourages agency staff to explore the impact of their proposed changes on the social service delivery system in the community network. Generalist social workers always keep in mind that they do not work with clients in isolation. Effective plans meet the client's goals, but good planning also anticipates and accounts for the responses of others.

Planning in Multiperson Systems

Planning means reaching agreement on what clients and social workers will do to accomplish their goals. This may not be such a difficult task for social workers and individual clients, who each have defined roles and clear areas of expertise for the process. But for client systems with two or more members, planning takes on the new dimension of negotiation. In other words, members of the client system must agree on what they seek and the methods they are willing to use. Dealing with differences, resolving conflicts, and facilitating decision making are additional skills necessary for planning with multiperson client systems.

Social workers function as facilitators in group planning to ensure the best efforts of the client system and, as much as possible, give each member a voice in the plan. Practitioners facilitate planning in groups of many sizes and types—couples, families, support groups, task groups, case management teams, program units in organizations, boards of directors, and community planning councils, to name just a few. Each group may benefit from a different kind of decision-making process depending on its particular needs, goals, and characteristics.

Decision making in groups

Group planning has advantages. It has profound effects on members, including encouraging higher motivation to achieve, increasing commitment to implement the decision, and initiating changes in behavior and attitudes (Johnson & Johnson, 2006). Groups have more resources than any one individual and can actually generate new perspectives and possibilities as members interact with one another. But combining the resources of individual group members also has drawbacks. Effective group decision making takes more time, requires a significant level of group development and maturity, and depends on effective and respectful interpersonal communication among members. Workers facilitating group planning processes may need to help groups develop and learn decision making before actually formulating action plans.

Johnson and Johnson (2006) classify group decision making into several types. Some types ultimately leave decisions in the hands of a single powerful group member. Three examples of individual members tapped to make decisions include members who are in designated authority roles, those respected as experts on the particular issues at hand, or those nominated to poll other members and make decisions based on the input they receive. Sometimes, groups vest this same kind of decision-making power in a subgroup such as an executive planning committee or a team of experts chosen from among the group's membership. At other times, the whole group makes decisions democratically by averaging the opinions of all members or by voting, thereby leaving the decision to the majority. Each of these styles—decision making by single members, subgroups, or the group as a whole—may be appropriate, depending on the unique qualities of the group and the decision to be made.

Consensus

When group members have the time and necessary skills, consensus decision making may be the most productive (Johnson & Johnson, 2006). Consensus decision making draws on the concept of the group as a social system. It activates all members to contribute to a mutual decision. Consensus does not imply total agreement among members. Rather, consensus decisions meld the variety of views and opinions held by those participating in the process. Although at times difficult to achieve, consensus results in creative decisions that garner participants' support for implementation, draw on their collective resources, and enhance future decision-making effectiveness.

GOALS AND OBJECTIVES

All social work practice is purposeful, directed toward clients' goals. Early in their dialogue with social workers, clients describe a preliminary direction for the work. This sense of purpose guides the assessment process and defines what may function as resources.

Now, in planning, workers and clients reconsider this original purpose in light of the assessment information; they translate this initial purpose into a concrete set of realistic goals and objectives. Therefore, as a beginning step in their planning tasks, clients stop, reflect on where they are, and focus clearly on a point in the future where they would like to be. This point of focus is the goal toward which clients and social workers plan a path of objectives and related activities.

Differentiating Goals and Objectives

Articulating goals is the prelude to preparing objectives and designing specific intervention activities. Setting goals is a process whereby clients consider the outcomes they hope to achieve, identify the specific objectives that lead them toward their goals, and delineate steps or actions ultimately to reach their goals. For simplicity, we define goals and objectives as having distinct meanings. *Goals* are broad, general statements of what clients want to accomplish. They express the desired outcomes, ideal conditions, or long-term aims of the helping relationship. Goals are not necessarily measurable. In contrast, *objectives* are explicit statements of concrete changes desired by clients in their behaviors or situations. Objectives are readily observable and measurable. Objectives are the smaller, incremental achievements required to reach goals. Workers and clients may set many objectives to achieve a single outcome goal.

Considering Goals

Research Based Practice

In planning, workers and clients develop plans that include goals, objectives, and action steps. How might action plans be useful in the evaluation of practice?

A goal is a simple concept, but how do social workers and clients actually develop goals? When there are a variety of issues, which one gets attention first? Can practitioners and clients work on several goals at once? What steps translate current difficulties into attainable outcomes? Should goals be long-term or immediate? Specific or global? Practitioners answer these questions differently depending on their own practice philosophies and the characteristics of their clients.

What goals should clients set?

Goals that client systems pursue vary greatly. Goldstein (1973) overviews five types of goals, including

1. Obtaining some concrete goods or services, or needed resources such as financial assistance, employment, health care, or housing

2. Making important life decisions, resolving crises, relieving immediate distress, or removing barriers to change

3. Modifying structures in social systems, such as a family, an organization, or a community by changing communication patterns, interactional behaviors, or roles and rules

4. Pursuing "foresight goals" or fulfilling some future aspiration through rational planning

5. Recognizing the basic value of growth and change, and seeking social work services to realize their fullest potential.

Social workers maintain flexibility to match their strategies and styles of work with the goals for which clients strive.

How far ahead?

Goals describe what we hope will happen in the future, but how far ahead do we look? Kisthardt (1992) cautions against goals that reach too far into the future. Social workers maintain flexibility between a long-term outlook as a general guide and a short-term view that clearly defines achievable tasks. A balance of long-term goals with discrete short-term steps keeps the relationship moving successfully forward while ensuring that each step leads in a productive direction.

Reflect for a moment on how you set goals for yourself. Do you have some general ideas about where you would like to be in the future? A 5-year plan? A 10-year plan? As you make daily decisions, do you take small steps in the general direction of your aspirations? Are you a social work student looking ahead to professional practice? What intermediate goals and objectives will you be accomplishing as you move toward your professional career? Likely, you have a clear goal to pass the final exam in this class, but your choice of a field of social work practice may remain vague until you explore the possibilities revealed in further course work and field experiences.

As we progress through a series of accomplishments, we assess, reassess, and decide where to go next. Sometimes we change direction. This same process works for clients, too. Clients benefit from the long-distance look ahead that long-term goals provide, but they also need a clear sense of interim steps.

How many goals?

Clients may desire many goals simultaneously. However, setting too many diverse goals may give the partners no direction at all. When clients have a lot they want to accomplish, social workers facilitate a sequential approach to help clients to organize and set priorities for issues and goals. Focusing on a reasonable number of goals facilitates their attainment. Social workers encourage clients to think broadly and optimistically about the future but guide them to move in one direction at a time.

Translating Goals into Objectives

Goal setting, as part of the planning process, functions as the initial step toward specifying concrete objectives. Siporin (1975) lays a foundation for understanding objectives and articulating their use for social work practice:

> Objectives express our values and intentions, and they also give direction and meaning to behavior. Objectives that are clear and explicit evoke investment and commitment. When accepted by the individual, there is also an acceptance of responsibility for action to implement them. They give to the individual a conscious sense of purpose and hope. They stimulate awareness of the interrelationships between purpose, choice, and activity and provide a standard against which to judge performance and progress. When shared with others, objectives provide means for communication, identification, and relationship with others. (p. 258)

Practitioners should formulate objectives in meaningful and realistic ways by considering objectives from many perspectives. According to Siporin, effective objectives are

- Steps toward goals
- Explicit and operational
- Realistic and attainable
- Discrete and time-limited
- Observable and measurable
- Acceptable to both clients and workers

The following paragraphs describe these attributes of objectives in further detail.

Steps toward goals

How can client systems achieve their goals? Each objective provides a part of the answer to this question. Although possible objectives are numerous and far ranging, those chosen as part of an action plan have one thing in common—each has the specific intent of moving client systems closer to their eventual goals. Objectives are not set to achieve random successes. Instead, they are focused attempts to chip away at the space between where clients are and their

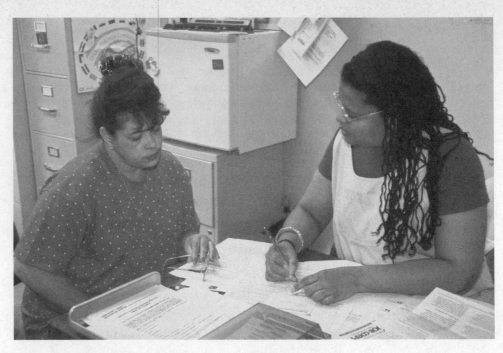

Clients and social workers collaborate to identify goals for change.

goals of where they would like to be. Workers and clients consider two general kinds of objectives

1. Small positive steps in the direction of goals

2. Removal of obstacles in the path toward goals

By continuing to achieve one step at a time and to remove each obstacle encountered, clients ultimately arrive at their desired goals.

Consider the example of a social worker facilitating a community task group whose members seek the goal of economic development for their deteriorating neighborhood. After a comprehensive assessment of the neighborhood, the social worker and task group are able to specify several objectives to work toward this goal. They set objectives to accomplish small positive steps, including obtaining the designation of "free enterprise zone" for the neighborhood, negotiating with the city council for property tax relief for new businesses, and accessing low-interest loans for neighborhood businesses from a local bank. But other objectives are also necessary to remove identified barriers, including the negative image of the neighborhood and the high rate of crime. Setting additional objectives to enhance the neighborhood's image as an historic district through a public relations campaign, to increase police patrols, and to institute a neighborhood watch program will take steps toward removing these obstacles. Overall, achieving each of these objectives either takes a direct step or clears the way for the task group to continue toward the goal of neighborhood economic development.

Explicit and operational

A comprehensive set of objectives that considers changes in clients and their environments may involve many persons and projects. Therefore, stating objectives in as precise and exact a manner as possible is essential. Clearly stated and mutually understood, objectives are prerequisites to establishing a common understanding and building consensus about courses of action. Frequently, failures to achieve objectives result from miscommunication. Making objectives explicit and understandable from the beginning effectively reduces this margin of error.

Objectives function as bridges from goals to the activities implemented to reach goals. In other words, objectives break down broad goals into small enough achievements that it begins to be obvious what actions social workers, clients, and others will take to accomplish their purposes. In the previous example of the community task group, the concrete objective to receive low-interest bank loans for neighborhood businesses already implies specific tasks. Obviously, the group will need to designate certain members to contact banks, business owners, and interested entrepreneurs about this project. Explicit objectives state the desired change and the direction of change in terms of specific target behaviors—who will accomplish what. In this example, the task group members will convince local banks to grant low-interest loans to neighborhood businesses. Workers and clients can quickly operationalize well-formed objectives into clearly defined strategies and action steps.

Realistic and attainable

Success builds on success. Clients need objectives that are realistic, given their present capabilities, opportunities readily available, and resources potentially accessible. This does not imply that clients should settle for less than they desire. It simply means that workers and clients should construct and prioritize objectives in such a way that each is possible to achieve and each achievement makes the next objective easier to accomplish. Objectives that, under present circumstances, require too big a leap or too much change set up clients for failure and disillusionment. For example, when a client who is unable to read sets an objective to pass a high school equivalency exam, disappointment is likely. Instead, when the worker helps this client set realistic, incremental objectives of enrolling in an alternative high school and beginning work with a tutor, the objective to pass the equivalency test becomes more realistic.

Structuring success into a plan of action is essential for maintaining client motivation and facilitating empowerment. Experiences with success lead to feelings of self-efficacy and beliefs in competence to achieve certain levels of performance (Bandura, 1984). Clients who perceive themselves as competent are likely to persist and exert greater efforts in their pursuit of goals. Conversely, clients who perceive themselves as ineffective may be reluctant to engage in change, may expect failure, and may view failures as evidence of personal deficiencies. Workers have responsibilities to work with clients to set attainable objectives, thereby instilling a sense of confidence and control to effect desired outcomes.

When clients experience success and view themselves as causal agents of the outcome, they approach future events with feelings of hopefulness. In other words, accomplishments empower clients with confidence and hope. Zimmerman (1990) states that "learned hopefulness suggests that experiences that provide opportunities to enhance perceived control will help individuals cope with stress and solve problems in their personal lives" (pp. 72–73). Experiencing or perceiving a lack of control over events or outcomes may evoke expectations that events in the future are out of reach and beyond control, resulting in symptoms of helplessness (Seligman, 1975). Setting and accomplishing realistic and attainable objectives initiates a chain of success that leads to hope, increased competence, and feelings of power and control.

Discrete and time-limited

Setting realistic objectives means taking small steps. Continuing success means dividing goals into discrete enough objective units to accomplish one step after another. For example, Sean, a client with profound developmental disabilities, may be overwhelmed by the singular objective of learning to brush his teeth. But when the worker breaks this objective into the discrete accomplishments of Sean picking up his toothbrush, applying toothpaste, wetting the brush, placing it in his mouth, and moving the brush across his teeth, success is now within reach. Sean and the worker can now focus on one objective at a time and celebrate each success as it occurs.

Redefining objectives as mini-objectives also opens up options of working on objectives sequentially (achieving one objective after another) or concurrently (attempting several objectives at one time). Sean, in the previous example, will likely benefit from a sequential approach. A task group, such as the one in the example working on economic development, has members that can work simultaneously and efficiently in several directions at once and therefore can use a concurrent approach. Achieving each small step, whether sequentially or concurrently, leads to quantum leaps as clients see results, experience success, and gain confidence. Research supports that "self motivation can be best created and sustained by attainable subgoals that lead to larger future ones" (Bandura & Schunk, 1981, p. 587). Feeling satisfied with their achievements of one objective, clients gain a sense of mastery and tend to persist in their change efforts.

Workers and clients also incorporate time considerations when formulating discrete objectives, usually by selecting objectives that can be achieved within a few weeks (Sheafor & Horejsi, 2006). If clients cannot accomplish an objective quickly, the objective is too broad or too long-term. Workers and clients should break it into smaller, sequential objectives. When meeting at designated intervals, such as once a week, workers and clients can easily consider what can be completed by the next time they meet in deciding what objectives to set. Quick accomplishments relieve immediate pressures and posture client systems toward further advancements.

Observable and measurable

In response to the press for accountability and for the evaluation of practice effectiveness, objectives serve an important function in assessing goal achievement. Objectives concretely articulate the path toward goals. Reaching various objectives provides a series of interim markers for checking progress and affirming success on the way to desired goals.

Well-formed objectives express desired outcomes in both behavioral and quantitative terms. To imagine an objective that is behavioral, envision what the outcome will look like. Ask yourself whether you and someone with you would agree on what you are seeing. If both you and the other observer would be likely to describe what you are observing in a similar way, then this observation could be set as a behaviorally observable outcome. If you can "see" when an objective is achieved, it is behavioral.

Objectives are measurable when they state specifically to what extent and how often the events or behaviors will occur. For example, when a family sets the objective to resolve differences through negotiation rather than conflict, they could evaluate the achievement of this objective by noting each time differences arise and recording the interaction that follows. Behaviorally observable and measurable objectives assist in evaluating outcomes.

Acceptable to client and worker

To be effective, any objective must relate to a particular client system, reflecting its strengths, distinct capabilities, current situation, and goals. Too often, workers clone somewhat standard objectives from one case plan to another without considering how a specific client would like to proceed. Rubber-stamp objectives do not account for a particular client's goals and values. They cannot replace objectives developed collaboratively and tailored to address a client's unique needs.

Effective objectives directly relate to changes that clients believe will improve their situations. Even when workers envision social or environmental

Box 11.1 **Ethic of Critical Thinking**

Critical thinking and reasoning skills are essential competencies for social work practice, so important for social workers that the Council on Social Work Accreditation (CSWE) has added a policy on critical thinking in its most recent revision of the standards by which Social Work Programs are evaluated for accreditation. Educational Policy 2.1.3 requires that social work students learn to be "knowledgeable about the principles of logic, scientific inquiry, and reasoned discernment" (CSWE, 2008, p. 16). Critical thinking involves creativity, curiosity, and the synthesis of information to "distinguish, appraise, and integrate multiple sources of knowledge, including research-based knowledge, and practice wisdom" (p. 16).

The ability to think critically is an asset for social workers working collaboratively with clients to evaluate resource capabilities and develop action plans. "Social work practice involves gathering information and analyzing information situations, but importantly requires that judgments and decisions be made and actions taken based on these. The process of critical thinking for social work is more than analysis, it is informed action" (Plath, et al., 1999, p. 208). Applying processes of critical thinking liberates clients and workers to go beyond "tunnel vision" to examine issues as multidimensional, opening many pathways to desired solutions. Critical thinking leads workers and clients to discover resources in unlikely places. It is a creative, reflective, and multidirectional assessment and planning process, sometimes referred to as "thinking outside the box."

Critical thinking involves a systematic evaluation of information, the analysis that accompanies the doing of social work practice. Critical examination processes place information in cultural, social, and political contexts. Social workers and clients reflect on the information they've gathered, apply theories of human behavior and knowledge about human variability to achieve a diversity-sensitive appraisal of

client functioning, estimate the capabilities of various environmental resources to respond to clients' needs, and consider various courses of action. Webb (2000) states that "the power behind discourse focuses on the orders of discourse, as dimensions of social institutions, structures or societies, and the way these are shaped and constructed by power relations" (¶13).

Baines (2000) emphasizes that practitioners should assume that race, class, and gender are organizing elements in every social work interaction and require attention in the processes of analysis and planning:

> We need to start from the premise that hierarchically raced, gendered and classed relations impact on every social work interaction. There is no way to diminish their presence in our everyday lives. Instead we need to work in tandem with our clients to understand how these forces organize the structures of emotion, culture, economics and politics in our ordinary lives and to intervene in ways that fundamentally reorder the relations of inequality that flow from these unjust structures. This includes analysis of the way that larger social structures impact on the resources and mandates that are available to us in our worksites, as well as the kinds of opportunities, expectations and choices that our clients have available to them (pp. 23–24).

Key questions guide a critical consideration of a client's situation and a proposed plan of action. What is the client's felt experience? In what physical and cultural environments does the client's situation occur? What social and political structures affect a client's experience with the situation? What resources and strengths do clients possess to address the situation? What resources do social workers bring? What gaps exist in meeting client goals? What changes in policy may contribute to achieving the client's solution? Critical thinking provides the necessary data and direction for planning future courses of personal and political action.

changes as beneficial for clients, ethical social workers recognize the client's privilege to select goals. Social justice cannot be achieved at the expense of people who are oppressed. Consider the example of the worker who wants to change the state's policy on distributing public assistance, knowing that it will help a specific client who is a single mother receiving welfare benefits. To set this objective, the client needs to understand clearly the implications of this macrolevel approach for her own situation to determine whether she wants to address her individual goals in this way. The product and process of this strategy must be something that this client truly believes is "new, improved, or enhanced" in her own life. Ethical social workers do not use a client as a springboard to larger issues that are of more concern to them than to the client.

Workers also consider whether clients can achieve their objectives without infringing on the rights of others or without coercing change in nonconsenting players. From a generalist perspective, implementing change activities usually involves others in addition to the client system. Even if people are not directly involved in the work, changes in the client system will likely affect others around the client. Social workers maintain professional ethics when they evaluate the potential impact of achieving the client system's objectives on the rights of the client and the rights of others.

CONSTRUCTING ACTION PLANS

Understanding goals and objectives prepares social workers to develop action plans. Designing action plans with clients at any system level is a deliberate and careful process involving sequential steps. For example, Figure 11.1 illustrates this process in planning with organizations. Plans build on the assessment information gathered and outline procedures for accomplishing purposes. To develop a relevant and workable plan of action, workers and clients complete the following steps.

1. Set positive and clear outcome goals that fit what clients want and that draw on assessment information
2. Write concrete and achievable objectives
3. Prioritize objectives
4. Generate possible intervention strategies using the broad perspective of generalist practice
5. Specify tasks, responsibilities, and actions necessary to meet objectives
6. Determine intervals and methods to review and modify the plan

Crystallizing Outcome Goals

As the beginning step in constructing action plans, workers and clients clarify goals. They consider what they have learned about clients' situations and capabilities during the assessment process in preparation for framing clear goals. Workers ensure that clients formulate goals in positive terms, stating what clients want and will be doing rather than what they don't want or will be avoiding.

Reorienting problems to outcomes
Social workers often help clients reorient their self-described problems into a vision of a desired outcome or solution. In other words, workers help turn clients around from looking back at their problems to facing forward and describing what their lives will be like when they have reached the solution.

Process	Answers	Questions
ORGANIZATIONAL ANALYSIS	Who we are	• What is our place in the organization? • What is our role in the organization?
STATING PURPOSE	What we do	• What is our mission? • What are our stated objectives?
STRATEGIC DIRECTION	What we ought to be	• Are we all that we want to be? • Are we all that we could be?
STRATEGIC PLANNING	What we need to do	• What short-term and long-range strategies do we want to accomplish? • What are our priorities?
TAKING ACTION	Who does what and when	• When do tasks/activities need to be done? • Who takes responsibility for implementing tasks?
EVALUATING SUCCESS	How effective our plan is	• Are our methods effective? • Did we achieve our expected outcomes?

Figure 11.1   Organizational Process Planning

Strategic planning exemplifies one planning process used with organizational clients. This type of planning is a systematic and interactive process used to realize long-term organizational objectives through the construction of short-term action plans. The process involves broad-base participation to examine organizational potential, set goals and priorities, and create a detailed plan of action for implementing the organization's vision for the future.

From *Visioning the Future: Organizational Strategic Planning by* B. L. DuBois (April, 1993). Used with permission of the author.

Policy Practice

Generalist social workers develop strategies that may include interventions at many system levels including the level of social policy. What questions should be considered when determining whether a social policy should be targeted for intervention in a specific client situation?

Social workers guide clients to state goals "in a linguistically positive form, that is in terms of what the client will be doing or thinking, rather than what they will not be doing or thinking" (Walter & Peller, 1992, p. 53).

Stated in positive language, goals reflect aims to enhance or strengthen, not to remediate or reduce. For example, an individual experiencing stress about a recent job loss may state a goal of obtaining other employment. Likewise, a family that seeks counseling because of concern about the constant yelling and bickering among family members may state a goal of finding new ways to resolve differences. Neighborhood residents distressed about gang activity may state the broad goal of creating a safe neighborhood. In each example, the worker helps the client system transform what has been into what will be.

Consider the example of Nate Hardy, a social worker with the Northside Development Association. Nate's primary client system is the Northside community itself. He works with various formal and informal groups in the community to meet his agency's mission of improving the quality of life in Northside. In the process of setting positive goals with a neighborhood group, Nate Hardy does two things. He strives for concreteness to describe the current concerns of the neighborhood residents and he works to reorient residents to consider the future.

To understand concerns concretely, Nate uses responding skills:

▶ When a resident says "I'm unhappy," Nate may respond by inquiring "With whom?" or "About what?"
▶ When another member of the neighborhood group says they are "falling apart," Nate can respond with, "What are you noticing that leads you to this conclusion?"
▶ When a neighborhood leader says things can't go on this way, Nate can ask, "What things? In what way?"

As the residents answer Nate's questions each will begin to offer a clearer view of what they are seeking. But these concrete views of the present are likely to be replete with visions of what is wrong or what should stop. Nate is likely to learn:

▶ The first resident wants others to stop ignoring his opinion.
▶ The second resident of the neighborhood group wants group members to stop arguing among themselves.
▶ The indigenous leader hopes to change the way the city budgets its money.

Each of these assertions begins to hint at goals, but they all stop short of defining them concretely and positively. On the contrary, each goal indicates what clients want to get rid of, not specifically what they would like to have happen instead. In other words, these tentative goals focus on negative outcomes—what needs to change, rather than positive ones—what will occur instead. Social workers encourage clients to positively frame their desired outcomes by describing what will be happening rather than what will be missing.

In order to set positive directions, Nate responds to each resident's negatively expressed goal to convert it to a positive statement by saying:

▶ So, if people stop ignoring you, how would you like them to respond instead? What will they be doing?
▶ You would like the group to stop arguing. Can you describe for me how it will be when group members handle their disagreements differently?
▶ What differences in the way the city allocates funds would you like to see?

Nate's continued prodding to consider the future leads each resident to visualize a positive outcome:

▶ I want this group to include my ideas in their neighborhood development plan.
▶ I want the group to negotiate decisions cooperatively.
▶ I would like to see the city adopt new procedures that access citizen's views at each step of the budgeting process.

Notice how Nate helps these residents construct visual descriptions of what they would like in their futures. Walter and Peller (1992) call this process "movie making." Many other contributors agree that positive visions of goals are most effective.

Building on positive momentum

Not all client systems who seek social work services experience situations characterized as problematic. Many others, after a strength-oriented assessment process, may see their situations in a new light. In these cases, goals set in planning may be to encourage something to occur more often or to stabilize an already improving situation. For instance, a newly formed stepfamily may discover that their increased expression of negative feelings is actually a good sign. It indicates that the family is becoming closer, blending together in a more intimate way. They may set goals to learn more about common transitions in stepfamilies in order to anticipate and resolve challenges likely to arise as the new family blends two distinct lifestyles and traditions into one.

Setting positive directions for goals is a straightforward affair when clients are optimistic and recognize existing strengths or recent improvements.

> ◗ When a woman says "Things have gotten better since I called you," the worker responds to identify what is working by asking, "What have you noticed that is better?"
> ◗ When a couple agrees they "feel hopeful," the worker asks for more details with the question, "What is happening that contributes to this feeling?"
> ◗ When the liaison from the agency says "We want to continue to make consensus decisions," the worker reflects and highlights the goal by saying, "I hear you saying that I am here to help you stabilize your abilities to make consensus decisions."

In each of these examples, the worker continues to clarify what works to set definitive goals that maintain and strengthen current productive functioning.

Sorting out possibilities

Translating problems into positive goals for the future is only one part of an effective goal-setting process. To ensure coherent goals, social workers also help clarify information by ordering it logically. Because too many goals may confuse the direction of the work, social workers assist clients in articulating what is most important to them. Helpful ways for social workers to organize information include two seemingly opposite skills. The first involves arranging complex and integrated information into separate compartments. The second involves grouping similar information around common themes.

Creating discrete units

Fant and Ross (1983) describe the analytic technique of "breaking it down." This technique of creating discrete units means taking issues that are complex and separating them into component parts to consider them one piece at a time. In contrast to the approach of clustering, which works to resolve several related issues at once, partializing takes seemingly insurmountable challenges and breaks them down into achievable units. Partializing relieves pressure on client systems and sets the stage for deciding which first step is likely to have the greatest impact on subsequent successes.

Grouping by similarity

In contrast, social workers can look for similarities among various issues. By finding the threads that run through several issues, social workers ascertain themes that have multiple ramifications. Clustering these issues leads to setting selective and efficient goals, the achievement of which can have multiple benefits. A mother's overprotectiveness, a son's anxious withdrawal, and a father's depression may all spring from the threat of the surrounding neighborhood. Identifying this central theme may lead to neighborhood change strategies or the family's move to a new location. Addressing this common issue brings relief to each of the family's members. Organizing issues coherently facilitates the planning process.

Writing Effective Objectives

Writing effective objectives is the heart of a good case plan. Well-formed objectives embody the realistic hopes of what clients will accomplish. Good objectives are rooted in concrete information about what clients need and the strengths and resources with which they have to work. Outcome objectives clearly lay out "who will achieve what when." They function as guides and give us markers to indicate if we are getting somewhere or if we need to reevaluate what we are doing and try another way.

Measurable objectives include a number of components. According to Sheafor and Horejsi (2006), a good intervention objective answers a five-part question:

- Who . . .
- will do what . . .
- to what extent . . .
- under what condition . . .
- by when?

This simple formula provides a useful tool for conceptualizing objectives. Applying it results in objectives that are specific, achievable, and measurable. Consider the following examples of objectives:

- Denise will receive a passing grade in math by the end of the semester
- Fernando will secure a teaching job within the next month
- The Patterson family will resolve each disagreement that arises in the next week by using the *stop, listen, and compliment* approach
- Each administrative staff member of Neighbors United will access a community action grant within the next fiscal year
- The task group will successfully persuade the city council to implement gang prevention activities within 3 months

Notice how each objective offers complete information, yet does so simply and clearly. To ensure that they are writing objectives in a meaningful way, workers can evaluate each objective by using the following criteria:

1. Is it active? Does it say what someone will achieve?
2. Does it specify one discrete accomplishment rather than many?
3. Does it include a time frame for completion?
4. Can you observe, measure, and evaluate it?
5. Do the social worker, client, and other participants understand it and what their particular part of it is?
6. Is it easy enough to accomplish yet significant enough to make it worth the effort?
7. Are both client and worker comfortable with it?
8. Does it fit with agency practices and social work ethics? (Sheafor & Horejsi, 2003)

Clearly written objectives lead clients directly to the goals they seek.

Determining measures

The true test of whether an objective is a concrete enough outcome to guide actions is whether the partners can measure its achievement. Realistically, if clients and workers are to know that they have been successful, they must be able to identify concretely achievement criteria for each objective in the action plan.

For example, consider the efforts of the Child Welfare Division of Northside Prevention Services. The Division has set an objective to increase child safety within the community during the next year. Measurable criteria for achieving this objective include:

- The reported incidence of child abuse will decrease by 25 percent over the same time period from last year
- Fifty percent of residents responding to a random telephone survey will indicate they would report child abuse if they suspect it
- The Public Health Department will report a 50 percent reduction in child injuries from poisoning and household accidents in the 3 months after the home-safety campaign

Determining ways to measure the attainment of objectives focuses the efforts of all involved in implementing the plan.

Prioritizing Objectives

After articulating objectives, clients and social workers examine them to establish priorities. This process assigns preference to certain objectives in light of critical needs and resource availability. Clearly, protecting a client's safety, relieving distress, and meeting basic human needs are always priority actions. But, beyond addressing these immediate needs, setting priorities poses a number of value decisions. Social workers and clients develop priorities by considering motivational factors, the likelihood of success, and the work that might have the greatest or most widespread effect. Logical sequencing may be inherent in the objectives themselves, since some things have a natural order. Questions that may help clients rank priorities include:

- Which objectives are most motivating to the client?
- Which will most likely lead to success?
- Which issues are most pressing?
- What does the client want to do first?
- Is there a logical order in which to proceed?
- Is anyone at risk?
- Are priority actions necessary?

Clients have privileges to define the priorities. Social workers have responsibilities to identify risks and take necessary actions to ensure the safety of clients and others.

Screening Generalist Intervention Strategies

Those who clearly recognize the voice of their own conscience usually recognize also the voice of justice

—Alexander Solzhenitsyn

Generalist social workers think broadly. Even though workers encourage clients to focus narrowly on concrete outcomes, they broaden clients' perspectives to recognize multiple strategies to achieve these goals and objectives. Systemically oriented social workers acknowledge and act on the principle that changes in one part of the system create changes in other parts of the system. This means that workers and clients can aim anywhere in their related ecosystems—inside or outside of the social work relationship system—to create changes in the direction of desired outcomes.

Considering multiple system levels as targets for change adds the generalist perspective to the planning process. During assessment, workers and clients trace the transactional nature of issues. As a result, they discover numerous locations toward which to direct their efforts, specifically, toward client systems, related environmental systems, or the transactions between systems. Interventions at any level may produce the desired change. Synchronizing actions at many system levels, sequentially or in concert, may have the greatest impact.

Relating outcomes to locations for change

Deciding on goals and objectives and locating places to direct attempts at change are companion processes. Considering what you want to accomplish has implications for where you need to work. Considering the places to which you have access to work has implications for the kinds of activities that are possible. Once clients articulate the outcomes they desire, planning how to reach those goals can begin in either place. In other words, workers and clients consider two general questions: What resource systems are available and how might they contribute to reaching the goal? Or, conversely, what are the steps to take and what locations are possible for achieving those steps? Each question starts from a different place but ends up with a realistic plan.

Monkman (1991) presents a framework of broad outcome categories for both persons and their environments, which illustrates the relationship between outcomes desired and locations for attempting changes. Each outcome category correlates with a specific system level or possible target for change.

Outcomes for Persons

Survival Outcomes	Obtaining and using resources defined as basic necessities for life activities
Affiliation outcomes	Forming close personal relationships or support systems
Growth and achievement	Expanding contributions to one's self and others
Information and skills	Increasing knowledge to acquire proficiency to deal effectively with life situations

Environmental Outcomes

Informal resources	Accessing extended kin and friendship networks for support, affection, advice, and services
Formal resources	Accessing services from membership organizations and associations
Societal resources	Accessing resources found in social institutions
Expectations	Seeking redefinition of normative behavior and changing role expectations by persons or institutions in the social environment
Laws, policies, customs, and rules	Seeking change by governing and legislative bodies and in administrative rules

The particular goals that clients seek lead workers and clients around the ecosystem to gather resources, forge new connections, or make necessary changes. Since clients' problems do not arise in isolation of their situations, solutions also are contextually based. As clients focus in on the objectives necessary to achieve their goals, the places they must direct their efforts become more obvious. For example, a teenage girl who wants to improve her academic performance may choose strategies that lead her to school to learn what teachers want from her, to her family to negotiate a quiet space and time away from chores in which to complete homework, to her social group to locate a study partner, and to her own self to increase her persistence in completing tasks. Each one of these systems influences her current functioning and can contribute to her goal of improved academic performance. The goals and objectives that clients set lead logically to the locations to consider for solutions.

Choosing targets for change

For each client system, there are four general locations to consider as targets for change. These areas include

- The client system
- Subsystems of the client system
- Environmental systems in the context of the client
- Transactional systems or the connections between clients and their environments

A change in any one of these areas of functioning may result in the achievement of clients' goals. Generalist social workers and their clients frequently use a multifaceted strategy by selecting and combining many targets for change into a unified approach.

Reconsider the example of Nate Hardy and his client system, the Northside community. In open forums, the community has set an objective to increase the availability of low-cost housing. Now, in beginning to formulate strategies, Nate and interested community members are scanning the resource systems of the neighborhood to determine where to direct their efforts at change. To facilitate this effort, Nate charts out the following ideas and locations for change to present for the citizens' review:

Client System

- Create a community newsletter which lists and compares costs of available rentals to encourage competition and lower rents
- Establish an annual festival to celebrate the history of the neighborhood and its current cultural diversity as a way to increase cohesion and affiliation among residents

Subsystems

- Organize a new group of community members with home-building and repair skills to volunteer to fix up currently uninhabited homes
- Initiate a program with the Northside Vocational High School to remodel abandoned homes as educational projects and sell them at cost to neighborhood residents

Environmental Systems

- Modify the local banking practices of lending only for new construction projects
- Change city ordinances which limit the number of "unrelated" persons in the same household to allow friends to live together and reduce housing costs through sharing

Box 11.2 Planning in Aging Services: A Policy–Practice Connection

In 2006, about 37 million people in the United States were 65 years of age or older USHHS-AoA, 2007). Projections indicate that the number of people over 65 in the United States in 2050 will expand to 81 million, or nineteen percent of the population (Passel & Cohen, 2008). In 2020, the number of those older than 85 will likely increase to 7.3 million Furthermore, the number of centenarians (people 100 years of age and older) has nearly doubled in the last decade. The population group over 65 is also becoming more diverse. The percentage of older adults described as members of minority population groups is expected to rise from 17.6 percent in 2003 to 26.4 percent in 2030 (Greenberg, 2003). Demographers anticipate the fastest rate of growth among Hispanic Americans resulting in a projected 342 percent increase in the numbers of Hispanic Americans older than 65 by 2030. This dramatic increase in the number of people who are 65 years of age and older focuses social work attention on developing policies that will accommodate the needs of older Americans (Bronstein & Admiraal, 2005; Freeman, 2005; Marshall & Altpeter, 2005; Wang, 2004).

Developing and implementing effective social policies to meet the needs of those 65 and older is complicated by the diversity and complexity of issues they face. Older adults of any age can be vigorous and healthy, or they may be dependent and physically or cognitively frail. Most older adults live independently or with assistance in the community, but some require the supports offered in specialized care settings. Although the rate of poverty among people older than 65 is lower than that of the general population, people in this age group tend to live on fixed incomes, challenged to meet rising costs in health care, energy, housing, and long-term care. More significantly, more than 80 percent of those whose annual income places them in the lowest quartile depend totally on Social Security.

Policy change is a critical component of addressing the needs of older Americans. Among the policy issues specifically identified by the NASW (1999c) are

▶ The urgency of developing and funding a coherent system of a long-term continuum of care that encompasses therapeutic, rehabilitative, and supportive goals in a variety of community and institutional settings

▶ The continued need for social supports, including but not limited to social services, housing, and nutrition to maintain older people in their homes and communities

▶ Inequalities in the availability of funding and provision of health, substance abuse, and social services the underutilization of older adults as a resource to society

▶ The need to educate the public, professionals, and service providers on issues surrounding aging

▶ Recognition of the mutuality of support now enjoyed by the multigenerational family and the need to provide supports that enhance these interrelationships

▶ Recognition of the cultural heterogeneity among the elderly population and the need to provide culturally sensitive and multilingual services

▶ Expand the work force with social workers trained to meet the needs of the aging population. (p. 324)

The dramatic changes in the numbers and proportion of people age 65 have profound implications for the infrastructures of social policy that support the full range of services for older adults. Members of the National Association of Social Workers, in their roles as policy makers, can give legislative testimony about the needs of an aging population and participate in drafting and implementing social policies that are responsive to the issues faced by persons in this cohort group.

Transactional Systems

▶ Organize a tenant's rights group to attend city council meetings and advocate for new rent control ordinances
▶ Obtain a federal grant to build scattered subsidized housing units throughout the neighborhood

All the options Nate lists are strategies involving different parts of the Northside community and its environment. Any one strategy works toward the goal of increasing available low-cost housing in the neighborhood. Choosing a combination of these approaches offers even greater possibilities for achieving a broad-based impact.

All client systems have component parts and environments that offer possible locations for change. Consider a family system. A worker could facilitate changes in the ways the family makes decisions. Another possible change could be in how the parents relate which, in turn, would affect the rest of the family. How much extended family support the family uses, how parents and children relate to jobs and school, how society views this family in terms of culture, race, socioeconomic status, and lifestyle—all contribute to what is happening with this family, and all also hold potential for how this family might change. When considering the places to intervene, clients and social workers look broadly to consider changes at many system levels.

Choosing Effective Strategies

To determine what strategies to implement requires a careful organization of available information and options. Workers can use many methods to generate options. Frequently, workers compile written lists with clients to ensure that they comprehensively consider everything that is necessary. Some recordkeeping procedures require such lists of identified strengths, needs, and possibilities for change.

Brainstorming

A helpful method to use in considering strategies is *brainstorming,* which generates discussion among many individuals to frame multiple potential solutions. In brainstorming, workers and clients list as many ideas as they can imagine without any evaluation of which would be best. The free-flowing nature of this process unleashes creativity and cooperation. This strategy is especially useful in planning with multiperson client systems because it encourages all to participate in the planning process with no fear that their ideas will be criticized.

Matching resources and needs

Matching resources available to client needs is another effective approach for developing intervention strategies. For example, Cowger and Snively (2002) recommend charting information to include client system strengths and needs on one side and environmental system resources and obstacles on the other. In this way, the partners delineate the strengths and resources available with respect to the challenges presented. Note how this charting emphasizes the transactional nature of client issues, highlighting possible strategies in the environment as well as those targeting changes in the client system itself.

Cowger and Snively's (2002) framework illustrates how the organizational processes chosen influence the planning that follows. This charting method focuses on both clients and environments and builds on strengths in the process. Consider the differences in the plan that would result from a procedure focusing only on a client's failures or inadequacies. How the partners organize the information makes a difference. Social workers help clients organize information in ways that motivate, encourage, and predict success. The questions to ask when matching challenges with resources include:

> ▶ What strengths and abilities does the client demonstrate in one area of functioning that might transfer to dealing with the challenge?

‣ What untapped resources are present in the environment to meet the client's defined needs?

‣ What does the client need that the worker can provide directly or access for the client?

‣ What resources need to be expanded or developed?

Answering all these questions orients workers and clients to the resources they currently have to meet objectives and what other resources might be necessary. Social workers also evaluate the usefulness of potential social service resources to choose effective strategies (see Table 11.1).

Emphasizing client strengths

The most empowering plans build on client strengths. To discover strength-oriented options, workers and clients ask themselves two questions:

‣ What are clients doing right that they should continue to do? In other words, what should they reinforce and strengthen?

‣ What strengths and resources of clients or their social and physical environments apply to the current situation?

Enhancing existing strengths and matching resources to needs are steps toward building action plans that clients can approach with feelings of confidence and expectations of success.

Table 11.1	Schema for Assessing Resources
Criteria	Description
Relevance	Does the resource offer services that are congruent with the client system's identified needs?
	Will the resource meet the client system's goals?
Availability	Will the resource be available when the client system requires it?
	Is there a waiting list?
	Do certain circumstances qualify for a quick response?
Accessibility	Is the office located on convenient travel routes?
	Does the resource offer services in the client's language? Sign language?
	Are the facilities accessible to those with disabilities?
Eligibility	What are the guidelines for receiving this service? Are there income, location, age, or other qualifiers?
Applications	Is there a formal application process? Who needs to fill out what form? What time frame is imposed on the application process? Are supporting documents required?
Fee	Is there a sliding fee scale?
	If fees are involved, has the client system been informed of the fee schedule?
	Will the client realistically be able to pay for the service? Under what circumstances can the fee be waived?
Feasibility	Considering all of the aforementioned factors, is this a viable resource?

Incorporating resources of social workers

Good action plans also anticipate what workers can bring to the process. What do workers know? What can workers do? To what resources do workers have connections? Some needs that clients bring may require these types of resources for successful resolutions, but be cautious here. Empowering social workers recognize the need to hold their own resources in check so as not to encourage dependency on the part of clients. Workers do not develop strategies that place themselves in central roles and leave the clients as passive observers. The best strategies place clients in charge and use workers' resources and skills as supplemental. Clients need as many opportunities as possible to experience their own effectiveness and to affirm their expertise.

Weighing costs and benefits

Not all available strategies are equal. It is likely that no perfect solution exists; there are pros and cons to each possibility. Before composing definitive objectives, workers and clients weigh the costs and benefits of each proposed strategy. Pertinent questions include:

- Is there an advantage to using one resource rather than another?
- What are the costs of each approach in terms of time and money?
- Are there possible hidden costs?
- Are some strategies easier to implement than others?
- What are the potential risks or consequences?
- Do certain combinations work better than others?
- Is there a logical order for proceeding? Should one approach be implemented first and another held back and used only if necessary?
- Should accessing multiple resources be gradual or simultaneous?
- Do clients think that certain strategies will work better for them than others?
- Which options are best based on the worker's practice experience?
- Does practice evaluation research offer suggestions about approaches?

The answers to these questions lead clients and workers to choose strategies that have the greatest likelihood of success.

Delineating Tasks and Responsibilities

Some strategies are so simple and direct that the way to achieve them may be obvious. At other times, additional specification is necessary so that all people involved know their roles and responsibilities in completing the task. Consider the example of a task group on gang prevention. To achieve their objective of influencing the city council to adopt their recommendations, the task group needs to complete more detailed planning. Tasks and responsibilities assigned may include: One member will call the city clerk to reserve a place on the council meeting's agenda. Another member will arrive at the meeting early to save a block of chairs so that task group members can sit together and be seen as a cohesive political unit. Someone will call the local newspaper to guarantee news coverage. The social worker will write a news release incorporating the group's recommendations to distribute to the representatives of the media. Delineating these specific roles and responsibilities ensures a coordinated effort in implementing the objective.

Setting Reviews and Evaluations

Effectively written objectives define intervals for reviewing progress. Because they specify time frames, workers and clients naturally will stop to review how they are doing at those times. Each review offers workers and clients an opportunity to proceed as planned or to make modifications.

Some social delivery systems structure intervals for review in their program procedures. For example, school social workers are very familiar with the Individual Education Plan (IEP), which is an annually updated plan outlining the program tailored for a student with special educational needs. To accommodate unanticipated events, rapid improvements, or changing needs, each IEP also offers opportunities to reconvene the planning body if necessary. Good planning requires periodic reviews and flexibility to modify plans as necessary.

CONTRACTING

The concept of contract underlies all phases of the social work process. Simply, a contract specifies the terms of service to which the client and social worker agree. Although formal contracts usually refer to the explicit agreements that social workers and clients forge to operationalize action plans, an implied contract secures the social worker–client relationship from the initial contact to the last. Contractual agreements vary from "assumed" to explicit. Clients and workers may either operate under an informal understanding or a more formal, written contract. The formality of the contract varies depending on the preferences of the worker, the client, and agency policy.

Clarity is essential for a contract's success. Workers ensure that all parties involved in the contract clearly understand what they are agreeing to do and hoping to achieve. The most effective contracts have flexibility, incorporate the views of clients, and concretely define the next step.

The Evolving Contract

Engage Assess
Intervene Evaluate

In theory the phases of engagement, assessment, intervention, and evaluation are distinct, but in practice they often overlap and occur simultaneously. How does the planning process incorporate each of these four phases of practice?

Describing the contract between social workers and clients as evolutionary makes sense in terms of the developmental nature of the social work process. The social work contract evolves through phases of agreeing to work together to agreeing to assess the situation to agreeing to the plan for change. Contracts also evolve in the context of work with groups. Members originally contract with themselves and the worker for their own individual purposes, but they change this contract to incorporate more group-centered content as they begin to function as part of the group. What members are working on, how they view themselves, and what seems possible changes as the work continues.

The contract changes as the professional relationship and focus of the work progresses over time (Table 11.2). Initially, workers and clients agree to meet and form a working alliance—the *contract for the relationship.* The initial dialogue leads to clarity about purpose and defines a direction for the partners to explore the situation further—the *contract for assessment.* Discovering available resources leads to an explicit plan to accomplish the concrete goals defined—the *contract for change.* When social workers and clients achieve their desired outcomes, they agree to dissolve the relationship—the *contract for resolution.* At each point of contracting and recontracting for their work together, social workers and clients have opportunities to redefine their collaboration.

Table 11.2	**The Evolving Contract**	
Phase	Type of Contract	Description
Dialogue Phase	Contract for Relationship	Agreement to form a working partnership to define direction
	Contract for Assessment	Agreement to further explore the situation and assess the resources available
Discovery Phase	Contract for Change	Agreement to a plan of action to activate and expand resources and opportunities
Development Phase	Contract for Resolution	Agreement to conclude the client–social worker relationship

Contracting for change

When social workers and clients agree to a comprehensive plan of action, this constitutes a contract for change. Contracting for change details the agreement between the client and social worker as to the roles and responsibilities with respect to such features as goals, objectives, strategies and activities, and methods and timing of evaluation. Creating an action plan clearly lays out the work that a client system and social worker will do. Forging an agreement to proceed with the plan is a contract for change. There is evidence that social work contracts for change, especially those that state objectives explicitly, enhance practice effectiveness. Contracts also give practitioners measurable criteria on which to base their evaluations of success.

Contracting as an Empowering Process

Contracting with clients has benefits beyond a simple clarification of current status and future direction. Contracts emphasize client participation, facilitate communication, improve commitment, foster a sense of autonomy and self-determination, and provide a framework for reflecting on outcomes. Contracting "reduces some of the power discrepancy between client and worker at a time when the client is under stress and vulnerable to manipulation" (Germain & Gitterman, 1980, p. 53).

Each time that social workers and clients renegotiate their working agreement, clients experience their power in the relationship. They have an opportunity to control what happens next. Renegotiating the contract also explicitly gives clients permission to change the direction of their work. It can rebalance the power when a social worker's expertise has encouraged the client to settle into a dependent pattern in their relationship. Explicitly discussing the evolving contract continues to share power with clients over the course of the relationship.

LOOKING FORWARD

Goal-directed planning focuses on outcomes. The ultimate measure of success is goal achievement. Some people question whether this emphasis on goals and end points represents a culturally biased view. Are concreteness and goal achievement Western precepts that ignore significant intangibles, such as relationship and process variables? Can purposeful change be guided by a process vision of relating the way you want to relate and approaching challenges in a deliberately ethical and proactive way?

Framing solutions means planning how client systems and workers intend to reach their goals. Planning accomplishes important tasks. It clarifies what the client is seeking, considers what aspects of the client system's functioning and context hold possibilities for solutions, and determines strategies necessary to succeed. The culmination of the planning process is a concrete action plan. Mutual planning produces a synergistic solution that reflects the expertise of both clients and workers. In the upcoming development phase, clients and workers implement the plan, evaluate its effectiveness, and wrap up their work together in a way that maintains progress.

Log onto **www.mysocialworklab.com** and select the **Interactive Skill Module** videos from the left-hand menu. Answer the questions below. (*If you did not receive an access code to* **MySocialWorkLab** *with this text and wish to purchase access online, please visit* www.mysocialworklab.com.)

1. **Watch pages 19, 20, and 24 of the school social work module** as worker Terry and client Michelle discuss plans to resolve Michelle's difficulties. Crystallize these ideas into an action plan by writing out the goal, objectives, and action steps to achieve desired results.

2. Read the previous question that asks you to write an action plan for school social work client Michelle. To measure the impact of your work, create an evaluation design that fits your plan. What data will you collect to evaluate your achievement?

PRACTICE TEST

1. A general statement about what a client hopes to accomplish is a _____,
   a. goal
   b. objective
   c. action plan
   d. vision statement

2. Social worker Chandell Williams structures success to maximize motivation and minimize failure and disillusionment by constructing objectives that are _____.
   a. specific and open-ended
   b. theoretical and speculative
   c. realistic and attainable
   d. global and abstract

3. Chandell develops effective objectives by ensuring that the objectives specifically state the extent and frequency of the events or behaviors. In other words, the objectives Chandell develops are _____.
   a. measurable
   b. qualitative
   c. closed-ended
   d. evaluative

Human Behavior

4. Analyzing the impact of larger social structures on the opportunities, expectations, and choices available to clients is one facet of _____.
   a. qualitative thinking
   b. ecosystemic analysis
   c. problem solving
   d. critical thinking

Professional Identity

5. Kendra's supervisor requested her to lead organizational planning process at Northside Aging Services, something she has never done. As a social work professional, she should tell her supervisor _____.
   a. I am a case manager, so that's not in my job description.
   b. I will need training on strategic planning before I begin.
   c. I will muddle my way through it.
   d. I don't think we need a strategic plan.

6. Which of the following objectives is LEAST likely to meet the criteria of a well-formulated objective?
   a. Ned will complete the independent study course within 6 weeks.
   b. Members of the coalition will present the proposal to their respective agency administrators before the next meeting of the coalition.
   c. Jordan will stop ignoring Carter.
   d. The Torres family will resolve each disagreement that occurs in the next week by using the stop, listen, and compliment approach.

Policy Practice

7. Working with the Northside Community Development group, Nate Hardy plans to design additional elder-friendly niches. One objective is to organize a group of older adults to attend city council meetings to advocate for safe walking paths. Which system is the target for change?
   a. client system
   b. subsystem
   c. environmental system
   d. transactional system

8. The type of contract in which parties agree to a plan of action is called a contract for _____.
   a. relationship
   b. assessment
   c. change
   d. resolution

9. Which of the following statements about goals and objectives is TRUE?
   a. Setting many diverse goals helps to broaden a client's options.
   b. Objectives are most effective when they focus on what clients will do rather than on things that clients won't do.
   c. Involuntary clients should not be consulted about goals to be included in an action plan.
   d. When members of a group disagree on goals and planning, workers should intervene to make the best decision considering the views of all group members.

Log onto **MySocialWorkLab** once you have completed the Practice Test above to take your Chapter Exam and demonstrate your knowledge of this material.

Answers

1) a 2) c 3) a 4) b 5) c 6) c 7) d 8) c 9) b

12

Activating Resources

CONNECTING CORE COMPETENCIES *in this chapter*

| Professional Identity | Ethical Practice | **Critical Thinking** | Diversity in Practice | **Human Rights & Justice** | Research Based Practice | **Human Behavior** | Policy Practice | **Practice Contexts** | Engage Assess Intervene Evaluate |

Donna Lester is the mother of 8-year-old twin boys whom the Child Protective Unit at the State Department of Social Services recently determined were beyond Donna's control. Donna herself initiated the chain reaction that led to the removal of her children by asking the local police department for help. The police then called in the Child Protective Unit. Donna's boys were placed in foster care, activating Jon Allen's role as a Case Advocate in the Foster Care Program at Northside Family Services.

Jon understands why some people see Donna as having little potential, as her challenges are considerable. Her moderate level of mental retardation, desperate financial situation, and recent separation from an abusive and alcoholic boyfriend on whom she still periodically depends for assistance could label Donna as "chronic" or "multiproblem." But Jon's strengths-oriented assessment has revealed Donna to be "multitalented" as well. Donna is good at recognizing her need for help. The call to the police is clear evidence of that. She succeeded in getting her boyfriend to move out and is no longer subsidizing his alcoholism, something she learned through her participation with Al-Anon. Donna is also extremely nurturing to her children, emotionally expressive, and loving. Besides, she's an excellent cook with a good sense of nutrition. Donna's needs are significant, but she is not without resources.

Donna is definite about her goal of having her sons return home. With this goal in mind, Jon and Donna develop a plan of action that targets three key objectives: Donna sets objectives to use effective and positive parenting methods, to stabilize her financial situation through public assistance and part-time employment, and to increase her abilities to function independent of her abusive boyfriend. These concrete objectives frame the work ahead.

Jon meets with Donna twice a week. At one meeting, Jon spends time with Donna alone to review her situation, discuss her options, encourage her progress, and plan activities for the week—small steps toward the outcomes she desires. He finds himself working directly to boost Donna's self-esteem, develop her sense of power, and maintain her motivation by listening to her story, highlighting her successes, congratulating her on progress, and designing readily achievable tasks.

During the second meeting each week, Jon monitors Donna's regular visit with the boys. Before visits, he and Donna collaborate to develop a plan for how she will handle the boys. During the visits, Jon sits back, creating space for Donna to test her parenting skills. Jon records his observations, particularly those parenting skills that he sees as effective so that he and Donna can review and discuss them after the visit. Once, Jon arranges for the visit to occur in the office so he can videotape the family's interaction. Watching the tape, Donna realizes how much of the time she is actually effective in handling her sons' behaviors.

Working with Donna alone is not enough. To increase productive transactions with others in her social environment, Jon works with Donna "to fill in her eco-map," as he and Donna name this activity. During assessment, they had drawn Donna's social and community support network as it existed. Now, during their meetings, they pull this eco-map out and target various connections to reinforce or change.

At Jon's suggestion, Donna meets with her public assistance worker to determine the extent to which her sons' foster care placement lowers her benefits and to find out when, after her sons return home, her benefits will increase. Donna obtains a copy of the rules describing how a part-time job will affect her assistance. In addition, Jon links Donna to the local community college's program for screening interests and skills to determine possible employment options. When the inventory reveals Donna's expertise in food preparation, Jon refers her to the State Employment Service where Donna locates a part-time job in the cafeteria of the local middle school—an opportunity that fits her skills and involves hours that will not require her to arrange for child care.

Jon also connects Donna to parenting classes at his own agency. When Donna's difficulty with reading interferes with her ability to keep up with the other parents in the class, Jon advocates within his agency to provide Donna with an individualized approach. He proposes to the agency's board of directors that they allocate funds to purchase videotapes on parenting skills. Jon's assertion that Donna has a right to access these educational services in a way that she can understand, as guaranteed under the American with Disabilities Act, strengthens his recommendation that the board approve the purchase.

Jon encourages Donna to maintain her attendance at Al-Anon meetings and participate in some of the family social events the program offers. He also coaches Donna on how to build on her work relationships at the school cafeteria to develop them into social relationships for her own enjoyment and to provide support in times of stress. This expanding social network gives Donna options other than her old boyfriend when she feels the need for friends or recreation.

Each of these activities contributes to Donna's successful achievement of her objectives. Jon's observations and suggestions about parenting, the newly acquired educational videotapes, and Donna's persistence in learning new parenting skills increase her effectiveness as a parent. Donna's meetings with public assistance workers and her new job stabilize her financial situation. Jon's nurturance, respect, and activities to build Donna's self-esteem along with Donna's newly developed network of friends increase her confidence to function independent of her previously abusive boyfriend. With these objectives accomplished, the goal of the boys' return home is within reach.

Jon's work with Donna activates her to develop her potential and attain her goals. To activate means to mobilize, energize, charge, stimulate, excite, arouse, start, trigger, and prompt. Notice the unifying thread of meaning in these words. Activating is a beginning, a "jump start," not a lifelong commitment. Activating resources means to take what is available within clients and their ecosystems and get it going. It does not mean to take care of, do for, drag to, control, fix, or treat. Both partners get things moving and keep things going in the direction of goals.

This chapter explores how social workers and clients intervene to activate resources to help clients reach their goals. It describes the processes and skills workers use to implement action plans in ways that respect, motivate, and empower clients. Specifically, this chapter

▸ Identifies generalist skills for activating resources within clients and their environments
▸ Details strategies for sustaining progress during the development phase
▸ Clarifies how workers recognize and enhance clients' experiences of power
▸ Delineates strategies for changing clients' perspectives and behaviors
▸ Explains key elements of effective resource management
▸ Describes educational activities for developing clients' knowledge and skills

By using these processes, a social worker can increase clients' experiences of power and efficient use of available resources.

APPLYING GENERALIST INTERVENTION SKILLS

This phase of development is when social workers and clients put their plans into action. Implementing plans requires generalist social workers to draw on an array of skills for working with both client systems and their environments. Workers use strategies to accentuate and develop client system strengths, experiment with changes in the ways clients do things, renegotiate the transactions of client systems with their environments, and modify environmental systems. These are mutual tasks in which clients and social workers play complementary roles.

Intervention Across System Levels

Generalist social workers, regardless of their practice setting, interweave generic practice skills with intervention skills specific to the level of client system. Because a client system may be an individual, couple, family, group, organization, neighborhood, or community, generalists must be adept at those skills that apply to the identified client system. In addition, regardless of the level of the client system, workers also intervene at other system levels on behalf of the current client. This chapter's opening example details how a worker collaborates directly with a client while also activating other resources in the client's environment to achieve the desired change. Generalist social work intervention involves work at multiple system levels.

Despite the diversity of human systems, certain social work practice skills have universal application. All clients, from individuals to communities, benefit from a social worker's interest, encouragement, and organized approach. Clients at all levels respond to an increased sense of power and new ways to look at their situations. All clients benefit from productive connections to resources, relevant information, and newly acquired skills. Generalist social workers can facilitate these benefits throughout the development phase as they carry out their roles associated with consultancy, resource management, and education. Throughout their work, practitioners use strategies for maintaining progress, developing power, changing perspectives, managing resources, and educating (Figure 12.1).

MAINTAINING PROGRESS IN THE ACTION PLAN

During the development phase, social workers consult with clients and others to keep moving as directly as possible toward goals. Workers maintain a positive, yet objective, stance on progress to monitor and facilitate the process of the work. To efficiently structure activities during this phase, practitioners draw on the plan that workers and clients have previously framed. To promote effective processes, workers intervene in ways to enhance the achievements of the client system and to maintain the client's motivation toward the goal.

Implementing Action Plans

Social workers keep the plan in the forefront of the development phase. The action plan prescribes what social workers and clients do when they are together and frames activities to accomplish between meetings. In those instances when the work gets somewhat off-track, social workers use the plan

Figure 12.1   Generalist Skills for Activating Resources

Maintaining Progress

- Implementing Action Plans: facilitating a productive, goal-seeking process; reviewing and updating plans as necessary
- Enhancing Interactions: encouraging participation; responding to clarify situations, refine goals, and locate resources; building alliances among participants
- Sustaining Motivation: validating client's views and feelings; providing nurturance; expressing optimism

Developing Power

- Promoting Leadership: asserting client privileges in the relationship; acknowledging leadership abilities
- Recognizing Choices: enhancing agency by recognizing existing options; locating areas of client's control
- Locating Genuine Options: expanding resource networks; overcoming oppressive conditions
- Magnifying Strengths: responding to highlight strengths; recognizing incremental steps

Changing Perspectives

- Offering Feedback: reflecting client actions; examining behavior with respect to goals
- Creating New Concepts: reframing; offering metaphors
- Reconstructing Narratives: externalizing; co-constructing; generating multiple interpretations
- Changing Behaviors: considering new ways to do things; experimenting with behavior change

Managing Resources

- Linking Clients with Resources: locating resources; maximizing client administration of resource network
- Client Advocacy: developing power within the service network; using professional influence on client's behalf
- Maximizing Clients' Rights: implementing a social justice agenda; ensuring clients' due process rights

Educating

- Teaching: modeling; role-playing; structuring educational experiences
- Sharing Information: sharing professional expertise; self-disclosing

---

to review progress and redefine directions. Social workers need not rigidly enforce previous agreements. Plans are flexible, yet they structure coordinated efforts for approaching challenges in goal-directed ways.

Collaborating on actions

The combination of in-meeting activities and between-meeting tasks keeps clients and workers actively moving toward goals. Each meeting provides direct opportunities to activate client resources. Social workers and clients generate new perspectives and review progress. Clients and workers use meetings to plan additional activities for each to implement. Between meetings, clients may experiment with new behaviors, observe the impact of change attempts, or connect to necessary resources in the environment. Social workers may investigate untapped community resources for their potential use, advocate with other systems, or consult with supervisors on a client's progress.

Over the course of time, as clients demonstrate their abilities to do more, social workers do less. As client systems become proficient in organizing and activating their own resources, workers modulate from being active interveners to becoming more reflective and encouraging facilitators. Enduring solutions are those clients discover within themselves and in the ways they manage their own worlds.

Enhancing Interactions

During the development phase, dialogue and discovery skills remain important. Clients continue to benefit from articulating thoughts and feelings, observing progress, and locating relevant strengths and resources. Workers strive to enhance clients' efforts by using their skills to maintain focus, encourage participation, and handle differences.

Maintaining focus

In the development phase, workers and clients already have agreed to a plan, complete with concrete objectives and definitive activities. With this information in mind, workers help clients "stay on course." For example, workers may say:

- I'm pleased to hear that your job is going well—I'm wondering if you had a chance to call your ex-wife like we talked about last week.
- I thought we were here to talk about your marriage and whether you wanted me to refer you to a marriage counselor. So far all we're talking about today is problems with the kids. Are you ready to talk about the referral or have you changed your mind?
- We certainly do have fun whenever this group gets together, and now we have some work to do. Who wants to report on their committee assignment first?

Notice how these practitioners encourage clients to talk about relevant issues and report on activities that are current. Social workers facilitate continuity by focusing conversations on the tasks at hand.

Workers also encourage clients to talk about one relevant issue in depth before moving on to another. Shifting from issue to issue often evades dealing intensively with feelings associated with a particular issue (Shulman, 1999). "Holding to focus sends the message to the client that the worker means to discuss the tougher feelings and concerns" (p. 173). When workers allow clients to skip around, they inadvertently conspire with clients to avoid troublesome issues. Clients may sense that workers are either uncomfortable or don't feel competent to handle what they need to discuss. Workers cannot force clients to talk about particular issues; nevertheless, workers should demonstrate that they can handle tough issues if clients choose to do so.

Larger systems multiply the difficulties that practitioners may experience in keeping the work on track. To focus many people at once, workers rely less on their interactional skills and more on structured processes. Examples include using written agendas, handouts, questionnaires, audiovisual materials, structured experiences, minutes of previous meetings, and mailings between meetings. Initiating more formal meeting procedures and using tangible materials can keep large groups focused on current issues.

Encouraging participation

Multiperson systems work best when they function in ways that allow all members to participate. Families, groups, and other larger systems activate more resources when each member feels free to contribute. This does not mean that every member must contribute equally to each interaction, but instead means that each member's ideas and expertise are considered in light of the issues and actions at hand (Toseland & Rivas, 2009). People need assurance that they have the right to their views, the privilege to express them, and the trust that others will listen and respect their ideas even when they disagree. In structural terms, members require some degree of power within the system's hierarchy and enough space to feel free to assert their opinions. Facilitative social workers interact directly with client systems to work toward this differentiated and respectful type of structure.

Social workers have many ways to ensure that all group members contribute. To coordinate conversational traffic, one might comment:

> ▶ Well, I've heard three opinions. Just two more to go. Who's next?

To ensure that group members hear each contribution, one might inquire:

> ▶ Could I ask you to tell me what you just heard Ryan say? Seems like you might have missed it.

To help members accept and appreciate divergent opinions, practitioners can point out the potential benefits of differences with comments such as:

> ▶ I really don't think that one of you has to be right and the other wrong. You're probably both right. You're two different people. You're bound to see things differently and that's okay; it gives us more to work with.

With each of these responses, workers encourage the participation of all group members.

Additionally, social workers can use more formal approaches. Situations such as conversations dominated by only one subgroup or members talking only with the worker hamper the full participation by other group members and require direct action by the worker (Toseland & Rivas, 2009). Implementing a structured experience disrupts this uneven pattern of participation. For example, the social worker could begin a meeting by individually inviting each group member to share. Dividing the time available into equal blocks safeguards time for exploring each member's issues. Structuring interactions to encourage participation activates dormant resources.

Stimulating support within client systems

With simple responses, workers can encourage support among group members. For example, highlighting similarities among members builds alliances:

> ▶ I guess the adults in this family see things in the same way.
> ▶ I noticed the three of you were nodding in agreement when Geena was talking.

Additionally, articulating underlying expressions of affection solidifies connections between group members:

> ▶ I'm seeing you express a strong commitment to working things out with Sharon when you say that.
> ▶ All this worry, concern, and nagging seems like love to me!

Recognizing alliances contributes to clients' feelings of support and power, encourages self-confidence, and increases abilities to risk changes.

Physical arrangements develop alliances, as well. Within a meeting, workers can purposefully arrange seating to encourage closeness. For example, perceptive practitioners create seating arrangements that remove physical barriers to interactions. Commonly, social workers intervening with family systems place parents together and children separately to facilitate the cooperative development of a parenting team and a supportive sibling subsystem.

Assignments of tasks and activities can also be used to create alliances. For example, to develop new subsystems of previously disconnected members, group leaders can implement exercises requiring subgroup activities. Likewise, community workers organize various task groups to involve individual members with each other more intensively.

Paradoxically, holding a separate meeting for selected subgroups within a client system is a powerful strategy for creating alliances. At the community level, consider the impact when the worker convenes a meeting between leaders of four different factions within a neighborhood organization. The effective alliance among leaders of these conflicting factions increases the respective power of each subgroup and of the entire neighborhood. In working with families, weigh the benefit of conducting a separate interview with parents when working with a family on issues of parental authority. A separate session with parents draws a clear generational boundary and gives the parents a chance to discuss parenting strategies as well as their own relationship.

Handling differences

Inevitably differences of opinion arise when systems have more than one member. When topics spark heated debate and divisive conflicts, workers can maintain collaboration among group members by asking each to represent the opposing view or summarize what others are saying (Johnson & Johnson, 2006). Rather than narrowly repeating singular viewpoints, this exercise facilitates listening to alternative views and builds on the unique contributions.

For example, consider this interaction at an interdisciplinary staffing. The facilitator intervenes in a potentially antagonistic disagreement by saying:

> I'm hearing several interesting and different perspectives. I guess that's the beauty of bringing people from different disciplines together. To make progress toward some kind of agreement though, we need to make sure that we are listening to everyone's input. It would probably help if we stopped for a minute and summarized the views we're hearing from each other to make sure that we're all on the same wavelength before we move on.

Notice how this social worker facilitates the way the team members communicate rather than simply adding information that could fuel the debate.

Sustaining Motivation

Social workers enter clients' lives at vulnerable times—times when clients need support. During times of change, clients are even more likely to be unsure of themselves. Although workers try not to foster dependency in clients, neither do they abandon clients. Instead they motivate clients with support, acceptance, and caring. Workers encourage clients as they risk new behaviors, experience setbacks, and celebrate successes. To sustain clients, workers strive to validate clients' experiences, reassure them about the uneven nature and the sometimes slow pace of change, respect their uniqueness, and provide emotional support.

Validating the client's reality

To maintain their efforts, clients need to know that someone else understands their experiences. The need for validation becomes especially important when clients are oppressed and see workers as unfamiliar with their particular stressors.

Human
Behavior

If all behavior is motivated, then there cannot be "unmotivated" clients. How might this understanding of motivation explain client resistence, inaction, and lack of follow through?

For example, "openly identifying and discussing institutionalized racism, discrimination, or economic disparities, can minimize clients' feelings of self-blame and helplessness and foster racial pride and identity" (Gibson, 1993, p. 391). This discussion cements the working relationship and energizes the client's participation.

Another way that workers can validate clients is to normalize their experiences. Considering a behavior in its environmental context means that workers convey their belief that, in these particular circumstances, most people would respond similarly. In other words, the client's behavior makes sense in context, especially in terms of the gender, lifestyle, and ethnic identity of the client. "Normalizing allows clients to stop blaming themselves, or someone else, and then to do something different" (Walter & Peller, 1992, p. 119).

Accepting the nature of change

Change occurs erratically. Sometimes clients leap forward. At other times, they stabilize or return to old ways. Resistance to change is a natural part of development; all human systems tend to maintain the comfort of habitual patterns in the face of changing situations. When things do change, humans take breaks to restabilize and see what things are like before they continue. It's natural for clients to slow down progress that is occurring, back up, and do it the old way again to find a sense of security before moving ahead.

Introducing the notion of "setbacks" normalizes the process of change:

> We tell clients that for every three steps forward there are two steps back. While we tell clients that the two steps backward are normal, we also tell them that we are concerned that they will mistakenly see the normal two steps back as failure and possibly give up on what is working. Often, after this type of normalizing, we give clients the assignment to notice how they get themselves back on track when the setback occurs. (Walter & Peller, 1992, p. 152)

Workers require patience to accept a client's pace and pattern of change. For example, discussing their work with persons who are homeless and mentally ill, Sheridan, et al., (1993) say that:

> Because service delivery to the homeless mentally ill is often a long, slow process, workers must be able to maintain a positive attitude about clients' progress even when it occurs in small but significant increments. In other words, workers must be patient, persistent, flexible, sincere, respectful, and, most important, committed to the well-being of their clients. (p. 417)

Clients benefit when workers demonstrate patience and enthusiasm for even the smallest incremental changes and remain optimistic when change is slow.

Respecting uniqueness

No two client systems change in the same way, have the same set of resources or constraints, or magically respond to the exact same strategy. Social workers take caution in applying "standard techniques" or "cookbook interventions" that fail to acknowledge the unique qualities of a particular client system. Certainly, social workers' general practice wisdom and knowledge of special populations contributes to their thinking. But even the most tried and true, research-supported strategies need modifications to suit specific situations.

Respecting uniqueness means that social workers acknowledge their differences from clients as well. Saying, "I know exactly how you feel," denies the reality of differences. To ask the client, "I guess I'm not really sure. How do potential employers in this area respond to someone who has recently immigrated?" shows respect by recognizing the client's first-hand expertise. Openly discussing and accepting differences transforms potential barriers into working alliances.

Matching the client's cultural experience   Social work strategies work best when they fit the worldviews and cultures of clients. One such example is the traditional Hawaiian family conflict resolution process known as *ho'oponopono*. Hurdle (2002) summarizes ho'oponopono as a highly structured process in which a clearly defined leader convenes all family members for a conversation governed by rules that limit emotional expression and conflict, assists them to discuss the problem and its impact, and encourages all members involved to ask for forgiveness from each other and consider restitution. "The formal nature of the ritual lends an aura of solemnity and importance to the process, which is crucial to many forms of traditional healing . . . reflective of the integration of spirituality with healing in many indigenous cultures" (p. 189).

Providing emotional support

Workers provide emotional support in two basic ways. First, they comment enthusiastically on a client's progress. Walter and Peller (1992) describe this as cheerleading, "emotional support that comes across through raised voice

---

Box 12.1 Ethic of Advocacy

Most social work clients experience oppression in some form. Among the most vulnerable populations and stigmatized groups of society, social work clients frequently have less leverage than others to obtain necessary resources and experience limited access to genuine opportunities. A social worker's efforts to advocate add professional punch to a client's attempts at acquiring resources. The ethic of advocacy means that social workers leverage professional resources as a way to champion the rights of individuals or causes (Aubrey, 2004; Freddolino, et al., 2004; Hoefer, 2006; Lens, 2004; Sherraden, et al., 2002). However, in the context of empowerment, advocacy as an ethical practice assumes social workers speak along with, not for, others.

The *Code of Ethics* of the National Association of Social Workers (1999a) emphasizes advocacy as a central activity of social work. According to the code:

> social workers should promote the general welfare of society, from local to global levels, and the development of people, their communities, and their environments. Social workers should advocate for living conditions conducive to the fulfillment of basic human needs and should promote social, economic, and cultural values and institutions that

are compatible with the realization of social justice. *(Section 6.01)*

Additionally, "social workers should act to prevent and eliminate domination of, exploitation of, and discrimination against any person, group, or class on the basis of race, ethnicity, national origin, color, sex, sexual orientation, age, marital status, political belief, religion, or mental or physical disability" (Section 6.04d).

Closely related to social justice, advocacy activities can be applied in the micro-, mezzo-, and macrolevel practice arenas. Client advocacy directs social workers to collaborate with clients to influence how social systems respond to a client's attempt to gather resources. Activities illustrating a client advocacy approach include educating clients on their rights, negotiating with agencies on behalf of clients, and teaching advocacy skills to clients (Ezell, 1994). As seasoned social workers begin to see similar constraints and frustrations in the experiences of many clients connecting with specific resources, they respond by expanding their efforts from case advocacy to cause advocacy. Arguing for more effective services for clients and educating the general public on an issue are examples of cause advocacy activities focused on larger system change.

tones, gestures, excited expressions, or the choice of words" (p. 106). Workers use compliments to reflect on the changes that clients have made and give them credit for these changes.

Workers can provide powerful emotional support by sharing feelings about their experience of working with clients. Sharing these feelings works in two important ways: "[It] effectively strengthens the working relationship (the process), while contributing important ideas for the client's work (the content)" (Shulman, 1999, p. 168). However, rather than serving the worker's own personal needs, Shulman cautions that the worker's "feelings should be shared in pursuit of professional purposes as the worker implements the professional function" (p. 199).

DEVELOPING POWER

Washing one's hands of the conflict between the powerful and the powerless means to side with the powerful, not to be neutral.

—Paulo Freire

People feel their own power when they become aware of their expertise, resources, and gifts. People have a sense of control when others allow and respect their views. People feel powerful when they connect to the power of others. Empowerment-based strategies provide clients with information, offer options and opportunities to make decisions, and help to build social support networks. Empowerment requires that workers help clients develop leadership, recognize choices, locate genuine options for solutions, and cultivate strengths and abilities.

Promoting Leadership

All human systems benefit from capable leadership. Workers can help client systems activate power by encouraging the evolution of effective leadership patterns. Consider social work practice with a community. To achieve broad-based participation in community change, an effective strategy develops leadership among diverse community constituents. For example, social workers facilitate the involvement of indigenous leaders to work efficiently toward the community's goals. Practitioners recognize and work with those leaders who have expertise for the task and who represent the views of their constituents.

Practitioners can also work to support leadership in a family system. An example of this is the worker in a shelter for homeless families. Ziefert and Brown (1991) describe how:

> The parenting role disintegrates quickly when a family becomes homeless. A primary task for shelter advocates is to reconnect family members to one another by strengthening their adaptive social role behaviors. Family boundaries are often fragmented and parent roles abdicated. (p. 217)

To empower these families, Ziefert and Brown (1991) suggest that workers support parental authority with rules that leave parents in charge but protect children from being hurt. Workers can also offer information on parenting skills such as the benefits of giving positive feedback to their children, using time outs, and modeling negotiation. Furthermore, they suggest that agencies budget money for workers to give parents so parents can take their children out for recreation and celebrate birthdays—activities that enhance parents in their children's eyes. Supporting the parenting role contributes to the whole family's sense of power and well-being.

Recognizing Choices

Clients frequently feel powerless, believing that events are beyond their control. Social workers counteract this immobilizing assumption by helping clients recognize those elements of a situation that clients could change. An ecosystemic view describes behavior as mutually determined rather than linearly caused, leaving both person and environment responsible for what's happening. The power to change any situation lies on both sides of the transaction. Workers help clients see the ways in which they participate, possibly revealing that clients have more influence than is readily apparent. Clients experience their own power when they see opportunities to make new choices in situations where they previously saw no options.

Locating Genuine Options

Assuming that clients share responsibility for their choices does not mean that workers blame clients for the actions of others. Rather, workers direct attention to the ways in which clients choose to participate and respond. Without question, a woman physically abused by her husband is not responsible for this violence and cannot be expected to change her spouse's behavior. No one has that kind of control over another person. However, the client does have choices about the way in which she responds to violence. The social worker's role is to help this client discover and access realistic choices—temporary shelter, an order of protection, an arrest warrant, referral for therapy—and to assure her freedom to choose among available options. "Empowerment and self-determination are dependent not only on people making choices, but also on people having available choices to make" (Cowger, 1994, p. 263).

Where exactly do workers and clients locate viable alternatives to submitting to oppressive relationships? There are two ways that systems can gain power in relationships where they feel powerless (Simons & Aigner, 1985). The first strategy is to find out the source of the dominant system's power and then help the client system find another way to meet those needs, circumventing the need for the powerful system and undermining its power base. For example, in abusive relationships, women may depend on their partners for financial support and shelter for themselves and their children. The availability of resources such as public assistance and transitional housing diminishes the abusive partner's power and control.

The second way to deal with oppressive power is to find out who else is oppressed by the powerful system and join them to form a united front (Simons & Aigner, 1985). For example, when a resident of an apartment complex is unable to get the owner to make necessary repairs, teaming with others in the same building may produce results. When all residents announce that they will withhold their rent, the financial incentive may work to rearrange the power between the residents and the owner and stimulate the owner to make the repairs. Limiting the owner's options enhances the residents' power base.

Magnifying Strengths

Magnifying strengths enhances a client's experience of power. Practitioners maintain attention to three areas to detect strengths, including clients' behaviors and accomplishments, distinguishing characteristics, and their base of tangible resources and support networks (Kirst-Ashman & Hull, 2006). The strategy of a "positive asset search" highlights this continual scanning for resources (Ivey & Ivey, 2006).

Even in apparently desperate circumstances, people demonstrate adaptive behavior and coping skills. For example, people who are homeless "display a remarkable capacity to cope and adapt to conditions that most of us would find intolerable" (Sheridan, et al., 1993, p. 413). Specifically, they have unique abilities, skills, and competence in

> learning how to eat any kind of food (from meal programs or garbage dumpsters), sleep anywhere (on a door stoop, in a park, or in a noisy, frightening shelter), and meet basic needs (through panhandling, recycling aluminum cans, or accepting a stranger's kindness). . . . (p. 413)

Social workers build their own abilities to recognize and activate clients' skills in the diverse forms in which clients demonstrate them.

Highlighting solutions

Social workers discover strengths by listening closely to what clients are saying. For example, when the social worker notices that a mother's efforts to gather updated information about her child's behavior at school accompanies her child's increased attendance, the social worker stops, analyzes, and reflects on what is working. Possibly, the mother's involvement with school shifted the child's attention in the same direction. Maybe the mother's attention to the child rather than her recent job loss relieved the child's anxiety about the family. Perhaps the mother's obvious commitment to the child's success in school is affecting the ways that teachers interact with the child, altering the school environment and learning experience for the child. Identifying what's working offers options with which to experiment to maintain the child's progress in attending school more consistently.

Shaping competence

Workers are more effective when they modify existing interactions rather than intervene as if clients are doing nothing right. This skill as it is used in family therapy is "shaping competence" (Nichols & Schwartz, 2001). "Shaping competence is like altering the direction of the flow. By highlighting and shaping the positive, structural therapists help family members use functional alternatives that are already in the repertoire" (p. 261).

This strategy adapts easily to other types of client systems. Place yourself in the position of a worker facilitating a support group and observing the responses of various members to one member's crisis. Your comment that you are impressed with a particular group member's ability to empathize without giving advice will likely influence other members to follow suit. In this way, you are able to guide the group toward a pattern of supporting each other's strengths without undermining their competence. Shaping competence acknowledges client systems' existing expertise and activates their resources in the direction of desired changes.

CHANGING PERSPECTIVES

Interventions to change perspectives involve examining, reframing, or reinterpreting behavior and circumstances. Workers may offer feedback to assist clients to step outside of their situations and look at them in more productive ways. Clients and social workers may also select strategies that offer opportunities for changing perspectives through behavioral change. Set in the context of trying new options, small-scale "experiments" investigate the effects of different behaviors.

Offering Feedback

By using effective feedback, workers help clients reflect on and change their behaviors. Practitioners witness how clients interact in the context of professional relationships. Through this type of observation, social workers can assess

- ♦ How client systems approach challenging situations
- ♦ What skills clients bring that work for them
- ♦ The ways clients involve others in building relationships and seeking solutions
- ♦ Which parts of the ecosystem help or hinder the progress

Additionally, workers observe a client's level of trust, ability to articulate ideas, awareness of feelings, patience, persistence, sense of humor, and creativity. Social workers are in positions to disclose their perceptions about clients by offering carefully constructed feedback.

Constructing Feedback

Critical Thinking

Feedback is a means for social workers to communicate professional judgments to help clients view their situations in more productive ways. When is communicating feedback to clients not constructive?

Examine the following examples of feedback:

- ♦ Could I give you some feedback? I just observed you talking to your daughter about her curfew for a full 5 minutes without yelling. I wonder what's working?
- ♦ I have an observation if you are ready for it. It seems to me that each time this agency has a funding crisis, the response is to expect workers to do more for less. It just happened this week when the board of directors decided to eliminate two positions, redistribute the workload, and freeze salaries.
- ♦ It's so encouraging to work with someone who takes risks like you. Just now, when I suggested we try something new, you immediately thought of three possibilities.

Notice how these practitioners carefully framed feedback, drawing on principles for constructive feedback:

- ♦ Describes rather than evaluates behavior
- ♦ Shares perceptions rather than offers advice
- ♦ Identifies specific current behaviors rather than recalls incidents from the past
- ♦ Reports positive behaviors as well as points to improve
- ♦ Keeps pace with the client's readiness

When workers offer feedback neutrally, clients can attach their own evaluations to the information. Because workers give feedback about specific behaviors rather than about the "person" of the client, clients have opportunities to behave in new ways that more clearly match their intent.

Confronting in a supportive way

Can you decide what you want, do something to obtain it, and end up getting it? If you can, you are, at least in this one instance, interpersonally effective. When clients articulate the intent of their behaviors, workers can observe and determine which behaviors net intended results and which miss their marks. Workers use this approach to highlight successful behaviors as well as those that may need changing.

To confront effectively, workers help clients articulate their actions in three parts—intent, behavior, and outcome. As workers carefully trace with clients the sequence of intent to behavior to outcome, clients often see things differently and choose new behaviors. Consider the following example. Support group member Tom has grown tired of the way that John monopolizes the conversation. Tom responds by disagreeing with everything that John offers, leaving other group members withdrawn and disinterested. When Tom complains that nothing seems to work to stifle John, the worker can lead Tom to see his own involvement by analyzing his behavior.

- The *intent*—Tom wants John to be less active and other group members to say more.
- The *behavior*—Tom argues with what John says.
- The *outcome*—the whole group revolves around John's issues and Tom's disagreement with John.

So, is Tom getting what he wants?

Workers use a confronting strategy selectively, usually after establishing a significant, respectful relationship and in an atmosphere of support. In observing and reporting their observations of clients' social effectiveness, workers do not need to blame or accuse but simply to lay out patterns for clients to review and take action.

Confronting works best when it fits the situation. It is particularly effective when confronting value issues. This helps clients "by making them aware they more or less chronically hold certain values and attitudes or behave in ways that are counter to their own expectations of competence or morality" (Grube, et al., 1994, p. 157). Cultural factors also determine whether to use this strategy. For traditional Asian American clients, confrontation and conflict "may violate their cultural rules. Asian culture says, 'It is good to have harmony and to be in sync with your environment.' Harmony is what Asians consciously or unconsciously seek and is evidenced by their behaviors" (Chung, 1992, p. 31).

Creating New Concepts

The way we respond to a situation may have more to do with the way we interpret it than the actual event itself. "Look on the bright side" may sound like a naïve approach, but the benefits of a positive outlook are well established. Workers can help clients to experience and describe events in helpful ways by using reframing, metaphors, and other narrative strategies.

Reframing

Clients who feel as if they are not getting anywhere benefit from views that they may, after all, be up to something constructive. Reframing examines a situation previously perceived as negative and takes a new look, describing it as somehow positive, functional, or useful. Toseland and Rivas (2009) describe the effect of using this strategy with group clients: "Once a member experiences a problem from a new perspective, the positive aspects of the situation are highlighted and the negative aspects of the situation have a better chance of being changed" (p. 266).

One way to reinterpret behavior is to consider the view that the response determines the meaning (Walter & Peller, 1992). Even apparently problematic behavior may be up to something good. Consider the following examples. The group member who monopolizes is helping other members to avoid dealing with difficult issues. The boy who constantly tests his Dad's authority is succeeding in getting his Dad closely involved. The depressed adolescent has discovered ways to elicit the support and nurturance of family and friends. The employee who files grievance after grievance is clarifying and developing the agency's policies and procedures.

Reframing also works to prevent problems from developing. Ben-Ari's (1995) study of coming out demonstrates that the way parents perceive a son's or daughter's disclosure of homosexuality makes a difference in their response. When social workers can lead parents to frame this disclosure as a means to gain intimacy rather than to shock or blame parents, parents adjust more easily to the information. When social workers consider the question, "What's good about it?," they give clients new perspectives on positive things that are already happening.

Using metaphors

Another way to reframe situations is to describe them in the form of a story or metaphor. Consider the parents frustrated over their child's slow progress in learning to read. When the social worker places this situation in the context of the traditional fable, "The Tortoise and the Hare," it transforms the behavior from lagging behind to steadily improving. The previous description stimulates feelings of anxiety and impatience. The new description recognizes success and leaves room for optimism.

Metaphors are ambiguous, letting clients make their own interpretations. This ambiguity makes metaphors particularly suitable for describing and working with feelings. When social workers and clients seek to articulate feelings, workers use phrases like:

▶ You feel as if you are out on a limb.
▶ So it's kind of like you're just drifting in the middle of a lake, not really getting anywhere.
▶ Seems as if you've hit rock bottom.

Building on these same metaphors social workers can offer hopeful directions, such as:

▶ Well, maybe, it's time to edge back toward the trunk.
▶ So as you are drifting, what do you see that catches your interest?
▶ Now that you're at the bottom, at least there's only one way to go— what's the first thing that needs to happen to pick yourself back up?

In activating client system resources, social workers introduce stimulating new perspectives, options, and interpretations to affect the way clients think, feel, and behave.

Using Narrative Strategies

"Reality is never experienced directly but is always filtered through human processes of knowing and creating meaning" (Laird, 1995, p. 151). People behave in ways consistent with what they believe is true rather than in keeping with some concrete reality to which we all subscribe. Such is the view of the social constructivist. We each have our own story to tell. These stories are resources that "need to be explored, to become valued, and to be rendered employable" (Saleebey, 1994, p. 352). Workers help clients take charge of their stories in ways that emphasize their strengths, experience their pride, and prepare them to narrate their way into a more desirable future. Workers can also affirm "clients' privilege to author their lives" by constricting new interpretations of their life stories (Freeman & Couchonnal, 2006).

To work with clients' narratives, social workers "serve as skillful facilitators, as editors searching for an undiscovered subtext, as conveners of groupings in search of problem-solving conversations, or as advocates for the inclusion of new characters and new resources" (Dyche & Zayas, 1995, p. 389). Social workers withhold any professional commentary to encourage clients to tell the stories of their lives. "By being too quick to translate a client's story into a theoretical construct, we may miss the nuances and unique qualities a particular client brings as well as the client's own creative efforts at problem solving" (Dean, 1993, p. 133). The example that follows illustrates how our own past experiences can also interfere with our ability to listen to clients' perspectives.

> In one situation, Mr. and Mrs. Evans, a White elderly couple from a poor rural community, lost their house and possessions in a fire. Mr. Evans had suffered a heart attack right after the fire. A young biracial practitioner (Japanese and White) in a veterans' hospital was assigned to work with the couple on discharge planning for Mr. Evans. When the practitioner contacted them, the couple continued to retell their story about the fire and their losses. During a supervision session focused on her work with the couple, the practitioner realized she had not listened to or acknowledged their loss narrative. This practice gap limited the couple's opportunity to process their narrative experience and its meaning to them and to cope with the related crisis. The practitioner also realized that the Evans's family narrative reminded her of her mother's story about an earthquake in her native Japan yeas before. The family lost several relatives as well as its home and was forced to migrate to another country. The practitioner had often ignored the retelling of her mother's narrative and had developed a cultural filter that denied the importance of such losses and relocations. That filter made it difficult for her to hear, acknowledge, and validate the Evans' painful narrative about loss. (Freeman & Couchonnal, 2006, p. 201)

Implementing a narrative strategy requires social workers to facilitate three activities during assessment and intervention—collaboration, reflexivity, and multiplicity (Laird, 1995). *Collaboration* is a familiar process in all empowering practice, requiring a specific focus on and respect for a client's experience rather than an externally accepted reality. *Reflexivity* means that social workers use responding skills that allow clients to view their stories more objectively—skills that separate stories out for joint reflection by both clients and workers. *Multiplicity* is accomplished by simply generating multiple ideas and interpretations. Both clients and workers can contribute to this "brainstorming." The use of reframing and metaphors described previously can be applied to this process. The more options clients have for viewing and interpreting their current story, the more opportunities they have for choosing empowering meanings to guide its future development.

Several techniques support a narrative approach. With individuals and families, workers can draw genograms to identify the "cast of characters" over the generations, and have clients narrate significant tales about the various family members. Workers respond by identifying dominant themes and strengths demonstrated over the years. Groups can construct their stories by using journaling (Brower, 1996). In this approach, each group member keeps independent logs of their responses to the group and reads them to each other at group meetings to contribute to "a narrative that gives their group experience coherence, history, rules, myths, and meaning" (p. 342). Considering even larger systems, Saleebey (1994) says that we must project individual client narratives toward agencies and institutions for mezzo- and macrolevel interventions. Techniques that encourage positive interpretations and increase a client's experience of power and importance are central to a narrative strategy.

Externalizing

Narrative strategies have the advantage of separating the story of someone's life from the actual person. In other words, the story is external to the person and can be modified or directed by the person. This is especially significant when people tell stories replete with problems, since the person and the problem become separate. Social work has already adopted this concept as evidenced in the politically correct description of a "person with a disability" rather than a "disabled person."

The process of separating people from their problems is "externalization" (White, 1989). First, help people talk about their problems as a separate entity—as something external to themselves. Then, look for "unique outcomes"—those times when people felt most in control of their problems. As clients describe these exceptions to problematic times, they simultaneously experience a sense of control and identify possible ways that they can repeat this success.

Trying Out New Behaviors

In many ways, action plans are carefully designed "experiments" for change. Experimentation always yields productive results. A "success" moves clients toward desired outcomes and a "failure" provides valuable information to guide future actions. Small-scale experiments, designed by workers and clients and implemented between meetings, can inform and change. To derive maximal benefit, each activity is mutually constructed, carefully implemented, and comprehensively evaluated (Figure 12.2).

Constructing experimental activities

Social workers and clients have an array of possible activities to choose from in constructing experiments. Four options include conducting observations, connecting and disconnecting, maintaining productive actions, and taking small steps toward goals.

Observations Observations are cautious experiments used to gather additional information. They ask for no direct change by the client system but often produce change since observing one's own or someone else's behavior frequently has impact. Clients observe when good things are happening or those times when problems are not occurring to decipher what might contribute to these successful events. For example, managers in an organization might observe closely when employees show regular attendance and positive attitudes to understand what works.

Connecting and disconnecting Clients can experiment with change by connecting to new people and resources or by disconnecting from previous relationships. For example, members of an adolescent group working to disassociate from gang membership may agree to keep away from areas of gang activity and refrain from talking with known gang members. These same group members may each also agree to choose a new person to eat lunch with in the school cafeteria to begin new peer relationships to replace their previous gang associations.

Figure 12.2   Guidelines for Between-Meeting Activities

Types of Activities

- Information gathering through observation
- Connecting to and disconnecting from persons, groups, services, and situations
- Maintaining and repeating productive behaviors
- Taking small steps in the direction of goals

Construction

- Determine client's willingness to participate
- Generate possible activities in mutual discussion
- Select activities based on:
  —Relevance to goals
  —Likelihood of success
  —Client's motivation to complete

Implementation

- Define as experimental
- Keep it clear, concrete, and simple
- Define roles of all participants
- Secure agreements to follow through
- Repeat agreement to ensure understanding

Follow-up

- When activity is completed:
  —Discuss outcomes
  —Access information from all members involved
  —Accept differences in perspectives
  —Validate each participant's perceptions
  —Highlight specific strengths and skills clients demonstrated in the activity
  —Note variations in expected outcome to detect unanticipated solutions
  —Construct follow-up activity
  —Encourage increased responsibility by client in constructing the next activity
- When activity is not completed:
  —Discuss obstacles
  —Determine how to overcome obstacles
  —Consider taking a smaller step
  —Implement the same activity
- If client chose not to complete activity:
  —Determine source of resistance
  —Change activity to match client's current motivation
  —Update client's outcome goals to ensure that worker and client are moving in the same direction

Maintaining productive actions   Encouraging clients to repeat productive actions is another useful technique. Consider the example of Nancy and her client Jerome. Jerome is a social worker, questioning his choice of profession since he frequently feels depressed and burned out. Recently, Jerome told Nancy about his angry outburst in an interdisciplinary team meeting when the group refused to consider changing the case plan of a client with whom he was working. Knowing that Jerome shows incredible patience and acceptance in his work with his clients, Nancy suggests that Jerome imagine the interdisciplinary team members are his clients rather than professional colleagues. In other words, Nancy asks Jerome to experiment with transferring his skills in a successful area of functioning to test their benefits in another.

Taking small steps   Taking a small step toward the goal is an experiment worth trying. Well-defined objectives in a comprehensive action plan will clearly indicate the options for these small steps. However, taking direct steps toward goals may seem risky, so social workers reassure clients that this step is only experimental. Once the results are in, clients can choose to take another step, or return to the previous ways of behaving.

Implementing activities

Some refer to these experiments as homework assignments or directives. Imagine your response to someone assigning or directing you to do something. Social workers circumvent resistance by framing these activities clearly as experiments and collaborating with clients to develop them. The social worker might say, "Are you interested in trying a little experiment?" "So those are my ideas, what do you think?" Clients are more likely to implement experiments that they help construct and agree to complete. "So we agree. You'll try this out and let me know what happened next week."

A well-designed experiment has several components. It describes "who will do what when." The best experiments are concrete, simple, and easily understood by clients and workers. With multiperson systems, all members need to understand what they are agreeing to do and know what their particular responsibilities are. Useful experiments also specify the time frame for completion and describe how to evaluate the impact. When experiments are relevant, clear, and collaboratively constructed, they are likely to produce the most positive results.

Following up

To complete a successful experiment, workers lead clients through a step-by-step process that evaluates the results. Workers may ask the following questions:

- Tell me the details. How did you carry it out?
- Did you implement the experiment as constructed or did you vary it? What led you to make these changes?
- What happened? Did it turn out like you expected? Did something unexpected happen?
- What did you learn that might help us decide what to do next?

When clients fail to follow through on completing assignments, workers also pursue additional information, by asking:

- So what got in the way? Was there no opportunity or did you decide it wasn't something you wanted to do? Did you understand what you were supposed to do?
- Are you willing to try to complete it again or do you think we're off base here?
- What would you like to do instead?

Well-designed experiments actively involve clients in the change process. When workers sequence experiments one after the other, they gradually pull back from the task in ways that increase clients' responsibilities for their development and implementation. Activating resources in this way prepares clients to function independently of the social worker.

MANAGING RESOURCES

All human systems from individuals to communities need environmental resources to sustain their functioning. During assessment, workers explore the various connections that clients have with their environments to see what works and should be reinforced, to detect what is not working and should be modified, and also to recognize what is missing and should be established. To

You have within you the strength, the patience, and the passion to reach for the stars to change the world.

—Harriet Tubman

Peer groups are a source of support for practicing new behaviors.

manage resources, social workers and clients collaborate to locate realistic options, make appropriate connections, and take steps to ensure that clients are successful in accessing resources.

Linking clients to necessary resources casts generalist social workers in the roles of brokers and advocates, mediators, activists, and catalysts. To play these roles effectively requires workers to know what the social delivery system has to offer, to learn current eligibility requirements for supportive services, to recognize indigenous resources that communities may possess, and to participate in resource development projects. Chapters 13 and 14 further explore managing resources at the mezzo- and macrolevel client system levels and in the context of professional relationships.

Linking Clients with Resources

Accessing resources confronts social workers with a common question. How much help do they give to clients in this process? The empowering answer is "as much as is necessary and as little as needed to be effective." Workers are supplemental in helping clients make connections. Whether workers simply inform clients about resources or take more direct actions, they consistently work for clients to understand the process of how clients might access the same resources directly without intervention by practitioners.

In linking clients with other services, social workers choose their methods based on the current capabilities of client systems with an eye toward how they might increase clients' own resource management skills. For example, consider Denise VanDeViere, an aftercare worker for Northside Hospital, and her client Cassie Carter, who is recovering from a serious head injury. Denise and Cassie have agreed that Cassie will apply for Social Security Disability Income (SSDI), supplemental financial assistance administered through the State Office of Public Assistance. To assist Cassie in this endeavor, Denise has a continuum of options varying from most supportive to least involved. These options, from most to least involved, include:

- Denise will call Louise Campbell, a caseworker she knows at Public Assistance (PA) to arrange an appointment. She will also gather the appropriate medical documentation to demonstrate Cassie's eligibility, pick up Cassie, and accompany her to the appointment
- Cassie will call Louise, mention that Denise has suggested the call, and arrange the appointment. Denise will gather the necessary medical records, pick up Cassie, and accompany her to the appointment
- Cassie will arrange the appointment, sign appropriate forms for release for information, gather up her medical records, and meet Denise at the PA office. Denise will guide Cassie through the application process and advocate only as necessary
- Denise will give information to Cassie about SSDI and the procedures for application through PA. Cassie will make the necessary arrangements to go to PA, apply for the assistance, and report the results of her efforts to Denise at the next meeting

Each option leads to the same outcome—Cassie applies for SSDI. But each option draws differently on the resources of the client and social worker. The best choice is the one in which clients feel confident in their abilities to succeed, use as much of their own capabilities as possible, and learn additional skills for the future. Considering these issues, Denise and Cassie decide that Cassie will make the necessary arrangements, that both will ride the bus together so that Denise can help Cassie learn to use the public transportation system, and that Cassie will do the talking at PA unless she directly seeks the assistance of Denise.

Client Advocacy

Policy Practice

Social workers often advocate on behalf of their clients in the bureacratic maze of the social service delivery network. What benefits can clients derive from participating in or at least observing the case advocacy efforts of the social worker?

Even when informed about other services, clients may experience unexpected obstacles or a lack of responsiveness, a situation calling on practitioners to add their professional power to ensure a successful connection. "Client advocacy is built upon a philosophy that seeks to protect, enforce, and ensure clients' *rights, entitlements, resources, services,* and *benefits*" (Schneider & Lester, 2001, p. 152). Although ideally designed to respond to clients' needs, the social delivery network is in reality economically strapped, short of staff, and bureaucratically complex. Frequently, clients need a social worker's guidance to traverse the bureaucratic red tape to access the services for which they are eligible. Advocacy in networking resources and services is essential to meet the needs of immigrant clients as determined in a qualitative study by Russell and White (2001). They describe worker responsibilities to provide "a range of practical services as well as 'being the voice' of the clients" (p. 89).

The way in which social workers advocate for their clients makes a difference, particularly with high-risk clients who have multiple challenges such as chronic mental illnesses, developmental disabilities, substance addictions, or major health issues such as AIDS. A client with multiple challenges needs to "personally witness the worker's advocacy on his or her behalf. There can be no empowerment without participation or, at least, presence and observation. By modeling this behavior, the client learns to become an active consumer/participant" (Klein & Cnaan, 1995, p. 205). All clients benefit more from working with rather than by being worked on by social workers.

Maximizing Clients' Rights

Clients have rights to resources in their communities and to those available within the social service delivery system. However, sometimes restrictive policies, guidelines, or procedures block clients' attempts to obtain services to which they are rightfully entitled. When interpretations of rules and regulations deny clients access to programs and services, they have rights to fair hearings, appeals, and due process.

Fair Hearings and Appeals

Clients' rights include their right to fair hearings. Fair hearings provide the mechanism for appealing decisions that have negatively affected clients' benefits or services (Chambers, 1993). Common to many types of programs and services, the Social Security Act stipulates the process for fair hearings and appeals as a mandated component of service delivery. As Chambers describes:

> A fair-hearing procedure is one in which a client or applicant is given the opportunity to appeal to an administrative tribunal or a judge (or a panel of judges) who hears arguments of both sides. This tribunal reviews agency policy, practices, and enabling legislation and then renders a decision for or against the agency or the complainant. The administrative judge is duty-bound to hold the agency to decisions and actions that are consistent with agency policy, tradition, or legislative mandate. The judge can require the agency to reverse its prior actions or decisions and/or change its policies and procedures. (p. 206)

Hearing procedures differ with respect to the independence of the hearing officer. In some instances, judges are subject to their peers' review of their actions. In other instances, the hearing officer is simply an administrator in charge of the program subject to the appeal. Social workers need to be familiar with their own employers' fair hearing and appeals policies and procedures as well as those in agencies to which they refer clients. When a client decides to appeal decisions about benefits and services, the worker advocates directly or links the client to a concerned professional who can advocate the client's position.

Due process

Due process of law protects individuals' rights in dealings with the government. Whether rules provide strict guidelines for implementation or whether they allow discretionary decision making, the U.S. Supreme Court regards constitutional due process as a central facet of welfare benefits (Chambers, 1993). Key features of due process involve clients' rights to

Human Rights & Justice

Clients have rights to appeals and fair hearings in adverse administrative decisions. Why is it important for social workers to inform clients of their due process rights?

- Be informed in a timely manner about the specifics of administrative actions, including the basis for these actions
- Argue their point of view at the hearing in writing or in person
- Be represented by legal counsel
- Face witnesses directly and question them in the context of cross examination
- Participate in an open or public hearing
- Have their appeal heard by an impartial, unbiased hearing officer or judge
- Have the facts of their record form the basis for the decision and obtain a written report that details the facts of their case and applicable laws (Handler, cited in Chambers, 1993)

Box 12.2 Natural Helping and Self-Help Resources: A Research–Practice Connection

Self-help groups, natural helpers, and informal networks are valuable supports to client systems, yet these resources are often unidentified and underused by social workers. Self-help groups "offer a vehicle for people with a common problem to gain support and recognition, obtain information on, advocate on behalf of, address issues associated with, and take control of the circumstances that bring about, perpetuate, and provide solutions to their shared concern." (Segal, 2008, p. 14).

Not only beneficial to individual functioning, informal resources are also integral to neighborhoods and communities (Breton, 2001). Moreover, natural helping networks are an important source of empowerment, including power over oneself to take control of addictions, cope with emotions and power in relation to the sociopolitical environment to take charge of care decisions, ensure accommodations for disabilities, and deal with social stigma, and confront structural barriers (Hardina, 2004b; Segal, 2008). Contemporary research documents the value of self-help and natural helping across cultures.

Just how much support and assistance do people access from their natural support networks? Even among groups in which the utilization of formal support services is low, research shows that people tap into the resources of natural helping networks such as family members, friends, and neighbors (Patterson & Marsiglia 2000). Williams and colleagues (2001) investigated perceived supports and barriers to the use of social and health services in communities plagued by violence. They discovered that language and cultural barriers interfere with access to formal services, although all groups studied, including African Americans, Latinos, and Vietnamese residents, identified various faith communities as significant sources of support.

Does natural support differ among cultural groups? By using a qualitative research design,

Patterson and Marsiglia (2000) studied community-based natural helping networks within the Mexican American community in the southwest United States. They interviewed 12 persons identified by community members as natural helpers and compared their responses with those from previous studies conducted with European American respondents. Similarities led the researchers to conclude that natural helping may be a cross-cultural phenomenon. Natural helpers in these cultural groups implemented combinations of task-related or facilitative roles, depending on the requirements of the situations. Interestingly, "the more polarized gender socialization process that is typically associated with Latinos and Latinas did not emerge" in their study; male natural helpers in their sample "used the facilitating style of helping more than women did" (p. 29).

What about the effectiveness of self-help groups? Mirroring the results of studies conducted in the United States, Mok's (2001) research on self-help groups in Hong Kong showed that participating in self-help groups "could lead to positive changes in individuals' outlook on life, personal ability, emotional control, and relationship and knowledge about society" (p. 82). Self-help groups stirred members' feelings to address social policy issues related to health, welfare, and housing, but did not necessarily prompt groups to take action. However, not all involvement in self-help groups leads to positive outcomes; it is possible that some members experience pressure to conform to group demands or feel overwhelmed in the context of the group.

Research suggests that social workers should value the involvement of nonprofessional helpers and view informal support systems as legitimate resources for clients. Informal supports are likely to be a good cultural fit for clients and to remain intact in clients' systems long after the professional social work relationship ends.

Social workers are not lawyers, but the advocacy practice of social work requires workers to know about laws, judicial process, and legal resources available.

EDUCATING

Clients and social workers sometimes select educational strategies. New information often leads to novel solutions. Learning strategies include role playing, implementing structured curriculums, and modeling. Workers also share information with clients by offering relevant professional knowledge and appropriately disclosing personal information.

Teaching

Like all effective social work practice, educational endeavors "begin where the client is." With respect to teaching, this means identifying the learner's objectives and learning style. Collaborative educational efforts involve both the facilitator and learners in the joint process of "assessing needs, setting objectives, selecting appropriate methodologies and materials, and developing evaluation procedures as well as actively participating in the facilitation of the learning" (Galbraith, 1991, p. 3). Collaborative teaching transforms educational processes so that learners become users rather than simply recipients of education. Possible educational experiences include role playing and structured training experiences.

Role playing

Role playing develops interpersonal skills. For example, when a client complains that an employer never listens, the worker may suggest a role play. First, the client describes the behaviors of the employer to guide the worker's portrayal. Then, the partners play out the scenario, discovering information about the client's approach and hypothesizing possible responses and feelings the employer may be having and exploring the client's perspective. Role playing provides an arena for trying out new behaviors without risking the consequences of failure (Johnson & Johnson, 2006).

Role playing also works with groups (Toseland & Rivas, 2009). There are numerous variations from structured experiences using scripts to unstructured experiences selecting various members for roles and facilitating extemporaneous interaction, observation, and feedback. Group members may play themselves to practice new behaviors or play another person's role to increase their empathy and understanding for the other person's position. Playing roles that require group members to represent views they themselves do not hold is particularly useful in developing skills in task groups, in teaching them to elucidate alternatives, and in reaching consensus in group decisions.

Structured training experiences

Curriculum-based learning strategies work best with some clients. Many agencies have brochures, manuals, or do-it-yourself skill development books for clients to use. Detailed skill development programs are packaged and offered commercially for nearly every kind of interpersonal development. Many social work groups focus on developing interpersonal skills such as anger management, assertiveness, or job interview skills. Examples of other educational topics include managing stress, dealing with caregiving issues, developing a strategic plan, working on a team, negotiating, and effective decision making.

As with any educational experience, material should be culturally sensitive and geared to identified learning objectives, levels, and learning styles of the participants (Figure 12.3). Cultural variations do exist in learning styles. For example: "A large proportion of European-Americans learn easily from details, a greater percentage of Native Americans learn most easily when watching, imagining, and reflecting" (Gilliland, 1992, as cited in Dykeman, et al., 1995, p. 153). Successful educational programs also consider participants' schedules to determine the best time frames and build in supports for attendance such as child care and transportation.

Technical supports for educational programming are expanding rapidly. For example, microwave transmitters interconnect multiple learning sites. Interactive teleconferences allow participants to interact with well-known

Figure 12.3 Developing Training Modules

Collaboratively, educators and learners:

- Assess the learning needs
- Identify the learning outcomes, that is, what knowledge or skills or attitudes will be achieved through the training
- Identify various types of learning experiences necessary to achieve learning outcomes such as existing curricula, role plays, films, speakers, lectures, or simulations
- Screen proposed learning strategies for cultural appropriateness
- Sequence the training agenda for a single session or schedule for multiple sessions
- Implement the training sessions
- Evaluate the learning outcomes and the methods used

---

experts. Video recording technology allows participants to record activities, play it back, and evaluate their responses. Computer-based programmed learning takes advantage of individualized instruction and immediate feedback.

Modeling

How many of us have heard a parent say, "Do as I say, not as I do"? How many of us have followed this advice? Unavoidably, social workers find themselves as models to clients on how to cope, communicate, and relate. Social workers acknowledge their responsibility as role models by monitoring their own behaviors to check for consistency with what they are saying.

Based on the social learning model developed by Bandura (1986), modeling promotes behavioral changes through the observation, imitation, and vicarious experience of the gains the modeled behavior attains. In social work practice, modeling occurs "when the client has an opportunity to observe the worker perform or when the worker encourages the client to observe the behavior of someone else" (Garvin & Tropman, 1998, p. 119). Being chosen as a model depends on perceived similarities between the model and the observer (Bandura). In other words, in the context of social work, the more clients identify with workers, the greater the likelihood they will learn through modeling.

Teaching by modeling works simply. If social workers want clients to listen to one another, workers must first demonstrate their own abilities to listen to what clients are saying. If a social worker wants clients to assert themselves, the practitioner responds enthusiastically when clients disagree with the worker's view. If social workers want clients to show patience, workers demonstrate how they expect change at a realistic and incremental rate. If practitioners discover they themselves are unable to do what they are asking from clients, workers re-examine their own expectations.

Sharing Information

One accessible resource all clients have is the social worker. Many writers describe the ways in which social workers develop their abilities to influence clients. "Studies have shown three characteristics to be important: expertise, trustworthiness, and likability" (Simons & Aigner, 1985, p. 117). Additional characteristics include the worker's legitimate authority, reputation, and control over resources, services, and the flow of information (Pincus & Minahan, 1973). Practitioners have influence with clients when

1. They are knowledgeable about the topic under consideration and will use that knowledge for the client's benefit

2. They have been granted the authority by some legitimate organization or licensing body to offer services, and will live up to the limits on their legitimate areas of influence included in the client-worker contract for intervention goals

3. They are warm and caring individuals who respect the client (Feld & Radin, 1982, p. 195)

To use influence effectively as an intervention, social workers develop their professional reputations and their skills in sharing expertise and self-disclosing.

Offering professional knowledge

Clients are experts, but acknowledging client expertise does not strip practitioners of their own. Social workers often offer clients theoretical information, practice wisdom, and research knowledge. Shulman (1999) says

> The client looks to the worker as a source of help in difficult areas. If the client senses that the worker is withholding data (facts, ideas, values, and beliefs), for whatever reason, the withholding can be experienced as a form of rejection. (p. 186)

The information shared should be consistent with the agreed-on contract, connected to the client's immediate concerns, and within the area of the worker's expertise.

Workers show caution when using their expertise, so as not to undermine clients' expertise. The most empowering way to share expertise is by responding to the client's request. Notice the style and kinds of expertise workers offer in the following examples:

- So, you're interested in what I know about stepfamilies. I did just read some research the other day that said parenting works best when both parent and stepparent discuss together what to do with children, but then the biological parent actually implements what they decide. The research reports that children are much more likely to accept the authority of the biological parent.
- It might help you decide what to do if I shared some information about what we generally see happen when someone first moves into our facility. Are you interested in that?
- I'm impressed with your interest in what we've learned about how foster children adjust to placement. Our observations support your experience as a foster parent; frequently, children do have difficulty eating and sleeping for the first few days.
- I've completed the research you requested, and I have located six foundations that are possible sources of funds for transitional housing.

Each example draws on some piece of the social worker's knowledge base—practice experiences, knowledge of human behavior, theoretical frameworks, or research outcomes. Each comment either responds to what the client seeks or asks permission from the client to continue. None of these examples presents the worker's expertise as absolute, but instead as a piece of information that *might* be helpful or *might* somehow explain. Clients can glean from it what they will. When these workers share their knowledge, they do so as participants in the process rather than as all-knowing and all-seeing expert professionals.

Social workers selectively use their expertise to inform and normalize, not to impress or undermine.

Sharing expertise requires cultural competence. Cultural awareness gives clues to how workers should present information, since people from different cultures tend to differ in their styles of learning. Varying cultural attitudes toward authority also have implications for the approach that workers might choose in sharing expertise. Finally, workers carefully screen the information they offer to ensure that the content is a "cultural fit."

Self-disclosing

Social workers are people, too. They have lives, relationships, families, jobs, successes, setbacks, embarrassments, and dreams. Sometimes, social workers carefully choose from among their own personal experiences to share something of benefit to clients. Note that this is a selective process. Workers screen personal information to ensure that it is relevant to clients' situations. For example, workers may share:

- I remember what a difficult time I had when my father died.
- I overcame my fear of talking in front of people by taking a speech class at a community college.
- I remember feeling so inadequate my first day on this job. I even got lost in the parking building that day.
- My husband and I fight sometimes, but we've learned what works for us is to take breaks, think about it, and come back to talk again in an hour or two.

Workers differentiate between self-disclosing and giving advice. Advice says, "This is how you ought to do it." Self-disclosure says, "This is what it is like for me. I don't know whether this is helpful to you or not. You'll have to decide for yourself." Workers can self-disclose most effectively by identifying the information as a personal sharing and acknowledging that it may or may not be useful to the client. This frees clients to respond in whatever ways they choose (Figure 12.4).

Figure 12.4 Checklist for Self-Disclosure

Before self-disclosing, workers carefully screen information to keep their personal sharing professional by asking themselves the following questions:

1. What experiences have I had that may offer new information, a different perspective, or demonstrate empathy?
2. Is this information relevant to the client's situation at this particular time?
3. Do I have a close enough relationship with the client to share personal information? Will personal sharing confuse or inhibit the client?
4. Is it culturally appropriate to disclose this information?
5. What is my motivation in sharing this information? To build the relationship? To inform? To impress?
6. In what way do I expect the client to respond to this information? To see new possibilities? To understand that we have similar experiences?
7. What is the best way to offer this information neutrally? Will the client experience this as advice, contributing to feelings of inadequacy or failure?
8. Can I share this information briefly enough to maintain the focus on the client's issues rather than my own personal life?

LOOKING FORWARD

Activating resources again tests the worker's ability to do enough, but not too much, for a client. Empowerment-oriented social workers temper their expertise out of respect for client self-direction and determination. Recent research shows that experienced social workers in many fields of practice actually implement a whole range of interventions that vary from nondirective reflection to determinative action taken without the knowledge or agreement of the client system (Rothman, et al., 1996).

To augment a client's experience of power and competence, workers use strategies to build confidence and encourage clients to oversee their own development. Practitioners work consistently for clients to recognize their own power to affect events in their current transactions, become aware of options, increase use of available resources, and strengthen skills for reaching goals. Social workers and clients collaborate to activate resources as they implement plans of action.

In an ideal world, efficiently and creatively working with what is available would be enough. Social workers would freely consult, manage resources, and educate. Clients would reach their goals. But, all social workers and clients confront situations in which they wish there were other options. The attempt to locate resources sometimes reveals gaps in service delivery and limited opportunities for clients. Simply dealing with existing resources is not adequate for meeting current and changing needs.

To respond to this resource scarcity, social workers strive to enrich environments. Chapter 13 describes how workers increase the available pool of resources by creating new alliances among clients, within the service delivery network, and in clients' natural support networks. Chapter 14 extends the view of possible interventions by describing the social worker's responsibilities for expanding opportunities in the environment. Workers may implement community development strategies, influence social policy, advocate legislative change, and initiate social action. Generalist social workers do not limit their intervention activities to changing clients themselves; they also modify the environment to enhance clients' choices and opportunities.

Log onto **www.mysocialworklab.com** and select the **Interactive Skill Module** videos from the left-hand menu. Answer the questions below. (*If you did not receive an access code to* **MySocialWorkLab** *with this text and wish to purchase access online, please visit* www.mysocialworklab.com.)

1. Pointing out client strengths is central to empowering practice. Sometimes, clients report discomfort with receiving compliments. **Watch page 10 of the group work module** to see a worker using compliments. Is she effective? What comprises a useful compliment?

2. **Watch page 18 of the group work module** to observe two clients rehearse new behaviors in a role-play. What are the advantages and disadvantages of this "member to member" role-play compared to one involving a group member with the group leader?

PRACTICE TEST

Human Rights & Justice

1. With respect to fair hearing procedures, which statement is LEAST accurate?
   a. Clients have a right to appeal adverse agency decisions before a judge or panel of judges.
   b. Both sides are represented at fair hearing procedures.
   c. The judge or panel of judges renders a decision after receiving testimony and reviewing relevant policies, procedures, and legislation.
   d. The agency is not bound to comply with the decision made by the judge or panel of judges.

Professional Identity

2. With respect to self-disclosure on the part of the social worker, _____.
   a. advice and self-disclosure are the same
   b. it is always unethical for social workers to disclose personal experiences
   c. the purpose of social workers' sharing of personal experiences is to create a friendly atmosphere
   d. social workers can self-disclose most effectively by identifying the information as personal and acknowledging that it may or may not be useful to the client

3. Members of the child abuse coalition engage in a heated debate about new program initiatives. How would you recommend the worker respond to handle these differences?
   a. "A range of opinions have been expressed. I wonder if the entire group would like to examine each view more closely for its merits."
   b. "We've heard from two members of the coalition so far, what about the rest of you?"
   c. "Could I ask you to repeat what you just heard as I think you might have missed it?"
   d. "Let's switch topics to an agenda item that's less controversial."

4. Social worker Monique Rogers wonders how to sustain clients' motivation. You recommend using a strategy called _____ because of the motivational power of communicating understanding.
   a. maintaining focus
   b. validating the client's reality
   c. encouraging participation
   d. stimulating support

5. Which of the following statements MOST accurately describes the nature of change?
   a. Change is always a smooth process.
   b. Change is a process of forward motion with infrequent "setbacks."
   c. Each client manifests a unique pace and pattern of change.
   d. After change occurs, it's unusual for people to experience a period of restabilization.

6. Describing an active child's behavior as exuberant rather than naughty is an example of _____.
   a. reframing
   b. paradoxical thinking
   c. a metaphor
   d. a cliché

Diversity in Practice

7. At Abilities Inc, social worker Aaron Goldfarb supervises the work of persons who have developmental disabilities. To maximize confidence in his clients' abilities, Aaron should _____.
   a. assist them by picking up the slack in their work
   b. give them less rigorous work activities
   c. encourage them by pointing out successes
   d. point out every mistake so the clients' can learn from them

8. Of the following statements, which MOST accurately describes a social worker's use of feedback?
   a. Giving feedback is a way of offering advice.
   b. Constructive feedback criticizes behavior.
   c. Feedback only focuses on the need to improve.
   d. Feedback is a strategy for sharing perceptions.

Log onto **MySocialWorkLab** once you have completed the Practice Test above to take your Chapter Exam and demonstrate your knowledge of this material.

Answers

1) d 2) d 3) a 4) b 5) c 6) a 7) c 8) d

Creating Alliances

CONNECTING CORE COMPETENCIES *in this chapter*

Professional
Identity

Ethical
Practice

Critical
Thinking

Diversity
in Practice

Human
Rights
& Justice

Research
Based
Practice

Human
Behavior

Policy
Practice

Practice
Contexts

Engage
Assess
Intervene
Evaluate

When the social work team of Consuela Diaz and Darrell Foster arrives at the community center, they feel as if they are late. The members of the Community Action Council are already talking among themselves, handing out various task group reports, and compiling an agenda for the official meeting. Marvella Harvey, chairperson of the Council, is talking to some members about the Council's new advocacy program, through which the Council represents the interests of citizens in their dealings with city officials, law enforcement officers, and state political representatives. Other members talk excitedly in small groups, pull out additional chairs from the storeroom to accommodate the overflow crowd, or snack on the coffee and cookies that someone has supplied. The workers see that the group has taken on a life of its own.

As social workers for the Northside Development Association, Consuela and Darrell worked with the Community Action Council from its inception as an informal group of interested citizens. Earlier in their work with the Council, Consuela and Darrell played facilitative roles in the group's operation, guiding the Council through various phases of organization, assessment, and analysis to create a comprehensive plan of action. But now, the plan is in motion, and so are the members of the Council. Both Consuela and Darrell recognize the signs. This group is sensing its power and learning to wield it. It's time for the two workers to take another step back. They greet the members of the Council and take seats on the side of the room.

After Marvella calls the meeting to order, Consuela and Darrell observe firsthand the abilities the group has developed. The members organize their interaction productively, actively seek each other's views, listen closely to one another, welcome differences of opinions as stimulating options rather than threats to unity, and focus on their goals. They even wrap up the meeting by posting a concrete list of the activities that each task group will complete by the next meeting. The members of the Community Action Council can see where they are, plan next steps, and know they have the capabilities to achieve their goals.

Clearly, the Community Action Council is activated—keeping in touch with its resources, feeling its power to make changes, and demonstrating the skills to do so. Do you sense the momentum building in this group? Do you notice how the group seems to be taking over the process of reaching its own goals? This client system is on the move! It is this kind of movement that social workers seek as they work to create and activate alliances.

This chapter discusses the activities of social workers and clients in building productive alliances in their respective environments. Specifically, this chapter

- Describes ways alliances empower clients and social workers
- Discusses how group alliances can foster mutual aid and social action
- Explores options for strengthening natural support networks
- Examines case management as an effective strategy for coordinating services
- Considers the role of organizational alliances in service delivery and resource development
- Surveys professional alliances as resources of support for social work practitioners

Social workers who create and facilitate alliances for their clients and for themselves will generate resources for service delivery and construct supportive environments for practice.

THE POWER OF ALLIANCES

When you add 1 + 1, what do you get? In the world of math, the answer is obviously 2. But in the world of empowering social work, 1 + 1 = 3! Think about the social worker–client system relationship as an example to understand this "new math." When you add the resources of the social worker to the resources of the client, you have two resources with which to begin. But as the social worker and client work together, a third resource emerges—the synergistic resource created through a collaborative alliance.

The possibilities for resource-generating alliances exist beyond the social worker–client relationship (see Figure 13.1). Social workers support clients'

Figure 13.1   Types of Alliances
Clients can benefit from many types of alliances including those with other clients who have similar concerns, supportive relationships within their natural support networks, alliances between clients and their service providers, organizational coalitions among agencies providing services, and the worker's own alliances within the professional network of support.

efforts to build productive connections with others. Alliances are possible among clients sharing the same issues and interests, such as those that develop when social workers facilitate client groups. Alliances are available within clients' natural support networks. And importantly, as in the example of case management, practitioners can cement collaborative partnerships among clients and their various service providers.

Even beyond the immediate context of the client, social workers build professional alliances that will have indirect benefits for clients. The organization-to-organization connections forged within interagency coalitions strengthen working relationships among service providers, reveal areas that require resource development, and provide muscle to influence political and legislative action. Finally, the connections that social workers make with each other and other professionals provide support and stimulation that will ultimately benefit clients through workers' feelings of support, increased motivation, and fresh ideas.

DEVELOPING ALLIANCES THROUGH GROUPS

All people benefit from supportive relationships with others. Such relationships contribute to feelings of confidence and security. Good relationships have synergy; they actually become resources—stimulating ideas, feelings, and experiences impossible for any individual to create independently. Social workers facilitate the development of alliances through their use of groups.

Groups and Empowerment

Social work groups are vehicles for personal growth, skill development, and environmental change. Through group work, group members may acquire new perspectives, be a support for one another, and also join forces for collective action. As such, group work may well be the method of choice for empowerment-oriented social work practice (Breton, 2002, 2006; DuBois & Miley, 2008; East, et al., 2002; Lee, 2001). Groups provide the forum for people to develop skills in critical thinking, receive information and validation, and organize a power base from which to advocate change in larger social systems. Group work characterizes the social work profession's tradition of empowerment with those persons who are oppressed.

In groups, members share resources with each other rather than depend primarily on the social worker's skills and expertise. From the perspective of empowerment, groups are vehicles for changing "oppressive cognitive, behavioral, social, and political structures or conditions that thwart the control people have over their lives, that prevent them from accessing needed resources, and that keep them from participating in the life of their community (Breton, 2004, p. 59).

Facilitating group functioning

Social workers have responsibilities to maximize the benefits of the group process. Workers use skills to (1) conceptualize and initiate the group, (2) develop the system of mutual aid essential to the group's success, and (3) mediate the interactions among group members and between the group and its environment to maintain and achieve the group's purpose.

Social workers complete many tasks to initiate an effective group. Often, workers decide on a group approach based on contacts with several individual clients who are expressing similar needs. At other times, the ideas for groups come from social issues identified by the worker or as suggestions from indigenous community leaders. Once the group is envisioned, workers engage in other pregroup activities that include taking steps to launch the group. These pregroup activities include developing a proposal, receiving sanction for the group from the sponsoring organization, accessing and screening potential members, and orienting members selected to the purpose and process of the group (Corey & Corey, 2006).

As the group begins, social workers as facilitators develop the system of mutual aid that characterizes the group approach. To accomplish this, workers direct members' interactions toward one another, help members respond to what other members are saying, foster the development of respectful and functional group norms, and highlight members' common characteristics and concerns (Germain & Gitterman, 1996). This phase of group work is the formation stage, a time when the group takes on its own unique identity. During this time, members begin to sense the power of the group alliance and recognize their place in the structure of the group.

Finally, to achieve the purposes of the group, social workers keep members on task, network appropriate resources and information to members, and help members implement goal-directed activities. Key skills for social workers during this phase of group operation include resolving conflicts, facilitating decision making, and stimulating creativity. For groups to be empowering, workers teach and model these skills so that members themselves can take responsibility for the group's interaction and success.

A group example

Irizarry and Appel (2005) describe their group work with inner-city youths—African American and Puerto Rican girls from 10 to 13 years of age. The authors describe these girls as experiencing a double marginality—coping with the developmental transitions to adolescence in the context of ethnic identity issues and poverty. The specific incident occurred on a subway trip to Coney Island. "The restraint of space and apparent scrutiny by passengers led to noisy behavior by the girls" (p. 178), which eventually led to their being ejected from the train. The worker indicated that the girls treated the event as a joke, even though their plans were ruined, and they had to return home. An excerpt from the case illustrates the girls' movement toward autonomy through their experience of mutual aid while discussing their experiences:

> The next day while we were eating cookies at the center, the whole episode was spontaneously reviewed. Judy remarked quite somberly, that she imagined passengers thought they were girls on a trip from a "loony house." Nilda added, without laughter, "We all looked crazy—no wonder people stared." Comments ensued about various crazy people from the neighborhood and how they acted. I asked if they wanted people to think that about them. Carmen instantly replied no but that it was my fault because I hadn't screamed at them and made them stop.
>
> I said I hadn't thought I was a policewoman to go around watching how they behaved, and that they were always telling me how much they didn't like their teachers bossing them around so much. Nilda said I could be in some ways like a teacher. Judy agreed to tell them to sit down. I said that I was willing to remind them to sit down if they wanted me to, but also asked them if they thought it would really stop them. Tata led the general response that no one could stop them when they got going "like that." I said that I thought one of the hardest things for anyone to learn in life was to act the way they really wanted. (pp. 178–179)

Demonstrating an important skill in group facilitation, the social worker in the example does not control the process or evaluate what the group members have done. Instead, she encourages the members themselves to interact and reflect on their own experiences.

Mutual Aid in Groups

Small groups provide opportunities for enhancing mutual aid among clients, a setting in which clients help themselves by helping each other. "The group is an enterprise in mutual aid, an alliance of individuals who need each other, in varying degrees, to work on certain common problems" (Shulman & Gitterman, 2005, p. 21). Workers facilitate interactions among members and stimulate processes which activate members' contributions to each other. Some examples of applications of mutual aid strategies include groups for older adults (Kelly, 2004; Lee & Ayón, 2005), professional women at midlife (Lesser, et al., 2004), drug-use prevention (Pinto & Queely, 2003), end-of-life care (Goelitz, 2004), and with a solution-oriented focus (Cohen, 2007, Cohen & Graybeal, 2007)

Mutual aid processes

Nine qualities of mutual aid processes empower group members (Shulman & Gitterman, 2005). *Sharing data* provides group members with opportunities to benefit from the knowledge and resources each member contributes. The *dialectical process* involves point-and-counterpoint discussions in which members articulate and synthesize divergent views. The abilities of some members to begin to talk about "*taboo subjects*" lend courage to others to do the same. Importantly, mutual exchanges also foster the sense of "*all being in the same boat.*" There is solace in knowing that others have similar experiences. *Mutual support* flows through individual members as well as the group as a whole and has reciprocal effects. Lending support to others benefits both the givers and the receivers. However, caring in and of itself is not enough to facilitate change. *Mutual demand* confronts the need to make changes and holds members accountable for taking action. *Individual problem solving* occurs when work in the group moves back and forth between specific cases and general issues. *Rehearsal* is a role play strategy for practicing new behaviors in a context where support and feedback can increase members' confidence in their abilities to change. Finally, there is *strength in numbers.* United with others, people will take actions that they dare not or cannot do alone.

Self-Help Groups

Workers are not always pivotal in constructing empowering groups. Self-help groups develop when individuals with similar concerns or problems join together to be helpful resources for one another. The caring that occurs in self-help or mutual support groups creates an empathic environment for exchanging ideas and providing relevant information, offers strategies for coping and problem resolution, and empowers group members to confront troubling issues (Segal, 2008). A recent study of 253 self-help groups in Kansas found that these groups had developed networks of connections with local professionals and alliances with related local, state, and national organizations, lending both credence and stability to these resources for support (Wituk, et al., 2000).

Diversity in Practice

Self-help groups are a source of social support for individuals who share common concerns or interests. What contributions do peers-helping-peers' strategies provide to persons from diverse or minority population groups?

These groups usually form around common concerns or problem areas such as substance abuse, intimate violence, grief issues, divorce, step-parenting, and health and wellness concerns. Typically, peers, who are participating group members themselves, facilitate the mutual support groups. Examples of nationally organized self-help groups include Alcoholics Anonymous, Parents without Partners, and the National Alliance for the Mentally Ill. Not only do these groups provide mutual exchange and support, but they often have a political agenda as well, seeking to change public attitudes and laws that affect their constituencies.

Working with self-help groups

Because of their potential role for providing clients with support and connections to others with similar difficulties, social workers develop skills for linking clients with self-help groups. To draw on these resources, social workers

- Develop a file that contains descriptions of the self-help resources
- Identify the key participants in local self-help groups
- Discuss the benefits of self-help groups with clients
- Give clients up-to-date information or brochures about the self-help group
- Provide clients with specific and accurate information about meeting times, locations, and contact persons

Self-help groups are part of a natural helping system within any community that supports the well-being of its members. When social workers draw on the resources of self-help groups, they help strengthen the client's sense of belonging to a community.

Self-help groups and empowerment

Self-help is integral to clients' experiences of empowerment (Cheung, et al., 2005; DeCoster & George, 2005; Mok, 2004; O'Connor, 2002; Yumiko, et al., 2003). Self-help groups provide emotional and social support, concrete assistance, a forum for learning new skills, and a base of power for collective action (Dodd & Gutiérrez, 1990). The self-help group members, by definition, help each other. The peers-helping-peers strategies of self-help are empowering because members are active participants in group discussions and activities rather than passive recipients of services (Sullivan & Rapp, 1994).

Participating in experiences where peers help peers has indirect effects as well. Cox and Parsons (1993) report the comments of a grandmother who describes the effect of her participation in a peer-counseling program for older adults:

> You know, one never knows what is in store for them. You just cannot plan things. I am taking care of my two granddaughters, one is 16 and one 20. Their mother, my daughter, is an alcoholic, and refuses to deal with them. I really have tried my best, but just haven't been able to reach them. They feel that I'm too old and removed from their world. The kids never shared their thoughts or feelings with me nor their doings in school. However, since I joined the peer counseling program, I started to apply some of the things I learned on my own grandkids. Do you know that now we sit around the table at suppertime and talk! The kids are now interested in what I'm doing and learning. They think it's great! Imagine at my age going to school and learning new things! I believe they think grandma is not so stupid after all. They even told their friends

Self-help groups provide the social support necessary to empower participants.

about me. Believe it or not, they have started thinking of aging and the attitudes that surround aging, including their own. Isn't it great! This program is my salvation! (pp. 132–133)

Social Action through Group Work

Tactics mean doing what you can with what you have.

—Saul Alinsky

Whereas mutual aid in groups supports individual change, social action in groups generates activities which aim toward mezzo- and macrolevel changes. Sometimes workers and clients initiate social action groups for the sole purpose of mezzo- and macrolevel change. At other times, social action emerges from the processes of mutual aid through which group participants identify the interconnections between personal difficulties and public issues. In either instance, participating in social action groups is often a pathway to a heightened sense of competence (Breton, 2004, 2006; Donaldson, 2004; Staples, 2004).

Gutiérrez (1991) describes her experiences of moving from mutual aid to advocacy and resource mobilization in her work with Latino and African American mothers in a community mental health center setting. The center ran a series of groups over a 9-month period. The initial group was a *support group* to address the concrete issues the women identified—"family stress, dangerous neighborhoods, and an inadequate school system" (p. 209). Gutiérrez observes that "for most of the women, this engagement toward changing concrete issues worked toward the resolution of personal problems as well" (p. 209). The second group was a *skills-building group,* primarily concerned with issues related to parenting. The group was designed to deal with issues the women identified in a supportive group atmosphere. At the group members' request for continued involvement, the graduates of the first skills building group became *mentors* for women who joined an open-membership parenting group. From this experience, the fourth group, a client-led *social support and social action group,* evolved. Topics for discussion included "how to budget their welfare allotment, how to make toys and gifts for children, understanding their children's behavior, and sex education" (p. 210). When educational concerns were a recurrent theme, the group took action to invite a representative from the local school board to their meeting. When the results of this conversation did not address their concerns, they initiated discussions with an attorney who spearheaded a class action directed at the lack of special education services in the community. "This example indicates how in less than a year, these women moved from feeling overwhelmed by their young children to feeling capable of confronting the city board of education" (p. 210).

Liddie (1991) also describes her work with a group for mothers whose children were enrolled in a day care program. Liddie and her colleagues used strategies that increased self-esteem and autonomy. Their intentional orientation toward empowerment placed the group members in charge of decisions about the group's activities—the agenda, guest speakers, meal preparation and clean-up, social and educational events, attendance at day care board meetings, and discussions with local politicians. Several interesting projects resulted from their increased self-confidence and their collaborative efforts in identifying common issues and strategizing action plans. They successfully organized a contingent of 500 community members to demonstrate at city hall about their objections to cuts in day care funding. The group also arranged meetings with the day care staff to express their desires to develop more mutually beneficial working relationships.

What began as a support group for mothers developed into a vehicle for addressing issues in the community and with the day care center. What began as women questioning their own worth and even denying their own strengths evolved to circumstances in which women experienced firsthand their individual and collective accomplishments.

STRENGTHENING NATURAL SUPPORT ALLIANCES

People may overlook the significant support they receive from social ties such as their relationships with family members, friends, colleagues, and their associations with churches, schools, or clubs (Table 13.1). However, support networks play an essential role in social functioning and are a potential resource in the social service delivery network.

Social Support

Social support includes those exchanges in our social networks that provide "emotional encouragement, concrete assistance or tangible aid, and advice and information" (Kemp, et al., 1997, p. 73). Family members, friends, neighbors, acquaintances, colleagues, self-help group members, and professionals are all potential sources of social support.

Numerous research findings underscore the significance of social support in protecting, moderating, and buffering the effects of crises and in contributing to peoples' resiliency in the face of ongoing stress (Campos, et al., 2008; Lietz, 2007; Nicholas, et al., 2007; Nicholas & Keilty, 2007; Owen, et al., 2008; Wong, 2008; Wood & Woody, 2007). Conversely, a lack of social support and a sense of social isolation often magnify the difficulties people experience and reduce the pool of resources that contributes to solutions.

Table 13.1   Social Support Networks

Informal Systems	Membership Systems	Professional Systems
Spouses	Churches and synagogues	Social workers
Partners	Informal social clubs	Mental health practitioners
Children	Clubs	Educators
Parents	Associations	Clergy
Siblings	Civic organizations	Lawyers
Extended family	Fraternities and sororities	Doctors and nurses
Friends	Athletic teams	Dieticians
Neighbors	Parent-teacher associations	Speech therapists
Classmates	Unions	Psychologists
Co-workers	Fraternal and social organizations	Elected officials
	Recreational memberships	
	Art and music groups	
	Hangouts (bars, the mall, supper clubs)	
	Mutual-aid groups	

Social support, by definition, involves connections with others. However, connections with others alone do not guarantee experiences of social support (El-Bassel, et al.,1998; Kemp, et al., 1997). The quality of these relationships makes a difference. Support occurs when relationships are based on reciprocity, mutuality, and shared power in an atmosphere where people can offer what they have to offer and receive the resources they seek.

Social support may provide resources for clients, yet workers should not expect naturally supportive networks to solve all dilemmas. Cautioning against viewing social support as a panacea, experts recommend defining social support as "a necessary but not sufficient component of a comprehensive service plan which likely will include family treatment, parent education, case management, and related services" (Whittaker & Tracy, 1991, p. 176). Social support networks play a significant role; however, they are best considered as complementary to rather than a substitute for professional social services. The strength of social support may be culturally based. Culturally responsive social workers recognize that extended family and community networks play a significant role in some cultures and geographic regions.

Workers' Roles in Encouraging Social Support

A person's social support network usually develops naturally, but workers can also encourage these networks to develop purposefully. Workers can participate in designing physical environments that create opportunities for interaction. They can also teach clients social skills to prepare them for new relationships. Finally, workers can access natural helpers in the community directly to ally them with clients who need support.

Designing environments

Our physical surroundings either enhance or inhibit the potential for developing social relationships. Research in social psychology shows that: "Just as it is possible to build oppressive environments that stifle social activity, it is also possible to design them to promote social activity and support" (Fleming, et al., 1985, p. 327). Research on which these authors draw indicates that the opportunities for social contact, the proximity of people to each other, and the appropriateness of space for group interaction all influence the formation of groups and other social networks.

The physical design of space—whether homes, offices, meeting rooms, apartment complexes, residential facilities, neighborhoods, or communities—influences the number of social exchanges people make, and likewise, the chances they have for becoming friends. Social workers can participate in designing spaces that support the development of social relationships and also in modifying the existing environments to promote social interactions.

Enhancing interactional skills

The advantage of physical environments that support social interactions is lost if people have not had an opportunity to develop their skills in relating to others. In the context of professional relationships, social workers have opportunities to observe clients in action in an "up-front and personal way." Workers' experiences with client systems offer information about how clients interact. Social workers draw selectively from this reservoir to provide feedback to clients about their skills.

When social workers notice a client's interpersonal skills, they mention them for the client's benefit. Giving compliments to clients about what social workers see has proven positive effects (Wall, et al., 1989). Clients who recognize their own interpersonal skills and abilities carry confidence into relationships with others. Workers say things such as:

- It's always good to talk with you. You have such a good sense of humor, and we all appreciate a good laugh.
- That's what I like about you! You listen so carefully when people talk, and you are so good at understanding how they feel.
- I appreciate your honesty about your feelings toward the child protective unit. It is so much easier to relate to people who are up front about their views.
- I admire the way you follow through. People can always count on you to keep your commitments to them.

Friendships are based on mutuality and exchange. Friendships are most likely to flourish in the context of shared interests, activities, and projects rather than concentrated efforts at "being friends." Enabling the development of social support networks requires creative use of clients' interests and existing connections. For example, social workers could encourage clients interested in the outdoors to join a hiking club or group interested in environmental causes, clients with school-age children to volunteer to assist with school activities or participate actively in school-based organizations, or clients who, by their age, qualify to take part in their community's programs for "seniors."

Activating natural helpers

All communities contain natural helpers, people known in their neighborhoods, workplaces, schools, or churches who function effectively on their own and who provide resources and support to others around them (Germain & Gitterman,

1996). Communities of faith offer significant sources of social support, contributing to resilience, wellness, and recovery (Ferguson, et al., 2007; Nelson-Becker, 2005; Netting et al., 2007; Pentz, 2005). Practitioners who focus their work in a particular community gradually become aware of people who play central roles as indigenous helpers. Indigenous leaders may reveal themselves through their community leadership and voluntarism, or social workers can discover their presence gradually as they hear about their activities in conversations with community members. Recent work in Hawaii describes the inclusion of indigenous Hawaiian helpers into a professional helping process. Kupana elders, from whom all tradition is conveyed within the extended family, have proven to be effective healers when participating in a substance abuse treatment program for women (Morelli & Fong, 2000). In this culturally sensitive model, Kupana provided child care, taught women Hawaiian ways and values, and participated in the traditional deep therapy process known as *ho'oponopono.*

CASE MANAGEMENT: CLIENT–SERVICE ALLIANCES

Case management creates and strengthens alliances among service providers and with clients. A popular, contemporary approach for networking health care and social services, case management coordinates relevant resources involved with a particular client system. The shift to social policies and funding protocols that endorse case management strategies ensures that case management will retain its pivotal role in the delivery of services (Roberts-DeGennaro, 2008). This section defines case management, describes its purpose, presents a case example, details case management activities, and examines key issues associated with the urgency to contain costs and the propensity to "manage cases" rather than provide effective service.

Case Management Defined

Case management services are delivered by an individual or team "who organizes, coordinates, and sustains a network of formal and informal supports and activities designed to optimize the functioning and well-being of people with multiple needs" (Moxley, 1989, p. 21). Case managers work with clients who need access to several types of resources. They also work with the members of interdisciplinary teams who are working with particular clients. Case managers seek "to assure that clients of human services systems receive the services, treatment, care, and opportunities to which they are entitled" (Weil & Karls, 1989, p. 1).

Origins of case management

One can trace the impetus for case management to six factors: deinstitutionalization, decentralization of services, clients with multiple needs, fragmentation of services, the nature of informal social supports, and the press to contain costs in the face of limited funds and scarce resources (Moxley, 1989).

- *Deinstitutionalization* is the trend to provide community-based rather than institution-based services. This means that clients with multiple challenges must sustain their ability to live independently by locating appropriate services among the complicated array of community-based programs.
- The trend toward *decentralization* intensifies the need for coordinating services among multiple community-based service providers. "From the

perspective of many clients and their families, accessing and using community services can be as difficult as untangling a Gordian knot" (p. 13).

▶ Without the benefits of case management, clients with *complex issues and multiple needs* must somehow piece together a "patchwork" of resources for themselves. Often they must access services from multiple providers, many of whom have never communicated with one another.

▶ The constraints of the requirements for services—including geographic boundaries, age restrictions, income guidelines, and categorical eligibility stipulation—*fragment* the delivery of social services. This fragmentation complicates the tasks of coordinating services and determining for which services clients are eligible.

▶ *Social support networks* can either enhance or reduce the positive effect of formal services. Case managers can play a unique role to ensure that formal and informal resources reinforce each other, maximizing the benefits of each.

▶ The *press to contain costs* and *conserve scarce resources* yet still meet the needs of clients requires the efficient processes that case management offers.

Expanding role for case management

Largely as a result of these trends, case management is rapidly acquiring a reputation as a major social work practice strategy with clients who have multiple needs. Case management is used extensively in the fields of mental health, addictions, developmental disabilities, health care, rehabilitation, corrections, public welfare, child welfare, and family-based and aging services. Within this array of fields, public, private not-for-profit, and private for-profit agencies provide case management services. Case management is the exclusive domain of some of the agencies; others offer case management services as one of several programs and services. Increasing numbers of generalist social workers will be employed as case managers or, at least, in practice settings that use case management for the delivery of programs and services

The Purpose of Case Management

Effective case management links clients to services, connects service providers with each other, and redresses shortcomings in service delivery. Based on the work of Applebaum and Austin, Quinn (1995) specifies a broad range of client-oriented and system-oriented objectives as an example of the purpose of case management in the field of case management in long-term care:

Client-Oriented Objectives

▶ To assure that services given are appropriate to client needs
▶ To monitor appropriateness of long-term care services
▶ To improve client access to the continuum of long-term care services
▶ To support the client's caregivers
▶ To serve as a bridge between institutional and community-based care systems

System-Oriented Objectives

▶ To facilitate the development of noninstitutional services
▶ To promote quality in long-term care service delivery

    ▶ To enhance the coordination of service delivery in long-term care

    ▶ To target individuals most at risk of nursing home placement to prevent inappropriate institutionalization

    ▶ To contain cost by controlling client access to services. (pp. 237–238)

Scan these objectives to note their general themes. Some of the objectives relate to initiating, planning, implementing, and evaluating services with a particular client. Others relate to the service delivery system itself—coordinating, evaluating, and containing costs, as well as revamping existing services and creating new ones. Although this list focuses on case management in long-term care, these same objectives readily adapt to other settings.

Case Management in Action: A Practice Example

Like other case managers, Kennedy Brown finds he is dealing with issues at all system levels. His responsibilities lead him to work with service providers, as well as clients and their families.

    When Sarah Martin calls to inquire about the availability of community-based services for her parents, Kennedy Brown hears a familiar story. As a case manager for OPTIONS, a Northside agency that provides services and programming for older adults, Kennedy recognizes the need for environmental supports as people become frail. Sarah's parents, Ida and George Palmer, are both 75. Until recently, they were able to maintain their normal routine, living in their own home, tending their yard, enjoying the neighborhood children, watching television, and reading. However, when Sarah had visited with her parents the day before, her mother confided that she had been keeping a nightly vigil for several weeks, guarding against George's wandering off during the night. Sarah was shocked to learn that her father, who always seemed so chipper when she visited, had been declining for some time and that her mother had been protecting their "secret." Sarah reports that Ida, although sick with exhaustion herself, is committed to caring for George. After all, they've been married for 55 years.

    Sarah feels torn. Both she and her husband work full-time, and their children have numerous work, school, and family commitments; however, she knows she must do something. The question Sarah poses to Kennedy Brown says it all: "Are there any services in our community that can help my parents?" Kennedy Brown sets up a meeting with Sarah and her parents to discuss their situation more fully and determine a course of action that will support the Palmers.

    Kennedy Brown's meeting with his new clients uncovers multiple concerns. Sarah and her parents concur that for George and Ida to remain in their own home they require supportive services as soon as possible to meet George's physical needs and to assist Ida in her caregiving role. Together they begin to generate some options:

    ▶ Medical evaluation at Northside Hospital's specialized program for older adults

    ▶ Meals on Wheels

    ▶ Homemaker services for assistance with household chores

    ▶ "Afternoon Out" respite program

Additional issues may surface after addressing the Palmer's immediate needs. Long-term goals will likely include expanding the family's understanding about disease processes and aging, as well as coping with their grief over George's declining health. For example, Sarah and her mother may want to join a caregiver support group or enroll George in the OPTIONS' Adult Care Center. Kennedy knows that depending on their assessment, the interdisciplinary medical team might recommend that George participate in the university-based research project to test the effectiveness of a new drug used to treat Alzheimer's disease.

Kennedy's work with the Palmers also means working with the resource network. Kennedy will convene meetings of service providers who will work with the Palmers as well as attend meetings of providers that focus on general issues of the client population he serves. Case managers are generalists, simultaneously working with microlevel clients and operating at the mezzolevel to coordinate service provisions, enhance interagency cooperation, identify gaps in services and problems with delivery, and increase the efficient use of scarce resources.

Three factors are essential for productive case management, including "an accurate assessment and recurring re-evaluation with the client of what is needed; the existence of the needed services; and the power to ensure that the services are in fact delivered in a timely fashion" (Dinerman, 1992, p. 4). Case managers coordinate the delivery of services, provide for continuity in their provision, seek fiscal accountability, and ensure service effectiveness. Their activities encompass work with case management clients and with various aspects of the delivery system itself.

Case Management Activities with Clients

Case managers rely on generic social work processes to carry out their case-management activities. Core functions include outreach, networking, assessment, planning, contracting, linking, advocacy, monitoring, and evaluation (Austin & McClelland, 1996; Roberts-DeGennaro, 2008). This section highlights four major case management activities—outreach, planning in case staffings, linking clients with resources, and advocacy.

Outreach

The intent of outreach is to heighten the visibility of programs and services by educating the general public and other service providers about available programs. A more focused activity, case finding, directs outreach efforts toward those who are likely to need the services the information is promoting. Case managers hope that, through the early identification made possible by outreach, their work with clients can prevent problems of a greater magnitude.

Community education initiatives include public speaking engagements, newspaper articles, brochures and pamphlets, and fund-raising campaigns. Contacts with key people in the community, such as indigenous leaders, clergy, visiting nurses, teachers, day care providers, lawyers, and physicians, often play a key role in outreach work, too. The client's first contact for assistance is often not with a social worker but, instead, with a community member or professional who is in a position of acting as a "bridge" to appropriate programs and services.

Planning in case staffings

Interdisciplinary staffings, a common planning strategy among service providers, coordinate work with client systems. Joint planning efforts synchronize services and avoid unnecessary duplications.

For empowerment-oriented social workers, the key issue in case staffings is ensuring an active role for clients. Many times, staffings exclude clients, ostensibly so professionals can "talk more openly." Carefully examine what this position reveals about professionals' communication with clients and the long-range effect of denying clients direct access to key information about their own situations. Decision-making processes that exclude clients usurp informed consent. Empowerment-based social work practice places clients genuinely in control over what happens in their lives by guaranteeing their participation in case staffings!

Social workers play various roles at case staffings. Sometimes they function as information givers, talking directly about their views of the client's situation. They may also be facilitators, guiding the group's interaction in such a way that clients have opportunities to offer their perspectives and other participants hear and respect what clients say. At other times, staffings require workers to switch their level of focus from their client to the interdisciplinary helping system itself. When focusing on the way the helping system functions, social workers support the effective development of the team. For example, a worker can facilitate a sense of rapport, nonjudgmental openness, and equal distribution of power by listening carefully and by encouraging participants to voice their opinions.

Linking clients with resources

Case managers are consummate information specialists. They offer technical assistance with respect to availability, benefits, eligibility requirements, application procedures, and other vital information about resources. In discussing the linking activities of her work with pregnant teens, Davis (1992) indicates she must weave "together people in agencies and programs dealing with adoption, dropouts, genetic counseling, job training, health, day care, equity, women's issues, fathers, family planning, child abuse issues, human growth and development, nutrition, parenting, and career planning" (p. 29).

By providing relevant information, case managers guide clients through the maze of the service network to assist them in acquiring suitable resources. Kaplan (1992) suggests several strategies for linking clients with resources. Effective case managers need to

- Be familiar with the resources, having, insofar as possible, firsthand information to draw on
- Plan ahead for emergency situations, anticipating, for example, the types of crises clients are likely to experience
- Create new resources when none exist
- Coordinate the services of multiple providers
- Modify the linkages with resources as the client's circumstances change

Advocacy

Advocates use their influence to compel the social service delivery system "to be more responsive to the unmet needs of clients" (Kisthardt & Rapp, 1992, p. 121). Questions to evaluate the necessity for initiating advocacy activities include:

- Is the resource *available?*
- Is the resource *accessible?*
- Is the provider willing to make the necessary *accommodations?*
- Will the resource be *adequate?*

To be culturally competent, case managers raise "awareness of discriminatory and oppressive practices and institutionalized forms of racism, sexism, ageism, ableism, and homophobia that create barriers to access" (Rogers, 1995, p. 65).

Rather than directing the advocacy process, case managers are most empowering when they support clients to advocate for themselves. Client-driven advocacy places clients in roles that control advocacy activities, leaving corollary roles for social workers to support clients' actions (Moxley & Freddolino, 1994). As initiators, clients define their own needs and select activities to address them. To facilitate this role, social workers as mentors model ways to solve problems, teach skills for dealing with institutions and bureaucracies, and suggest ways to network with others. Clients as implementors act on their own behalf, whereas social workers as coaches guide clients in their advocacy activities. Clients determine whether they should continue, modify, or halt their advocacy activities. Through their support role, social workers bolster clients' advocacy efforts and back their decisions. Clients as educators inform professionals about what they want to achieve, how they want to achieve it, and what they are willing to accept from a provider, telling the social worker when to act as the client's representative "to resolve disputes through mediation and negotiation, or through more assertive actions such as administrative hearings or formal legal action" (p. 99).

This client-driven model of advocacy does more than help clients gain access to services. It also "promotes the values of self-determination and client control over intervention activities" and "addresses the basic needs and resources of clients from the perspectives of clients themselves" (Moxley & Freddolino, 1994, p. 104).

Case Management Activities with the Delivery System

Case managers also work with other professionals in the delivery system itself, both to coordinate the work of various programs and professionals involved with particular clients and to build a more-responsive social service delivery network.

Coordinating services

The purpose of coordinating services is to ensure "that services are being implemented in harmonious and compatible ways by the human service providers and social network members who have been organized by the case manager to respond to client needs" (Moxley, 1989, p. 101). In coordinating services, the case manager reviews the service provisions to ensure that their goals are congruous, that the services delivered correspond with the agreed-on plan, and that opportunities for service providers to communicate exist. Factors that impede coordination include turf issues, competition among service providers, disagreements about priorities and intervention strategies, and the lack of a common vision for the plan.

Collaboration reaps the same benefits with service providers as it does with clients. Sheridan et al. (1993) indicate that cooperating with service providers "is most challenging for workers who tend to perceive the system as unresponsive, unworkable, or even as 'the enemy.' For various reasons, barriers exist in the service delivery system and agencies differ in their responsiveness to client needs" (p. 416). These authors describe their case management efforts with homeless clients and the success they experience with providers by beginning "with the assumption that personnel wanted to be helpful, that they knew their jobs, and that they cared about client service" (p. 416).

Relating to other professionals

Sometimes connections between clients and potential resource systems need to be modified. In these situations, workers use skills to enhance the relationships of clients with resource systems. This requires a sorting out of responsibilities between family systems and larger system helpers. Clarifying roles reduces conflicting messages to the client, prevents overlaps in service delivery, and alleviates turf battles among various service providers. When clients renegotiate their connections to larger systems, they can shift the distribution of power—getting larger systems to work for them rather than on them.

The way in which social workers approach other systems has an impact on the ensuing success. Representatives of resource systems are people, too. They respond to the same respectful treatment, appreciate the same consideration, and need the same validation as clients. Effective social workers empower environmental systems as well as clients in their work to reach clients' goals.

Building responsive networks of services

Even the best plans are inadequate when resources are unavailable or inaccessible. A prime function of case managers is to advocate changes within the delivery system to make its services more appropriate, adequate, and accessible. Case managers are in key positions for building more responsive networks of social services. "The daily practice of case management provides ample opportunity to identify and document service delivery effects, barriers, and obstacles originating at the system level, especially in fiscal and operational policies" (Austin, 1993, p. 457). Case managers can address service delivery issues by

- Creating changes in organizations or the networks of service delivery providers
- Participating in capacity building or "strengthening the network of community resources so that it will be responsive to other clients in the future"
- Finding ways to "influence the development of new resources and programs" (Moxley, 1989, p. 94)

However, case management is no panacea for an inadequate social service delivery system that is badly in need of structural reform and financial investment. "By itself, case management services cannot alter biases and shortages in the delivery system. . . . In the absence of adequate funding, case managers cannot create services that do not exist" (Austin, 1992, p. 64).

Workers' Resources for Case Management

Social work knowledge and skills support case management activities. Effective case management builds on a sound base of knowledge about the consumers such as key developmental issues, cultural backgrounds, and the community context. A resourceful case manager also knows about relevant programs and services—their eligibility requirements, costs, restrictions, application procedures, and availability. Being prepared with information helps workers coach clients to deal more successfully with service providers.

Case managers use skills to build relationships, exchange information, use the telephone productively, and manage time (Quinn, 1995). Skills in listening are important for relating to both clients and colleagues. Gathering and conveying information to clients and around the helping system is also pivotal to competent case management. When communicating over the phone, case managers have "facts in hand," respond to messages in a timely fashion, inquire about the best time to return a call, and craft succinct, yet informative, messages. Time-management skills help case managers balance countless demands such as responding to crises, coordinating the activities of multiple service providers, and meeting deadlines. Effective organization is the key. Marking appointments, meetings, forms to fill out, calls to make, deadlines, and follow-up work on a daily calendar effectively organizes a workload.

Critical Issues and Ethical Dilemmas

Ethical Practice

In many ways, case management is actually care management. What are the ethical obligations of social workers to their clients in a managed care environment?

Although many clients benefit from case management services, this area of practice is also laden with critical issues and ethical dilemmas. Among them are:

▶ Who's in charge of decision making?
▶ What are the implications of managed care for the delivery of social services?
▶ Who needs to know and who actually has permission to receive information about a parsticular client?
▶ Can clients access the services they want or do they have to settle for what they can get?

Who's in charge of case management?

Who is responsible for making decisions? The client? The client's family? The case manager? The team of service providers? The representative of the funding body? The case monitor? The empowering answer to these questions is that workers and clients collaborate as "co-managers" in assessing what they need and agreeing on what is to be done (Dinerman, 1992).

Dinerman (1992) warns workers against the seduction of "management" in case management positions, particularly when working with clients whom society labels dependent—such as those who are frail, in ill health, or have chronic mental illness. This type of case management is control that is disguised as care, "not from malevolence but simply from the dynamic of powerful and resourceful professionals interacting with vulnerable and resource-weak clients. . . . Precisely when care is beneficent, intrusions upon autonomy can go unchecked, unscrutinized, even unobserved behind the curtain of good intentions" (Collopy, 1992, p. 56). The more case managers manage decisions for clients, the less involved clients are likely to be. "Non-compliance is one likely response to such situations. Effectiveness in case management in any event requires joint and participatory planning by clients and case managers" (Dinerman, 1992, p. 7).

An ethical dilemma occurs when the client's choice is dramatically different from that of the case manager, and it is the case manager's opinion that the client's choice will create problematic risks for the client:

Clearly, case managers should not impose their own views of acceptable risk on clients and families. But what are a case manager's rights when he or she cannot in good conscience accede to the plan the client prefers? Does the case manager have a duty to refer the case to another case manager? If several case managers and their supervisors agree that the client's choices are dangerous to self or society, is this a test of truth? (Kane, 1992, p. 224)

In this instance, the case manager must balance the benefits of supporting the client's autonomous decision-making against the risks of harming the client through passive neglect (Austin, 1996). An open discussion with the client about the worker's views maintains the collaborative relationship and helps to inform the client's and the worker's choice.

Box 13.1 Case Management: A Research–Practice Connection

Case management is a prominent casework method applied in the fields of child welfare, mental health, substance abuse, and aging services. Much research has been conducted on the utility and effectiveness of case management models and methods in helping clients access the complex array of services available within the social service delivery network.

To study the experience of clients receiving substance abuse services through a strengths-based case-management model, Brun and Rapp (2001) conducted a qualitative study that focused on the experience of ten individuals. They posed questions to ascertain clients' perceptions about the strengths-based approach and to compare their responses to the principles of strength-based case management. Results indicated that strengths-based work was valued by the clients who participated, but that not all clients accepted the worker's focus on strengths. Some reported they were reluctant to accept strength based feedback because it made them feel vulnerable. Clients also saw value in some kind of reflection on problems, at least problems related to substance use. Clients with addictions cited the quality of the professional relationship with the worker as significant in helping them make productive life changes.

Results of other studies on substance abuse service delivery demonstrate a correlation between a strengths-based approach to case management and positive client outcomes. In a quantitative study of 632 clients, Siegal and colleagues (1996) found that clients who participated in strengths-based case management showed improved functioning at their places of employment and increased likelihood of following through with aftercare treatment. In a follow-up study with this same group of clients, researchers found that lessened severity of drug use was associated with strengths-based case management (Rapp, et al., 1998).

The potential benefits of including a peer consumer advocate on the case management team was the focus of research by Nwakeze and colleagues (2000). Studying how case management services affected soup kitchen guests, these researchers compared the results of an individual case-manager model with the results of a team-based approach that allied a case manager with a paraprofessional peer helper functioning as a peer consumer advocate. Pre- and postservice interviews with clients and service providers were used with 86 participants to track clients' progress. Findings indicated that the presence of a peer advocate likely contributed to increases in follow-up by clients in keeping appointments with the case manager, in connecting clients to more service referrals, and in accessing entitlements and services. The partnership of the client and peer advocate freed the case manager to focus on interaction within the professional service network, useful in "screening clients for eligibility before referring them to a given service and remaining updated concerning which community providers were open to new clients" (p. 33).

In another field of practice, mental health, Johnson (2000) adds to the understanding of what works in case management with a qualitative study of families of 180 people with chronic and persistent mental illness. Participants were socioeconomically and ethnically diverse. By analyzing interviews with various family members, Johnson identified three key themes to guide the development of case management services. First, results confirmed earlier studies that a family's response to a member with a mental illness varies depending on ethnic identity. The need for a culturally differentiated approach is clear. Second, with respect to a collaborative approach, Johnson concluded "family members want (and deserve) to be treated as team members by the professional community" (p. 132). Finally, family members emphasized consensus among team members, religious faith, and connections with support groups using a self-help model as factors contributing to competence in coping with the family members with chronic and persistent mental illness.

Issues of autonomy become more complicated when individuals rely on the support of others to exercise their chosen options. In the case of older adults who are frail, self- determination may be limited by the abilities of their life partners, adult children, friends, and neighbors to support their decisions (Kane, 1992). Furthermore, the "right" decision for the client may not be the best decision for family members or, for that matter, the taxpayers. An ecosystemic perspective considering the client in social context helps case managers and clients generate solutions that fit their circumstances.

Managed care

Managed care is a means for determining the type of behavioral, health, and mental health services provided and for regulating the costs of these services. Lauded by some as a strategic way of controlling costs, managed care is criticized by others as provider-driven care regulated by restrictive cost-controlled policies rather than by concern for healthcare consumers.

For the most part, services controlled by care management organizations have been located in the private sector, particularly those services reimbursed by private health insurance carriers. As more government entities strive to contain costs, public sector services are contracting with managed care groups to oversee the allocation of entitlements. People question whether the safety net historically provided by public sector services will be lost when for-profit managed care companies restrict or deny service claims. In some cases, already overburdened voluntary agencies are called on to provide services without remuneration for those clients denied access to public sector services.

Managed care has widespread implications for service delivery. For example, Hopps and colleagues (1995) observe that "multilevel, multisystem intervention is becoming less and less feasible in this day of managed care, which reinforces the segmenting of problems and the achievement of limited goals" (p. 138). Because cost is central to decision making in managed care systems, guidelines for the approval of evidence-based treatments emphasize cost containment (Bolen & Hall, 2007).

Many raise issues regarding the appropriateness of a managed care environment for social work professionals and their clients (Beaudin & Kramer, 2005; Egan & Kadushin, 2005; Galambos, et al., 2004; Kramer & Auer, 2005; Lee & Rock, 2005). According to Davidson and Davidson (1996), issues in the managed care environment with respect to legal, professional, and fiscal dilemmas include

- Unfettered access to information with vague parameters for confidentiality
- Legal liability for unforeseen client outcomes
- Subrogation of client interests for that of managed care
- Role shift for social workers toward social control
- Potential abridgement of client rights to service
- Exclusion of "uncooperative" social workers as designated preferred providers

Preserving confidentiality

Confidentiality issues abound in case management. Even when clients have signed release-of-information forms, the basic quandary is "Who exactly has permission to know what when?" For example:

- To what extent does the release of information detail the precise circumstances of sharing information?
- How much information must the case manager share to initially secure service provisions?
- Are all service providers privy to all of the confidential details or is sharing of information selective, based on relevance and the desires of the client?
- If the client chooses to limit disclosure, will providers, likewise, limit or even refuse to provide services?
- If a client signs releases early in the case management process, does this cover new information revealed during the course of service delivery or is it necessary to secure updated releases?

⬧ What are the implications for confidentiality if case managers enter confidential information into the managed care data base?

⬧ Can we assume confidentiality if case management services are provided under mandated auspices such as an entitlement program, Medicaid, public child welfare, or the criminal justice system?

⬧ What confidentiality issues are raised if case management team members who are present during a case review are not involved with the particular client?

⬧ Does sharing information with multiple providers negate the client's right to claim legal privilege?

Case managers and clients should clarify the rules of confidentiality before clients choose to disclose sensitive information and revisit issues about disclosure periodically to keep pace with the changing base of information.

Accessing services

In the face of limited funds and rising costs, case managers must be ingenious financial managers to stretch their budgets to meet clients' needs. Caps on spending drive case managers to create plans that work effectively for the least amount of money. Gatekeeping secures the road to fiscal accountability, but does it guarantee clients' rights? Denying access to services often means that clients have to settle for services that are least expensive and available rather than being able to secure the best fit for what they want and need.

To resolve the ethical dilemma posed by being gatekeepers as well as advocates, case managers must define their role as serving a population group rather than an individual client (Kane, 1992). "The case manager becomes an advocate for identifying and meeting the needs of the entire group fairly and well, as well as for meeting the needs of any given individual" (p. 221). The perspective of the case manager is "to allocate services appropriately in a community, use resources wisely for those most in need, document inadequacies of total resources for planning purposes, and introduce system-wide incentives to improve the quality of all care providers in the community" (p. 220). Case managers also participate in social and political actions to enlarge the pool of resources available to potential consumers.

ORGANIZATIONAL ALLIANCES FOR SERVICE DELIVERY

Federal programs, state bureaucracies, community service networks, multiservice agencies, and coalitions of nongovernmental organizations are all locations in which social workers and clients might find necessary resources. But for the uninformed, these potential resource networks can be tangled webs that frustrate, disappoint, and disempower. To avoid this tangle and to function effectively as service brokers, social workers educate themselves about resource systems. They learn policies, eligibility requirements, referral procedures, and appeal processes of the systems that may be important to their clients.

An effective way to learn about other programs and to increase the effectiveness of the network itself is through creating service delivery alliances. Social workers use a variety of strategies to connect with other service organizations. These strategies include building interagency coalitions, developing effective working relationships with other professionals, working on teams, and leading meetings.

Building Interagency Coalitions

Interagency coalitions form as a way for agencies with common interests and concerns to leverage more power by working in concert to achieve agreed-on outcomes. Representatives of the agencies come to some agreement about how they can work on a joint initiative to address a particular community issue or an aspect of social service delivery. Several conditions are necessary for building successful coalitions among agencies. Each agency must participate on a voluntary basis, retain its autonomy, share common goals with other potential coalition members, and discern the benefits of participating in the coalition (McInnis-Dittrich, 1994).

Those leading the effort toward interagency collaboration draw on numerous skills for the outcome to be successful. Leaders create an appropriate climate, forge members' commitment to the purpose of the collaboration, envision a positive outcome, mediate conflicts effectively, and build consensus among members. An effective leader simultaneously maintains a vision of the whole alliance while understanding the intricacies of the constituent parts.

Interagency coalitions benefit from a broad base of ownership and a diverse pool of expertise. Working with other agencies distributes the costs and responsibilities of new ventures among the coalition members. Successful collaborative efforts are likely to improve the overall communication and linkages between and among agencies. Coalitions also present a united front, with more power to influence decision makers, legislators, the media, and the general public.

Bringing together a variety of stakeholders, collaborative practice creates multifaceted approaches to complex social problems (Lawson, 2008). Effective collaborations

- Develop equitable relations amid difference in their power and authority
- Negotiate their differences and resolve their conflicts
- Reinforce awareness that they fundamentally depend on each other
- Identify shared interests, responsibilities, and action-oriented theories
- Promote norms of reciprocity and trust
- Reconfigure and realign rules, roles, boundaries, governance systems, and jurisdictions
- Develop shared language
- Promote a collective identify
- Share resources
- Take into account salient features of local context
- Pursue opportunities to develop joint accountability for results. (Claiborne & Lawson, 2005, p. 94)

Working on Teams

Social workers implement teamwork skills to activate professional alliances and to collaborate effectively with other professionals. Effective teamwork is essential for maximizing the expertise of various professionals (Abramson & Bronstein, 2008). When the various components of a service-delivery system are working as a team, clients benefit from the harmonious operation of helping systems. Teams comprise persons who share a common purpose, contribute their

Practice Contexts

Social workers are integral members of multidisciplinary teams and interagency coalitions. What unique perspectives and expertise do social workers bring to these organizational alliances?

expertise to the work at hand, and collaborate to achieve some mutually agreed-on outcome. Professionals often work in teams to design programs and services, plan community-action efforts, and develop social action strategies. Teams also convene to coordinate work with individual clients or families when several professionals are involved. Efficient team meetings require responsible preparation, effective organization, economical use of time, and respectful participation by team members. Characteristics of effective team members include listening skills, respect for differences, and the abilities to manage conflict and build consensus (Abramson & Bornstein), Additional factors promoting effectiveness uncovered by a recent study on teams in child welfare settings include respect and unity of purpose, clear communication, and agency support (Lewandowski & GlenMaye, 2002). Steps for efficient teamwork include

- Identifying the problem, including its dimensions and boundaries
- Stating the team's purpose with respect to the defined problem
- Agreeing on goals
- Delineating tasks and specifying which team member "will do what when" for each of these tasks
- Evaluating the outcome, including the achievement of goals as well as the process of work as a team (Brill & Levine, 2002)

Leading Effective Meetings

Well-conducted meetings begin with a stated purpose, follow an agenda, and complete business within the specified time. Effective meeting facilitators help participants articulate short- and long-term objectives and delineate clear expectations for the tasks to be accomplished between meetings by individuals, officers, standing committees, ad hoc committees, or staff members. The person leading the meeting also takes responsibility for focusing discussions, encouraging participants to contribute their perspectives, and guiding the discussion toward decisions and actions.

Agendas structure meetings by listing the order of business and specifying items for discussion and action. An agenda serves as a physical reminder of the purpose of the meeting. Typically, it identifies the date and time of the meeting and lists items of business including committee reports, carryover or "unfinished business," and topics under "new business," and specifies points the group will need to act on through discussion, consensus, or a formal vote.

Wrapping up a meeting is critical for maintaining motivation and progress toward goals. Several activities end meetings effectively:

- Reviewing decisions and plans to help participants reflect on the actions taken and the plans made during the meeting, offering an opportunity to ensure that those who have committed to follow-up tasks know what they are to do
- Agreeing on a date and time for the next meeting and requesting members' input in regard to the agenda
- Incorporating the successes of the present meeting into the future work of the group by encouraging participants to critique accomplishments and suggest areas for improvement (Schwartz, 1994)

Box 13.2 Ethic of Collaboration

Collaboration is a fitting concept to describe an empowering style of social work implemented with individual, couple, family, and small group clients. Collaboration is also the guiding theme for empowerment-based social workers as they work in concert with national and international organizations, professional groups, and local and world communities to facilitate social change. "Creating partnerships, working with and in communities, and integrating personal, interpersonal, and social action practice facilitates dealing with major social problems, meaning that issues of public policy, and therefore of social justice, can be placed, as they should, at the core of social work practice" (Breton, 2002, p. 31).

Professional organizational alliances are created primarily to expand opportunities to enhance social functioning, to improve social service delivery practices, to develop comprehensive community-based services, and to create avenues for changes in social policies. "A collaborative alliance can be described as an interorganizational effort to address problems too complex and too protracted to be resolved by unilateral organizational action. Collaboration refers to the process; collaborative alliances are the forms" (Gray & Wood, 1991, p. 4). Organization-to-organization collaboration involves the same partnership principles as those found in worker–client partnerships. Creating alliances involves joining forces of "stakeholders of a problem domain" in a common effort (Wood & Gray, 1991) by synchronizing mutual activities and designing conjoint strategies.

Coalition building among national and international nongovernmental organizations is an example of professional collaboration. Nongovernmental organizations (NGOs) are legally constituted, nonprofit, voluntary organizations created by private persons or organizations. NGOs exclude government representatives from membership. Although independent from direct government control, as "people organizations," NGOs may work in tandem with the world's governments to resolve problems or to accomplish specific goals of the NGO. Many international NGOs serve in a consultative capacity in concert with the United Nations on humanitarian issues. They are reputedly outspoken advocates on such issues as human rights, refugee resettlement, social programs and policies, sustainable environments, poverty alleviation, and peace efforts, to name a few (Healy, 2001; Reichert, 2006; Smith, 2003). "The IASSW and IFSW are making efforts to strengthen their consultative status as NGOs. NASW is now a member of Interaction, a coalition of more than 150 U.S.-based development agencies that engages in advocacy on global issues" (Healy, 2008, p. 486). In addition to preparing position statements on advocacy issues, some NGOs may assume a more operational role in designing and implementing relief efforts or social, educational, and economic development projects. Oftentimes, to achieve their goals, NGOs join with other organizations to strengthen their initiatives.

Such collective action requires collective resources. The ethic of collaboration is thus twofold: the ethic inherent in the process of collective action (individual versus group benefits) and the ethic regarding sharing resources and using political power necessary to effect social change (group versus universal good). Going beyond autonomy, the collaborative nature of collective action features interdependence (Ramon, 1999). The common issues addressed by the collective and the social or institutional systems targeted for change define the scope, impact, and ethics of the work.

At its core, creating alliances through collaboration involves joining power resources in a planned change effort. In group and community work, "the power of alliances with others gives voice to unspoken feelings and unites people in common struggles against privileged views and norms" (O'Melia, 2002). Equitable structures and participatory processes to engage service users in community or organizational collaboration are essential to apply an empowering approach in planning, implementing, and evaluating service delivery (Alameda-Lawson & Lawson, 2002; Hardina, 2004b; Keys & Factor, 2001; Peterman, 2004).

To the extent that formal meetings are conducted effectively, participants are likely to continue to invest their time and effort. Conducting effective meetings requires the leader to prepare carefully (see Figure 13.2).

Figure 13.2 Tips for Leading an Effective Meeting

- Develop an orderly agenda
- Send out timely meeting notices including minutes from the last meeting and the agenda for the upcoming meeting
- Arrange the meeting space to ensure comfort and participation
- Review the agenda before the meeting begins
- Welcome participants as they arrive
- Pace the meeting to complete tasks within the agreed upon time
- Draw upon listening and skills to facilitate discussion
- Thank participants for their involvement in the group's activities and acknowledge the group's accomplishments

PROFESSIONAL SUPPORT NETWORKS

Social workers frequently ally themselves with other professionals for support. Supportive professional relationships are usually available within the worker's immediate organizational environment. These relationships are a worker's best ally to avoid burnout. Beyond the agency setting, the resources of professional memberships and connections via computers can also stimulate a worker's professional development and provide a web of support.

Alliances within Organizations

Work settings provide important alliances to support social workers as people and as practitioners. A "one-step removed" perspective offers a fresh look when workers are stumped. Sometimes, the client–social worker relationship falls into unproductive patterns, failing to work efficiently toward goals or to envision a broad range of solutions. In these situations, the social worker has several options for assistance. Supervisors provide seasoned expertise and a more objective look at the information workers bring. A review by a team of peers offers a synergistic resource created by group interaction. Consultants can provide a technical view and offer specific information that is unavailable in the worker's knowledge base or particular practice setting.

Supervision

Most social workers, especially beginning practitioners, function in settings that provide ongoing supervision. At a minimum, supervision requires the worker to be accountable. In its most effective form, supervision accomplishes three purposes: (1) to structure practice by asking the worker to report and reflect on the work with the client system, (2) to provide a support system to reinforce and encourage the work, and (3) to create a forum to identify the worker's strengths and set goals for professional development.

Supervisors use a variety of helpful analytic tools with workers. Supervisors use techniques such as: modeling, role-playing, concept identification, and forecasting (Fant & Ross, 1983). *Modeling* draws on the similarities of the supervisor–worker relationship with the worker–client relationship. Workers become more sensitive to a client's perspective when having experiences that parallel those of the client. *Role plays* function in a similar way with supervisors taking the roles of workers and workers acting out specific aspects of the client's situation, experientially increasing the worker's empathy and awareness.

This also allows the worker to observe the more experienced supervisor in action. Moreover, supervisors integrate the theory and knowledge base of the profession into the unique client information brought by the worker. By using *concept identification,* the supervisors connect their specific observations to the theory that supports them. "This kind of knowledge helps the worker to become creative, use his or her own ideas to demonstrate these principles, and generalize the learning" (p. 243). Finally, supervisors use a technique called *forecasting* to alert workers to what might be coming up by drawing on the supervisor's knowledge of human system behavior and practice experience.

Peer review

Frequently, social workers participate as members of teams that provide professional support. There are many advantages to peer review. Presenting a client's situation to the team compels the worker to organize information coherently. The questions that team members ask often reveal information gaps for the worker and client to fill. Team members may also notice similarities between the situation presented and experiences with clients of their own and offer suggestions on what they have tried with success in these other situations. Finally, the careful review afforded by the peer consultation process accentuates for clients the importance of their situations.

Consultation

The complexity of human behavior extends beyond the knowledge base of any single professional. Sometimes, workers and clients need more information for a comprehensive assessment, or they need specific expertise to implement an intervention strategy. In these cases, workers seek the assistance of consulting specialists. Useful outside perspectives may include consultants who are psychologists, neurologists, dieticians, attorneys, indigenous healers, and clergy. For macrosystem clients, these specialists may be economists, demographers, urban planners, engineers, or sociologists. Consultation usually moves beyond the worker's organizational setting and requires the worker to gain the client's explicit approval and written permission to do so.

Job Stress and Burnout

Professional Identity

Worker burnout negatively impacts the quality of client care and the expression of genuine concern for clients. What proactive steps can practitioners and organizations take to reduce job stress and worker burnout?

Empowerment-based social workers function best when their work environments empower them as professionals, support a focus on strengths, and encourage their efforts to collaborate with clients as partners. Work settings designed to cushion stress involve employees in decision making, compliment their success, and enhance their self-efficacy, competence, and sense of professional empowerment. In contrast, when workers lack a sense of control, experience insufficient collegial and supervisory support, and receive little recognition for their accomplishments, such work environments become hotbeds of burnout. High job stress combined with few rewards and scanty involvement in decision-making have profound repercussions for professionals (Maslach & Leiter, 2008). Research studies demonstrate that a lack of hopefulness also leads to burnout (McCarter, 2007; Schwartz et al., 2007). Furthermore, practitioners who work with persons who have experienced trauma are vulnerable to compassion fatigue (Adams, et al., 2008; Figley, 1995).

Strict rules and regulations, unreasonable amounts of paperwork, overbearing workloads, and unfavorable physical work environments all increase pressures that can disempower social workers. These work conditions are likely to intensify workers' feelings of immersion in the physical, social, financial, and psychological problems of their clients (Maslach, 2003). When accumulating demands exceed a worker's tolerance, the likelihood of job burnout increases dramatically. When social workers experience burnout, their personal and professional sense of power dwindles along with their practice competence. Research indicates that workers experiencing burnout are more likely to apply coercive and expert influence strategies (McCarthy & Frieze, 1999).

Burnout takes its toll on workers, clients, and the delivery of social services. Maslach (2003) reports research evidence of three dimensions of burnout among human service workers, including "an overwhelming exhaustion, feelings of cynicism, and detachment from the job, and a sense of ineffectiveness and lack of accomplishment" (p. 190). Practitioners experiencing burnout become less objective, less positive, and less concerned about their clients. Moreover, burnout curtails creativity. The aftermath includes petty and dogmatic thinking as well as oppressive, rigidly bureaucratic behavior (Maslach, 2003). Burnout can also lead to a worker's "loss of idealism, feelings of hopelessness, lowered morale, lack of initiative, absenteeism, alcohol and drug use, and physical and emotional exhaustion" (Dressel, 1992, p. 216). All these consequences are polar opposites of empowerment-based practice.

Responses to job stress and burnout

Workers can counter the effects of work stress and the tendency toward burnout. Social workers can learn to work effectively within bureaucracies, using skills "to capitalize on the possibilities of organizational life" as well as "to neutralize its stresses and dangers" (Pruger, 1978, p. 154). A feminist orientation considers the political context of the worker's practice: "When workers act on a political understanding of their client's problems, they are also more likely to make a political analysis of their own workplace and personal situations and are less prone to self-blame" (Gottlieb, 1992, p. 316). Taking an active role in shaping the work environment is an antidote to burnout.

Stress management experts also recommend numerous personal strategies to counter the effects of stress, including relaxation exercises, guided imagery, meditation, exercise, hobbies, recreational activities, and supportive relationships with family and friends. Cognitive strategies include reframing one's understanding of stressful circumstances as challenges, maintaining a perspective of optimism and hope, and sustaining a keen sense of humor. Studies indicate resiliency-enhancing factors include such characteristics as personal self-efficacy and sense of mission, social support, and recognition for job-related capabilities (Zunz, 1998). Radley and Figley's (2007) work on the social psychology of compassion argues in favor of a paradigm shift toward identifying characteristics associated with *compassion satisfaction,* including affect, work resources, and self-care. Professional education, in itself, mitigates some of the effects of job stress. For example, in spite of the challenges inherent in child welfare, particularly child protective services, workers who hold BSW or MSW degrees have higher job performance and lower turnover rates than those employees without these professional degrees (NASW, 2004b).

Professional Memberships

Social workers augment their immediate networks of support through their affiliations with professional associations, such as the National Association of Social Workers (NASW) and other special interest organizations. These affiliations enhance professional identity, provide opportunities to exchange ideas, and encourage professional growth through conferences, publications, newsletters, and funding for research. Professional organizations also create opportunities for interdisciplinary coalitions and alliances solidifying a united force for policy and legislative advocacy at the local, state, and federal levels.

More than 150,000 social work professionals hold membership in the NASW, the world's largest social work professional association (Clark, 2008). Full membership in the NASW is contingent on graduation from a baccalaureate or master's degree program accredited by the Council on Social Work Education (CSWE). Students in these programs also qualify for membership at a reduced rate. Associate membership is available to human service providers with other educational backgrounds.

The NASW has 56 chapters, one in each state and in Washington, D.C., New York City, Puerto Rico, the Virgin Islands, Guam, and an international chapter that serves members in Europe and other parts of the world. Special interest groups within the NASW, such as the National Committees on Minority Affairs, Lesbian, Gay, and Bisexual Issues, and Women's Issues provide opportunities to emphasize the diverse views of the Association's members. To support its membership, the NASW develops standards for various fields of practice, endorses a code of ethics, sponsors local and national conferences and workshops, publishes numerous books and journals, and advocates on Capitol Hill and in state legislatures.

In addition to the NASW, numerous other professional organizations and special interest groups provide support to social workers. Like the NASW, these groups shape professional identity, set standards and monitor practice, provide opportunities for exchanges of ideas and collective endeavors, and foster interdisciplinary relationships. Many publish journals and newsletters (see Figure 13.3).

Colleague assistance

Collegial support cushions the effects of stress, provides a reduction of isolation along with a sense of connection with others, and assuages the effects of burnout. In addition to providing for collegial exchange, professional social support networks offer a safety net for professionals who experience difficulty with stress, drug addiction, or alcohol abuse. Estimates indicate that at least 20 percent of social work practitioners experience drug addiction or alcohol abuse (Peebles-Wilkins, 2008). Consequences of social workers' difficulties with

Figure 13.3   Examples of Professional Organizations

American Association of Industrial Social Workers
Baccalaureate Program Directors (BPD)
Child Welfare League of America (CWLA)
Commission on Gay Men/Lesbian Women
Council on Social Work Education (CSWE)
International Association of Schools of Social Work
International Federation of Social Workers (IFSW)
International Council on Social Welfare
National Network for Social Work Managers
National Federation of Societies of Clinical Social Work
National Association of Puerto Rican/Hispanic Social Workers
National Association of Oncology Social Workers (NAOSW)
National Indian Social Workers Association
National Association of Black Social Workers
National Association of Social Workers (NASW)
North American Association of Christians in Social Work
The Society for Social Work Administrators in Health Care

alcohol and other drugs extend beyond the personal into their professional interactions with clients and colleagues (Siebert, 2005).

The NASW (1999b) policy statement on "Professional Impairment" recommends lending assistance through programs organized by local NASW chapters. Colleague assistance programs offer peer support and encourage workers troubled by psychological stress or chemical dependency to seek professional assistance.

Connections in Cyberspace

There are alliances to support social workers beyond the macrosystem level. A rising global consciousness coupled with advances in communication technology give social workers stimulating new alliances to explore in the "megasystem." The concept of the megasystem expands our consciousness to consider accessing and sharing resources in the international community. It also begins to explore the relevance of the realm of the "person:global social and physical environment."

New computer technology broadens the possibilities for social workers to create alliances with other professionals around the world. Social workers can take advantage of this technology to correspond with others via e-mail or participate in listserv discussion groups or other bulletin board systems on the Internet or commercial online services. Accessing information on the World Wide Web is another advantage of computer technology. Web sites contain a wealth of material—U.S. Census Bureau data, financial information, online electronic libraries with full-text articles, research databases, directories of local programs and services, notices of conferences and workshops, and information about various colleges and universities.

LOOKING FORWARD

The impetus for managed care has moved from promoting cost-effectiveness in the case plan, to imposing cost-containment criteria on the service package, to restricting service provisions to the least costly service. The effect of managed care on case planning raises a number of concerns. For example, how should social workers respond to the reliance on off-site managed care consultants to approve intervention strategies, to prescribe the term of service, and to require labeling of client behavior for third-party reimbursement?

To be empowering, social workers themselves must experience empowerment in the context of their workplace, relationships with colleagues, and everyday professional practice. Workers apply their understanding of power and powerlessness to their own agency system, the service delivery network, and social institutions. In this way, they model effective behaviors for clients, encourage empowerment of staff through worker-led peer-support groups, create innovative programs and a more responsive system for the delivery of services, and engage in social and political action.

Working within the context of the delivery system reveals gaps in service delivery and limited opportunities for clients. Simply dealing with existing resources does not adequately meet current and changing needs. To respond to this scarcity in resources and opportunities, social workers strive to redress social injustices and oppression and enrich the pool of environmental resources. Chapter 14 describes these macrolevel strategies to change policy and legislation, neighborhoods and communities, and social institutions.

Log onto **www.mysocialworklab.com** and select the **Interactive Skill Module** videos from the left-hand menu. Answer the questions below. (*If you did not receive an access code to* **MySocialWorkLab** *with this text and wish to purchase access online, please visit* www.mysocialworklab.com.)

1. **Watch page 16 of the group work module** to analyze the group worker's facilitation of mutual aid within a client group. What does the worker do to facilitate a mutual aid process within the group? What else could she do?

2. Case management is a key skill when working with domestic violence survivors. **View pages 7, 16, 18, and 19 of the domestic violence module.** Determine what services you might manage with Faye so she can return to secure functioning in the community.

PRACTICE TEST

1. Client groups, natural support networks, case management teams, and agency coalitions are all _____.
   a. effective sources of social support
   b. types of alliances
   c. microlevel systems
   d. likely to be dysfunctional

2. Which type of group most likely has mezzolevel change as its purpose?
   a. mutual aid group
   b. self-help group
   c. social action group
   d. skills building group

3. When social workers facilitate interactions among group members and stimulate processes which activate members' contributions to each other, they are encouraging _____.
   a. self-help activities
   b. social action responses
   c. mutual aid processes
   d. coalition building

4. Self-help groups _____.
   a. form around divergent concerns or problems
   b. are different from the natural helping systems of a community
   c. operate on the principle of "peers-helping-peers"
   d. benefit from leadership by professionals

Human Behavior

5. The Burnetts have had a difficult year given economic hardships, damage to their home caused by floodwater, and the addition to their family of five with the early birth of their triplet sons. When medical social worker Kristine Goldman meets with them in the Neonatal Intensive Care Unit, she notes their strength in managing stress. Based on research about social functioning and natural helping networks, what has most likely contributed to their resiliency?
   a. participation in a self-help group
   b. consultation with a professional counselor
   c. denial of their difficulties
   d. support from their families, friends, and neighbors

Practice Contexts

6. Managed care in long term care includes both client-oriented and system-oriented objectives. Of the following objectives, which is most likely a system-oriented objective?
   a. To monitor appropriateness of long-term care services
   b. To support the client's caregivers
   c. To contain cost by controlling client access to services
   d. To assure that services given are appropriate to client needs

Ethical Practice

7. Shirley Quinn, a case manager at OPTIONS, sometimes runs into situations where older adults and their adult children and grandchildren disagree about "mom" or "dad" remaining in their own home. Which ethical dilemma applies to Shirley's challenge?
   a. Does the cost-containment objective of managed care abridge client's rights to service?
   b. Who has the right to make decisions?
   c. What are the bounds of confidentiality?
   d. What is the proper balance between advocacy and gatekeeping?

8. Social worker Gina Howell is employed at a family agency that uses teams to build alliances of support among professional staff. Each week teams hold case conferences to review critical cases and discuss strategies. The process of this professional support network is most aptly called _____.
   a. peer review
   b. supervision
   c. group work
   d. consultation

9. Natalie's colleagues are encouraging her to join them as members in the largest professional organization for social workers. If Natalie takes their advice, she will join the _____.
   a. CSWE
   b. ACOSA
   c. CWLA
   d. NASW

Log onto **MySocialWorkLab** once you have completed the Practice Test above to take your Chapter Exam and demonstrate your knowledge of this material.

Answers

1) b 2) c 3) c 4) c 5) d 6) c 7) b 8) d 9) d

Expanding Opportunities

CHAPTER OUTLINE

CONNECTING CORE COMPETENCIES *in this chapter*

| Professional Identity | Ethical Practice | Critical Thinking | **Diversity in Practice** | **Human Rights & Justice** | Research Based Practice | Human Behavior | **Policy Practice** | Practice Contexts | Engage Assess Intervene Evaluate |

All human systems—individuals, families, groups, organizations, and communities—depend on internal resources and environmental opportunities to survive, develop, and change. The interconnections among micro-, mezzo-, and macrosystems give generalist social workers many intervention options to expand opportunities and work for social change. Think back on some of the practice examples presented in earlier chapters. Damon Edwards and Nate Hardy are two social workers who operate principally with larger systems in ways that ultimately benefit individuals. Damon Edwards facilitates changes in community policy through his work with the residents of Franklin Courts. By successfully changing the city's response to the crisis of lead contamination, Damon and the residents' group will improve the quality of life for the people of Franklin Courts. These policy changes at the community level will benefit other public housing residents in the city as well. Also, consider the example of Nate Hardy of the Northside Development Association. His work to increase the availability of low-cost housing has far-reaching benefits for the entire Northside community. Typical of larger system interventions, many people draw from changes made and resources developed at the macrolevel.

Even those workers whose practice focuses primarily on microlevel clients demonstrate concern for expanding opportunities at other system levels. For example, Andrea Barry, who works in family preservation services, is active in the child welfare lobby in her state. Mark Nogales, who works in the field of mental health, represents his agency on a panel of providers who are planning a more coordinated service network for persons with chronic mental illness. Paul Quillin, a social worker in a family agency, is writing a grant to fund a family life education project to implement in the local school district. Kay Landon and Karen McBride, both outreach health care providers, serve on their state NASW chapter's political task force. Each of these generalist social workers puts ecosystemic principles into action by working simultaneously on issues in personal and public domains.

This chapter identifies options for environmental change and offers concrete strategies for social workers and clients to work together to expand opportunities. Specifically, this chapter

- Clarifies the interrelationship between opportunities and empowerment
- Explains methods for expanding resources by mobilizing resources, educating the public, and writing grant proposals
- Explicates strategies for community change through community organization and community development
- Discerns social work as a political profession
- Discusses how to create more responsive social institutions through policy development
- Describes social action and advocacy as strategies for expanding opportunities
- Delineates processes for legislative advocacy

All generalist social workers may draw on these methods and strategies whether they work directly with mezzo- or macrolevel client systems or they look broadly for options to assist microlevel client systems.

OPPORTUNITIES: KEYS TO EMPOWERMENT

Expanding opportunities in the social structures of society is both ethical and effective social work practice. The profession's mandate for social justice and the NASW *Code of Ethics* (1999a) charges social workers to extend opportunities and resources to all citizens, particularly those who are disenfranchised and oppressed.

To meet these ethical responsibilities in the broader society, practitioners develop expertise for modifying social and physical environments, drawing on existing community resources, linking clients with natural helping networks, and creating new resources (Acevedo-Garcia, et al., 2008; Kemp, et al., 2002). Social workers remain faithful to the core purposes of the social work profession when they return to their social function of linking people with needed resources, solidifying the network of available resources, and involving themselves in community education and community development (Specht & Courtney, 1994). However, many obstacles exist to locating resources for clients. Among these are constraints in social institutions, economic policies, political practices, ideologies, and the legacy of history. Social workers strive to overcome the risks of these environmental obstacles to enhance environmental opportunities for clients.

Empowerment and Opportunities

Human Rights & Justice

Empowerment social workers advocate for resources in the socio-economic-political environment. How does the lack of resources for vulnerable client population groups perpetuate oppression and social injustice?

Expanding opportunities means promoting client self-sufficiency through social, economic, educational, and political change. It also means eliminating discriminatory barriers that deny access to resources. The NASW *Code of Ethics* (1999a) stipulates "Social workers should act to expand choice and opportunity for all persons, with special regard for vulnerable, disadvantaged, oppressed, and exploited persons and groups" (Section 6.04b). To expand opportunities in ways that facilitate empowerment, workers and clients implement strategies that enhance clients' sense of mastery as well as their participatory or political competence. This includes activities that expedite clients' access to services by maximizing their rights and removing obstacles in social service delivery. Likewise, at the community level, workers team with clients to expand public services such as transportation, affordable housing, social service outreach, and community education. Most important, social workers assertively advocate social change to provide institutional supports in the sociopolitical environment.

An economically and socially stratified society distributes its wealth unequally and systematically denies opportunities for some people to participate in decisions about resource allocations. Breton (1994) explores this disempowering cycle—the lack of resources coupled with the lack of power to affect decisions about resource distribution, describes how this perpetuates oppression, and offers ideas for change:

> There would be no need for empowerment work if there was a just distribution of power and resources in the society, and a just distribution of the opportunities to participate in the allocation of existing resources and the creation of needed resources, in other words, if we lived in a just society. In a just society, by definition, power and resources would be shared equitably. People who did not know how to exercise their power or were psychologically unable to exercise it, would be taught and/or helped to do so; people who did not access the resources they need or participate in decisions as to their creation and allocation would be encouraged and helped to access these resources, or would be educated to participate in the democratic process whereby decisions are taken by citizens on the creation and allocation of resources.(p. 32)

For those persons who are powerless or oppressed, choices are limited and, too often, control over opportunities and resources rests with the actions of "others."

Social workers must be cautious to avoid being one of those "others" who are limiting their clients' choices. Empowerment-oriented social workers maximize clients' involvement in efforts to influence social policy decisions. Clients take their rightful place in controlling their own opportunities through

- ▶ Collective action to achieve a just balance of power targeting socioeconomic, political, and structural systems change
- ▶ Awareness of political responsibilities, recognizing that socioeconomic and political forces shape people's lives and a class-stratified society creates problems for members of marginalized classes
- ▶ Consciousness of the right to have a voice and to exercise that voice
- ▶ Recognition of their own competence, trust in their knowledge and abilities and, in turn, acknowledgment of their competence by others
- ▶ Use of different sources of power—personal, collective, and political—to produce desired results (Breton, 1994)

Empowerment in Groups and Communities

Powerlessness in groups and communities may be defined as the inability to use resources to achieve collective goals.

—Barbara Solomon

Group and community methods are particularly important for addressing issues of powerlessness with those who have experienced oppression (Breton, 1994; DuBois & Miley, 2008; Everett, et al., 2007; Lee, 2001; Miley & DuBois, 1999; To, 2007). The group is "the instrument through which members can develop that sense of community and mutual support which is needed in the process of social change" (Lewis, 1991, p. 32). Social change

requires the active engagement of members of the vulnerable population, as well as "helpers," professionals, religious groups, and educators, in this exploration and action. It necessitates a critical mass of adherents working toward a reconstruction of the social fabric, a praxis for change. Member participants in social work groups are a vital part of the praxis for change, and may have the greatest stake in defining and working toward that change. (p. 28)

Group intervention is a prelude to critical consciousness. Developing a critical consciousness is a process of learning to perceive and question social, economic, and political contradictions and take action against oppression. For Freire (1993, 1997), the development of critical awareness, or conscientization, transforms people from a naive state to critical consciousness. Freire views critical education as a form of networking knowledge. Praxis, or the combination of reflection and action, is a central theme. Critical learning and thinking generate power within individuals; whereas, the process of critical education—reflecting on one's reality, critically examining the world, and engaging in dialogue with others—leads to collective action for social change.

Consciousness raising is the process of developing a heightened sense of awareness and increased knowledge about oppression and its effects. Consciousness raising and self-awareness are key components of empowerment at the individual and the interpersonal levels. Individuals who experience similar issues can join, develop a critical consciousness about their status, and believe that their collective voice can influence change. This same critical consciousness is a prerequisite to collective action and social change (Carr, 2003; Gutiérrez, 1995). Thus, empowerment-based practice through work with groups and communities addresses issues of oppression at the personal or interpersonal level and institutes corrective actions at the collective or social policy level.

RESOURCE EXPANSION

Social workers wield their power and encourage clients to do the same in accessing necessary services to meet clients' needs. Sometimes, what people require is simply not there, but needs must be met one way or another!

Identifying Resource Shortages

The network of social service delivery agencies, organizations, and private practitioners offers significant resources for its clientele. However, given the diversity of human problems and social issues, the ever-changing needs of human systems, and the complexities of organizational structures, it is no surprise to discover that gaps and barriers exist in the panorama of services and resources in most communities. Figure 14.1 offers guidelines for analyzing a community's human service delivery system.

Mobilizing Resources

To fill gaps and overcome service delivery barriers, workers mobilize resources in the private and public arenas. Social workers exercising the role of mobilizer assemble people and organizations and marshal their combined energies to achieve mutual goals. As partisans in social conflict, mobilizers act "to animate one's client group to advocate for itself collectively and, at the same time, to advocate as vigorously as possible for that group's interest" (Simon, 1994, p. 164). Mobilizers bring together diverse constituencies, open lines of communications, develop a common agenda, clarify the direction of goals, and outline strategies for action. By responding to mobilization strategies, clients can become influential political forces.

Educating the Public

Mindful of the importance of educating citizens about a wide range of subjects—including social issues, social policy development, and the availability of social service resources—social workers disseminate information through community

---

Figure 14.1   Framework for Human Service Delivery System Analysis

Part I Continuum of Needs

1. Identify health and human service needs
2. Delineate the service needs of special populations and ethnic minorities
3. Describe the patterns of needs among various population groups

Part II Continuum of Services

1. Inventory informal and formal support services
2. Describe the program parameters and eligibility requirements for each service
3. Describe the structures and opportunities for interagency planning and collaboration
4. Characterize the service delivery network as comprehensive or fragmented; driven by client needs or resource availability

Part III Gaps and Barriers in the Service Delivery System

1. Assess unmet needs of target population groups in the service delivery system
2. Identify gaps in service delivery
3. Assess physical and social barriers to accessing services
4. Evaluate the effectiveness of the service delivery network as a coordinated system

---

education. Community education includes such diverse outreach activities as media promotions, television and radio appearances, public service announcements, newsletter mailings, educational brochures, staffing information booths at community fairs, speaking engagements, and video productions. Community education promotes a broader use of social services and raises community consciousness about issues of concern to social workers and the population groups with whom they work.

Box 14.1 Social Service Delivery Network: A Policy–Practice Connection

Reflecting a conservative trend, current public policy limits agencies' abilities to respond to the social service needs of communities. Budget cuts, retrenchments of services, and competition for scarce resources characterize social service delivery systems at all levels. Simply, "there is a glaring absence of a national policy defining the need, significance, and role of social services in the United States" (NASW, 2002d, p. 328). Other issues also contribute to the gaps and barriers in service delivery. DuBois and Miley (2008) detail them as follows:

▶ Fragmentation of services results from ineffective or inefficient planning for programs and services. Clients frequently experience fragmentation when they are involved with multiple providers. Lack of coordination, conflicting recommendations, and confusing rules, regulations, and procedures create unnecessary burdens with which clients must contend.

▶ Agency turf battles ensue when agencies protect their service territories and exert their domains of authority. Competition for clients and funding, and therefore survival, complicates cooperative working relationships among service providers and delimits coordinated planning in the overall delivery of services.

▶ Social triage classifies clients as "treatable" or "untreatable" and, therefore, judges clients as either qualified or unqualified for particular programs and services. Triage, too often, responds to the pressures of insufficient funding by attempting to sift out those persons who would least likely benefit from the provision of services.

▶ Privatization is the trend toward decreasing the spectrum of public-sector social services, encouraging instead the development of services in the private sector. At issue is the likelihood of differential services—those for the rich and those for the poor, those for persons with adequate health insurance and those for persons without insurance benefits.

▶ Accessibility of services is fundamental. Transportation and child-care constraints, fees for services, limited times for appointments, waiting lists, and the lack of multilingual professionals seriously limit resource accessibility.

The NASW (2002c) policy statement, "Social Services," identifies principles to guide policy analysis and development in an effort to redress limitations in the current social service–delivery network:

▶ Universal access advocates that services be "accessible, attainable, and offered in a way that encourages voluntary use" (p. 329).

▶ Comprehensive services, including a continuum of services for both short- and long-term needs in public and private venues.

▶ Informed consent, including stipulations to "ensure that each consumer has informed self-determination regarding choice of services, protection of individuality, and ability to participate in policy matters" (p. 329).

▶ Simplicity and efficiency of procedures and administrative regulations to create transparent systems of accountability.

▶ Stakeholder involvement in establishing social service delivery network policies and priorities.

▶ Planning and evaluation processes that include social work practitioners, managers, community members, and consumers to ensure accountability.

▶ Advocacy activities to promote social justice.

▶ Education of the funding community to broaden their base of knowledge about the "nature and necessity of social services" (p. 330).

Responding to the social justice mandate of the profession, social workers take on leadership roles with respect to influencing and implementing equitable social policies. Social policies changes at the national, state, and local levels will be necessary to shape the philosophy, scope, regulations, and funding to improve the social service delivery network in the United States.

Writing Grant Proposals

Often the burning question with respect to creating opportunities through innovative social service programs is, "Where will we get the money?" Agencies face tough choices in expanding service delivery. They can either economize within the current budget, switch the program's emphasis from established programs to new services, or expand the agency's funding base. Although any of these financial strategies can yield money for new programs, acquiring new sources of funding through grants frequently gains top priority. When agencies receive grants for new programs, they expand resources rather than simply shift them around.

Preparing proposals for grant funding requires the same kind of thinking social workers apply to working with client systems, including conducting assessments, developing plans that incorporate measurable objectives, implementing strategies, and evaluating outcomes. Five sections typical of various types of grant applications are:

- The *statement of the problem* and needs assessment section details the identified problem. It answers questions such as who is involved, the extent of the problem, and its financial implications at the federal, state, and local levels. This section of the application also describes the problem as addressed in professional journals, reports, and other relevant documents and discusses what other programs have already tried.
- Grant applications incorporate a section on measurable *goals and objectives* or outcomes the proposed program aims to achieve. The proposal also establishes a baseline from which to measure change.
- The third section specifies the *program activities* designed to meet the stated goals and objectives. In other words, it delineates the "who, what, when, where, and how" for implementing the program.
- The *evaluation plan* typically includes a timeline; describes data-collection procedures, names those responsible for collecting the data, and details the methods to be used for analyzing the data; and specifies who will receive the report.
- Grant applications explicate a *budget* for the program proposal, noting sources of additional revenue and "in kind" matches, as well as line-item expenditures. (Wolk, 1994)

Successful grant writers follow the instructions for the grant application "to the letter" and consult with designated staff from the funding organization for clarifications.

COMMUNITY CHANGE

All of us live and work within communities. As community residents, we draw on the opportunities that our community offers and, in turn, contribute to its economic, political, educational, social, and cultural resources. How well a community supports life within the community and the extent to which its members enrich community life attests to the competence of the community. The nature of this reciprocal exchange between a community and its members determines its need for change and further development: At times, forces such as a weak economy, restrictive federal and state policies, prejudice and discrimination toward special population groups, and limited health and social service resources mitigate the competence of neighborhoods and communities (Breton, 2001).

These external and internal forces become targets of change as social workers focus their efforts to enhance community competence. Practitioners who apply their generalist skills to macrolevel systems as community practitioners can initiate work community and organizational leaders to strengthen social network bonds, expand the availability of resources, and foster sociopolitical changes "to improve the quality of life for their residents in ways that enhance inclusions and social justice and decrease the barriers of exclusion, racism, and classism" (Weil, 2005, p. 20). With the trend toward applying community-based models in a variety of fields of practice, such as family, mental health, faith-based, and aging services, social work leaders call for direct practice workers to prepare themselves for a community-based approach (Weil). The purposes of community practice include

- ▶ Improving the quality of life
- ▶ Extending human rights
- ▶ Advocacy
- ▶ Human social and economic development
- ▶ Service and program planning
- ▶ Service integration
- ▶ Political and social action
- ▶ Social justice (Weil & Gamble, 2005, p. 126)

Processes for Working with Communities

Community practice, then, is work to improve quality of life and increase social justice, through social and economic development, community organizing, social planning, and progressive social change. It is a cooperative effort between practitioners and affected individuals, groups, communities, and coalitions. Improving the quality of life for impoverished and vulnerable persons and communities requires helping people help themselves to build resources and develop social and political power. (Weil, 2005, p. 10)

Empowerment-based social workers tailor the same generalist processes for working with individuals, families, and groups to structure their community change efforts. These processes, detailed throughout this text, are easily applied to community work, including

- ▶ *Forming partnerships* with community residents, local governmental officials, and other community leaders
- ▶ *Articulating situations* that interfere with the competence of the community
- ▶ *Defining* the purpose and direction of the community-change strategies
- ▶ *Identifying* relevant community strengths
- ▶ *Assessing* community resource capabilities
- ▶ *Framing solutions* to address community challenges and unmet needs by planning strategies to facilitate change
- ▶ *Activating and mobilizing* existing community resources—people, services, support base
- ▶ *Creating alliances* among and between formal and informal community structures
- ▶ *Expanding opportunities* in community institutions through advocacy, policy changes, and resource development

> ▶ *Recognizing and measuring the successes* of the community involvement in the organizing effort
> ▶ *Integrating and stabilizing the gains* made within the social networks and sociopolitical structures of the community

Working with Communities through Organizing

Community organizing is a method social workers use to bring together people from a community who share common interests and goals for addressing social problems through collective action. As community organizers, social workers promote the interpersonal and political development of constituency groups and facilitate change at the neighborhood, community, and societal levels. Community organizers today initiate many of the same activities they have in the past: they bring diverse constituencies together to dialogue about issues they have in common; they bridge differing agendas; they promote grassroots leadership development; they use empowering strategies to develop a critical consciousness; and they encourage collective action.

The role of community organizer includes that of practice researcher, if we understand community as "the agent of change, the target of change, or the context for change" (Couoton, 2005, p. 74). Couoton challenges social workers to adopt a more rigorous approach to community-based research, moving beyond psychometrics to ecometrics. "Social work has deep roots in community and has given voice to the importance of local communities for human development and social justice. Therefore, social work should be the leader in advancing scientific knowledge about how and why communities can change" (p. 84). Community organizers in the new social movement arena, like their historic counterparts, question the status quo. They call for reexamining the assumptions that stabilize social structures and the societal values that perpetuate them. Furthermore, they draw on research-based evidence to inform their practice and promote community change.

Community organizing in minority communities

Minority communities have a long history of activating informal supports of families and neighbors, as well as formal networks of churches and fraternal organizations to meet individual and community needs through self-help programs. To redress institutional racism, confront oppression, and secure civil rights, professional organizers build on the self-help traditions in minority communities. Rivera and Erlich (1998) summarize important qualities for the success of organizers in racially and culturally diverse communities. In addition to sharing similar cultural and racial characteristics with the community with which they are working, organizers

> ▶ Are familiar with the culture of the community including its values, belief systems, and traditions
> ▶ Possess linguistic competence in language style and subgroup slang of the ethnic community members
> ▶ Convey collaborative leadership styles
> ▶ Are adept in analyzing the power dynamics, mediating influences, and the economic relationship between the ethnic community and the wider community
> ▶ Bring practice wisdom and professional knowledge about the record of success and failures of organizing activities

Diversity in Practice

Minority communities have a history of using self-help traditions to address community needs. How can professional organizers who do not share the minority-status of target communities be effective in their organizing efforts?

- Are skillful in using conscientization and empowerment strategies in disenfranchised communities
- Are capable of analyzing the psychological makeup of the community
- Understand the dynamics of organizational functioning and decision making
- Are adept at evaluating community problems and trends and involving community members in participatory research
- Are skillful administrators in planning, developing, and managing programs
- Recognize their own abilities, intentions, and limits

Working with Communities through Development

In contrast to community organization, which focuses on community structures and functions, community development focuses on the sociopsychological functioning of a community. Community development enhances community competence by increasing the involvement of citizens in community life. Lane and Henry (2004) assert "community development—as an empowering, participatory, 'bottom-up' process of change—has considerable potential also, to contribute to the prevention of crime and violence" (p. 209).

People require opportunities: a practice example

As a way to understand the impact of community development, consider the two very different scenarios that explore how Raymond meets his needs in ways that match what the community environment has to offer. First, think of Raymond as a young man who is really moving up in the world. His success in working security has led to his position in sales. His skill in sales has shown the top brass his growing abilities in management. Clearly, Raymond is a natural leader who has opportunities to exercise and develop his potential. Less than a year ago, Raymond was just another poor kid from the wrong part of town. Fifteen years old, confined by poverty, and intimidated by the roving gangs in his Northside neighborhood, Raymond looked as if he had no future. There seemed to be no way out. But, then, "opportunity" fell into his lap when Terrence introduced him to the War Lords.

Raymond knew about the War Lords before he became acquainted with Terrence. The War Lords were one of three gangs that roamed and ruled Raymond's neighborhood. Raymond thought that the gangs had always been a part of his neighborhood, but his mother told him that the gangs showed up recently, just when people thought things couldn't get any worse. But the gangs made it worse, or so Raymond's mother said.

Raymond had his own ideas about the War Lords; they were his ticket out. Before the War Lords, Raymond felt trapped. Now, Raymond felt a sense of belonging and some control over his life. Running with the War Lords, he was enjoying money from illegal ventures, the safety of tough and loyal friends, and the power of gang membership. Raymond believed his mother didn't really understand the realities of life when she said that she trusted her faith, hard work, and the family to get her "somewhere." After all, that "somewhere" was a cramped unit of public housing in a neighborhood that was under siege each time the sun went down.

From the outside looking in, joining a gang doesn't make much sense. But Raymond's view of life holds little promise elsewhere. Like all human beings, Raymond seeks emotional and economic security, the freedom to develop his abilities, and the chance to be a success. The way Raymond sees it, the War

Lords provide the only path to those goals. Whereas gangs are certainly antisocial and threatening, viewed from another perspective, they provide what their members perceive as plausible opportunities for security and success. Given other genuine choices, Raymond may be able to avoid the lure of gang membership. Social workers have responsibilities to create those choices. The press for social justice compels workers to develop opportunities, particularly for those who, like Raymond, are disenfranchised and oppressed.

Now, imagine a different scenario for Raymond's story, one in which other opportunities are available, where Raymond has choices, and the neighbors have hope. Here, too, Raymond is really moving up in the world. His good work as a cashier at Northside Center Grocery has led to his new position as the night manager. His position as night manager pays more than running the register and gives Raymond opportunities to show the store manager his talents in public relations and the quick way he masters new responsibilities. He is developing marketable skills, building a good job record, and making money, too. Raymond is beginning to feel as if he has some control over his life. Just 1 short year ago, Raymond didn't see a future for himself. Stuck in a deteriorating Northside neighborhood with no money and no plans—even joining a gang had started to seem like his only real option. But that was before Northside Center opened and Raymond discovered he has some real choices.

A community development effort generated the original idea for Northside Center. After receiving a parcel of land, city leaders polled residents in Raymond's neighborhood for ideas about what to do with the property. Results revealed an overwhelming need for convenient neighborhood businesses and services, as families had to travel long distances just to take care of basic needs—like buying groceries, filling prescriptions, and doing laundry. Community groups, social agencies, and city leaders combined their efforts to make the neighborhood's dream a reality in the opening of Northside Center, a small mall with a grocery store, a pharmacy, and a laundromat.

These early businesses were just the beginning. Last summer, business expanded to include a farmer's market. A startling success, the market drew customers and vendors from all parts of the city and the surrounding rural areas, bringing together people who otherwise would be leading totally separate lives. Northside Center also added a community service agency that coordinates neighborhood social services and recreational activities and provides local residents with information and referral services. It was at the drop-in center that a group of neighbors initiated plans for a watch program to deter gang activity.

Developed as a partnership of local businesses, city leaders, social service agencies, and community members, Northside Center does more than bring the convenience of groceries, medicine, and laundry back to the neighborhood. It expands opportunities for employment, builds relationships among neighbors, and reconnects the Northside neighborhood to the larger community. Raymond is reaping the benefits of this new opportunity, too. He has a job and plans for the future.

Empowerment and community development

Empowerment-oriented community development incorporates two core strategies: "promoting the participation of community members in the change process with a focus on self-initiative and providing technical assistance to enable leadership development" (Zippay, 1995, p. 263). Clearly, it is important to organize with members of a community in a collaborative sense, rather than for them in a patriarchal sense. Community members participating in development efforts acquire a critical consciousness about the needs of the community as a whole and the benefits of collective action. Community practitioners facilitate indigenous leadership, provide leadership development training, and apply a range of strategies to enhance community capacities (Austin, et al., 2005; Franco, et al., 2007; Harvey, et al., 2007; Ohmer, 2007; Wituk, et al., 2007).

SOCIAL WORK AS A POLITICAL PROFESSION

Social work by nature is a political profession. Social workers use the political strategies of consensus building, compromise, negotiation, and even conflict to resolve inequities in the allocation of social welfare services and to achieve social justice. Methods to achieve the profession's mandate for social justice

---

Box 14.2 Ethic of Politicized Social Work

Social work is inherently political. "A decision to act apolitically is a decision to support the status quo, impede opportunities for change, and further participate in the oppression of vulnerable client system" (Long, 2002, p. 57). This charge for political practice is particularly important in times of policy devolution (Sherraden, et al., 2002), managed care (Dietz, 2000), new federalism (Linhorst, 2002), the new significance of state policy-making levels (Ortiz, et al., 2004; Schneider, 2002), electronic advocacy (McNutt, 2000; McNutt & Menon, 2004; 2008), and the renewed emphasis in social work on social justice and macrolevel practice (Cox, 2001; Finn & Jacobson, 2003; Haynes & Mickelson, 2003; Mizrahi, 2001).

Jane Addams once remarked that the cure to what ails democracy is more democracy. Democratic principles are founded on maximizing participation, including the voices of all population groups in the democratic process, and exercising influence over political processes. Consistent with social work's roots in the democratic ideal, the ethic of politicized social work is detailed in the section of the NASW *Code of Ethics* (1999a) that describes social workers' responsibilities for social and political action:

a. Social workers should engage in social and political action that seeks to ensure that all people have equal access to the resources, employment, services, and opportunities they require to meet their basic human needs and to develop fully. Social workers should be aware of the impact of the political arena on practice and should advocate for changes in policy and legislation to improve social conditions in order to meet basic human needs and promote social justice.

b. Social workers should act to expand choice and opportunity for all people, with special regard for vulnerable, disadvantaged, oppressed, and exploited people and groups. (Section 6.04)

The ethical responsibilities that social workers have for social and political action are too often neglected in contemporary practice. Bureaucratic self-interests, organizational goal displacement, work overload, confining job descriptions, and resource scarcity constrain the political actions of social workers. Workers who take a political stance risk being marginalized within their own organizational and service delivery contexts. Theoretical perspectives can block workers' application of a politicized practice. Overemphasizing psychological and emotional difficulties of clients can obscure workers' recognition of the social factors of poverty, oppression, and inequality that profoundly afflict many social work clients (Millar, 1999).

Today, most social work professionals work in direct practice settings, sometimes viewed as separate from the macrolevel practice that carries a distinct political emphasis. However, policy practice is readily integrated into a microlevel service context. Long (2002) notes that social workers can politicize their direct practice by

▶ Making the connections between the "personal and political"

▶ Considering common needs and issues among clients for policy change action

▶ Critically evaluating practice theories and models for their tendencies to maintain privilege and social injustice

▶ Reviewing organizational policies and procedures for issues of equity, justice, and inclusive participation

Ultimately, political practice attends to issues of power in relationships at all levels. As Dietz (2000) says, "To politicize micro practice, it is necessary to support people in reconnecting and experiencing their power at the individual and group levels and in joining with others in a process of political transformation" (p. 387).

draw from divergent political, economic, and social ideologies. Although social workers are not expected to adopt a singular viewpoint, clarifying their particular ideological and political positions is essential to professional practice.

Political Perspectives

Our perception of problems as either personal or public, how we assign blame and responsibility, and our preferences for change strategies all depend on our political ideals. At the societal level, social welfare policy and social change activities are shaped by the tension among factions representing the liberal, conservative, and radical perspectives.

Liberal

Liberals vigorously campaign for social policies that champion fundamental human rights and social equality. Key priorities include safeguarding political and civil liberties through economic freedom and democratic participation. Liberals believe that all citizens should have opportunities to participate fully in society but also recognize how social problems that disrupt personal social functioning sometimes curtail citizen participation. Advocating public responsibility for addressing root causes of social injustice, liberal ideology promotes governmental solutions. Thus, liberals view social welfare programs as a citizen's right and a legitimate function of the government.

Neoliberalism surfaced in response to the resounding defeat of liberal politicians in the 1970s and 1980s. Neoliberalism favors reducing government expenditures and encouraging partnerships with private entrepreneurs to accept increased responsibility for ensuring citizens' welfare (Karger & Stoesz, 2008). Neoliberals advocate privatization or the administration of social welfare programs by private businesses and corporations rather than the government.

Conservative

The conservative position reveals an individualistic perspective based on Western values such as rugged individualism and the work ethic. Conservatism embraces a capitalistic free-market economy and the preservation of social stability through existing institutional structures. This view deems problems public only when the stability of societal structures is threatened and, even then, offers solutions that foster individual rather than social change. Because conservatives believe that problems result from personal failure, they limit governmental support of social welfare to temporary services so as not to destroy individual initiative. Like the neoliberals, conservatives support privatization of social services through efforts such as voluntary charities, self-help organizations, and business corporations.

Neoconservatives actively oppose welfare programs (Karger & Stoesz, 2008). They propose a needs-based approach that requires workfare, compels familial responsibility for dependents, and switches responsibility for welfare from the federal government to state and local governments and the private sector. This view faults megastructures, such as big government and big business, for social problems. Neoconservatives want to contain government programs, increase private-sector responsibility for the welfare burden, and use mediating structures such as neighborhoods, voluntary associations, and churches as sources of change (Berger & Neuhaus, 1977).

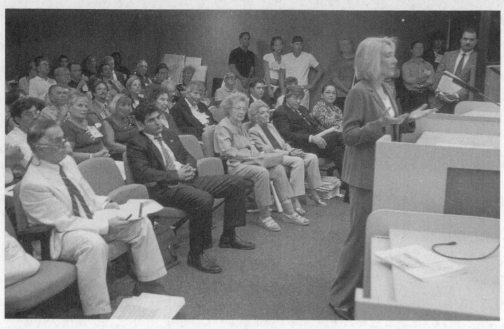

Community forums provide a venue for social action.

Radical

The radical perspective holds society responsible for social inequities and advocates redressing these inequities through change in the institutional fabrics of society. Radicals believe that problems in living generate from social structures rather than from within individuals themselves. Furthermore, radicalism posits that, instead of contributing to social justice, conventional public social welfare oppresses, stigmatizes, and regulates the poor and disadvantaged (Piven & Cloward, 1971). Changing these oppressive conditions requires sweeping macrostructural reform to construct a noncapitalistic welfare state in which all citizens share societal benefits equally.

Political Perspectives Applied to Social Work

No one political ideology represents the social work position. Social workers' duties of social control often conflict with their pursuits of social reform. Regarding this conflict, workers "need to understand and utilize both control and reform types of strategies, principles, and procedures, as they are appropriate in helping situations. Social work practice needs both conservative and radical contributions" (Siporin, 1980, p. 524). Although we may be tempted to forge our ideas about social policy into one political mold, the dialogue that results from various political perspectives generates creative tension, clarifies positions, and revitalizes the social work profession.

POLICY DEVELOPMENT

Throughout their careers, social work professionals discuss policy issues, and social workers, on their own and collectively through professional associations like the NASW, are in positions to frame public policy and debate the consequences of policy directives. Direct service practitioners have at their fingertips key information about social problems gleaned from their frontline experiences. They also have ideas about causes of and solutions to those problems. Because of their close proximity to consumers of social services, workers witness the intentional and unintentional effects of policies on social service delivery in general and their clients in particular. In committing to social justice and expanding opportunities, social workers use the information they accrue to make policy concerns an integral aspect of their professional practice.

Policy Analysis and Change

Social policy analysis involves studying and evaluating those public policies that are intended to address citizens' needs or to redress identified social problems. Social workers monitor legislation or other forms of policy during its development to analyze its intent and anticipate its potential consequences. During the phase of policy development, workers can offer critical data to shape the direction of the policy. After the implementation of a policy, social workers can assess its actual impact on targeted populations, measure the degree to which it achieves its goals, examine its short- and long-term consequences, evaluate its social implications, and determine its cost-effectiveness.

As policy analysts, social workers examine the social, economic, political, and global variables evident in the process of formulating policies, study the values and preferences that those policies reflect, and analyze the legalities as well as the costs and benefits of implementing the policies (Gilbert & Terrell, 2005; Midgley, 2007). Many authors propose comprehensive models for policy analysis (Chambers & Wedel, 2009; DiNitto & Cummins, 2007; Gilbert & Terrell, 2005; Karger & Stoesz, 2008). Figure 14.2 highlights the major components of a policy analysis.

Consumer Participation in Policy Development

As identified stakeholders in social welfare policy and agency services, social workers and their clients must find meaningful ways to participate in the policy

Figure 14.2 Framework for Policy Analysis

Part I Policy Specification

1. Detail the history of the policy under study and related policies
2. Describe the problems that the policy will redress
3. Identify the social values and ideological beliefs embedded in the policy
4. State the goals of the policy
5. Summarize the details of the policy regarding implementation, funding, eligibility criteria, and other stipulations

Part II Policy Feasibility

1. Identify projected outcomes of the policy
2. Discuss the political and economic feasibility of the policy
3. Characterize the support or dissent for the policy
4. Assess the ramifications of the policy for the existing health and human service delivery structures

Part III Policy Merits

1. Assess the effectiveness and efficiency of the implementation of the policy
2. Weigh the social costs and consequences of the policy
3. Evaluate the differential effects of the policy on diverse population groups
4. Judge the merits of the policy

Policy Practice

Empowering social workers believe that clients' voices should be heard in policy development. What are some meaningful ways for social work clients to speak in their own voices in policy development processes?

process—from clarifying issues to setting priorities to formulating, implementing, and evaluating policies. Empowerment-based practice presupposes that consumers will be directly involved in developing policies at all levels—from those of local agencies to those of national organizations and the federal government.

The responsibility of social workers to see that clients' voices are heard and understood by policymakers and to work for inclusion of clients in policy-making becomes clear when the focus is put on the strengths rather than the deficits of the people for whom the policies and programs are developed. (Chapin, 1995, p. 509)

Many opportunities exist for active citizen participation. Broad-based constituent involvement in strategic planning, community forums, brainstorming sessions, and consumer advisory groups are all mechanisms for involving a variety of interested parties, including clients, in policymaking. Interested individuals and public-interest groups contact political leaders to share information and experiences about a policy issue.

Agency policy and consumer participation

When consumers participate in developing agency policy, it safeguards their rights as clients, secures the relevancy of program services, and holds agencies accountable to their constituencies. Individual consumers who participate in policy development benefit from the self-growth, increased feelings of personal control, and networks of cooperative relationships that develop. Factors that increase the likelihood of consumers' successful participation include a clear mandate for their participation, a power base from which to assert their right to participate, and recognition of their legitimacy as spokespersons.

Social service consumers can be involved in several aspects of organizational development, including

- Defining service delivery procedures and setting agency policies
- Participating in program evaluation
- Influencing the direction of strategic planning
- Presenting testimony on proposed social policy and legislative changes
- Helping in fundraising activities
- Identifying new areas for service initiatives
- Participating on staff and administrative hiring committees
- Serving on advisory committees and boards of directors

Involving clients in making policy decisions requires that social workers provide technical knowledge rather than direct the process. For example, workers support effective group decision making to analyze the situation, refine goals and objectives, and develop plans of action. Workers and clients function as partners, recognizing that the authority for decision making in this process rests with clients.

SOCIAL ACTIVISM AND SOCIAL ADVOCACY

Accessible and equitable resources in the social, economic, educational, and political institutions of society directly affect persons' ability to achieve an optimal level of social functioning. Social activism is a strategy to redress the inequities that result from differential social status, resource distribution, and power. The NASW *Code of Ethics* (1999a) makes clear the expectation that social workers will use social and political action as a means to guarantee access to resources and opportunities for all persons. To ensure fair access to existing rights, entitlements, and resources, generalist practitioners work toward creating opportunities in macrolevel systems through social action and advocacy.

A Heritage of Social Reform

Social action and social advocacy permeate the early history of the social work profession. Seeking to address social problems associated with industrialization, urban overcrowding, and immigration, settlement house workers utilized their research and community organizing skills to initiate social change.

> By the turn of the century, the South End Settlement House in Boston, Henry Street in New York, and university settlements in both New York and Chicago had become centers for research, discussion, and political agitation to improve urban conditions. They led fights for better housing laws, shorter work hours, and improved working conditions. They also conducted surveys and distributed research reports that became the intellectual basis for some of the period's social legislation. (Franklin, 1990, p. 62)

Even the micro-oriented Charity Organization Society recognized the effects of environmental conditions and focused attention on public issues such as unemployment and housing and their effect on individuals.

Throughout the twentieth century, many professionals carried on this tradition of social action and social reform. Among the most noteworthy is Bertha Capen Reynolds, a social activist and advocate who instilled in her students and colleagues the necessity for political activity, social advocacy, and other pursuits of social justice. Writing about social casework, Reynolds (1951) described it as helping "people to test and understand their reality, physical, social and emotional, to mobilize resources within themselves and in their social environment to meet their reality or change it" (p. 131).

With the recent trend toward privatization, some people question whether activism remains central to social work practice. Many social workers say "Yes!" A study of activism among social work professionals found that social workers who identify strongly with their profession are likely to reflect social work's heritage of social action (Reeser, 1991).

Promoting Social Action

A strong commitment to social justice, egalitarian values, and the ability to take risks are professional ingredients that prompt social workers to social action. Successful advocates

- Build a consensus among stakeholders regarding the need for change
- Develop agreement among stakeholders as to the nature of the desired outcome
- Explore issues in the context of the whole community system
- Recognize that community problems are interrelated, and that solutions in one arena may lead to solutions in others
- Find pathways for working outside of adversarial systems
- Adopt a strengths-focused perspective that identifies assets, capacities, and opportunities, rather than a problem-focused perspective that restricts its vision to liabilities, issues, and limitations (Flower, 1998)

Advocacy Role

Advocates work to achieve social justice by empowering people to speak out and exercise their influence to correct inequity. Achieving social change through advocacy that empowers requires the active partnership of citizens who are vulnerable or disenfranchised with professionals who recognize the public issues inherent in personal troubles. Advocates speak on behalf of clients and encourage clients to speak for themselves when situations deny their rights and entitlements.

Advocacy efforts can focus either on protecting the interests of individual clients or on the general issues of collective causes. As you recall from Chapter 12, client advocacy refers to working on behalf of one's client or client group to obtain needed services or social welfare entitlements. In contrast, class or cause advocacy seeks to redress collective issues through championing social reform and developing responsive social policies.

On the surface, these two types of advocacy seem separate and distinct in purpose and action. Indeed, client advocacy is usually associated with microlevel practice, whereas cause advocacy is an important component of macrolevel practice. Yet it is often the experience of microlevel work that provides the impetus for macrolevel change. There is an essential relationship between micro- and macrolevel practitioners in successful advocacy efforts.

Essential to empowerment-based advocacy is the continual involvement of stakeholders. Workers who ignore the potential and power of clients as resources in social action waste resources and risk alienating those who are in the best position to inform the process. To involve clients in advocacy efforts, workers provide them with pertinent information, use consciousness-raising strategies to help clients understand the impact of the sociopolitical and economic systems on their situations, ensure client access to existing agency services and entitlements, and argue with decision makers for expanded client entitlements and new services. Importantly, workers help them organize into groups to push for their rights and entitlements en masse, because supportive alliances of people with similar concerns provide a sense of power. With the increased prominence of technology, advocates can take advantage of the Internet and cyberactivism (Hick & McNutt, 2002; McNutt & Menon, 2004, 2008)

Designing advocacy interventions

Whether client or cause advocacy, the process begins by identifying the particulars of the injustice:

> The decision to pursue the advocacy of a case or a cause, or a combination of both, will usually have been preceded by the identification of an injustice which it is felt cannot be rectified simply by efficient administration or negotiation. The identification of an injustice and the sense of conviction that the removal of this injustice should become a priority, even in a congested workload, goes hand in hand with the advocacy process. It is not sufficient merely to recognize an injustice. You have to believe that this issue should be fought for, and if necessary over a long period of time. (Rees, 1991, p. 146)

The knowledge, skills, values, and processes of generalist practice apply to a social worker's advocacy efforts regardless of the particular system targeted for change. In designing advocacy interventions, social workers consider numerous variables, including:

▶ At what social system level do advocates *define the problem?* For instance, does the problem reflect a personal need, a relationship difficulty, a social service delivery gap, an interorganizatonal conflict, or an inequitable social policy?

▶ What is the *objective* of the intervention? For example, is the purpose of the advocacy effort to entitle clients to available services or to expand the pool of resources?

▶ What is the *target system* for the advocacy intervention? In some situations, this may be the advocate's own agency, another organization, or a social institution. Advocates evaluate the positive or negative nature of their relationship with decision makers in the system targeted for change.

▶ What *sanction*, right, or authority does the worker have to intervene in a targeted system? Legal rights, judicial decisions, and client entitlements all provide leverage for advocacy efforts.

▶ What *resources* are available? Sound advocacy requires resources such as the worker's professional expertise, political influence, credibility, and negotiating skills as well as clients' expertise and supports.

▶ How likely will the target system be *receptive* to the advocacy effort? Typically, when target systems consider the advocacy "legitimate," reasonable, or lawful, they are more receptive to negotiating change.

▶ What *level of intervention* is necessary to achieve the desired outcome? Different levels include policy changes, procedural or administrative modifications, and alterations in discretionary actions taken by management or staff.

▶ Who is the *object of the advocacy* intervention? Depending on the cause, individuals with whom the advocate intervenes may range from the direct service worker, to an agency administrator, to a regional organization, to a legislative body.

▶ What *strategies or modes of intervention* are appropriate to achieve the desired objectives? Advocates may assume roles as adversaries, negotiators, or collaborators. They use a variety of intervention techniques such as mediating disputes, building coalitions, negotiating differences, and exchanging information.

▶ What can advocates *learn from the outcomes* of prior advocacy efforts? Advocates glean information from both their successes and failures. (McGowan, 1987)

LEGISLATIVE ADVOCACY

Pressing for change in public policies requires advocacy in the context of legislative activities. In today's political and economic climate, everything social workers and their clients do is affected by legislation and social policies. Ortiz and colleagues (2004) note that legislative casework involves the intersection of policies and social work practice. They call for an increased presence of social workers in this policy arena. The dearth of funding, the glut of problems, and the competition among programs make legislative advocacy skills vital to everyday practice. Strategies and skills for legislative advocacy include legislative analysis, lobbying, and legislative testimony.

Legislative Analysis

Legislation and social policies undergird all aspects of social work in every field of practice. What can social workers do at state and federal levels to create policy agendas and set funding priorities to address the unmet needs of disadvantaged client population groups and to redress gaps and barriers in the public welfare system?

Numerous pieces of legislation interest social work professionals including diverse laws related to child welfare, health care reform, education, public welfare, mental health, and emergency relief services. Social workers focus on five areas to analyze legislative proposals: substantive issues, committee structure, fiscal requirements, political dimensions, and support and opposition relative to the legislative initiative (Kleinkauf, 1989).

To *analyze substantive issues,* legislative advocates consider the status of current laws and regulations, extent of proposed changes, constituency affected, potential ramifications, and the inherent social work value issues. Because proposed legislation is assigned to specific legislative committees that hold hearings, social workers identify the members of relevant committees and ascertain their positions on social work issues. The *fiscal analysis* of the proposed legislation reviews the results of the findings of the committee on the costs of implementing the sources of funds. Social workers ensure that sound fiscal analysis considers "human" as well as monetary costs. Estimating the likelihood that the bill will gain enough support to pass means scrutinizing its *political status.* This involves reviewing the way in which it was initiated, surveying the position of key legislators, and evaluating plans supporting its passage. Social workers identify which governmental agencies are affected, list those individuals and systems which *support or oppose* the bill, and summarize the major points of their positions. By thoroughly investigating these key areas, workers can evaluate a bill's chances for passage and estimate the impetus for mobilizing political action to support or oppose it.

Lobbying

Lobbying is any political activity that seeks to sway the plans of lawmakers and government officeholders for legislative and public policy. Lobbyists attempt to persuade lawmakers to draft legislation favorable to their special interest positions.

Professional staff lobbyists employed by the NASW carry out many of the lobbying functions for the social work profession. The Educational Legislative Action Network (ELAN) serves as a communication and action network for the congressional districts of the NASW's various chapters. Another NASW-sponsored initiative, Political Action for Candidate Election (PACE), tracks the voting records of legislators and promotes political awareness and lawful action by the NASW membership.

Social workers take five basic steps to prepare for lobbying activities:

1. Assess strengths and limitations with respect to commitment, time, sponsors, alliances, and information regarding the policy context and related strategic processes.

2. Set the action agenda by estimating goals for change, priorities, and fallback positions.

3. Identify target policymakers, including their motivations and the values that underlie their definition of issues.

4. Gather and evaluate evidence by checking the credibility of one's sources.

5. Prepare a case that describes the issue; argues from a definition, cause-effect, or action perspective; and presents a rebuttal. (Richan, 1996)

Successful lobbying encompasses diverse activities and tasks (Mahaffey, 1982). Workers first must keep track of pertinent legislation as well as legislative committee activities, plans, and decisions. Workers may even offer legislators technical assistance and expertise. Most important, lobbyists build coalitions. They cultivate liaisons between organizational sponsors and legislators. To accomplish this connection, lobbyists train and organize a cadre of social workers to become politically involved by writing letters, making phone contacts, and testifying at legislative hearings.

Too often the public policy debate frames issues as struggles between competing interests, pitting the middle class against the poor or care for the aged against care for children. Blecher and Hegar (1991) advocate advancing empowerment-based social welfare by featuring the values that underlie policy options rather than a competing struggle for limited resources. They say: "By emphasizing a collective role in meeting common human needs that cut across class lines, social work can help demonstrate that empowerment for anyone is linked with the empowerment of others" (p. 50).

Legislative Testimony

At public hearings sponsored by legislators or public officials, social workers and their clients can ask questions about newly proposed or adopted policies and express opinions on important social issues. Public hearings are often mandated by law. Additionally, the general public may demand a hearing be held to discuss controversial issues if one has not been scheduled.

When presenting testimony before legislative committees and at public hearings, clients and social workers may share written or oral statements about their own experiences and expertise. More often than not, clients who tell their own stories have the most powerful effect on lawmakers. Speaking in their own voices from their own experiences and on their own behalf, clients can effectively address the merits of particular social service programs and the probable impact of proposed bills. Jackson-Elmore (2005) conducted a key informant study of twelve states to learn about sources of information state legislators relied on for policy-making decisions. Findings indicated that state legislators from various communities all regarded feedback from local grassroots organizations as important. What was most appreciated was direct personal contact by individuals and organizational representatives, particularly constituents. This research provides evidence that involving clients in legislative testimony and action is, indeed, a valuable strategy.

To maximize the desired impact of legislative testimony, social workers follow these guidelines:

- Conduct substantive and procedural research on pending bills or policy by reviewing existing related statutes, gathering information that refutes or supports it, figuring the costs of its implementation, learning the position taken on the bill by those governmental offices or organizations that will ultimately be affected by its passage, and tracking its passage through committees
- Analyze the committee's membership, political affiliations, and constituencies for sources of influence and support
- Prepare factual testimony or a position paper that expresses the general opinion of the group or organization that you represent
- Testify calmly and with straightforward information
- Answer questions directly and from an informed knowledge base without claiming more expertise on the issue than you possess

▶ Follow up by providing promised additional materials or documentation, and continue to track the bill through the various assigned committees. (Kleinkauf, 1981)

When social workers prepare written testimony, their finished documents should be clear and understandable, free of jargon, based on facts and logic.

LOOKING FORWARD

Some scholars charge that social work practitioners pay little attention to macrosystems change in their practices. Because social work has a dual focus—on both enhancing individual functioning and expanding opportunity structures in society—practitioners are well advised to give due regard to facilitating change in social environments. The empowerment approach to social work practice holds that macrolevel change is integral to client empowerment.

Expanding opportunities during the development phase enhances the availability and accessibility of needed resources. Resources in client systems' personal, interpersonal, organizational, and societal domains afford options and accord power for resolving challenges. Social workers and clients join together to activate individual and collective energies to initiate social reform and work toward community development.

How effective are the resources, including the professional relationship and social work strategies, in satisfying the client's expressed goals? Chapter 15 explores evaluation and research as empowering processes for assessing the effectiveness of intervention methods and the accomplishment of goals. Only when clients recognize their success and determine what worked do they truly experience their own power.

Log onto **www.mysocialworklab.com** and select the **Interactive Skill Module** videos from the left-hand menu. Answer the questions below. (*If you did not receive an access code to* **MySocialWorkLab** *with this text and wish to purchase access online, please visit* www.mysocialworklab.com.)

1. **Watch page 19 of the child welfare module** in which a worker explains the policy of family preservation that guides her practice. What services and opportunities does this client need and how would you advocate to achieve the goals explicit in this policy?

2. **Analyze pages 4, 5, and 11 of the domestic violence module** in which client Faye describes her situation. If you were called as an expert witness to provide legislative testimony about expanding services to survivors of domestic violence, what would you say?

PRACTICE TEST

1. Social worker Suzanne Castro works arduously on behalf of clients to secure benefits to which they are entitled. Her activities are most likely called _____.
   a. legislative advocacy
   b. client advocacy
   c. policy advocacy
   d. cause advocacy

2. Social worker Berlinda Brown is employed by the state chapter of NASW to sway lawmakers' plans for legislation to benefit the welfare of disadvantaged citizens. Berlinda is most likely involved in _____.
   a. legislative analysis
   b. lobbying activities
   c. legislative testimony
   d. legislative debate

Human Rights & Justice

3. Social worker Jeremiah Price believes in democratic participation and governmental solutions to address root causes of social injustice. His political perspective is most likely _____.
   a. conservative
   b. neo-conservative
   c. radical
   d. liberal

4. A talk show host is a proponent of rugged individualism, the free market economy, and limited governmental involvement in social welfare. This political perspective is most likely _____.
   a. conservative
   b. neo-liberal
   c. radical
   d. liberal

5. Which of the following is LEAST accurate with respect to grant applications?
   a. Applications include measurable goals and objectives.
   b. Applications include a budget, including "in kind" matches
   c. Applications include a description of program activities, designed to meet the stated goals and objectives.
   d. Applications do not include the evaluation plan.

Policy Practice

6. Which is NOT an application of policy practice to direct practice?
   a. making the connections between the personal and political
   b. critically evaluating practice theories for their tendencies to maintain privilege and social injustice
   c. organizing political rallies to "fight city hall"
   d. reviewing organizational policies for issues of equity, justice, and inclusive participation

7. Of the following, which most accurately reflects a stated purpose of community practice?
   a. extend human rights and social justice
   b. ensure personal development
   c. enhance the self-esteem of individuals
   d. facilitate organizational change

8. _____ is an important strategy for organizing in minority communities.
   a. Passive leadership style
   b. Collaborative leadership style
   c. Aggressive leadership style
   d. Top-down leadership style

Practice Contexts

9. Social worker Colleen O'Hare is concerned about the uncoordinated service delivery system in her community. Her concern revolves around _____.
   a. agency turfism
   b. bureaucratic disentitlement
   c. fragmentation of services
   d. social triage

Log onto **MySocialWorkLab** once you have completed the Practice Test above to take your Chapter Exam and demonstrate your knowledge of this material.

Answers

1) b 2) b 3) d 4) a 5) d 6) c 7) a 8) b 9) c

Recognizing Success

CONNECTING CORE COMPETENCIES *in this chapter*

| Professional Identity | Ethical Practice | Critical Thinking | Diversity in Practice | Human Rights & Justice | Research Based Practice | Human Behavior | Policy Practice | Practice Contexts | Engage Assess Intervene Evaluate |

Are clients achieving their goals? Is our work with clients making a difference? Are we selecting the most effective and efficient practice techniques? Does the practice research support our selection of intervention strategies and program delivery models? These are important questions that social workers and clients ask themselves throughout the development phase of the intervention process. Social work evaluation and research answers these questions and provides information to enrich future attempts. In empowerment-based social work, the purpose of evaluation goes beyond simply measuring outcomes and processes. It also affirms the accomplishments made by clients and confirms the effectiveness of social service programs and social policies. The phrase, "recognizing success," frames evaluation research as a process that empowers by highlighting the positive achievements of clients.

Certainly, the emphasis on recognizing success does not diminish the accountability function of measurement in evaluation research. Social workers do need to acknowledge that not all strategies lead to successful solutions. If social work programs and practices fall short of their stated outcomes, their utility should be questioned, and, if the level of goal achievement does not satisfy their expectations, clients may lose confidence. Monitoring activities during a social work intervention affords opportunities to make necessary changes. Ongoing review and evaluation allow workers to modify their approaches and give clients opportunities to redirect their efforts.

Research is central to all generalist social work practice. Workers evaluate their own practice continuously to increase the effectiveness of their work with clients. Additionally, practitioners participate in more global projects to evaluate programs within their agencies. Some social workers practice as research specialists, evaluating theories, approaches, and methods to contribute their scientific findings to the knowledge base of social work.

This chapter examines the methods social workers use to evaluate their own practice and to contribute to the research base of the profession. In detail, this chapter

- Describes the purposes of social work evaluation and research as integral to social work practice
- Applies evidence-based practice to generalist social work
- Differentiates strategies for practice evaluation
- Explicates the research process, research terminology, and key ethical issues related to research
- Delineates elements and types of single-system design

Skills in conducting research and evaluation as well as in applying the results are essential for competent generalist practice.

SOCIAL WORK EVALUATION AND RESEARCH

Research was paramount to the work of early social work pioneers. At the turn of the century, settlement house workers documented adverse societal conditions through research studies that ultimately led to legislative and social policy reforms in child labor practices, housing, sanitation, and the juvenile court. In that same era, principles of social investigation and "scientific charity" guided the casework of friendly visitors of the charity organization societies. Throughout the remainder of the century, practitioners continued to apply research methods to address social problems and to use evaluation techniques to demonstrate the effectiveness of social work practice.

Today, social workers continue the tradition of integrating research and evaluation into their practice. Consider the various ways that the generalist social workers featured in previous chapters can carry out research and evaluation projects.

▶ Mark Nogales conducts a needs assessment to determine whether there is a need for more community-based services for persons with chronic mental illnesses. Mark gathers information from clients and their families, mental health advocates, human service practitioners, employers, and other key informants to document gaps in services and identify the types of services most needed.

▶ Kay Landon routinely administers client satisfaction surveys to access clients' perceptions of the quality and usefulness of the home health services they receive.

▶ Paul Quillin prepares a paper for publication on his empirical research about the relationship between the degree of parental involvement and the level of children's self-esteem.

▶ Karen McBride, along with four of her clients, participates in a regional study, the purpose of which is to identify the characteristics of practitioners that clients perceive as most empowering. As a research participant, Karen uses process recording to document her actions and behaviors; her clients complete research surveys to evaluate Karen's approach.

▶ As a "research consumer," Tony Marelli reads professional journals and attends conferences to learn about evidence-based strategies and "best practices" that he can apply to his addictions recovery work.

▶ Damon Edwards collects data on the incidence and severity of the lead-poisoning problem at Franklin Courts and prepares a position paper to influence the housing authority's action on lead abatement.

▶ Rita Garcia uses single-system case monitoring designs to help clients in the family reunification program evaluate their progress and identify areas that require further work.

▶ OPTIONS, the agency for which Kennedy Brown works, is a lead agency in the State Department of Aging Services case management pilot program. OPTIONS will implement an innovative assessment component that directs workers to seek specific information about clients' preferences for the delivery of home-based services—including how, when, and by whom. Another agency that is not implementing the new component will serve as the control. After a 6-month period, researchers will evaluate the data to determine whether increased personal choice results in a lower rate of nursing home admission.

▶ In his work with the Northside Development Association, Nate Hardy prepares a cost–benefit analysis of a public–private partnership between the city and owners of apartment complexes in the community. His findings lend Nate support to influence the city council to consider his proposal to increase the availability of low-income housing through a viable alternative to costly new construction.

These examples illustrate how generalist social workers participate in a variety of research and evaluation activities in their day-to-day practice. Social work professionals, as active researchers, develop and test the theory base of their practice and contribute to the growing body of evidence-based practice through their own research activities.

Integrating Practice and Research

Research Based Practice

Social workers in all fields of social work practice, select, and use best evidence interventions for their work with clients at all system levels. For a value-based profession, how can practitioner–researchers develop evidence-based interventions that are infused with social work values?

Social work practice and research are interdependent. The practice arena offers many opportunities to engage in research and evaluation. Research, in turn, is an important tool for conducting ethical and effective practice.

Social work practice generates social research—a knowledge-building function. Held accountable for their actions by clients, agencies, and funders, social workers evaluate the changes made by clients, the effectiveness of specific intervention strategies, and the overall outcomes of programs and services. To demonstrate accountability, social workers evaluate these various components of their practice to determine whether client systems' situations improve during the course of social work interventions. To generate practice knowledge, social workers use research to ascertain what specific strategies account for clients' improvements (Corcoran, 2003; Macdonald, 2001; McNeece & Thyer, 2004; Nathan & Gorman, 2002). In this way, social work research expands the knowledge base of practice and provides a way to evaluate practice effectiveness.

Similarly, *social research informs social work practice*—a solution-seeking function. Social work requires research-based knowledge to understand human behavior as well as social processes and social problems that differentially affect client systems. Practitioners make numerous professional judgments in their day-to-day practice activities. As such, their decisions and actions need a firm foundation of research evidence rather than merely intuition and untested assumptions.

EVIDENCE-BASED PRACTICE

With its roots in evidence-based decision-making in medicine and health care professions, evidence-based practice is increasing in prominence in social work practice internationally (Macdonald, 2001; Plath, 2006; Regehr, et al, 2007). The evidence-based approach applies to all fields of social work practice, including mental health, criminal justice, child welfare, and aging services. Additionally, it extends to all facets of generalist practice, including work with individuals, families, groups, organizations, communities, and policy practice.

Gibbs and Gambrill (2003) define evidence-based practice as "the conscientious, explicit, and judicious use of current best evidence in making decisions about the care of clients" (p. 452). Social workers adopting evidence-based practice incorporate salient research about the efficacy of interventions into their decision-making processes (Jenson & Howard, 2008). Evidence-based practice is a process for combining "well-researched interventions with practice experience, ethics, client and community preferences and culture, to guide and inform the delivery of treatments and services, that can be applied at the individual, family, group, organization or policy level" (IASSR, 2008, p. 1).

Steps for Evidence-Based Decision-Making

In essence, evidence-based practice is a process of informed decision-making. Applying this approach follows five structured steps first developed in the field of medicine:

1. Converting need for information into an answerable question.

2. Tracking down the best evidence with which to answer that question.

3. Critically appraising that evidence for its validity (closeness to the truth), impact (size of effect), and applicability (usefulness in practice).

4. Integrating the critical appraisal with our clinical expertise and with our [client's] unique biology, values, and circumstances.

5. Evaluating our effectiveness and efficiency in executing steps 1 to 4 and seeking ways to improve them the next time. (Straus, et al., 2005, pp. 3–4)

Answerable questions

Developing an explicit, answerable question is critical for all types of research. With respect to evidence-based practice, well-framed questions are more efficient in directing the search for answers toward relevant research studies. Social workers are likely interested in a range of topic areas, including effective methods and assessments, prevention, factors related to risk and resilience, costs, potential drawbacks, and harm (Gambrill, 2006). Effective questions delineate the specific parameters of the information needed to obtain answers.

Tracking down evidence

Although the steps in evidence-based practice seem straightforward, locating research evidence requires sophisticated information literacy skills, including *knowing where* to locate such information, and *knowing how* to use effective search strategies. With the increased popularity of this approach, more resources are being developed, many of which are available on the Internet (See Table 15.1). One such resource is the Campbell Collaboration (campbell collaboration.org.), an international, nonprofit organization that reviews and synthesizes research about interventions and public policies in social, behavioral, and educational arenas. Research teams conduct and disseminate systematic reviews through a meta-analysis of research studies on interventions and public policies in social welfare, criminal justice, and education. The primary focus is to disseminate information about policy and practice effectiveness and variables that influence outcomes. These reports are available to policy makers as background for their decision making, to practitioners for selecting research–practice methods, to researchers for accessing databases of meta-analyses, and to the general public for ensuring accountability.

The skills required for finding relevant evidence are similar to the Boolean strategies we use when searching for scholarly articles on an academic library's electronic databases or for more general web-based information. Most of us quickly discover the power of well-defined search terms!

Critically appraising evidence

Critical appraisal involves assessing the authority of the research and determining whether the research findings are relevant to the situation about which

---

Table 15.1   Selected Internet Resources for Evidence-Based Practice

California Evidence-Based Clearinghouse for Child Welfare www.cachildwefareclearinghouse.org

Campbell Collaboration www.campbellcollaboration.org

National Initiative for the Care of the Elderly http://nicenet.aging.utornonto.ca/

Social Care Institute for Excellence www.scie.org.uk

SAMHSA Guide to Evidence-based Practices www.samhsa.gov/ebpwebguide/index.asp

Swedish Institute for Evidence-based Practice www.socialstyrelsen.se/en/

Practitioners make effective use of research-based theory and technique, but some situations are confusing "messes" incapable of technical solution.

—Donald A. Schön

we have the question. The Institute for the Advancement of Social Work Research (IASWR, 2008) categorizes research studies according to the following hierarchy: "surveillance data, systematic reviews of multiple intervention research studies, expert opinion/narrative reviews, a single intervention research study, program evaluation, word of mouth/media/marketing, and personal experience" (p. 2). Underlining the importance of consumer involvement, the Social Care Institute for Excellence in London incorporates evidence provided by consumers, family members, and volunteers, in addition to the knowledge from practitioners, organizations, policy implementation, and research (Pawson, et al., 2003, cited in Johnson & Austin, 2006). Plath (2006) cautions social workers not to accept research at face value and not to generalize the findings automatically to different contexts.

Applying the evidence

To apply the research-based evidence to a particular facet of practice, social workers use "critical thinking skills, sensitive interpersonal skills, insights into personal and contextual factors, awareness of political and power issues and a strong value base" (Plath, 2006, p. 70). Considerations include the similarities and differences between the research and the specifics of the practice question as well as the potential effects of any potential modifications. In other words, social workers must critically evaluate the particulars of the practice context as well as the details of the research evidence.

Evaluating effectiveness

As with the application of any strategy, practitioners are more likely to make improvements to the process when they assess its effectiveness. Evaluating each step of the process creates a cycle of continuous quality improvement. Examining how closely strategies and programs replicate the research findings provides a measure of fidelity. For example, Substance Abuse and Mental Health Services Administration (SAMSHA) has developed fidelity scales, which are essentially goal attainment scales to assist agency personnel in assessing how closely their programs adhere to SAMSHA's specifications for the evidence-based model.

Implications for Social Work Practice

Evidence-based practice has many benefits as well as indicators for caution. An evidence-based approach to social work practice enhances the scientific foundation of the social work profession and legitimizes practice strategies. Given the standard for accountability in the NASW *Code of Ethics* (1999a), it makes sense to select practice strategies, initiate programs, and develop policies based on high-quality research evidence. Improvements in the quality of social work practice follow from the feedback loops embedded in practice evaluation. With respect to notes of caution, social workers could fall into a trap of privilege in relation to expertise in research unless they are committed to involving clients as full partners in analyzing and selecting strategies that are most appropriate to the client's situation.

The increased emphasis on research calls for increased skills for understanding, interpreting, and conducting research. As Plath (2006) says, "the effective integration of critical reflection with an evidence-based practice approach requires curiosity, preparedness to question and willingness to explore alternatives" (p. 69). Building on the premise that private troubles emanate from public issues, Bolen and Hall (2007) warn that "much research, by targeting a social problem and then considering only individual-level variables related to it (e.g., individual factors contributing to homelessness), appears to focus on public issues as private troubles" (p. 474). To address these concerns, they call on social workers to "develop rigorous, evidence-based, social work models of practice that reverberate with the values of social work" (p. 474).

PRACTICE EVALUATION

Practice evaluation is a method of assessing the outcomes and measuring the effectiveness of social work strategies. Practitioners and clients monitor *progress*—to assess what clients *achieve* and to evaluate what programs *accomplish* rather than what they fail to do. Recognizing success during evaluation infuses the strengths perspective into practice. It increases the client system's energy and motivation for further change, directs the partners to repeat effective strategies, and acts as a catalyst for improving social services.

Three types of practice evaluation predominate in social work—progress evaluation, outcome assessment or client goal attainment, and program evaluation. *Progress evaluation* refers to continually monitoring and evaluating the success of the action plan. *Outcome assessment* involves measuring a client's achievement of goals and the effectiveness of the methods used in the change process. *Program evaluation* evaluates the effectiveness of a particular program or service in accomplishing programmatic goals. General evaluative criteria apply to each (Table 15.2).

Progress Evaluation

Action plans direct clients' and practitioners' activities during the development phase. These plans include well-defined goals, concrete objectives, and specific activities for social workers and clients to carry out to reach the desired outcomes. However, the most comprehensive plan can only suggest strategies that social workers and clients believe have the best possibility of attaining a successful outcome. Throughout the social work intervention, a client and a practitioner periodically take stock of what is happening to determine what is and what is not working. In light of this, the social worker has responsibility for participating in the implementation of the plan and also for monitoring, evaluating, and updating the plan.

Monitoring and evaluating action plans

Workers monitor and evaluate action plans as they are implemented to detect positive movements and steer activities in the direction of the desired outcomes. When workers and clients discover success, they stay the course. If a plan is ineffective or unworkable, the worker stops to discuss the situation

Table 15.2	**General Evaluative Criteria**
Criteria	Key Questions
Effectiveness	Was the desired outcome attained?
Efficiency	Was the outcome reached in the most direct way?
Equity	Were the client's rights protected? Were the rights of others ensured?

with the client to revise the plan. As social workers oversee the implementation of the plan, they look for answers to several evaluation questions:

- Are both clients and workers doing what they have contracted to do?
- Are some parts of the plan working and other parts running into roadblocks or dead ends?
- What activities have the greatest impact? What activities take a lot of effort but realize a minimal return?
- Is the plan on the right track, or is it falling short of expectations?
- Are clients actively involved in carrying out their part of the plan?
- If they are not, what is getting in the way?
- Do clients understand their roles or do they lack confidence that implementing the plan is worth the effort?
- Have clients' goals and motivations changed?

Updating plans

After considering this new evaluative information, workers and clients modify action plans to incorporate recent changes and emerging strengths. Before considering a new approach, workers caution clients not to discard previously planned activities until they have had a chance to be successful. Sometimes, progress is slow and requires patience for success. However, it doesn't make sense to repeat strategies that fail to produce desired outcomes.

Client Outcome Assessment

Research Based Practice

Social workers are held accountable by their clients, funders, and the public for the achievement of client outcomes. What are the implications of this mandate of professional accountability in the design of client outcome assessments?

In client outcome assessment, workers simultaneously evaluate the degree of goal achievement and the effectiveness of the strategies implemented. In short, social workers apply this type of practice evaluation to gain answers to two basic questions: "Were the desired client outcome goals reached?" and "In what ways did the social work methods used contribute to the desired change?" Additional information workers and clients can gain from outcome assessments includes the identification of the client's strengths and resources that contribute to goal achievement, the degree of change, the stability of the change, the unintended or unanticipated consequences of the change, and the efficiency of the change effort.

Questions that focus on client outcome assessment include:

- To what extent did the client system accomplish its goals?
- Can the changes be attributed to the intervention?
- Are there other factors that can account for the changes?
- Which client strengths and environmental resources were most significant in achieving results?
- Does the situation warrant further intervention?
- In what ways should workers modify their strategies?
- How does this information apply to follow-up work with this client and to work with future clients?
- To what degree was the client system involved in the evaluation process?

In spite of its name, outcome assessment is not a "tag on" last step in the helping process. Rather, workers conduct outcome assessments in their earliest contacts with clients and repeat these assessments throughout the process. Each time clients and social workers meet, they clarify the current situation, discuss goals and objectives, and examine progress. Each discussion involves a "mini" outcome assessment to evaluate progress and plan the next step.

For many, graduation marks achievement of an important personal goal.

Outcome assessment has four practical uses in social work. First, it provides concrete, continuous feedback on progress toward goals. This information is invaluable as clients and practitioners refine goals and develop further plans. Second, measuring the level of the achievement of goals and objectives, documents outcomes and promotes accountability. Third, results of evaluations provide vital information that social workers can incorporate in planning with other clients. Finally, practitioners use the results of outcome assessment for their own professional development. These four benefits—continuous feedback, accountability, transferability, and professional development—make outcome assessment an essential part of every social worker's professional practice.

Goal attainment scaling

Goal attainment scaling (GAS) is an evaluation design that measures client achievement levels. In this evaluation, practitioners use clients' statements of their goals as the criteria for measurement. Thus, GAS is individualized and tailored for each client system. Social workers can apply GAS at all client system levels.

Framed around explicit and measurable goal statements rather than problem areas, goal attainment scaling typically uses a 5-point scale of predicted levels of attainment. These levels range, for example, from "much less than expected" to "much more than expected," or from "least favorable outcome" to "most favorable outcome." For each point on the scale, the client specifies a behavioral outcome appropriate to the designated levels of outcome achievement. To achieve a quantitative GAS score, social work researchers assign a numeric weight to each point in the scale.

For example, the Northside Community Action Council has identified three goals: (1) to form a Neighborhood Watch Program; (2) to demolish abandoned buildings; and (3) to propose an ordinance to limit on-street parking to residents only. Table 15.3 illustrates the goal attainment scale for this case example.

Program Evaluation

Because many meritorious social programs compete for limited funding, funding agents expect assurances that programs for which they provide money do make a difference. The Substance Abuse and Mental Health Services Administration funds major program initiatives related to drugs and alcohol and mental health. For funding and evaluation purposes, SAMHSA identifies three categories of evidence-based programs: promising programs, effective programs, and model programs. Meeting rigorous standards of research for program evaluation as reviewed by the National Registry of Evidence-based Programs and Practices (NREPP), model programs, by design, are developed for replication and nationwide implementation (modelprograms.samhsa.gov/template_cf.cfm?page=model_list).

Program evaluations determine the value of the particular program under review. Moreover, the *Code of Ethics* (NASW, 1999a) sets forth standards for accountability: Social workers should not promise what they cannot deliver. Program evaluation provides the tangible evidence required for fiscal responsibility and ethical accountability. Additionally, program evaluation tracks the achievement of programmatic goals and objectives and identifies gaps to address in services and areas of service delivery.

Program evaluation asks the question: "Is the program accomplishing what it set out to do?" Social workers use a number of methods to secure data to discover the answer. Considering each client's outcome and compiling the results helps to determine whether a particular program has met its goals. Agencies

Table 15.3   Northside Community Action Council: Goal Attainment Scale

Goal Attainment Level	Goal 1: Form a Neighborhood Watch Program	Goal 2: Demolish Abandoned Buildings	Goal 3: Establish an Ordinance to Limit On-Street Parking to Residents Only
Much less than expected outcome achievement	No neighborhood support for program	Lawsuits ensue over target properties	Residents object to the proposed ordinance
Less than expected outcome achievement	Participation by a few households	Agreement to demolish but postponed two years	Proposed ordinance defeated
Expected level of outcome achievement	Half of the households participate	A scheduled plan for demolition approved	Ordinance considered by city council
More than expected outcome achievement	Household participation and commitment to weekly meetings	Funds for neighborhood rehabilitation and renovation considered	Ordinance passed by city council
Much more than expected outcome achievement	Full neighborhood participation and private security	Full funding for building renovations	Off-street parking lot constructed

may also administer consumer satisfaction surveys to ascertain clients' perspectives on the effectiveness of workers and services. Follow-up surveys of former clients and referral agencies are other sources of valuable information regarding the effectiveness and reputation of a particular program. Periodic reviews of case files by agency staff reveal client progress in relation to the overall program goals and agency mission. Finally, formalized processes such as quality-assurance checks by peers and supervisors provide internal mechanisms for program evaluation. Each method of program evaluation examines services from a different angle. A combination of approaches leads to a more comprehensive view of service delivery.

Program evaluation measures the effects that programs have on the clientele served, the agency organization, and the general public. Examples of researchable questions for program evaluation include:

- Does the program cause desired changes for clients?
- Is the program sensitive to diverse populations?
- Did the program meet the expectations of funding organizations?
- Are the program objectives consonant with the agency mission?
- What are the strengths and weaknesses of the program?
- Is staffing for the program adequate?
- How accessible is the program to potential clientele?
- Does the program alter public attitudes or awareness?
- Does this program continue to satisfy a need in the community?
- Is this program viable?

Program evaluation design

An evaluation design is a written plan for administering the evaluation study, including ways to obtain the information and report the results. The evaluation design specifies both when to collect data, what data to collect, and how to collect that data. Specifically, it

- Details the evaluative questions
- Identifies the required informational data
- Describes the data collection instruments
- Delineates data collection procedures, including sampling, who will collect the data, and the timeline
- Specifies techniques for analyzing data
- Provides guidelines for interpreting the data and reporting the results (Worthen, et al., 1997)

Evaluators may communicate the results of their program evaluation studies as in-house written reports, as executive summaries, as on-line communications, and as journal articles. Whatever form reports take, evaluators carefully attend to both content and format. With respect to content, well-written reports include the evaluation findings and the implications for the various stakeholders, such as program constituencies, funding bodies, and accrediting agencies. A clear, visually pleasing, and consistent format creates an impression of competence and credibility. Additionally, narrative explanations complement the technical presentation of the data and enhance reports' readability. In writing evaluation reports, evaluators also consider their intended audience. The written report should be understandable and maintain readers' interest.

Agency personnel use program evaluation data to make administrative decisions. These research findings provide information useful for formulating agency policy, especially with respect to planning programs, developing services, setting priorities, and allocating resources. Program managers also use program evaluation research to identify ways to streamline agency procedures and replicate successful strategies in other program areas.

Consumer satisfaction surveys

Program evaluators often poll clients to determine their satisfaction with services. Consumer satisfaction surveys assess clients' perceptions or attitudes about an agency's delivery of services. These surveys solicit clients' views about the relevance of the services received, the extent to which the services actually resolved their presenting problems, and their satisfaction with the social work process. Although they are valuable sources of information, client satisfaction instruments measure the subjective experiences of clients. Alone, they are not sufficient to evaluate the quality of services. They are important from an empowerment perspective, as client satisfaction surveys ensure that clients have opportunities for feedback that can influence agency policies and program development.

Empowerment evaluation

Empowerment implies that many competencies are already present or possible, give niches and opportunities.

—Julian Rappaport

Empowerment evaluation is an alternative approach to the more conventional program evaluation methods; its purposes are to foster ongoing self-assessments and promote continuous program improvements (Andrews, et al., 2005; Fetterman, 1996, 2002; Secret, et al., 1999). In actualizing participants' self-determination, empowerment evaluation emphasizes participant learning and capacity building. Empowerment evaluation also uses evaluation to influence policy development.

Five facets frame the method of empowerment evaluation—training, facilitation, advocacy, illumination, and liberation (Fetterman, 1996). *Training* refers to teaching program participants to internalize evaluation principles and practices, to conduct their own evaluation, and through the process, to become more self-sufficient as evaluators and to create opportunities for capacity building. *Facilitation* characterizes the role of empowerment evaluators "as coaches or facilitators to help others conduct a self-evaluation" (p. 11). As coaches, evaluators offer general direction and guidelines, provide suggestions about process, and help participants create evaluation designs. *Advocacy* refers to assisting disenfranchised people to become empowered through their participation in evaluation processes and subsequent recommendations for program improvements. Advocacy includes both helping others to advocate on their own behalf, and advocating on behalf of disempowered groups. Advocacy extends to advocating policy and legislative change as well as economic development. *Illumination* means promoting insight or framing new understanding "about roles, structures, and program dynamics" (p. 15). In this way, program participants acquire confidence in their abilities to assess problems and frame workable solutions. Finally, *liberation,* which is an outgrowth of illumination, refers to the emancipation of one's self and the corollary action to take charge of one's life. In other words, "empowerment evaluation enables participants to find new opportunities, see existing resources in a new light, and redefine their identities and future roles" (p. 16).

The empowerment evaluation model protects the voices of consumers, customers, or client from being inadvertently silenced or reinterpreted by professional or managerial voices. By design, empowerment evaluation requires that client systems play a prominent role in all facets of the evaluation process, from defining the focus of the evaluation to interpreting the results.

RESEARCH

Research is a method of systematic investigation or experimentation. In the context of social work, research both informs practice and adds to the knowledge base of the profession. Social workers conduct research to test theories about human behavior and the social environment and to document evidence of the effectiveness of intervention strategies. To conduct formal research for purposes of practice evaluation, program development, and policy analysis, generalist social workers learn about the research process, research terminology, and related ethical issues.

Box 15.1 Ethic of Inclusion

Issues of privilege surface in many aspects of social work practice. The ethic of inclusion presses empowerment-oriented social workers to redress issues of exclusivity in practice processes by working collaboratively with clients in all facets of practice, policy, and research (Beresford, 2003; Beresford & Croft, 2003; Boehm, & Staples, 2004; Braye & Preston-Shoot, 2005; Evans, 2004; McLaughlin, 2005; MHRN, 2005; Walsh & Lord, 2003).

Within the domain of social work research, the effect of professionals "objectively" studying clients is particularly insidious, as research done on, rather than with, people creates an exclusive base of knowledge that privileges the views and values of expert professionals. Ristock and Pennell contend that from a political perspective, the traditional "researcher as expert" approach perpetuates hegemony, or a power imbalance, that privileges the researcher rather than the researched, imposing thinking or conclusions that ultimately serve the interests of the dominant group and "homogenizing differences" within the non-dominant group (1996, as cited in Altpeter, et al., 1999, p. 35).

Identified variously as action research, participatory action research, community action research, or empowerment evaluation, this research "is founded on the principle that those who experience a phenomenon are the most qualified to investigate it" (DePoy, et al., 1999, p. 561). Rather than excluding those who are objects of studies from research processes, the research subjects are actively included in all steps of the process (Evans & Jones, 2004; Fisher, 2002). Rather than presupposing that a single expert can generate knowledge, the process incorporates the knowledge of multiple knowers (Levin, 1999). Researchers

identify themselves as "equal partner[s] with the participants, assisting in, rather than leading, the identification of the research questions, management of the data collection, and the data analysis" (Altpeter, et al., 1999, p. 34).

Essentially, the researcher's role is one of learner, learning from people who are experts on their own situations (White, et al., 2001). Ensuring participants' involvement in all phases of the research process, the role of the practitioner as researcher, like their involvement in other social work processes, validates clients' voices and generates knowledge based on principles of inclusion. According to DePoy and colleagues (1999), "interest groups that have been silenced can be empowered with resources such that traditional models of knowledge generation and thus of services delivery can be challenged, with systems change being an outcome" (p. 568). Participatory research emphasizes the integral relationship among practice, research, and a commitment to social change (Altpeter, et al., 1999).

Principles of inclusion are salient in anti-oppressive social work. Anti-oppressive research joins workers and clients in a process of collaborative inquiry by "making explicit the political practices of creating knowledge. It means making a commitment to relating with the people you are working with, personally and professionally in order to mutually foster conditions for living and thriving" (Potts & Brown, 2002, p. 2). Anti-oppressive research has characteristics and goals similar to community action research and empowerment evaluation, one of several "alternative research methodologies that share similar political agendas and attend to relationships with the goal of empowerment and emancipation" (p. 16).

The Research Process

Research is a meticulous and organized process that follows a logical progression of steps. Most often these interdependent steps include

1. Specifying the research problem
2. Reviewing the professional literature
3. Relating the research problem to theory
4. Formulating a testable hypothesis
5. Selecting the research design
6. Gathering data
7. Analyzing the data
8. Interpreting the results
9. Identifying implications for practice
10. Preparing the research report

The research process begins by identifying a problem and formulating a hypothesis. *Problem identification* evolves from a general concern or curiosity. From a general interest, the researcher narrows the field of study to formulate a researchable question. Through a *review of the literature,* the researcher locates and studies research related to the research question to determine the status of knowledge and viewpoints about this and similar problems. The researcher then explores the *relationship of the research problem* to theory, examines alternative theories, and formulates the problem into a testable hypothesis by expressing the problem in precise terms. A *hypothesis* is a tentative statement of the relationship that exists between two variables, such as the social work intervention and the client outcome. Sometimes hypotheses specify the nature of the relationship between the independent and dependent variables.

Conducting research also involves designing the research plan for collecting, analyzing, and interpreting the data. The *research design* conceptualizes the sequence of strategies necessary to test the hypothesis and details the methods for gathering and analyzing data. *Gathering data* is the process of systematically collecting information pertinent to the research question. A researcher may locate data in existing data or generate original data through observations, surveys, interviews, tests, or experiments. *Data analysis* uses techniques such as scaling, graphical presentations, or statistical manipulations to examine and evaluate the data. *Data interpretation* gives meaning and understanding to the research results. The researcher is then in a position to infer or project the *implications* for practice of the research findings and suggest subsequent courses of action. Finally, researchers compile their findings in *research reports* and disseminate the information through publications or presentations. The empowerment-oriented practitioner–researchers must be sensitive to client participation throughout the research process.

Research Terminology

Research has a vocabulary of its own. Explaining all the nuances of social work research and practice evaluation is beyond the scope of this chapter. The following sections briefly highlight fundamental concepts relevant to a beginning understanding of research. For in-depth information, consult a specialized book on social work research and statistics (Bloom, et al., 2006; Royse, 2008; Rubin & Babbie, 2008; Sirkin, 2006; Weinbach & Yegiddis, 2009).

Variables

Research variables are concepts that vary in ways that can be observed, recorded, and measured. Examples are variations in behaviors among different client systems or in the behaviors of the same client system at different points in time. Research variables may also be differences among types of social work interventions or variations within a single intervention. Practice evaluation research examines the relationship between the variables of the social work "intervention" and the "client outcomes" to monitor and evaluate a client's progress and to guide decisions about a social worker's method.

Independent variables   Social work researchers typically designate the intervention as the *independent variable.* As such, the intervention is the causal or influencing variable that affects change. For example, consider a home visitor prevention program that offers support and child development information to new parents. The home visitor program is the independent variable when evaluating whether the program reduces the incidence of child abuse and neglect in a community. Likewise, the program is the independent variable when measuring participants' increased knowledge of infant care.

Any social work intervention may itself have numerous variations. For instance, an intervention can vary in type, intensity, and length of time. The home visitor program can offer in-home visitation by a trained volunteer twice a week for 6 months or once a week for a year; or parents may or may not attend parenting skills classes conducted by a child development specialist in conjunction with the visitation component; or the program may involve all new parents or only those defined as at risk. Consequently, research practitioners make conscious choices about which interventions to select, how to arrange and implement them, and over what period of time to administer them.

Dependent variables   The outcome of the intervention, that is, changes in the incidence, severity, or degree of the targeted problems, solutions, or changes in the client system's behaviors, attitudes, or feelings *depends* on the intervention. Hence, the problem or behavior being measured is called the *dependent variable.* The primary goals of many home visitor programs are to reduce child abuse and neglect and enhance parenting effectiveness. In this instance, two variables—the incidence of abuse and the level of parenting skills—are dependent variables. Carefully formulated research designs accurately measure the changes in the dependent variable. Clearly, positive change in the dependent variable is the goal of social work intervention and is of utmost importance in practice evaluation.

Intervening variables   Frequently, researchers are unable to conclude that the outcomes are entirely the result of the action of the independent variable. Sometimes other factors interject their influence. These factors are *intervening variables.* An intervening variable is any other variable that inadvertently affects the outcome, either positively or negatively. Suppose, in the home visitor program, that the reports of child abuse decrease over time. Evaluators should question whether the home visitor program is solely responsible and consider other possibilities for this positive outcome. Examples of intervening variables may be a lower birth rate, the improvement of the economic climate in the community, or the increased availability of affordable child care. Researchers strive to design research studies in ways that, insofar as possible, control for the effects of intervening variables.

Graphing the variables   In social work research, the relationship between the influencing and resulting variables are framed in terms of X and Y. X denotes the independent variable or the "influencing" intervention; whereas Y denotes the dependent variable or the "resulting" change. To represent data pictorially, the researcher locates the independent variable (X) on the horizontal axis of a graph and places the dependent variable (Y) along the vertical axis. The graph plots the relationship between the independent (X) and dependent (Y) variables. Each point on the graph represents the position at which the X and Y variables intersect. In this way, the graph portrays the effect of the intervention on the direction of change, either positive or negative.

Hypotheses

Hypotheses state the connection between the independent and dependent variables. A hypothesis is a tentative statement of the relationship between these two variables. In practice evaluation, the variables are the intervention variable and the outcome variable. Simply, the research hypothesis in outcome assessment states that if X (the intervention) occurs, then Y (the outcome) results. In the example about the home visitor program, one hypothesis postulates that if a community implements a home visitor program (X), then the incidence of child abuse and neglect (Y) will decrease. Another possible hypothesis states that new parents who participate in the program (X) are likely to follow up with well-baby appointments (Y) and immunization schedules (Y) at a higher rate than do nonparticipants. The research process subjects the hypotheses to tests or comparisons to either prove or disprove the supposition that a relationship exists between the intervention and outcome variables. Here are several examples of hypotheses:

- If the Acme company sponsors on-site child-care provisions, then workers' absenteeism will decrease.
- Foster parents who complete the intensive training program are less likely to experience placement disruptions.
- The incidence of residential burglary will decrease after implementing the neighborhood watch program.
- Julie's score on the self-esteem scale will increase as she participates in counseling.

Measurement

In evaluating practice effectiveness, researchers assign meaningful labels or numeric values to the observations made and the data collected about client progress and the intervention methods. *Measurement* is an objective process by which the evaluator collects data. One uses measures to assess the status or the "what is" of the object under study or to evaluate the value of the "what should be." In terms of the relationship between evaluation and measurement, one measures first, and then uses the measures to assess or evaluate. For example, researchers can label the degree of achievement of client goals on a continuum from fully achieved to unachieved, or they can calculate actual behaviors into percentages. Likewise, workers can evaluate interventions by classifying successful or unsuccessful attempts or by simply counting the number of sessions.

Reliability and validity

Researchers consider issues of reliability and validity in choosing measuring instruments such as questionnaires, surveys, structured observations, and diagnostic scales. A measuring instrument is *reliable* when its measures are similar or consistent over time or with repeated applications. A measuring instrument has *validity* when it measures accurately the variable it intends to measure.

To be effective, measuring instruments must be both reliable and valid. Reliability and validity are two distinct yet interrelated issues. It is possible for an instrument to be reliable, that is, consistently to result in same measures over time, and not be valid by failing to measure what it's supposed to measure. In short, if a measuring instrument or variable used to represent the concept is not valid, don't bother to test for reliability, as a lack of validity automatically nullifies reliability. Conversely, if a measuring instrument is valid, that is, it measures what it's supposed to measure, then it may prove reliable. Reputable measurement tools have passed appropriate tests and statistical analyses for reliability and validity. Typically, documentation about reliability and validity accompanies published scales.

All social work practitioners should understand the concepts of reliability and validity. First and foremost, social workers, as research consumers, draw on the published research findings of others to guide their practice. In this capacity, social workers consider reliability and validity information to examine the research critically for its accuracy and usefulness. Second, in their role as research practitioners, social workers often develop their own tools for use with various clients and routinely collect data from clients to evaluate client outcomes and practice methods. Well-constructed research designs and reliable and valid data collection instruments are necessary for practitioners to have confidence in their research results. And finally, for the research specialist whose primary function is building theories or conducting practice research, measures of reliability and validity are central to designing research instruments, constructing diagnostic scales, and making statistical inferences.

Qualitative and quantitative data analysis

Social workers collect information, or data, about their clientele. *Data* are the facts gathered about the client system's situation. The data collected either describe qualities of the variables being studied, or measure their quantity. For instance, in conducting a community study on the plight of those who are homeless, practitioners may gather qualitative information through verbal descriptions or written accounts by persons who are homeless or from providers of services to these clients. The data collected in this example are qualitative because they *describe* the conditions of homelessness. If, however, a social worker was researching the effectiveness of shelter programs on reducing the number of homeless families in the community, the data gathered are quantitative. In this instance, quantitative data involve *a numerical measurement* of the homeless population before and after the program's implementation. Both qualitative and quantitative data inform social work practice.

Data and research methods are interdependent: The nature or type of data—whether qualitative or quantitative—dictates the method most applicable for the data analysis. Simply put, if the data consist of words, researchers select qualitative methods; if the data are numeric, researchers select quantitative methods. *Qualitative data* usually result in descriptive analysis, although researchers can still assign numeric representations to the words and apply limited statistical analyses. Examples of qualitative research in social work include case studies, document research, surveys, and key informant studies. Researchers may analyze *quantitative data* mathematically by using more powerful statistical applications. Experimental, quasi-experimental, and other studies involving statistical analysis are examples of quantitative research.

The role of hypotheses differs in qualitative and quantitative research. In qualitative studies, researchers can construct hypotheses and make generalizations about the relationship of the independent and dependent variable after collecting and analyzing the data. Quantitative studies are hypothesis-driven studies; in these studies, researchers develop the design to test hypotheses and draw conclusions about specific causal relationships. Each type of research makes a unique contribution to the research base of social work practice.

Ethics in Research

Research Based Practice

Ethical principles for research include informed consent, confidentiality, anonymity, voluntary participation, objectivity, careful research design, and accurate reporting of findings. What guidelines does the NASW *Code of Ethics* delineate regarding ethical practice in research?

As with other aspects of social work practice, ethics influences the ways practitioners conduct social work research. Practitioners are responsible for designing and carrying out research and evaluation both knowledgeably and ethically (Anastas, 2008). This includes considering diversity in each aspect of the research process. Relevant ethical principles include:

- *Informed Consent*—Research subjects give their consent to participate only after researchers fully disclose the purpose of the research, what it entails, and its potential effects or consequences
- *Confidentiality*—Researchers assure the privacy of clients' responses
- *Anonymity*—Researchers carefully guard the identity of the respondents
- *Voluntary Participation*—Clients' involvement in research is strictly by their choice. Researchers never coerce respondents into participating
- *Objectivity*—Researchers conduct studies and report results impartially
- *Careful Research Design*—Researchers construct designs that are unobtrusive so as not to conflict with practice priorities
- *Accurate Reports of Findings*—Researchers report their findings accurately to avoid misrepresenting the data

Guidelines for ethical research endeavors are set forth clearly in the NASW's *Code of Ethics* (1999a) with respect to obtaining voluntary and written informed consent from participants without any penalty for refusal; informing participants about their rights to withdraw from the research project at any time; protecting participants from distress, harm, danger, or deprivation as a result of participating in research; and safeguarding confidentiality of participants. Following ethical guidelines for research not only protects clients' rights, but it also ensures the integrity of the results.

SINGLE-SYSTEM DESIGNS

One of the most practical ways for social workers to assess client change and evaluate practice effectiveness is through the use of single-system evaluation designs. Also called single-subject or single-case designs, this typically involves evaluating and monitoring the effects of interventions on a client system's target problem. The term "single-system" indicates this design applies the same research principles to evaluating interventions in multiperson systems such as families, groups, organizations, neighborhoods, and communities.

To be implemented successfully, single-system designs must meet three requirements. They must

- State the change objective in measurable terms
- Evaluate the achievement with reliable and valid outcome measures (that is, the observations, verbal reports, and physiological measures) that produce quantitative data
- Display the data graphically. (Grinnell & Unrau, 2005)

For applications of single-system designs to be empowering, clients must be actively involved in all aspects of design, implementation, data analysis, and interpretation. Empowerment-oriented practitioners take caution to avoid the role of "analytical expert" in interpreting behaviorally driven, single-system outcome evaluations. This collaboration may heighten clients' motivation for change and promote self-direction in change activities.

Elements of Single-System Designs

One distinguishing characteristic of single-system designs is the planned comparison of measurements made in a preintervention period with measurements completed during or after the intervention. The periods of time during which observation of the client systems' behavior or evaluation of the client systems' progress occurs are called phases. To compare the "before" and "after," practitioners need to understand the concepts of baseline and intervention phases.

Baseline phase

To implement a single-system design, practitioners first establish a baseline. Taken in the preintervention period, baseline measurement involves a series of observations of the naturally occurring frequency of the behaviors under study. Workers measure the behavior that reflects the client's problem or observe the client's situation as it presently exists for a specified period.

Carefully constructed research establishes a baseline measure before introducing intervention strategies. However, ethical researchers consider the detrimental effects of counting adverse behaviors to acquire baseline data with clients who need immediate relief. Sometimes the choice to gather baseline information gives way to the need for immediate intervention.

Intervention phase

In a single-system research design, an intervention is what practitioners do to affect or change the identified target behaviors. As such, the intervention under study may be a single practice technique, a combination of several strategies, or an entire program with multiple components (Bloom, et al., 2006). Possible interventions may include such differing practice techniques as marriage counseling, a 12-step program, advocacy, mediation, a support group, neighborhood development, or a community action. Recall that, in social work research, the intervention is the independent variable, meaning that it is within the control of the worker and the client. They may apply an intervention, change its intensity, or withdraw it.

Alphabetic notation

Researchers use alphabetic notation to represent the phases in single-system designs. The letter A denotes the baseline or preintervention phase, and subsequent letters designate the intervention phases. So an AB design indicates a baseline phase (A) followed by an intervention phase (B). Likewise, the ABC design includes a baseline phase (A), followed by an intervention phase (B), which in turn is followed by another, yet different, intervention (C). How the baseline and intervention phases are arranged determines the type of single-system research design being implemented.

Types of Single-System Designs

Single-system designs commonly used in social work include case study or monitor design (B design), the basic baseline-intervention design (AB design) and other variations of the AB design, notably, the successive intervention design (ABC design), the withdrawal or reversal design (ABAB design and the BAB design), and multiple baseline designs.

Using the B design or the AB design answers the evaluative question: Did the client's situation improve during the course of treatment? The reversal designs are experimental designs and answer the question of causation: Did the client system improve because of social work intervention? Social workers are more likely to seek answers to evaluative questions in their practice by using the B or AB design, as these designs are more practical to implement than the more ambitious experimental designs that require rigorous controls.

AB design

The AB design is a useful and popular single-system design that social workers use to observe and measure change in target problems. It is simple to apply because it includes only one baseline period (A) and one intervention period (B). In many ways, it is one of the least-intrusive evaluative measures in terms of preserving social work practice priorities. It naturally fits into an organized practice process—observing first what is and then implementing and evaluating efforts to change.

In the AB design, workers introduce a single independent variable or intervention technique after the baseline phase. Practitioners monitor the shifts in the data from the baseline phase to the intervention phase to determine whether the client's situation is improving. From this information, the practitioner can draw only tentative conclusions about whether the intervention led to the improvement or whether changes were caused by some extraneous event, an intervening variable, or by chance. Despite this limitation, the AB design does provide immediate feedback about the direction of change during the intervention phase. As a result, practitioners and clients can discuss the possible explanations for the change and modify their strategies if necessary.

Consider the following case example that uses an AB design:

> The Millwork Company discontinued Mr. Jones' job position, resulting in termination of his employment. His unemployment benefits are insufficient to meet his family's income needs. He wants to find new employment, but he is hesitant to seek other jobs and lacks confidence in his job-seeking and interviewing skills. To feel prepared and confident for a job interview, Mr. Jones role-played a simulated interview with his employment counselor. Together, they analyzed the videotaped interview and noted points of strengths and areas for improvement.

As depicted in Figure 15.1, during the 5-week baseline or preintervention phase, Mr. Jones applied for a total of seven jobs. Following the role-play intervention, Mr. Jones significantly increased the number of employment applications.

B design

The B design is often referred to as the case-study method or the monitoring design. With this design, clients and practitioners apply an intervention and monitor the client's target problem to see if it is changing in the desired direction. This design does not stipulate taking baseline measurements before implementing the intervention strategy. However, in some situations, practitioners can ascertain

Client System: Individual—Mr. Jones
Target Problem: Hesitancy to Apply for Jobs
Intervention: Videotaped Role Play of a Job Interview

Figure 15.1   AB or Baseline and Intervention Design
Evaluation: The number of job applications Mr. Jones placed each week increased after the role play of the simulated interview.

a retroactive baseline from preexisting records or verbal reports from the client system. The lack of a baseline for comparing before and after measures is a significant drawback of this design method, as the design offers no way to decipher what accounts for observed changes.

The following case example illustrates the B design:

> Polly Martin, a 14-year-old, displays symptoms of anorexia, an eating disorder resulting in weight loss. At the start of the intervention phase, she weighs 92 pounds, 20 percent less than her original body weight of 115 pounds. Polly participated in an eating disorder program that included self-esteem counseling, nutritional counseling, and self-monitoring of food intake through the use of food cards.

As Figure 15.2 shows, Polly gradually gained a total of 10 pounds over the course of the eating-disorder intervention program. In Polly's situation, a baseline period or measurement was inadvisable given the potential seriousness of her eating disorder.

ABC design

Workers use successive intervention phases after the baseline period when implementing the ABC single-system design. Like the basic AB design, the ABC design establishes a pattern of data in the baseline phase (A), followed by introducing an intervention in the first intervention phase (B), and then adding a different, or perhaps modified, intervention (C). If workers add even more interventions, they would label subsequent intervention phases D, E, and so on.

ABC designs apply when practitioners introduce multiple intervention components in sequence, or when they modify one intervention in frequency

Client System: Individual—Polly Martin
Target Problem: Anorexia
Intervention: Healthy Eating Program

Figure 15.2   B or Case Study or Monitor Design
Evaluation: By the 10th week in counseling, Polly gained a total of 10 pounds.

or intensity because it doesn't appear to be working as planned. Because practitioners introduce several interventions during the change process, they are uncertain which specific intervention created the desired effect.

The ABC design is used in the following case example:

> For the past 6 months, the Kanton metropolitan community saw a rising unemployment rate, as local industry experienced severe cutbacks, subsequent layoffs, and manufacturing plant closings. The Kanton Economic Development Group recognized a need for a two-part approach to the problem—a job retraining program and a job placement program. The EDG contracted with the W. O. R. K. organization (Work, Opportunities, and Resources for Kanton) to design and implement community-based programming for the displaced workers.

Figure 15.3 shows the decreasing unemployment rate over the course of the year as each of the programs was being implemented.

ABAB design

Simply, the ABAB design is a string of AB designs used to evaluate changes in the same client system after reapplying the same intervention technique. After the initial baseline and intervention phases, the ABAB design adds a second baseline phase, after which workers reintroduce the intervention. They establish the second baseline by discontinuing or withdrawing the intervention for a period. Social workers and clients may plan this withdrawal or may simply experience an unexpected pause in the intervention.

Client System: Community—Kanton
Target Problem: High Unemployment Rate
Interventions: 1. Job Retraining Program
                       2. Job Placement Program

Figure 15.3   ABC or Successive Intervention Design
Evaluation: The community unemployment rate steadily decreased as both the job retraining program and job placement program were being implemented.

The ABAB single-system design is a *reversal* or withdrawal design. Logically, we presume that if the target behavior improves during the first intervention phase, reverts when the intervention is withdrawn, and improves again during the second intervention phase, the improvement is likely to result from the intervention. Thus, the ABAB design offers more evidence of the causal effects of the intervention on the behavior or target problems.

Clearly, ethical issues emerge with planned withdrawals of interventions, especially when an intervention appears to be helpful. Concerned social workers question whether clients will suffer unnecessarily if their situation reverts to the preintervention level. After all, the well-being of client systems is a priority concern of social work practice. In some cases, social workers and clients purposely discontinue services temporarily to test whether clients can independently sustain the gains. At other times, an unexpected time-out from intervention caused by either clients' or social workers' circumstances offers an opportunity for establishing the second baseline.

BAB design

The BAB design is also a reversal design, without establishing an initial baseline pattern. Instead, the social worker immediately introduces an intervention (Phase B). Later, the worker withdraws the intervention and observes changes in the behavior, establishing a postintervention baseline (Phase A). Subsequently the worker reapplies the intervention (Phase B).

Changes in the patterns of data observed and measured during the first intervention period (B), the withdrawal period (A), and the second intervention period (B) provide valuable information about the effectiveness of the intervention on the target problems. If, after the intervention is withdrawn, the behavior gains are lost during Phase A, and then later improve when reintroducing the intervention, the social worker can make a stronger inference about the causal influence of the intervention. Again, ethical social workers carefully explore the potential consequences of withdrawing services that appear to be working.

Multiple-baseline designs

Another variation of the AB design establishes baselines with and observes changes in multiple clients, in multiple settings, and for multiple target problems. This multiple-baseline design allows social workers to monitor three types of situations. Workers can track (1) more than one client system that shares the same problem and uses the same intervention, (2) a client system that experiences the same problem in more than one setting, or (3) a single subject who exhibits more than one problem situation in the same setting.

Evaluating multiple client systems with the same problem allows the practitioner to generalize findings with different clients. Monitoring the effects of the intervention on one client system in two or more settings looks for a generalization of the outcomes within the client's functioning. The multiple-baseline design also allows practitioners simultaneously to evaluate changes in multiple problem situations presented by a single client system.

Limitations of Single-System Designs

Research Based Practice

In developing single-case evaluation techniques, social workers need to accommodate the research role without violating their service role. What ethical issues emerge when the research mandate collides with practice priorities?

Single-case evaluations and single-system research designs are gaining a degree of acceptance by social work practitioners to evaluate practice effectiveness and to contribute to the knowledge base of practice. However, these designs may not fit all practice situations.

Single-case designs readily adapt to measuring behavioral change, but not all social workers use behavioral or task-centered models that specify problems in the ways necessary to implement single-case designs. Thus, methodological issues arise in applying single-subject research by those practitioners who use other approaches. To apply single-system designs in these situations, researchers carefully delineate and operationally define client outcome goals in ways that can be measured objectively. Researchers should identify intermediate progress indicators to monitor the achievement of short-term objectives in long-term interventions.

Agencies hold direct service practitioners accountable for assessing client outcomes and evaluating the effectiveness of the interventions they use. Practitioners are also in positions to conduct empirical or experimental practice research. Certainly, research should not intrude on the client–practitioner relationship, nor should research dominate the intervention process. The social work profession needs to continue to develop single-case evaluation techniques that fit more naturally with practice; view evaluation as a process to enhance practice rather than an exercise in accountability; and adopt a variety of formats to accommodate diverse client populations, intervention goals, and practice methods (Gingerich, 1990).

Box 15.2 Action Research: A Practice-Research Connection

Through research, we develop theories about social problems, human behavior, and client population groups. From traditional research findings, we acquire information to guide decisions at the levels of policy, programs, and direct practice. In contrast, practical solutions to everyday problems result from action research, with its emphasis on stakeholders' participation in both action and reflection (Reason & Bradbury, 2008). Reitsma-Street and Brown (2002) contend that with respect to expertise for conducting action research, those who experience situations are most qualified to investigate their situations.

By definition, action research is participatory and empowering (Brown, 1994; Hanley, 2005). The relationship of the researcher and participants provides the foundation for successful implementation. They work together collaboratively throughout the process as co-learners, from developing the design, to collecting the data, to implementing plans for change. Action research gives voice to the participants, reveals their worldviews, affirms their humanity, leads to a heightened critical consciousness, and uses processes of reflection and action. Action research incorporates elements of research, education, and action. Research cycles through a series of recurring steps—planning, acting, observing, and reflecting. Critical reflection, similar to conscientization, plays an integral role, as it lends vision to subsequent cycles of planning, acting, observing, and reflecting.

Given its roots in the work of Freire (1973; 1993) and the outcome potential of emancipation and liberation, action research is especially appropriate with those who are in some way disadvantaged or oppressed (Healy, 2001; Patel, 2005; Strier, 2007). Because research, action, and outcomes intertwine, one "can expect participant and community empowerment, capacity building, and change to result" (Gutiérrez, et al., 1996, p. 506). One such example is the Sexual Minority Youth Action Research Project sponsored by the Institute for Community Research:

> Through this two-community study, project participants gathered information on a critical issue that youth identified as facing urban—particularly African-American and Puerto Rican—LGBTQ youth. In past years youth have explored issues such as: supports for LGBTQ youth, available resources and their accessibility to youth; and identifying barriers for youth access to these resources. Project staff recruited two teams of six high school age Community Youth Researchers who received intensive training in participatory action research. The teams met separately for 8 to 10 hours/week to conduct research in their communities. The two teams came together periodically to discuss progress, share ideas and receive joint trainings as needed. Using research results, Community Youth Researchers worked with project staff to develop and begin implementation of action strategies based on their research findings, which were designed to affect change and to build resources for urban LGBTQ youth (http://www.incommunityresearch.org/research/smy.htm).

Other examples include giving voice to unemployed women in China (Sung-Chan & Yuen-Tsang (2008), identifying service needs among Pakistani families with children who have disabilities (Kramer-Roy, 2007), and building international and interdisciplinary community partnerships to address domestic violence (Ritchie & Eby, 2007). Working on the assumption that a picture is worth a thousand words, an innovative technique, photovoice, supplements written reports with photographs to heighten sensitivity to social justice issues (Molloy, 2007). Action research can also be applied within the social service delivery network to create changes by working *within* an organization, giving voice and status to service users (Bailey, 2005; Cassano & Dunlop, 2005; Evans, 2004; Evans & Jones, 2004).

LOOKING FORWARD

The shifting paradigm to participatory evaluation and action research in social work raises a number of issues. Among these issues are the efficacy of moving from the use of external evaluators to internal evaluators, the effects of involvement by community stakeholders and social service consumers in all parts of evaluation or research design, and the changing role of the evaluator from evaluation expert to policy advocate.

Social work research and evaluation support effective generalist practice. Practitioners and policy makers rely on sound research methods and evaluative processes to identify ways to enhance social service delivery. The evolutionary nature of social work requires practitioners, as clinicians, to contribute to the knowledge and skill base of the profession.

Recognizing client and program successes in social work practice suggests progress, achievement, and accomplishment. Thus, the process of recognizing success cues the client and social worker whether it is time to conclude their work together. If clients are sufficiently satisfied with their level of goal achievement, social workers and clients prepare to bring closure to the professional relationship. Chapter 16 explores how social workers and clients wrap up their work together in ways that credit clients with success and stabilize the progress achieved.

Succeed with PEARSON mysocialworklab

Log onto **www.mysocialworklab.com** and select the **Interactive Skill Module** videos from the left-hand menu. Answer the questions below. (*If you did not receive an access code to* **MySocialWorkLab** *with this text and wish to purchase access online, please visit* www.mysocialworklab.com.)

1. **Watch pages 4, 5, and 11 of the domestic violence module** to observe a client describe spousal abuse, a report mirroring current research about domestic violence. What would you do to find additional relevant research?

2. **Watch page 19 of the child welfare module** in which a worker explains the goal of family preservation sought by the Department of Social Services. Propose a social work research project to evaluate the extent to which the department is meeting this goal?

PRACTICE TEST

1. Which method of evaluation answers the question, "Is the program accomplishing what it set out to do?"
   a. program evaluation
   b. client outcome assessment
   c. process evaluation
   d. progress evaluation

2. Jessica wants to assess clients' perceptions about the service delivery. You suggest that she develop a ___.
   a. citizen perception poll
   b. goal attainment scale
   c. needs assessment instrument
   d. consumer satisfaction survey

3. ___ refers to the explicit and judicious use of current best evidence in making decisions about social work practice.
   a. Outcome assessment
   b. Evidence-based practice
   c. Practice evaluation
   d. Single-system research

4. Larry is conducting research on the effectiveness of a stress management technique for reducing clients' levels of anxiety. In this design, the stress management technique is the ___ variable.
   a. dependent
   b. intervening
   c. independent
   d. nominal

Ethical Practice

5. When a researcher ask subjects to participate in a research study only after the researcher fully discloses the purpose of the research, what it entails, and its potential effects or consequences, the researcher is complying with the ethical principle of ___.
   a. voluntary participation
   b. confidentiality
   c. informed consent
   d. careful research design

6. Juan has been asked to assess how closely the new program being implemented adheres to the evidence-based model on which the program is based. Juan needs to use a ___.
   a. fidelity scale
   b. program evaluation
   c. outcome assessment
   d. goal attainment scaling

7. Amy wants to apply an evidence-based approach to her family practice. What do you recommend as her first step?
   a. searching the Internet for research evidence
   b. appraising the evidence
   c. evaluating the effectiveness of the model
   d. constructing an answerable question

Research Based Practice

8. Sharea is gathering information for her research on the effects of unemployment through intensive interviews with key informants. Sherea is MOST likely conducting a ___ study.
   a. quantitative
   b. goal attainment
   c. consumer satisfaction
   d. qualitative

9. Of the following, which will MOST likely be used to assess client change?
   a. program evaluation
   b. single-system designs
   c. qualitative research
   d. fidelity scaling

Research Based Practice

10. School social worker Jude Lawson is working with Billy Martin, a third grader who frequently picks fights with his peers. Jude decides to use a single-system design to graph the results of the intervention strategy. Which design should he select if he wants to monitor Billy's behavior only during the intervention period?
   a. A
   b. B
   c. AB
   d. ABAB

Log onto **MySocialWorkLab** once you have completed the Practice Test above to take your Chapter Exam and demonstrate your knowledge of this material.

Answers
1) a 2) d 3) b 4) c 5) c 6) a 7) d 8) d 9) b 10) b

16

Integrating Gains

CHAPTER OUTLINE

CONNECTING CORE COMPETENCIES *in this chapter*

| Professional Identity | Ethical Practice | Critical Thinking | Diversity in Practice | Human Rights & Justice | Research Based Practice | Human Behavior | Policy Practice | Practice Contexts | Engage Assess Intervene Evaluate |

The rule in personal relationships is that as long as things are going well they will continue to evolve and intensify. The rule in social worker–client relationships is that even when things are going well, relationships will end. Practitioners work themselves out of a job with each successful practice endeavor. Simply, the common goal of all social work is for client systems to operate independent of the social worker, drawing instead on their own competence, support networks, and the resources of a just society.

Social work literature sometimes refers to the final step in the social work process as "termination." To others, like Gutheil (1993), the word "terminate" has nefarious connotations. Whereas "terminate" does mean discontinue or conclude, it also evokes more negative undertones associated with death, dismissal, and being fired. Who can avoid the "terminator" video image of automatic weapons, violence, and destruction? Other writers offer the alternative description of this phase as "endings" (Maluccio, 1979; Shulman, 2009; DuBois & Miley, 2008; Walsh, 2007).

Whatever words or phrases practitioners choose, their words should reflect the reality that when workers and clients resolve their professional relationships, they don't encapsulate their work and put it aside. Paradoxically, social work practice "endings" are also beginnings. Wrapping up "signifies both an ending of the working relationship and the beginning of life without the professional helping person" (Gutheil, 1993, p. 163). Clients go on, empowered to incorporate what they have learned into how they continue to cope. Social workers also move on, enriched with yet another professional relationship experience and additional practice wisdom.

Describing this last process as "integrating gains" emphasizes the importance of client growth, development, and change beyond the professional relationship. Within the context of each successful social work endeavor, clients have discovered the power available in the strengths within themselves and in the resources of their environments. A social worker's task in ending the relationship is to sustain the client's ability to draw on and amplify this power independently. Endings are crucial for the success of the process as a whole. Adept endings help client systems integrate the work of earlier phases, recognize achievements, build a sense of mastery, consolidate gains, and provide a springboard into the future.

This chapter describes what social workers and clients do to resolve their work together in ways that integrate and apply what each has gained from the experience. Specifically, this chapter

- Describes social work endings
- Details endings that involve completing contracts
- Specifies circumstances leading to referrals and specifies procedures for making referrals
- Guides social workers on how to respond when clients discontinue services
- Reflects on issues associated with grief, end-of-life care, and the deaths of clients
- Discusses endings in the context of group-, organization-, and community-level clients

Social workers end their work with clients in ways that stabilize desired changes and empower client systems to continue functioning competently.

SOCIAL WORK ENDINGS

Generally, three situations define exit points for most client systems (Table 16.1). Workers celebrate with clients who reach their goals, refer clients to other professionals when necessary, or acknowledge the rights of clients to withdraw from services as they see fit. Each type of resolution requires a unique process to end the work in a way that benefits clients and provides workers with information to further their continuing professional development.

The actions a worker takes at closure vary, depending on the preferences and behaviors of clients and the specific situation. In planning effective closure processes, workers consider many issues, among them

- The degree of success that has been achieved so far
- The potential benefits of continuing the work
- The duration and intensity of the relationship with the client system
- The resources available to continue the work in this particular setting
- Whether the client is voluntary or mandated
- The client's plans
- The role the social worker may play in the client's life after the closure

Endings also differ depending on the level of client system. Work with individuals and families has a degree of intimacy that may reveal itself in the intensity of feelings during the closure process. In group work, individuals are likely to be facing the loss of relationships with other group members as well as the discontinuation of the relationship with the social worker. Work within organizations and communities may be ongoing rather than short term, redefining the closure process as a transition to the next task or project rather than signaling the end of the professional relationship itself.

Table 16.1	**Types of Closure**	
Categories	Description	Social Work Processes
Completing Contracts	Clients made significant progress or achieved success in the plan of action and no longer need social work services	Preparing for resolution Discussing readiness Reviewing progress Sharing feelings Generalizing outcomes
Closing with Referral	Clients require continued services beyond the contracted work with the practitioner that may involve more specialized provider expertise or agency programming	Acknowledging limited resources Smoothing the transition Tracking clients' progress
Responding to Client Withdrawal	Clients, on their own initiative, conclude the helping relationship	Preparing for early withdrawal Recognizing exiting clues Pursuing mutual resolution

COMPLETING CONTRACTS

The first and most preferred resolution is when clients have made significant progress toward the goals they have set. Planning for this kind of ending begins early in the relationship with the negotiation of a specific contract for services. Recognizing that it is time to resolve the relationship "according to plan" hinges on the clarity of the observable and measurable outcomes contained in this contract. Resolving a social work relationship by successfully completing the contract is the culmination of a collaborative effort. Both social workers and clients deserve credit. Both benefit from an opportunity to reflect on their work and incorporate what they have learned for their future endeavors. To maximize the benefits of their experience, workers and clients examine where they are, review where they've been, and predict where they are going after their work together ends.

Specific steps in successful resolutions include

- Thorough preparation throughout the entire process, especially in terms of contracting, and periodic reminders of the time-limited nature of the relationship
- Open discussion about the client's readiness for closing, including a concrete evaluation of success, drawing on both client and worker perspectives
- Comprehensive review of the relationship highlighting the client's contributions, significant achievements, and methods used to achieve results
- Mutual sharing of feelings about the relationship and the upcoming closure
- Anticipating the future, projecting upcoming challenges, and predicting the client's continuing success
- Clear agreement on the point of transition from "active" to "closed," description of how the client accesses additional service if necessary, and discussion of possible follow-up contacts

Preparing for Resolution

Social workers prepare for closures in professional relationships even from the beginning of the work. Social workers foreshadow successful resolutions by defining a purposeful and professionally oriented relationship from the outset (Hess & Hess, 1999). They continue to hone the specificity of this purpose as they create action plans with concrete enough outcomes to clearly indicate that the work is complete.

Throughout the entire process, social workers remind clients of the transitory nature of the relationship by using direct and indirect messages. Social workers may say:

- I noticed that this is the end of our third month of working together—halfway through the 6-month period that our program permits.
- By my count, this is group meeting number 8 out of 12. Just four meetings left on our agreement. I guess that means if there's anything you've been putting off that you'd like to talk about, this might be the time.
- You've been coming up with great ideas about how to proceed. This demonstrates that you are probably ready to handle things on your own.

Social workers intersperse these comments selectively early in the process, but interject them more frequently as the ending becomes imminent. By the time only a few meetings are left and clients are clearly finishing up, the discussion of endings becomes central in conversations between clients and workers. Although workers cannot control whether clients choose to drop out of service suddenly, ethical social workers never abruptly withdraw service from clients without explanation or direction.

Recall the flexibility of the social work contract and how it keeps pace with the current focus of the work during the course of the relationship. Through this continuous renegotiation of the contract, clients clearly experience their power to continue or end the work. These discussions offer clients legitimate exit points, acknowledging their rights to self-determination about how they would like to pursue their goals. Choosing to wrap up their work with the social worker in favor of proceeding on their own may signal that clients are empowered with their own sense of efficacy.

Stopping short of goals

Sometimes clients and workers make significant progress yet don't quite attain predetermined goals. Clients have reached a plateau where continued joint efforts are producing no appreciable benefit. Perhaps the goals were overly ambitious. Maybe the immediate crisis has passed, leaving clients comfortable with where they are and with limited motivation for continuing their change efforts. When workers see few possibilities for productivity in future sessions, they may suggest renegotiating the original goals to those outcomes clients have already achieved. In other words, they ask, "Is this good enough?" If clients agree, social workers proceed with closure activities that acknowledge what clients have achieved thus far, and suggest that clients may return for additional work in the future.

Discussing Readiness

Human Behavior

Research indicates that clients withdraw from services for many different reasons. What clues might signal a client's intent to discontinue services and how should social workers respond to this possibility?

Social workers observe carefully for signs that the work is done. They monitor progress toward goals and assess clients' developing abilities to manage independently. Workers are not alone in "looking for the end." Although most of the social workers in Maluccio's (1979) study asserted the decision to end the professional relationship was mutual, most of the clients indicated that they themselves initiated the closure.

As clients near their goals, social workers engage them in conversations about their readiness to finish up the work. Periodically evaluating progress in carrying out the action plan is one way that workers measure a client's preparedness for ending the relationship. Workers also keep an eye on other behavioral indicators that clients are moving from interdependent work with the social worker to independent work of their own. Behaviors that signal clients may be outgrowing the need for professional assistance include when clients

- Use meetings with the worker as a forum to bounce off their ideas about what to do rather than passively seeking the worker's suggestions and expertise
- Take the initiative between meetings to modify and improve on plans developed with the social worker
- Begin to manage the process of change by organizing their own assessment, analysis, planning, and intervention activities to modify situations they desire to change
- Acknowledge their own abilities openly, demonstrate confidence, and express optimism

When workers believe that the time to end the professional relationship is approaching, they share their observations directly with clients. Workers keep the progress toward goals in the forefront of discussions, not the relationship itself.

Reviewing progress

Social workers and clients retrace their progress to identify and reinforce client strengths and abilities. Reviewing progress solidifies changes and reinforces clients' sense of achievement. As clients review their progress, they are likely to attribute success or failure to their own efforts or to forces outside themselves. Dispositional attributions are those in which clients believe they themselves created the improvement and experience their own competency. Situational attributions are those in which clients credit workers or other forces outside themselves with creating the change. When clients make situational attributions, workers get the credit, and clients do "not expect the behavior to continue when contacts with the worker are ended" (Feld & Radin, 1982, p. 481). By making dispositional attributions, clients acknowledge their part in creating the change, and "they are more likely to anticipate the improvement will remain after termination" (p. 481). A review process encouraging dispositional attributions helps clients believe they have the power to sustain change.

Evaluating

Although evaluation is integral to successful work throughout the entire social work process, it functions in a very important way near the end. As part of the closure process, a comprehensive evaluation identifies what worked and clarifies the methods and strategies that the client used most effectively. In effect, engaging in evaluation processes can empower the client with information that might be useful in meeting future challenges and brings a sense of completion to the current work. Evaluative questions that facilitate closure include:

- What did you like best about our work together?
- What did you like least about our work together?
- What will you miss about our work together?
- What do you look forward to when we stop working together? (Gutheil, 1993, p. 171)

Many techniques are available for evaluating outcomes. Chapter 15 provides an overview of some of these approaches, including single-system design, goal attainment scaling, and qualitative methods. Workers and clients choose evaluation methods that fit their particular situation the best and actively involve clients. For example, with individual and family clients, Gutheil (1993) suggests using comparative eco-maps. Clients compare their support networks at the beginning of the work with their networks as they exist at the end. Imagine the impact on a client of viewing the differences between an earlier eco-map, sparse with connections compared with a subsequent one, rich with community and social supports developed during the course of the social work endeavor.

Responding to evaluations

Both workers and clients benefit from evaluating their work nondefensively. Honest appraisals can be empowering. Openly considering what worked and what didn't gives concrete information on which to build future solutions. To elicit such information, workers ask directly for feedback about their work and respond nondefensively by thanking clients for information whether it compliments or criticizes.

Some practitioners are reluctant to acknowledge their good work, fearing that they will take away from a client's sense of achievement. Acknowledging mutual accomplishments should represent no problem for collaborative social work partnerships, because both partners have contributed to their success. Social workers accept their part of the credit while continuing to highlight those aspects of the work for which clients deserve praise.

Sharing Feelings

To bring closure to the relationship, social workers and clients share their feelings about completing their work. Practitioners can anticipate the possible range of feelings clients may experience by considering the intensity and length of the relationship, content of the work, size of client system, the client's past experiences with transitions, and the reason for ending.

Often, when we think about endings, we think of the feelings related to grief and sadness. However, this is not necessarily the case when workers focus on a client's potential mastery, adaptation, and maturation process. Endings can be positive events. Consider the findings of a study by Fortune, Pearlingi, and Rochelle (1992) as evidence of the positive feelings clients and workers may experience as they complete their work. These researchers surveyed 69 respondents (both workers and clients together for at least 10 sessions, having completed their work within 6 months before the survey) to gather information about client and practitioner reactions to closure. They report that

> Practitioners responding to the questionnaire reported strong positive reactions to termination for both their clients and themselves. Negative reactions were weak or absent. Among clients, the strongest reactions were positive affect (pride, accomplishment, independence), evaluation of success, evaluation of the therapy experience, and positive flight. Least strong were nihilistic flight, regression, denial, recapitulation, and expression of a need for further treatment. Among practitioners, the strongest reactions were pride in the client's success and pride in their own skill; least strong were relief, doubt about their effectiveness, doubt about the client's progress, and reexperiencing of previous losses. (p. 176)

Research like this reorients workers from merely empathizing with their clients' feelings of loss at closure to joining clients in their celebrations of success.

Social workers' personal experiences with transitions combined with their sense of competence as professionals and their feelings toward clients influence how they respond as the working relationship ends (Hess & Hess, 1999). Questions to spark self-awareness about endings include:

- What are my experiences with separations and transitions including high school graduation, moving, divorce, death, loss of friendships, job promotion, or leaving home?
- How have I reacted to transitions? Have they been marked by anxiety, ambivalence, optimism, or a sense of challenge?
- What helps me through transitions?
- How do I view myself as a professional? How do I respond to negative evaluations of my work? Can I accept compliments about my work?
- How do I feel about my work with this particular client system?
- What did I do right? What could I have done differently?

Self-awareness helps us to differentiate our own experiences from those of our clients, supports a forthright evaluation of our work, and leads to constructive resolutions of our relationships with client systems.

Generalizing Outcomes

Even though closure means that the work is "winding down," social workers are not quite finished yet, as there is evidence that the carryover of gains is most effective when gains generalize into everyday functioning.

Accomplishments are more likely to generalize when social workers have helped clients continually focus on relevant issues and situations, as well as practice new skills and behaviors in a variety of situations and settings, and when clients have gained confidence in their own abilities rather than in those of the worker (Toseland & Rivas, 2005). The most enduring work is that which is consistently integrated into the client's functioning throughout the entire process. The increase of community-integrated programs, work with natural support networks, in-home treatment, and policies of deinstitutionalization reflect attempts to make and keep social work practice immediately relevant in clients' natural settings.

Changes also endure when clients not only experience the results of the success, but also when they learn the process by which the success has been achieved. To teach process, workers openly collaborate with clients to define problems clearly, complete comprehensive assessments, articulate concrete action plans, and actively implement change strategies. At closure, workers can help clients take knowledge of these processes with them by reviewing the processes implemented and discussing how to apply these processes to issues that may arise in the future.

Stabilizing success

An important activity in closure is for workers and clients to make connections between what they have done together and how clients might approach upcoming issues. A comprehensive review that emphasizes client strengths facilitates this connection and empowers clients to move on with an objective understanding of their ability to resolve issues on their own. Clients benefit from an appraisal of their strengths and how they might work in the future, but Shulman (2006) cautions workers to avoid reassuring clients who express doubts about their own competence. He adds that even though workers can display confidence in clients, they should stop short of minimizing the difficulties that may lie ahead. Clients transition to independent functioning best with an honest view of their competencies and how these abilities might help them in the future.

Kacen (1999) studied the effects of closure on participants in seven support groups designed to reduce anxiety in members recovering from heart attacks. Findings revealed a temporary increase in anxiety at closure that was positively related to the cohesiveness of the group. In other words, the greater the group's success in providing support, the more traumatic is its loss for members. In contrast, the cohesiveness of the support group offered resources to workers and clients to address these negative reactions directly in a supportive manner in preclosure group meetings. Kacen also suggests follow-up meetings as a way to counteract the increased anxiety of group members at closure.

In their work with clients with schizophrenia, Walsh and Meyersohn (2001) also describe the potential benefits of closure if clients' needs are met. They recommend that practitioners (1) normalize endings as part of a natural occurrence of coming together and moving apart that occurs in most human relationships; (2) accept ambivalence and contradictory feelings as normal responses to impending separation; and (3) review the past, present, and future to integrate the current experience into a coherent sense of client identity in dealing with significant loss and change.

Firming Up Social Supports

Clients function most effectively after discontinuing their work with practitioners if they have ongoing support from others. Self-help groups, natural helping networks, clubs, neighborhoods, and churches are other places that clients and workers can explore for ongoing support.

Earlier work in which workers helped clients assess and activate resource systems on the client's behalf may already leave clients closely involved with supports that will help maintain their stability. To facilitate further access to supports, workers can help clients plan what events will require the support of others, determine ways that they will contact supports if necessary, or even invite significant others into closing sessions (Simons & Aigner, 1985).

Celebrations and Ritualized Endings

What traditions does your family have to mark passages, transitions, and achievements? Do you have family gatherings, picnics, suppers, or ceremonies? Do certain family members play particular roles in giving toasts, lighting candles, singing songs, giving gifts, or preparing special food? Are passages recorded in your family albums, books, or other treasures? Individuals and families as well as groups frequently mark normal life passages, milestones, and achievements by rituals and ceremonies. Rituals provide human systems with structured ways to deal with emotions, vehicles for communication, and means to celebrate accomplishments (Imber-Black & Roberts, 1998).

Box 16.1 Ethic of Change

Change is a core theme that punctuates social work practice. When clients seek social work assistance, their actions represent a change in the way they are dealing with their situations that will perhaps result in something new or different—change to produce change. When clients adapt to shifting circumstances in their social and economic environments, such changes can lead to increased security and well-being—change to produce stability. From an ecosystemic perspective, change is continuous and multidimensional, as all humans experience the interplay of change and stability perpetuated through systemic interaction.

The challenge for social workers and clients is to understand and guide this continuous change process. "Empowerment is a process of change with the service user at the centre, and social workers must facilitate this change rather than direct it" (Jupp, 2005, Conclusion section, ¶1). Throughout their work together, workers and clients examine and deliberately interact with systems affecting a client's situation. As workers and clients close their work, the ability of clients to sustain progress depends on whether the desired changes were embedded in the ecosystem, including relevant organizational, community, policy, and institutional structures.

To endure beyond the end of a social work process, supportive changes must occur at several system levels. Increases in a client's personal capacity, effective interaction with their family and friends, responsive community organizations and institutions, and socially just policies all combine to reinforce and perpetuate achievements. To experience sustainable and integrative change, clients must return to a "different" or enhanced environmental system, that is, one flexible enough to embrace and support the changes made. The ethic of change charges social workers to effect long-term contextual change.

Sustainable change is multisystemic. At the intrapersonal level, enduring change occurs in an individual's beliefs, attitudes, and values about self-identify and personal competence. At the interpersonal level, increases in power and support within significant relationships can sustain development. Qualities at the macrosystem level that stabilize changes include community responsiveness to fundamental and critical needs and opportunities for social support and enjoyment. Clients succeed in sustaining positive changes when their contexts nourish and reinforce their success.

Evidence indicates that rituals function positively for the endings of social worker–client relationships as well (Gutheil, 1993). Rituals provide a definitive transition point for both social workers and clients. "Such procedures, by framing the termination and making it stand out as a special part of the work help underscore the important role of this phase in putting closure on the work and consolidating gains" (p. 167). Rituals mark progress, celebrate strengths, and anticipate the possibilities of the future. By providing structure for communicating thoughts and emotions about endings, ceremonies help us cope with ambiguous and sometimes contradictory feelings.

In designing meaningful ceremonies to mark endings, workers and clients create experiences that are symbolic of the achievements of the work. "Graduation" ceremonies with music, processionals, and "diplomas" may successfully signify the end of a training group. Collaborating on creating a mural or collage may signify a stepfamily's successful blending into a cohesively functioning unit. Each event integrates the gains of the work completed and clearly indicates the transition in the client system and the professional relationship.

Looking to the Future

History, despite its wrenching pain, cannot be unlived, but if faced with courage, need not be lived again.

—Maya Angelou

Constructive resolutions look to the future. To encourage competent functioning beyond the relationship, social workers and clients envision plans and future successes as well as anticipate upcoming challenges. Workers inquire

Social workers encourage ongoing support by family members.

how clients will approach potential issues, develop plans for follow-up including specifying resources for continued support, possibly suggest the idea of a follow-up appointment, or simply acknowledge that reincidence does not represent failure.

Social workers' knowledge of human behavior in general and their experiences with specific clients may allow workers to formulate hunches about what might be coming up. Expected life transitions, particular risk factors in clients' lives, previous patterns likely to resurface—all may be worth mentioning so that clients are not blindsided by their optimism in having accomplished current tasks.

Read the following examples of how social workers help clients anticipate upcoming challenges:

- I have been so impressed with your ability to figure out how to balance giving Hank the freedom to be with his friends with your concerns about the safety of the neighborhood. But I also see that Celia is approaching that age where she will want to do the same. What have you learned from this experience with Hank that you think might help you with Celia's transition to adolescence?
- This neighborhood really did dodge the wrecking ball just in the nick of time. Your abilities to organize, target key people in the city's administration, and generate public support have been amazing. I also recognize that some of the same concerns that prompted the city's actions still exist—the high crime, sporadic maintenance, and abandoned buildings. Have you thought what you might do with the resources you've developed to head off the city's next move before it happens?
- You really do seem set for now. Your skill in managing all of those services to keep Howard at home is nothing short of miraculous. But we both know that Alzheimer's is a progressive disease. What sort of plans are you making for the future?

Each of these comments reflects workers' confidence in their clients yet indicates the reality that things don't stand still; clients will have to continue to cope as time goes on. Workers can guide clients to apply the skills and processes they have learned to each of these upcoming situations.

Following Up

For successful resolution, workers and clients also clarify exactly where the relationship goes from here. The practitioner's posthelping responses can ensure that this process remains empowering (Dunst, 1993). Will there be additional contacts? Should clients schedule a check-up visit for 3 months to monitor whether they are still on track? Will someone from the agency contact clients to check their continuing progress as part of the agency's outcome evaluation procedure? How will clients access their records if they choose to do so? What if clients really feel the need to contact the worker again—how do they do it? Is it acceptable for clients to get back in touch? Can they call with good news or are contacts limited to those requests for additional assistance? What are clients supposed to do if they coincidentally run into workers in other contexts, at the mall, the grocery store, or the movies?

These questions deserve attention to alleviate clients' concerns about the future. As workers and clients discuss the answers to these issues they modify their working agreement to formulate a "contract for closure" that specifies how clients will continue without workers and the conditions under which clients or workers may reinitiate contact. Clients need information about policies and procedures for reconnecting to the worker. Clarity about these issues gives clients the information they need to make sound decisions about managing their own resources in the future.

CLOSING WITH REFERRAL

Practice Contexts

Generalist social workers frequently need to refer clients to other agencies and organizations for specialized assistance. What situations might necessitate a referral to a practitioner in a speciality field of social work?

Sometimes relationships between social workers and clients end before reaching the desired goals. For a variety of reasons, workers identify the need to refer clients elsewhere for continued service. This decision may be prompted by the agency's restrictions on length of service or client eligibility, the worker's move to a new position, or the worker's lack of qualifications to continue working with the client's issues that have surfaced. Changes in clients' needs, crisis events in their lives, or lack of continuing progress may also precipitate a referral and subsequent resolution of the professional relationship.

Previous chapters describe processes for linking clients with available resources while clients continue to work with the current agency and worker. But when referring clients at closure, workers attempt to smooth the transition, maintain client motivation, and incorporate any progress achieved so far into the work of the subsequent helping relationship. In closing with clients by referring to another service, workers are simultaneously ending and beginning—wrapping up a phase of the work and orienting clients toward a successful start somewhere else.

Acknowledging Limited Resources

When practitioners contract with clients for social work services, they are guaranteeing that what clients appear to need is a good fit for what the agency offers. To honor this agreement, workers monitor three systems—the agency, the client, and the worker. Changes in any of these systems may create a gap between what the client seeks and what the agency or worker can provide. Social workers know that it is time to end the professional relationship with an appropriate referral when these systems are unable to mesh in ways effective to reach clients' goals.

When client needs exceed worker limits

Sometimes, workers discover that their practice abilities or settings can offer nothing further. Workers may recognize this situation in their own inability to respond to what clients want or when updated assessment information reveals that clients need something that workers do not have available. Ethical social workers accept their limits and refer clients when the situation moves beyond the worker's role or expertise.

Discovering the need to refer is not unusual. Some challenges surface more slowly than others. When clients withhold significant information, workers may blame themselves or clients. However, this does not mean that workers are inadequate or that clients have been "lying." Sensitive subjects may require extensive testing of the worker and a trusting, established professional relationship for the client to come forward. Examples where clients are reluctant to quickly share "what is really happening" often involve alcoholism, drug addiction, sexual abuse, or criminal behavior. When clients have developed enough trust to disclose these issues, workers respond in a trustworthy manner by referring clients to the most appropriate service.

Dale Storonski is well acquainted with the constraints that sometimes lead him to end his work with clients by referring them to others for continued assistance. Dale, a delinquency prevention worker at Northside Youth Services, recently closed a case that provides such an example. Todd, a client referred to Dale after his arrest for shoplifting, continued his illegal activity in spite of their work to focus Todd on more productive activities. When Todd finally admitted to Dale that he was using cocaine daily, Dale explained his inability to work with addiction in his particular setting and referred Todd to the Addictions Recovery Center. In this situation, the indications for referral were explicit. The priority actions necessary for the best interests of this client required Dale to close out his work and refer Todd elsewhere for continuing service.

Service restrictions

At other times, organizational constraints prescribe endings rather than leaving the actual choice to social workers or clients. Agencies may impose time limits based on guidelines from fund sources or policies about the distribution of services. Managed care policies often delimit the length of service for which the third-party providers will pay. Service restrictions also occur when agency policies target clients in a particular age range, feature time-limited interventions, or emphasize crisis resolution rather than long-term work. Consider a delinquency prevention program that may only work with juveniles under the age of 18, because older clients are no longer at risk of "delinquency" according to the laws of the particular state. As a part of developing a service continuum, the agency can mitigate any disruptions by negotiating "working agreements" with adult-oriented services to accept referrals when the delinquency prevention program's clients turn 18.

Other organizational stipulations affect the nature and duration of service as well. For example, many workers practice in host settings, where social work services are supplementary to the organization's primary mission. Such organizations include hospitals, schools, or private businesses. Organizational factors, including discharge from the hospital, the end of the school year, or termination of employment, can force social workers to finalize their work quickly (Hess & Hess, 1999). Although social workers can anticipate these endings, they may not represent "natural" conclusions or resolutions. For successful closure with these clients, workers clarify the limits of their services at the outset, negotiate only goals that fit the setting, and provide referral options at closure.

Finally, internal changes in an agency's structure or mission may shift a worker's responsibilities and create other personnel and programmatic changes that affect the continuity of services. Fiscal constraints all too often determine parameters for services. Social workers assess what impact these changes will have on clients and apprise them of what they can expect. When agency practices, guidelines, or changes force clients out before they are ready, ethical social workers build bridges to other assistance to sustain client motivation, safety, and progress.

Implementing Legal Mandates

All social workers are mandated to report incidents that threaten clients' safety or the safety of others. High-risk situations including child abuse, elder abuse, intimate violence, and potential suicide or homicide require that workers take immediate steps to secure the safety of those involved. This may entail actions to report concerns to state protective services, local police, or potential victims, or to arrange for clients to be evaluated at community mental health centers. Chapter 8 describes these circumstances and the priority actions that social workers must take to prevent harm.

Moreover, complying with legal mandates may interrupt a practitioner's work with a client. Mandated service providers are likely to have service arrangements that make preexisting services unnecessary or shift previous goals to a secondary importance in the face of the current crisis. In some cases, clients themselves may respond to the worker's actions negatively, feeling betrayed or undermined and refuse to continue the relationship. As a result, a social worker's contract with a client may be preempted by the mandated report of a dangerous situation.

Social workers cannot be swayed by the potential for service disruption in handling such events. A social worker's ethical responsibility to report harm takes precedence over the preference for service continuance. However, workers should also be careful not to abandon clients at these times of crisis. Clients benefit from workers who stay involved for a sufficient period to make the necessary transition. A worker's goals at this time are similar to other situations in which the client transfers to a new service provider or withdraws prematurely from service. The worker attempts to consolidate the progress from the work thus far and facilitate the success of the subsequent plan.

As an example, consider the case of Linda, a client who reveals to youth worker Dale Storonski that her grandfather has been sexually abusing her. Dale's mandated report to the Child Protective Unit results in Linda's removal from her grandparents' home and emergency placement in a foster home across town. The web of services offered by the child welfare system usurps Dale's role with Linda, requiring that he close out his work and prepare Linda to work successfully within the new service arena. To facilitate this transition, Dale arranges a conjoint meeting with Linda, her new caseworker, and her foster family to discuss his previous work with Linda and participate in updating Linda's case plan for implementation under these new circumstances.

Making Referrals

When workers reach the limit of what they can offer, they have an ethical obligation to discuss this with clients openly and to offer clients other resource possibilities. Failure to offer honest information about the worker's or agency's limitations may leave clients with feelings that they are being "dumped." To avoid misunderstandings, workers may say:

- As we discussed when we first got together, the crisis service we offer only allows us 30 days per client. Things seem a little calmer now, but you've told me that you still would like to build on the progress you are making. I have several possibilities about where to go next that I think we should discuss.
- You have been great at figuring out how to deal with the kids and avoid using physical punishment, but now you are asking me for assistance with your marriage, and I don't really feel qualified as a marriage therapist. There are, however, several excellent programs that I could recommend to you.
- I need to let you know that I'll be leaving my position in 3 weeks. I got a promotion, but that moves me out to the regional office. I know we're right in the middle of things, so would you like me to refer you to the new worker immediately so you don't lose any ground?

▶ I know that you are still facing a big challenge in confronting the school board about some of its discriminatory suspension policies. But guidelines set by my board of directors prevent me from participating in the kind of protest against the school that you are planning. I do know that the Center for Citizens' Rights has dealt with some similar concerns. Would you be interested in contacting them for continued support?

Notice how, in each example, workers directly acknowledge their limitations, offer honest expectations, reinforce the progress already made, and clearly indicate where clients might go next.

Recognizing interim success

Resolving a professional relationship by referring clients elsewhere is not a defeat, but a step on the way to success. Identifying a more appropriate service clearly moves clients toward the solutions they seek. When making the transition to a new service, workers reflect this perspective by reviewing the client's successes so far in a positive way. So, workers guide clients to discuss their readiness to discontinue, highlight achievements, encourage the exchange of feelings, and anticipate future development.

Smoothing the transition

Workers have a double dilemma in referring clients to others for continuation of the work. If the work has been successful, clients have probably developed a sense of confidence in the relationship and will be reluctant to transfer. If the work has run into obstacles, clients may be discouraged about continuing with anyone. Recognizing these potential hazards in closing a case by referral, practitioners work carefully on transitions that keep clients moving forward toward goals.

Imagine yourself in the role of a client for a minute. You finally take a risk of getting some assistance. Things are going pretty well until your social worker starts talking about running out of time—something about eligibility and agency policy. What would help you pick up with a new worker where you left off with the old one? Clearly the transition would be easier if you didn't have to start all over. You would want the new worker to be informed. You would also want the new worker to be someone you could relate to easily. And you might want to circumvent all the red tape that some agencies put you through before you actually get into one of the inner offices or get the direct service worker into your home.

Facilitating client control

By following a few simple suggestions, the social worker can assist client and the referral worker in building on the progress already made. For example, it works best to refer clients to another human being with a name, description, and set of qualifications rather than an agency, program, or department. If possible, provide clients with alternatives from which to choose. Inform clients of the entry procedures so they can navigate those sometimes confusing and uncomfortable beginning processes. Collaborate with clients on how to transfer information and secure their written consent to facilitate the transfer of case records. A referral conference that includes the client, the former worker, and the referral worker allows all of the participants to discuss the work already completed in a format that allows for clarification and questioning. When time or organizational restraints prevent this direct type of transfer, social workers and clients still work cooperatively toward a smooth transition.

RESPONDING TO CLIENTS' DISCONTINUATION OF SERVICES

Clients conclude their work in different ways, sometimes earlier than social workers would prefer. Many reasons prompt clients to withdraw from services prematurely—reasons that vary widely, from clients' feelings of disillusionment to their feelings of success and empowerment. Regardless of the reason, workers recognize that clients have the privilege to withdraw from services as they see fit. Even involuntary clients can choose to stop and then experience the consequences for their refusal to continue. One recent qualitative study about terminations in an adolescent mental health treatment program found that most endings were "unplanned, unannounced, and unilaterally initiated" by the adolescent clients (Mirabito, 2006).

Preparing for Early Discontinuation

Practitioners work actively to resolve relationships successfully even with clients who drop out of services. First, workers structure each meeting with clients in such a way that if clients fail to return, they have still gained something from the work. Second, workers learn to recognize signs that clients are drifting away to invite an open discussion about the direction of the work. Finally, workers follow up with clients who drop out to clarify the status of the relationship, receive feedback on the reasons that clients discontinued the service, and let clients know how to return in the future if they so desire.

The dynamic nature of social work practice demands that workers attend to all facets of the process simultaneously, regardless of the specific phase that time factors may indicate. As social workers, we assess clients as we build partnerships with them; we observe clients change and develop even while we are still discovering what they can do; we continue to build relationships as we implement changes; and we *anticipate the end of the relationship even as we are beginning.* Preparing for the inevitable ending, workers "integrate gains" throughout the entire process. To do so, workers consistently guide clients in the direction of their strengths, their goals, and their power. Clients will then leave the work with greater confidence in their abilities even if they exit prematurely.

"Every session is the first and every session is the last" (Walter & Peller, 1992, p. 140). This phrase depicts a here-and-now style of practice, and also says that social workers help clients best when they function as if each session could be the last. When workers end each meeting with a summary of the progress made and concretely plan the next step to take, clients leave with a sense of accomplishment and direction whether or not they return for their next scheduled meeting.

Recognizing Exit Clues

Social workers attend to clients' clues of pending departure. Many times clients reveal their tendency to discontinue services in behavioral rather than verbal ways. Clients begin to show up late for meetings, cancel sessions frequently because more important events are occurring, or miss appointments altogether. They neglect to carry out activities as planned in previous sessions. Clients may seem inattentive or fail to present important issues during meetings. All of these behaviors may indicate early withdrawal. However, these signals are ambiguous, leaving workers to share their observations and ask clients about their motivation to continue.

When workers see evidence that client involvement is waning, they bring these observations to the forefront. Workers do not accuse clients of hidden agendas. Instead, they convey acceptance and acknowledge that clients have choices to stop early. In the example that follows, notice the worker's up-front, yet accepting tone in sharing observations with a client showing exiting behaviors:

> I'm a little unclear about what's going on. This is the second week you've come late to our appointment. You're also telling me that you really don't have much to talk about, haven't gotten around to completing the experiment we designed, and you need to leave early today. I'm wondering if you're thinking that we've gone about as far as you want to and you'd like to wrap up or take a break.

Clarifying what clients are saying with "withdrawing" behaviors works whether or not the worker's hunches are correct. If clients are indeed preparing to depart, workers can initiate processes to wrap up the work more productively. If clients are unaware that they are losing focus, a worker's comments may bring them back to task. If clients are indirectly communicating other issues, such as their dissatisfaction with the worker or the present plan, the worker's feedback invites direct discussion and redirection. When workers share their observations that clients are not keeping their commitments to the process, they remind clients they have the privilege to take charge of where the relationship goes next.

Resolving Unplanned Exits

Engage Assess
Intervene Evaluate

Social workers should follow-up with clients who unexpectedly drop services. Why is it important to bring some type of formal resolution and closure to the helping relationship?

Sometimes workers miss the clues that indicate clients are leaving. Other clients leave no clues. When clients simply "don't show" or call and cancel not only the next appointment but the work altogether, the professional relationship is left unresolved. The reasons clients withdraw abruptly probably vary. Some may feel angry or hopeless. Some may feel that things are good enough. Others may perceive that the worker isn't really interested. Still others may assess that the effort in time, transportation, and cost does not justify the limited benefits they are receiving, or factors totally unrelated may interfere.

Good social work requires that practitioners follow up with clients who make "unplanned" exits (Hepworth, et al., 2006). Workers have several purposes in doing so, including

- Understanding a client's reasons for withdrawing
- Validating a client's right to withdraw
- Inviting the client back for future work if desired
- Reinforcing any client progress thus far
- Evaluating and improving the worker's own skills in "reading" client messages, and resolving relationships effectively
- Clarifying the "open" or "closed" status of clients for agency accountability purposes

Most important, this follow-up contact reassures clients they can feel comfortable in pursuing their goals in their own way and at their own pace. Workers should not leave clients with thoughts that they have somehow done something wrong.

WHEN CLIENTS DIE

The realm of social work reflects the human seasons of birth through death. Social workers in medical settings and gerontological services are most likely to experience a client's death. But social workers in other settings may also be confronted with the realities of death. As a result, all social workers need fundamental knowledge about grief and its impact as well as skills to support those who have survived the loss of someone they loved.

Grief

Classic studies of grief by Kübler-Ross (1969) offer a paradigm for understanding the emotional dimensions of our experiences with death and dying. These emotions may include denial, anger, bargaining, depression, and acceptance. More recent research on grief describes the idiosyncratic response of each individual to loss and casts doubt on the abilities of any worker to assess and treat a client's grief accurately by applying a predetermined model. This collaborative approach matches the reality that people may experience only some of the emotions Kübler-Ross identifies, experience these emotions in various sequences, or respond completely differently.

A person's age, gender, health, coping style, cultural background, religious beliefs, previous experiences with death, and availability of familial and social support all contribute to feelings of vulnerability, resiliency, or loss when people die (Berk, 2007; Nakashima, 2003). Some people may talk readily about their sorrow; others may feel a greater need for privacy and withhold their feelings from the scrutiny of others. Still others may disavow their loss, separating themselves from consciously considering their feelings, feelings that may emerge in other ways such as physical affliction, anger, depression, or acting out behavior. Being able to anticipate the loss provides opportunities to work on unfinished business prior to death (Zilberfein, 1999).

To respond in a supportive way to those who are grieving, workers accept the diverse methods people use to deal with loss and allow survivors to cope at a pace that fits the person and the situation. Supportive workers extensively use good listening skills even when clients repeat information, accept both direct and indirect expression of feelings, and encourage adaptive coping strategies. Responsible social workers also update their information on the array of community services available for grief support, including those specialty services such as support groups for parents who have lost children, people losing partners to AIDS, and people who have lost loved ones to violence.

End-of-Life Care

Paradoxically, resilience is an important characteristic when people are at the ends of their lives. Resilience involves discovering meaning in life and living a meaningful life that extends beyond the experience of illness. Based on a small-scale qualitative study of older individuals in hospice care, Nelson-Becker (2006) identified four major themes, including (1) redefining self-image, (2) drawing on the strength of religion or grappling with uncertainty of meaning, (3) investing in social relationships, and (4) wanting to maintain independence. Excerpts from this study reveal the measures respondents were taking to come to terms with their illnesses:

> One woman, a retired social worker, talked about her struggle with different forms of cancer over the past decade. "I call it the invader. I've given it a name, because it's come into my life uninvited, unannounced and its decided it's going to camp here. I can't get rid of it. It's like a houseguest you don't want." She viewed the illness as something separate from herself. It is significant that she named it thereby creating a psychological distance between the illness and herself. The disease,

within her and around her, was not who she was. A man with a background in the arts, spoke about the progression of the illness and his growing ability to accept the constraints it placed on his life, while viewing himself as separate from his disease. "I couldn't do the simplest thing and I was angry. I began to think about how I am going to die rather than if. I know from last week to this week how much I've lost. I've accepted everything that came along and incorporated it in my living. But my illness is not who I am. "Don't make a religion of your illness," is my advice. (pp. 95–96)

In end-of-life care work, social workers provide support for "dying well," so that their clients, like those represented in this example, can engage in living as fully as possible in whatever way they choose. "Dying well is ultimately about living fully and consciously in whatever way one chooses until the moment of death" (p. 88).

Advance care planning

Evolving in importance in health care and gerontological social work, advance care planning (ACP) involves both advance directives and planning for end-of-life care (Black, 2007). The Patient Self-Determination Act (PL 101-508) requires Medicare and Medicaid providers to ask everyone using their health care services if they have advance directives, such as a living will or durable power of attorney (Csikai, 2008). Living wills provide instructions with respect to the application of life sustaining measures. Durable powers of attorney for healthcare are legal documents that assign the responsibility for following directives if individuals are no longer able to make decisions for themselves. ACP also involves "using a long-range, holistic perspective of examining care needs throughout the end of life" (Black, p. 39). Among the areas of focus are needs in psychological, social, spiritual, medical, physical, and financial domains.

Grieving the Death of a Client

Although experiencing the death of a client certainly differs from enduring the loss of a family member or friend, personal and professional grief have common elements. Emotional responses of workers vary, depending on the unique qualities of the worker, the client, and the nature of the professional relationship. Kramer (1998) articulates four factors influencing the way a social worker copes with a client's death, including the worker's

- Sense of preparedness to deal with personal losses
- Feelings of competence to assist clients and family members with death and dying
- Perception of confidence in professional knowledge and skills for helping clients with the grieving process
- Degree of cognitive and emotional assimilation of the inevitability of his or her own death

The particular circumstances of the client's death—whether it was sudden, lingering, or marked by suffering, as well as the impact on the client's family and significant others— also influence the worker's experience and response.

The recollections of Emily Carter, a Northside Hospital hospice social worker, convey the emotional experience of working with death and dying:

Faces of clients and their stories fill my memory. Knowing them, I've learned about myself. I remember 8-year-old Amanda whose rage was

Box 16.2 End-of-Life Care: A Policy–Practice Connection

End-of-life care involves "multidimensional assessment and interventions provided to assist individuals and their families as they approach the end of life" (NASW, 2004c, p. 9). Social workers in many fields of practice are involved in end-of-life care (Kramer, et al., 2003). Medical social work settings in which social workers are likely to confront end-of-life issues include home health care, hospice services, and hospital units such as the emergency room, oncology, intensive care, pediatrics, and critical care. Social workers practicing in other settings, particularly schools, child welfare, and aging services, are also likely to encounter issues related to death and illness in their day-to-day work.

The psychological, cultural, and social ramifications of death, grief, and bereavement for both social workers and their clients are further complicated by numerous legal and ethical challenges. The NASW (2002a) policy statement on hospice care, for example, identifies several concerns related to end-of-life care:

- Access to insurance coverage for hospice services is not available to at least 15 percent of the population in the United States. Additionally, some persons who are insured may not have benefits that fully cover medications.
- Although more people are receiving end-of-life care through hospice services, the length of time they receive services is shorter.
- Ethnic minorities are underrepresented among those served by end-of-life care programs and services.
- Increasing costs and limited services often results in rationing scarce resources. Concerns surface as to "how to determine appropriateness of health care choices and who should make those decisions" (p. 191).

- End-of-life care services such as hospice often rely on the presence of family caregivers to provide day-to-day support to the person who is dying, but geographic mobility of family members and employment obligations of caregivers create barriers to intensive family involvement.
- Changes in health care and medical technology result in variations in the trajectory of death and dying. Death may be imminent or in the future; treatment may involve high-tech or traditional palliative care.

With respect to empowerment and advocacy, the NASW (2004c) *Standards on Palliative and End-of-Life Care* indicates that "the social worker shall engage in social and political action that seeks to ensure that people have equal access to resources to meet their bio-psycho-social needs in palliative and end-of-life care" (pp. 22–23). This includes "identifying and defining needs from the client's perspective, including cultural and spiritual beliefs, and communicating the concerns and needs of the client to decision makers and providers of care" (p. 23).

The principle of self-determination guides social workers in assisting clients with end-of-life decisions. Two factors have played a significant role in ushering in a new era of formalized documentation of personal choice—the legal press for personal involvement in decision making coupled with the financial reality of prolonging life through extraordinary interventions. Social workers play a role in implementing and complying with the legal requirements of advance directives, such as living wills and durable power of attorney for health care, while ensuring that clients' preferences are heard and honored (Black, 2004; Buchanan, et al., 2004).

fueled by incurable cancer and fear of loneliness, and her parents whose anguish choked their ability to communicate openly with their daughter. I recall Seth, the plucky 3-year-old boy with leukemia who brought laughter to the hospital unit and bittersweet joy to his parent's heart. And there is Irene, from the skilled care unit, with whom I had worked for several months. We were talking about my going on vacation when she abruptly said, "Let me put on my glasses so I can see your face clearly one more time!" And, then we talked about my leaving and her dying. She thanked me for being someone who did not judge her for being angry, someone who would sit with her in silence, someone who would listen to her reminiscing about her past and musing about the future, someone who helped her to discover hope even in the face of sorrow. I remember crying with Irene that day and later grieving her death. Mostly,

> I remember the power of her affirmation and the meaningfulness of our work together.

Self-awareness and support are key components in handling issues of death and dying. Workers who cope successfully with the deaths of clients are honest in their appraisal of impact. It is not "unprofessional" to grieve the loss of a genuine relationship. Practice settings such as hospitals, extended care facilities, hospice programs, and caregiver support programs frequently develop staff support services to deal with the significant effects of working in situations in which clients die. Beside self-care and institutional support, Strom-Gottfried and Mowbray (2006) recommend preparation, review and debriefing, and memorial rituals as beneficial supports for professionals working through grief issues.

Death by accident or intention

One of the most difficult experiences that workers may confront is when clients die in ways that workers believe might have been prevented. When clients die of drug overdoses, are murdered participating in gang activity, or take their own lives, workers may be left with guilt that somehow they could have done more or done something different. Shulman (1999) emphasizes the importance of the practice setting in helping workers cope. He offers a three-step model for responding to such events: first, to encourage the worker to grieve; second, to elicit support from other workers with similar experiences or whose positions put them at risk of the same experience; and finally, to refocus the worker toward other clients who still need assistance.

RESOLVING RELATIONSHIPS WITH LARGER SYSTEMS

Closure skills with larger systems incorporate all those processes already discussed. Workers perform tasks to help members express feelings, evaluate progress, function independently, plan for the future, and maintain progress. But ending the work with a multiperson client system requires additional actions to stabilize the functioning of the system as a whole and to ensure the continuing well-being of its members. Consider the special circumstances of resolving relationships with groups, organizations, and communities.

Small Group Endings

Social workers facilitate small group clients with many different purposes. The specific purpose affects the interaction, development, intensity, duration, and character of the group. To plan appropriately for closure, workers analyze each group's particular characteristics, examine important events that have transpired during the life of the group, and consider where the group and its members will go next.

Whether the group is closed- or open-ended is a significant feature that affects closure activities. A closed-ended group meets for a predetermined number of meetings or long enough to reach a desired goal. At closure, the group disbands, and all members leave at once. Conversely, an open-ended group continues to meet as some members "graduate." At any given time, a worker may be wrapping up with some group members while simultaneously initiating new members into the group's activities. The different meanings of "ending" in these two types of groups lead workers to facilitate closure activities to fit each situation.

Closed-ended groups

Closed-ended groups may work to raise consciousness among people who are oppressed, implement social action strategies in the larger environment, provide mutual aid, or increase members' skills in communication, assertion, parenting, or other areas of functioning. By the time the group moves toward closure, all members have worked together to create a shared experience and history with one another. They have convened simultaneously, learned to communicate and relate with one another, worked collaboratively on common tasks, and now face the reality that the group as a resource will soon cease to exist for them.

The similar experiences of members in closed-ended groups allow workers to steer the focus toward shared concerns. All members will benefit from conversations that review and evaluate the work, share feelings, and look ahead toward how the group's benefits can be integrated into each member's functioning outside of the group. Adapting closure activities to a group client, workers also recognize the additional complexity that each group member is actually ending multiple relationships at once. Members are resolving their relationships with the worker, with each other, and with the group itself. Workers guide members to express their thoughts and feelings concerning each of these relationships as the work ends. Particularly, members should consider that the group as an entity will not exist past the closure, leaving them without the group as a resource "to fall back on."

Open-ended groups

Groups structured in an open-ended style may include treatment groups to modify behaviors, addiction recovery groups, and support groups such as those focused on grief, caregiving stress, or survival from violence. Similar to participation in other groups, members will progress through phases defining their relationship to, comfort in, and work with the group. But because members are entering and leaving the group at different times, each member is constructing an idiosyncratic and unique history with the group—sharing common experiences with some group members but having very little interaction with others. In facilitating closure activities with an open-ended group, workers face a collection of members at various developmental levels with very diverse needs.

Even when only one member leaves an open-ended group, every other group member also experiences the closure, yet this event holds a different significance for each. All group members can benefit from an open exchange of the different perspectives they hold. New members are able to imagine themselves completing their work as they listen to others describe their progress and success. Members who are now leaving can "see" their own progress more vividly through the eyes of new members. When a member leaves, workers simultaneously wrap up with that member while also using this success to activate other members who may be only beginning their work.

Session endings

Each group meeting contains elements of the entire social work process combining beginning, middle, and ending phases or, in the language of empowering practice, phases of dialogue, discovery, and development. Beginning phases reinforce the group's cohesion and identify the meeting's goals. Middle phases complete tasks in ways that activate group member resources. Ending phases of a group meeting solidify and integrate the group's success for that session and anticipate the impact for the future work of the group.

Birnbaum and Cicchetti (2000) describe the ending phase of a group encounter as the "most neglected" part of the session. They recommend that successful sessional endings allow reflection on the group's work and its application in members' lives, anticipate the issues and challenges of the upcoming session as a way to create continuity, and ensure that members have a sense of completion, satisfaction, and accomplishment about the work completed. Session endings are most important for an open-ended group because, for some members, this may be their final group meeting.

Resolving Intermember Relationships

When practitioners complete their work with group clients, the worker–client relationship is not the only one to resolve. Members of larger client systems also have relationships with each other—relationships from which members have benefited and on which they have grown to depend. Workers must also provide opportunities for members of multiperson client systems to wrap up their work with each other in ways that acknowledge and support the benefits of relationships among group members.

If you are a proficient math student, you can readily calculate the incredible number of relationship combinations in a client system with many members. In a small group of 5 people, there are 10 dyadic relationships and many small group combinations. In a group of 10 members there are 45 dyadic relationships and enough subgroup possibilities to boggle the mind. Imagine the complexity of relationships in a large organization or community! Obviously, there is not enough time to resolve all of these relationships individually or even know the significance of each one. To cope with closing these multiple relationships, workers initiate structured processes to meet members' needs in a time-efficient and productive way.

Structured endings

Workers plan final meetings with larger client systems to provide all members with opportunities to share their thoughts and feelings about the work completed and to consider the future. For example, workers may solicit written feedback from members and present summary information to the group. Practitioners may also use structured experiences in which members take turns responding to similar questions, such as "What was the most important thing you learned?" or "How do you anticipate using what you have learned in the future?"

A rotating dyadic experience in which each group member talks briefly one-on-one with each other group member also offers opportunities for members to wrap up with each other. Workers may leave the topic of these dialogues to the discretion of the members. As an alternative, workers can suggest that members thank each other for the benefits that have accrued based on the relationship or reminisce about positive interactions and events that have occurred in the life of the group.

Endings with Organizations and Communities

Much work with organizations and communities involves face-to-face human interaction working with people in various leadership roles, task groups, or teams. Therefore, resolving relationships with these larger client systems draws on the same skills that workers implement with individuals, families, and small groups. But integrating gains in work with mezzo- and macrolevel systems additionally requires substantive changes in organizational or community structures, policies, procedures, and operations. Workers see a larger system's readiness for closure when the system has institutionalized the desired changes by incorporating them into the functioning of the organization or community itself. To wrap up their work, organizational- and community-level workers also strive to support the continuing development of leadership, intrasystem alliances, and widespread collaboration in decision making.

Institutionalizing change

To maintain the stability of progress initiated in a larger system client past the point of closure, workers target changes in policies and practices that will endure. "When the change in an organization's purpose, structure, and procedures or service arrangements is no longer perceived as change, but as an integral part of its ongoing activities, the innovation is institutionalized" (Germain & Gitterman, 1996, p. 395). A social system's tendency to maintain equilibrium works in favor of sustaining desired changes that become a routine part of the system's functioning.

Consider the example of Damon Edwards, first presented in Chapter 10, as he wraps up his work with the residents of Franklin Courts. The residents have achieved their goals. The children with lead poisoning are receiving medical treatment, the source of the contamination has been discovered, and city work crews are renovating buildings to ensure their safety. To stabilize these changes, the members have also initiated policy changes in the housing authority's code that ensure monitoring of materials used in public housing work projects. Organizing annual blood screenings is another institutionalized accomplishment that will monitor the health of those children already exposed to lead. These embedded changes in policy and practices are institutional changes that will have enduring benefits after Damon and the residents of Franklin Courts complete their work together.

Sustaining empowered functioning

The ultimate goal for any level of client system in empowerment-based social work practice is the sustained empowered functioning of the client after the contracted work is completed. With larger system clients this "may include developing organization or community ability to make decisions based on a representational influence, gaining and maintaining political power, and ensuring the decisions are implemented for the benefit of the organization or community" (Harrigan, et al., 1998, p. 76). Key elements necessary to sustain this empowered functioning include leadership development, collegial collaboration, and consensus-building skills such as negotiation and mediation.

Drawing on the Franklin Courts example, Damon Edwards can work to enhance the leadership of Fiona Grant. Having identified Mrs. Grant's leadership abilities early in the work, Damon has always found ways to create plenty of space for her to lead, leaving himself in a consulting role. The group's success has activated Mrs. Grant's motivation further, and she has now expanded her activities to focus on other neighborhood issues. At closure, Damon directly states his confidence in Mrs. Grant's abilities and offers honest feedback on her strengths as he sees them.

To encourage powerful alliances within the group, Damon also helps group members establish a resident council that meets regularly to review conditions at Franklin Courts, maintains a presence at city council meetings, and monitors the activities of the housing authority, even after the initial crisis fades. Developing leadership and maintaining effective structures and alliances will empower the residents to continue their efforts without needing Damon's involvement. Through his work with this council, Damon has also facilitated the development of decision-making skills. Members work toward consensus by accessing each participant's views, respecting differences of opinion, and creating plans that incorporate the strengths of everyone involved.

Professional Identity

Professional community organizers often work in the communities in which they reside. What issues arise for these macropractice social workers as they transition from resident to organizer and vice versa?

Termination or transition?

An important consideration in closure activities with organizations and communities is the role that the social worker will play with the system after the point of closure. In organizational practice, the worker is often a member of the client system itself and will continue to be so when the project at hand is complete. In community practice, the worker is likely to have a long-term, ongoing relationship with the community, wrapping up one project and moving on to the next. In these situations, closure will not mark the end of the relationship with the client system but instead signifies a change in the worker's role.

For such a transition to be successful, the "closure" must be clearly understood, and the client system must be able to sustain the desired changes without the continuing efforts of the social worker. "If the practitioner is an ongoing member of the organization or community in which the change took place, future activity must be restricted to an ongoing, established role and responsibility to ensure that change is fixed with some other individual, position, group, or unit" (Harrigan, et al., 1998, p. 75). Damon Edwards' successful work in supporting Fiona Grant and the resident council as leaders in Franklin Courts allows him to return to his previous role in the Northside Community. He will still interact with the Franklin Courts residents, but refrain from doing for them what they can now do for themselves.

To increase clarity about the role changes that occur at these points of transition, macrolevel practitioners discuss them openly. Workers may also use symbolic means to mark the turning point in their involvement. Work with groups, task forces, committees, organizations, and communities has long been known for its use of ritualized endings. Parties, ceremonies to recognize accomplishments, certificates of merit, voting approval of the final committee report, and notifications of grant funding all affirm accomplishments, mark endings, and serve as bridges to new beginnings. In planning closure ceremonies, workers seek to offer members opportunities to reflect on their work together and define their future relationships with each other in addition to wrapping up with the social worker.

ENDINGS ARE BEGINNINGS

An effective closing process does not end the client's development. Instead, it is a beginning for the client to stabilize the progress achieved, to integrate the skills learned, and to function independently. The success of this transition not only rests on the closing activities, but it also requires a process that encourages client self-direction throughout the entire social work relationship. A collaborative social worker and client partnership that recognizes client strengths, creates productive alliances, and increases opportunities empowers clients with the resources to continue to function competently after the professional relationship is finished.

Social workers also move beyond the partnership, enriched by another practice experience. An ending that carefully reviews the process and includes an open exchange of thoughts and feelings offers workers important feedback about their professional skills and interpersonal qualities. The practice wisdom gained by workers from each client stimulates the worker's professional development and becomes a resource on which workers draw for each client system yet to come.

Succeed with **PEARSON mysocialworklab**

Log onto **www.mysocialworklab.com** and select the **Interactive Skill Module** videos from the left-hand menu. Answer the questions below. (*If you did not receive an access code to* **MySocialWorkLab** *with this text and wish to purchase access online, please visit* www.mysocialworklab.com.)

1. **Watch page 24 of the group work module** to observe the end of a group session. What if this were the last meeting of the group? What else should the leader do to end the group in a way that would stabilize group members' progress and resolve their feelings?

2. **On page 19 of the child welfare module** social worker Cheryl describes the option of referring her client for supportive services. What steps should Cheryl take to ensure successful linkage to substance abuse treatment?

PRACTICE TEST

Diversity in Practice

1. Social worker Jake Stein recognizes that he is not prepared to work effectively with clients who are refugees. When he learns that his new client is dealing with an immigration issue, Jake should _____.
   a. read the latest research on immigration law and continue to work with the client
   b. ask his colleagues about how to work effectively with this client
   c. refer his client to a professional with expertise in this area
   d. conclude that lack of preparation is inconsequential and continue to work with the client

2. Social worker Carly Quinn learns from her supervisor that preparation for ending professional relationships _____.
   a. starts with the first contact with clients
   b. commences with the beginning of the discovery phase
   c. originates at the beginning of the development phase
   d. begins after the outcomes have been evaluated

3. The purpose of social workers' final activities is to stabilize success and _____ clients' everyday functioning.
   a. generalize outcomes into
   b. prevent recidivism in
   c. alleviate problems in
   d. restrict options for

4. Cecilia Adams believes she is has gained competency and is the one responsible for the improvements in her situation. Her conclusion exemplifies a(n) _____ attribution.
   a. dispositional
   b. situational
   c. personal
   d. interpersonal

5. When social worker Sherrie Olstean tells you that one of her clients has developed a pattern of showing up late or missing appointments, you suggest she _____.
   a. confront her client directly about having a hidden agenda
   b. ignore the client's behavior

   c. transfer the client to another social worker in the agency
   d. clarify the meaning of the client's exiting behaviors

Policy Practice

6. _____ is a document that provides instructions for the application of life sustaining measures, whereas _____ assigns the legal responsibility for decision-making if individuals are no longer able to make decisions for themselves.
   a. A health care self-determination plan; a living will
   b. A living will; a durable power of attorney
   c. An end-of-life care plan; an advance directive
   d. A living will; an end-of-life care plan

7. Social worker George Lester and his client conclude that the client had made significant progress and no longer needs social work services. From this we can conclude that _____.
   a. a referral for additional service is appropriate
   b. the client will never return for additional services
   c. the client will withdraw from services before the work is complete
   d. the contract with the client was completed

8. The strategy social worker Rose Hernandez should select to solidify changes and reinforce her client's sense of achievement is to _____.
   a. discuss termination with the client
   b. highlight the errors the client has made recently
   c. reformulate the objectives of the service plan
   d. review the client's progress with the client

Engage Assess Intervene Evaluate

9. Which of the following statements about endings of professional relationships is LEAST true?
   a. Social workers' experiences with separation and loss can influence their response to endings.
   b. Social workers' views of themselves as professionals can influence their response to endings.
   c. Social workers' reactions to transitions can influence their response to endings.
   d. Although an important component of professional practice, self awareness is irrelevant to the endings of professional relationships.

Log onto **MySocialWorkLab** once you have completed the Practice Test above to take your Chapter Exam and demonstrate your knowledge of this material.

Answers

1) c 2) a 3) a 4) a 5) d 6) b 7) d 8) d 9) d

Epilogue

Andrea Barry walked out into the summer evening. She felt energized, enthused, and content, all at the same time. The Northside Network's annual conference always seemed to leave her with feelings of confidence, a sense of support, and something new to try. Following each conference of the last 2 years, Andrea had experienced similar feelings. It felt good to get together with Northside's other social workers.

The idea to start the annual conference had come up at one of the Northside Network's brown-bag lunches. With each meeting of the Network, members were seeing more clearly that they were all "in this together." In spite of their differences in agency settings and clientele, all workers used similar practice processes. Each Northside social worker also drew resources from the Northside community. What benefited the work of one held potential benefits for them all. It seemed only logical that they should pool their efforts. The annual conference was one way they did that.

The conference was a multidimensional experience. Each member of the Network facilitated a workshop, presentation, or task-oriented session. From Mark Nogales, Andrea had learned about the integration of the strengths perspective into working with clients with mental illnesses. Andrea had also participated in writing a position paper about the need for more low-cost and transitional housing. She had really enjoyed the "Tune In, Don't Burn Out" workshop, where Tony Marelli had taught relaxation skills and stress-reduction techniques. She attended a panel discussion of several clients discussing what services, approaches, and workers' styles they felt were most helpful. Andrea herself had presented the results of her research on the impact of cultural sensitivity training on worker–client relationships.

But it was the closing ceremony that had left Andrea with the afterglow that she would carry into the evening and back to work tomorrow. Kay Landon was the facilitator. She led those attending through a series of reflections on the work of the past year, an update of current conditions in the Northside community, and a guided fantasy experience of where they could be 1 year from now. As the experience drew to a close, Kay invited participants to share what being a social worker meant to them. It was Damon Edwards' words that still rang in Andrea's thoughts.

> We are in a beautiful place here. We are social workers. We have the opportunity to know people. Some are people similar to others we might have run into anyway. But many are people that we would never know in any other way. They all fascinate us, because each of them brings his or her own unique way. They are resources to us. They have taught us more about human diversity than we have learned in textbooks.
>
> We are in an important place here. We sit at the crossroads, because, as social workers we connect to people at all different levels. We are the elevators of society's people. We pick them up in one place and go with them to where they want to go. We understand the connections and the connectors.

We are in a challenging place here. We weave science and art, because social work practice needs spontaneity with precision. Because people aren't simple, and neither are we. And all that is gold does not glitter.

We are in a vulnerable place here. People show us their pain. They share their reality and shake our beliefs. They swamp our perspectives as we work for their goals. And just when we get there, we let them go.

We are in the right place here. Somehow we've always been on the way. The world has nurtured us, and now we nurture it in return. Just as all universes seek balance, we too work as part of our world's solution. We are naturals. We revel in the opportunities for the world and for us.

Appendix A

CLIENT EMPOWERMENT: SURVIVING DOMESTIC VIOLENCE

A Case Study about Niki Lindstrom

Prepared by Michael O'Melia

This case example illustrates the empowering approach to generalist practice as explained in the text. It exemplifies the wide-angle view of the generalist practitioner, assessing situations in environmental context, and considering all system levels in designing interventions to activate resources, create alliances, and expand opportunities. The case narrative is divided into four sections to correspond to the four units in the book. Focus questions follow each section.

Key Facts:

- Niki Lindstrom is a young single mother affected by domestic violence, poverty, and social policy limiting welfare assistance. A public service announcement on TV prompts Niki to take action to resolve her predicament and leads to a series of changes that sets Niki on a path toward success.
- Sandy Weber is a social worker for the Domestic Violence Advocacy Program who assists survivors of domestic violence through legal advocacy, counseling and support, and referral services.
- Evelyn Mackey is a social worker with the Transit Program, a transitional housing program for single parents and their children in the Northside community, a program assisting Niki in transitioning to self-sufficiency.
- Gabe Thomas is a social worker employed as a workforce development counselor with the Northside Employment and Training Program (NET), an agency with goals to move Temporary Assistance for Needy Families (TANF) recipients toward independence through employment.

UNIT 1: SOCIAL WORK PRACTICE PERSPECTIVES

Things had been tough for Niki Lindstrom most of her life. Not long ago, Niki's mother Marie had kicked her out when she found out that the 17-year-old was pregnant. Marie even forbade Niki's 15-year-old sister Liza to have any contact with Niki. Niki hadn't heard from her own father Mark since her parents' divorce 8 years before. To complicate things, Niki had lost contact with most of her friends when she left high school and completed her GED. With her mother's edict to move out and no other support from friends or family, Niki felt she had no alternative except to move into her own apartment.

A few months after the move, Jared was born. Caring for an infant, Niki found herself even more isolated and lonely. It was only natural that she would begin to depend more and more emotionally on 22-year-old Jerome. After all, Jerome was Jared's father! Sometimes during his frequent visits, Jerome was loving and helpful, leaving Niki hopeful that things might work out between them. Other times, Jerome seemed angry and demanding. Niki recalls her "mixed feelings" when Jerome informed her that he had decided to move in, but she felt the decision was out of her hands.

Despite Niki's attempts to please Jerome, the relationship deteriorated quickly as Jerome used crack more frequently. Jerome's crack habit led to unpredictable outbursts of anger and paranoia—times during which Jerome would belittle Niki, criticize her mothering, and accuse her of being unfaithful to him. Jerome would also bully her into giving him money, money from Niki's TANF benefits that she was trying to stretch to meet household expenses. Niki grew increasingly depressed as the bills piled up and Jerome's behavior remained erratic. She felt powerless and increasingly hopeless.

It was only a public service announcement on TV, but it launched Niki into a whole new direction. She had never really seen herself as an abuse victim before—after all, Jerome had never actually hit her, even though he had threatened to at times. But as the people on the TV described the symptoms of an abusive relationship, Niki could actually feel what they were saying. She was experiencing the recurring cycle of control and abuse that trapped her with Jerome. That day, Niki called the Domestic Violence Advocacy Center and talked with social worker Sandy Weber.

Talking with Sandy helped Niki to clarify her thinking about the situation with Jerome. Niki concluded that she needed to get away from him. She also felt afraid about doing so, wondering how Jerome might respond. This dilemma was something that Sandy Weber had seen before, and she carefully helped Niki consider her ambivalent thoughts and feelings about the situation. Sandy also shared relevant legal information and described community services that might be able to provide assistance to someone in Niki's situation.

Together, Niki and Sandy developed a plan to maximize Niki's feelings of safety and give her support as she left Jerome. Sandy accompanied Niki to the courthouse to get a no-contact order. She provided transportation and direct assistance to help Niki pack up items that she and Jared would need after leaving the apartment. Sandy also arranged for Niki to stay at an emergency shelter run by the Domestic Violence Advocacy Center. The move out of her own apartment gave Niki the chance to break the pattern of Jerome dropping over at will, to prevent Jerome's extortion of money from her, and to ensure Niki's safety as she extricated herself from the relationship. She remained at the shelter until an apartment in one of Northside's transitional housing programs—the Transit Program for single parents and their families—became available.

That was 4 months ago, and things had gotten better for 19-year-old Niki ever since. Her individual consultations with Transit Program social worker Evelyn Mackey had helped Niki feel good about herself again. She had changed from thinking about herself as a victim and began to experience the new identity of "survivor." What Evelyn said was true. Niki had taken charge to resolve her situation with Jerome. It reinforced what Niki had already learned about herself from her achievements at school—she was a smart woman who was coping with her situation rather than becoming a victim of it. Evelyn Mackey had also connected Niki to an academic counselor to discuss plans for continuing her education and arranged child care while Niki attended her various appointments. From Evelyn, Niki was also learning about proper nutrition for Jared and had picked up some new skills in parenting.

As part of the Transit Program, Niki met weekly with other women in a support group that Evelyn Mackey facilitated. During these meetings, Niki began to see herself differently. She experienced how her situation was not unique but similar to other women. Each woman in the group shared stories of oppression in intimate relationships complicated by limited opportunities in employment, low wages, and short-circuited educational attainment. Niki saw the need to take care of her own needs emotionally and financially to avoid falling back into another dependent relationship, such as her life with Jerome.

As a result of her discussions with the academic counselor, Niki applied to school to become a registered nurse (RN), a position with job opportunities, mobility, and a decent salary. Her acceptance to nursing school had arrived the same day as a scheduled meeting with her TANF worker. Niki had found out that she could start the RN program in 2 months. However, when Niki discussed her educational plans at the meeting, the welfare worker patiently explained that the state no longer saw itself as a "scholarship program." Going to school was fine, but first and foremost, Niki needed to get a job. Obtaining employment had to happen quickly because Niki's benefits would be coming to an end. The TANF worker suggested it might be more realistic for Niki to enroll in a certification program to become a Certified Nursing Assistant (CNA)—a 10-week program that Niki could even complete on-line. Despite Niki's protests, the TANF worker simply repeated that "policy is policy, and you need to get a job." The worker wrapped up the meeting by informing Niki that she was being referred to the Northside Employment and Training Program (NET) for assistance in gaining immediate employment.

The appointment with the TANF worker left Niki angry. A job as a CNA would not hold the benefits that a position as an RN promised. Working enough hours to pay for nursing school on her own while also caring for Jared could make it impossible to succeed in school. She shared her frustration with other support-group members. They agreed it was just another way that the system worked to get in your way rather than actually help you become self-sufficient. Niki was a "welfare mother," an identity that stigmatized her and left her trapped in a vicious cycle of poverty and dependence. She felt determined to assert her opinion when she met with the counselor at the employment program.

Niki was initially thrown off balance when she met NET counselor Gabe Thomas. How possibly could this man—a middle-aged African American social worker dressed in a coat and tie—ever understand her, a young Caucasian mother who was young enough to be his daughter?

Questions that Focus on Unit 1

1. Evelyn Mackey, Niki Lindstrom's worker in the Transit program, is a generalist social worker. What evidence supports this conclusion? What other activities would you expect Evelyn to carry out in her work as a generalist practitioner?

2. As a generalist social worker, Evelyn functions in many roles. Identify the functions and roles that Evelyn implements in her work with Niki.

3. Apply the ecosystems perspective to describe Niki's situation at the time of her emotional abuse by Jerome. Using the household of Niki and her son Jared as the focal system, describe what is happening

inside this system, how this system is relating to its environment, and how it is progressing through time. Consider Niki's situation at the present time. What has changed since Niki entered the Transit program? Apply the same ecosystemic perspective to account for these changes.

4. The core values of "human dignity and worth" and "social justice" guide all social work practice. Apply these value concepts to consider the policy that will pay for Niki to become a CNA but not fund her efforts to become an RN. Is Niki being treated with dignity? Is this policy just?

5. Analyze the cultural characteristics of the upcoming relationship between Niki and NET counselor Gabe Thomas. What elements may inhibit the development of a productive partnership? What may contribute to its effectiveness? How might Gabe prepare himself to work with Niki?

6. The strengths perspective recognizes that all people have strengths and resources. What strengths and resources are evident in Niki's life?

7. Many changes have occurred in Niki's life recently. Explain these changes in terms of empowerment. Consider personal, interpersonal, and sociopolitical dimensions of empowerment. Identify the situations that have increased Niki's feelings of power and control.

8. Gabe Thomas uses an empowering approach to social work practice. In a general way, describe the phases and processes that he and Niki will accomplish in their work together.

UNIT 2: THE DIALOGUE PHASE: BUILDING RELATIONSHIPS AND ASSESSING CHALLENGES

Although Niki Lindstrom was prepared to give Gabe Thomas a "piece of her mind" about the unfairness of the system in which she felt trapped, Gabe's wide smile and friendly demeanor softened her attitude. Gabe began the meeting by explaining who he was, the purpose of the NET Program, and Niki's rights and responsibilities as a participant. Gabe explained that it was his task to guide Niki toward self-sufficiency to prepare her for the termination of her TANF benefits, which would occur 6 months from now.

The NET Program could offer counseling support, planning, referral services, child care assistance, and funds for short-term training. As Gabe explained, Niki didn't actually have to cooperate with him—she could find her own means of support. But if Niki refused to cooperate with NET or find a job on her own, Gabe would be obligated to report this to her TANF worker, an action that could result in an immediate reduction of benefits. Although Gabe's work with Niki would be "pretty much confidential," Niki's TANF caseworker would have open access to all information exchanged and any case records kept during the process of working with Gabe.

Gabe's remark *"Do you have any questions about what we are doing here today?"* shifted the focus of the conversation to Niki.

Niki: Let me get this right. What you are saying is that you are cutting off my benefits. I have to get a job either through you or on my own.

Gabe: Basically that's it. The goal is to move you from welfare to a work situation where you will no longer need payments.

Niki: Do I have anything to say about this?

Gabe: About what part specifically?

Niki: About you cutting off my benefits?

Gabe: The new policy limits the time you can collect benefits. The goal is to move you toward self-sufficiency through work.

Niki: Just like that—you're going to cut me off—just when I was starting to pull my life together.

Gabe: Pulling your life together?

Niki: Yes! Before you and your policy so rudely interrupted, I was accepted and about ready to go to nursing school. I want to be an RN.

Gabe: Congratulations on getting into nursing school. That's a big step toward self-sufficiency. Tell me more about your plan.

Niki: My "plan," as you put it, was to keep getting assistance until I got my nursing license, get a decent-paying job, and then get you people off my back once and for all.

Gabe: Seems like you and I have the same goal.

Niki: Not exactly. I want to be an RN, but my caseworker already told me that I should think about getting training to be a CNA.

Gabe: That's true—there are no NET funds available for nursing school nor will your benefits last long enough for you to complete training to be an RN. It's also true that we recommend short-term vocational training that results in quicker employment, such as the CNA program. But, I'm hearing that you're not interested in certification as a CNA.

Niki: You've got that right. I don't want to be stuck as a CNA for the rest of my life.

Gabe: Becoming a CNA feels more like a dead end to you than a career opportunity.

Niki: Like my opinion really matters. You're going to tell me that's the only choice I've got.

Gabe: Seems like you're feeling somewhat powerless to make your own decisions. But let me clarify that I'm not here to tell you what to do. That choice is yours. I'm here to discuss options that the NET program offers to see if there is any way that we can help you get where you want to go. And from what I've heard so far, you want to go to nursing school to be an RN.

Niki: Right! So how can you help me?

Gabe: What kind of help do you need?

Niki: Right now I have a decent place to live and someone to take care of my son Jared.

Gabe: So, you've got housing and child care covered.

Niki: What I need is a regular income for a couple of more years and some money for nursing school. It'll take me that long to get through the RN program and by that time, you can cut off my benefits. I know I'd make a great nurse. Couldn't you people bend the rules a little?

Gabe: I'm not really in a position to bend the rules, but that might not be the only way to get where you want to go. Let me make sure I'm understanding you. You have a clear direction—to become an RN. You've been accepted into a nursing program. You have housing and someone to take care of Jared. And what you want from me is to help you figure out a way that you can afford to get through nursing school.

Niki: You've got it. Where do we go from here?

Questions that Focus on Unit 2

1. Social worker/client relationships combine professional and personal qualities. Identify the ways in which Gabe negotiates a professional partnership. What contributes to the personal side of the relationship?

2. The case example does not address the cultural differences that are obvious in the partnership between Niki Lindstrom and Gabe Thomas. Should these differences be addressed? If so, when and how? Are there any ways in which Niki and Gabe are culturally similar?

3. To discuss an issue from a "challenge" rather than a "problem" perspective, workers implement a three-pronged approach to define: (1) what is currently happening, (2) where the client wants to go, and (3) what strengths and resources are available to get there. Analyze the dialogue between Niki and Gabe to identify these three elements. What methods does Gabe used to steer the dialogue in this way?

4. Empowering social work dialogue maintains a responding rather than initiating stance. Identify the various responses from the response continuum (as described in Chapter 7) that Gabe uses to leave Niki in charge of the direction of the conversation.

5. Through dialogue social workers validate feelings as well as clarify what clients are saying. Note examples when Gabe identifies and accepts what Niki is feeling.

6. Niki's participation with the NET program is involuntary, which may lead her to resist Gabe's efforts. What actions does Gabe take to build a more collaborative working relationship and move away from a resistant style of interaction? What is the key to maintaining Niki's motivation to work toward the mandated goal of economic self-sufficiency?

7. Social work principles are evident in effective social work practice. Examine the dialogue to identify examples of the principles of acceptance, individuation, nonjudgmentalism, objectivity, self-determination, and confidentiality.

8. A key component in the initial dialogue between worker and client is to establish a mutual direction. Clearly state the direction that Niki and Gabe establish to guide the upcoming work.

UNIT 3: THE DISCOVERY PHASE: ASSESSING, ANALYZING, AND PLANNING

Gabe Thomas: You want to know where we go from here? Well, it seems to me that we are at the point of deciding how we can get you through nursing school. We are stuck with two roadblocks, though—you only have a maximum of

6 months of eligibility left on TANF, and the NET program has no funding for becoming an RN. But, as my mother always says "there's more than one way to get to heaven."

Niki Lindstrom: OK. What should I do?

Gabe: I'm not exactly sure, but I'm wondering if you'd feel comfortable telling me some more about your situation to see what plan we can develop that is a good fit for you.

Niki: What do you need to know?

Gabe: Let's start with the things about you that you think are important for me to know.

Niki began to relate her story. She described her relationship with Jerome, the unexpected pregnancy, her estrangement from her parents, and the birth of Jared. Gabe encouraged her sharing through his attentive posture, selective responses, and accepting tone. Niki grew visibly depressed as she described the problems with Jerome. Gabe's response of "*Why did you stay with him for so long?*" brought Niki's anger and resistance to the forefront. Gabe was reminded by Nikis response that "why questions" frequently activate a client's resistance, reorienting him to examine how Niki survived and where she intended to go from here.

Niki: Are you saying that I should have done something different? I had Jared to think about, you know. I had no one to turn to, nowhere to go.

Gabe: I see what you mean—must have been tough to feel trapped in the relationship with Jerome out of your love for Jared. Where did you find the strength to endure that situation?

Niki: I knew I was better than that. At first, I thought that Jerome would change, but later I started to plan my own way out. I would have gotten rid of him eventually I think, but when I saw that ad, it moved my plans up.

Gabe: How were you able to get out?

Niki relaxed again as she continued her story of the involvement with Sandy Weber and the Domestic Violence Advocacy Program, staying at the shelter, her move into the Transit program, the help that Evelyn Mackey had been, and how much she benefited from the support group. Gabe's enthusiastic responses showed that he was genuinely impressed.

Gabe: I see that you're right! You certainly do deserve better than you were getting with Jerome. And it seems like you're on the way toward getting it. You have a lot of personal strengths, and you seem to be building a strong base of social support. I'd like to look more carefully at that support if you don't mind.

Niki: What do you mean?

Gabe: I'd like to draw a genogram and eco-map.

Niki: I don't know what you're talking about.

Gabe: Genograms and eco-maps are diagrams that illustrate information about your life. A genogram looks at family relationships. An eco-map looks at relationships you have with other people, social services, and environmental resources. It might help us to identify what in your life can help you succeed in working your way off welfare as well as target issues that might get in the way.

Niki: OK. Go for it.

Gabe rose from his chair and moved to a marker board that hung in his office. He began with the genogram, carefully discussing each member of Niki's family, including her parents, sister, Jared, and even Jerome. As he learned about Niki's family, Gabe drew them out on the board. He concluded the genogram by drawing a circle around Niki and Jared before seeking information to complete the eco-map that would describe Niki's relationships with other people and systems outside of this two-person household.

Niki found herself more and more intrigued with this process. Although the diagrams contained only information with which she was very familiar, looking at them in this way gave her a new perspective. She felt lonely when she saw her lack of familial support as indicated by the genogram. But she was comforted by the eco-map showing her current connections to Evelyn Mackey, her support group, and other resources available to her via the Transit program.

With the genogram and eco-map complete, Gabe drew a chart next to them. He titled the chart "Niki Lindstrom, RN" and then drew two columns underneath. He labeled the first column "needs" and the second one "resources." Together Niki and Gabe reflected on the information they had gathered to fill in the columns. Organizing the information in this way revealed important facts about Niki's quest to become an RN. The needs for housing, child care, and transportation were currently met through her participation in the Transit program. Niki's recent acceptance into the RN program also was in the resources column. Money for living expenses and tuition for nursing school loomed large in the needs column.

This analysis also revealed several unanswered questions. If Niki decided to go to nursing school instead of directly to work, would the TANF program reduce her benefits immediately or let her collect payments for the remaining 6-month period? How much did nursing school cost? Were scholarships or loans available? What about the dormant resources of her family relationships? Niki's connections to her mother, father, sister, and Jerome were clearly not working, but was there any potential for them to help Niki reach her goals?

As their discussion continued, a plan begin to evolve. Gabe pulled out a required NET form entitled "Plan for Self-sufficiency" and worked with Niki to fill in the blanks.

Self-sufficiency Goal: Obtain licensure as an RN.

Objective #1: Niki will acquire sufficient funds to pay for nursing school tuition within 2 months.

Objective #2: Niki will maintain her current level of income to meet living expenses during the 2 years necessary to complete the RN program.

Objective #3: Niki will access additional resources to provide child care, transportation, and social support to decrease her dependence on those available through the Transit Program within 6 months.

To continue planning, Gabe and Niki teamed to brainstorm possible activities and select strategies to meet each objective. They ended their meeting with an agreement or "contract" to implement the plan, decided what actions each needed to accomplish before their next meeting, and set a time to meet again.

Questions that Focus on Unit 3

1. Within the discovery phase, social workers and clients search for available strengths and resources. What actual and/or potential resources did Niki and Gabe discover? What methods were effective in this discovery process?

2. Gabe uses a strength-oriented approach. Examine the conversation to identify examples of this approach. Now, identify the one deficit-oriented response that Gabe uses. Compare the effects of strengths-versus deficit-oriented responses. What is the impact on the dialogue and on the relationship between Niki and Gabe?

3. Draw the genogram that fits the information offered about Niki and her family. Include all information available throughout the entire case study.

4. Draw the eco-map that fits the information offered about Niki's household and its relationships with environmental resources. Include all information available throughout the entire case study. Annotate the eco-map to indicate the flow of resources in and out of this household.

5. Examine the genogram, eco-map, and the case study narrative. Apply the ecosystemic framework described in Chapter 10 of the text to analyze what's happening inside this system, what's happening outside of this system, how the inside and outside relate, and how the system is progressing through time.

6. Study the objectives that Niki and Gabe have written. An effective objective answers the question "who will accomplish what when?" Are these effective objectives? Identify the key elements of each.

7. Brainstorm possible activities that may work to reach each of these objectives. Think broadly like a generalist practitioner by including activities that target changes in the client, the client's transactions with others, the helping system, and the social environment.

8. Niki and Gabe agree to a "contract" to implement their plan. List the key elements of their agreement that should be included in such a contract. In what ways does the process of contracting affect the relationship of social worker Gabe with his client Niki?

UNIT 4: THE DEVELOPMENT PHASE: IMPLEMENTING, EVALUATING, AND STABILIZING CHANGE

When the next meeting began, Gabe Thomas could sense Niki Lindstrom's excitement. Niki had completed her task of visiting the nursing school to find out how much it would cost and talked with an admissions counselor about financial assistance. She had already applied for a student loan and was considering applying for a scholarship offered by an area hospital in exchange for an agreement to work for a period of time after graduation. Gabe congratulated Niki on her initiative, pointed out her abilities to get things done fast, and noted her particular strength in activating people on her behalf. Niki was clearly taking steps toward meeting her first objective to secure funds for school.

Gabe also reported on his activities since their last meeting. He had checked to see how long Niki could continue to receive TANF benefits if she chose to enter nursing school rather than cooperate with efforts to obtain immediate employment. The news here was not so good. The TANF Program supervisor Gabe had consulted interpreted the rules rigidly, saying that Niki needed to make efforts to get a job now. A 2-year training program did not represent immediate progress toward employment. Unless Niki looked for a job, her benefits would likely be reduced immediately and completely eliminated before the end of 6 months. Meeting the objective of maintaining a livable income while attending nursing school was obviously going to be difficult.

Gabe and Niki discussed her possible choices. Niki could change her plans to be an RN, enter short-term training leading to immediate employment, or try to combine work and nursing school. Another option was to look for other sources of income, go off TANF, and do whatever she wanted. Or, she could fight the unfair policy either by appealing the individual decision about her own case or by addressing the policy itself at another level—yet neither she nor Gabe was hopeful about those ideas. Having clarified these possibilities, Niki wanted to think it about for a week before moving in any direction.

At the next week's meeting, Niki told Gabe that she had made her choice to go to nursing school one way or the other. Niki also decided not to file an appeal about the cut-off of her benefits, saying that she "could see the hand-writing on the wall," and it was time to get ready to support herself. She accepted Gabe's offer to assist her to find part-time employment, saying that a part-time job would still allow her to enter the nursing school's part-time program. Niki left Gabe's office with a list of job possibilities and instructions to bring back proof of the applications she submitted to meet TANF rules documenting job-seeking attempts.

During that week of decision, Niki had also shared her frustrations with the other women in the support group at the Transit Program. Each of them reported similar roadblocks on their journeys out of violent intimate relationships and toward self-sufficiency. Some reported difficulties in dealing with courts that seemed more responsive to protecting the rights of domestic violence perpetrators than to ensuring the safety of victims. Others recounted their feelings of helplessness as their own voices and preferences were subdued by legal processes that seemed to be beyond their control. Still others described the lack of support they had received from their own extended families, who seemed to blame the women themselves for their own victimization. They all agreed that public ignorance about domestic violence was the norm, and this lack of awareness contributed to social policy ineffective in meeting the needs of survivors of domestic violence.

Fueled by indignation, Niki functioned as a catalyst in the support group. She worked closely with group facilitator Evelyn Mackey to move the group's focus from social support to develop a critical consciousness about domestic violence as a prelude to social action. At Evelyn's suggestion, Niki contacted similar groups operating in other transitional housing programs and began to develop a larger coalition to raise consciousness about the issues surrounding domestic violence and the need for progressive social policy to assist domestic-violence survivors toward independence. In this way, the Women's Political Action Coalition (WOPAC) was born.

So many women became involved that WOPAC had resources to work in several directions at once. One committee coordinated a public information campaign, teaming with the Domestic Violence Advocacy Program to establish a speaker's bureau for survivors to share their stories at area schools and social organizations. A second subgroup launched a letter writing campaign targeting local legislators to increase funds for extended stays in transitional housing to accommodate those pursuing higher education and for evening child care to allow parents to attend night classes. A third committee submitted a grant proposal to a local foundation interested in women's issues to fund WOPAC's efforts. Niki herself testified at a legislative forum evaluating the impact of the state's mandatory arrest statute in domestic violence situations, working to carve out ways that victims would maintain more influence on the disposition of their cases.

Meanwhile, Niki continued her regular meetings with Gabe focused on securing Niki a part-time job that would allow her to continue her TANF benefits for her remaining 6 months of eligibility. In each meeting, they would discuss how the job search was going. She also reported that she had entered nursing school financed by a combination of scholarships and student loans. Niki would also talk about her activities with WOPAC. In response, Gabe would highlight her successes, encourage her efforts, and normalize brief setbacks as a natural occurrence in any change process. At times, Niki mentioned how proud she thought her mother would be if she knew what Niki was accomplishing. Sensing Niki's need for familial support, Gabe suggested that this might be a time for reconciliation with her mother. With Niki's consent, Gabe referred her to a Northside Family Services family counselor to discuss ways to reconnect with her mother.

Gabe maintained a consistent focus on Niki's objectives to guide the content of their meetings and to monitor and evaluate Niki's progress. One meeting in particular, he helped Niki stop and look at how far she had progressed. He chose the third objective as an example and drew a graph illustrating the dramatic increase in Niki's social support since they had begun their work together. Niki also described her progress in meeting the other objectives.

Niki and Gabe were accomplishing what they set out to achieve. Even though Niki was not yet an RN, she had secured a part-time job, and that meant her professional relationship with Gabe must end. Gabe and Niki discussed their progress, reviewed their accomplishments, and decided to wrap up their work together. Gabe emphasized the positive things that had happened in their work together and thanked Niki for teaching him to work with "stubborn young women." They both laughed about that, Niki knowing that Gabe appreciated her dogged determination. Gabe's warm handshake that wrapped up the session was accompanied by the invitation to "give me a call sometime to let me know how you're doing." Niki assured him that she would.

Questions that Focus on Unit 4

1. Activities in the development phase are guided by goals and objectives articulated in the action plan. Review the actions implemented by Gabe Thomas and Niki Lindstrom during this time. Are they goal directed? Which activities work to achieve which objectives?

2. Generalist social workers perform many tasks to "activate client resources" by functioning as consultants, resource managers, and educators. Carefully examine the case study to identify actions that Gabe takes to function in these various ways. What other possible actions could Gabe have taken?

3. Alliances are empowering. The Women's Political Action Committee (WOPAC) is a clear example of that. Imagine that you are in Transit Program social worker Evelyn Mackey's position. Evelyn works to transform the woman's support group to a social action group and to facilitate this group's alliance with other similar groups in the Northside community. What processes, activities, and skills would you use to facilitate the development of these alliances?

4. WOPAC used a legislative forum, community outreach, and grant writing as strategies to effect social change. Define and give examples

of each of these strategies. What other interventions to expand opportunities could WOPAC have used to reach its goals?

5. Gabe used a single-system design to evaluate Niki's progress toward meeting her objectives. Develop a single-system research design that would apply to evaluate the achievement of objective number 3. In doing so, answer the following:
   a. What research design are you using?
   b. Describe what is happening during each observational phase of your design.
   c. Identify the dependent variable(s).
   d. Identify the independent variable(s).
   e. Describe what measures you will use to evaluate success and produce quantifiable data.
   f. Draw a graph to illustrate how you could display your results.

6. Gabe and Niki wrapped up their work before Niki actually achieved her goal. Is this acceptable practice? What actions did Gabe take to ensure an empowering resolution of the relationship? Gabe's work with Niki demonstrates closure processes with an individual client. How might these processes differ when a social worker closes with a larger client system such as in the example of Evelyn Mackey when she wraps up her work with the WOPAC organization?

Appendix B

ASSESSING YOUR COMPETENCE

Chapter 1

Use the scale below to rate your current level of achievement on the following concepts or skills associated with each competency presented in the chapter:

1. I can accurately describe the concept or skill.
2. I can consistently identify the concept or skill when observing and analyzing practice activities.
3. I can competently implement the concept or skill in my own practice.

Articulates the value base and purposes of the social work profession

_____ Human dignity and worth as a value of social work
_____ Social justice as a value of social work
_____ The purposes of social work
_____ Professional identity

Defines generalist social work as an integration of practice, policy, and research

_____ Social work from a generalist perspective
_____ The policy–practice connection
_____ The role of research in generalist social work practice

Explains social work intervention activities at each system level of practice—micro-, mezzo-, and macrolevel, and the social work profession

_____ Microlevel system interventions
_____ Mezzolevel system interventions
_____ Macrolevel system interventions
_____ Interventions with the social work profession

Differentiates the multiple functions and roles of generalist social workers at various system levels

_____ Roles associated with the consultancy function of generalist social work: enabler, facilitator, planner, colleague/monitor
_____ Roles associated with the resource management function of generalist social work: broker and advocate, convener and mediator, activist, and catalyst
_____ Roles associated with the education function of generalist social work: teacher, trainer, outreach, researcher/scholar

Chapter 2

Use the scale below to rate your current level of achievement on the following concepts or skills associated with each competency presented in the chapter:

1. I can accurately describe the concept or skill.
2. I can consistently identify the concept or skill when observing and analyzing practice activities.
3. I can competently implement the concept or skill in my own practice.

Describes the contributions of multidisciplinary theories and perspectives that support the knowledge and skill base of generalist social work

_____ how research from various disciplines informs social work practice

_____ framework to evaluate theories of human behavior for social work practice

Summarizes the relationship between the person and environment as foundational to the ecosystems perspective for social work practice

_____ the influence of the social environment on human development

_____ the adaptive goodness-of-fit between the person and environment

_____ how environmental stress and press create problems in social functioning

Explains concepts from social systems theory for generalist social work practice

_____ the concepts of a structural view of human systems

_____ the concepts of an interactional view of human systems

_____ the concepts of a biopsychosocial view of human systems

_____ the concepts of a cultural view of human systems

Applies the steps of an ecosystems framework as a tool for generalist social work practice

_____ Step 1: identify a focal system

_____ Step 2: analyze what's happening inside the client system

_____ Step 3: analyze what's happening outside the client system

_____ Step 4: determine how the inside and outside connect

_____ Step 5: evaluate how the client system moves through time

Chapter 3

Use the scale below to rate your current level of achievement on the following concepts or skills associated with each competency presented in the chapter:

1. I can accurately describe the concept or skill.
2. I can consistently identify the concept or skill when observing and analyzing practice activities.
3. I can competently implement the concept or skill in my own practice.

Describes how expectations and personal perspectives influence perceptions, interactions, and relationships

_____ examine one's frame of reference with respect to understanding clients' experiences and shaping our expectations

_____ appraise one's style for effectively communicating in empowering ways

Delineates the values and principles of social work practice that guide practitioners to build ethical relationships with clients

_____ acceptance
_____ individualization
_____ nonjudgmentalism
_____ objectivity
_____ self-determination
_____ access to resources
_____ confidentiality
_____ accountability

Considers the influences of a social worker's personal resources and self-awareness on professional practice

_____ personal values and assets for engaging with social work clients
_____ use-of-self in professional interactions with social work clients

Explores multicultural competence for social work practice

_____ cultural competence, cultural sensitivity, and cultural responsiveness
_____ one's own level of multicultural competence

Assesses cultural competence at the personal, agency, and community levels

_____ cultural self-inventory to identify professional development goals toward becoming a competent cross-cultural social worker
_____ cultural inventory for agency settings to improve responsiveness to culturally diverse clients
_____ inventory cultural assets in a community

Chapter 4

Use the scale below to rate your current level of achievement on the following concepts or skills associated with each competency presented in the chapter:

1. I can accurately describe the concept or skill.
2. I can consistently identify the concept or skill when observing and analyzing practice activities.
3. I can competently implement the concept or skill in my own practice.

Describes the strengths perspective and discusses the implications of this view for social work practice

_____ the practice assumptions of a strengths perspective
_____ the ways in which an asset-based approach transforms social work practice orientation from problem focused to strengths focused

Defines empowerment as a process and desirable goal of social work intervention to address issues of social injustice

_____ the personal–interpersonal, sociopolitical continuum of empowerment social work
_____ the consequences of powerlessness, oppression, and victim blaming
_____ the prejudicial "isms" that contribute to oppression and social injustice

Explains how an orientation to strengths and empowerment shapes the practice of social work

_____ how collaboration and partnership define an empowering practitioner–client relationship

_____ characteristics of empowerment-centered social work
_____ empowerment strategy of integrating clinical and political practice
_____ empowerment strategy of using group modalities
_____ empowerment strategy of developing a critical consciousness
_____ empowerment strategy of engaging in praxis
_____ empowerment strategy of taking social action

Chapter 5

Use the scale below to rate your current level of achievement on the following concepts or skills associated with each competency presented in the chapter:

1. I can accurately describe the concept or skill.
2. I can consistently identify the concept or skill when observing and analyzing practice activities.
3. I can competently implement the concept or skill in my own practice.

Summarizes the perspectives that support an empowering generalist approach to social work practice
_____ infusing an ecosystems perspective
_____ reflecting a social justice commitment
_____ applying a strengths perspective
_____ collaborating with clients
_____ constructing an empowering reality

Describes the phases of dialogue, discovery, and development that guide the activities of generalist social workers
_____ relationship building in the dialogue phase of the empowering model of generalist social work
_____ examining resources in the discovery phase
_____ implementing plans of change in the development phase

Details processes and skills for each phase of the empowerment method
_____ forming partnerships in the dialogue phase
_____ articulating situations in the dialogue phase
_____ defining directions in the dialogue phase
_____ identifying strengths in the discovery phase
_____ assessing resource capabilities in the discovery phase
_____ framing solutions in the discovery phase
_____ activating resources in the development phase
_____ creating alliances in the development phase
_____ expanding opportunities in the development phase
_____ recognizing success in the development phase
_____ integrating gains in the development phase

Offers examples that apply the generalist model to practice with clients at the micro-, mezzo-, macrolevels of social work practice
_____ microlevel examples of the empowerment model of generalist social work
_____ mezzolevel examples of the empowerment model of generalist social work
_____ macrolevel examples of the empowerment model of generalist social work

Features a full-length integrative case example for multilevel generalist social work practice
_____ multilevel intervention in generalist practice

Chapter 6

Use the scale below to rate your current level of achievement on the following concepts or skills associated with each competency presented in the chapter.

1. I can accurately describe the concept or skill.
2. I can consistently identify the concept or skill when observing and analyzing practice activities.
3. I can competently implement the concept or skill in my own practice.

Describes the qualities and structure of an empowering worker–client partnership

_____ Worker expertise
_____ Client expertise
_____ Agency influences on partnership

Articulates the initial steps of developing a working partnership with a client

_____ Recognizing what clients bring
_____ Initiating collaboration
_____ Clarifying the purpose

Lists the characteristics that distinguish a worker–client relationship from a social relationship

_____ Genuineness
_____ Acceptance and respect
_____ Trustworthiness
_____ Empathy
_____ Cultural sensitivity
_____ Purposefulness

Guides workers to consider how power, privilege, and culture influence the achievement of a worker–client partnership

_____ Rights and responsibilities
_____ Oppression and powerlessness
_____ Voluntary and involuntary clients

Explains confidentiality and its impact on worker–client relationships

_____ Absolute confidentiality
_____ Relative confidentiality
_____ Informed consent
_____ Privileged communication

Chapter 7

Use the scale below to rate your current level of achievement on the following concepts or skills associated with each competency presented in the chapter.

1. I can accurately describe the concept or skill.
2. I can consistently identify the concept or skill when observing and analyzing practice activities.
3. I can competently implement the concept or skill in my own practice.

Frames an empowering style of communication to meet the purposes of social worker–client conversations.

_____ Describing the current situation
_____ Orienting toward goals
_____ Searching for strengths

Analyzes communication and processes that influence effective communication

_____ Verbal communication
_____ Nonverbal communication
_____ Culture
_____ Emotion
_____ Previous experiences

Demonstrates various ways for social workers to elicit and organize information offered by clients

_____ Allowing space
_____ Nonverbal responses
_____ Single word responses
_____ Restatement
_____ Clarification
_____ Summary clarification
_____ Questions

Identifies how workers effectively respond to client feelings expressed verbally and nonverbally

_____ Identifying feelings
_____ Verbalizing feelings
_____ Validating feelings

Delineates specific approaches for workers to communicate in difficult conversations

_____ Anger
_____ Silence
_____ Questions
_____ Feedback

Contrasts the skills necessary for responding to individuals with those necessary for responding to larger groups

_____ Facilitating discussion
_____ Respecting existing functioning

Chapter 8

Use the scale below to rate your current level of achievement on the following concepts or skills associated with each competency presented in the chapter.

1. I can accurately describe the concept or skill.
2. I can consistently identify the concept or skill when observing and analyzing practice activities.
3. I can competently implement the concept or skill in my own practice.

Demonstrates skills that guide a worker and client to reformulate a problem statement into a goal

_____ Orienting forward

_____ Framing the search for resources
_____ Considering transactional dimensions

Uses methods to understand and activate a client's motivation

_____ Defining motivation
_____ Learned helplessness
_____ Synchronizing worker and client motivation
_____ Motivating larger systems

Explains how a collaborative social worker interprets and responds to a client's resistance

_____ Resistance as motivation
_____ Cooperating with resistance
_____ Environmental resistance
_____ Mandated clients

Summarizes effective social worker responses to crisis events that require immediate action

_____ Trauma
_____ Threats of suicide
_____ Threats toward others
_____ Child abuse
_____ Elder abuse
_____ Intimate partner violence
_____ Survival needs
_____ Addiction

Chapter 9

Use the scale below to rate your current level of achievement on the following concepts or skills associated with each competency presented in the chapter.

1. I can accurately describe the concept or skill.
2. I can consistently identify the concept or skill when observing and analyzing practice activities.
3. I can competently implement the concept or skill in my own practice.

Argues the value of focusing on client strengths in social work practice

_____ Defining strengths
_____ Purposes of identifying strengths
_____ Balancing strengths and challenges

Gives examples of strengths potentially present in various human systems

_____ Individuals
_____ Families
_____ Groups
_____ Organizations
_____ Communities

Exhibits dialogue skills for social workers to shape conversations to discover client strengths

_____ Creating a solution-saturated atmosphere
_____ Searching for exceptions
_____ Detecting incremental steps

Analyzes strengths shown by ethnic group members as discovered through social work research

_____ African Americans
_____ Latino Americans
_____ Asian Americans
_____ Native Americans

Delineates strengths unique to various population groups

_____ Women
_____ Gays and lesbians
_____ Older adults
_____ Those with religious affiliations
_____ Persons with disabilities

Identifies strengths developed by clients in coping with adversity

_____ Oppression
_____ Violence
_____ Family disruption

Chapter 10

Use the scale below to rate your current level of achievement on the following concepts or skills associated with each competency presented in the chapter.

1. I can accurately describe the concept or skill.
2. I can consistently identify the concept or skill when observing and analyzing practice activities.
3. I can competently implement the concept or skill in my own practice.

Explains social work assessment from a strengths-based generalist perspective

_____ Recognizing environmental resources
_____ Finding resources in challenging situations
_____ Collaboration

Frames assessment from an ecosystemic perspective

_____ Assessing structures
_____ Assessing interactions
_____ Assessing thoughts and feelings
_____ Assessing cultural influences
_____ Assessing spiritual dimensions
_____ Assessing physical environments

Articulates the use of social work tools relevant to each level of social work practice

_____ Social histories
_____ Genograms
_____ Eco-maps
_____ Culturally sensitive assessment
_____ Social-network maps
_____ Group assessment
_____ Organizational assessment, including force field analysis
_____ Neighborhood and community assessment, including focus groups

Describes techniques for social workers to enhance assessment

_____ Interviewing significant others
_____ Contacting professionals
_____ Observation

Defines procedures for workers to record information

_____ Recordkeeping formats, including note-taking, activity logs, process recording, summary recording
_____ Legal and ethical issues in record keeping

Chapter 11

Use the scale below to rate your current level of achievement on the following concepts or skills associated with each competency presented in the chapter.

1. I can accurately describe the concept or skill.
2. I can consistently identify the concept or skill when observing and analyzing practice activities.
3. I can competently implement the concept or skill in my own practice.

Identifies appropriate roles for workers and clients in a collaborative planning process

_____ Worker–client distribution of expertise
_____ Issues affecting collaboration
_____ Planning in multiperson systems

Distinguishes goals from objectives

_____ Goals
_____ Objectives
_____ Incremental steps
_____ Explicitness
_____ Attainability
_____ Measurability
_____ Acceptability

Articulates processes for constructing actions plans

_____ Crystallizing outcome goals
_____ Writing effective objectives
_____ Prioritizing objectives
_____ Screening effective intervention strategies
_____ Delineating responsibilities
_____ Setting reviews

Analyzes contracting as a dynamic and empowering process

_____ Evolving contract
_____ Empowering contract

Chapter 12

Use the scale below to rate your current level of achievement on the following concepts or skills associated with each competency presented in the chapter:

1. I can accurately describe the concept or skill.

2. I can consistently identify the concept or skill when observing and analyzing practice activities.

3. I can competently implement the concept or skill in my own practice.

Identifies generalist skills for activating resources within clients and their environments

_____ Intervention across system levels

Details strategies for sustaining progress during the development phase

_____ Implementing action plans
_____ Enhancing clients' involvement
_____ Sustaining motivation

Clarifies how workers enhance clients' experiences of power

_____ Promoting leadership
_____ Recognizing choices
_____ Locating options

Delineates strategies for changing clients' perspectives and behaviors

_____ Offering feedback
_____ Constructing feedback
_____ Creating new concepts
_____ Using narrative strategies
_____ Trying out new behaviors

Explains key elements of effective resource management

_____ Linking clients with resources
_____ Advocating clients' rights
_____ Maximizing clients' rights

Describes educational activities for developing clients' knowledge and skills

_____ Teaching, including role playing, structured training, and modeling
_____ Sharing information: professional knowledge and self-disclosure

Chapter 13

Use the scale below to rate your current level of achievement on the following concepts or skills associated with each competency presented in the chapter:

1. I can accurately describe the concept or skill

2. I can consistently identify the concept or skill when observing and analyzing practice activities

3. I can competently implement the concept or skill in my own practice

Describes ways alliances empower clients and social workers

_____ Power of alliances

Discusses how group alliances can foster mutual aid, social action, and self-help

_____ Groups as vehicles for empowerment
_____ Facilitating groups
_____ Mutual aid in groups
_____ Social action groups
_____ Self-help groups

Explores options for strengthening natural support networks

_____ Role of social support
_____ Encouraging social support by designing environments, enhancing inter-action skills, and activating natural helpers

Examines case management as an effective strategy for coordinating services

_____ Purpose of case management
_____ Case management activities with clients, including outreach, planning, linking clients with resources, and advocacy
_____ Case management activities with the delivery system, including coordinating services, relating to other professionals, and building responsive networks of services
_____ Critical issues and ethical dilemmas

Considers the role of organizational alliances in service delivery and resource development

_____ Interagency coalitions
_____ Working on teams
_____ Leading effective meetings

Surveys professional alliances as resources of support for social work practitioners

_____ Using alliances within organizations for support, including supervision, peer review, and consultation
_____ Recognizing signs of burnout and ways to respond
_____ Professional memberships

Chapter 14

Use the scale below to rate your current level of achievement on the following concepts or skills associated with each competency presented in the chapter:

1. I can accurately describe the concept or skill.
2. I can consistently identify the concept or skill when observing and analyzing practice activities.
3. I can competently implement the concept or skill in my own practice.

Clarifies the interrelationship between opportunities and empowerment

_____ Opportunities as empowerment
_____ Empowerment in groups and communities

Explains methods for expanding resources

_____ Identifying shortages of resources
_____ Mobilizing resources
_____ Educating the public
_____ Writing grant proposals

Explicates strategies for community change through community organization and community development

_____ Elements of community organizing, including processes, models, and roles
_____ Empowerment and community development

Discerning social work as a political profession

_____ Differentiating political perspectives
_____ Social work and political perspectives

Discusses how to create more responsive social institutions through policy development

_____ Policy analysis as vehicle for change
_____ Consumer participation in policy development

Describes social action and advocacy as strategies for expanding opportunities

_____ Promoting social action
_____ Advocacy role
_____ Designing advocacy interventions

Delineates processes for legislative advocacy

_____ Legislative analysis
_____ Lobbying
_____ Legislative testimony

Chapter 15

Use the scale below to rate your current level of achievement on the following concepts or skills associated with each competency presented in the chapter:

1. I can accurately describe the concept or skill.
2. I can consistently identify the concept or skill when observing and analyzing practice activities.
3. I can competently implement the concept or skill in my own practice.

Describes the purposes of social work evaluation and research as integral to social work practice

_____ Integrating practice and research

Applies evidence-base practice to generalist social work

_____ Steps for evidence-based decision-making
_____ Implications for social work practice

Differentiates strategies for practice evaluation

_____ Progress evaluation
_____ Outcome assessment, including goal-attainment scaling
_____ Program evaluation

Explicates research

_____ Research process
_____ Research terminology, including variables, hypotheses, reliability, validity, and qualitative and quantitative data analysis
_____ Key ethical issues

Delineates single-system design

_____ Elements of single-system designs, including phases and notation
_____ Types of single-system design, including AB, B, ABC, ABAB, BAB, and multiple baseline designs
_____ Limitations of single-system designs

Chapter 16

Use the scale below to rate your current level of achievement on the following concepts or skills associated with each competency presented in the chapter:

1. I can accurately describe the concept or skill.
2. I can consistently identify the concept or skill when observing and analyzing practice activities.
3. I can competently implement the concept or skill in my own practice.

Describes social work endings

_____ Types of closure

Details endings that involve completing contracts

_____ Preparing for resolution
_____ Discussing readiness
_____ Evaluating work
_____ Sharing feelings
_____ Generalizing outcomes
_____ Firming up social supports
_____ Celebrations and rituals for groups and organizations

Specifies circumstances leading to referrals and procedures for making referrals

_____ Acknowledging limited resources
_____ Implementing legal mandates
_____ Making referrals

Guides social workers on how to respond when clients discontinue services

_____ Preparing for early discontinuation
_____ Recognizing exit clues
_____ Resolving unplanned exits

Reflects on issues associated with the deaths of clients

_____ Grief
_____ End-of-life care
_____ Grieving the death of a client

Discusses endings in the context of group-, organization-, and community-level clients

_____ Small group endings
_____ Resolving intermember relationships
_____ Endings with organizations and communities, including institutionalizing change, sustaining empowered functioning, and making transitions

References

Abramson, J., & Bronstein, L. (2008). Teams. In T. Mizrahi & L. E. Davis (Eds.), *Encyclopedia of social work: Vol. 4* (20th ed.) (pp. 199–204). Washington, DC: NASW Press.

Abramson, L. Y., Seligman, M. E. P., & Teasdale, J. C. (1978). Learned helplessness in humans: Critique and reformulation. *Journal of Abnormal Psychology, 87,* 49–74.

Acevedo-Garcia, D., Osypuk, T. L., McArdle, N., & Williams, D. R. (2008). Toward a policy-relevant analysis of geographic and racial/ethnic disparities in child health. *Health Affairs, 27*(2), 321–333.

Ackerson, B.J., & Harrison, W.D. (2000). Practitioner's perceptions of empowerment. *Families in Society, 81*(3), 238–244.

Adams, P., & Krauth, K. (1994). Empowering workers for empowerment based practice. In L. Gutiérrez, & P. Nurius (Eds.), *Education and research for empowerment practice* (pp. 183–194). Seattle, WA: University of Washington Press.

Adams, R. (1997). Empowerment, marketization, and social work. In B. Lesnick (Ed.), *Change in social work* (pp. 69–87). Aldershot, England: Arena.

Adams, R. E., Figley, C. R., & Boscarino, J. A. (2008). The compassion fatigue scale: its use with social workers following urban disaster. *Research on Social Work Practice, 18*(3), 238–250.

Aguilera, D. C., & Messick, J. M. (1982). *Crisis intervention: Theory and methodology* (4th ed.). St Louis, MO: Mosby.

Aho El Nasr, M. (1989). The term "client" in the social work profession. *International Social Work, 32,* 311–318.

Ainslie, J., & Feltey, K. (1998). Definitions and dynamics of motherhood and family in lesbian communities. In J. M. Schriver, *Human behavior and the social environment* (pp. 327–343). Boston: Allyn & Bacon.

Akamatsu, N. (1998). The talking oppression blues: Including the experience of power/powerlessness in the teaching of "cultural sensitivity." In M. McGoldrick (Ed.), *Revisioning family therapy: Race, culture, and gender in clinical practice* (pp. 129–143). New York: Guilford Press.

Akamatsu, N., Basham, K., & Olson, M. (1998). Teaching a feminist family therapy. *Journal of Feminist Family Therapy, 8*(2), 22–36.

Alameda-Lawson, T., & Lawson, M. A. (2002). Building community collaboratives. In M. O'Melia & K. K. Miley (Eds.), *Pathways to power: Readings in contextual social work practice* (pp. 108–127). Boston: Allyn & Bacon.

Alexander, R. (1997). Social workers and privileged communication in the federal legal system. *Social Work, 42*(4), 387–391.

Altpeter, M., Schopler, J. H., Galinsky, M. J., & Pennell, J. (1999). Participatory research as social work practice: When is it viable? *Journal of Progressive Human Services, 10*(2), 31–53.

American Psychiatric Association. (1994). *Diagnostic and statistical manual of mental disorders* (4th ed.). Washington, DC: Author.

Amundson, J., Stewart, K., & Valentine, L. (1993). Temptations of power and certainty. *Journal of Marital and Family Therapy, 19*(2), 111–123.

Anastas, J. W. (2008). Ethics in research. In T. Mizrahi & L. E. Davis (Eds.), *Encyclopedia of social work: Vol. 2* (20th ed.) (pp. 151–158). Washington, DC: NASW Press.

Anderson, C. M., & Stewart, S. (1983). *Mastering resistance: A practical guide to family therapy.* New York: Guilford Press.

Anderson, R. E., Carter, I., & Lowe, G. (1999). *Human behavior in the social environment: A social systems approach* (5th ed.). New York: Aldine de Gruyter.

Andrews, A. B., Motes, P. S., Floyd, A. G., Flerx, V. C., & Lopez-DeFede, A. (2005). Building evaluation capacity in community-based organizations: Reflections of an empowerment evaluation team. *Journal of Community Practice, 13*(4), 85–104.

Aubrey, J. (2004). The roots and process of social action. *Groupwork, 14*(2), 6–23.

Austin, C. D. (1992). Have we oversold case management? *Journal of Case Management, 1*(2), 61–65.

Austin, C. D. (1993). Case management: A systems perspective. *Families in Society, 74,* 451–458.

Austin, C. D. (1996). Aging and long term care. In C. D. Austin & R. W. McClelland (Eds.), *Perspectives on case management practice* (pp. 1–16). Milwaukee, WI: Families International.

Austin, C. D., Des Camp, E., Flux, D., McClelland, R. W., & Sieppert, J. (2005). Community development with older adults in their neighborhoods: The elder friendly communities program. *Families in Society, 86*(3), 401–409.

Austin, C. D., & McClelland, R. W. (1996). Introduction: Case management—Everybody's doing it. In C. D. Austin & R. W. McClelland (Eds.), *Perspectives on case management practice* (pp. 1–16). Milwaukee, WI: Families International.

Bailey, D. (1994). Organizational empowerment from self to interbeing. In L. Gutiérrez & P. Nurius (Eds.), *Education and research for empowerment practice* (pp. 37–42). Seattle, WA: University of Washington Press.

Bailey, D. (2005). Using an action research approach to involving service users in the assessment of professional competence. *European Journal of Social Work, 8*(2), 165–179.

Baines, D. (1997). Feminist social work in the inner-city: The challenges of race, class, and gender. *Affilia, 12*(3), 297–317.

Baines, D. (2000). Everyday practices of race, class and gender: Struggles, skills, and radical social work. *Journal of Progressive Human Services, 11*(2), 5–27.

Balgopal, P. R. (2000). Social work practice with immigrants and refugees: An overview. In P. R. Balgopal (Ed.), *Social work practice with immigrants and refugees* (pp. 1–29). New York: Columbia University Press.

Bandler, R., & Grinder, J. (1975). *The structure of magic.* Palo Alto, CA: Science and Behavior Books.

Bandura, A. (1984). Recycling misconceptions of perceived self-efficacy. *Cognitive Therapy and Research, 8*(3), 231–255.

Bandura, A. (1986). *Social foundations of thought and action: A social-cognitive theory.* Englewood Cliffs, NJ: Prentice Hall.

Bandura, A., & Cervone, D. (1983). Self-evaluative and self-efficacy mechanisms governing the motivational effects of goals systems. *Journal of Personality and Social Psychology, 45,* 1017–1028.

Bandura, A., & Schunk, D. H. (1981). Cultivating competence, self-efficacy, and intrinsic interest through proximal self-motivation. *Journal of Personality and Social Psychology, 41*(3), 586–598.

Baradell, J. G., & Klein, K. (1993). Relationship of life stress and body consciousness to hypervigilant decision making. *Journal of Personality and Social Psychology, 64*(2), 267–273.

Bargal, D. (2000). The future development of occupational social work. *Administration in Social Work, 23*(3/4), 139–156.

Barker, R. L. (2003). *The social work dictionary* (5th ed.). Washington, DC: NASW Press.

Barker, R. L., & Branson, D. M. (1992). *Forensic social work: Legal aspects of professional practice.* New York: The Haworth Press.

Barnes, C., & Mercer, G. (2004). *Implementing the social model of disability: Theory and research.* Leeds, England: Disability Press.

Barnes, S. L. (2001). Stressors and strengths: A theoretical and practical examination of nuclear, single-parent, and augmented African American families. *Families in Society, 82*(5), 449–460.

Bartlett, H. (1970). *The common base of social work practice.* New York: National Association of Social Workers.

Beaudin, C. L., & Kramer, T. L. (2005). Evaluation and treatment of depression in managed care (Part II): Quality improvement programs. *Disease Management & Health Outcomes, 13*(5), 307–316.

Beavers, W. R., & Hampson, R. B. (1990). *Successful families: Assessment and intervention.* New York: Norton.

Beavers, W. R., & Hampson, R. B. (1993). Measuring family competence: The Beavers Systems Model. In F. Walsh (Ed.), *Normal family processes* (2nd ed.) (pp. 73–103). New York: Guilford Press.

Behnia, B. (2004). Trust building from the perspective of survivors of war and torture. *Social Service Review, 78*(1), 26–40.

Belenky, M. F., Clinchy, B. M., Goldberger, N. R., & Tarule, J. M. (1986). *Women's ways of knowing: The development of self, voice, and mind.* New York: Basic Books.

Bem, S. L. (1993). *The lenses of gender: Transforming the debate on sexual inequality.* New Haven, CT: Yale University Press.

Ben-Ari, A. (1995). Coming out: A dialectic of intimacy and privacy. *Families in Society, 76,* 306–314.

Beresford, P. (1999). Towards an empowering social work practice: Learning from service users and their movements. In W. Shera & L. Wells (Eds.), *Empowerment practice in social work: Developing richer conceptual foundations* (pp. 259–277). Toronto, Canada: Canadian Scholars' Press.

Beresford, P. (2003, February). Where's the evidence? *Mental Health Today,* pp. 31–34.

Beresford, P., Brough, P., & Turner, M. (2001). Where do you stand with service users? *Journal of Social Work, 1*(1), 119–120.

Beresford, P., & Croft, S. (2003). Service users and practitioners reunited: The key component for social work reform. *British Journal of Social Work, 34*(1), 53–68.

Berg, I. K. (1994). *Family based services: A solution-focused approach.* New York: Norton

Berg, I. K., & De Jong, P. (1996). Solution-building conversations: Co-constructing a sense of competence with clients. *Families in Society, 77,* 376–391.

Berg, I. K., & Miller, S. D. (1992). *Working with the problem drinker: A solution-focused approach.* New York: Norton.

Berger, P., & Neuhaus, J. R. (1977). *To empower people: The role of mediating structures in public policy.* Washington, DC: American Enterprise Institute.

Berk, L. E. (2007). *Development through the lifespan* (4th ed.). Boston: Allyn & Bacon.

Berlin, S. (2005). The value of acceptance in social work direct practice: A historical and contemporary view. *Social Service Review, 79*(3), 482–510.

Bernal, G., & Shapiro, E. (1996). Cuban families. In M. McGoldrick, J. Giordano, & J. K. Pearce (Eds.), *Ethnicity and family therapy* (2nd ed.) (pp. 155–168). New York: Guilford Press.

Bethea, L. (1999). Primary prevention of child abuse. *American Family Physician, 59*(6), 1577–1597.

Bhul, K., King, M., Dein, S., & O'Connor, W. (2008). Ethnicity and religious coping with mental distress. *Journal of Mental Health, 17*(2), 141–151.

Biestek, F. P. (1957). *The casework relationship.* Chicago: Loyola University Press.

Bilingsley, A. (1992). *Climbing Jacob's ladder: The enduring legacy of African American families.* New York: Simon & Schuster.

Birdwhistell, R. (1955). Background to kinesics. *Etc., 13,* 10–18.

Birnbaum, M., & Cicchetti, A. (2000). The power of purposeful sessional endings in each group encounter. *Social Work with Groups, 23*(3), 37–52.

Bisman, C. (2004). Social work values: The moral core of the profession. *British Journal of Social Work, 34,* 109–123.

Black, K. (2004). Advance directive communication with hospitalized elderly patients: Social workers' roles and practices. *Journal of Gerontological Social Work, 43*(2/3), 131–145.

Black, K. (2007). Advance care planning throughout the end-of-life: Focusing the lens for social work practice. *Journal of Social Work in End-of-Life & Palliative Care, 3*(2), 39–58.

Blecher, J. R., & Hegar, R. L. (1991). Social work and the casualties of capitalism: Empowerment of the urban poor. *Journal of Progressive Human Services, 2*(1), 39–53.

Bliss, M., Oglery-Oliver, E., Jackson, E., Harp, S., & Kaslow, N. (2008). African American women's readiness to change abusive relationships. *Journal of Family Violence, 23*(3), 161–171.

Bloch, D. S. (1999). Adolescent suicide as a public health threat. *Journal of Child and Adolescent Psychiatric Nursing, 12*(1), 26–38.

Bloom, M., Fischer, J., & Orme, J. G. (2006). *Evaluating practice: Guidelines for the accountable professional* (5th ed.). Boston: Allyn & Bacon.

Bloor, R., & Pearson, D. (2004). Brief solution-focused organizational redesign. *International Journal of Mental Health, 33*(2), 44–53.

Blount, M., Thyer, B. A., & Frye, T. (1996). *Social work practice with Native Americans.* In D. F. Harrison, B. A. Thyer, & J. S. Wodarski (Eds.), *Cultural diversity and social work practice* (2nd ed.) (pp. 257–298). Springfield, IL: Charles C Thomas.

Boehm, A., & Staples, L. H. (2002). The functions of the social worker in empowering: The voices of consumers and professionals. *Social Work, 47*(4), 449–461.

Boehm, A., & Staples, L. H. (2004). Empowerment: The point of view of consumers. *Families in Society, 85*(2), 270–280.

Bolen, R. M., & Hall, J. C. (2007). Managed care and evidence-based practice: The untold story. *Journal of Social Work Education, 43*(3), 463–479.

Book, H. E. (1988). Empathy: Misconceptions and misuses in psychotherapy. *American Journal of Psychiatry, 145*(4), 420–424.

Bower, G. H. (1981). Mood and memory. *American Psychologist, 36*, 129–148.

Boyd-Franklin, N. (1989). *Black families in therapy: A multisystems approach.* New York: Guilford Press.

Boyd-Franklin, N. (1992, July). *African American families in therapy.* Presentation for the Illinois Chapter of the National Association of Social Workers, Springfield, IL.

Boyd-Franklin, N. (1993). Race, class, and poverty. In F. Walsh (Ed.), *Normal family processes* (2nd ed.) (pp. 361–376). New York: Guilford Press.

Braye, S., & Preston-Shoot, M. (1995). *Empowering practice in social care.* Philadelphia, PA: Open University Press.

Braye, S., & Preston-Shoot, M. (2005). Emerging from out of the shadows? Service user and carer involvement in systematic reviews. *Evidence and Policy, 1*(2), 173–193.

Breton, M. (1993). Relating competence-promotion and empowerment. *Journal of Progressive Human Services, 5*(1), 27–44.

Breton, M. (1994). On the meaning of empowerment and empowerment-oriented social work practice. *Social Work with Groups, 17*(3), 23–37.

Breton, M. (1999). Empowerment practice in a post-empowerment era. In W. Shera & L. Wells (Eds.), *Empowerment practice in social work: Developing richer conceptual foundations* (pp. 222–233). Toronto, Canada: Canadian Scholars' Press.

Breton, M. (2001). Neighborhood resiliency. *Journal of Community Practice, 9*(1), 21–36.

Breton, M. (2002). Empowerment practice in Canada and the United States: Restoring policy issues at the center of social work. *The Social Policy Journal, 1*(1), 19–34.

Breton, M. (2004). An empowerment perspective. In C. D. Garvin, L. M. Gutiérrez, & M. J. Galinsky (Eds.), *Handbook of social work with groups* (pp. 58–75). New York: Guildford Press.

Breton, M. (2006). Path dependence and the place of social action in social work practice. *Social Work with Groups, 29*(4), 25–44.

Bricker-Jenkins, M. (1991). The propositions and assumptions of feminist social work practice. In M. Bricker-Jenkins, N. R. Hooyman, & N. Gottlieb (Eds.), *Feminist social work practice in clinical settings* (pp. 271–303). Newbury Park, CA: Sage.

Briggs, H. E., Briggs, A. D., & Leary, J. D. (2005). Promoting culturally competent systems of care through statewide family advocacy networks. *Best Practices in Mental Health, 1*(2), 77–99.

Brill, N. I., & Levine, J. (2002). *Working with people: The helping process* (7th ed.). Boston: Allyn & Bacon.

Bronstein, L. R., & Admiraal, K. (2005). Implications of an aging population on the delivery of public sector social services. *Families in Society, 86*(1), 47–54.

Brower, A. M. (1988). Can the ecological systems model guide social work practice? *Social Service Review, 62*, 411–429.

Brower, A. M. (1996). Group development as constructed social reality revisited: The constructivism of small groups. *Families in Society, 77*, 336–343.

Brown, E. G. (1982). Rationale for a generalist approach to social work practice. In D. S. Sanders, O. Kurren, & J. Fischer (Eds.), *Fundamentals of social work practice* (pp. 119–130), Belmont, CA: Wadsworth.

Brown, P. A. (1994). Participatory research: A new paradigm for social work. In L. Gutiérrez & P. Nurius (Eds.), *Education and research for empowerment practice* (pp. 293–303). Seattle, WA: Center for Policy and Practice Research, School of Social Work, University of Washington.

Browne, C., & Broderick, A. (1994). Asian and Pacific Island elders: Issues for social work practice and education. *Social Work, 39*, 252–259.

Brun, C., & Rapp, R. C. (2001). Strengths-based case management: Individuals' perspectives on strengths and the case manager relationship. *Social Work, 46*(3), 278–289.

Buchanan, R. J., Chakravorty, B., Bolin, J., Wang, S., & Kim, M-S. (2004). Decision making and the use of advance directives among nursing home residents at admission and one year after admission. *Journal of Social Work in Long-term Care, 3*(2), 3–12.

Burgoon, J. K., Buller, D. B., & Woodall, W. G. (1996). *Nonverbal communication: The unspoken dialogue* (2nd ed.). New York: Harper & Row.

Busby, D. M., Glenn, E., Stegell, G. L., & Adamson, D. W. (1993). Treatment issues for survivors of physical and sexual abuse. *Journal of Marital and Family Therapy, 19*, 377–392.

Burke, A. C., & Gregoire, T. K. (2007). Substance abuse treatment outcomes for coerced and noncoerced clients. *Health and Social Work, 32*(1), 7–15.

Campos, B., Schetter, C. D., Abdou, C. M., Hobel, C. J., Glynn, L. M., & Sandman, C. A. (2008). Familialism, social support, and stress: Positive implications for pregnant Latinas. *Cultural Diversity and Ethnic Minority Psychology, 14*(2), 155–162.

Canda, E. R. (1988). Conceptualizing spirituality for social work: Insights from diverse perspectives. *Social Thought, 14*(1), 30–46.

Canda, E. R. (2001). Transcending through disability and death: Transpersonal themes in living with cystic fibrosis. *Social Thought, 20*(1/2), 109–134.

Canda, E. R. (2002). The significance of spirituality for resilient response to chronic illness: A qualitative study of adults with cystic fibrosis. In D. Saleebey (Ed.), *The strengths perspective in social work practices* (3rd ed.) (pp. 63–79). Boston: Allyn & Bacon.

Canda, E. R., & Furman, L. (1999). *Spiritual diversity in social work practice: The heart of helping.* New York: The Free Press.

Carr, E. W. (2003). Rethinking empowerment theory using a feminist lens: The importance of process. *Affilia, 18*(1), 8–20.

Catalano, S. (2007). *Intimate partner: Violence in the United States.* U. S. Department of Justice, Bureau of Justice Statistics. Retrieved May 15, 2008, from www.ojp.usdoj.gov/bjs/pub/pdf/ipvus.pdf

Carter, B., & McGoldrick, M. (1989). Overview: The changing family life cycle: A framework for family therapy. In B. Carter, & M. McGoldrick (Eds.), *The changing family life cycle: A framework for family therapy* (2nd ed. (pp. 3–28). Boston: Allyn & Bacon.

Carter, B., & McGoldrick, M. (2005). *The expanded family life cycle: Individual, family, and social perspectives* (3rd ed.). Boston: Allyn & Bacon.

Cartledge, G., Kea, C., & Simmons-Reed, E. (2002). Serving culturally diverse children with serious emotional disturbance and their families. *Journal of Child and Family Studies, 11*(1), 113–126.

Cassano, D. R., & Dunlop, J. (2005). Participatory action research with South Asian immigrant women: A Canadian example.

Critical Social Work, 6(1). Retrieved June 5, 2008, from www.criticalsocialwork.com/units/socialwork/critical.nsf/inToc/8B8307415348655A85256FD7007474D9

Castex, G. (1994a). The function of stereotyping processes: A challenge for practice. In L. G. Gardella, R. Daniel, M. C. Joyner, N. Mokuau, & J. M. Schriver (Eds.), *In memory of Ronald C. Federico: A BPD Festschrift* (pp. 8–16). Springfield, MO.

Castex, G. M. (1994b). Providing services to Hispanic/ Latino populations: Profiles in diversity. *Social Work, 39*, 288–297.

Centers for Disease Control and Prevention [CDC]. (2006). *Understanding intimate partner violence: Fact sheet.* Retrieved May 15, 2008, from www.cdc.gov/ncipc/dvp/ipv_factsheet.pdf

Chambers, D. E. (1993). *Social policy and social programs: A method for the practical public policy analyst* (2nd ed.). New York: Macmillan.

Chambers, D. E., & Wedel, K. (2009). Social policy and social programs. In *A method for the practical public policy analyst* (5th ed.). Boston: Allyn & Bacon.

Chapin, R. K. (1995). Social policy development: The strengths perspective. *Social Work, 40*, 506–514.

Chau, K. (1989). Sociocultural dissonance among ethnic minority populations. *Social Casework, 70*, 224–239.

Cheung, Y. W., Bong-Ho, M., & Tak-Sing, C. (2005). Personal empowerment and life satisfaction among self-help group members in Hong Kong. *Small Group Research, 36*(3), 354–377.

Child Welfare League of America [CWLA]. (2001). *Alcohol, other drugs, & child welfare.* Retrieved June 5, 2008 from www.cwla.org/programs/bhd/aodbrochure.pdf

Choi, K-H., & Wynne, M. E. (2000). Providing services to Asian Americans with developmental disabilities and their families: Mainstream service providers' perspectives. *Community Mental Health Journal, 36*(6), 589–595.

Chung, D. K. (1992). Asian cultural commonalities: A comparison with mainstream American culture. In S. M. Furuto, R. Biswas, D. K. Chung, K. Marase, & F. Ross-Sheriff (Eds.), *Social work practice with Asian Americans* (pp. 27–44). Newbury Park, CA: Sage.

Claiborne, N., & Lawson, H. (2005). An intervention framework for collaboration. *Families in Society, 86*(1), 93–103.

Clark, E. J. (2008). National Association of Social Workers. In T. Mizrahi & L. E. Davis (Eds.), *Encyclopedia of social work: Vol. 3* (20th ed.) (pp. 292–295). Washington, DC: NASW Press.

Clark, P. G. (1989). The philosophical foundation of empowerment. *Journal of Aging and Health, 1*(3), 267–285.

Clements J. A., & Rosenwald M. (2007). Foster parents' perspectives on LGB youth in the child welfare system. *Journal of Gay and Lesbian Social Services, 19*(1), 57–69.

Clowes, L. (2003). Cultural competence in services to children and families. *Focal Point: A National Bulletin on Family Support and Children's Mental Health, 17*(1), 21–23. Retrieved June 5, 2008, from www.rtc.pdx.edu/PDF/fpS03.pdf

Coates, D., Renzaglia, G. J., & Embree, M. C. (1983). When helping backfires: Help and helplessness. In J. D. Fisher, A. Nadler, & B. M. DePaulo (Eds.), *New directions in helping, Vol 1: Recipient reactions to aid* (pp. 251–279). New York: Academic Press.

Cohen, M. B. (1998). Perceptions of power in client/worker relationships. *Families in Society, 79*(4), 433–442.

Cohen, M. B. (2007). Using solution-oriented techniques in mutual aid groups. *Social Work with Groups, 30*(4), 41–58.

Cohen M. B., & Graybeal C. T. (2007). Using solution-oriented techniques in mutual aid groups. *Social Work with Groups, 30*(4), 41–58.

Collopy, B. J. (1992). Autonomy in long term care: Some crucial distinctions. In S. M. Rose (Ed.), *Case management and social work practice* (pp. 56–76), New York: Longman.

Congress, E. (1994). The use of culturagrams to assess and empower culturally diverse families. *Families in Society, 75*, 531–540.

Cooper, B. (2001). Constructivism in social work: Towards a participative practice viability. *British Journal of Social Work, 31*, 721–738.

Corcoran, J. (2003). *Clinical applications of evidence-based family interventions.* New York: Oxford.

Corcoran, J., & Nichols-Casebolt, A. (2004). Risk and resilience ecological framework for assessment and goal formulation. *Child and Adolescent Social Work Journal, 21*(3), 211–235.

Corey, M. S., & Corey, G. (2006). *Groups: process and practice* (7th ed.). Pacific Grove, CA: Brooks/Cole.

Council on Social Work Education [CSWE]. (2008). *Educational policy and accreditation standards.* Retrieved May 27, 2008. from www.cswe.org

Couoton, C. (2005). The place of community in social work practice research: Conceptual and methodological developments. *Social Work Research, 29*(2), 73–86.

Cowger, C. D. (1992). Assessment of client strengths. In D. Saleebey (Ed.), *The strengths perspective in social work practice* (pp. 139–147). New York: Longman.

Cowger, C. D. (1994). Assessing client strengths: Clinical assessment for client empowerment. *Social Work, 39*, 262–268.

Cowger, C. D., & Snively, C. A. (2002). Assessing client strengths: Individual, family, and community empowerment. In D. Saleebey (Ed.), *The strengths perspective in social work practice.* (3rd ed.) (pp. 106–123). Boston: Allyn & Bacon.

Cox, E. O. (1991). The critical role of social action in empowerment oriented groups. *Social Work with Groups, 14*(3/4), 77–90.

Cox, E. O. (2001). Community practice issues in the 21st century: Questions and challenges for empowerment-oriented practitioners. *Journal of Community Practice, 9*(1), 37–55.

Cox, E. O., & Parsons, R. J. (1992, March). *Building community through empowerment-oriented groups.* Paper prepared for Council on Social Work Education's Annual Program Meeting. Kansas City, MO.

Cox, E. O., & Parsons, R. (1993). *Empowerment-oriented social work practice with the elderly.* Pacific Grove, CA: Brooks/Cole.

Crystal, D. (1989). Asian Americans and the myth of the model minority. *Social Casework, 70*, 405–413.

Csikai, E. L. (2008). End-of-life decisions. In T. Mizrahi & L. E. Davis (Eds.), *Encyclopedia of social work: Vol. 2* (20th ed.) (pp. 126–132). Washington, DC: NASW Press.

Cummings, S. M., & MacNeil, G. (2008). Caregivers of older clients with severe mental illness: Perceptions of burdens and rewards. *Families in Society, 89*(1), 51–59.

Daniel, C. A. (2004). Social work with West Indian families: A multilevel approach. *Journal of Immigrant and Refugee Services, 2*(3/4), 135–145.

David, G. (2001). Aging, religion, and spirituality: Advancing meaning in later life. *Social Thought, 20*(3/4), 129–140.

Davidson, T. & Davidson, J. (1996). Confidentiality and managed care: Ethical and legal concerns. *Health and Social Work, 21*, 208–215.

Danis, F. S. (2004). Domestic violence: An overview. In F. S. Danis & L. L. Lockhart (Eds.), *Breaking the silence in social work education: Domestic violence modules for foundation courses* (pp. 1–8). Alexandria, VA: Council on Social Work Education.

Davis, I. L. (1992). Client identification and outreach. In B. S. Vourlekis & R. R. Greene (Eds.), *Social work case management* (pp. 27–34). New York: Aldine de Gruyter.

Dawson, K., & Berry, M. (2002). Engaging families in child welfare services: An evidence-based approach to best practice. *Child Welfare, 82*(2), 293–317.

Dean, R. G. (1989). Ways of knowing in clinical practice. *Clinical Social Work Journal, 17*(2), 116–127.

Dean, R. G. (1993). Constructivism: An approach to clinical practice. *Smith College Studies in Social Work, 63*(2), 127–146.

Dean, R. G. (2001). The myth of cross-cultural competence. *Families in Society, 82*(6), 623–630.

Dean, R. G., & Rhodes, M. L. (1998). Social constructionism and ethics: What makes a "better" story? *Families in Society, 79*(3), 254–262.

DeAngelis, T. (2002). New data on lesbian, gay and bisexual mental health. *Monitor On Psychology, 33*(2). Retrieved June 5, 2008, from www.apa.org/monitor/feb02/newdata.html

DeCoster, V. A., & George, L. (2005). An empowerment approach for elders living with diabetes: A pilot study of a community-based self-help group: The Diabetes Club. *Educational Gerontology, 31*(9), 699–713.

De Jong, P., & Berg, I. K. (2002). *Interviewing for solutions* (2nd ed.). Belmont, CA: Wadsworth.

De Jong, P., & Miller, S. D. (1995). How to interview for client strengths. *Social Work, 40*, 729–736.

Delgado, M., & Barton, K. (1998). Murals in Latino communities: Social indicators of community strengths. *Social Work, 43*(4), 346–356.

Dempsey, I., & Dunst, C. J. (2004). Helpgiving styles and parent empowerment in families with a young child with a disability. *Journal of Intellectual & Developmental Disability, 29*(1), 40–51.

Dennison, S. T., Poole, J., & Qaqish, B. (2007). Students' perceptions of social work: Implications for strengthening the image of social work among college students. *Social Work, 52*(4), 350–360.

Department of Defense Task Force on Mental Health [DOD]. (2007). *An achievable vision: Report of the Department of Defense Task Force on Mental Health.* Falls Church, VA: Defense Health Board. Retrieved June 10, 2008, from www.taps.org/download/DOD%20Mental%20Health%20Task%20Force%20Report.pdf

DePoy, E., Hartman, A., & Haslett, D. (1999). Critical action research: A model for social work knowing. *Social Work, 44*(6), 560–569.

de Shazer, S. (1982). *Patterns of brief family therapy: An ecosystemic approach.* New York: Guilford Press.

de Shazer, S. (1985). *Keys to solution in brief therapy.* New York: W. W. Norton.

de Shazer, S. (1988). *Clues: Investigating solutions in brief therapy.* New York: W. W. Norton.

de Shazer, S. (1989). Resistance revisited. *Contemporary Family Therapy, 11*(4), 227–233.

Dessel, A., Rogge, M. E., & Garlington, S. B. (2006). Using intergroup dialogue to promote social justice and change. *Social Work, 51*(4), 303–315.

Devore, W. (1987). Developing ethnic sensitivity for the counseling process: A social work perspective. In P. Pedersen (Ed.), *Handbook of cross-cultural counseling and therapy* (pp. 93–98). New York: Praeger.

Devore, W., & Schlesinger E. G. (1999). *Ethnic-sensitive social work practice* (3rd ed.). Boston: Allyn & Bacon.

Dewees, M. (2001). Building cultural competence for work with diverse families: Strategies from the privileged side. *Journal of Ethnic and Cultural Diversity in Social Work, 9*(3/4), 33–51.

Dickson, D. T. (1998). *Confidentiality and privacy in social work: A guide to the law for practitioners and students.* New York: The Free Press.

Dietz, C. A. (2000). Responding to oppression and abuse: A feminist challenge to clinical social work. *Affilia, 15*(3), 369–389.

Dinerman, M. (1992). Managing the maze: Case management and service delivery. *Administration in Social Work, 16*(1), 1–9.

DiNitto, D., M., & Cummins, L. K. (2007). *Social welfare policies and public policy* (6th ed.). Boston: Allyn & Bacon.

Diwan, S., Jonnalagadda, S. S., & Balaswamy, S. (2004). Resources predicting positive and negative affect during the experience of stress: A study of older Asian Indian immigrants in the United States. *Gerontologist, 44*(5), 605–614.

Dodd, P., & Gutiérrez, L. (1990). Preparing students for the future: A power perspective on community practice. *Administration in Social Work, 14*(2), 63–78.

Dolgoff, R., Loewenberg, F. M., & Harrington, D. (2004). *Ethical decisions for social work practice* (7th ed.). Pacific Grove, CA: Brooks/Colo.

Donaldson, L. P. (2004). Toward validating the therapeutic benefits of empowerment-oriented social action groups. *Social Work with Groups, 27*(2/3), 159–175.

Dore, M. M., & Alexander, L. B. (1996). Preserving families at risk of child abuse and neglect: The role of the helping alliance. *Child Abuse and Neglect, 20*, 349–361.

Drake, B. (1994). Relationship competencies in child welfare services. *Social Work, 39*, 595–602.

Dressel, P. (1992). Patriarchy and social welfare work. In Y. Hasenfeld (Ed.), *Human services as complex organizations* (pp. 205–223). Newbury Park, CA: Sage.

DuBois, B., & Miley, K. K. (2004, February). *Ethical principles for empowerment social work.* Council on Social Work Education Annual Program Meeting, Anaheim, CA.

DuBois, B., & Miley, K. K. (2008). *Social work: An empowering profession* (6th ed.). Boston: Allyn & Bacon.

DuBois, B., Miley, K., & O'Melia, M. (1993, April). *Applying an empowerment process in social work practice.* Paper presented at the Central Midwest Conference on Child Abuse, Moline, IL.

Dunst, C. J. (1993, April). *Empowerment strategies in human services programs.* Paper presented for the Central Midwest Conference on Child Abuse, Moline, IL.

Dunst, C. J., Boyd, K., Trivette, C. M., & Hamby, D. W. (2002). Family-oriented program models and professional helpgiving practices. *Family Relations, 51*(3), 221–229.

Dunst, C. J., & Trivette, C. M. (1988). Helping, helplessness, and harm. In J. C. Witt, S. N. Elliot, & F. M. Gresham (Eds.), *Handbook of behavior therapy* (pp. 343–376). New York: Plenum Press.

Durrant, M., & Kowalski, K. (1992). Enhancing views of competence. In S. Friedman (Ed.), *The new language of change* (pp. 107–137). New York: Guilford Press.

Dyche, L., & Zayas, L. H. (1995). The value of curiosity and naivete for the cross-cultural psychotherapist. *Family Process, 34*, 389–399.

Dykeman, J., Nelson, R., & Appleton, V. (1995). Building strong working alliances with American Indian families. *Social Work in Education, 17*(3), 148–158.

Dziegielewski, S. F., Campbell, K., & Turnage, B. F. (2005). Domestic violence: Focus groups from the survivors' perspective.

Journal of Human Behavior in the Social Environment, 11(2), 9–23.

East, J. F., Manning, S. S., & Parsons, R. J. (2002). Social work empowerment agenda and group work: A workshop. In S. Henry, J. East, & C. Schmitz (Eds.), *Social work with groups: Mining the gold.* (pp. 41–53). New York: Haworth Press.

Egan, G. (2002). *The skilled helper: A problem-management approach to helping* (7th ed.). Pacific Grove, CA: Brooks/Cole.

Egan, M., & Kadushin, G. (2005). Managed care in home health: Social work practice and unmet client needs. *Social Work in Health Care, 41*(2), 1–18.

Ekman, P., & Friesen, W. V. (1975). *Unmasking the face.* Englewood Cliffs, NJ: Prentice Hall.

El-Bassel, N., Chen, D-R., & Cooper, D. (1998). Social support and social network profiles among women on methadone. *Social Service Review, 72*(3), 379–401.

Ely, G. E. (2004). Domestic violence and immigrant communities in the United States: A review of women's unique needs and recommendations for social work practice and research. *Stress, Trauma, and Crisis, 7,* 223–241.

Erikson, E. H. (1963). *Childhood and society* (2nd ed.). New York: Norton.

Evans, C. (2004). Reflections on a model of empowered user involvement. *Journal of Integrated Care, 12*(6), 22–27.

Evans, C., & Jones, R. (2004). Engagement and empowerment, research and relevance: Comments on user controlled research. *Research Policy and Planning, 22*(2), 5–13.

Evans, E. N. (1992). Liberation theology, empowerment theory and social work practice with the oppressed. *International Social Work, 35,* 135–147.

Evans, G., & Farberow, N. L. (1988). *The encyclopedia of suicide.* New York: Facts on File.

Everett, J. E., Homstead, K., & Drisko, J. (2007). Frontline worker perceptions of the empowerment process in community-based agencies. *Social Work, 52*(2), 161–170.

Ezell, M. (1994). Advocacy practice of social workers. *Families in Society, 75,* 36–46.

Falicov, C. J. (1996). Mexican families. In M. McGoldrick, J. Giordano, & J. K. Pearce (Eds.), *Ethnicity and family therapy* (2nd ed.) (pp. 169–182). New York: Guilford Press.

Fant, R. S., & Ross, A. L. (1983). Supervision of child care staff. In H. Weissman, I. Epstein, & A. Savage (Eds.), *Agency-based social work: Neglected aspects of clinical practice* (pp. 238–250). Philadelphia: Temple University Press.

Farley, Y. R.(2007). Making the connection: Spirituality, trauma and resiliency. *Journal of Religion & Spirituality in Social Work, 26*(1,), 1–15

Faver, C. (2001). Rights, responsibility, and relationship: Motivation for women's social activism. *Affilia, 16*(3), 314–336.

Federal Interagency Forum on Aging-Related Statistics [Forum]. (2008). *Older Americans 2008: Key indicators of well-being.* Retrieved May 12, 2008 from agingstats.gov/agingstatsdotnet/Main_Site/Data/2008_Documents/OA_2008.pdf

Feld, S., & Radin, N. (1982). *Social psychology: For social work and the mental health professions.* New York: Columbia University Press.

Ferguson, K. M., Wu, Q., Dyrness, G., & Spruijt-Metz, D. (2007). Perceptions of faith and outcomes in faith-based programs for homeless youth: A grounded theory approach. *Journal of Social Service Research, 33*(4), 25–43.

Ferriter, M. (1993). Computer aided interviewing in psychiatric social work. *Computers in Human Services, 9*(1/2), 59–72.

Fetterman, D. M. (1996). Empowerment evaluation: An introduction to theory and practice. In D. M. Fetterman, S. J. Kaftarian, & A. Wandersman (Eds.), *Empowerment evaluation: Knowledge and tools for self-assessment and accountability* (pp. 3–46). Thousand Oaks, CA: Sage.

Fetterman, D. M. (2002). Empowerment evaluation: Building communities of practice and a culture of learning. *American Journal of Community Psychology, 30*(1), 89–102.

Figley, C. R. (1995). *Compassion fatigue: Coping with secondary traumatic stress disorders in those who treat the traumatized.* New York: Brunner/Mazel.

Figueira-McDonough, J., Netting, F. E., & Nichols-Casebolt, A. (2001). Subjugated knowledge in gender-integrated social work education: Call for a dialogue. *Affilia, 16*(4), 411–431.

Finn, J. L., & Jacobson, M. (2003). Just practice: Steps toward a new social work paradigm. *Journal of Social Work Education, 39*(1), 57–78.

Fischer, J. (1973). An eclectic approach to therapeutic casework. In J. Fischer (Ed.), *Interpersonal helping: Emerging approaches for social work practice* (pp. 317–335). Springfield, IL: Charles C Thomas.

Fischer, J. (1978). *Effective casework practice: An eclectic approach.* New York: McGraw Hill.

Fisher, M. (2002). The role of service users in problem formulation and technical aspects of social research. *Social Work Education, 21*(3), 305–312.

Fleming, R., Baum, A., & Singer, J. E. (1985). Social support and the physical environment. In S. Cohen, & S. L. Syme (Eds.), *Social support and health* (pp. 327–345). New York: Academic Press.

Flower, J. (1998). A toolkit for building a healthy city. *National Civic Review, 87*(14), 293–310.

Flowers, P., & Buston, K. (2001). "I was terrified of being different": Exploring gay men's accounts of growing-up in a heterosexist society. *Journal of Adolescence, 24,* 51–65.

Fook, J. (2002). *Social work: Critical theory and practice.* Thousand Oaks, CA: Sage.

Fong, R. (1997). Child welfare practice with Chinese families: Assessment issues for immigrants from the People's Republic of China. *Journal of Family Social Work, 2*(1), 33–47.

Fong, R., & Mokuau, N. (1994). Not simply "Asian American": Periodical literature review on Asians and Pacific Islanders. *Social Work, 39,* 298–306.

Fortune, A. E., Pearlingi, B., & Rochelle, C. D. (1992). Reactions to termination of individual treatment. *Social Work, 37,* 171–178.

Frame, M. W. (2001). The spiritual genogram in training and supervision. *The Family Journal, 9*(2), 109–115.

Franco, L. M.; et al. (2007). Voices from the community: Key ingredients for community collaboration. *Social Work in Mental Health, 5*(3/4), 313–331.

Franco, L. M., Mckay, M., Miranda, A., Chambers, N., Paulino, A., & Lawrence, R. (2007). Voices from the community: Key ingredients for community collaboration. *Social Work in Mental Health, 5 (3/4),* 313–331.

Franklin, A. J. (1993). The invisibility syndrome. *The Family Therapy Networker, 17*(4), 32–39.

Franklin, C., & Gerlach, B. (2007). Solution-focused brief therapy in public school settings. In T. S. Nelson & F. N. Thomas (Eds.), *Handbook of solution-focused brief therapy* (pp. 167–189). New York: Haworth Press.

Franklin, C., Waukechon, J., & Larney, P. S. (1995). Culturally relevant school programs for American Indian children and families. *Social Work in Education, 17*(3), 183–193.

Franklin, D. L. (1990). The cycles of social work practice: Social action vs. individual interest. *Journal of Progressive Human Services, 1*(2), 59–80.

Freddolino, P. P., Moxley, D. P., & Hydak, C. A. (2004). A differential model of advocacy in social work practice. *Families in Society, 85*(1), 119–128.

Freedenthal, S. (2008). Suicide. In T. Mizrahi & L. E. Davis (Eds.), *Encyclopedia of social work: Vol. 4* (20th ed.) (pp. 181–186). Washington, DC: NASW Press.

Freeman, E. M., & Couchonnal, G. (2006). Narrative and culturally based approaches in practice with families. *Families in Society, 87*(2), 198–208).

Freeman, I. C. (2005). Advocacy in aging: Notes for the next generation. *Families in Society, 86*(3), 419–423.

Freeman, M. L., & Valentine, D. P. (2004). Through the eyes of Hollywood: Images of social workers in film. *Social Work, 49*(2), 151–161.

Freire, P. (1973a). *Education for critical consciousness.* New York: Continuum.

Freire, P. (1973b). *Pedagogy of the oppressed.* New York: Seabury.

Freire, P. (1990). A critical understanding of social work. *Journal of Progressive Human Services, 1*(1), 3–9.

Freire, P. (1993). *Pedagogy of the oppressed* (New rev. 20th anniversary ed.). New York: Continuum.

Freire, P. (1997). *Pedagogy of the heart.* New York: Continuum.

Freisthier, B., Merritt, D. H., & Lascala, E. A. (2006). Understanding the ecology of child maltreatment: A review of the literature and directions for future research. *Child Maltreatment, 11*(9), 263–280.

Freud, S. (1999). *Keynote Presentation at Annual Psychology Conference.* Black Hawk College, Moline, Illinois.

Friedman, B. D. (2000). Building a spiritual based model to address substance abuse. *Social Thought, 19*(3), 23–38.

Furman, B., & Ahola, T. (1992). *Solution talk: Hosting therapeutic conversations.* New York: W. W. Norton.

Galambos, C. M. (2005). Natural disasters: Health and mental health considerations. *Health & Social Work, 30*(2), 83–86.

Galambos, C., Rocha, C., McCarter, A. K., & Chansuthus, D. (2004). Managed care and mental health: Personal realities. *Journal of Health & Social Policy, 20*(1), 1–22.

Galbraith, M. W. (1991). The adult learning transactional process. In M. W. Galbraith (Ed.), *Facilitating adult learning: A transactional process* (pp. 1–32). Malabar, FL: Krieger.

Gall, T. L. (2006). Spirituality and coping with life stress among adult survivors of childhood sexual abuse. *Child Abuse & Neglect, 30*(7), 829–844.

Gambrill, E. (2006). Evidence-based practice and policy: Choices ahead. *Research on Social Work Practice, 16*(10), 336–357.

Garbarino, J. (1983). Social support networks: Rx for the helping professions. In J. K. Whittaker & J. Garbarino (Eds.), *Social support networks: Informal helping in the human services* (pp. 3–28). New York: Aldine de-Gruyter.

Garcia-Preto, N. (1996). Puerto Rican families. In M. McGoldrick, J. Giordano, & J. K. Pearce (Eds.), *Ethnicity and family therapy* (2nd ed.) (pp. 183–199). New York: Guilford Press.

Garcia-Preto, N. (1998). Latinas in the United States: Bridging two worlds. In M. McGoldrick (Ed.), *Revisioning family therapy: Race, culture, and gender in clinical practice* (pp. 330–344). New York: Guilford Press.

Garrett, J. T. (1993–1994). Understanding Indian children. *Children Today, 22*(4), 18–21, 40.

Garvin, C. D., & Tropman, J. E. (1998). *Social work in contemporary society* (2nd ed.). Boston: Allyn & Bacon.

Gelman, S. R. (1992). Risk management through client access to case records. *Social Work, 37*, 73–79.

Gelman, S. R., Pollack, D., & Weiner, A. (1999). Confidentiality of social work records in the computer age. *Social Work, 44*(3), 243–252.

Gerdes, K. E., & Benson, R. A. (1995). Problems of inner-city schoolchildren: Needs assessment by nominal group process. *Social Work in Education, 17*, 139–147.

Gergen, K. J. (1994). *Realities and relationships: Soundings in social construction.* Cambridge, MA: Harvard University Press.

Germain, C. B. (1979). Ecology and social work. In C. B. Germain (Ed.), *Social work practice: People and environments.* (pp. 1–22). New York: Columbia University Press.

Germain, C. B. (1983). Using social and physical environments. In A. Rosenblatt & D. Waldfogel (Eds.), *Handbook of clinical social work* (pp. 110–133). San Francisco: Jossey-Bass Publishers.

Germain, C. B., & Gitterman, A. (1980). *The life model of social work practice.* New York: Columbia University Press.

Germain, C. B., & Gitterman, A. (1996). *The life model of social work practice: Advances in theory and practice.* New York: Columbia University Press.

Gewirth, A. (2001). Confidentiality in child-welfare practice. *Social Service Review, 75*(3), 479–489.

Gibbs, L., & Gambrill, E. (2002). Evidence-based practice: Counterarguments to objections. *Research on Social Work Practice, 12*, 452–476.

Gil, D. G. (2002). Challenging injustice and oppression. In M. O'Melia & K. K. Miley (Eds.), *Pathways to power: Readings in contextual social work practice* (pp. 35–54). Boston: Allyn & Bacon.

Gilbert, M. C. (2000). Spirituality in social work groups: Practitioners speak out. *Social Work with Groups, 22*(4), 67–84.

Gilbert, N., & Terrell, P. (2005). *Dimensions of social welfare policy* (6th ed.). Boston: Allyn & Bacon.

Gilson, S. F., Bricout, J. C., & Baskind, F. R. (1998). Listening to the voices of individuals with disabilities. *Families in Society, 79*(2), 188–196.

Gingerich, W. J. (1990). Rethinking single-case evaluation. In L. Videka-Sherman & W. J. Reid (Eds.), *Advances in clinical social work research* (pp. 13–24). Silver Spring, MD: NASW Press.

Gitterman, A., & Germain, C. B. (2008). Ecological framework. In T. Mizrahi & L. E. Davis (Eds.), *Encyclopedia of social work. Vol. 1* (20th ed.) (pp. 97–102). Washington, DC: NASW Press.

Gitterman, A., & Shulman, L. (2005). Preface. In A. Gitterman & L. Shulman (Eds.), *Mutual aid groups, vulnerable and resilient populations, and the life cycle* (3rd ed.) (pp. ix–xv). New York: Columbia University Press.

Goelitz, A. (2004). Using end of groups as an intervention at end-of-life. *Journal of Gerontological Social Work, 44*(1/2), 211–221.

Gold, N. (1990). Motivation: The crucial but unexplored component of social work practice. *Social Work, 35*(1), 49–56.

Goldman, J., & Salus, D. (2003). *A coordinated response to child abuse and neglect: The foundation for practice.* Children's Bureau, Office on Child Abuse and Neglect. Retrieved May 15, 2008, from www.childwelfare.gov/pubs/usermanuals/foundation/foundation.pdf

Goldstein, H. (1973). *Social work practice: A unitary approach.* Columbia, SC: University of South Carolina Press.

Goldstein, H. (1987). The neglected moral link in social work practice. *Social Work, 32*, 181–186.

Gomez, A. (2002). Measuring the cultural pulse of service providers. *Focal Point: A National Bulletin on Family Support and Children's Mental Health, 16*(2), 13–15. Retrieved June 5, 2008, from www.rtc.pdx.edu/PDF/fpF02.pdf

Gothard, S. (1995) Legal issues: Confidentiality and privileged communication. In R. L. Edwards (Ed.), *Encyclopedia of social work. Vol 2* (19th ed.) (pp. 1579–1584). Washington, DC: NASW Press.

Gotterer, R. (2001). The spiritual dimension in clinical social work practice: A client perspective. *Families in Society, 82*(2), 187–193.

Gottlieb, N. (1992). Empowerment, political analyses, and services for women. In Y. Hasenfeld (Ed.), *Human services as complex organizations* (pp. 301–319). Newbury Park, CA: Sage.

Graham, M. (2002). Creating spaces: Exploring the role of cultural knowledge as a source of empowerment in models of social welfare in Black communities. *British Journal of Social Work, 32,* 35–49.

Gray, B., & Wood, D. J. (1991). Collaborative alliances: Moving from practice to theory. *Journal of Applied Behavioral Science, 27*(1), 3–22.

Graybeal, C. T. (2007). Evidence for the art of social work. *Families in Society, 88*(4), 513–523.

Graybeal, C. T., & Ruff, E. (1995). Process recording: It's more than you think. *Journal of Social Work Education, 31,* 169–181.

Green, J. W. (1999). *Cultural awareness in the human services: A multi-ethnic approach* (3rd ed.). Boston: Allyn & Bacon.

Greenberg, S. (2003). *A profile of older Americans: 2003.* Administration on Aging, U.S. Department of Health and Human Services. Retrieved November 21, 2005, from www.aoa.gov/prof/Statistics/profile/2003/2003profile.doc

Greene, G. J., Jensen, C., & Jones, D. H. (1996). A constructive perspective on clinical social work practice with ethnically diverse clients. *Social Work, 41*(2), 172–180.

Greene, G. J., & Lee, M. Y. (2002). The social construction of empowerment. In M. O'Melia & K. K. Miley (Eds.), *Pathways to power: Readings in contextual social work practice* (pp. 175–201). Boston: Allyn & Bacon.

Greene, G. J., Lee, M. Y., & Hoffpauir, S. (2005). The languages of empowerment and strengths in clinical social work: A constructivist perspective. *Families in Society, 86*(2), 297–277.

Greene, R. R. (2002). Holocaust survivors: A study in resilience. *Journal of Gerontological Social Work, 37*(1), 3–18.

Greene, R. R. (2007). *Social work practice: A risk and resilience perspective.* Monterey, CA: Brooks/ Cole.

Greene, R. R., & Cohen, H. L. (2005). Social work with older adults and their families: Changing practice paradigms. *Families in Society, 86*(3), 367–373.

Greene, R. R., & Ephross, P. H. (1999). *Human behavior theory and social work practice* (2nd ed.). New York: Aldine De Gruyter.

Greif, G. L. (1986). The ecosystems perspective "Meets the press." *Social Work, 31,* 225–226.

Griffin, R. E. (1991). Assessing the drug-involved client. *Families in Society, 72,* 87–94.

Grimm, L. L. (1992). The Native American child in school: An ecological perspective. In M. J. Fine & C. Carlson (Eds.), *The handbook of family-school intervention* (pp. 102–118). Boston: Allyn & Bacon.

Grinnell, R. M., & Unrau, Y. A. (2005). *Social work research and evaluation* (7th ed.). New York: Oxford University Press.

Grube, B., & Chernesky, R. H. (2001). HIV/AIDS case management tasks and activities: The results of a functional analysis study. *Social Work in Health Care, 32*(3), 41–63.

Grube, J. W., Mayton, D. M., & Ball-Rokeach, S. J. (1994). Inducing change in values, attitudes, and behaviors: Belief system theory and the method of value self-confrontation. *Journal of Social Issues, 50*(4), 153–173.

Gruber, J., & Trickett, E. J. (1987). Can we empower others? The paradox of empowerment in the governing of an alternative school. *American Journal of Community Psychology, 15,* 353–371.

Gummer, B. (1983). Consumerism and clients rights. In A. Rosenblatt & D. Waldfogel (Eds.), *Handbook of clinical social work* (pp. 920–938). San Francisco: Jossey-Bass.

Gutheil, I. A. (1992). Considering the physical environment: An essential component of good practice. *Social Work, 37,* 391–396.

Gutheil, I. A. (1993). Rituals and termination procedures. *Smith College Studies in Social Work, 63*(2), 163–176.

Gutiérrez, L. M. (1989, March). *Empowerment in social work practice: Considerations for practice and education.* Paper presented at the Council on Social Work Education Annual Program Meeting, Chicago, IL.

Gutiérrez, L. M. (1991). Empowering women of color: A feminist model. In M. Bricker-Jenkins, N. R. Hooyman, & N. Gottlieb (Eds.), *Feminist social work practice in clinical settings* (pp. 199–214). Newbury Park, CA: Sage.

Gutiérrez, L. (1992). Empowering ethnic minorities in the twenty-first century: The role of human service organizations. In Y. Hasenfeld (Ed.), *Human services as complex organizations* (pp. 320–338). Newbury Park, CA: Sage.

Gutiérrez, L. M. (1994), Beyond coping: An empowerment perspective on stressful life events. *Journal of Sociology and Social Welfare, 21*(3), 201–219.

Gutiérrez, L. M. (1995). Understanding the empowerment process: Does consciousness make a difference? *Social Work Research, 19,* 229–237.

Gutiérrez, L., Alvarez, R. A., Nemon, H., & Lewis, E. A. (1996). Multicultural community organizing: A strategy for change. *Social Work, 41*(5), 501–508.

Gutiérrez, L., DeLois, K., & GlenMaye, L. (1995a). Understanding empowerment practice: Building on practitioner-based knowledge. *Families in Society, 76,* 534–542.

Gutiérrez, L., GlenMaye, L., & DeLois, K. (1995b). The organizational context of empowerment practice: Implications for social work administration. *Social Work, 40,* 249–258.

Gutiérrez, L. M., & Lewis, E. A. (1998). A feminist perspective on organizing with women of color. In F. G. Rivera & J. L. Erlich (Eds.), *Community organizing in a diverse society* (pp. 97–115). Boston, MA: Allyn & Bacon.

Gutiérrez, L., Moxley, D. P., Alvarez, A., & Johnson, A. K. (2005). The complexity of community empowerment. *Journal of Community Practice, 132,* 1–3.

Gutiérrez, L., & Nagda, B. A. (1996). The multicultural imperative in human services organizations: Issues for the twenty-first century. In P. R. Raffoul & C. A. McNeece (Eds.), *Future issues for social work practice* (pp. 203–213). Boston: Allyn & Bacon.

Gutiérrez, L. M., & Ortega, R. (1991). Developing methods to empower Latinos: The importance of groups. *Social Work with Groups, 14*(2), 23–43.

Haight, W. L. (1998). "Gathering the Spirit" at First Baptist Church: Spirituality as a protective factor in the lives of African American children. *Social Work, 43*(3), 213–221.

Hanley, B. (2005). *Research as empowerment?: Report of a series of seminars organised by the Toronto Group.* York, England: Joseph Rowntree Foundation. Retrieved June 8, 2008, from www.chsrf.ca/kte_docs/Research%20as%20Empowerment.pdf

Hardiman, E. R. (2004). Networks of caring: A qualitative study of social support in consumer-run mental health agencies. *Qualitative Social Work, 3*(4), 431–448.

Hardina, D. (2004a). Guidelines for ethical practice in community organization. *Social Work, 49*(4), 595–604.

Hardina, D. (2004b). Linking citizen participation to empowerment practice: A historical overview. *Journal of Community Practice, 11*(4), 11–37.

Harold, R. D., Mercier, L. R., & Colaross, L. G. (1997). Eco maps: A tool to bridge the practice-research gap. *Journal of Sociology and Social Welfare, 24*(4), 29–44.

Harrigan, M. P., Fauri, D. P., & Netting, F. E. (1998). Termination: Extending the concept for macro social work practice. *Journal of Sociology and Social Welfare, 25*(4), 61–80.

Harris, P. B. (2008). Another wrinkle in the debate about successful aging: The undervalued concept of resilience and the lived experience of dementia. *International Journal of Aging & Human Development, 67*(1), 43–61.

Hartman, A. (1978, reprinted in 1995). Diagrammatic assessment of family relationships. *Families in Society, 76,* 111–122.

Hartman, A. (1992). In search of subjugated knowledge. *Social Work, 37,* 483–484.

Hartman, A., & Laird, J. (1983). *Family centered social work practice.* New York: Free Press.

Harvey, M. R., Mondesir, A. V., & Aldrich, H. (2007). Fostering resilience in traumatized communities: A community empowerment model of intervention. *Journal of Aggression, Maltreatment, & Trauma, 14*(1/2), 265–285.

Hawkins, L. Fook, J., & Ryan, M. (2001). Social workers' use of the language of social justice. *British Journal of Social Work, 31,* 1–13.

Haynes, K. S., & Mickelson, J. S. (2003). *Affecting change: Social workers in the political arena.* Boston: Allyn & Bacon.

Healy, K. (2001). Reinventing critical social work: Challenges from practice, context and postmodernism. *Critical Social Work, 2*(1). Retrieved June 8, 2008, from www.criticalsocialwork.com/units/socialwork/critical.nsf/inToc/E603FCB05B70F07385256EA5006E72E0

Healy, L. M. (2001). *International social work.* NY: Oxford University Press.

Healy, L. M. (2008). International social work. In T. Mizrahi & L. E. Davis (Eds.), *Encyclopedia of social work: Vol. 2* (20th ed.) (pp. 483–488). Washington, DC: NASW Press.

Hensley, L. G. (2002). Treatment for survivors of rape: Issues and interventions. *Journal of Mental Health Counseling, 24*(4), 431–448.

Hernandez, P., Almeid, A. R., & Dolen-Del-Vecchio, K. (2005). Critical consciousness, accountability, and empowerment: Key processes for helping families heal. *Family Process, 44*(1), 105–119.

Hepworth, D. H., Rooney, R. H., Rooney, G. D., Strom-Gottfried, K., & Larsen, J. (2006). *Direct social work practice: Theory and skills.* (7th ed.). Pacific Grove, CA: Brooks/Cole.

Hess, H., & Hess, P. M. (1999). Termination in context. In B. R. Compton & B. Galaway, *Social work processes* (pp. 489–497). Pacific Grove, CA: Brooks/ Cole.

Hick, S., & McNutt, J. (2002). *Advocacy and activism on the internet: Perspectives from community organization and social policy.* Chicago: Lyceum.

Hick, S. F. (2002). Anti-oppressive practice: Challenges for social work. *Critical Social Work, 3*(1). Retrieved June 5, 2008, from www.criticalsocialwork.com/units/socialwork/critical.nsf/inToc/89D3BC12CC4FA6DB85256E5006E7EC3

Hill, R. B. (1997). *The strengths of African American families: Twenty-five years later.* Washington, DC: R & B Publishers.

Hines, P., & Boyd-Franklin, N. (1996). African American families. In M. McGoldrick, J. Giordano, & J. K. Pierce (Eds.), *Ethnicity and family therapy* (pp. 66–84). New York: Guildford Press.

Hingsburger, D. (1990). *i to I: Self concept and people with developmental disabilities.* Mountville, PA: VIDA Publishing.

Ho, M. K. (1987). *Family therapy with ethnic minorities.* Newbury Park, CA: Sage.

Hodge, D. R. (2000). Spirituality: Towards a theoretical framework. *Social Thought, 19*(4), 1–20.

Hodge, D. R. (2001a). Spiritual assessment: A review of major qualitative methods and a new framework for assessing spirituality. *Social Work, 46*(3), 203–214.

Hodge, D. R. (2001b). Spiritual genograms: A generational approach to assessing spirituality. *Families in Society, 82,* 35–48.

Hodge, D. R. (2003). The challenge of spiritual diversity: Can social work facilitate an inclusive environment? *Families in Society, 84*(3), 348–358.

Hodge, D. R. (2004). Working with Hindu clients with a spiritually sensitive manner. *Social Work, 49*(1), 27–38.

Hodge, D. R. (2005a). Social work and the House of Islam: Orienting practitioners to the beliefs and values of Muslims in the United States. *Social Work, 50*(1), 162–173.

Hodge, D. R. (2005b). Spiritual ecograms: A new assessment instrument for identifying clients' strengths in space and across time. *Families in Society, 86*(2), 287–296.

Hodge, D. R. (2005c). Spiritual lifemaps: A client-centered pictorial instrument for spiritual assessment, planning, and intervention. *Social Work, 50*(1), 77–87.

Hodge, D. R. (2006). A template for spiritual assessment: A review of the JCAHO requirements and guidelines for implementation. *Social Work, 51*(4), 317–326.

Hodge, D. R. (2007). Social justice and people of faith: A transnational perspective. *Social Work, 52*(2), 139–148.

Hoefer, R. (2006). *Advocacy practice for social justice.* Chicago: Lyceum.

Hollis, F. (1967). Principles and assumptions underlying casework principles. In E. Younghusband (Ed.), *Social work and social values* (pp. 22–38). London: George Allen & Unwin Ltd.

Holzman, C. G. (1994). Multicultural perspectives on counseling survivors of rape. *Journal of Social Distress and the Homeless, 3*(1), 81–97.

Home, A. (1999). Group empowerment. In W. Shera & L. Wells (Eds.), *Empowerment practice in social work: Developing richer conceptual foundations* (pp. 234–245). Toronto, Canada: Canadian Scholars' Press.

Hopps, J. G., Pinderhughes, E., & Shankar, R. (1995). *The power to care: Clinical practice effectiveness with overwhelmed clients.* New York: The Free Press.

Huang, L. N. (2002). Reflecting on cultural competence: A need for renewed urgency. *Focal Point: A National Bulletin on Family Support and Children's Mental Health, 16*(2), 4–7. Retrieved June 5, 2008, from www.rtc.pdx.edu/PDF/fpF02.pdf

Hurdle, D. E. (2002). Native Hawaiian traditional healing: Culturally based interventions for social work practice. *Social Work, 47*(2), 183–192.

Houston-Vega, M. K., Neuhring, E. M., & Daguio, E. R. (1997). *Prudent practice: A guide for managing malpractice.* Washington, DC: NASW Press.

Hyam, V. (2003). Inalienable rights: Anti-racist social work, as part of social reconstruction in the Czeck Republic. *Social Work in Europe, 10*(2), 47–53.

Hyde, C. A. (2008). Feminist social work practice. In T. Mizrahi & L. E. Davis (Eds.), *Encyclopedia of social work. Vol. 2* (20th ed.) (pp. 216–221). Washington, DC: NASW Press.

Imber-Black, E., & Roberts, J. (1998). *Rituals for our time: Celebrating, healing, and changing our lives and relationships.* Northvale, NJ: Aronson.

Imre, R. W. (1982). *Knowing and caring: Philosophical issues in social work.* Lanham, MD: University Press of America.

International Federation of Social Work. (2000). *Definition of social work.* Retrieved June 5, 2008, from www.ifsw.org/en/p38000208.html

International Federation of Social Work & International Association of Schools of Social Work [IFSW & IASSW]. (2004). *Ethics in social work, Statement of principles.* Retrieved June 10, 2008, from www.ifsw.org/en/p38000324.html

Institute for the Advancement of Social Work Research [IASSR]. (2008, January). *Evidence-based practice: A brief from the Institute for the Advancement of Social Work Research.* Washington, DC: IASSR.

Irizarry, C. & Appel, Y. H. (2005). Preteens in double jeopardy: supporting developmental growth through a natural friendship group. In A. Gitterman & L. Shulman (Eds.), *Mutual aid groups, vulnerable and resilient populations, and the life cycle* (3rd ed.) (pp. 165–202). New York: Columbia University Press.

Itzhaky, H., & Schwartz, C. (2000). Empowerment of parents of children with disabilities: The effect of community and personal variables. *Journal of Family Social Work, 5*(1), 21–36.

Ivanoff, A. M., Blythe, B. J., & Tripodi, T. (1994). *Involuntary clients in social work practice: A research-based approach.* New York: Aldine de Gruyter.

Ivey, A. E., & Ivey, M. B. (2006). *Intentional interviewing and counseling: Facilitating client development in multicultural society.* (6th ed.). Pacific Grove, CA: Brooks/Cole.

Jackson, A. P., & Sears, S. J. (1992). Implications of an Africentric worldview in reducing stress for African American women. *Journal of Counseling & Development, 71,* 184–190.

Jackson, H., Hess, P. M., & van Dolen, A. (1995). Preadolescent suicide: How to assess and how to respond. *Families in Society, 76,* 267–279.

Jackson-Elmore, C. (2005). Informing state policy makers: Opportunities for social workers. *Social Work, 50*(3), 251–261.

Jacobson, M., & Rogeley, C. (2007). Community-based participatory research: Group work for social justice and community change. *Social Work with Groups, 30*(4), 21–39.

Janis, I., & Rodin, J. (1980). Attribution, control and decision making: Social psychology and health care. In G. Stone, F. Cohen, & N. Adler (Eds.), *Health psychology* (pp. 487–521). San Francisco: Jossey-Bass.

Jenson, J. M., & Howard, M. O. (2008). Evidence-based practice. In T. Mizrahi & L. E. Davis (Eds.), *Encyclopedia of social work. Vol. 2* (20th ed.) (pp. 158–165). Washington, DC: NASW Press.

Johner, R. (2006). Dual relationship legitimization and client self-determination. *Journal of Social Work Values and Ethics, 3*(1). Retrieved May 20, 2008, from www.socialworker.com/jswve/content/view/30/44/#Mittendorf

Johnson, A. K. (2004). Social work is standing on the legacy of Jane Addams: But are we sitting on the sidelines? *Social Work, 49*(2), 319–322.

Johnson, D. W. (2006). *Reaching out: Interpersonal effectiveness* (9th ed.). Boston: Allyn & Bacon.

Johnson, D. W., & Johnson, F. P. (2006). *Joining together: Group theory and group skills* (9th ed.). Boston: Allyn & Bacon.

Johnson, E. D. (2000). Differences among families coping with serious mental illness: A qualitative analysis. *American Journal of Orthopsychiatry, 70*(1), 126–134.

Johnson, L. C., & Yanca, S. (2007). *Social work practice: A generalist approach* (9th ed.). Boston: Allyn & Bacon.

Johnson, M., & Austin, M. J. (2006). Evidence-based practice in the social services: Implications for organizational change. *Administration in Social Work, 30*(3), 75–104.

Johnstone, M., & Kanitsaki O. (2008). Cultural racism, language prejudice and discrimination in hospital contexts: An Australian study. *Diversity in Health and Social Care, 5*(1), 19–30.

Jupp, V. (2005). Issues of power in social work practice in mental health services for people from Black and minority ethnic groups. *Critical Social Work, 6*(1), retrieved June 5, 2008, from www.criticalsocialwork.com/units/socialwork/critical.nsf/inToc/8B8307415348655A85256FD7007474D9

Kacen, L. (1999). Anxiety levels, group characteristics, and members' behaviors in the termination stage of support groups for patients recovering from heart attacks. *Research on Social Work Practice, 9*(6), 656–672.

Kadushin, A., & Kadushin, G. (1997). *The social work interview.* New York: Columbia University Press.

Kagle, J. D. (1987). Recording in direct practice. In A. Minahan (Ed.), *Encyclopedia of social work. Vol 2* (18th ed.) (pp. 463–467). Silver Spring, MD: National Association of Social Workers.

Kagle, J. D. (1990). Teaching social work students about privileged communication. *Journal of Teaching in Social Work, 4*(2), 49–65.

Kagle, J. D. (1991). *Social work records* (2nd ed.). Belmont, CA: Wadsworth.

Kagle, J. D., & Kopels, S. (1994). Confidentiality after Tarasoff. (*Tarasoff v. Board of Regents of the University of California.* 1976). *Health and Social Work, 19*(3), 217–222.

Kane, R. A. (1992). Case management: Ethical pitfalls on the road to high-quality managed care. In S. M. Rose (Ed.), *Case management and social work practice* (pp. 219–228). New York: Longman.

Kaplan, K. (1992). Adult protective services case management. In B. S. Vourlekis & R. R. Greene (Eds.), *Social work case management* (pp. 89–105). New York: Aldine de Gruyter.

Karger, H. J., & Hernandez, M. T. (2004). The decline of the public intellectual in social work. *Journal of Sociology & Social Welfare, 31*(3), 51–68.

Karger, H. J., & Stoez, D. (2008). *American social welfare policy: A pluralist approach* (5th ed.). Boston: Allyn & Bacon.

Keenan, E. K. (2004). From sociocultural categories to socially located relations: Using critical theory in social work practice. *Families in Society, 85*(4), 539–548.

Keith-Lucas, A. (1972). *The giving and taking of help.* Chapel Hill, NC: University of North Carolina Press.

Kelly, T. B. (2004). Mutual aid groups for older persons with a mental illness. *Journal of Gerontological Social Work, 44*(1/2), 111–126.

Kemp, S. P., Whittaker, J. K., & Tracy, E. M. (1997). *Person-environment practice: The social ecology of interpersonal helping.* New York: Aldine de Gruyter.

Kemp, S. P., Whittaker, J. K., & Tracy, E. M. (2002). Contextual social work practice. In M. O'Melia & K. K. Miley (Eds.), *Pathways to power: Readings in contextual social work practice* (pp. 15–34). Boston: Allyn & Bacon.

Kettner, P. M., Daley, J. M., & Nichols, A. W. (1985). *Initiating change in organizations and communities: A macro practice model.* Monterey, CA: Brooks/ Cole.

Keys, C. B., & Factor, A. R. (2001). Building community coalitions with people with disabilities and their families: An empowerment approach. *Journal of Prevention & Intervention in the Community, 21*(2), 91–112.

Kieffer, C. (1984). Citizen empowerment: A developmental perspective. In J. Rappaport, C. Swift, & R. Hess (Eds.), *Studies in empowerment: Toward understanding and action* (pp. 9–36). New York: Haworth Press.

Kirst-Ashman, K. K., & Hull, G. H. (2006). *Understanding generalist practice.* (4th ed.). Belmont, CA: Brooks/Cole.

Kisthardt, W. E. (1992). A strengths model of case management: The principles and functions of a helping relationship with persons with persistent mental illness. In D. Saleebey (Ed.), *The strengths perspective in social work practice* (pp. 59–83). New York: Longman.

Kisthardt, W. E., & Rapp, C. A. (1992). Bridging the gap between principles and practice: Implementing a strengths perspective in case management. In S. M. Rose (Ed.), *Case management and social work practice* (pp. 112–125). New York: Longman.

Kivnick, H. Q. (1988). Grandparenthood, life review, and psychosocial development. *Journal of Gerontological Social Work, 12*(3/4), 63–81.

Kivnick, H. Q., & Murray, S. V. (2001). Life strengths interview guide: Assessing older clients' strengths. *Journal of Gerontological Social Work, 34*(4), 7–32.

Kivnick, H. Q., & Stoffel, S. A. (2005). Vital involvement practice: Strengths as more than tools for solving problems. *Journal of Gerontological Social Work, 46*(2), 85–116.

Klein, A. R., & Cnaan, R. A. (1995). Practice with high risk clients. *Families in Society, 76*, 203–211.

Kleinkauf, C. (1981). A guide to giving legislative testimony. *Social Work, 26*, 297–303.

Kleinkauf, C. (1989). Analyzing social welfare legislation. *Social Work, 34*, 179–181.

Kondrat, M. E. (2002). Actor-centered social work: Revisioning "person-in-environment" through a critical theory lens. *Social Work, 47*(4), 435–448.

Kopels, S., & Kagle, J. D. (1993). Do social workers have a duty to warn? *Social Service Review, 67*, 101–126.

Kopels, S., & Kagle, J. D. (1994). Teaching confidentiality breaches as a form of discrimination. *Arete, 19*(1), 1–9.

Kosmin, B. A., Mayer, E., & Kaysar, A. (2002). *American religious identification survey.* Retrieved June 5, 2008, from www.gc.cuny.edu/faculty/research_briefs/aris.pdf

Kramer, B. J. (1998). Preparing social workers for the inevitable: A preliminary investigation of a course on grief, death, and loss. *Journal of Social Work Education, 34*(2), 211–227.

Kramer, B. J., & Auer, C. (2005). Challenges to providing end-of-life care to low-income elders with advance chronic disease: Lessons learned from a model program. *Gerontologist, 45*(5), 651–660.

Kramer, B. J., Pacourek, L., & Hovland-Scafe, C. (2003). Analysis of end-of-life content in social work text books. *Journal of Social Work Education, 39*, 299–300.

Kramer, T. L., Jones, K. A., Kichner, M. D., Miller, T. L., & Wilson, C. (2002). Addressing personnel concerns about school violence through education assessment and strategic planning. *Education, 123*(2), 292–204.

Kramer-Roy, D. (2007). Researching the support needs of Pakistani families with disabled children in the UK. *Research Policy and Planning, 25*(2/3), 143–153.

Kretzmann, J. P., & McKnight, J. L. (1993). *Building communities from the inside out: A path toward finding and mobilizing a community's assets.* Chicago: ACTA Publications.

Krill, D. F. (1988). Existential social work. In R. A. Dorfman (Ed.), *Paradigms of clinical social work* (pp. 295–316). New York: Brunner/Mazel.

Kübler-Ross, E. (1969). *On death and dying.* New York: Macmillan.

Kuehl, B. P. (1995). The solution-oriented genogram: A collaborative approach. *Journal of Marital and Family Therapy, 21,* 239–250.

Kulis, S., Marsiglia, F. F., Elek, E., Dustman, P., Wagstaff, D., & Hecht, M. L. (2005). Mexican/ Mexican American adolescents and *keepin' it REAL:* An evidence-based substance use prevention program. *Children & Schools, 27*(3), 133–145.

Kurzman, P. (1995). Professional liability and malpractice. In R. L. Edwards (Ed.), *Encyclopedia of social work. Vol. 1* (19th ed.) (pp. 1921–1927). Washington, DC: NASW Press.

Labassi, M. F., & Maluccio, A. N. (1986). Competence centered social work: Prevention in action. *Journal of Primary Prevention, 6,* 168–180.

Laird, J. (1990). Creating the world, or, watch your language! *Smith College Studies in Social Work, 60*(3), 213–215.

Laird, J. (1993). Women's secrets: Women's silences. In E. Imber-Black (Ed.), *Secrets in families and family therapy* (pp. 243–267). New York: W. W. Norton & Company.

Laird, J. (1995). Family-centered practice in the postmodern era. *Families in Society, 76*(3), 150–162.

Lamb, J. M. (1990). The suicidal adolescent. *Nursing, 90,* 20(5), 72–76.

Lane, M., & Henry, K. (2004). Beyond symptoms: Crime prevention and community development. *Australian Journal of Social Work, 39*(2), 201–213.

Langlery, J. (2001). Developing anti-oppressive empowering social work practice with older lesbian women and gay men. *British Journal of Social Work, 31,* 917–932.

Lawson, H. (2008). Collaborative practice. In T. Mizrahi & L. E. Davis (Eds.), *Encyclopedia of social work. Vol. 1* (20th ed.) (pp. 341–346). Washington, DC: NASW Press.

Lazar, A., & Bjorck, J. P. (2008). Religious support and psychosocial well-being among a religious Jewish population. *Mental Health, Religion & Culture, 11*(4), 403–421.

Lee, C. D., & Ayón C. (2005). The power of groups for older adults: A comparative study of European American and Latino senior mutual aid groups. *Social Work with Groups, 28*(2), 23–39.

Lee, J. A. B. (2001). *An empowerment approach to social work practice: Building the beloved community* (2nd ed.). New York: Columbia University Press.

Lee, J. S., & Rock, B. D. (2005). Challenges in the new prospective payment system: Action steps for social work in home health care. *Health & Social Work, 30*(1), 48–55.

Lee, M-Y., & Greene, G. J. (1999). A social constructivist framework for integrating cross-cultural issues in teaching clinical social work. *Journal of Social Work Education, 35*(1), 21–37.

Lee, M-Y., Sebold, J., & Uken, A. (2007). Solution-focused treatment with domestic violence offenders. In T. S. Nelson & F. N. Thomas (Eds.), *Handbook of solution-focused brief therapy* (pp. 135–166). New York:Haworth Press.

Leigh, J. W. (1998). *Communicating for cultural competence.* Boston: Allyn & Bacon.

Leight, A. K. (2001). Transpersonalism and social work practice: Awakening to new dimensions for client self-determination, empowerment, and growth. *Social Thought, 20*(1/2), 63–76.

Lenrow, P. B., & Burch, R. W. (1981). Mutual aid and professional services: Opposing or complementary? In B. H. Gottlieb (Ed.), *Social networks and social supports: Vol. 4, Sage studies in community mental health* (pp. 233–257). Beverly Hills, CA: Sage.

Lens, V. (2004). Principled negotiation: A new tool for case advocacy. *Social Work, 49*(3), 506–513.

Leonardsen, D. (2007). Empowerment in social work: An individual vs. a relational perspective. *International Journal of Social Welfare, 16,* 3–11.

Lesser, J. G., O'Neill, M. R., Burke, K. W., Scanion, P., Hollis, K., & Miller, R. (2004). Women supporting women: A mutual aid group fosters new connections among women in midlife. *Social Work with Groups, 27*(1), 75–88.

Lester, H., & Tritter, J. G. (2005). "Listen to my madness": Understanding the experiences of people with serious mental illness. *Sociology of Health & Illness, 27*(5), 649–669.

Levin, R., (1999). Participatory evaluation: researchers and service providers as collaborators versus adversaries. *Violence Against Women, 5*(10), Retrieved November 11, 2002, from EBSCOhost ContentSelect Helping Professions.

Lewandowski, C. A., & GlenMaye, L. P. (2002). Teams in child welfare settings: Interprofessional and collaborative processes. *Families in society, 83*(3), 245–256.

Lewin, K. (1951). *Field theory in social science.* Westport, CT: Greenwood Press.

Lewis, E. (1991). Social change and citizen action: A philosophical exploration for modern social group work. *Social Work with Groups, 14*(3/4), 23–34.

Lewis, R. G., & Ho, M. (1975). Social work with Native Americans. *Social Work, 20,* 379–382.

Libassi, M. F., & Maluccio, A. N. (1986). Competence-centered social work: Prevention in action. *Journal of Primary Prevention, 6*(3), 168–180.

Liddie, B. W. (1991). Relearning feminism on the job. In M. Bricker-Jenkins, N. R. Hooyman, & N. Gottlieb (Eds.), *Feminist social work practice in clinical settings* (pp. 131–146). Newbury Park, CA: Sage.

Lietz, C. A. (2007). Uncovering stories of family resilience: A mixed methods study of resilient families, part 2. *Families in Society, 88*(1), 147–155.

Linhorst, D. M. (2002). Federalism and social justice: Implications for social work. *Social Work, 47*(3), 201–208.

Linhorst, D. M., Hamilton, G., Young, E., & Eckert, A. (2002). Opportunities and barriers to empowering people with severe mental illness through participation in treatment planning. *Social Work, 47*(4), 425–434.

Little, M., Axford, N., & Morpeth, L. (2004). Research review: Risk and protection in the context of services for children in need. *Child and Family Social Work, 9,* 105–117.

Loftus, E. (1979). *Eyewitness testimony.* Cambridge, MA: Harvard University Press.

Long, P. (2002). Ethical and inescapable: Politicized social work practice. In M. O'Melia & K. K. Miley (Eds.), *Pathways to power: Readings in contextual social work practice* (pp. 55–73). Boston: Allyn & Bacon.

Longres, J. F. (1995). *Human behavior in the social environment.* Itasca, IL: F. E. Peacock.

Longres, J. F. (2000). *Human behavior in the social environment.* (3rd ed.). Itasca, IL: F. E. Peacock.

Lorenzo, M. K., Frost, A. K., & Reinherz, H. Z. (2000). Social and emotional functioning of older Asian American adolescents. *Child and Adolescent Social Work Journal, 17*(4), 289–304.

Lowenthal, B. (1999). Effects of maltreatment and ways to promote children's resiliency. *Childhood Education, 75*(4), 204–209.

Lukes, C. A., & Land, H. (1990). Biculturality and homosexuality. *Social Work, 35,* 155–161.

Lum, D. (2004). *Social work with people of color: A process-stage approach* (5th ed.). Pacific Grove, CA: Brooks/Cole.

Macdonald, C., Harris, J., & Wintersteen, R. (2003). Contingent on content? Social work and the state in Australia, Britain, and the U.S.A. *British Journal of Social Work, 33,* 191–208.

Macdonald, G. (2001). *Effective interventions for child abuse and neglect: An evidence-based approach to planning and evaluating interventions.* New York: Wiley.

Macleod, J., & Nelson, G. (2000). Programs for the promotion of family wellness and the prevention of child maltreatment: A meta-analytic review. *Child Abuse & Neglect, 24*(9), 1127–1149.

Madden, R. G. (2003). *Essential law for social workers.* New York: Columbia University Press.

Mahaffey, M. (1982). Lobbying and social work. In M. Mahaffey, & J. Hanks (Eds.), *Practical politics: Social workers and political responsibility* (pp. 69–84). Silver Spring, MD: National Association of Social Workers.

Maluccio, A. N. (1979). Learning from clients. New York: The Free Press.

Maluccio, A. N. (1981). Competence-oriented social work practice: An ecological approach. In A. N. Maluccio (Ed.), *Promoting competence in clients: A new/old approach to social work practice* (pp. 1–24), New York: The Free Press.

Maluccio, A. N., & Libassi, M. F. (1984). Competence clarification in social work practice. *Social Thought, 10,* 51–58.

Malekoff, A. (2008). Transforming trauma and empowering children and adolescents in the aftermath of disaster through group work. *Social Work with Groups, 31*(1), 29–52.

Marsh, P., & Fisher, M. (1992). *Good intentions: Developing partnerships in social services.* York, England: Joseph Rowntree Foundation.

Marshall, V. W., & Altpeter, M. (2005). Cultivating social work leadership in health promotion and aging: Strategies for active aging interventions. *Health & Social Work, 30*(2), 135–144.

Martinez Jr., C. (1988). Mexican-Americans. In L. Comas-Diaz & E. E. H. Griffith (Eds.), *Clinical guidelines in cross-cultural mental health* (pp. 182–203). New York: John Wiley & Sons.

Maslach, C. (2003). Job burnout: New directions in research and intervention. *Current Directions in Psychological Science, 12*(5), 189–192.

Maslach, C., & Leiter, M. P. (2008). Early predictors of job burnout and engagement. *Journal of Applied Psychology, 93*(3), 498–512.

Maslow, A. H. (1970). *Motivation and personality.* New York: Harper & Row.

Masten, A. S. (2005). Children who overcome adversity to succeed in life. *Just in Time Research: Resilient Communities.* Minneapolis, MN: University of Minnesota. Retrieved June 5, 2008, from www.extension.umn.edu/distribution/familydevelopment/components/7565_06.html

Mattaini, M. A. (1993). *More than a thousand words: Graphics for clinical practice.* Washington, DC: NASW Press.

May, R. (1972). *Power and innocence: A search for the sources of violence.* New York: W. W. Norton.

Mayer, L. M. (2005). Professional boundaries in dual relationships: A social work dilemma. *Journal of Social Work Values and Ethics, 2*(2). Retrieved May 20, 2008, from www.socialworker.com/jswve/content/view/25/37/

McAuaide, S., & Ehrenreich, J. H. (1997). Assessing client strengths. *Families in Society, 78*(2), 201–212.

McCarter, A. K. (2007). The impact of hopelessness and hope on the social work profession. *Journal of Human Behavior in the Social Environment, 15*(4), 107–124.

McCarthy, W. C., & Frieze, I. H. (1999). Negative aspects of therapy: Client perceptions of therapists' social influence, burnout, and quality of care. (Social influence and social power: Using theory for understanding social issues). *Journal of Social Issues, 55*(1), 33–50.

McCoullough-Chavis, A., & Waites, C. (2004). Genograms with African American families: considering cultural context. *Journal of Family Social Work, 8*(2), 1–19.

McGill, D. W. (1992). The cultural story in multicultural family therapy. *Families in Society, 73,* 339–349.

McGoldrick, M. (1989). Ethnicity and the family life cycle. In B. Carter & M. McGoldrick (Eds.), *The changing family life cycle: A framework for family therapy* (2nd ed.) (pp. 69–90). Boston: Allyn & Bacon.

McGoldrick, M., & Gerson, R. (1985). *Genograms in family assessment.* New York: Norton.

McGoldrick, M., & Gerson, R. (1989). Genograms and the family life cycle. In B. Carter & M. McGoldrick (Eds.), *The changing family life cycle: A framework for family therapy* (2nd ed.) (pp. 164–189). Boston: Allyn & Bacon.

McGowan, B. G. (1987). Advocacy. In A. Minahan (Ed.), *Encyclopedia of social work, Vol 1* (18th ed.) (pp. 89–95). Silver Spring, MD: National Association of Social Workers.

McInnis-Dittrich, K. (1994). *Integrating social welfare policy and social work practice.* Pacific Grove, CA: Brooks/Cole.

McIntosh, P. (1998). White privilege: Unpacking the invisible knapsack. In M. McGoldrick (Ed.), *Revisioning family therapy: Race, culture, and gender in clinical practice* (pp. 147–152). New York: Guilford Press.

McLaughlin, H. (2005). Young service users as co-researchers: Methodological problems and possibilities. *Qualitative Social Work, 4*(2), 211–228.

McLaughlin, L. A., & Braun, K. L. (1998). Asian and Pacific Islander cultural values: Considerations for health care decision making. *Health and Social Work, 23*(2), 116–126.

McNeal, C., & Perkins, I. (2007). Potential roles of Black churches in HIV/AIDS prevention. *Journal of Human Behavior in the Social Environment, 15*(2/3), 219–232.

McNeece, C. A., & Thyer, B. A. (2004). Evidence-based practice and social work. *Journal of Evidence-Based Social Work, 1*(1), 7–25.

McNicoll, P. (2008). A group worker response to 'A mission-based model for social work'. *Social Work with Groups, 31*(1), 25–28.

McNutt, J. G. (2000). Coming perspectives in the development of electronic advocacy for social policy practice. *Critical Social Work, 1*(1), Retrieved June 5, 2008, from www.criticalsocialwork.com/units/socialwork/critical.nsf/inToc/EBC1FE35DA22CBF485256EA5006E510D

McNutt, J. G., & Menon, G. (2004). Electronic democracy and social welfare policy: A look at Internet resources. *Social Policy Journal, 2*(3), 87–91.

McNutt, J. G., & Menon, G. M. (2008). The rise of cyberactivism: Implications for the future of advocacy in the human services. *Families in Society, 89*(1), 33–38.

Meer, D., & VandeCreek, L. (2002). Cultural considerations in release of information. *Ethics & Behavior, 12*(2), 143–156.

Mental Health Research Network [MHRN]. (2005). *Guidance for good practice: Service user involvement in the UK Mental Health research network.* London: Mental Health Research Network. Retrieved June 5, 2008, from www.mhrn.info/index/library/surge-docs.html

Mercier, L., & Harold, R.(2003). A feminist approach to exploring the intersections of individuals, families and communities: An illustration focusing on lesbian mother research. *Journal of Human Behavior in the Social Environment, 7*(3/4), 79–95.

Merighi, J. R., & Grimes, M. D. (2000). Coming out to families in a multicultural context. *Families in Society, 81*(1), 32–41.

Meyer, C. (1993). *Assessment in social work practice.* New York: Columbia University Press.

Middleman, R. R., & Wood, G. G. (1990). *Skills for direct practice in social work.* New York: Columbia University Press.

Midgley, J. (2007). Perspectives on globalization, social justice and welfare. *Journal of Sociology & Social Welfare, 34*(2), 17–36.

Miles, M. S., Holditch-Davis, D., Pederson, C., Eron, J. J., Schwartz, T. (2007). Emotional distress in African American women with HIV. *Journal of Prevention & Intervention in the community, 33*(1/2), 35–50.

Milewski-Hertlein, K. A. (2001). The use of a socially constructed genogram in clinical practice. *The American Journal of Family Therapy, 29,* 23–28.

Miley, K. K. (1992, April). *Religion and social work practice.* Paper presented at the Midwest Conference on Social Work Education, LaCrosse, WI.

Miley, K., & DuBois, B. (1999). Empowering processes for social work practice. In W. Shera & L. Wells (Eds.), *Empowerment practice in social work: Developing richer conceptual foundations* (pp. 2–12). Toronto, Canada: Canadian Scholars' Press.

Miley, K. K., & DuBois, B. (2004, May). *Ethical preferences for the clinical practice of empowerment social work.* Presented at the Fourth International Conference on Health and Mental Health, Quebec City, Quebec, Canada.

Miley, K. K., & DuBois, B. (2005, February). *Social work image: Drawing on the traditions of social work.* Presented at Council on Social Work Education Annual Program Meeting, Anaheim, CA.

Miley, K. K., & DuBois, B. (2007a). Ethical preferences for the clinical practice of empowerment social work. *Social Work in Health Care, 44*(1/2), 29–44.

Miley, K. K., & DuBois, B. (2007b). Ethical preferences for the clinical practice of empowerment social work. In S. Dumont & M. St-Onge (Eds.), *Social work, health, and international development: Compassion in social policy and practice* (pp. 26–44). New York: Haworth Press.

Millar, M. (1999). Psychology and anti-oppressive social work: Understanding the complexity of individual lives. *Social Work and Social Sciences Review, 8*(1), 25–41.

Miller, O. A., & Gaston, R. J. (2003). A model of culture-centered child welfare practice. *Child Welfare, 82*(2), 235–250.

Millstein, K. (2000). Confidentiality in direct social work practice: Inevitable challenges and ethical dilemmas. *Families in Society, 81*(3), 270–282.

Mirabito, D. M. (2006). Revisiting unplanned termination: Clinicians' perceptions of termination from adolescent mental health treatment. *Families in Society, 87*(2), 171–180.

Mizrahi, T. (2001). The status of community organization in 2001: Community practice context, complexities, contradictions, and contributions. *Research on Social Work Practice, 11*(2), 176–179.

Mok, B-H. (2001). The effectiveness of self-help groups in a Chinese context. *Social Work with Groups 24*(2), 69–89.

Mok, B-H. (2004). Self-help group participation and empowerment in Hong Kong. *Journal of Sociology & Social Welfare, 31*(3), 153–168.

Molloy, J. K. (2007). Photovoice as a tool for social justice workers. *Journal of Progressive Human Services, 18*(2), 39–55.

Monkman, M. M. (1991). Outcome objectives in social work practice: Person and environment. *Social Work,* 36(3), 253–258.

Moore, V. R., & Miller, S. D. (2007). Coping resources: Effects on the psychological well-being of African American grandparents raising grandchildren. *Journal of Health & Social Policy, 22*(3/4), 137–148.

Moos, R. H. (2003). Social contexts: Transcending their power and their fragility. *American Journal of Community Psychology, 31*(1/2), 1–13.

Morales, A. T., & Salcido, R. (1998). Social work practice with Mexican Americans. In A. T. Morales & B. W. Sheafor (Eds.), *Social work: A profession of many faces* (8th ed.) (pp. 513–539). Boston: Allyn & Bacon.

Morelli, P. T., & Fong, R. (2000). The role of Hawaiian elders in substance abuse treatment among Asian/ Pacific Islander women. *Journal of Family Social Work, 4*(4), 33–44.

Morrison, L. L., & L'Heureux, J. (2001). Suicide and gay/lesbian/bisexual youth: Implications for clinicians. *Journal of Adolescence, 24,* 39–49.

Moxley, D. P. (1989). *The practice of case management.* Newbury Park, CA: Sage.

Moxley, D. P., & Freddolino, P. P. (1994). Client-driven advocacy and psychiatric disability: A model for social work practice. *Journal of Sociology and Social Welfare, 21*(2), 91–108.

Mullaly, B. (2002). *Challenging oppression: A critical social work approach.* Ontario, Canada: Oxford University Press.

Mulroy, E. A. (2003). Theoretical perspectives on the social environment to guide management and community practice: An organization-in-environment approach. *Administration in Social Work, 28*(1), 77–98.

Nakanishi, M., & Rittner, B. (1992). The inclusionary cultural model. *Journal of Social Work Education, 28,* 27–35.

Nakashima, M. (2003). Beyond coping and adaptation: Promoting a holistic perspective on dying. *Families in Society, 84*(3), 367–376.

Napoli, M. (1999). The non-Indian therapist working with American Indian clients: Transference-countertransference implications. *Psychoanalytic Social Work, 6*(1), 25–47.

Nathan, P. E., & Gorman, J. (Eds.). (2002). *A guide to treatments that work* (2nd ed.). New York: Oxford.

National Association of Social Workers [NASW] (1981). *Standards for the classification of social work practice: Policy statement 4.* Silver Spring, MD: Author.

National Association of Social Workers (1999a). *Code of ethics of the National Association of Social Workers.* Washington, DC: Author.

National Association of Social Workers. (1999b). Professional impairment. In author. *Social work speaks: National Association of Social Workers policy statements 2006–2009* (7th ed.) (pp. 296–304). Washington, DC: NASW Press.

National Association of Social Workers. (1999c). Senior health, safety, and vitality. In author. *Social work speaks: National Association of Social Workers policy statements 2006–2009.* (7th ed.) (pp. 341–347). Washington, DC: NASW Press.

National Association of Social Workers. (2001a). *National standards for cultural competence in social work practice.* Washington, DC: NASW Press.

National Association of Social Workers. (2001b). *What social workers should know about the HIPPA Privacy Regulations.* Retrieved June 5, 2008, from www.socialworkers.org/practice/behavioral_health/mbh0101.asp

National Association of Social Workers. (2002a). Hospice. In author. *Social work speaks: National Association of Social Workers policy statements 2006–2009* (7th ed.) (pp. 211–216). Washington, DC: NASW Press.

National Association of Social Workers. (2002b). Pippahpack: Promoting positive youth environments. Washington, DC: NASW Press.

National Association of Social Workers. (2002c). Social Services. In author. *Social work speaks: National Association of Social Workers policy statements 2003–2006* (6th ed.) (pp. 327–336). Washington, DC: NASW Press.

National Association of Social Workers. (2004a). *HIPPA for social work employers and administrators.* Retrieved June 9, 2008, from www.socialworkers.org/ldf/legal_issue/200405.asp

National Association of Social Workers. (2004b). *If you're right for the job, it's the best job in the world: The National Association of Social Workers' Child Welfare Specialty Practice Section members describe their experiences in child welfare.* Retrieved June 9, 2008, from www.naswdc.org/practice/children/NASWChildWelfareRpt062004.pdf

National Association of Social Workers. (2004c). *NASW standards for palliative and end of life care.* Washington, DC: National Association of Social Workers. Retrieved June 5, 2008, from www.naswdc.org/practice/bereavement/standards/standards0504New.pdf

National Association of Social Workers. (2005a). *Assuring the sufficiency of a frontline workforce: A national study of licensed social workers, preliminary report.* Washington, DC: National Association of Social Workers, Center for workforce Studies. Retrieved June 5, 2008, from www.socialworkers.org/resources/workforce/files/NASW_SWCassuring_3.pdf

National Association of Social Workers. (2005b). Client self-determination in end-of-life decisions. In author. *Social work speaks: National Association of Social Workers policy statements 2006–2009* (7th ed.) (pp. 129–135). Washington, DC: NASW Press.

National Association of Social Workers. (2005c). *Practice update: Multiculturalism.* Retrieved June 5, 2008, from www.socialworkers.org/practice/equity/multiculturalism-PU0505.pdf

National Association of Social Workers. (2005c). Disasters. In author. *Social work speaks: National Association of Social Workers policy statements 2006–2009* (7th ed.) (pp. 88–93). Washington, DC: NASW Press.

National Association of Social Workers. (2005d, May). *Social Work Congress sets future course.* NASW News. Retrieved June 5, 2008, from www.socialworkers.org/pubs/news/2005/05/swCongress.asp

National Association of Social Workers. (2005e). *Social workers and duty to warn.* Retrieved June 9, 2008, from www.social-workers.org/ldf/legal_issue/200502.asp

National Association of Social Workers. (2005f). *Social workers and HIPPA security standards.* Retrieved June 9, 2008, from www.socialworkers.org/ldf/legal_issue/200504.asp

National Association of Social Workers. (2005g). *Social workers and Psychotherapist-patient privilege:* Jaffee v. Redmond revisited. Retrieved June 9, 2008, from www.socialworkers.org/ldf/legal_issue/200503.asp

National Association of Social Workers. (2005h). *The power of social work.* Retrieved September 9, 2005, from www.naswdc.org/images/new_look/membershipMap.gif

National Center for Health Statistics [NCHS]. (2007). *Health, United States, 2007 with chartbook on trends in the health of Americans.* Hyattsville, MD: DHHS Publication No. 2007-1232. Retrieved May 15, 2008, from www.cdc.gov/nchs/data/hus/hus07.pdf

National Center for Injury Prevention and Control [NCIPC]. (2006). *Understanding intimate partner violence: Fact sheet.* Center for Disease Control. Retrieved June 5, 2008, from www.cdc.gov/ncipc/dvp/ipv_factsheet.pdf

National Center on Elder Abuse [NCEA]. (2005). *Fact sheet: Elder abuse prevalence and incidence.* Retrieved June 5, 2008, from www.ncea.aoa.gov/ncearoot/Main_Site/pdf/publication/FinalStatistics050331.pdf

National Clearing House on Child Abuse and Neglect. (2003). *Substance abuse and child maltreatment.* Retrieved October 11, 2005, from/nccanchacf.hhs.gov/pubs/factsheets/sub-abuse_childmal.pdf

National Institute of Mental Health [NIMH]. (2004). *In harms way: Suicide in America.* Bethesda, MD: National Institute of Mental Health, National Institutes of Health, U.S. Department of Health and Human Services. NIH Publication Number: NIH 5124. Retrieved June 5, 2008, from, www.sprc.org/library/event_kit/nimh_harmsway.pdf

Nelson, G., Lord, J., & Ochocka, J. (2001). Empowerment and mental health in community: Narratives of psychiatric consumer/survivors. *Journal of Community & Applied Social Psychology, 11,* 125–142.

Nelson-Becker, H. (2005). Religion and coping in older adults: A social work perspective. *Journal of Gerontological Social Work, 45*(1/2), 51–67.

Nelson-Becker, H. (2006). Voices of resilience: Older adults in hospice care. *Journal of Social Work in End-of-Life & Palliative Care, 2*(3), 87–106.

Netting, R. E., O'Connor, M. K., & Singletary, J. (2007). Findings homes for their dreams: Strategies founders and program initiators use to position and sustain faith-based programs. *Families in Society, 88*(1), 19–29.

Neuman, K. M., & Friedman, B. D. (1997). Process recordings: Fine-tuning an old instrument. *Journal of Social Work Education, 33*(2), 237–243.

Newman, B. S. (1989). Including curriculum content on lesbian and gay issues. *Journal of Social Work Education, 25,* 202–211.

Newman, B. S. (1994). Diversity and populations at risk: Gays and lesbians. In F. G. Reamer (Ed.), *The foundations of social work knowledge* (pp. 346–392). New York: Columbia University Press.

Newsome, W. S. (2005). The impact of solution-focused brief therapy with at-risk junior high school students. *Children & Schools, 27*(2), 83–90.

Nicholas, D. B., & Keilty, K. (2007). An evaluation of dyadic peer support for caregiving parents of children with chronic lung disease requiring technology assistance. *Social Work in Health Care, 44*(3), 245–259.

Nicholas D. B., Darch, J., McNeill, T., Brister, L., O'Leary, K., Berlin, D., & Koller, D. F. (2007). Perceptions of online support for hospitalized children and adolescents. *Social Work in Health Care, 44*(3), 205–223.

Nichols, M. P., & Schwartz, R. C. (2001). *Family therapy: Concepts and methods* (5th ed.). Boston: Allyn & Bacon.

Norlin, J. M., & Chess, W. (1997). *Human behavior and the social environment: A social systems model* (3rd ed.). Boston: Allyn & Bacon.

Norris, F. H., Stevens, S. P., Pfefferbaum, B., Wyche, K. F., & Pfefferbaum, R. L. (2008). Community resilience as a metaphor, theory, set of capacities, and strategy for disaster readiness. *American Journal of Community Psychology, 41*(1/2), 127–150.

North, C. S., & Hong, B. A. (2000). Project CREST: A new model for mental health intervention after a community disaster. *American Journal of Public Health, 90*(7), 1057–1058.

Nwakeze, P. C., Magura, S., Rosenblum, A., & Josephs, H. (2000). Service outcomes of peer consumer advocacy for soup kitchen guests. *Journal of Social Service Research, 27*(2), 19–38.

Oatts-Chandler, J., & Nelstrop, L. (2008). Listening to the voices of African-Caribbean mental health service users to develop guideline recommendations on managing violent behaviour. *Diversity in Health and Social Care, 5*(1), 31–41.

O'Connor, D. L. (2002). Toward empowerment: Revisioning family support groups. *Social Work with Groups, 25*(4), 37–56.

O'Donnell, J., & Giovannoni, J. M. (2006). Consumer perceptions of family resource center service delivery strategies. *Families in Society, 87*(3), 377–384.

Office of Applied Studies. (2003). *The NHSDA report: Children living with substance-abusing or substance-dependent parents.* Retrieved June 5, 2008, from www.oas.samhsa.gov/2k3/children/children.pdf

Ogunwole, S. U. (2006). *We the people: American Indians and Alaska Native in the United States: Census 2000 special reports.* U. S. Census Bureau. Retrieved May 26, 2008, from www.census.gov/prod/2006pubs/censr-28.pdf

Ohmer, M. L. (2007). Citizen participation in neighborhood organizations and its relationship to volunteers' self- and collective efficacy and sense of community. *Social Work Research, 31*(1), 109–120.

Oliver, M. (1996). *Understanding disability: From theory to practice.* London: Macmillan Press.

Oliver, M. (1997). The Disability movement is a new social movement. *Community Development Journal, 32*(3), 244–251.

Olson, D. H., & DeFrain, J. (2006). *Marriage and family diversity and strengths* (5th ed.). Boston: McGraw Hill.

Olson, J. J. (2007). Social work's professional and social justice projects: Discourses in conflict. *Journal of Progressive Human Services, 18*(1), 45–69.

O'Melia, M. (1991). *Generalist Perspectives in case coordination.* Workshop presentation at The Association for Retarded Citizens of Rock Island County, Rock Island, IL.

O'Melia, M. (October, 1998). *Proactive responding: Paths toward diverse strengths.* Paper presented at BPD 16th Annual Conference, Albuquerque, NM.

O'Melia, M. (2002). From person to context: The evolution of an empowering practice. In M. O'Melia & K. K. Miley (Eds.), *Pathways to power: Readings in contextual social work practice* (pp. 1–14). Boston: Allyn & Bacon.

Orme, J. (2002). Social work: Gender, care and justice. *British Journal of Social Work, 32,* 799–814.

Ortiz, L., Villereal, S., & Engel, M. (2000). Culture and spirituality: A review of the literature. *Social Thought, 19*(4), 21–36.

Ortiz, L. P., Wirtz, K., & Rodriguez, C. (2004). Legislative casework: Where policy and practice intersect. *Journal of Sociology and Social Welfare, 31*(2), 49–68.

Osmo, R., & Landau, R. (2001). The need for explicit argumentation in ethical decision-making in social work. *Social Work Education, 20*(4), 483–492.

Owen, A., Thompson, M., Mitchell, M., Kennebrew, S., & Paranjape, A. (2008). Perceived social support as a mediator of the link between intimate partner conflict and child adjustment. *Journal of Family Violence, 23*(4), 221–230.

Oyserman, D., & Sakamoto, I. (1997). Being Asian American: Identity, cultural constructs, and stereotype perception. *Journal of Applied Behavioral Science, 33*(4), 435–453.

Palmer, N., & Kaufman, M. (2003). The ethics of informed consent: Implications for multicultural practice. *Journal of Ethnic & Cultural Diversity in Social Work,* 12(1), 1–25.

Papernow, P. (1993). *Becoming a stepfamily: Patterns of development in remarried families.* San Francisco: Jossey-Bass.

Papp, P. (1983). *The process of change.* New York: Guilford Press.

Pardeck, J. T. (1988). Social treatment through an ecological approach. *Clinical Social Work Journal, 16,* 92–104.

Parker, L. (2003). A social justice model for clinical social work practice. *Affilia, 18*(3), 272–288.

Parsons, R. J. (2001). Specific practice strategies for empowerment-based practice with women: A study of two groups. *Affilia, 16*(2), 159–179.

Parsons, R. (2008). Empowerment practice. In T. Mizrahi & L. E. Davis (Eds.), *Encyclopedia of social work: Vol. 2* (20th ed.) (pp. 123–126). Washington, DC: NASW Press.

Passell, J. S., & Cohen, D. (2008). U. S. population projections 2005–2050. *Pew Research Center; Social and Demographic Trends.* Retrieved May 12, 2008, from pewhispanic.org/files/reports/85.pdf

Patel, T. (2005). The usefulness of oral life (hi)story to understand and empower: The case of transracial adoption. *Qualitative Social Work, 4*(3), 327–346.

Patten, S., Gatz, Y. K., Jones, B., & Thomas, D. (1989). Posttraumatic stress disorder and the treatment of sexual abuse. *Social Work, 34,* 197–203.

Patterson, S. L., & Marsiglia, F. F. (2000). "Mi casa es su casa": Beginning exploration of Mexican Americans' natural helping. *Families in Society, 81*(1), 22–31.

Pease, B. (2002). Rethinking empowerment: A postmodern reappraisal for emancipatory practice. *British Journal of Social Work, 32,* 135–147.

Peebles-Wilkins, W. (2008). Professional impairment. In T. Mizrahi & L. E. Davis (Eds.), *Encyclopedia of social work: Vol. 3* (20th ed.) (pp. 423–425). Washington, DC: NASW Press.

Peled, E., Eisikovits, Z., Enosh, G., & Winstok, Z. (2000). Choice and empowerment for battered women who stay: Toward a constructivist model. *Social Work, 45*(1), 9–25.

Pentz, M. (2005). Resilience among older adults with cancer and the importance of social support and spirituality-faith: "I don't have time to die." *Journal of Gerontological Social Work, 44*(3/4), 3–22.

Perlman, H. H. (1957). *Social casework: A problem solving process.* Chicago: University of Chicago Press.

Perlman, H. H. (1976). Believing and doing: Values in social work education. *Social Casework, 57,* 381–390.

Peterman, W. (2004). Advocacy vs. collaboration: Comparing inclusionary community planning models. *Community Development Journal, 39*(3), 266–276.

Pew Forum on Religion and Public Life. (2008). *U. S. religious landscape survey 2008.* Retrieved May 12, 2008, from religions. pewforum.org/pdf/report-religious-landscape-study-full.pdf

Pew Research Center for the People and the Press. (2003). *Evenly divided and increasingly polarized: 2004 political landscape.* Retrieved June 5, 2008, from people-press.org/reports/pdf/196.pdf.

Pew Research Center for the People and the Press. (2001). *Faith-based funding backed, but church-state doubts abound: Section IV–Religion in American life.* Retrieved June 5, 2008, from people-press.org/reports/display.php3?PageID=115

Pierson, J. (2002). *Tackling social exclusion.* London: Routledge.

Pincus, A., & Minahan, A. (1973). *Social work practice: Model and method.* Itasca, IL: Peacock Publishers.

Pinderhughes, E. B. (1979). Teaching empathy in cross-cultural social work, *Social Work, 24,* 321, 316.

Pinderhughes, E. B. (1982). Afro-American families and the victim system. In M. McGoldrick, J. K. Pearce, & J. Giordano (Eds.), *Ethnicity and family therapy* (pp. 108–122). New York: Guilford Press.

Pinderhughes, E. (1995). Empowering diverse populations: Family practice in the 21st century. *Families in Society, 76,* 131–140.

Pine, B. A., & Drachman, D. (2005). Effective child welfare practice with immigrant and refugee children and their families. *Child Welfare, LXXXIV*(5), 537–562.

Pinto, R. M., & Queely, T. (2003). Parents and children come together to prevent drug use: A mutual aid approach. *Social Work with Groups, 26*(3), 77–92.

Pippard, J. L., & Bjorkland, R. W. (2004). Identifying essential techniques for social work community practice. *Journal of Community Practice, 11*(4), 101–116.

Piven, F. F., & Cloward, R. A. (1971). *Regulating the poor: The functions of public welfare.* New York: Vintage Books.

Plath, D. (2006). Evidence-based practice: Current issues and future directions. *Australian Social Work, 59*(1), 56–72.

Plath, D., English, B., Connors, L., & Beveridge, A. (1999). Evaluating the outcomes of intensive critical thinking instruction for social work students. *Social Work Education, 18*(2), 207–217.

Polack, R. J. (2004). Social justice and the global economy: New challenges for social work in the 21st Century. *Social Work, 49*(2), 281–290.

Potts, K., & Brown, L. (2002, May). *Becoming an anti-oppressive researcher.* Paper presented at the Canadian Association of Schools of Social Work. Toronto, Canada.

Pray, J. (1991). Respecting the uniqueness of the individual: Social work practice within a reflective model. *Social Work, 36,* 80–85.

Proctor, C. D., & Groze, V. K. (1994). Risk factors for suicide among gay, lesbian, and bisexual youth. *Social Work, 39,* 504–512.

Proctor, E. K., & Davis, L. E. (1994). The challenge of racial difference: Skills for clinical practice. *Social Work, 39,* 314–323.

Professional impairment. (1999, March). *NASW News, 44*(3), p. 16.

Pruger, R. (1978). Bureaucratic functioning as a social work skill. In B. Baer & R. Federico, *West Virginia undergraduate social worker curriculum development project: Educating the baccalaureate social worker* (pp. 149–168). Cambridge, MA: Ballinger Publishing.

Pyles, L., & Kim, K. M. (2006). A multilevel approach to cultural competence: A study of the community response to underserved domestic violence victims. *Families in Society, 87*(2), 221–229.

Quible, Z. K. (1998). A focus on focus groups. *Business Communication Quarterly, 61*(2), 28–36.

Quinn, J. (1995). Case management in home and community care. *Journal of Gerontological Social Work, 24*(3/4), 233–248.

Radley, M., & Figley, C. R. (2007). The social psychology of compassion. *Clinical Social Work Journal, 35*(3), 207–214.

Raheim, S. (2002). Cultural competence: A requirement of empowerment practice. In M. O'Melia & K. K. Miley (Eds.), *Pathways to power: Readings in contextual social work practice* (pp. 95–107). Boston: Allyn & Bacon.

Ramon, S. (1999). Collective empowerment: Conceptual and practice issues. In W. Shera & L. Wells (Eds.), *Empowerment practice in social work: Developing richer conceptual foundations* (pp. 44–53). Toronto, Canada: Canadian Scholars Press.

Ramon, S. (2000). Participative mental health research: Users and professional researchers working together. *Mental Health Care, 3*(7), 224–228.

Ramos-McKay, J. M., Comas-Diaz, L., & Rivera, L. A. (1988). Puerto Ricans. In L. Comas-Diaz & E. E. H. Griffith (Eds.), *Clinical guidelines in cross-cultural mental health* (pp. 204–232). New York: Wiley.

Rapp, C. A. (1998). *The strengths model: Case management with people suffering from severe and persistent mental illness.* New York: Oxford University Press.

Rapp, R. C., Siegal, H. A., Li, L., & Saha, P. (1998). Predicting post-primary treatment services and drug use outcome: A multivariate analysis. *American Journal of Drug and Alcohol Abuse, 24,* 603–615.

Rappaport, J. (1981). In praise of paradox: A social policy or empowerment over prevention. *American Journal of Community Psychology, 9,* 1–25.

Rappaport, J. (1985). The power of empowerment language. *Social Policy, 17,* 15–21.

Rappaport, J. (1987). Terms of empowerment/exemplars of prevention: Toward a theory for community psychology. *American Journal of Community Psychology, 15*(2), 121–144.

Rappaport, J., Reischl, T. M., & Zimmerman, M. A. (1992). Mutual help mechanisms in the empowerment of former mental patients. In D. Saleebey (Ed.), *The strengths perspective in social work practice* (pp. 84–97). New York: Longman.

Reamer, F. G. (1993). *The philosophical foundations of social work.* New York: Columbia University Press.

Reamer, F. G. (1994). *Social work malpractice and strategies for prevention.* New York: Columbia University Press.

Reamer, F. G. (1998). *Ethical standards in social work: A critical review of the NASW Code of Ethics.* Washington, DC: NASW Press.

Reamer, F. G. (2001). Moral philosophy meets social work: Commentary on Alan Gewirth's "Confidentiality in child-welfare practice." *Social Service Review, 75*(3), 490–496.

Reamer, F. G. (2003a). Boundary issues in social work: Managing dual relationships. *Social Work, 48*(1), 121–133.

Reamer, F. G. (2003b). *Social work malpractice and strategies for prevention* (2nd ed.) New York: Columbia University Press.

Reamer, F. G. (2005). Update on confidentiality issues in practice with children: Ethics risk management. *Children & Schools, 27*(2), 117–120.

Reamer, F. G. (2008). Ethics and values. In T. Mizrahi & L. E. Davis (Eds.), *Encyclopedia of social work. Vol. 2* (20th ed.) (pp. 143–151). Washington, DC: NASW Press.

Reason, P., & Bradbury, H. (2008). Introduction. In P. Reason & H. Bradbury (Eds.), *The handbook of action research participative inquiry and practice* (pp. 1–10). Los Angeles: Sage.

Red Horse, J. (1982). Clinical strategies for American Indian families in crisis. *Urban and Social Change Review, 15*(2), 17–19.

Rees, S. (1991). *Achieving power: Practice and policy in social welfare.* North Sydney, Australia: Allen & Unwen.

Reese, D. J. (2001). Addressing spirituality in hospice: Current practices and a proposed role for transpersonal social work. *Social Thought, 20*(1/2), 135–162.

Reeser, L. C. (1991). Professionalization, striving, and social work activism. *Journal of Social Service Research, 14*(3/4), 1–22.

Regehr, C., Stern, S., & Shlonsky, A. (2007). Operationalizing evidence-based practice: The development of an Institute for Evidence-Based Social Work. *Research on Social Work Practice, 17,* 408–416.

Rehabilitation Research and Training Center on Disability Demographics and Statistics. (2007). *2006 Disability Status Report.* Ithaca, NY: Cornell University. Retrieved May 12, 2008, from www.ilr.cornell.edu/edi/disabilitystatistics/StatusReports/2006-PDF/2006-StatusReport_US.pdf?CFID=2609519&CFTOKEN=91812979

Reichert, E. (2006). *Understanding human rights.* Thousand Oaks, CA: Sage.

Reisch, M. (2002). Defining social justice in a socially unjust world. *Families in Society, 83*(4), 343–354.

Reisch, M., & Andrews, J. (2004). *The road not taken: A history of radical social work in the United States.* New York: Brunner-Routledge.

Reitsma-Street, M., & Brown, L. (2002). Community action research. In M. O'Melia & K. K. Miley (Eds.), *Pathways to power: Readings in contextual social work practice* (pp. 74–94). Boston: Allyn & Bacon.

Revheim, N., & Greenberg, W. M. (2007). Spirituality matters: Creating a time and place for hope. *Psychiatric Rehabilitation Journal, 30*(4), 307–310.

Reynolds, B. C. (1951). *Social work and social living.* New York: Citadel Press.

Richan, W. C. (1996). *Lobbying for social change.* New York: Haworth Press.

Ringel, S., Ronell, N., & Getahune, S. (2005). Factors in the integration process of adolescent immigrants. *International Social Work, 49*(1), 63–76.

Ringstad, R. (2008). The ethics of dual relationships: Beliefs and behaviors of clinical practitioners. *Families in Society, 89*(1), 69–77.

Ritchie, D. J., & Eby, K.K. (2007). Transcending boundaries: an international, interdisciplinary community partnership to address domestic violence. *Journal of Community Practice, 15*(1/2), 121–145.

Rivera, F. G., & Erlich, J. L. (1998). A time of fear: A time of hope. In F. G. Rivera & J. L. Erlich (Eds.), *Community organizing in a diverse society* (pp. 1–24). Boston: Allyn & Bacon.

Robbins, S. (2002). The rush to counsel: Lessons of caution in the aftermath of disaster. *Families in Society, 83*(2), 113–116.

Roberts-DeGennaro, M. (2008). Case management. In T. Mizrahi & L. E. Davis (Eds.), *Encyclopedia of social work. Vol. 1* (20th ed.) (pp. 222–227). Washington, DC: NASW Press.

Rock, B., & Congress, E. (1999). The new confidentiality for the 21st century in a managed care environment. *Social Work, 44*(3), 253–262.

Rogers, G. (1995). Educating case managers for culturally competent practice. *Journal of Case Management, 4*(2), 60–65.

Rooney, R. H. (1992). *Strategies for work with involuntary clients.* New York: Columbia University Press.

Rosenthal, R., & Jacobson, L. (1968). *Pygmalion in the classroom.* New York: Holt, Rinehart and Winston.

Ross, L., Holliman, D., & Dixon, D. R. (2003). Resiliency in family caregivers: Implications for social work practice. *Journal of Gerontological Social Work, 40*(3), 81–96.

Rothman, J., Smith, W., Nakashima, J., Paterson, M. A., & Mustin, J. (1996). Client self-determination and professional intervention: Striking a balance. *Social Work, 41*(4), 396–405.

Royse, D. (2008). *Research methods in social work* (5th ed.). Pacific Grove, CA: Brooks/Cole.

Rubin, A., & Babbie, E. (2008). *Research methods for social work* (6th ed.). Pacific Grove, CA: Brooks/ Cole.

Ruch, G. (2002). From triangle to spiral: Reflective practice in social work education, practice and research. *Social Work Education, 21*(2), 199–216.

Russell, M. N., & White, B. (2001). Practice with immigrants and refugees: Social worker and client perspectives. *Journal of Ethnic & Cultural Diversity in Social Work, 9*(3/4), 73–92.

Ryan, W. (1976). *Blaming the victim* (Rev. ed.). New York: Vintage Books.

Sakamoto, I., & Pitner, R. O. (2005). Use of critical consciousness in anti-oppressive social work practice: Disentangling power dynamics at personal and structural levels. *British Journal of Social Work, 35*(4), 435–452.

Saleebey, D. (1990). Philosophical disputes in social work: Social justice denied. *Journal of Sociology and Social Welfare, 17*(2), 29–40.

Saleebey, D. (1992). Introduction: Power in the people. In D. Saleebey (Ed.), *The strengths perspective in social work practice* (pp. 3–17). New York: Longman.

Saleebey, D. (1994). Culture, theory, and narrative: The intersection of meanings in practice. *Social Work, 39*(4), 351–359.

Saleebey, D. (2002a). The strengths approach to practice. In D. Saleebey (Ed.), *The strengths perspective in social work practice* (3rd ed.) (pp. 80–94). Boston, MA: Allyn & Bacon.

Saleebey, D. (2002b). The strengths perspective: Possibilities and problems. In D. Saleebey (Ed.), *The strengths perspective in social work practice* (3rd ed.) (pp. 264–283). Boston, MA: Allyn & Bacon.

Saleebey, D. (2002c). Introduction: Power to the people. In D. Saleebey (Ed.), *The strengths perspective in social work practice* (3rd ed.) (pp. 1–22). Boston, MA: Allyn & Bacon.

Saleebey, D. (2004). "The power of place": Another look at the environment. *Families in Society, 86*(1), 7–16.

Saltzman, A., & Furman, D. M. (1999). *Law in social work practice.* (2nd ed.). Chicago, IL: Nelson-Hall.

Salzinger, S., Feldman, R. S., Ng-Mak, D. S., Mojica, E., Stockhammer, T., & Rosario, M. (2002). Effects of partner violence and physical child abuse on child behavior: A study of abused and comparison children. *Journal of Family Violence, 17*(1), 23–52.

Sapey, B., Stewart, J., & Donaldson, G. (2005). Increases in wheelchair use and perceptions of disablement. *Disability & Society, 20*(5), 489–495.

Saulnier, C. F. (1996). *Feminist theories and social work: Approaches and applications.* New York: Haworth Press.

Schafer, C. M. (1969). Teaching social work practice in an integrated course: A general systems approach. In G. Hearn (Ed.), *The general systems approach: Contributions toward an holistic conception of social work* (pp. 26–36). New York: Council on Social Work Education.

Scheyett, A., & Diehl, M. J. (2004). Walking our talk in social work education: Partnering with consumers of mental health services. *Social Work Education, 23*(4), 435–450.

Schiele, J. H. (1996). Afrocentricity: An emerging paradigm in social work practice. *Social Work, 41*(3), 284–294.

Schlosser, L. Z. (2003). Christian privilege: Breaking a sacred taboo. *Journal of Multicultural Counseling and Development, 31*, 44–51.

Schneider, R. (2002). Influencing "state" policy: Social work arena for the 21st century. *The Social Policy Journal, 1*(1), 113–116.

Schneider, R. L., & Lester, L. (2001). *Social work advocacy.* Belmont, CA: Brooks/Cole.

Schorr, A. L. (1985). Professional practice as policy, *Social Service Review, 59*, 178–196.

Schott, S. A., & Conyers, L. M. (2003). A solution-focused approach to psychiatric rehabilitation. *Psychiatric Rehabilitation Journal, 27*(1), 43–51.

Schriver, J. M. (2004). *Human behavior and the social environment* (4th ed.). Boston: Allyn & Bacon.

Schroeder, L. O. (1995). *The legal environment of social work.* Washington, DC: NASW Press.

Schwartz, R. H., Tiamiyu, M. F., & Dwyer, D. J. (2007). Social worker hope and perceived burnout: The effects of age, years in practice, and setting. *Administration in Social Work, 31*(4), 103–119.

Schwartz, R. M. (1994). *The skilled facilitator: Practical wisdom for developing effective groups.* San Francisco: Jossey-Bass.

Scommegna, P. (2004). *U.S. Growing bigger, older, and more diverse.* Population Reference Bureau. Retrieved June 5, 2008, from www.prb.org/Articles/2004/USGrowingBiggerOlderand-MoreDiverse.aspx

Scurfield, R. M. (2002). Commentary about the terrorist acts of September 11, 2001: Posttraumatic reactions and related social and policy issues. *Trauma, Violence & Abuse, 3*(1), 3–14.

Searing, H. (2003). *The crisis in social work: The radical solution.* Retrieved June 5, 2008, from www.radical.org.uk/barefoot/crisis.htm

Secret, M., Jordan, A., & Ford, J. (1999). Empowerment evaluation as a social work strategy. *Health and Social Work, 24*(2), 120–127.

Segal, S. P. (2008). Self-help groups. In T. Mizrahi & L. E. Davis (Eds.), *Encyclopedia of social work. Vol. 4* (20th ed.) (pp. 14–17). Washington, DC: NASW Press.

Seligman, M. E. P. (1975). *Helplessness.* San Francisco, CA: Freeman Press.

Sewpaul V. (2006). The power of bibliography: Shifting the boundaries of knowledge through emancipatory pedagogy and critical consciousness. *Social Work/Maatskaplike Werk, 42*(2), 101–116.

Sheafor, B. W., & Horejsi, C. R. (2006). *Techniques and guidelines for social work practice* (7th ed.). Boston: Allyn & Bacon.

Sheridan, M. J., Gowen, N., & Halpin, S. (1993). Developing a practice model for the homeless mentally ill. *Families in Society, 74*, 410–421.

Sherraden, M. S., Slosar, B., & Sherraden, M. (2002). Innovation in social policy: Collaborative policy advocacy. *Social Work, 47*(3), 209–221.

Shulman, L. (1999). *The skills of helping individuals, families, groups, and communities* (4th ed.). Itasca, IL: F. E. Peacock Publishers, Inc.

Shulman, L. (2009). *The skills of helping individuals, families, groups, and communities* (6th ed.). Pacific Grove, CA: Wadsworth.

Shulman, L. & Gitterman, A. (2005). The life model, oppression, vulnerability and resilience, mutual aid and the mediating function. In A. Gitterman, & L. Shulman (Eds.), *Mutual aid groups, vulnerable and resilient populations, and the life cycle* (3rd ed.) (pp. 3–37). New York: Columbia University Press.

Siebert, D. C. (2005). Help seeking for AOD misuse among social workers: Patterns, barriers, and implications. *Social Work, 101*, 65–75.

Siegal, H. A., Fisher, J. A., Rapp, R. C., Kelliher, C. W., Wagener, J. H., O'Brien, W. F., & Cole, P. A. (1996). Enhancing substance abuse treatment with case management: Its impact on employment. *Journal of Substance Abuse Treatment, 13*, 93–98.

Simon, B. L. (1990). Rethinking empowerment. *Journal of Progressive Human Services, 1*, 27–39.

Simon, B. L. (1994). *The empowerment tradition in American social work: A history*. New York: Columbia University Press.

Simons, R. L., & Aigner, S. M. (1985). *Practice principles: A problem solving approach to social work*. New York: Macmillan.

Simmons, T., & O'Connell, M. (2003). *Married-couple and unmarried-partner households: 2000*. U.S. Census Bureau. Retrieved June 5, 2008, from www.census.gov/prod/2003pubs/censr5.pdf

Siporin, M. (1975). *Introduction to social work practice*. New York: Macmillan.

Siporin, M. (1980). Ecological systems theory in social work. *Journal of Sociology and Social Welfare, 7*, 507–532.

Siporin, M. (1983). Morality and immorality in working with clients. *Social Thought, 9*(4), 10–28.

Siporin, M. (1985). Current social work perspectives on clinical practice. *Clinical Social Work Journal, 13*, 198–217.

Sirkin, R. M. (2006). *Statistics for the social sciences*. (3rd ed.). Thousand Oaks, CA: Sage.

Slonim-Nevo, V. (1996). Clinical practice: Treating the non-voluntary client. *International Social Work, 39*, 117–129.

Smalley, R. (1967). *Theory for social work practice*. New York: Columbia University Press.

Smith, L. A. (1996). Unique names and naming practices among African American families. *Families in Society, 77*, 290–297.

Smith, R. K. M. (2003). *International human rights*. NY: Oxford University Press.

Solomon, B. B. (1976). *Black empowerment: Social work in oppressed communities*. New York: Columbia University Press.

Solomon, B. B. (1987). Human development: Sociocultural perspectives. In A. Minahan (Ed.), *Encyclopedia of social work. Vol 1* (18th ed.) (pp. 856–866). Silver Spring, MD: National Association of Social Workers.

Specht, H. (1983). Policy issues in clinical practice. In A. Rosenblatt & D. Waldfogel (Eds.), *Handbook of clinical social work* (pp. 721–730). San Francisco: Jossey-Bass Publishers.

Specht, H., & Courtney, M. E. (1994). *Unfaithful angels: How social work has abandoned its mission*. New York: The Free Press.

Spencer, J. H., & Le, T. N. (2006). Parent refugee status, immigration stressors, and Southeast Asian youth violence. *Journal of Immigrant Health, 8*, 359–368.

Stacey, K. (2001). Achieving praxis in youth partnership accountability. *Journal of Youth Studies, 4*(2), 209–231.

Staples, L. (2004). Social action groups. In C. D. Garvin, L. M. Gutierrez, & M. J. Galinsky (Eds.), *Handbook of social work with groups* (pp. 344–359). New York: Guilford Press.

Starratt, R. J. (1994). *Building an ethical school: A practical response to the moral crisis in schools*. Washington, DC: The Falmer Press.

Strier, R. (2007). Anti-oppressive research in social work: a preliminary definition. *British Journal of Social Work, 37*(5), 857–871.

Strom-Gottfried, K. (1999). Professional boundaries: An analysis of violations by social workers. *Families in Society, 80*(5), 439–449.

Strom-Gottfried, K. (2003). Understanding adjudication: Origins, targets, and outcomes of ethics complaints. *Social Work, 48*(1), 85–94.

Strom-Gottfried, K., & Mowbray, N. D. (2006). Who heals the helper? Facilitating the social worker's grief. *Families in Society, 87*(1)9–15.

Substance Abuse and Mental Health Services Administration [SAMHSA]. (2007). *Results from the 2006 National Survey on Drug Use and Health: National Findings*. Rockville, MD: Office of Applied Studies, NSDUH Series H-32, DHHS Publication No. SMA 07-4293). Retrieved May 15, 2008, www.oas.samhsa.gov/nsduh/2k6nsduh/2k6results.pdf

Sue, D. W. (2004). Whiteness and ethnocentric monoculturalism: Making the "invisible" visible. *American Psychologist, 59*(8), 761–769.

Sue, D. W., & Sue, D. (2003). *Counseling the culturally different* (4th ed.). New York: John Wiley & Sons.

Sullivan, T. R. (1994). Obstacles to effective child welfare service with gay and lesbian youths. *Child Welfare, 73*, 291–304.

Sullivan, W. P. (1992). Reclaiming the community: The strengths perspective and deinstitutionalization. *Social Work, 37*, 204–209.

Sullivan, W. P., & Rapp, C. A. (1994). Breaking away: The potential and promise of a strengths-based approach to social work practice. In R. G. Meinert, J. T. Pardeck, & W. P. Sullivan (Eds.), *Issues in social work: A critical analysis* (pp. 83–104). Wesport, CT: Auburn House.

Swift, C. (1984). Empowerment: An antidote for folly. *Journal of Prevention in Human Services, 3*, xi–xv.

Sung-Chan, P., & Yuen-Tsang, A, (2008). Our journey nurturing the voices of unemployed women in China through collaborative-action research. *Qualitative Social Work, 7*(1), 61–80.

Swift, C., & Levin, G. (1987). Empowerment: An emerging mental health technology. *Journal of Primary Prevention, 8*(1/2), 71–94.

Szente, J., Hoot, J., & Taylor, D. (2006). Responding to the special needs of refugee children: Practical ideas for teachers. *Early Childhood Education Journal, 34*(1), 15–20.

Tang, K-I. (2003). Internationalising anti-racism efforts: What social workers can do. *Journal of Ethnic and Cultural Diversity in Social Work, 12*(3), 55–71.

Tarasoff v. *The Regents of the University of California*, 551, P.2d 334 (Calif. 1976).

Tatara, T., & Kuzmeskus, L. M. (1997). *Reporting of elder abuse in domestic settings: Elder abuse information series No. 3*. Retrieved December 1, 2002, from www.elderabusecenter.org/basic/index.html

Tillich, P. (1962). The philosophy of social work. *Social Service Review, 36*(1), 13–16.

Timberlake, E. M., Sabatino, C. A., & Martin, J. A. (1997). Advanced practitioners in clinical social work: A profile. *Social Work, 42*(4), 374–385.

Tjaden, P., & Thoennes, N. (2000). *Full report of the prevalence, incidence, and consequences of violence against women*. Retrieved June 5, 2008 from www.ncjrs.gov/pdffiles1/nij/183781.pdf

To, S-M. (2007). Empowering school social work practices for positive youth development: Hong Kong experience. *Adolescence, 42*(167), 555–567.

Toseland, R. W., & Rivas, F. F. (2009). *An introduction to group work practice* (6th ed.). Boston: Allyn & Bacon.

Toth, S. L., & Cicchetti, D. (2005). Promises and possibilities: The application of research in the area of child maltreatment to policies and practices. *Journal of Social Issues, 63*(4), 863–880.

Tower, K. D. (1994). Consumer-centered social work practice: Restoring client self-determination. *Social Work, 39*, 191–196.

Tracy, B., & DuBois, B. (1987, September). *Information model for generalist social work practice.* Paper presented at the meeting of the Baccalaureate Program Directors of Social Work Programs, Kansas City, KS.

Tracy, E. M., & Whittaker, J. K. (1990). The social support network map: Assessing social support in clinical practice. *Families in Society, 71,* 461–470.

Trevithick, P. (2003). Effective relationship-based practice: A theoretical exploration. *Journal of Social Work Practice, 17*(2), 163–176.

Trotter, C. (1999 reprinted in 2004). *Working with involuntary clients: A guide to practice.* Thousand Oaks, CA: Sage.

Turner, M. (1997). Reshaping our lives. *Research, Policy and Planning, 15*(2), 23–25.

United Nations High Commission on Refugees [UNHCR]. (2007). Statistical yearbook 2006: Trends in displacement, protection, and solutions. Retrieved June 9, 2008, from www.unhcr.org/statistics/STATISTICS/478cda572.html

U.S. Census Bureau. (2007). The American community– Blacks: 2004. *American Community Survey Reports.* Retrieved May 12, 2008 from www.census.gov/prod/2007pubs/acs-04.pdf

U.S. Department of Health and Human Services [USHHS]. (2005). *Trends in the well-being of America's children and youth 2003: Section 3: Health conditions and health care.* Retrieved October 2, 2005 from aspe.hhs.gov/hsp/03trends/HC2.pdf

U.S. Department of Health and Human Services, Administration on Children, Youth and Families [USHHS, ACYF]. (2008). *Child Maltreatment 2006.* Washington, DC: U.S. Government Printing Office. Retrieved May 12, 2008, from http://www.acf.hhs.gov/programs/cb/pubs/cm06/cm06.pdf

U.S. Department of Health and Human Services, Administration on Aging [USHHS-AoA]. (2007). A profile of older Americans 2007. Retrieved June 9, 2008, from www.aoa.gov/prof/Statistics/profile/2007/2007profile.pdf

Valokivi, H. (2004). Participation and citizenship of elderly persons: User experiences from Finland. *Social Work in Health Care, 39*(1/2), 181–207.

Visher, E. B., & Visher, J. S. (1996). *Therapy with step-families.* New York: Brunner/Mazel.

von Bertalanffy, L. (1968). *General system theory.* New York: George Braziller.

Wagner, R., van Reyk, P., & Spence, N. (2001). Improving the working environment for workers Waldrop, D. P. (2006). Caregiving systems at the end of life: how informal caregivers and formal providers collaborate. *Families in Society, 87*(3), 427–437.

Walker, J. S. (2001). Caregivers' views on the cultural appropriateness of services for children with emotional or behavioral disorders. *Journal of Child and Family Studies, 10,* 315–331.

Walker, J. S., & Cook, J. (2002). Caregivers' perspectives on cultural competence. *Focal Point: A National Bulletin on Family Support and Children's Mental Health, 16*(2), 35–37. Retrieved June 5, 2008, from www.rtc.pdx.edu/PDF/fpF02.pdf

Walker, R., & Staton, M. (2000). Multiculturalism in social work ethics. *Journal of Social Work Education, 36*(3), 449–462.

Wall, M. D., Kleckner, T., Amendt, J. H., & Bryant, r. d. (1989). Therapeutic compliments: Setting the stage for successful therapy. *Journal of Marriage and Family Therapy, 15,* 159–167.

Walsh, F. (1999a). Opening family therapy to spirituality. In F. Walsh (Ed.), *Spiritual resources in family therapy* (pp. 28–58). New York: Guilford Press.

Walsh, F. (1999b). Religion and spirituality: Wellsprings for healing and resilience. In F. Walsh (Ed.), *Spiritual resources in family therapy* (pp. 3–27). New York: Guilford Press.

Walsh, J. (2007). *Endings in clinical practice: Effective closure in diverse settings* (2nd ed.). Chicago, IL: Lyceum Books.

Walsh, J., & Meyersohn, K. (2001). Ending clinical relationships with people with schizophrenia. *Health and Social Work, 26*(3), 188–195.

Walsh, T. (2002). Structured process recording: A comprehensive model that incorporates the strengths perspective. *Social Work Education 21*(1), 23–34.

Walsh, T., & Lord, B. (2003). Client satisfaction and empowerment through social work intervention. *Social Work in Health Care, 38*(4), 37–55.

Walter, J. L., & Peller, J. E. (1992). *Becoming solution-focused in brief therapy.* New York: Brunner /Mazel.

Walton, E., & Smith, C. (1999). The genogram: A tool for assessment and intervention in child welfare. *Journal of Family Social Work, 3*(3), 3–20.

Wang, D. (2004). Service delivery and research considerations of the 85+ population. *Journal of Gerontological Social Work, 43*(1), 5–17.

Washington, J., & Paylor, I. (2000). Social exclusion and inequalities in the United Kingdom. *Critical Social Work, 1*(2). Retrieved September 26, 2005, from www.criticalsocialwork.com/units/social-work/critical.nsf

Watzlawick, P., Bavelas, J. M., & Jackson, D. D. (1967). *Pragmatics of human communication.* New York: W. W. Norton.

Waugh, C. E., Fredrickson, B. L., & Taylor, S. F. (2008). Adapting to life's slings and arrows: Individual differences in resilience when recovering from an anticipated threat. *Journal of Research in Personality, 42*(4), 1031–1046.

Weaver, H. (1999). Indigenous people and the social work profession: Defining culturally competent services. *Social Work, 44*(3), 217–225.

Weaver, H. N. (2000). Culture and professional education: The experience of native American social workers. *Journal of Social Work Education, 36*(3), 415–428.

Weaver, H. N., & Burns, B. J. (2001). 'I shout with fear at night': Understanding the traumatic experiences of refugees and asylum seekers. *Journal of Social Work, 1*(2), 147–164.

Weaver, H. N., & White, B. J. (1997). The Native American family cycle: Roots of resiliency. *Journal of Family Social Work, 2*(1), 67–79.

Weaver, H., & Wodarski, J. S. (1996). Social work practice with Latinos. In D. F. Harrison, B. A. Thyer, & J. S. Wodarski (Eds.), *Cultural diversity and social work practice* (2nd ed.) (pp. 52–86). Springfield, IL: Charles C Thomas.

Webb, S. A. (2000). The politics of social work: Power and subjectivity. *Critical Social Work, 1*(2), Retrieved June 15, 2008, from www.criticalsocialwork.com/units/socialwork/critical.nsf/inToc/63888CFF2F58ABA085256EA5006E6966

Webster, B. H., & Bishaw, A. (2007). Income, earnings, and poverty data from the 2006 American Community Survey. *American community survey reports ACS-08.* Washington, DC: US government Printing Office. Retrieved May 22, 2008, from www.census.gov/prod/2007pubs/acs-08.pdf

Weick, A. (1980). Issues of power in social work practice. In Weick & S. T. Vandiver (Eds.), *Women, power, and change* (pp. 173–185). Washington, DC: NASW Press.

Weick, A. (1983). Issues in overturning a medical model of social work practice. *Social Work, 28,* 467–471.

Weick, A. (2000). Hidden voices. *Social Work 45*(5), 395–402.

Weick, A., & Chamberlain, R. (2002). Putting problems in their place: Further explorations in the strengths perspective. In D. Saleebey (Ed.), *The strengths perspective in social work practice* (3rd ed.) (pp. 95–105). Boston: Allyn & Bacon.

Weick, A., Rapp, C., Sullivan, W. P., & Kisthardt, W. (1989). A strengths perspective for social work practice. *Social Work, 34,* 350–354.

Weick, A., & Saleebey, D. (1995). Supporting family strengths: Orienting policy and practice toward the 21st century. *Families in Society, 76,* 141–149.

Weil, M. (2005). Introduction: Contexts and challenges for 21st century communities. In M. Weil (Ed.), *Handbook of community practice* (pp. 3–34). Thousand Oaks, CA: Sage.

Weil, M., & Gamble, D. N. (2005). Evolution, models, and the changing context of community practice. In M. Weil (Ed.), *Handbook of community practice* (pp. 117–150). Thousand Oaks, CA: Sage.

Weil, M., & Karls, J. M. (1989). Historical origins and recent developments. In M. Weils & J. M. Karls (Eds.), *Case management in human service practice* (pp. 1–28). San Francisco, CA: Jossey-Bass Publishers.

Weiman, K., Dosland-Hasenmiller, & O'Melia, J. (2002). Shutting off that damn bell: Raising the voices within. In M. O'Melia, & K. K. Miley (Eds.), *Pathways to power: Readings in contextual social work practice* (pp. 156–174). Boston: Allyn & Bacon.

Weinbach, R. W., & Yegidis, B. L. (2009). *Statistics for social workers* (6th ed.). Boston: Allyn & Bacon.

Wheeler, D. P., & Bragin, M. (2007). Bringing it all back home: Social work and the challenge of returning veterans. *Health and Social Work, 32*(4), 297–300.

White, G. W., Nary, D. E., & Froehlich, A. K. (2001). Consumers as collaborators in research and action. *Journal of Prevention & Intervention in the Community, 21*(2), 15–34.

White, M. (1989). The externalizing of the problem and the re-authoring of lives and relationships. In M. White (Ed.), *Selected papers* (pp. 5–28). Adelaide, Australia: Dulwich Centre Publications.

Whittaker, J. K., & Tracy, E. M. (1991). Social network intervention in intensive family-based preventive services. *Prevention in Human Services, 9*(1), 175–192.

Williams, C. C. (2002). A rationale for an anti-racist entry point to anti-oppressive social work in mental health. *Critical Social Work, 2*(2), 20–31. Retrieved March 4, 2003, from www.criticalsocialwork.com/CSW_2002_2.html

Williams, C. C. (2006). The epistemology of cultural competence. *Families in Society, 87*(2), 209–220.

Williams, J. H., Pierce, R., Young, N. S., & Van Dorn, R. A. (2001). Service utilization in high-crime communities: Consumer views on supports and barriers. *Families in Society, 82*(4), 409–417.

Williams, N. R (2004). Spirituality and religion in the lives of runaway and homeless youth: Coping with adversity. *Journal of Religion & Spirituality in Social Work, 23*(4), 47–66.

Williams, N. R., Davey, M., & Klock-Powell, K. (2003). Rising from the ashes: Stories of recovery, adaptation and resiliency in burn survivors. *Social Work in Health Care, 36*(4), 53–77.

Wilson, S. J. (1980). *Recording: Guidelines for social workers.* New York: The Free Press.

Wilson, S. J. (1978). *Confidentiality in social work.* New York: The Free Press

Wilson, S. J. (1980). *Recording: Guidelines for social workers.* New York: The Free Press.

Wituk, S., Shepherd, M. D., Slavich, S., Warren, M. L., & Meissen, G. (2000). *Social Work, 45*(2), 157–165.

Wituk, S., Pearson, R., Bomhoff, K., Hinde, M., & Meissen, G. (2007). A participatory process involving people with developmental disabilities in community development. *Journal of Developmental and Physical Disabilities, 19,* 323–335.

Wolin, S. J., & Wolin, S. (1993). *The resilient self: How survivors of troubled families rise above adversity.* New York: Villard Books.

Wolk, J. L. (1994). Grant writing: Linking the social work program to the community. *Journal of Teaching in Social Work, 10*(1/2), 83–97.

Wood, D. J., & Gray, B. (1991). Toward a comprehensive theory of collaboration. *Journal of Applied Behavioral Science, 27*(2), 138–162.

Wood, D., & Woody, D.J. (2007). The significance of social support on parenting among a group of single, low-income, African American mothers. *Journal of Human Behavior in the Social Environment, 15*(2/3), 183–198.

Woody, D. J., & Green, R. (2001). The influence of race/ethnicity and gender on psychosocial and social well-being. *Journal of Ethnic & Cultural Diversity in Social Work, 9*(3/4), 151–166.

Woolfson, L. (2004). Family well-being and disabled children: A psychosocial model of disability-related child behaviour problems. *British Journal of Health Psychology, 9*(1), 1–13.

Wong, D. F. K. (2008). Differential impacts of stressful life events and social support on the mental health of mainland Chinese immigrant and local youth in Hong Kong: a resilience perspective. *British Journal of Social Work, 38*(2), 236–252.

Worthen, B. L., Sanders, J. R., & Fitzpatrick, J. L. (1997). *Program evaluation: Alternative approaches and practical guidelines.* White Plains, NY: Longman.

Wright, O. L., & Anderson, J. P. (1998). Clinical social work practice with urban African American families. *Families in Society, 79*(2), 197–205.

Yamato, G. (1993). Something about the subject makes it hard to name. In V. Cyrus (Ed.), *Experiencing race, class, and gender in the United States* (pp. 206–213). Mountain View, CA: Mayfield.

Yellow Bird, M., Fong, R., Galindo, P., Nowicki, J., & Freeman, E. M. (1995). The multicultural mosaic. *Social Work in Education, 17*(3), 131–138.

Yumiko, M., Kiyomi, A., & Sachiyo, M. (2003). A trial to support family caregivers in long-term care insurance in Japan: Self-help groups in small communities. *Home Health Care Management & Practice, 15*(6), 494–499.

Zide, M. R., & Gray, S. W. (2000). The solutioning process: Merging the use of genograms and the solution-focused model of practice. *Journal of Family Social Work, 4*(1), 3–19.

Ziefert, M., & Brown, K. S. (1991). Skill building for effective intervention with homeless families. *Families in Society, 72,* 212–219.

Zilberfein, F. (1999). Coping with death: Anticipatory grief and bereavement. *Generations, 12*(1), 69–74.

Zimmerman, M. A. (1990). Toward a theory of learned hopefulness: A structural model analysis of participation and empowerment. *Journal of Research in Personality, 24,* 71–86.

Zippay, A. (1995). The politics of empowerment. *Social Work, 40,* 263–267.

Zugazaga, C. B., Surette, R. B., Mendez, M, & Otto, C. W. (2006). Social worker perceptions of the portrayal of the profession in the news and entertainment media: An exploratory study. *Journal of Social Work Education, 42*(3), 621–636.

Zunz, S. J. (1998). *Resiliency and burnout: Protective factors for human service managers. Administration in Social Work, 22*(3), 39–54.493

Photo Credits

Author Index

Abramson, J., 352, 353
Abramson, L. Y., 144, 187
Acevedo-Garcia, D., 363
Ackerson, B. J., 86
Adams, P., 69
Adams, R., 88
Adams, R. E., 356
Admiraal, K., 292
Aguilera, D. C., 199
Aho El Nasr, M., 88
Ahola, T., 229
Aigner, S. M. 311, 325, 419
Ainslie, J., 226
Akamatsu, N., 66
Alameda-Lawson, T., 354
Alexander, L. B., 140
Alexander, R., 149
Altpeter, M., 292, 396
Amundson, J., 144, 238
Anastas, J. W., 401
Anderson, C. M., 190
Anderson, J. P., 209, 221
Anderson, R. E., 35, 37, 40, 44
Andrews, A. B., 395
Andrews, J., 11
Appel, Y. H., 334–335
Aubrey, J., 91, 309
Auer, C., 350
Austin, C. D., 193, 344, 347, 348, 372
Austin, M. J., 389
Axford, N., 34
Ayon C., 335

Babbie, E., 397
Bailey, D., 68, 408
Baines, D., 29, 59, 283
Balaswamy, S., 163
Balgopal, P. R., 163
Bandler, R., 159, 160
Bandura, A., 188, 281, 282, 325
Baradell, J. G., 162
Bargal, D., 258
Barker, R. L., 7, 10, 15, 16, 52, 136, 193, 266
Barnes, C., 228

Barnes, S. L., 221
Bartlett, H., 31
Barton, K., 215
Baskind, F. R., 228
Beaudin, C. L., 350
Beavers, W. R., 214
Behnia, B., 163
Belenky, M. F., 176–177
Bem, S. L., 67
Ben-Ari, A., 315
Benson, R. A., 189
Beresford, P., 213, 396
Berg, I. K., 186, 216, 217, 221
Berger, P., 373
Berk, L. E., 428
Berlin, S., 50, 136, 219
Bernal, G., 222
Berry, M., 140
Bethea, L., 202
Bhul, K., 228
Biestek, F. P., 50, 193
Bilingsley, A., 209, 221
Birdwhistell, R., 160
Birnbaum, M., 433
Bishaw, A., 225
Bisman, C., 11
Bjorck, J. P., 228
Bjorkland, R. W., 258
Black, K., 429, 430
Blecher, J. R., 381
Bliss, M., 221
Bloch, D. S., 198
Bloom, M., 397, 402
Bloor, R., 216
Blount, M., 224
Boehm, A., 396
Bolen, R. M., 350, 389–390
Book, H. E., 139
Bower, G. H., 162
Boyd-Franklin, N., 161, 209, 221, 230
Bradbury, H., 408
Bragin, M., 231–232
Branson, D. M., 266
Braun, K. L., 223

Subject Index